# Performance Practices of the Seventeenth and Eighteenth Centuries

# Performance Practices of the Seventeenth and Eighteenth Centuries

## Frederick Neumann
### Prepared with the Assistance of Jane Stevens

SCHIRMER BOOKS
An Imprint of Macmillan Publishing Company
New York

Maxwell Macmillan Canada
Toronto

Maxwell Macmillan International
New York  Oxford  Singapore  Sydney

Schirmer Books
An Imprint of Macmillan Publishing Company
866 Third Avenue
New York, NY 10022

Maxwell Macmillan Canada, Inc.
1200 Eglinton Avenue East, Suite 200
Don Mills, Ontario M3C 3N1

Macmillan Publishing Company is part of the Maxwell Communication Group of companies.

Library of Congress Catalog Card Number: 92-33205

Printed in the United States of America

printing number
1 2 3 4 5 6 7 8 9 10

Library of Congress Cataloging-in-Publication Data
Neumann, Frederick.
    Performance practices of the seventeenth and eighteenth centuries
  / Frederick Neumann ; prepared with the assistance of Jane Stevens.
      p. cm.
    Includes bibliographical references and index.
    ISBN 0-02-873300-2
    1. Performance practice (Music)—17th century.   2. Performance
practice (Music)—18th century. I. Stevens, Jane. II. Title.
ML457.N46 1993
781.4'3'09032—dc20
                                            92-33205
                                              CIP
                                              MN

The paper used in this publication meets the minimum requirements of American National Standard for Information Sciences—Permanence of Paper for Printed Library Materials. ANSI Z39.48-1984. ∞™

*For BRENDA and TOM*
*whose devoted, giving friendship in times of adversity gave me the*
*strength to carry the work on this book through to its completion,*
*with profound gratitude and love*

# Contents

# PART III

## *Dynamics*

# PART IV

## *Articulation*

# PART V

## *Phrasing*

# PART VI

## *Ornamentation*

# Preface

We have been witnessing a vogue of "early music" performances that use period instruments and lay claim to being "historically informed"—a term now widely used in place of yesterday's "authentic." It signifies, roughly, an interpreter's attempt to reconstruct a performance that would have met with the composer's approval. Such speculative reconstruction involves not only every detail of interpreting the score but also such matters as the numbers and distribution of the performers, the voice production of the singers, the sound and technique of the instruments used, and their pitch and tuning. All these concerns, singly or in combination, are aspects of historical performing practice—the subject addressed by the present book.

Since offering information on *all* of these matters would be a task of encyclopedic proportions beyond my—and maybe any individual's—capacity, I had to narrow the range of enquiry. I do not address issues of vocal and instrumental sonorities and techniques, numbers of performers, pitch, tuning, conducting, or realization of a thorough bass. What I do address is what could be called the tactical issues of interpretation: tempo, rhythm, dynamics, articulation, phrasing, and ornamentation, with an all-too brief introductory discussion of the strategic issues of expression and taste.

On matters of ornamentation I have already published two books: *Ornamentation in Baroque and Post-Baroque Music: With Special Emphasis on J. S. Bach* (hereafter *OrnB*) and *Ornamentation and Improvisation in Mozart* (hereafter *OrnM*); on matters of rhythm I have written many articles that are collected, with articles on other subjects, in two volumes of essays: *Essays in Performance Practice* (*Essays 1982*) and *New Essays on Performance Practice* (*Essays 1989*). In discussing these two subjects in the present book, I shall lean heavily on my previous work. The present treatment, however, is substantially condensed and does not by any means supersede the far more detailed earlier presentations (the two books on ornamentation together comprise close to a thousand large pages). Readers interested in more detailed information regarding these two subjects are referred to these publications.

A "historically informed" performance is by necessity a mixture of factual knowledge and educated guesses. While we must never cease to search for all available historical information, this information remains fragmentary and often ambiguous. The performer's artistry, taste, and musical intelligence must always supplement the scaffolding of historical information in order to bring an "early" work to life.

In every chapter I focus first on all the factual information that I have been able to garner and provide an evaluation of these data. After that I occasionally offer performance suggestions when they help in clarifying a point. Whenever possible I have inserted a short horizontal rule, such as follows this paragraph, to separate sections containing factual statements from those containing subjective statements. Often, however, such a neat separation was not practicable. One entire chapter, "Phrasing in Practice," is subjective and advisory in character.

---

Eight years have gone into the preparation of this book, and I am offering it now to the public in the hope that it may be found useful. It does not call for previous knowledge and is addressed primarily to performers and students of performance. In addition, it is hoped that anybody concerned with the art of musical interpretation, including discriminating listeners, will find in it matters of interest.

Some of the findings of this book, notably on questions of rhythm and ornamentation, contradict long-standing traditional views. Yet traditions can be treacherous, and it behooves us every so often to take a probing look at such received wisdoms.

I apologize for not a few cases where instead of printing a lengthy music example I refer to it in another easily accessible source. I have done so not for my convenience but in order to keep down expenses and the price of this volume.

Translations are mine unless otherwise indicated.

Finally, a word on the collaboration of Jane Stevens, whom I thank in the Acknowledgments for her outstanding role in the preparation of this book. She had a vital part in all matters of form: from what was discussed, what left out, how materials were arranged, and how thoughts were expressed to the overall tone, style, and character of the presentation; moreover, by her probing questions she had me every so often rethink matters of content. But by and large, for all factual statements, performance suggestions, and opinions expressed, it is I who have to take full responsibility.

# Acknowledgments

For financial help with the research expenses I wish to thank the National Endowment for the Humanities for its grant of a (second) fellowship.

I am indebted to the staffs of all the libraries mentioned in this book for their unfailing helpfulness.

I wish to express my sincere thanks to Princeton University Press for the generous permission to make extensive use of materials from my two ornamentation books.

As to individuals, I owe my deepest gratitude to Professor Jane Stevens, whose pivotal role in the making of this book is reflected on the title page, while the nature of her contribution is explained in the Preface. Without her assistance this book would have been much poorer.

I am very grateful to Professor Alejandro E. Planchart, who read the problematic first three chapters and gave me the benefit of detailed comments and invaluable advice. I wish to thank my friend Max Rudolf, who read a few sections and favored me with learned and wise counsel.

I am indebted to Barbara Anderson, who has again, as twice before, prepared for me a fine bibliography and index. My thanks go also to Bonlyn Hall, who helped me secure materials on interlibrary loan, and to David Severtson for a copyediting performance of extraordinary care and thoroughness.

# Performance Practices of the Seventeenth and Eighteenth Centuries

# Introduction

A composition remains for most of us a dead letter until performance transforms it into living sound. Certainly, trained musicians can, to varying degrees, read a score and hear the music in their minds. But for the overwhelming mass of music lovers, performance is indispensable for getting to know, enjoy, and appreciate the artistic values of a musical work.

The performer has the task of "interpreting" the composition, that is, of conveying faithfully to the listener the spirit and meaning of the musical text. To do so properly involves an act of artistry comparable to the translation of a poem, not just an act of technical skill comparable to the translation of a business report. Ideally, the interpreter should know the work in question thoroughly in all its aspects, grasp its style, its structure, its spiritual or emotional content, the interplay of the various elements of the musical language, the relationship of the parts to the whole: in short, its artistic essence. On the basis of such knowledge the interpreter is then to arrive at the kind of execution that will best illuminate the aesthetic values of the work.

Over the last few hundred years the role of performance has undergone remarkable changes that stemmed from two main roots. One was the gradual growth of the composer's control over the execution of his works by ever greater accuracy and specificity in the score. The second was the changing attitude toward music of the past. Roughly speaking, up to around 1800—that is, to the end of the patronage system in music and the arts—both patrons and public were interested mainly in the music of the present, hardly in that of the past. Hence, for practical purposes, the problem of historical performance did not exist.

The Romantic age, with its interest in national cultural heritage, was the first to revive older music systematically. The performers, though, were not concerned with historical appropriateness; instead they filled the older music spontaneously with the spirit of their own style. The idea of a "performance practice," other than their own, was foreign to them. As a consequence of this attitude, the age produced a mass of corrupt "romanticized" editions of 18th-century masters, many of which, unhappily, are still in wide circulation today.

Interest in historically appropriate performance awoke gradually at the end of the 19th century with the revival of antique instruments. In 1894 Charles Bordes and Vincent d'Indy founded the Schola Cantorum in Paris, which at its beginning focused on the revival of old church music. In 1901 Henri Casadesus, supported by Camille Saint-Saëns, founded the Société des Instruments Anciens, which organized concerts of music played on old instruments. In 1903 Wanda Landowska gave her first harpsichord recital, and a year later she published her book *Musique ancienne*, in which she pleads for the use of the harpsichord where historically called for. A further important landmark was the publication, in 1915, of Arnold Dolmetsch's well-known, truly pioneering book *The Interpretation of the Music of the Seventeenth and Eighteenth Centuries*, the fruit of many years of study and experimentation. In the era between the world wars, presumably inspired by the spreading enthusiasm for old instruments, more harpsichordists followed Landowska's example, while gambists and recorder players also began to appear on the musical scene. But after World War II the fuse they had lit set off an eruption of enthusiasm so widespread and so intense that we can well speak of a revolution in the history of musical performance.

While the causes for this development await the enquiry of cultural historians, the events themselves are known to every music lover: the widespread reproduction of harpsichords and other old instruments that heretofore have been confined to museums; the building of "Baroque organs"; the emergence all over the Western world of organizations devoted to the cultivation of early music on period instruments; the rising flood of recordings and tapes of pre-1800 music in what were at first proudly proclaimed as "authentic" interpretations on "authentic" instruments.[1]

The intense preoccupation with historical sound and style has led to a vast increase in the volume of research on the subject of the performance practices of various historical periods. Since the present book tries to make a contribution to this field, it behooves us now to take a look at this relatively new discipline, to examine its nature, its problems.

The term "performance practice" (or its de facto synonym "historical performance") most often refers to the search for a historically appropriate interpretation of "early music."[2] Such was not always the case. In 1931, in his great book *Aufführungspraxis der Musik* (the origin of our term "performance practice"), Robert Haas dealt with the historical facts of musical performance from antiquity to the present but neither said nor implied that his findings should serve as models for today's performances. By way of contrast, today's search in this field is pragmatic: we probe the historical facts to provide proper guidelines for our own playing and singing. Today we aim at performances that come close to the composer's concept of the work.

How to approach this aim is the fundamental problem of our task. The biggest hurdle we encounter is the inadequacy of musical notation. Even the sophisticated scores of today's composers are far removed from the precision of an architect's blueprint and consequently leave many interpretive decisions to the judgment of the performer. But the more we go back in time the more fragmentary becomes the notation, the greater grows the gap between the composer's intentions and his ability—or willingness—to specify them in writing. To fill these gaps is the formidable task we face. The attempt to do so is what performance practice is all about.

In trying to solve the mysteries of a fragmentary score, we must, like detectives, gather all the evidence we can and follow any promising lead. What we cannot fill in with genuine evidence we must in the end fill in with speculation. The score, whatever it says and fails to say, is still the most important body of evidence. Hence we must try to establish a reliable text, one that ideally shows what the composer has actually written and separates it from later editorial accretions. Here the so-called Urtext editions are helpful, provided they live up to the meaning of their designation as authoritative texts.

All the elements of music that combine in the composition of a work have to be similarly combined to achieve a desirable interpretation. They are—not necessarily in the order of their importance—the melody, with its articulation, its phrasing, its ornamentation and improvisation; meter, rhythm, and tempo; and dynamics (loudness and softness), sonorities, and balance. As they are integrated in the composer's thought, and ought to be integrated in the replay of interpretation, they combine to yield the envisaged "spirit" or "expression" of the work. This is probably the most vital quality of proper interpretation and at the same time the most elusive one.

Some of these elements are more important than others, and some are more problematic than others. The melody, in its essence of pitch and rhythm, is given in the score, as is the combination of melodies in contrapuntal textures. What may be missing from the scores, partially or completely, is ornamentation, dynamics, articulation, and phrasing; and where improvisation is expected, it is missing by definition.

Rhythm is, theoretically, defined by the score; but in practice it can deviate from the mathematics of notation, either as a consequence of notational shortcomings or in deference to particular conventions of "rhythmic alterations."

Tempo, prior to the invention of the metronome in the early 19th century, is at best only roughly suggested by various notational means. In view of the enormous importance of tempo for the desired expression, tempo is one of the most vexing problems of interpretation.

Dynamics had to wait for the 19th century to be indicated with much specificity in the score. For our era, help from the score ranges from fragmentary in the 17th century to more detailed (yet occasionally no more than a general outline) in the second half of the 18th century.

The score can yield some other valuable information as well, if we know how to extract it. Most important in this respect is musical evidence of two kinds: external, when derived from the composer's autograph or a reliable scribe's manuscript, and internal, when derived from the logic of melody, harmony, counterpoint, rhythm, or other musical elements. For just one illustration of external evidence: when Haydn, in the first movement of his Symphony No. 90, writes the same motive haphazardly a few times like this and a few times like this we can conclude from the second, slurred version that the three ornamental notes (a "turn") are to be played in the time of the preceding, not the following, note. For one illustration of internal evidence, an onbeat placement of an ornamental note is unlikely when it would result in offensive parallels. Evidence from these sources is particularly valuable because its pertinence to the specific work and composer involved is not in question.

There are a number of other fruitful avenues outside of the score. One has to do with sonorities. We are familiar with many of the old instruments and have a good idea of their old playing techniques. We also know the basic strength of many instrumental and choral organizations and in some cases know their seating arrangements and the way they were directed. But interesting as these insights are, they are only peripheral since they tell us little about the central question of our task: the particular *interpretation* of specific works.

For information bearing on this central question, scholars have for a long time turned to old treatises that deal with questions of performance. Many of these treatises are of great value, but they have to be used with the greatest of care. They generally contain rules and principles; the question is to whom and to what these formulations do or do not apply. It is thus impossible to classify a book *in toto,* say, Quantz's famous treatise *On Playing the Flute.* If we ask to whom and to what it applies we probably have to say that some of it is timeless and was valid five hundred years ago and is still valid today; that some of it may be valid for Bach, some of it for Mozart, some only for the galant music of the mid-18th century, and some perhaps only for Quantz himself and his immediate circle. Some scholars have let themselves be swayed by a convenient but fallacious belief in a "common practice" of an extended era, leading them to assume that such important mid-century books like those of Quantz, C. P. E. Bach, or Leopold Mozart could be safely and automatically "applied" in their entirety not only to all contemporaries but backward and forward in time to encompass J. S. Bach along with Mozart.

There are other dangers in old tracts. One is the too literal, too rigid interpretation of principles that were meant to be flexible. A classic case of this danger is ornament tables. The modern French organist and scholar Geoffroy-Dechaume coined a felicitous phrase when he spoke of the "inanity of ornament tables" because they seem to suggest a single rigid design for an ornament that can and should assume a multitude of shapes in performance.[3] The ornament tables themselves are usually not inane, since many of them were written by eminent musicians. They become inane when we mistake, as we so often do, their pure abstraction for models to be applied literally in every concrete circumstance. When so treated, ornaments become instruments of hardness and rigidity while their artistic function calls for them to be agents of liquidity and flexibility.

Thus while old tracts are indispensable for our task, we must treat them with great circumspection. We must screen them for their possible pertinence to a specific composer by considering stylistic kinship and by cross-checking their principles against musical evidence derived from the scores. We must also be constantly alert to the danger of mistaking the abstract for the concrete, the relative for the absolute.

As a consequence of an inappropriate use of these treatises, many questionable beliefs have entered the canon of principles regarding "historically informed" performance, beliefs that are in need of careful revision. Some of these principles will be familiar to readers of my earlier writings. Here is a list of the more important dubious tenets for the 17th and 18th centuries:

Every ornament starts on the beat, every trill starts on the upper note.

The French overture style with its sharp rhythmic contractions and synchronizations had a wide range of application.

The French *notes inégales* had international currency.

Binary–ternary conflicts have to be resolved by assimilation of one mode to the other.

The "basic" articulation was clear detachment.

Instrumental vibrato was only minimally used, vocal vibrato not at all.

Long notes should be rendered with a swell and taper (*messa di voce*).

The old keyboard fingerings were intended to cause two-by-two articulation and two-by-two inequality.

These and a few other scattered items of received wisdom are in need of critical review. In the fields of ornamentation and rhythm I have already attempted such a revision, largely through a far more extensive use of musical evidence than has been practiced so far and through the inclusion of many hitherto untapped theoretical writings. In addition to summarizing my findings in these two fields, the present book attempts a new look also at the questions of tempo, articulation, phrasing, and dynamics. These are the six important issues that will be discussed in the six parts into which the thirty-three chapters of this book are divided. As explained in the Preface, I do not deal here with such matters as voices and instruments and their techniques, nor with pitch, tuning, or accompaniment.

Two important matters, those of expression and taste, need to be discussed, however, because they are perhaps the most critical problems of interpretation. Yet it is difficult to find a proper place for them in the body of the book since they are not issues on a par with the six mentioned but permeate them all. Here seems to be the best place to remark on these matters.

"Expression" sums up the spirit that inhabits a musical work. In the 17th century this spirit, or "affection" as it was called, had to be guessed from a bare score that contained little more than pitches and their relative length. In vocal works the words, provided they were properly set, could offer further guidance. Early on some composers began to suggest the basic tempo (with its strong impact on expression) by such words as *adagio, allegro,* and *presto,* to which in the 18th century were added occasional qualifying adjectives such as *cantabile, grazioso, maestoso.* An expression mark like *dolce* begins to make sporadic appearances in the late 18th century, while *espressivo* may have been Beethoven's innovation. The French used words that more directly focused on expression— words such as *noblement, tendrement, audacieusement.* All these terms can at best suggest tempo and expression by a subtle process of association.

Perhaps because the concept of expression is so elusive yet obviously so important to performance, theorists in the 17th and 18th centuries compared a musical performance to an orator's delivery, the *pronuntiatio* of classical rhetoric, in which skillful articulation is the counterpart to musical expressiveness. The art of delivery can make the difference between a speech that falls flat and one that can arouse the audience to passionate response.

In 1619 Michael Praetorius devotes an eloquent paragraph on this comparison: "Just as it is an orator's role not only to grace a speech with beautiful, graceful, and lively words, and with splendid figures of speech, but also to deliver it properly so as to arouse the emotions: by raising his voice here, lowering it there, speaking alternately with powerful, with gentle, with full and resonant voice; so it is the duty of the musician not simply to sing, but to sing with artistry and grace, so as to stir the heart of the listeners and move their emotions and thus allow the song to fulfill the purpose for which it was destined" (*Syntagma musicum,* 3:229).

Some 130 years later Johann Joachim Quantz opens the important Chapter 11 of his *Versuch* with the sentence: "Musical performance can be likened to an orator's delivery." He continues this comparison in the very spirit of Praetorius. The orator and the musician, he says, both aim to touch the hearts of the listeners, to arouse or calm their passions, and to transport them now to one, now to another emotion. The orator should have a clear and pure voice, a distinct and proper pronunciation; his voice and speech should be well modulated to avoid monotony; he should vary the loud and the soft, the fast and the slow; he should raise the voice for words that call for emphasis, lower it for others, adjust the tone to the changing sentiments, and in general take into account the locale, the content of the speech, and the character of the audience. Quantz stresses that all these desiderata apply equally to musical performance and then proceeds to elaborate the parallels in considerable detail.

All these elements of good musical delivery are subsumed under the term "expression." Musicians, writers, and critics, all tend to use this term whenever they speak of desirable musical performance.

Jean Jacques Rousseau, philosopher also of music, writes in 1768 (*Dictionnaire*, s.v. "Exécution"): "Nothing is as rare as a good performance. It means little to read the music exactly note by note; one must penetrate all the ideas of the composer, feel and render the *fire of expression*" (emphasis added). He defines expression as that quality with which the musician senses intelligently, and renders energetically, all the ideas he is to render and all the feelings he is to express. "First you have to know the character of the piece that you are to perform . . . then abandon your being [livrez vos organes] to all the fervor that these thoughts [considérations] have inspired; do what you would do if you were at the same time the poet, the composer, the actor, and the singer, and you will have found all the expression that you are capable of giving to the work you are to perform." Here we see how even Rousseau with his astonishing eloquence has difficulty in getting a firm hold on the slippery concept of expression while at the same time succeeding in pointing to the centrality of its role in performance.

A related concept, equally elusive and equally vital, is "taste" (*Geschmack, gusto, goût*). Taste in the arts in general is a central concern of 18th-century aesthetics. Johann Georg Sulzer, in his *Allgemeine Theorie der schönen Künste* of 1773–75, has a long article on "Geschmack," a longer one yet in the edition of 1792–94 (I owe this information to Max Rudolf). In music, taste is the combination of stylistic knowledge, musical intelligence, and the keen sensitivity that grants an insight into the nature of a composition. We find it extolled in a number of important treatises as the key to desirable expression. In his letters, Mozart refers time and time again to "Gusto" as a guide to performance. And the French in particular, composers and theorists alike, from at least the 17th century on, consistently subjected any rule to the higher authority and veto power of *le bon goût*. By emphasizing the critical role of taste, composers silently surrender its exercise to the performer, who is thereby authorized, indeed obligated, to use judgment where the score leaves off.

Expression and taste are the truly *strategic* issues of performance; they will not yield their secrets to any rules. Only enlightened insight can be our guide, and in the end we have to rely on our own musical sensitivity and intelligence in trying to grasp the spirit of a work prior to communicating it in performance to the listeners.

Whether the spirit of a work can be properly communicated only with period instruments and their authentic techniques, in lower pitch and with numbers of players and singers corresponding to historical models, is of course the question that underlies the present schism between "mainstream" performances and those that aspire to the epithet of being "historically informed." It is not within the purpose of this book to take a stand on this controversy, and I shall limit myself here to a brief comment. First, let it be said that the question has no self-evident answer. Such an answer will depend on what we conceive to be the touchstone of a historically appropriate performance. If the test is the quasi-archeological pursuit of re-creating an original acoustical phenomenon, then of course period instruments are indispensable; if the test is the effective communication of a work's essence to today's listener, the answer is less certain. After all, musical performance has to be above all *musically* satisfying, and any master's spirit can be revealed only in *musical* terms. Such questions as tone color or number of performers should not be subjected to a moral judgment of right and wrong but only to the artistic one of being in rapport with the style and spirit of the work; of being more or less compelling, moving, exciting, engrossing, enchanting, exhilarating, edifying, or whatever other adjective we can summon to describe the appropriate response to an artistic experience. Such artistic judgment would be in harmony with 18th-century aesthetic ideas that a desirable performance is one that expresses the "affections" inherent in the music and moves the listener's emotions (*die Leidenschaften erregen*) accordingly.

What *is* within the purpose of this book is the attempt to give an account of what can be established with a good degree of probability about the way composers of the era under scrutiny intended their music to be interpreted and, where facts are elusive, what educated guesses may be reasonably made. The emphasis here is on the core issues of interpretation—on tempo, rhythm, dynamics, articulation, phrasing, and ornamentation.

Throughout the book the presentation will be descriptive, *not prescriptive:* it is meant to give today's interpreter a foundation of historical insights as a basis for making artistic decisions, not to offer a rule book of what the performer must and must not do. The final authority must be handed to the musically gifted and stylistically knowledgeable performer who is informed of available facts and of the best guesses that modern scholarship can provide.

---

## A Note on the Literature

The literature on performance practice is huge and keeps growing at an accelerating pace. At the time of writing (1991) no less than three journals were devoted entirely or predominantly to this subject—*Early Music,* a quarterly published in London, was founded in 1973, and in 1988 two American semiannuals began publication: *Historical Performance,* the Journal of Early Music America, and *Performance Practice Review,* published by the Claremont Graduate School in California. Many articles on the subject have of course appeared and keep appearing in other, less specialized music journals. Their huge number alone forbids a survey in this limited space. I shall comment here only on some of the more important books on the subject.

Only a few books deal with a wide range of subjects in performance. The first was *The Interpretation of the Music of the Seventeenth and Eighteenth Centuries* by Arnold Dolmetsch, which appeared in 1915. With its publication Dolmetsch became the true founder of the discipline and strongly influenced its future course. He studied old tracts and determined in a manner that now seems rather simplistic and arbitrary which of them are (*in toto*) applicable to which composers. He cited individual passages, from which he then deduced a number of principles; although some of his conclusions are questionable, they have continued to exert great influence to the present. Among them are his theory about the so-called French overture style (not his term) with its drastic rhythmic contractions, which he said ought to be applied "to all old music," and his idea that the French convention of *notes inégales* ought to be applied to Bach and Handel and other non-French composers.

In 1931 Robert Haas published his magisterial study *Aufführungspraxis der Musik,* a history of performance from antiquity to the end of the 19th century. As has already been mentioned, it was not intended as a manual for today's performers.

After Dolmetsch's death the much younger Thurston Dart (1921–71) assumed the leadership of the movement striving for historical reconstruction. Self-taught, he built on Dolmetsch's foundations, the only ones available at the time. He wrote many articles but exerted his greatest influence with his small book of some 170 pages, *The Interpretation of Music* (1954). Written in an easy conversational style and carrying its scholarship lightly, it was translated into various languages and has remained popular to the present day. With a chronological range from the Middle Ages to 1800 and with a substantial section on the sound of old instruments, there was space for only rather fragmentary (and often unreliable) documentation. By and large the book issues directives without making too strenuous an effort to justify them.

The true heir to Dolmetsch is his student Robert Donington, a thorough and painstaking scholar. His large book *The Interpretation of Early Music,* originally published in 1962 and revised in 1974, is essentially an extended catalog of quotations from old tracts. They often juxtapose one country to another, one era to the next. Many of these passages are of great interest, but by transforming them into instant prescriptions the author is treading a dangerous path.

In 1990 the Norton/Grove Handbooks in Music series published *Performance Practice,* a two-volume handbook edited by Howard M. Brown and Stanley Sadie, with the expressed intention of bringing up to date Thurston Dart's *The Interpretation of Music* of 1954. The first three parts (319 pages) of the second volume, which treats of music after 1600, deal with the 17th and 18th centuries. These volumes are a collective effort of a large number of scholars, each writing on a specific topic. For music after 1600 the main emphasis is on sonorities: on voices, instruments and their techniques, pitch, and tunings. Other subjects that have traditionally been more closely associated with historical performance are treated only peripherally if at all. Thus, for Baroque music, the discussion of ornamentation is limited to six pages, rhythm to nine; for the Classical era, instrumental ornamentation, improvisation, and cadenzas are allotted a single chapter, vocal ornamentation part of a chapter, whereas tempo, articulation, phrasing, and dynamics are hardly mentioned. Thus the subject matter of the sections dealing with the 17th and 18th centuries overlaps only minimally with the present book.

In 1988 Roland Jackson, editor of *Performance Practice Review,* published *Performance Practice, Medieval to Contemporary: A Bibliographic Guide.* With its 1,392 annotated entries, which are regularly brought up to date in the journal just mentioned, it is a remarkable accomplishment and an indispensable tool for research.

Among books that deal with more specialized topics, studies of keyboard music are most numerous. Eva and Paul Badura-Skoda's *Interpreting Mozart on the Keyboard,* published in 1962, has the considerable distinction of considering the music first, the rules second. Paul Badura-Skoda's new, important book, *Bach Interpretation: Die Klavierwerke Johann Sebastian Bachs* (1990; an English translation is being prepared), similarly emphasizes musical considerations, despite its occasional dependence on a traditional "application" of C. P. E. Bach's rules.

Hans Klotz, in his 1984 book *Die Ornamentik der Klavier- und Orgelwerke von Johann Sebastian Bach,* seems to have set out to demonstrate the orthodox position that all of Bach's ornaments have to start on the beat and that all the trills have to start with the auxiliary.[4]

Sandra Rosenblum, in her 500-page book *Performance Practices in Classic Piano Music* (1988), takes yet a different approach: she presents and analyzes a multitude of musical passages, offering individual performance suggestions, but without attempting to extract from them more generalized guidelines. While still in part indebted to traditional interpretations, her suggestions often offer musically satisfying solutions.

In his 1988 book *Beethoven on Beethoven: Playing His Piano Music His Way*, William S. Newman summarized and expanded on his earlier preliminary studies, providing a great deal of valuable information and performance advice.

Jean-Pierre Marty's *The Tempo Indications of Mozart*, from 1988, is impressive in its all-inclusive survey and analysis of every single tempo marking in Mozart's works. Marty makes a truly revolutionary attempt to standardize all of Mozart's tempi by establishing a number of categories formed by tempo words plus meter signature, such as "Allegro ₵." Then he further subdivides these categories according to the prevailing prominence of quarter notes or eighth notes and their relationship as "main" or "secondary" impulses, forming such categories as "₵a" or "₵b," each of which is assigned a single "correct" tempo. Allegro ₵b appears more than two hundred times in works ranging from operatic recitatives, arias, and ensembles to overtures, symphonies, string quartets, sonatas, and so forth. Such a grouping of the most disparate forms, media, and numbers of performers raises questions about the fitness of exactly the same tempo for all. While Marty's is a masterful study that offers many a fresh perspective on Mozart's tempi, careful thought is in order before applying his standardized prescriptions.

Neil Zaslaw includes a chapter on orchestral performance practice in his important book on *Mozart's Symphonies* (1989). Here he deals interestingly and often provocatively with questions of string–wind balance, seating arrangements, localities, techniques including vibrato, tempo— including an interesting if unproven theory that there was a definite tempo relationship between the four movements of a symphony—and repeats, which Zaslaw insists should be respected (even in the da capo of a minuet). Max Rudolf had earlier made a case for such repeats ("Inner Repeats").

Regarding John Butt's *Bach Interpretation: Articulation Marks in the Primary Sources of J. S. Bach*, see chapter 18 of this book.

While not all the conclusions embodied in the studies just listed will withstand a critical enquiry, by and large, all this recent scholarly activity augurs well for the future of historical performance.

The present attempt at a broad and summary view of 17th- and 18th-century performance practices can make no claim to having all the answers. Nobody has and nobody will ever have them. But I do hope to have taken a few steps in the right direction and to have shed light on some gray areas. I have tried to find and correct earlier misconceptions, to extend the use of external and internal musical evidence, and to interpret theoretical data in a more cautious and I hope more discriminating manner than have some of my predecessors. And as to the educated guesses that are indispensable in filling the voids of knowledge, I hope to have proceeded correctly in handing a larger share of authority than many have to musical sense, taste, and intelligence at the expense of a strict adherence to rules derived from sundry old tracts. It is precisely such strict adherence to rules, in both theory and practice, that keeps dominating today's historical performances, often in defiance of musical common sense. While we must always reverently weigh and evaluate any principles formulated by eminent authorities, we might gain a better perspective on our present idolization of rules by recalling the irreverent thoughts that Johann Mattheson (1681–1764) had expressed on this very subject. On repeated occasions this remarkable diplomat-author-composer-theorist railed at the tyranny of rules and berated pedants who worshiped them as the supreme law of music. In 1713 he ridiculed as know-nothings "such would-be luminaries who believe that music has to follow their rules, when in truth their rules have to follow the music" (*Das neu eröffnete Orchestre*, 3). In 1722 he opined that "rules are valid as long as I consider it well and sensible to abide by them. They are valid no longer than that"; then in epigrammatic summary: "The rule of nature in music is nothing but the ear" (*Critica musica* 1:302, 338 n. z).

In sympathy with this spirit of Mattheson, the guiding idea of the present study was to go, in the many doubtful situations we shall encounter, by the music rather than "by the book."

# Part I

# Tempo

# 1

# TEMPO AND ITS ROOTS IN MENSURAL NOTATION

If we were to rank the various elements that combine to achieve a desirable performance of any work, the choice of the right tempo would easily occupy first place. Its preeminence can perhaps best be seen in the negative: nothing can distort a work or ruin its effect more completely than a tempo that is far off the mark. When what should be exhilarating turns out by faulty choice of tempo to be ennervating, what should be spirited turns dull, what should be contemplative or moving turns tedious and soporific, no amount of authentic sonorities and techniques will be able to compensate for such a defect. Frescobaldi already had stressed the primacy of tempo for the perfection of performance, and among later masters who come to mind having gone on record with the same opinion are Mozart, Beethoven, and Gustav Mahler; there are unquestionably many more.

Unfortunately, the problem of tempo is as difficult as it is important. Of all the major components of performance, the tempo, certainly for the two centuries of our main concern, may be the most elusive one. In the 19th and 20th centuries, the problem of tempo has been eased by the metronome but by no means solved. Brahms, Wagner, and Mahler used the metronome in early works, then gave it up in disenchantment with its shortcomings. Brahms explained with a rhetorical question: "Do you believe that I play the same every day?" Interesting is what Mahler had to say (at the time of his Third Symphony). Speaking of notation, he lamented that it is desperately inadequate in determining "by far the most important thing: the tempo and the total conception of a work, because here we have to do with something living, flowing, that can never be completely the same, not even twice in a row. Therefore metronome markings are inadequate and almost worthless, because the tempo must change already after the second measure if the work is not to be rattled off in a miserable hurdy-gurdy manner" (Killian, *Gustav Mahler*, 42). Beethoven had voiced a similar thought—namely, that after the first measures are passed, feeling must decide the tempo (Newman, *Beethoven on Beethoven*, 113).

The problem of tempo grows bigger the further we go back in time. For Mozart and Haydn we lack the crutch of the metronome and have to contend with the intrinsic vagueness of tempo words and the uncertainty of their connection with meter signatures. With Bach, Handel, and their contemporaries, we face a huge body of works, especially those for the keyboard, that have no tempo words at all. For the 17th century we meet the enormous difficulty posed by the slow, irregular, confusing, and near-chaotic transition from the mensural system of notating rhythm, which was still in use in 1600, to the modern metrical system. This transition occurred over the span of the whole century. During that period some composers had forgotten the original meaning of some of the symbols and by using them inappropriately added to the difficulties of interpretation. The muddle resulting from the intermingling of the two systems may never be resolved; but in order to grasp the problems of tempo in the 17th century, we need at least to understand the fundamentals of the mensural system. The following pages try to provide a basic overview.

## Mensural Notation and the Tactus

In the 16th century, with its mensural notation, the tempo was *theoretically* regulated by a standard beat, the tactus, its length referred to as *integer valor* (meaning the untouched, unchanged, and by implication unchangeable value). Theorists linked it with such natural rhythms as the heartbeat or a leisurely walk or defined it by the pronunciation of certain words in a simple manner. Whatever the definitions, they all seem to approximate the value of MM ca. 60–75. Though valuable as a rough reference point, the tactus was variable in practice and far from stable as some believe it to have been.

For the better part of the 16th century, the tactus referred to a semibreve (◇) but then gradually descended to smaller units; in the early part of the 17th century it often was the minim (𝅗𝅥) and by the end of the century occasionally the semiminim (♩), the modern quarter note. The tactus beat was composed of two motions, down and up, of equal duration for binary rhythms, unequal for ternary ones (namely, down for one–two and up for three).

"Mensuration" refers to the way a large note, beginning with the breve (◫), is divided into the smaller units, first into semibreves and they in turn into their subunits, the minims. The "mensuration signs" placed at the start of a piece specify these relationships between larger and smaller note values. Whereas in modern notation a regular note is always divided by two (a whole note into two half notes, a half note into two quarter notes, etc.), in mensural notation a breve as well as a semibreve can be divided into either two or three of its subunits. If a unit is divided in three, it is called "perfect," if in two, "imperfect," as shown in Fig. 1.1.

FIGURE 1.1

The division into three, which yields the equivalent of a ternary meter, was called perfect because the number three was hallowed by its reference to the Holy Trinity. The mensuration sign for the subdivision of the breve into three semibreves was appropriately a circle ( o ), the most perfect of geometrical figures. If the breve was subdivided into two semibreves, this relationship was imperfect and indicated by the imperfect half circle ( c ). The same principle holds on the next lower level: a semibreve is perfect (also called "major") when subdivided into three minims and imperfect (also called "minor") when subdivided into only two minims. The symbols used to designate these subdivisions are explained below.

Now, a perfect breve can be subdivided into either perfect semibreves or imperfect semibreves. Where a perfect (ternary) breve is subdivided into perfect (ternary) semibreves, this mensuration is indicated by the sign of a circle with a dot in its middle ( ⊙ ). It may be rendered into modern notation as $\frac{9}{8}$, in which three dotted quarters, each carrying a beat, are subdivided into three eighth notes each (Fig. 1.2).

FIGURE 1.2

The disparity of denominations in the equation shown in the figure is not so unreasonable as it might appear at first glance. A beat of approximately MM 70, which is appropriate for the perfect semibreve tactus, is reasonable as well for the modern dotted quarter note. Thus the minim of the original notation becomes a modern eighth note.

In the same way, when the perfect (ternary) breve is divided into imperfect (binary) semibreves, this mensuration is indicated by the plain, undotted circle. It is the equivalent of the modern $\frac{3}{4}$ meter, with a dotted half note divided into three quarter notes, each in turn divided into two eighth notes (Fig. 1.3).

FIGURE 1.3

The same two combinations are possible for the imperfect breve and semibreve: the imperfect breve can be divided into imperfect (binary) semibreves, as indicated by the plain half circle, in an equivalent of the modern $\frac{2}{4}$ meter; or it can be divided into perfect (ternary) semibreves, indicated by the sign of the half circle with a dot ( ͼ ), corresponding to the modern $\frac{6}{8}$ (Fig. 1.4).

FIGURE 1.4

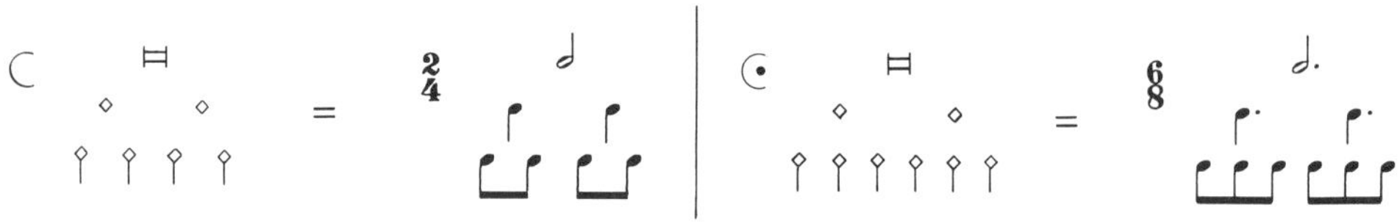

Because of the relative speed of the 16th-century semibreve, most modern transcriptions resort to reductions in note values, usually by two, but sometimes by four, in which case the semibreve, the carrier of the beat, becomes a quarter note (some modern editions of Lasso, Marenzio, and even Josquin tend to use unreduced values).

Minims and all smaller note values are always imperfect, that is, subject only to binary division. The composer had another alternative to these small note values, however: he could make use of diminution, the halving of the value of the notes with a corresponding doubling of the speed. Indicated by a vertical stroke through either the circle ( ⦶ ) or the half circle ( ¢ ), diminution shifts the tactus—at least theoretically—from the semibreve to the breve; hence the term *alla breve*. Yet in practice the cut half circle ₵ had by 1520 become the routine sign for duple meter with hardly any tempo implication.

Two more terms should be mentioned here simply because they show up frequently in discussions of this notation: *tempus* and *prolatio*. *Tempus* refers to the mensuration of the breve, its perfect or imperfect nature, referred to as *tempus perfectum* or *tempus imperfectum*. *Prolatio* refers similarly to the mensuration of the semibreve: "perfect (or major) prolation" (*prolatio perfecta*) and "imperfect (or minor) prolation" (*prolatio imperfecta*) refers respectively to the division of the semibreve into three or two minims. The dot that is placed within a circle or semicircle and that signifies the perfect nature of the semibreve is the "dot of prolation."

Although there were many more signs that greatly added to the complexity of the system, including combinations of symbols with numbers, the ones shown here are by far the most important ones. The **C** and the ₵ are of course still common today as the only survivors from mensural notation. But the circular signs, as well as the signs with a dot, still make frequent appearances in the 17th century and need to be understood.

The mensural system also provided for a variety of changes in metric meaning for single notes during the course of a piece. A perfect note could be changed into an imperfect one, for example, or could be otherwise reduced in value, through the use of "black" notation. This black notation, which was originally both complex and controversial (it could reduce note values by one-fourth, one-third, one-half, or not at all), survived in simplified form into the 17th century. Should a reader face these or other problems of mensural notation, it would be best to consult the standard work by Willi Apel, *The Notation of Polyphonic Music, 900–1600*, especially pages 96–185.

## *The Proportions*

As long as the mensural system lasted, the tactus continued to indicate a standard tempo, something later called a *tempo giusto* or *tempo ordinario*. It stands to reason, however, that music cannot live with just a single tempo. The necessary tempo changes could be effected in various ways. One was the use of smaller or larger denominations. Another was the change of the beat on the part of the director or, in the absence of a director, of the performers, who could modify the standard tactus, in deviation from textbook rules, when they felt it would serve the music better (Heinrich Glareanus, in his *Dodecachordon* of 1547, recommends tempo changes from section to section to avoid fatigue [quoted by C. Sachs, *Rhythm and Tempo*, 216]). The third and most important was the method called the "proportions," a system of equations that related the length of note values that preceded to those that followed. Not only could the tempo be changed in an exact mathematical ratio in this fashion, but the meter could be shifted from binary to ternary or vice versa.

The theory of the system of proportions was enormously complicated: from Gafurius in the mid-15th to Morley at the end of the 16th century, and even to Gregorio Strozzi as late as 1683, we find tables of extraordinary complexity. In practice, however (as Morley himself admits), only a handful of proportions were in common use. Five proportions were most important. The dupla ($\frac{2}{1}$) indicated that two of the following notes of equal nominal value corresponded to one of the preceding ones, thus doubling the tempo; the tripla ($\frac{3}{1}$) and the rarer quadrupla ($\frac{4}{1}$) tripled and quadrupled the tempo, with the tripla having the added effect of forming a triple meter. Intermediate tempo changes, both also attended by shifts in meter, were achieved by the sesquialtera ($\frac{3}{2}$), in which a binary meter was changed into a somewhat faster ternary meter by the substitution of three new notes for two old ones, and the sesquitertia ($\frac{4}{3}$), which caused a ternary meter to be changed into a slightly faster binary one. Other proportions did occur (Ganassi in his famous recorder treatise of 1535 used the $\frac{5}{4}$ and $\frac{7}{4}$ proportions) but became rarer as the 16th century progressed. Any of these proportions could be canceled by reversing the equation: thus $\frac{2}{3}$ after $\frac{3}{2}$ restores the original value of the notes. In Frescobaldi we often find the sesquialtera proportion written as $\frac{12}{8}$—i.e., twelve new notes of the same kind in the time of eight previous ones—which is then canceled by the sign of $\frac{8}{12}$, eight new notes in the time of twelve preceding ones.)

With its many signs (of which only the simplest have been shown here), its proportions, its rules for imperfection and alteration, and its black notation of many meanings, the mensural system was not only extremely complex but shot through with ambiguities. Arthur Mendel concludes his penetrating analysis of some of these uncertainties ("Some Ambiguities of the Mensural System") with "An Outline of Possible Alternatives or Conflicting Interpretations of Features of the Mensural System." This outline alone, covering seven pages, reveals the extraordinary intricacy of the system together with its inconsistencies and contradictions, showing why the system was destined to break down and make room for the far simpler, and by and large unambiguous, modern metrical notation. This process of dissolution, which started well before 1600 and perhaps even as early as 1520, took most of the 17th century to complete. During this transition period, the interweaving of the old with the new system created many uncertainties for both rhythm and tempo.

# 2

# Tempo and Proportions During the Transition to Modern Notation

## *Steady versus Flexible Tempo*

Essential to the concept of the *integer valor* as tactus, explained in the preceding chapter, was a standard, stable pulse. While proportions caused an instant change of rhythm and pulse, they did not affect the principle of stability: the new pulse proceeded with comparable steadiness.

Sixteenth-century vocal polyphony, the glory of the late Renaissance, culminating in the works of Palestrina and Lasso, is admiringly called by some the *ars perfecta*. This music was a citadel of steady tempo, as it had to be. In genuine and consistent polyphony—the earmarks of this style—steadiness of the beat is a logical requirement since tempo fluctuations prompted by the expressive needs of one voice are bound to conflict with similar needs of the simultaneous, independent voices. Free, elastic tempo modulations are generally practicable only in homophonic settings in which freedoms of tempo can be taken without disturbing vital parts of the musical texture. Much instrumental music also required a steady beat: by their very nature, dances, marches, military music, and music for ceremonial functions needed to maintain a steady movement.

But not all 16th century music was either consistently polyphonic or destined for dance or march. As in all times, there were solo songs that were not bound to a steady pulse. More important, during the 16th century there began to surface some stylistic mutations that were eventually (around 1600) to usher in the new Baroque style with its recitative, monody, and opera.

*Das Mottettische und das Madrigalische.* The new tendencies manifested themselves largely in connection with the relationship between words and music. Practiced during decades of solo song with lute accompaniment, these tendencies came to the fore most characteristically in the madrigal, first perhaps in the works of Cipriano de Rore (1516–65), whom Monteverdi identified as the pioneer of a new style. The characteristic feature of this new style is a far tighter link between the music and the text, a link that reflects closely the rhetorical and affective structure of the poem, that follows the rise and fall of its emotional tension, and that in the process often resorts to musical word painting. The ensuing word-directed ebb and flow strongly affected form, texture, and tempo. The form became freer and was sometimes sectionalized, with homophonic passages alternating with polyphonic ones. As a consequence the tempo lost its unity and became highly elastic as it adjusted to the momentary demands of the text. It was understandably the homophonic passages that most readily permitted and invited fluctuations of tempo. This new flexibility of form and tempo was carried to an extreme by Gesualdo in a fashion that is sometimes referred to as "manneristic."

The result of this development was a polarity of styles that Praetorius, writing in 1619, called "das Mottettische" and "das Madrigalische," the first referring to the classical *ars perfecta*, with its steady tempo and unity of form and character, the second to the new style that was flexible in form, tempo, rhythm, and texture (*Syntagma musicum*, 3:80). Thus the 17th century inherited from the stylistic dualism of the 16th both the convention of a steady tempo, associated with the "motet style," and the freely changing tempo, associated with the new "madrigal style."

This dualism is manifest in Monteverdi, who used the terms *prima prattica* for the motet style and *seconda prattica* for the madrigal style as well as for recitative and monody. Straddling both stylistic camps, he was the most eminent of the practitioners of the new style; yet he also composed masses, motets, vespers, and other sacred works in the style of the *prima prattica* and in many other works mixed the old and the new. Such a mixture is beautifully represented in his *Madrigali guerrieri et amorosi* (1638) in the piece "Non havea Febo ancora": here the first and third parts are to be sung *al tempo della mano*, meaning with a steady beat, whereas the middle section, the enchanting "Lamento della ninfa," is to be done *al tempo del'affetto del animo e non a quello della mano*, meaning that the tempo must not be steady but freely follow the expressed emotions. What we see here is a mixture of Praetorius's motet style with his madrigal style, a mixture that Praetorius recommends as a means of bringing variety to many types of music (*Syntagma musicum*, 3:80).

***Disintegration of the Mensural System.*** Near the end of the 16th century, mensural notation began to undergo a gradual transformation into the modern metrical system. Whereas the mensuration signs (theoretically) indicated—with reference to the *integer valor* of MM ca. 70—the absolute length of notes, and hence the tempo of a work, the new meter signatures had no built-in link with a standard beat but indicated rather the inner structure of the measures, which were organized in patterns of heavy and light beats. Yet the link between denomination and actual length of notes was not completely broken in the new system. Rather, it continued in a qualified, more casual form up to about the mid-18th century in the sense that long note values were meant to be rendered fairly long and short values fairly short. This link was not broken until the time of Beethoven, when a sixteenth-note *lento* could become the equivalent of a whole note *presto*.

The transition from mensural to metrical notation was a complex process that created uncertainty and confusion. In keeping with the "cultural lag" observed by sociologists for all periods of transitions, the old mensural symbols continued to be used; but their original meanings were evaporating, and they gradually passed from the consciousness of practicing musicians. Though a number of theorists continued for almost another century to expound the principles of mensural notation, composers became unsure of, or lost interest in, the complexities of the many symbols; and, by using them improperly, they confounded their contemporaries as well as today's scholars and musicians. The fact that many passages in, say, Monteverdi or Schütz are given discrepant rhythmic interpretations by various modern editors suggests that the mensural textbook solutions have become unreliable.[1] As Professor Alejandro E. Planchart points out, composers such as Gabrieli, Monteverdi, Praetorius, or Schütz, in trying to cope with the disintegration of the mensural system, developed their own ad hoc solutions (letter to author). Since the ensuing notational mannerisms understandably differed from one another, they have to be individually explored and interpreted.

The resulting disarray of the mensural system is described in a number of documents. Banchieri writes in 1614 of composers who create admirable works but "resort to great abuses in matters of proportions, using the figures indiscriminately; and we see others who contradict themselves in one and the same work" (Altri [conpositori] poi vi sono che nelle conpositioni riescono mirabili, ma nelle proportioni usano grandi abusi segnando gli numeri indeferentemente, & alcuni vediamo che in un opera istessa si contradiscono [*Cartella*, 168]).

Johann Kretschmar writes in 1605: "Nowadays musicians use these [mensural] signs indiscriminately" (Heutigen Tages brauchen die Musici diese Zeichen gantz und gar ohne Unterscheid), pointing among others at the signs   o𝟐̸, c𝟑̸ , ₃ (*Musica latino-germanica*, fol. 8r).

Praetorius, speaking in 1619 of proportions in unequal tactus (see chap. 1, p. 17, about the meaning of "unequal tactus"), tells us that many composers do not follow their own prescriptions but indiscriminately use one sign for another ("Verum tamen plurimos sua ipsorum praecepta non observare, & indiscretè unum [signum] pro altero usurpare video" [*Syntagma musicum*, 3:53]). Speaking of proportions in equal (i.e., binary) tactus, he not only calls those signs of the "old timers" useless but declares them to be nothing but "an aberration and confusion that disturbs, obstructs, and confuses the young people in the schools along with even experienced vocal and instrumental chapel musicians."[2]

Daniel Friderici in 1624 confirms this state of confusion when he says that composers do not any more observe the difference between tripla ($\frac{3}{1}$) and sesquialtera ($\frac{3}{2}$). It is then up to the director, he says, to beat either of them slower or faster according to the meaning of the text (*Musica figuralis* [1624], chap. 6, n. p.). In other words, the signs $\frac{3}{1}$ and $\frac{3}{2}$ —and other signs as well—have lost their proportional meaning.

Christoph Demantius in 1611 points to the synonymity of various signs for ternary rhythm when "three semibreves or three minims are sung in one tactus." This mensuration, he says, is indicated by the figure **3**, which "is sometimes written by itself, sometimes in combination with other signs: ₃, ⊘𝟑̸, ⊙𝟐̸, c𝟑̸, ¢₃, c₃ , *but all these different signs indicate the same tact [meter] and the same mensuration*" (einerley Tact und gleiche Mensur); furthermore, there is no difference in the relationship between the notes: "Tactus and note values . . . are identical" (Der Tact und der Valor oder die Geltung derselben ist einerley [*Isagoge artis musicae*, n. p.]).

To get a better perspective on the profusion and confusion of mensural signs after 1600 we must recall that, as mentioned in the preceding chapter, there were already uncertainties during the 16th century about the meaning of some signs as well as contradictions within the system. And, as has been pointed out, the tempo fluctuations of the madrigal had begun to undermine the whole system. Thus while some modern writers have assumed, based on theorists' continuing descriptions of the principles of proportions, that an elaborate system was still fully operational in the 17th century, genuine proportions in fact survived only in fragmentary fashion.

## The Emergence of the Modern Metrical System

Composers in Italy, who were in the musical avant-garde, were apparently the first to begin to discard the proportions. The spreading use of tempo words is by itself a clear indication that the proportions were not functioning properly any more.

In the preface to his *Il primo libro di capricci canzon Francese e recercari* (1624), containing works in strict style, Frescobaldi writes that sections in ternary rhythm ("in tripla or sesquialtera") are to be played adagio when in semibreves (◇ ◇ ◇); "somewhat faster" when in minims (♩♩♩); faster still in semiminims (♩♩♩), and allegro in 𝄴 (i.e., in fusae, the modern eighth notes). This passage is incompatible with a continued authority of the proportions and thus proclaims their de facto demise. Tempo is now no longer indicated by the mensural signs but is suggested by the prevalence of certain denominations whose guidance is, of course, only vague and far from mathematical.

Friderici's observations in 1624 about the confusion of tripla and sesquialtera (see p. 24) had similar implications; and Praetorius makes the remarkable statement that the director will choose a slow or fast beat "with regard to word meaning and musical context"(ex consideratione textus et harmoniae), hence *not* with regard to proportions (*Syntagma musicum*, 3:51).

Small wonder that at the dawn of the 17th century, with the rise of a new style in full swing, the old order, with its elaborate system of symbols, found itself in the state of dissolution so vividly portrayed by the above quotations. Not surprisingly, the *New Grove Dictionary of Music and Musicians* (s.v. "Notation") points out—echoing the above quotation from Demantius—that in the 17th century the signs ¢, o, c3, c⅜, ¢⅜, 3, and ⅜ were often used interchangeably for quick triple time. Professor Planchart points out, however, that the Grove article makes the situation look worse than it actually was in the 17th century: "Some of those signs, in my experience, are *never* used for a *fast* triple meter." He then comments on these signs and their meanings around 1600:

**3** by itself is already by 1600 a problematic sign and can mean either tripla or sesquialtera of the preceding duple meter.

¢⅜ indicates a very fast triple meter; "this is a way composers could make sure that everyone understood they meant a true tripla."

c⅜ was used by "a composer taking no chances in indicating a true sesquialtera."

¢3: "since the middle of the 16th century this is the one safe sign to indicate 'keep the same ¢ pulse but subdivide each beat in three.'"

c**3** means the "same as the preceding sign but at a slow tempo (though [by now] no longer twice as slow as ¢ )." (letter to author)

In binary measure tactus and beat were theoretically represented by a semibreve in c and by a breve in ¢ . But in practice, as Professor Planchart points out, ¢ had become by 1520 the standard duple meter with no tempo implications and with a semibreve, not a breve, tactus. For more on the use and meaning of c and ¢ , see chapter 5.

In the 17th century, a further step away from the old and toward the modern system is the growing custom of placing proportional signs such as $\frac{3}{1}$, $\frac{3}{2}$, $\frac{6}{4}$, or just **3** at the start of a work instead of at the point of rhythmic change. Placed at the start, they cease to be proportions since they do not relate to what precedes and are de facto meter signatures. The same is true of the French signs **2**, ¢ , **3**, or $\frac{3}{2}$, common around 1600 at the beginnings of pieces in lute tablatures, in *airs de cour*, or in the royal ballets (see for the latter the Collection Philidor in the Bibliothèque Nationale [fonds du conservatoire]); like the Italian mensuration signs, these are similarly indistinguishable from modern meter signatures. Modern in concept, too, are Lully's signs  c , ¢ , **2**, **3**, **4**, $\frac{3}{2}$, $\frac{6}{4}$, $\frac{3}{8}$, $\frac{6}{8}$ for his dances, overtures, airs, and so forth.

Even where proportional fractions occurred in mid-piece, where they may have been meant to be read as genuine proportions, they functioned simultaneously to indicate the rhythmic organization of the following section. In other words, those fractions have the Janus face of old proportions and new meter signatures, and more and more the latter.

Such overlapping of meanings explains why, in the 17th century, we find so many instances of triple meters that are so difficult to interpret. Should a new signature of, for instance, $\frac{3}{1}$ be treated strictly according to the proportional rules, or should it be read as $\frac{3}{2}$ or be handled freely as an unmathematical change of rhythm and tempo? In such doubtful cases it might be advisable first to try out the literal meaning of $\frac{3}{1}$ and see whether it makes for a logical connection. Such a connection is necessary when the proportional sign occurs in mid-phrase, so to speak. If the $\frac{3}{1}$ seems too abrupt, without a textual cue that would suggest such abruptness, then the $\frac{3}{2}$ might make better musical sense. Where the sign occurs after a full cadence, the exact ratio will often be of minor importance.

The metrical implications of the fractions show, furthermore, how the modern notational system could gradually infiltrate the old and could become functional before theorists could catch up with the evolution and explain the structure of the new system. It is not possible to give a definite date for this transformation, first because the change was gradual and second because there were, as was to be expected, progressives and conservatives in every country. If, as we have seen, Frescobaldi at the start of the century was progressive in linking tempo changes to denominations and affect rather than to proportions, Georg Muffat in Germany, at the century's end, was conservative in still writing certain works with mensural procedures of imperfection, alteration, and blackened notes at a time when such methods partook of antiquarianism.

Clearly, the 17th century was a confusing age, with its bewildering mixture of the old and the new, the fading of traditions, and the emergence of new principles. The resulting uncertainties have provided a fertile ground for modern scholarly controversies about the continuing role of the proportions and of other elements of the mensural inheritance, such as the *integer valor*.

*Praetorius's Average Tactus.* Praetorius, who was one of very few writers to provide clock measurements for tempi, lists for an average tempo ("einen rechten mittelmässigen Tact") 640 *tempora* (i.e., breves) per hour (*Syntagma musicum,* 3:87–88). This calculation amounts to an approximate length of 5½ seconds for a breve and thus (assuming duple division of both breve and semibreve) 2¾ seconds for a semibreve, 1⅜ seconds for a minim, and slightly less than ¾ second for a semiminim. The semibreve would be equivalent to MM 21—too slow for a practical beat. For such "mittelmässigen Tact," the beat could have fallen either on the minim at MM ca. 42 or on the semiminim at MM ca. 84, which would be the closest value to the old *integer valor*.

*The Frequent Need for Exact Ratios in Changing Rhythms.* In order better to understand the problems of proportional signs, we must realize that in certain circumstances an exact ratio between successive meters is a musical necessity, a matter of musical logic as cogent today as it was then. The circumstances in question are metrical changes that occur within a musical continuum, notably those that happen in mid-phrase. The difference between now and then is only in notation: what was written in the 17th century as a proportion symbol is now written in the form of an equation of metronome markings or of note values (such as $\downarrow. = \downarrow$), with words like *l'istesso tempo* or *doppio movimento,* or by spelling out binary–ternary transitions with triplets or duplets. (See, for instance, the *alla breve* in the middle of the "Eroica" Scherzo, where the metronome markings clearly equate the whole note to the former dotted half in a pure $\frac{4}{3}$ sesquitertia proportion.)

Whenever we encounter such mid-phrase changes in 17th-century music, we have to assume a proportional meaning but one that does not necessarily conform to the orthodox formulas for the symbols notated. Since, as we have seen, various ternary symbols were often used indiscriminately, we have to be alert to the possibility that $\frac{3}{1}$, for instance, may have been intended to indicate not the tripla but the sesquialtera, and once in a while even the sextupla $\frac{6}{1}$. Often, however, the literal meaning will make good musical and declamatory sense, while occasional minor adjustments seem to be called for.

A case of textual and musical continuum across a mensuration change is shown in Ex. 2.1a, from Schütz's "Verbum caro" (*Kleine geistliche Concerte* II/9). At the change from $\frac{3}{1}$ to C  the exclamation "Alleluja" continues and so does its motive (with the thirds filled in) while the tempo slows, if we observe the proportional ratio. There is a temptation to read the change to C not as $\frac{1}{3}$ but as $\frac{1}{2}$, as ⬦ ⬦ = ⬦, which would keep the rhythm of the motive intact. But to do so would be presumably wrong because it would illogically speed the tempo of the recurrent "et habitavit." Later in the piece we find a mensuration change to C in mid-word (Ex. 2.1b), where the literal meaning of ⬦ ⬦ ⬦ = ⬦ makes the best sense. In Ex. 2.1c, from "Wohl dem" (*Kleine geistliche Concerte* I/9), the signature change occurs in the middle of the same repeated words ("it succeeds well") and the same motive, but here the slowing of the motive with the C meter makes good sense as an emphatic reassertion.

In Ex. 2.1d, from "Ich liege" (*Kleine geistliche Concerte* II/5), the initial C meter has to be beaten slowly so that on its later occurrence in the piece (Ex. 2.1e) the melisma on "Zähne" has sufficient space to be rendered clearly. The slow beat fits the initial words: "I am lying down and sleeping." In the brief $\frac{3}{1}$ episode the words "and awaken, and awaken" might suggest a slight hurrying beyond the proportion. That Schütz did not expect mathematical precision is shown in a number of cases where he uses tempo words both at proportional signs and in mid-meter. They all point to freely chosen tempo changes.[3]

EXAMPLE 2.1.    Schütz, *Kleine geistliche Concerte*

a. II/9, "Verbum caro"

Sop. II

et ha - bi - ta - - - - - vit in no - bis    Al - le - lu - ja

Al - le - lu - ja   Al - le - lu - ja    Al - le - lu - ja et ha - bi - ta - - - -

Sop. I

b. II/9, "Verbum caro"

Sop. I

(ta) - vit in no - bis      et ve - ri - ta - - te

c. I/9, "Wohl dem"

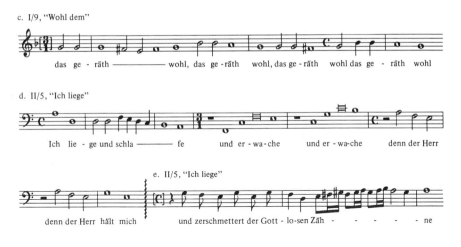

d. II/5, "Ich liege"

e. II/5, "Ich liege"

Some scholars propose that the sequence $c-\frac{3}{1}-c$ should be rendered according to the orthodox rule of $c \diamond = \frac{3}{1} \diamond \diamond \diamond$. Arthur Mendel, among others, argues for this ratio and adduces striking proof from one passage in Schütz's *Musicalische Exequien,* shown in Ex. 2.2. A sole surviving part book for the quintus (a fifth voice part added to the four standard ones) of this work has no change of signature where the tenor has the change from $c$ to $\frac{3}{1}$. Instead it continues in $c$ with forty-seven semibreve rests. This makes sense only if the beat for the semibreve remains unchanged for the section in $\frac{3}{1}$. Mendel, however, registers a small "hedge": since the strict mathematical ratio would slow the declamation for the $\frac{3}{1}$ section, he suggests a slight speeding up. Such adjustments of the beat, he says, are not excluded by the notation.[4]

FIGURE 2.2.  Schütz, *Musicalische Exequien*

* Here the black notation does not alter the note values. It simply shows syncopation.

This kind of textbook solution, with or without minor adjustments, makes good sense when the beat comprises a semibreve, as it mostly did: then the beat remains the same, and three new semibreves take the place of one old one and vice versa on return to $c$: $c \diamond \quad \frac{3}{1} \diamond \diamond \diamond \quad c \diamond \diamond \diamond$.

When, however, the beat had descended to the minim (half note) or even the semiminim (quarter note), as it occasionally did in the 17th century, an exact proportional transition is harder. In this case, given the era's casual attitude toward tempo, the director or individual performer is likely to have made an approximate, rather than a mathematical, adjustment of the beat.

***Modern Meter Signatures.*** In Carissimi's *Ars cantandi,* which, although it survives only in an anonymous German translation of 1689, probably dates from mid-century, we find such signs as $\frac{3}{4}$ and $\frac{3}{8}$ described with a clear metrical meaning. The author clarifies the break with mensural traditions by rejecting for modern use the many signs and figures of the "ancients" and their "queer" (wunderliche) terms such as dupla, tripla, quadrupla, hemiola, subdupla, and many others. For binary meters Carissimi lists only c for a slow ("gravitätisch") tempo and ¢ for one twice as fast. For the ternary meters he declares the ternary mensural symbols of o and φ as unnecessary and outdated. He lists in their stead the following types of tripla with the meter–tempo relations that became a standard pattern later in the century: (1) the "whole triple" (gantzer Tripel), $\frac{3}{1}$ with three semibreves (whole notes) in a measure, used in slow works; (2) the "half triple" (halber Tripel), $\frac{3}{2}$ with three half notes in a measure, for somewhat livelier pieces; (3) the "quarter triple" (viertels Tripel), $\frac{3}{4}$ with three quarter notes in a measure, for a faster tempo than $\frac{3}{2}$, as used in "Arieten" and for gay, amusing materials; and (4) the "eighth triple" (Achtels Tripel), $\frac{3}{8}$ with three eighth notes per measure for still faster tempos. Carissimi further lists the "six-eighth triple" (sechsachtels Tripel), $\frac{6}{8}$ with two even beats that in turn have ternary subdivisions (*Ars cantandi,* 14–15).

In 1656 the French theorist de La Voye Mignot, like Carissimi, declares the signs o, ⊙, o$\frac{3}{2}$, and φ$\frac{3}{2}$ to be old and obsolete ("antien et non usitez") and explains meter according to its strictly modern meaning. There are, he says, only two kinds of meters: binary and ternary. The binary signs are c for a slow, ¢ for a fast beat, while **2** occasionally takes the place of either. As ternary signatures he lists c3 for slow, ¢$\frac{3}{3}$ (meaning $\frac{3}{2}$) for a fast beat, while **3** can be either slow or fast (*Traité de musique,* 11–12).

Michelangelo Rossi, in his *Toccate e corrente d'intavolatura d'organo e cimbalo* (1657), begins all the toccatas in c. A few have sections in $\frac{6}{4}$ or in **3**, with no obvious need for specific proportional ratios. The correntes are all in **3**, with a clear modern meaning of $\frac{3}{4}$.

# Summary

It will be advisable to take a more relaxed and undoctrinaire approach to 17th-century proportions regardless of contemporary theorists' continuing explanation of them and several modern theorists' strict interpretation of them. Theorists are often retrospective and also have the inveterate tendency to make matters appear more complicated than they are. Thus theory frequently lags behind the times while composition moves forward to new procedures. It will be well to be alert to the probability that the old mensural and proportional signs were in fact often used in modern metrical meaning.

Especially when proportional signs occur between distinct, thematically independent sections within a piece, as for instance in a toccata, capriccio, or canzona, there will hardly ever be a need for mathematical ratios. When proportions do occur within the far more sensitive context of a musical continuum, then it behooves us to try to explore the composer's intention by considering which of the following alternatives make the best musical sense: (1) the orthodox meaning of the fraction; (2) the substitution of sesquialtera for tripla; (3) a free, nonmathematical choice of tempo. In other words, we have to figure out how to satisfy the need for coherence in a way that is logical, musical, and practical.

# 3

# FLEXIBLE TEMPO
# AFTER 1600

## The Recitative and Related Forms

The epitome of flexible tempo is recitative, which is free from the confines of a steady beat and follows instead the free rhythm of prose declamation. The antecedents of recitative can be traced, as intimated in the preceding chapter, to the madrigals of the second half of the 16th century, which were intensely responsive to word meanings and in which homophonic sections often contained passages in pure speech rhythms.

The recitative proper was born, or rather invented, in late 16th-century Florence. With the madrigal as pathfinder, recitative issued from humanistic endeavors to re-create Greek drama. Girolamo Mei, a philologist who had thoroughly researched all available surviving documents on Greek music, arrived at the conclusion that Greek dramas were not spoken but sung. Mei communicated his conclusions to like-minded musicians, amateurs, and scholars who regularly met with artists, philosophers, and writers, all of whom were united in their enthusiasm about the reconstruction, the *renaissance,* of classical theater and drama. It was in its way a 16th-century counterpart to our present-day search for "authentic" performance practices. Out of these deliberations arose the theory that a musical style that lay between speech and song was the answer they had been searching for. Musicians like Cavalieri, Peri, and Caccini realized such a style in the recitative (*stile recitativo* or *rappresentativo*). The answer was historically incorrect, since Greek music did not know any accompaniment and was limited to melody alone. But the product of this flawed research, the recitative, has remained a powerful force in music ever since.

The hallmark of the recitative is the supremacy of the word and the striving for a musical line that, in melody and in rhythm, conforms to the declamatory inflections of speech. The Italians spoke of *recitare cantando* (roughly, to recite in pitch). Throughout the history of recitative, freedom from an exact beat—a freedom that permits such adaptation—has been one of its chief characteristics. In Monteverdi's *Lettere amorose* we encounter the instruction "senza battuta" (without a beat).

In the early years of the 17th century, recitative was closely linked both with monody (i.e., solo song accompanied by the recently developed basso continuo) and the newly invented opera. In both monody and opera, recitative leaned toward oratorical delivery, which meant that tempo fluctuations, which were unquestionably practiced, were presumably only modest. In monody such fluctuations created no problem, and in opera too they were practicable because the orchestra was small and the players of the continuo instruments probably had the words written into their parts.

As arioso sections, which sprouted from the recitative, developed into regular arias, the arias were increasingly set apart from the recitatives. Now the recitative came to serve as a narrative link between arias that expressed feelings rather than reported events. In the ensuing polarity of aria and recitative, the latter became less and less oratorical, until in the Italian opera buffa it turned into the *parlando* manner of fast exchanges patterned on everyday speech with hardly a trace of a distinct beat left. Accompanied by keyboard and basses, this type of recitative was called *semplice* and is today better known by the later term of *secco* (meaning dry).

Alongside this *recitativo secco*, the end of the 17th century saw the emergence of a different type, the *accompagnato*, with the whole orchestra, or at least the strings, participating in the accompaniment. Such larger participation limited the freedom of tempo but did not eliminate it. Notably in passages framed by orchestral interjections, the singer was free to follow the lead of diction rather than that of the beat.

***Recitative in Germany.*** The Italian recitative style only slowly made its way into Germany. In the *Psalmen Davids* of 1619, Heinrich Schütz introduced what he called the "stylo recitativo," which as he writes in his preface was "up to now almost unknown in Germany." Here the style is still limited to choral declamation in speech rhythm. Schütz urges the singers not to hurry the tempo ("sich im Tact ja nicht obereylen") but to maintain a happy medium that will permit them to recite the words in a comprehensible manner. Four years later, in his *Historia der . . . Auferstehung* (Resurrection Story), Schütz resorts for the Evangelist's narration to the genuine soloistic Italian recitative. In the preface he instructs the Evangelist "to recite his part without any steady beat, just as he thinks it proper, without sustaining any syllable more than is done in usual slow and comprehensible orations" (Der Evangelist nimpt seine *partey* für sich, und *recitiret* dieselbe ohne einigen *tact,* wie es ihm bequem deuchtet, hinweg). For the four viols that accompany the Evangelist, Schütz urges thorough rehearsal and careful attention not to the beat but to the words that are written into their parts.

Schütz's only opera, *Dafne,* is unfortunately lost. In it he unquestionably used the Italian style of recitative. But apart from Schütz, recitative remained largely unknown in Germany. The devastations of the Thirty Years War (1618–48) had a paralyzing effect on Germany and effectively disrupted any artistic intercourse with Italy or other countries. For the same reason, opera was very slow to gain a foothold in Germany before the end of the 17th century. Around the turn of the century, however, Reinhard Keiser adopted the Italian recitative in his operas, and Johann Philipp Krieger (1649–1725), who had studied for two years in Italy, introduced the recitative into his church music (he wrote no less than 2,000 cantatas!). Krieger may have served as a model for Bach's methodical and consistent use of recitative in his vocal music. Bach's genuine recitatives ought to be rendered with a flexible tempo yielding to the declamatory demands of the words. I said "genuine" because Bach names many a movement "Recitative" in which a declamatory melody has an obbligato accompaniment of a kind that calls for a steady beat (for two out of many examples, see Cantata No. 40/5, Cantata No. 42/2).

Mozart's use of the recitative, both *accompagnato* and *secco,* in his Italian operas is well known. In his German operas, he uses the *accompagnato* on a few special occasions only. Haydn, who used recitative in his operas in a manner identical to Mozart's, introduced the recitative in his two great German oratorios.

According to J. A. Westrup (*MGG,* s.v. "Rezitativ"), Handel was the first to introduce the recitative in England, first in his operas and later in his oratorios, and served there as a model for such English masters as William Boyce, Thomas Arne, and others.

*The French Recitative.* The French were not receptive to the Italian-type recitative, which they believed was unsuited to the nature of the French language. Italian prosody, like its German and English counterparts, is based on accentuation; French prosody, in view of a lack of distinct accentuation, is based primarily on length and shortness of syllables (like that of the classical languages). It was the Italian-born Lully, the father of French opera (*tragédie lyrique*), who invented a new type of recitative that was uniquely fitted to the character of French declamation. He studied the diction of tragic actors at the Comédie Française and made a conscious effort to translate it into musical terms by reflecting both the pitch inflections and the quantitative ratios between syllables.

He devised an ingenious system in which frequent changes of meter, mainly between c, ¢, **2**, **3**, and $\frac{3}{2}$, allowed for a smoothly flowing execution.

The meter changes create beat equivalence problems that do not always have simple answers. Étienne Loulié, in manuscript additions to his treatise of 1696, discusses the problem and writes: "When a composition changes meter because of the words, in order that certain long syllables coincide with the downbeat, the time value of a beat [in one meter] should be equal to that of [a beat in] the other, even though the note values are not equal."[1] He illustrates this principle with a passage from an air in Lully's *Roland* where in the sequence

the half note in c equals the quarter note in **3** meter. Generally, a similar beat equivalence is likely also for the recitative, and Lois Rosow, in a fine paper, "The Metrical Notation of Lully's Recitative," supports this view for "the vast majority of passages of recitative."[2] But problems remain, for instance when both **2** and ¢ occur in the same recitative, occasionally in neighboring measures: whereas the **2** was always beaten in two, the c could be sometimes beaten in fast four, which alone can create ambiguities. Also, there are passages in which the theoretical beat equivalence does not make for the best melodic-rhythmic-prosodic flow; in such cases adjustments seem to be called for. Since the French recitative did not have a steady beat either and, as Rosow points out (411), was not conducted but left to the singer's judgment, the ensuing rhythmic flexibility allowed adjustments to suit the declamatory and musical logic of the situation.

The Lullian type of recitative remained alive at least until and including Rameau. The next generation of French masters simplified the meter: throughout Mondonville's *Les fêtes de Paphos* (1758), for example, long recitatives in **3** meter are interspersed with passages marked *mesuré*, which in turn reflect on the unmetrical nature of the remainder. For a broadening at the final cadence Mondonville often goes into the **2** meter, with the clear equivalence of **3** ♩.=**2** ♩ .

The continuing elasticity of tempo is confirmed in 1769 by Lécuyer, who writes that in "scènes" and "monologues" (containing recitatives) the tempo is not strict; that one can allow certain notes and ornaments to stretch out ("se pavaner"), but one must clearly articulate the musical lines—that is, clearly distinguish the long and the short, mark the rests, and dwell only on verbs that signify an action or a movement; and that above all one must always reflect the meaning of the words ("aller droit au sens"). In *airs mesurés et de caractère* one must never alter the tempo (*Principes du chant*, 22–23).

Like its Italian counterpart, the French recitative must speak, even though it speaks in the elevated prose of dramatic declamation. Yet its tempo seems to have been on the whole rather fast. On that point we gain a fascinating insight in a letter from Telemann to Carl Heinrich Graun, who had criticized the French recitative with its frequent changes of meter. In his answer, Telemann defends the French manner by writing that "the changes in meter cause no difficulty for the French. [The recitative] keeps rapidly flowing along [as smoothly] as champagne" (Es läuft alles nacheinander fort, wie Champagnerwein [quoted by Rosow, "French Baroque Recitative," 468]).

## *Other Vocal Forms*

While recitative is the most striking instance in vocal music for great freedom of tempo, there were other types of compositions that called for greater or lesser flexibility of tempo. As early as 1555, Nicola Vicentino asks for free changes of the tempo ("muovere la misura") in order better to express words, passions, and harmonies. "And sometimes one uses a certain way of proceeding in the composition that cannot be written down—such as to sing *piano* and *forte,* and to sing *presto* and *tardo,* moving the measure according to the words to demonstrate the effects of the passions of the words and of the harmony. . . . And the composition sung with changes of tempo is more pleasing in its variety than that which is sung without being varied all the way to the end."[3] Vicentino then refers to the orator, who speaks now loud, now soft, now slower, now faster. Most likely he had the madrigal in mind without necessarily limiting his remarks to that genre. One page before (fol. 88r), he stresses the importance of recognizing the character of the music and points to singers who betray their poor judgment and understanding ("poco giuditio, & poca consideratione") when they sing a sad passage joyfully and a joyful passage sadly.

Lodovico Zacconi in 1592 speaks of *stringere* and *allargare*—that is, speeding up and slowing down "con maniera" (with taste), without referring to any specific type of music (*Prattica di musica,* fol. 22r).

Michael Praetorius devotes a chapter to variations of tempo and dynamics. In principle, he says, the beat should be steady. But with a view to the text, the alternation of faster and slower "miraculously adorns the song by its singular majesty and grace" (singularem majestatem & gratiam habet, & cantum mirificè exornat [*Syntagma musicum,* 3:79]).

As mentioned before, Praetorius distinguishes the motet and the madrigal styles, of which the first had a steady tempo, the second a flexible one. Now he states as a general principle that the motet and the madrigal styles should be mixed and that motets as well as vocal concertos should be given more charm and grace ("Lieblich- und Anmütigkeit") by many changes from slow to fast, accompanied by changes from loud to soft in order to avoid monotony ("damit nicht allzeit in einem Tono und Sono fortgehe" [*Syntagma musicum*, 3:80]). Such tempo changes, he says, are a matter of discriminating judgment: "Anyone can reflect on these matters and upon considering text and music conclude where the tempo should be fast and where slow" (Es kann aber ein jeder den Sachen selbsten nachdenken, und ex consideratione Textus & Harmoniae observiren, wo ein langsamer oder geschwinder Tact gehalten werden müsse [3:51]).

In 1624 Daniel Friderici writes: "In vocal works the beat must not be uniform but adjust to the words of the text. Those cantors err who measure the beat as mechanically as a clockwork measures its minutes and ignore the decorum and needs of text and music [observiren ganz kein decorum und convenientz des Textus und der Harmonie], because some places call for a fast, others for a slow beat" (*Musica figuralis*, [1624], Regula 19, n. p.).

In France, Marin Mersenne in his *Harmonie universelle* of 1636 allows for acceleration or retardation in accord with the words or the different emotions of the subject. But he advises the composer who wants to have several notes or measures to be played faster or slower than the rest to indicate it with special signs in order to insure compliance with the composer's intentions (*Harmonie universelle: Traitez des consonances*, 2:359).

Bénigne de Bacilly in 1668 expresses an idea similar to Friderici's: "I don't doubt that the variety of tempo of fast and slow contributes much to the expression of a song" (*Remarques sur bien chanter*, 200).

Toward the end of the 17th century and throughout the late Baroque period, the increasing textural enrichment of vocal genres by polyphonic penetration limited, and largely excluded, tempo variations. Choruses by Handel, Bach, or, say, Charpentier or De La Lande should probably not have their tempi tampered with; nor is it likely that duets or arias with orchestral accompaniment deviated markedly from the established beat.

In arias with continuo, however, subtle freedoms taken by the soloist that did not threaten the ensemble must have been rather commonplace. Johann Mattheson, who sees the main responsibility of the director to be in the establishment of the proper tempo, writes that it should be steady but also flexible enough to accommodate a soloist's tastefully executed ornament by a slight slowing down or by a slight speeding up in response to the demands of expression (*Vollkommene Capellmeister*, pt. 3, chap. 26, par. 13). Here, too, texture will matter a great deal. In homophonic works, including those of the Classical masters, *subtle* shadings of tempo will often be called for and, if done with sensitivity, will not be a stylistic misdemeanor, whereas in richly polyphonic choral movements tempo changes in mid-stream that transcend the scope of nuance can be objectionable if not specified in the score.

# Instrumental Works

Freedom of tempo in 17th-century vocal works found its counterpart in certain instrumental works as well, notably those that were improvisatory in nature, such as toccatas, preludes, and related forms of idiomatic keyboard music. In their declamatory character all these works had a kinship to both the madrigal and the recitative.

*Italy.* From Italy we have a fascinating account in Frescobaldi's preface to his first book of toccatas of 1615–16, which might well be the most important theoretical document on 17th-century instrumental performance practice. While this preface touches on several aspects of interpretation, I shall cite in the following those sections that have a bearing on tempo.

After an opening preamble Frescobaldi gives a series of performance directives in numbered paragraphs, including the following. (In view of the importance of this document, the original text of the quoted sections is shown side-by-side with its translation.)

1. First, this playing style must not be subjected to a steady beat; [instead] it should follow the performance of modern madrigals, which, though difficult, are well served by tempo variations: now languid, now fast, now sustained in keeping with the prevailing expression or the meaning of the words. . . .

1. Primieremente; che non dee questo modo di sonare stare soggetto à battuta, come ueggiamo usarsi ne i Madrigali moderni, i quali quantunque difficili si ageuolano per mezzo della battuta portandola hor languida, hor ueloce, è sostenendola etiando in aria secondo i loro affeti, ò senso delle parole. . . .

3. The beginnings of toccatas should be played slowly and arpeggiando; in suspensions or [other] dissonances and in the middle of the piece [the notes] should be struck together in order not to leave the instrument empty, and they may be so restruck at the player's choice. . . .[4]

3. Li cominciamenti delle toccate sieno fatte adagio, et arpeggiando: e così nelle ligature, ò uero durezze come, anche nel mezzo del opera si batteranno insieme, per non lasciar uoto l'Istromento: il qual battimento ripiglierassi à beneplacito di qui suona. . . .

5. Even when cadences look fast on paper, it is proper to sustain them strongly; in approaching the ends of sections or cadences the tempo should be held back. . . .

5. Le cadenze benche sieno scritte veloce conuiene sostenerle assai; e nello accostarsi il concluder de passaggi ò cadenze si anderà sostendendo il tempo più adagio. . . .

9. When we find [florid] passages or expressive sections in
variation works [nelle Partite]
it is advisable to play them
slowly; the same applies to
toccatas. Sections devoid of
passage work can be played
somewhat faster. The good
taste and fine judgment of the
player determine the tempo;
and it is in the tempo that is
embodied the spirit and the
perfection of this playing
manner and style. (*Toccate e
partite,* preface)

9. Nelle Partite quando se trou-
eranno passaggi, et affetti sarà
bene di pigliare il tempo largo;
il que osseruarassi anche nelle
toccate. L'altre non passeggi-
ate si potranno sonare alquanto allegre di battuta,
rimettendosi al buon gusto è
fino giuditio del sonatore il
guidar il tempo; nel qual consiste lo spirito, e la perfettione
di questa maniera, e stile di
sonare.

Several points in these paragraphs of Frescobaldi's preface are of great significance to our subject: first, the central role this master assigns to tempo for conveying the spirit of these works and (implicitly) of others as well; second, the view that the choice of the right tempo is a matter of individual taste and judgment; third, the need, in order to arrive at this judgment, to probe the prevailing expression and, in the madrigal style, the meaning of the words; fourth, the great freedom of tempo with the emphasis on strong retards at the ends of sections.

Some of these principles apply to works in a stricter style as well, as we can gather from Frescobaldi's preface to his *Primo libro di capricci canzon francese e recercari* of 1624. Referring specifically to the capricci, Frescobaldi stresses again the need to search for the right expression for each passage and for the intentions of the author. Admitting the difficulty of such a probe, he formulates a timeless principle in saying that after thorough study of a piece one ought to become aware of its spirit. For centuries to follow, this dictum was to be restated by eminent composers and theorists.

Once again, Frescobaldi recommends a slow start in order to brighten the following contrasting section, for which he also requests a substantial slowing down for cadences before starting subsequent phrases. A similar contrasting effect is desirable for certain dissonances that should be stressed by slowing them down and arpeggiating them to add spirit to what follows.[5] Apart from asking the performer to judge the proper tempo according to the character of the piece, Frescobaldi points to the link with notation when the change of the beat from semibreves (whole notes) to semiminims (quarter notes) parallels a change of tempo from adagio to allegro.

The freedoms of tempo that Frescobaldi specified for his toccatas remained valid for the lifetime of this form and still applied to the many Bach works in this genre. In the *adagio* of the Toccata in D Major for

Clavier (BWV 912), Bach actually spelled out his wish for tempo fluctuations with the words *con discrezione*. With Buxtehude we find the telltale *con discrezione* even in works in a strict style, such as the Fugue in E Major for Organ (BB mus. MSS. 2681 and 2683). These freedoms were generally valid for any work of a rhapsodic or improvisatory character. Froberger, for instance, was reported to have played many of his pieces with great freedom. He himself specifies for the *Tombeau . . . de M. Blacheroche* that it be played "fort lentement à la discrétion sans observer aucune mesure" (very slow, at will and without abiding by a beat).

*France.* In French lute music the *style luthé* implied considerable freedom of rhythm and implicitly—because of the frequent absence of a beat—of tempo as well. Thomas Mace, an English exponent of the French lute school, writes in 1676: "Masters . . . can command all manners of time . . . sometimes faster and sometimes slower, as we perceive the nature of the thing requires." (*Musick's Monument*, 81).

An extreme case of freedom is that of the French unmeasured preludes, which were apparently first composed by the lutenists around 1600 and taken over by the clavecinists beginning in the second half of the 17th century, from Louis Couperin and Chambonnières to Le Roux and the young Rameau. Some of these preludes give pitches only in whole notes, while others distinguish groups of different note values, but all are open to the most varied temporal interpretations.

In the 18th century we have François Couperin's testimonial about the proper style of preludes, referring to the eight specimens in his clavecin treatise. They are, he writes, conceived in the vein of improvisation and unless marked as *mesuré* should be played in an easy manner without clinging too strictly to the regularity of the tempo ("sans trop s'attacher à la précision des mouvements" [*L'art*, 60]).

Rameau sees "feeling" (le sentiment) as the dominant object of French music, but feeling "has no definite tempo, hence cannot be subjugated by a strict beat without losing the truthfulness that is its charm."[6]

Jean Jacques Rousseau contrasts the vagueness of the French beat with the precision of the Italian one ("le mouvement ayant toujours moins de précision dans la musique Françoise . . . que dans la musique Italienne" [*Dictionnaire*, s.v. "Mouvement"]).

*Germany.* Turning to Germany of the mid-18th century, we find C. P. E. Bach first stressing the need for precision in holding notes and rests for their exact value, except in fermatas and cadenzas, then giving an additional exception: every so often ("öfters"), he writes, one can intentionally commit "the most beautiful infractions against the beat [Tackt]." Provided that one plays alone or with but few and sensitive partners, one can do some violence to the tempo itself ("der ganzen Bewegung zuweilen einige Gewalt [anthun]") and expect that the accompanists, instead of being confused, will be alerted and will follow the soloist's intentions. When playing with a large accompanying group made up of players of unequal competence, however, one can still take some freedoms with the solo part but must do so against the background of a steady beat (*Versuch über Art das Clavier* [1753], chap. 3, par. 8).

Fluctuations of tempo are often referred to as *tempo rubato*. When using the term in this sense it is well to distinguish it from *rubato* pure and simple. This latter term has the literal meaning of "robbed," in the sense that one takes away from one note and gives to another so that in the end the time values come out even. In other words, the beat remains steady, but within beats the inner rhythm of a phrase is subtly manipulated. Thus, whereas *tempo rubato* is genuinely a matter of tempo where no compensations are due for fluctuations, the simple *rubato* is a matter of rhythm and will be discussed in chapter 9. (In the passage just quoted, C. P. E. Bach lucidly juxtaposes the *tempo rubato* with its tempo fluctuations and the *rubato* in the narrow sense of rhythmic flexibility against a strict beat, while listing the favorable conditions for the respective use of each.)

In 1789 Daniel Gottlob Türk describes special cases where expression can be enhanced by *extraordinary* means. Among these are playing without a steady beat; hurrying and hesitating; and *tempo rubato*. All of these he says can be very effective, provided they are used rarely and at the proper time. Playing according to feeling rather than strict measure is proper in free fantasias, cadenzas, fermatas, and in passages marked "Recitativo" (Türk speaks only of keyboard performance). The hurrying and hesitating can be used only when playing alone or with very alert accompanists. For appropriate contexts he mentions pieces of violent, angry feeling where the strongest spots can be somewhat hurried, as can lively passages that interrupt tender moods. Holding back is appropriate for spots in which a tender or sad feeling seems to come to a climax, for approaching a fermata or the end of a piece, or for whenever the composer writes *diminuendo, smorzando,* or other indications for slowing or softening. For tender spots that are inserted between lively thoughts, a sudden, not gradual, but very modest slowing down can be fitting. Finally, what Türk calls *tempo rubato* involves no change of tempo but rhythmic freedom within a steady beat. This is the *rubato* in the narrow, literal sense (*Klavierschule,* chap. 6, pars. 63–72).

***Late 18th-Century Trends.*** Late Baroque Italian music, notably with its *opere buffe,* its sonatas, symphonies, and concertos, was the decisive ingredient in the subsequent international pre-Classical style that invaded France and all other European countries. This Italian triumph and the demise of innate French musical traditions may well be the reason that, in the latter part of the 18th century, freedom of tempo played a diminishing role. In the Classical era *subtle* adjustments of tempo between energetic and lyrical passages were unquestionably practiced, but *major* freedoms were mainly restricted to recitative, cadenzas, and similar improvisatory passages.

From that period we have a significant testimonial by Mozart stressing the importance of maintaining the tempo and condemning the misuse of its alterations. In a letter to his father (October 23, 1777), he criticizes the little daughter of the piano maker Stein for her inability to remain in the same tempo by getting slower and slower on every repeat of a theme. She will, he writes, "never acquire the most essential, the most difficult, and the chief requisite in music, which is time, because from her earliest years she has done her utmost not to play in time." And later: "Everyone is amazed that I can always keep strict time" (*Letters*, 497). This last quotation is a fitting reminder that any freedom of tempo, to justify this term, must be the outcome of musical judgment, not of deficient control.

## Summary

In vocal music flexibility of tempo became significant after the mid-16th century in the Italian madrigal, where in homophonic passages rhythm and tempo responded to the meaning of the words. This tendency toward adaptation to the text found its climax in the recitative, invented in Italy shortly before 1600. In it tempo is dictated by the free, declamatory speech rhythm. The degree of freedom varied and was smaller in rhetorical, larger in narrative passages; smaller in sacred, larger in secular topics; smaller in the *accompagnato,* larger in the *secco* type, largest in the fast conversational exchanges of the opera buffa, where often any semblance of a beat disappeared.

Beginning with Schütz, German composers adopted the Italian recitative; Bach did likewise and so did Handel, who introduced it to England. Recitative remained a vital structural element of Italian opera from its beginnings well into the 19th century and was used by the Classical composers consistently in their Italian works and on occasion in their German ones.

French recitative, pioneered by Lully, adapted the form to French prosody, which is based on length and shortness of syllables, not—like the Italian and German—on accents. Lully and his followers up to Rameau resorted to constant changes of meter to accommodate the patterns of long and short while allowing for a smooth, flowing execution. Here, too, the tempo responded to the rhythm dictated by spoken declamation.

Flexibility of tempo extended to other vocal forms as well. We have documents from Italy, France, and Germany that point to tempo variations in response to the character of a section or to the need for variety.

Toward the end of the 17th century, however, the growing contrapuntal enrichment of the texture limited freedom of tempo.

In instrumental music flexibility of tempo found its chief home in keyboard works of an improvisatory character, such as toccatas and fantasias, that have a kinship to the recitative. Generally, freedom of tempo was the province of the soloist. The larger the ensemble, the stricter the form, and the more contrapuntal the work, the more the tempo had to be steady. Up to the mid-18th century there was, for the keyboard, generally more freedom in France than in Italy and Germany. In the Classical period the range of tempo flexibility narrowed and resided mainly in cadenzas, fermata embellishments, fantasies, and works of similar character.

# 4

# METER,
# DENOMINATIONS,
# AND TEMPO

## *Mensural Heritage*

Mensural signs such as o or $\phi$, alone or in combination with numbers, such as o$\frac{3}{2}$, or with prolation dots, as ꜿ , faded from the collective memory of composers when the original meanings of these symbols fell into disuse in the course of the 17th century. The combination of the half circle c with numbers seems to have lasted longer, yet here, too, toward the end of the century the prefix c became meaningless. Except for c**3**, which, at least in France, denoted a slower tempo than the solitary **3**, in most of the combination signs of ternary meters the prefix gradually disappeared. Brossard, in his *Dictionnaire* of 1703, lists many such combination signs (s.v. "Tripola") and in each case provides for the optional omission of the c .

In addition to such fractional signs as $\frac{3}{2}$, $\frac{3}{4}$, $\frac{3}{8}$, and so forth, the symbols C and ₵, just as well known, remained in use up to today. Mainly, though not exclusively, in France a **3** could stand for $\frac{3}{1}$, $\frac{3}{2}$, $\frac{3}{4}$, or $\frac{3}{8}$; a **2** usually for $\frac{2}{2}$ or, more rarely, for $\frac{2}{4}$. With the fading of the proportions the fractional signs assumed their modern meanings, whereby the denominator indicated the metrical unit, the numerator their number in a measure.

Once theorists acknowledged the new system, they proceeded to relate the meters to tempo. The meter–tempo relationship is clearly an inheritance from the mensural system, where the mensural signs, by way of the *integer valor* (the basic beat), had an implication for the absolute length of the various denominations and hence on the tempo of the piece.

The *integer valor,* as discussed before, was never an unerring yardstick of tempo, but its principle remained alive for a surprisingly long time and became known as *tempo giusto,* the standard tempo that is neither fast nor slow. That such a concept survived, like an incarnation of the *integer valor,* is understandable because it has a foundation in human nature. Our physiological rhythms, like walking or breathing, may not have an exact standard of normalcy: but it is not difficult to characterize walking speeds as fast or slow with an intermediate zone that would correspond to the *tempo giusto.* As will be presently seen, such an average tempo, when expressed in tempo words, will usually range from andante to moderato (*modéré* in French, *mässig bewegt* in German).

Another trait that survived from the mensural system until about the end of the 18th century is a continuing link between denominations and absolute time values. By and large, note values of whole and half notes were not used for fast passages, nor could small note values be understood to move sluggishly. This link, as mentioned before, was not fully severed until Beethoven's time. It is precisely because composers chose meters to accommodate short or long values with congenial denominations that meter remained an important guide to tempo. This in turn explains why until roughly the end of the Baroque period composers often dispensed with tempo words, relying on the clue of meter and denominations to provide guidance.

*Meter–Tempo Link in France.*  In France more than in any other country, theoretical tracts from the mid-17th century to well past the mid-18th century offer an almost routine representation of the meter–tempo link and do so in tabulations that are remarkable for their overall agreement. They list for each meter the number as well as the speed of the beats. The French sources on this matter are so abundant and basically repetitious that I show in Table 4.1 only a few select but representative examples covering the span of close to a century.

Charles Masson, writing in 1699, stands apart in this respect. For certain meters he sees so wide a tempo range that the implications of these meters for tempo seem strongly diluted. The four-beat measure (C), he says, can be beaten in two ways: *lent* or *léger.* The two-beat measure (**2** or ₵) can be beaten in four ways: *lent, léger, vite,* or *très vite.* But $\frac{3}{2}$ is always *fort grave* (*Nouveau traité,* 6–7).

In his important harpsichord treatise of 1702, Saint Lambert first establishes the theoretical tempo equivalents for each meter with mathematical precision, then in effect repudiates these equations for actual

TABLE 4.1.    Number and Character of Beats in Various Meters

| Meter | Nivers 1670 | J. Rousseau 1683 | Montéclair 1709 | Denis 1747 (1762) |
|---|---|---|---|---|
| C | 4* graves | 4 graves | 4 lents | 4 graves |
| ₵ | } 2 graves<br>} 4 vistes | } 2 lents<br>} 4 légers | } 2 lents<br>} 4 légers | 2 graves |
| **2** | 2 légers** | 2 vites | faster than ₵ | |
| $\frac{2}{4}$ | | | 2 très légers | 2 très vifs |
| $\frac{2}{8}$ | | | | 2 très vifs |
| $\frac{6}{4}$ | | | | 2 graves (related to ₵) |
| $\frac{6}{8}$ | | faster than $\frac{6}{4}$ | | 2 gays (related to **3**) |
| C3 | 3 lents | 3 lents | | |
| $\frac{3}{2}$ | 3 lents | 3 lents | 3 lents | 3 lents |
| **3** | 3 vistes | 3 légers | 3 gays | } 3 graves<br>(passacaille sarabande)<br>3 gays (chaconne vilanelle)<br>3 très légers (menuet) |

*Insert *tem[p]s*, meaning beats, after each number.
**léger: literally "light," meaning moderately fast, the approximate equivalent of allegro moderato.

praxis (*Principes de clavecin*, 15–23). His basic beat is established by the step of a man who walks one and a quarter leagues (lieues) within an hour. The length of the league was changeable, and hence the exact measurement is uncertain; but the description of the C meter as consisting of "4 temps graves" establishes the slowness of the basic beat. The ₵ meter is beaten in two and is twice as fast. Next, the **2** meter is twice as fast as ₵, and $\frac{2}{4}$ twice again as fast as the **2** meter, "hence very fast."

Turning to the triple meters, the $\frac{3}{2}$ is beaten in "3 temps graves" wherein the half-note beat corresponds to the quarter note in C meter. The **3** meter is twice as fast as $\frac{3}{2}$, and $\frac{3}{8}$ twice as fast as the **3** meter. The latter, says Saint Lambert, is beaten in one and used, for example, for minuets to be danced (as opposed to minuets to be played on the harpsichord at a lesser speed). The $\frac{6}{4}$ meter has either two beats equivalent to those in the **2** meter or three "temps gays." The $\frac{6}{8}$ is twice as fast as $\frac{6}{4}$.

This tabulation, with its mechanical doubling of the tempo from one meter to the next faster one, is mathematically very neat but hardly realistic in either its precision or its up to eightfold acceleration of speed. So it is not surprising that Saint Lambert, one of the finest and most penetrating of the old theorists, strongly qualifies his principles by writing: "These are the rules, but among all the rules of this art they are the ones least observed by its practitioners" (*Principes de clavecin*, 23–24). The performer has the privilege of choosing the tempo he considers fitting, provided it does not directly contradict the meter signature, is suitable for the piece, and brings out its values. Because the meter signs determine the tempo only imperfectly, composers add such words as *legerement, gayement, vîte, fort vîte, lentement,* and *gravement* to supplement the incapacity of the meter to express their intentions. As an example of the meter's unreliable guidance, Saint Lambert reports that Lully took the $\frac{6}{4}$ section of the overture to *Armide* very fast yet a later air in the same meter very slow. He sees in this an example of how praxis disowns theory ("la théorie est démentie par la pratique" [25]). (We have seen in Table 4.1 that Denis acknowledges a wide range for the **3** meter, from the slowness of a sarabande to the fastness of a menuet, echoing the vast flexibility shown by Masson fifty years earlier.)

I have reported on Saint Lambert's rules in some detail because his qualifications offer us another object lesson on the danger of taking theoretical rules at face value. We must, however, not underrate the importance of the meter. In France, for example, a **C** meter hardly ever had a fast beat but might have ranged from very slow to moderately slow; the quarter note in **2** meter could range from fast to moderate, but not slow; the $\frac{3}{8}$ was invariably lively; and so on. In fact, before 1700, when a **C** was added to a sign, such as in the **C3** combination, it indicated slowness of the beat; a **₵** in such combination suggested a livelier tempo. Saint Lambert's point was not a total upsetting of the theoretical meter–tempo relationships he had listed, but their flexible adjustment to the character of the music.

In France a further reason for preserving the basic characteristics of a meter lay in the very definite meter– *inégalité* relationship (on this see chap. 11). Since *inégalité* makes musical sense only within a certain tempo range, the tempo within a specific meter can vary only within a fairly limited scope.

***Meter–Tempo Link in England and Germany.*** Outside of France, the theoretical discussions of meter–tempo relationships are less specific, though the various meters and the patterns of their beats (though not usually their speed) is routinely explained.

Christopher Simpson, in a 1667 treatise so influential that it was reedited and republished nine times in the course of over one hundred years, writes that "in all Triplas" the notes are sung or played much faster than they are in common time; that in **3** meter each of three half notes approximates the value of a quarter note in **C** meter. The inverted **C** ( **Ɔ** ) indicates diminution to half the values, hence twice the speed, and so does the synonymous ₵, though many, he writes, dash it so without any intention of doubling the speed (*Compendium of Practical Musick*, 32–33).

In Germany in 1704, Johann Baptist Samber writes that C means not only a binary meter but also a slow and solemn tempo. The sign ₵, he says, is twice as fast, yet many copyists write ₵ instead of C because they think it is the same. Generally, he adds, meter signs are given to "show whether the song should be slow, moderate, or fast and hurried" (*Manuductio ad organum*, 9, 13).

Johann Philipp Kirnberger, a student of Bach's and his great admirer, comes closest to the French in giving in 1776 a detailed tabulation of meters and their meanings for denominations and tempo. Generally, he says, the larger meters such as alla breve, $\frac{3}{2}$, and $\frac{6}{4}$ are heavier and slower than the shorter meters such as $\frac{2}{4}$, $\frac{3}{4}$, and $\frac{6}{8}$, and these in turn are slower than $\frac{3}{8}$ and $\frac{6}{16}$. Besides the meter sign there are two other determinants of tempo. One is the denomination of the shortest notes in a piece. Thus dances with sixteenth and thirty-second notes are slower than those with eighth and only occasional sixteenth notes as the fastest denominations. For this reason a sarabande (with its many small note values) is slower than a minuet, though both are in $\frac{3}{4}$ meter. The third determinant is the tempo word. Where the simple terms *largo, allegro*, and so on are not specific enough, one should add qualifying words: *allegro assai, allegro moderato*, and others.

Kirnberger speaks somewhat confusingly of a "large" $\frac{4}{4}$ and a "small" $\frac{4}{4}$ meter, both of which were indicated by the C symbol. It seems that the first, "large" type is marked *largo* and is emphatic ("nachdrücklich") and serious; the "small" $\frac{4}{4}$ is lively, though with some emphasis (here he differs from the French as well as from Samber). The $\frac{2}{4}$ is lively with lightness; the $\frac{4}{8}$ is very fleeting ("ganz flüchtig") with no more trace of the emphatic character of the $\frac{4}{4}$ meter (*Kunst des reinen Satzes*, 2:106–36).

One can summarize his ideas as follows: other things being equal, the larger the denominator of the meter sign, the faster the tempo; and the smaller the fastest notes, the slower the tempo; tempo words have to be used for clearer definition.

Johann Abraham Peter Schulz, Kirnberger's student, writing in Sulzer's *Allgemeine Theorie*, follows his teacher's lead in linking meter to tempo and expression (s.v. "Tact"). Among two-beat measures, he writes, the alla breve ₵ is to be rendered heavily but twice as fast as the note values suggest. It has no notes smaller than eighths. The $\frac{2}{4}$ has the same speed but is to be rendered much more lightly ("weit leichter"); it can have all denominations and, in an adagio or andante, even a few thirty-seconds. The $\frac{2}{8}$ is to be used only for the most vivacious expression. The $\frac{6}{4}$ is heavy, like the ₵, and has sixteenths as the fastest notes. The $\frac{6}{8}$ is light and pleasant ("leicht und angenehm"), comparable to the

$\frac{2}{4}$ with sixteenths as fastest notes. The $\frac{6}{16}$ calls for the very lightest character and tempo and therefore rarely has notes faster than sixteenths. Schulz points to its characteristic use by Couperin and J. S. Bach.

Among four-beat measures he distinguishes, like Kirnberger, two types of the ₵ meter, the "large" (der große) and the "small" (der kleine) $\frac{4}{4}$ meter. The "large" one has eighths as shortest notes, is of serious and pathetic character, is usually marked *grave,* and is proper for the church. The "small" type calls for a lighter rendition, is twice as fast, and can have all types of notes. It is still serious and poised but not grave. The $\frac{4}{8}$ meter, often used by Couperin, is faster than ₵ but slower than $\frac{2}{4}$. The triple meters, $\frac{3}{2}$, $\frac{3}{4}$, and $\frac{3}{8}$, follow the same pattern, proceeding from heaviness to greater lightness. Their related meters with ternary subdivision, $\frac{9}{4}$, $\frac{9}{8}$, and $\frac{9}{16}$, are much lighter than their counterparts. Only the $\frac{9}{4}$ is still sedate; the $\frac{9}{8}$ has a leaping quality ("hüpfender"), mainly for gigue-like pieces; while the $\frac{9}{16}$ is extremely playful ("tändelnd") and vivacious.

## Denominations and Other Tempo Guides

Besides the meter, J. A. P. Schulz, like Kirnberger before him, sees other determinants of tempo in the denominations of the notes and in the character and style of the work. An allegro for the church is slower than one for the chamber or the theater. It is faster in symphonies than in vocal works or in a polyphonic ("gearbeiteten") trio. The tempo must never be so fast as to impair clarity nor so slow that it becomes difficult to sense the beat. Summing up, he says that the experienced performer who has carefully studied a piece will be able to find its correct tempo (Schulz, in Sulzer, *Allgemeine Theorie,* s. v. "Vortag").

Other German theorists of the 18th century treat of tempo in a more general way. Johann Mattheson in 1739 cautions that tempo can hardly be determined by dos and don'ts because it depends first on the sentiment of the composer, then on that of the performer (*Vollkommene Capellmeister,* pt. 2, chap. 7, par. 18).

Friedrich Wilhelm Marpurg in 1755 lists tempo words but gives no meter–tempo connection: "It happens every so often that whole notes are played as fast as quarter notes, and quarter notes as fast as whole notes." Experience, he says, will guide us in finding the right tempo (*Anleitung zum Clavierspielen,* 15–17).

C. P. E. Bach devotes only one brief paragraph to the question. Tempo, he says, is to be judged by the content of the piece, as indicated by Italian tempo words and especially as suggested by the fastest notes and figurations. Such orientation will permit us neither to rush the *allegro* nor to get too sleepy in the *adagio* (*Versuch über Art das Clavier* [1753], chap. 3, par. 10).

Johann Joachim Quantz deals with tempo at greater length. Following an old tradition, he refers to the normal pulse (which he clocks at 80) as the fundamental beat and relates all other speeds to this point of reference. Thus he lists four basic tempos, all expressed in terms of his basic beat in **C** meter: (1) the allegro assai ($\bar{\phantom{}}$ = MM 80); (2) the allegretto ($\bar{\phantom{}}$ = 80); (3) the adagio cantabile ($\flat$ = 80); and (4) the adagio assai ($\flat$ = 80). In **₵** meter the values are shifted to the next higher category by doubling the note values: **o** = MM 80 for the allegro assai and so on. Similar relationships are given for $\frac{3}{4}$ and other meters (*Versuch einer Anweisung*, chap. 17, pars. 49ff.).

It hardly needs to be mentioned that these equations are at best useful in a first approach. Quantz himself, like C. P. E. Bach, mentions the fastest notes in connection with tempo words as further guidelines. Arias, he says, are slower than instrumental works, sacred music slower than operas (pars. 52–53). Very interesting is his remark that repeats call for a faster tempo (par. 55).

Johann Samuel Petri, in 1782, questions a meter–tempo relationship by pointing out that the same meter is to be played sometimes fast and sometimes slow. Tempo words have to serve as guides (*Anleitung zur Musik* [1782], 156).

In 1756 Leopold Mozart cautions against reliance on tempo words that are by themselves inadequate. The proper tempo has to be deduced from the piece itself. In this connection he makes the important and helpful statement that each work has at least *one phrase* that discloses the tempo with certainty: "often [this phrase] pushes with forcefulness into the natural tempo" (*Versuch einer Violinschule*, chap. 1, sec. 2, par. 7). More about this presently.

Daniel Gottlob Türk, in 1789, sees little value in rules. A fairly experienced performer, he says, can judge the right tempo from the prevalent denominations, figurations, and passages (*Klavierschule*, chap. 1, par. 76).

*The Fastest Notes As Guide.* The clue provided by the fastest notes and figurations, mentioned in the previous quotations from C. P. E. Bach and Quantz, is one that can be of great help for works that call for unity of tempo. The tempo must then be such that the fastest notes are technically reasonable and, though they should be fast, must not be blurred, let alone sound frenzied.

Irmgard Herrmann-Bengen cites several instances where Monteverdi admonishes the continuo player to a slow tempo in order to accommodate the short note values of the upper voices. For instance, in the Magnificat from the Vespers (1610), he writes at the start of a movement: "to be played slowly, because the two tenors are singing in sixteenth notes" (va sonato tardo perchè li doi tenori cantano di semicroma [*Tempobezeichnungen*, 41–42]).

## Practical Applications

Taking an illustration from Bach, the opening theme of the Fifth "Brandenburg" Concerto (Ex. 4.1a) has no built-in natural tempo. Its allegro ¢ could be done as fast as perhaps ♩=50. But the thirty-second-note passages in measures 47–49 in the clavier, of which the first measure is given (Ex. 4.1b), put an effective lid on speed since the ritornello theme, which returns in measure 49, calls for an unwavering tempo throughout. The thirty-second notes recur in measures 139–53 against other thematic fragments that call for a constant tempo. As a consequence the maximum tempo for the movement seems more likely to be in the neighborhood of ♩=40–44.

EXAMPLE 4.1.   Bach, Fifth "Brandenburg" Concerto, BWV 1050

We find a similar situation in the Fourth "Brandenburg" Concerto. Its first thematic idea (Ex. 4.2a) could, by itself, be played as fast as ♩.=69, but the passages of thirty-seconds in the solo violin (of which Ex. 4.2b gives a brief excerpt) can hardly accommodate a tempo faster than ♩.=ca. 58.

EXAMPLE 4.2.   Bach, Fourth "Brandenburg" Concerto, BWV 1049

In the Fugue in A Minor of *WTC II*, the theme (Ex. 4.3a), in its intervallic abstractness, gives no clue to tempo; but the numerous passages in thirty-seconds (Ex. 4.3b) would seem to provide an upper speed limit of roughly ♩=69, "roughly" because the touch and speed of response varies from one type of keyboard instrument to another (be it harpsichords of different makes, clavichord, fortepiano, or modern piano) and between different specimens within the same type. But with such variants the principle is the same.

EXAMPLE 4.3.   Bach, Fugue in A Minor, *WTC II*, BWV 889/2

a.                                          b.

In the Fugue in G Major of the same volume, too (Ex. 4.4), the passages in thirty-seconds of measures 62–64 will probably limit the tempo to a maximum of ♩.=ca. 50.

EXAMPLE 4.4.   Bach, Fugue in G Major, *WTC II*, BWV 884

*The Clue of Ornamentation.* In a slow movement, the fastest notes will often surprisingly act to guard against undue slowness. Passages of thirty-second notes in an adagio carry the strong presumption of being ornamental figurations, and as such they must not be rendered as if they consisted of structural pitches from the melodic line. True to their ornamental nature, they should flow easily and lightly, and to permit them to do so the tempo has to move at a sufficiently fluent pace. Often such figurations are of the kind that many composers of the time did not specify in writing but left to the improvisatory talent of the performers. Examples 4.5–4.8 show some Bach passages in which performers often fail to recognize the purely ornamental nature of such thirty-second figurations and as a consequence select tempi that are too slow for the true nature of the musical texture.

The Sonata in G Minor for Violin Solo (Ex. 4.5) might best be played in slow four, not in eight. If the beat is not slower than ♩=36, the ornamental thirty-second notes will be able to flow without disturbing the adagio character of the underlying melody.

EXAMPLE 4.5.  Bach, Sonata in G Minor for Violin Solo, BWV 1001/1

In the organ chorale "Wenn wir in höchsten Nöten sein" (Ex. 4.6), the ornamental nature of the thirty-seconds suggests a tempo not slower than ♩=38–40.

EXAMPLE 4.6.  Bach, "Wenn wir in höchsten Nöten sein," BWV 641

In the Fifth Sonata for Organ (Ex. 4.7), the same considerations seem to favor a beat not slower than ♪=84.

EXAMPLE 4.7.  Bach, Fifth Sonata for Organ, BWV 529/2

In the first duet from the Cantata No. 140 (Ex. 4.8), the violin figurations are again purely ornamental. A beat of ♪=ca. 92 seems thus to be the slowest acceptable tempo, giving sufficient flow to the coloraturas while preserving the adagio character of the main theme.

EXAMPLE 4.8.   Bach, Cantata No. 140/3

***Leopold Mozart's Principle.*** Leopold Mozart's above-mentioned maxim about the usual presence of a theme that spontaneously reveals the natural tempo has special relevance for the pre-Classical and Classical period, in whose sonata, symphony, or concerto movements we find many polythematic works that call for unity of tempo. While there are many themes and phrases that by themselves could make musical sense at a variety of speeds, there are others that seem to demand a tempo within a narrow range; and these are presumably the ones to which Leopold Mozart refers.

In sonata-form movements we find clues of this kind more frequently in the subsidiary and closing themes, which tend to be more songful, popular, or dancelike and more fully unfolded than the principal statement, which tends to be more abstract, more compact, more "symphonic." For these reasons the more songful themes are more likely to "push into the natural tempo." If more than one theme is of such tempo sensitivity, then, as in a triangulation, the search for the right tempo is greatly helped.

Take for an illustration the terse, martial signals of the opening of the "Jupiter" Symphony (Ex. 4.9a). Even with their brief contrasted sequel they could make musical sense within a fairly wide range of tempo: they could be done as fast as ♩=160 or as slow as ♩=112 without sounding irrational. Not so the second, subsidiary theme (Ex. 4.9b) that, within the frame of 𝄵 meter, allegro vivace, would seem to accommodate a much smaller tempo range, perhaps of ♩=ca. 144–52. Still more clearly defined is the dancelike closing theme (Ex. 4.9c), which to me seems to favor the lower limit of ♩=ca. 144. Jean-Pierre Marty, in his study of Mozart's tempi, gives ♩=152 as a desirable speed for this movement while noting that it is often performed much faster (*Tempo Indications*, 155).

EXAMPLE 4.9.   Mozart, "Jupiter" Symphony, K 551/1

Similarly, in Haydn's Symphony No. 97 in C, the military fanfares of the first allegro theme (Ex. 4.10a) are by themselves ill-defined as to tempo, but the second theme (Ex. 4.10b), with its dancelike lilt in vivace $\frac{3}{4}$, seems to point to a tempo of ♩ = ca. 134–44.

EXAMPLE 4.10.   Haydn, Symphony No. 97 in C, 97/1

## *Summary*

The proportions faded in the 17th century, but as a carry-over from mensural notation there remained a clear link between the nominal values and the actual lengths of the notes: large values were not fast, while small values were not sluggish. Similarly, when mensural signs changed into meter signatures, the latter were associated with different types and speeds of the beat and thereby carried strong implications for the tempo. Until late in the 18th century, theorists listed these meter–beat relationships in fairly definite terms, but these rules often had to be strongly qualified by consideration of the proper expression and by the use of tempo words. A number of eminent musicians stressed the impossibility of giving rules about an unmarked tempo and emphasized instead the need to explore the basic character—the "affect"—of a piece while considering the value of the shortest notes. For polythematic works that call for unity of tempo, Leopold Mozart gives the wise counsel to look for a phrase that "pushes with forcefulness into the natural tempo."

# 5

# THE SPECIAL CASE OF
# C AND ₵

In the meter–tempo relationship the difference between C and ₵ meter presents a special problem. In mensural notation, whence these symbols derived, they either had proportional meaning or were simple tactus signs. When one followed the other in the same voice, or when both occurred in simultaneous voices, they were proportional signs with the ₵ a synonym for $\frac{2}{1}$, the dupla proportion, calling for doubling the tempo. When used at the beginning of a work as tactus signs, the relationship of one to the other was much more vague: generally, the ₵ was taken at a somewhat faster, but not usually a much faster, speed.

In the discussion of faster or slower speed, confusion threatens when no clear differentiation is made between the *motus,* the speed with which different pitches follow one another, and the *tempus* or *tactus,* the speed of the beat. Thus Praetorius writes that madrigals are usually written in C because they have many semiminims (quarter notes) and fusae (eighth notes) and hence move at a faster pace ("celeriori motu") than motets, written in ₵, in which breves and semibreves predominate and therefore move at a slower pace. But to accommodate the many fast denominations in madrigals, he continues, the C calls for a slower beat; conversely the faster ₵ beat in motets prevents them from getting too sluggish. In the first case fast *motus* combines with slow *tactus*; in the second, slow *motus* with faster *tactus* (*Syntagma musicum,* 3:50–51).

Whenever a motet or related work has many "black notes" (meaning modern quarters and eighths), it will, says Praetorius, best be set in C to signal a slower beat. Whereupon he makes the significant statement (quoted above) that verbal and musical context rather than the tactus sign determines whether a faster or slower beat is in order (*Syntagma musicum*, 3:51).

Praetorius then points to the different usages of various composers, among whom Giovanni Gabrieli uses the ¢ exclusively, while others use the c exclusively. Monteverdi writes ¢ in motet-like works, c in those that contain more black than white notes; Viadana reserves the ¢ for vocal, the c for instrumental works. Others, again, have no method, and their use of either sign seems indiscriminate with regard to both the character of the work and the prevalent denominations. Praetorius himself prefers ¢ for motets but c for other works that, being in a mixed style (notably concertos), usually call for a slower beat.

The relatively small difference between the barred and unbarred Cs and the vagueness of their respective meanings emerge also from the texts of other German theorists of the 17th century. Christoph Demantius in 1611 refers to the ¢ as the "common" (der gemeine oder schlechte) tactus—a term reserved in the 18th century for the C meter—whereas the c without a bar means "somewhat slower" (*Isagoge artis musicae*, chap. 5, n. p.). In 1673 Johann Rudolf Ahle calls C the "great and slow" (großer und langsamer) tactus, whereas ¢ means that the beat should move "a little faster" (etwas geschwinder) [*Brevis introductio*, "Von den Signis," n. p.]. Johann Peter Sperling in 1705 writes that some theorists and composers make a difference between the unbarred and the barred Cs, with the first intended to be slower and the second faster, but that this contrast is not observed by many who mark the tempo with such "curious" (absonderliche) terms as "*tardo, presto, alla breve*, etc." (*Principia musicae*, 66).

Daniel Merck, for one, makes a clear differentiation. The C, he writes, stands for slow four, the ¢ "noch so geschwind," meaning probably twice as fast and beaten in two (*Compendium musicae* [1695], pt. 1, chap. 3, n. p.).

The relationship of the barred and unbarred Cs has undergone interesting changes over the last few hundred years. Beginning with the occasionally distinct proportional meaning in mensural notation, the difference between the two began to blur as early as the 16th century, when, as pointed out, the signs were used not as proportions but as tactus signs. At least in Italy and Germany the difference remained vague throughout the 17th and, for some masters, even through the 18th centuries, while it became more distinct with Bach and still more so with Haydn and Mozart. Then, coming around almost full circle, the clear contrast, mainly in terms of four versus two beats, became the rule in the 19th century in a relationship that has remained valid to the present day.

In France, as was shown, the C had, seemingly already in the 17th century, the distinct meaning of four rather slow beats; the ¢ was definitely faster and beaten either in slow two or in fast four. Since the typically French **2** signature was always beaten in two, it is usually explained as being somewhat faster than ₵. Yet Montéclair says in 1710 that the latter's meaning has not yet been clearly determined (*Petite méthode*, 48).

In Bach's usage we find occasional vestiges of the proportional meaning of C and ₵ (the latter sometimes written as barred **2: ₹**) when one follows the other. In Cantata No. 34, as well as in its secular model, Cantata No. 34a, the choral movement "Friede über Israel" (no. 4) starts in C meter, marked *adagio* in No. 34 (unmarked in 34a), and then in measure 3, with presumed doubling of the tempo, changes into ₹ for No. 34, ₵ for 34a. In the first movement of Cantata No. 41, the change from ₵ presto to C is also strictly proportional, as evidenced by the rhythmic and motivic identity between the sections when the tempo is halved. An exact doubling of the tempo occurs in Cantata No. 29 at the transition from the recitative no. 6 to the alto aria no. 7, as shown in Ex. 5.1.

EXAMPLE 5.1. Cantata No. 29/7

In a few situations the evidence would seem to point to indifference regarding these symbols when Bach used them interchangeably. In the autograph of the early Cantata No. 71, the last section of the last chorus (no. 7) has the upper seven staves in C and the lower eight staves in ₵; the (autograph) voice, flute, cello, and organ parts have C throughout. In the Christmas Oratorio, pt. 2, no. 21 (chorus), instruments and continuo in the autograph score are in C, the voice parts in ₵. In the original performance parts, soprano, tenor, and all instruments except the continuo are in ₵, while alto, bass, continuo, and organ are in C. In Cantata No. 13/5 the autograph violin solo part is in ₵, the autograph basso and flute parts are in C (St. 69).

The meaning of these cases must not be exaggerated. They seem to be exceptions due to haste or oversight; by and large Bach seems to have used the two symbols very carefully. The C is much more frequent than the ₵, perhaps at a ratio of 20:1 throughout his entire oeuvre. Whenever he writes the C we are generally on safe ground to beat it in moderate to slow four. We find the ₵ in vocal works almost exclusively in movements that contain no, or only very few, notes smaller than eighths. Generally they are meant to be beaten in two. In his instrumental works the same principle applies in most cases, too, though there, owing to the greater agility of the instruments, we find occasional movements that contain sixteenth and even thirty-second notes. Some movements in ¢ that contain many black notes may not have been beaten in two. As so frequently happened in French music, the symbol then indicated a fairly fast beat in four. Examples are the first movements of many concertos that call for a lively speed but would, at least today, be more comfortably beaten in fast four than in two: for instance, the First, Second, Third, Fifth, and Sixth "Brandenburg" concertos, the Violin Concerto in E, the Double Violin Concerto in D Minor, and the clavier concertos in D minor and A major.

The continuing uncertainty with regard to the barred and unbarred C signs is reflected in the following quotations from Marpurg and Agricola. Whereas Friedrich Wilhelm Marpurg in 1755 still upholds the proportional meaning of the two signs by saying that the half note in ¢ has the same length as the quarter note in C, he adds that "concerning notation, the error arises fairly often of confusing the simple C with the barred C, in which case one has to examine the character of a piece with regard to its fastest notes and its phrases [Einschnitte] in order to determine whether it has two or four beats" (*Anleitung zum Clavierspielen,* 20).

In an anonymous polemical essay of 1749, Johann Friedrich Agricola criticizes Marpurg's doctrine of the barred C as "disorderly and confused" (unordentlich und verworren). "It is true," he continues, "that the bar through the C usually indicates a fast tempo; but one also finds the bar in pieces that move very slowly and, conversely, no bar in fast pieces." A better formulation of the rule, he says, would be that the barred C means alla breve and that, whether the tempo is fast or slow, the notes in it are held only half as long as in the common meter with the unbarred C (*Schreiben an Herrn,* 45).

It would seem that Agricola, rather than Marpurg, was confused in not distinguishing Praetorius's *motus* and *tempus:* since the notes in the barred ¢ are twice as fast, the *tempus* is twice as fast, but if the denominations are large, then the actual unfolding of the movement (*motus*) can be slower than in a common meter with slower beat but smaller denominations.

With the Classical composers the difference between the barred and unbarred C meters becomes on the whole very distinct. Mozart was usually very precise in his tempo instructions: his tempo words combined with the meter seem usually to circumscribe the tempo within a fairly narrow range. His allegro ¢ will never be in four, always in two. An allegro in C should be thought of as being in four beats, especially when there is a distinct quarter-note pulse present, in which case the four beats should be felt as such even when the piece is more conveniently beaten in two.

## Practical Illustrations

The allegro C from the first movement of Mozart's "Prague" Symphony K 504, if beaten and felt in two, is often taken too fast. If it is beaten instead in fast four at ♩=ca. 136–44, the resulting moderation of its speed combined with the quarter-note pulse will bring out the martial aggressiveness of the episode initiated by the theme in measures 55–70 (Ex. 5.2a) and in its many recurrences. A beat felt in two may also deprive the "secondary" theme in the dominant (Ex. 5.2b) of its ingratiating, soothing eloquence. Marty, listing the movement in his huge category of "Cb," assigns the tempo ♩=126 (*Tempo Indications*, 39).

EXAMPLE 5.2. Mozart, "Prague" Symphony, K 504/1

Mozart wrote a presto in C only infrequently. (Although this combination is found in the finale of the "Haffner" Symphony in the sixth edition of Köchel and in most editions prior to the NMA, the autograph has clear ¢s on every staff.) An outstanding example of a presto in C meter is the *Figaro* Overture, which is, however, misrepresented in most editions as ¢. Another is the Overture to *The Impresario* K 486. Since both are unlikely candidates for being beaten in four, the meter signature in both cases should be taken as a warning against excessive speed. A tempo of approximately ♩=118–22 might be fitting for *Figaro*, one of ca. 120–24 for *The Impresario*. Marty wants the *Figaro* Overture felt in quarter notes at the speed of ♩=276 (*Tempo Indications*, 169) and *The Impresario* Overture at the "correct tempo" of 200/400 (♩/♩ [p. 170]), both of which seem hardly practicable. Mozart had in fact provided a further caveat against the breakneck speed so frequently heard today when in the autograph catalog of his works he listed the tempo of each overture not as "Presto" but as "Allegro assai" while retaining the C meter of the score (*Verzeichnüss* [1786]).

The same catalog reveals that on occasion the difference between C and ¢ may have been blurred in Mozart's mind: the first movement of the String Quartet in F, K 590 is allegro C in the score but ¢ in the catalog.

Andantes and adagios that are written in ¢ are special problems. Perhaps because they are at odds with modern practice, they cause many a performer and conductor either to ignore or to misunderstand the vertical bar. Türk in 1789 speaks of this combination: although the alla breve proper is more common in allegro than in adagio, so he writes, the latter does occur. "If the fastest notes in an adagio ¢ are only eighths or occasional sixteenths, the tempo must be taken a little faster" (*Klavierschule,* chap. 1, par. 70 n. **).

In these circumstances it is important to find the right balance between the adagio (or andante) character of the piece and the need for distinctly faster tempo than would be indicated without the bar through the C. An adagio alla breve will best be done in four, not in eight. The pace of the four will depend on the shortest notes and the overall character of the piece.

An especially challenging problem is offered by the adagio ¢ introduction to Mozart's E-Flat Symphony No. 39 K 543, because it contains phrases and passages of such disparate character: there are the solemn opening fanfares that must have splendor and majesty without ponderousness; there are the thirty-second-note descending scale passages in the violins, later inverted in the low strings, that must flow in anticipation of the related scales in the following allegro, but not so fast that they sound breathless or become murky in the basses; there are the ominously threatening dotted rhythms that must not be so slow as to lose their dramatic power; there are the syncopated quarter notes in measures 7–8, and still more the mystic half notes of the last four measures that must not be so slow as to lose a sense of cohesion. We have to compromise between the demands of these divergent phrases, and an approximate tempo of ♩=50–54 might be a reasonable solution. Marty assigns to it (and to many companions in his category "Adagio ¢b") the tempo of 30/60 (♩/♩ [*Tempo Indications,* 29]). Marty stipulates, with special regard to similar adagio or andante movements, that "if the alla breve sign is to have any meaning at all, the half-note pulse must be felt" (28). I do not believe that this can be categorically stated: it may apply often but probably not always. As an absolute principle it can easily promote too fast a tempo, one that would lose its connection with the *adagio* or *andante* markings. Thus I believe that the better part of the adagio introduction to the E-flat Symphony No. 39, notably measures 9–21 with their pervasive quasi-dotted eighth-note figures, seems to suggest a quarter-note rather than a half-note pulse. But Marty certainly has a case when he objects to beating this introduction in eight (29).

The andante ¢ of the *Don Giovanni* Overture (as well as the corresponding climactic scene with the Commendatore's statue) must not be so slow that the undulating scales with their crescendos and sudden pianos, which seem to evoke gusts of infernal winds, would be deprived of their breathtaking imagery. A tempo in the range of ♩=69–72 might be appropriate. Marty's tempo of 88/44 (♩/♩ for what he classified as "Andante ¢c" again seems rather fast (*Tempo Indications*, 22).

Another andante ¢ that is sometimes taken more like an adagio is the second movement of the Piano Concerto in C Major K 467. To preserve its ethereal serenity, I would suggest a tempo in the rage of ♩=76–79. Marty places it in the same category as the opening of the *Don Giovanni* Overture and consequently lists the tempo of 88/44 (♩/♪) [*Tempo Indications*, 22]).

For a larghetto in ¢, such as the slow movement of the B-flat concerto K 595, an approximate tempo of ♩=76 might be proper. Marty, who classifies it as "Larghetto ¢b," gives for this category the tempo of ♩=72 (*Tempo Indications*, 59).

In all related cases of andante, larghetto, or adagio alla breve, it is imperative that the chosen tempo be compatible with the character suggested by the *tempo word*, which is the leading determinant; the bar through the C then indicates that within the frame staked out by the word, the tempo should be on the fast side and be beaten in four, probably never in eight, and once in a while (perhaps in an andante or larghetto) even in two.

The same problems arise in Haydn's use of the two signatures C and ¢ in combination with tempo markings from *presto* to *adagio*, and it appears that the answers are similar. Haydn, too, seems to have been very deliberate in choosing the two alternative markings, as evidenced by the prevalent denominations: his C meters in allegro contain many more sixteenth notes than his alla breve meters, and his alla breve signatures in adagios are quite certainly also meant as hedges against excessive slowness. For Haydn, too, neither the presence nor the absence of the bar through the C must be ignored: its presence in slow movements advises against dragging the tempo, while its absence in fast movements warns against excessive speed.

# 6

# TEMPO WORDS

## The Emergence of Tempo Words

As described in previous chapters, the basic tempo of mensural notation, the *integer valor,* began to be undermined in a process that began in
the mid-16th century but gained momentum during the 17th. With the
resulting loss of clear tempo direction, the need arose for supplementary
guidance.

The necessary help came chiefly from tempo words. They show up
first in the 16th century, in connection with the various note values and
their meanings for tempo. Vicentino in 1555 characterizes the longa as
"tardo," the brevis as "ne presto, ne tardo," the semibrevis as "mediocre," the minim as "più mediocre," the semiminim as "presto," the
fusa as "veloce," and the semifusa as "velocissimo" (*L'antica musica,* fol.
42v). The idea was presumably that a composition in which one of these
note values predominates will have the character of the respective speed
term.

Speed terms like these may have first appeared as regular tempo
indications in Spanish guitar (vihuela) tablatures of the 1530s. We find
them in Luis Milán's *El maestro* of 1535, the first Spanish instrumental
tablature. It was a didactic work addressed to beginners, which explains
the attempt to give more specific directives than was the norm. Milán
marks most of the pieces as either "fast" (apriesa) or "slow" (a espacio)
with occasional qualifications such as "with somewhat accelerated beat"
(conel compas algun apressurado) and similar ones such as "somewhat
gaily," "neither fast nor slow," and others.

During the next decade or so, other Spanish vihuela players followed Milán's example in their own didactic works. Elsewhere such

tempo markings were very rare for the rest of the 16th century but began to appear more frequently shortly after 1600. Banchieri, in the *Battaglia* from the second edition of his *Organo suonarino* of 1611, used such terms as *adagio, allegro, presto,* and *veloce.* Other masters began to use a pair of contrasting terms either in lieu of or in support of proportions. Thus we find Frescobaldi using the "adagio–allegro" contrast, Schütz that of "presto–tarde." Around mid-century the terms seem to have emancipated themselves from their dualistic function as pseudo-proportions and to have taken on the same kinds of independent tempo meanings as had the terms of the Spanish vihuelists a century before.

Dances had, by and large, definite, well-known tempo meanings, and in vocal music there was still the text to give a clue to the character of a work, hence to its approximate tempo. So it might be understandable that the need for tempo words seems to have been felt most keenly in what we now call the "absolute music" of Italian sonatas and concertos. In these works tempo markings became a standard feature by the end of the 17th century.

The Germans and the English took over the Italian tempo words. The French used their own words for French-style music, but they too adopted the Italian ones for sonatas and concertos. The French, more often than the Italians, used terms that often define feelings, attitudes, and moods rather than an abstract speed. François Couperin has terms such as *noblement, audacieusement, languissament, voluptueusement sans langueur,* and *nonchalamment,* evoking with striking eloquence a musical character that often defines the proper tempo more tangibly than any speed word could.

Bach is consistent in giving tempo words for practically all his chamber music and concertos. Occasional exceptions are first movements, where *allegro* was understood (for instance in the First, Second, Third, and Sixth "Brandenburg" concertos). In his suites and partitas the titles of the dances suggested the tempo, and every so often he implied a speed by referring to a dance: for example, "Tempo di borea, di sarabanda, di gavotta," and so on. In his vocal music he uses tempo words very sparingly, relying, so it seems, on the clues offered by the text and the character of the music in those places with the fastest notes. Surprising is the fact that Bach's non-dance-related keyboard music is by and large devoid of tempo markings. The reason for this neglect—which, as we shall see, has a counterpart in articulation—probably lies in the realization that the keyboard player who sees the full score has a better chance to judge the nature of a work than do other executants.[1] By the time of the Classical composers, tempo words have become ubiquitous to a point where their occasional omission is likely a matter of simple oversight. Only the minuets of symphonies and chamber music were often not further defined, in which case *allegretto* or *moderato* was understood.

## Problems with Tempo Words

Tempo words present us with several problems. First, they are by nature vague; second, they have been differently interpreted in different countries and regions; and third, they have changed their meanings over the years.

Whereas some of the Italian tempo words directly indicate speed (among them *lento, moderato,* and *presto*), others imply a speed by indicating an action such as walking (*andante*), or a state of mind, (*grave,* meaning serious, grave; *adagio,* meaning at ease; *allegro,* meaning joyful; *vivace,* meaning lively, vivacious), or a general character (*largo,* meaning broad). At first the mood words were interpreted at face value, and in many cases the literal meaning lingered on. Thus when Bach writes *Vivace e Allegro* in measure 147 of the Confiteor in the Mass in B Minor, the meaning is clearly "fast and joyful." Gradually, however, these mood words assumed abstract tempo meaning: *adagio* meant very slow, *allegro* meant fast, its diminutive *allegretto* meant moderately fast.

The basic vagueness of these words then prompted composers, as early as the latter part of the 17th century, to aim for a clearer tempo indication by adding qualifiers: adverbs such as *molto, poco, più, meno,* or *assai;* suffixes such as *-ino* or *-etto* for diminutives, *-issimo* for amplified meaning; or adjectives such as *cantabile, espressivo, sostenuto, grazioso,* and so forth. Such qualifiers have proved very helpful in clarifying a composition's character and, when combined with the meter signature, can provide a more secure bearing on the desirable tempo.

As to the regional differences, Georg Muffat writes in 1701 in the preface to his Concerti Grossi (*DTÖ,* XI/2) that the Italians play adagio, grave, and largo much more slowly than do "our musicians." By contrast they play allegro, vivace, presto, più presto, and prestissimo "incomparably faster" than is common in Germany.

Half a century later, in 1762, C. P. E. Bach writes of the tempi practiced in Berlin, "where the adagios are rendered much slower, the allegros much faster than customary in other regions" (*Versuch über Art das Clavier* [1762], chap. 36, par. 7). Meanings of the terms were not only flexible, they were also relative with regard to the locale.

A further problem is that these terms changed their meanings over the years. At first, *presto* simply meant fast as opposed to the slowness of *tarde* or *adagio,* although the contrast was not necessarily sharp. In the 17th century and after, *presto* meant less fast than *vivace* and was a de facto synonym of *allegro.* Even in Bach's time a presto movement must not be played too rapidly and should be thought of as "fast" rather than as "very fast." Gradually its meaning began to suggest greater speed, but it does not seem to have reached its present meaning until Mozart's time.

*Largo* is another ambiguous word. Today it is at the extreme slow end of the tempo scale. For a long time, certainly including the period of Bach and Handel, it was taken in its literal meaning of broad, or sustained, and therefore slow, but not as slow as adagio. Handel clarified this meaning with terms such as *Largo ma non adagio* or *Largo andante*. In Bach's Mass in B Minor it is equally clear that when the four majestic opening measures marked *Adagio* lead to the long fugal section marked *Largo ed un poco piano*, the tempo has to increase. Only by the second half of the 18th century did the meaning of *largo* slow down, overtaking *adagio* in slowness for Haydn and Mozart and moving toward the end of the scale, where it shared the extreme position with *grave*. Yet there was by no means a consensus about this order, and for some musicians of Mozart's time (Clementi among others) *adagio* kept the meaning it had held in Bach's time, as the slowest tempo.

In the Classical era, *larghetto*, the diminutive of *largo*, meant faster than the latter and faster too than adagio; it was generally considered to be a shade slower than andante and as such closely related to the pre-1800 meaning of *andantino*, which will be explained presently.

*Lento*, a term used by Praetorius in the 1620s, occurs once in a while in Bach (in the Sixth Organ Sonata for instance) but not in Mozart. In the 18th century it was more frequent in France (as *lent*). In either form it has no exact niche in the scheme of tempo gradations: its tempo hovers around the adagio range and may be somewhat faster or, more frequently, somewhat slower than the latter, but it is less slow than largo or grave. Its use increased after 1800.

*Andante*, too, presents problems. Literally, it means walking, which is normally done at a deliberate, unhurried pace; thus the term had a neutral connotation at the boundary between fast and slow but leaning originally slightly toward the fast side with an emphasis on movement. As a consequence, up to about the end of the 18th century, such terms as *poco andante* or *andantino*, meaning a little andante, had the meaning of less movement, hence a little slower than andante—opposite the way we understand it now. Conversely, the term *più andante*—that is, more walking or faster walking—meant an accelerated tempo. This meaning is clear in the finale ("Vaudeville") of Mozart's *Die Entführung*, in which the andante tempo is changed to *Più andante* at the start of a rapid acceleration to *Allegro assai*, expressing Osmin's mounting fury at the pardon of the prisoners. By the same token, the *Molto andante* in the second act finale of *Le nozze di Figaro*, at Susanna's surprise emergence from the cabinet, indicates a tempo that is nimble and graceful, not sluggish and heavy: it means a fast, not a slow, andante of perhaps $\eighthnote = 98$; Marty's "right tempo" is $\eighthnote = 108$ (*Tempo Indications*, 121). (Herrmann-Bengen opts here, I believe erroneously, for "very slow" [*Tempobezeichnungen*, 190]).

Up to the time of Haydn and Mozart, *andante* was closely related to *moderato*, both words indicating the truly centrist tempo. (J. J. Rousseau, in his *Dictionnaire* of 1768, equates the French *modéré* with the Italian *andante*.) But the term gradually shifted to the slow side of the spectrum, a change that was bound to affect the diminutive form of *andantino* as well. The shift was taking place at the time of Beethoven, who as a consequence was bewildered about the meaning of *andantino*. In a letter of February 19, 1813, to George Thomson, his Edinburgh editor, he wrote: "that word [*andantino*] is of such imprecise meaning that on one occasion *andantino* can be close to *allegro* and on another almost like *adagio*" (*Letters*, vol. 1, p. 405). J. J. Rousseau in 1768 (s.v. "Andante") and Türk in 1789 (*Klavierschule*, chap. 1, par. 70) still considered *andantino* to refer to a tempo slower than andante, in accord with Mozart and Haydn. On the other hand, in 1802 Koch already lists it in the modern sense as being faster (*Musikalisches Lexicon*, 143).

On the fast end of the spectrum there are fewer problems, except for the previously mentioned change in the meaning of *presto*. Yet even though *presto* meant very fast for the Classical composers, it was not associated with the same breakneck speed with which it is so often associated today. A speed that obscures delicate figurations is too fast, regardless of the tempo marking. When Mozart wrote his father that the finale of the "Haffner" Symphony, which is marked *Presto* ₵, should be played "as fast as possible," he meant as fast as the mediocre Salzburg orchestra, not the New York Philharmonic, could negotiate it clearly and cleanly. That *presto* did not imply precipitate speed is clear from the *Figaro* Overture, which—as previously noted—is so marked in the score but listed as "Allegro assai" in Mozart's autograph catalog of works—its speed further qualified by its ₵ meter (not ₵, as erroneously printed in most editions). The same disparity between "Presto" in the autograph and "Allegro assai" in the catalog also obtains for the Overture to *The Impressario*.

That the meaning of tempo words was far from settled by the end of the 18th century can be seen in Türk's treatise of 1789, where he lists with his usual thoroughness the Italian tempo words, adding modifications by means of suffixes (such as *-issimo*, *-etto* or *-ino*) or adverbs. Assuming that he arranged the words in the sequence of speed, *allegro* would be faster than *vivace*, *adagio* slower than *grave*. It is a testimonial to the problematic nature of tempo words that the schoolmasterly Türk, who liked to formulate rules, was forced to admit their inadequacy in matters of tempo and instead placed his trust in the ability of the experienced performer to deduce the right tempo from the nature of the work itself (*Klavierschule*, chap. 1, par. 76). This is the old and ever new refrain voiced for the last four hundred years by eminent composers and theorists alike.

# 7

# THE FINAL
# RITARDANDO

Many of today's performers slow down, without the prompt of a *ritardando* sign, at final cadences in music of all ages. They do so spontaneously in order to prepare the listener for the impending end of the piece. In the middle of certain works a ritardando can be similarly suggested by fermatas that signal a temporary stopping place.

Such a retardation, however, is not always indicated. It will not be needed when composers announce the approaching end of a piece by structural means. They can slow the rhythm by lengthening the note values, by inserting rests, or by emphatically repeating the tonic chord and ending with a strong masculine cadence. For an illustration, see the last measures of the *Figaro* Overture, where a *ritardando* would be redundant. Similar examples are legion. Another structural means for clarifying the end is the procedure, so frequent in Handel, of attaching an abrupt adagio ending to an allegro movement.

Other contexts that generally do not favor a retard are dance pieces or works of the perpetual-motion type, where steadiness and continuation of rhythmical drive are more important than preparation for ending the work. A special emphasis on the final note, or a slight hesitation before the last downbeat, will often be all that is needed to clarify the end.

Where, however, the melodic, harmonic, or rhythmic configuration of a terminal passage does not by itself speak loudly enough to herald the imminent end, a ritardando suggests itself. The question is whether such retards are historically justified in pre-1800 music.

A number of eminent scholars (among them Curt Sachs and Paul H. Lang), along with many historically oriented performers, object to final retards, which they ascribe to a 19th-century mentality. Paul Badura-Skoda, in his book on Bach's keyboard works, cites approvingly the total lack of final retards on an 18th-century barrel organ and adds that "final retards, *if they existed at all,* were certainly smaller than done today" (*Bach Interpretation,* 24 and 32 [emphasis added]). Are these objections valid?

## *Theoretical Sources*

I have been able to find only *one* theoretical statement that could conceivably be construed to have an antiritardando meaning. Georg Muffat writes that one should maintain the tempo in a cadence: the last measure must not be faster than the first but "rather held back than hurried" (pencher à retenir qu'à précipiter la mesure" [*Florilegium secundum,* iii]). Apart from this statement, which seems to favor rather than forbid a retard, there is a sizeable amount of both theoretical and musical evidence in unambiguous support of a final ritardando.

Lodovico Zacconi in 1592 has the singer dwell on the penultimate note, provided the other parts can be made to follow the example ("Allóra su la penultima figura a tanto si hà da fermare quanto que tutte l'altre parte vogliano, & si contentano; & poi salire all'ultima figura" [*Prattica di musica,* fol. 79r]).

Praetorius in 1619 considers singers, organists, or other instrumentalists as betraying provincialism ("musici oppidani") if they hurry into the final note without delaying the motion. Only after a delay should the ultima be rendered (*Syntagma musicum,* 3:80).

Giovanni Maria Trabaci, in his *Secondo libro de ricercare, & altre varij caprici* of 1615, writes "Allarga la battuta" (broaden the beat) in several places, each time before a cadence—for instance in *veno nono* primo tono; in *veno quarto* secondo tono; in *veno ottavo,* terzo tono (here four measures before the end!).

As mentioned before, Frescobaldi, in the prefaces to both his toccatas of 1615 and his capricci of 1624, stresses the need for considerably slowing down ("sostenerle assai") the cadences of sections before staring the next sections.

In Germany, Daniel Friderici writes: "Toward the end of the song, in *penultima consonantia* . . . all the voices must wait and make a finely drawn *Confinal,* and not abruptly attach the *Final* to the song. To do so strikes the listener as very annoying and disagreeable. It deprives the song of much amenity and grace if one breaks off the song abruptly and cuts it off short."[1]

Wolfgang Caspar Printz writes in 1678: "At the end of a piece some extend the penultimate note, whereas others fall immediately into the final one, but the latter should be somewhat, though not too much, extended, to give the ear at the end a complete pleasure" (*Musica modulatoria*, 22).

Georg Falck in 1688 speaks of a retard prior to a fermata. The fermata symbol, he says, either indicates an ending ("dass Final gemacht werden soll") or the need to slow down meter and beat for the sake of the implied heaviness ("um sonderbarer Gravität willen, mit Mensur und Tact ein wenig umgehalten werden soll" [*Idea boni cantoris*, 83–84]). The "Final" clearly calls for a retard.

In France, André Raison writes in 1688 that in *Grand plein jeu* the last measure must always be very long ("la dernière mesure soit toujours fort longue" [*Livre d'orgue*, Preface]).

François Couperin, in "L'ingénue" (*Pièces de clavecin*, 19th *ordre*), has inserted a six-note ornament between the first and second beat of the penultimate measure of the Seconde Partie, and this ornament is playable only in the frame of a ritardando. Rameau, in the third concert, "La La Poplinière" (*Pièces de clavecin en concerts*), has four eighth notes notated *marqué* in the penultimate measure; their implied pesante rendition seems equivalent to a retard. Lécuyer contrasts the *scène* and the *monologue* of French opera, in both of which one can stretch out certain tones or *agréments*, with *airs mesurés et de caractère*, in which one must not under any circumstances alter the tempo *except in a final cadence* (*Principes du chant*, 22f.).

In 18th-century Germany, Marpurg writes in 1750 that ornaments must neither change nor interrupt the tempo, except in cadences in a solo, where it is customary on the last repeat to dwell beyond the beat on the appropriate ornament (meaning presumably the trill or perhaps a brief cadenza [*Des critischen Musicus*, 1:55]).

C. P. E. Bach has interesting comments in his treatise on accompaniment (*Versuch über Art das Clavier* [1762], chap. 29, pars. 20–21). In slow or moderate tempo, he writes, one dwells longer on phrase endings than is indicated, especially when the bass rhythm is rhythmically synchronized with the other voices or with the principal part in a solo. The same is the case with fermatas and cadences, where one intentionally drags a little and where the accompanist has to yield somewhat to the strictness of the beat. The final trill of a piece is often held longer, regardless of tempo. If there are repeats, the ritardando should be made only at the last repeat, at the end. Thus, he says, one gives weight to the end and lets the listener know that the piece is over. He does list exceptions, though. A fiery or sad idea can demand that one keep up the beat and not extend the final trill. He gives some excellent examples in paragraph 21. Later, in chapter 31, paragraph 3, he gives instructions to the accompanist on what to do when the soloist slows down before a fermata.

J. F. Agricola has a theory about the final retard. Originally, he thinks, cadences were played as written; then trills were made on the middle note; later, ornaments were added to the note preceding the trill; then the last measure of the voice part was slowed down; and finally this measure was embellished by passages that signaled the birth of the modern cadenza. According to this theory the cadenza is an ornamented final retard (*Anleitung zur Singkunst*, 195–96)!

The documentation seems abundant and international enough to disprove the notion that the final retard is unhistorical.

## Evidence for Retard in Bach

Concerning J. S. Bach, a few items of musical evidence to the same effect might be of interest. In the autograph of the *Orgelbüchlein* (P 283) we find the word *adagissimo* two times at the end of BWV 622 ("O Mensch, bewein"), starting exactly one eighth note before the last measure—that is, in a place where a sudden shift of tempo would hardly be logical.

In the alto aria "Qui sedes" from the Mass in B Minor, the term *adagio* is found in the autograph score in different spots: exactly at the start of measure 74 for the alto part, exactly one eighth note before the barline for oboe and continuo. In Kirnberger's copy in the Amalienbibliothek we find the identical discrepancy.

In Cantata No. 82/3 (bass aria "Schlummert ein"), the last two measures are marked *adagio*. Yet in the original parts (St 54) the entries vary in location as much as a whole measure. In the autograph organ part (#4) the *adagio* is placed at the start of the penultimate measure; in the autograph oboe da caccia part (#3) it is placed at the start of the last measure, and we find the same location in the two first violin parts (#7 and #9) and in the second violin part (#11 with autograph additions); in the second violin part (#12) the entry *pianissimo e adagio,* seemingly by Bach, starts half a measure earlier, in mid-penultimate measure; in the autograph viola part (#15) the words *pianissimo e adagio* start in the penultimate measure right after the first dotted quarter note. The inference of gradualism is inescapable. Moreover, in the earlier autograph version of the aria in Anna Magdalena's second notebook the *adagio* is missing altogether, which would hardly be the case if a structural, sudden change of tempo rather than a gradual slowing down had been intended.

In the tenor aria (no. 3) of Cantata No. 215, as given in Ex. 7.1, *Adagio* is written in the tenor part over the last eighth note of measure 57, where the last beat is set against four sixteenth notes in the bass. Since a sudden break in tempo that would split the four sixteenth notes

EXAMPLE 7.1. Bach, Cantata No. 215/3

in the middle is unthinkable, the ritardando meaning appears obvious. An analogous situation exists before the da capo, where *Adagio* is written for the tenor on the last two eighth notes in measure 97 while there are even eighth notes in all the other parts.

In the Concerto in E for Clavier (BWV 1053/1, m. 113), the tutti drops out at the cadence before the recapitulation, ostensibly to facilitate the soloist's ritardando to the *adagio* for the last two beats. In the Fugue in E Minor from *WTC II*, the fermata over the eighth triplet in measure 83 makes little sense without a preceding retard. The spot is marked *Adagio* in Altnikol's copy of 1744.

In Bach's arias it is, so it seems, a standard procedure for accompanying instruments other than the continuo to drop out at the full cadences of the vocal parts. This happens not only at the final singer's cadence but also in mid-aria, and its purpose is most probably to allow the soloist the rhythmic freedom of a slight retard. If this inference is correct, it would suggest that in soloistic situations emphatic full cadences not only at the end but also in the middle of a piece could, and maybe should, be underlined by a subtle slowing down. For a few illustrations, taken from just a single volume of the NBA (I/27), see Cantatas No. 60/3, duo ("Aria") with oboe d'amore and violin solo, tenor cadences in measures 27–28, 51–52, 80–81; No. 26/2, tenor aria with flute and violin solo, measures 76–78, 93–94; No. 26/4, bass aria with three oboes, measures 101–3; No. 90/1, tenor aria with strings, measures 55–60, 102–5; No. 90/3, bass aria with trumpet and strings, measures 50–52; No. 116/2, alto aria with oboe d'amore, measures 31–35, 70–73; No. 70/8, tenor aria with oboe and strings, measures 38–40; No. 140/6, duo with oboe, measures 72–73.

The slowing down in all these and similar circumstances should be subtle, unless an *adagio* directive calls for a substantial tempo change.

From the foregoing we can gather that today's musicians who instinctively slow down at the end of certain works, be they by Frescobaldi, Bach, or Mozart, do so in full accord with historical practice. Furthermore, we see that in some important matters our modern musical instincts can well agree with those of musicians of times long past.

# 8

# Tempo of Dances

*The Role of the Dance.* In the social life of the 17th and of a good part of the 18th century, dance occupied a preeminent place. As a consequence, dance rhythms entered the collective consciousness of the age and permeated to a remarkable extent much of the music, sacred and secular, of the Baroque era. Whether we find such rhythms in a Bach chorus, in a Lully aria, or in a Corelli sonata, the wide extent of this fertilization is hard to overestimate. France was the model in all fields of civilized intercourse and polished manners, and France was also the homeland of the theatrical dance, the great *ballet de cour* and the *opéra ballet.* For these reasons it was French dances that made the strongest international imprint on the art music of the period.

The role of specific dance types began to wane with the decline of the Baroque and became less conspicuous with the total victory of the galant style. For the second half of the 18th century only one specific dance, the minuet, survived the turmoil of the stylistic break and lingered on with its name intact, in symphonies and chamber music as well as in dance halls. The genius of dance, however, distilled to its rhythms and spirits, continued to reverberate through much of the music of the Classical era and beyond: in addition to the minuet the "Deutsche" (the nascent valse) and the widely popular contredanse took the place vacated by the obsolete French court dances.

Important as the dance no doubt was for, say, Mozart, it was not, I believe, as all-encompassing as suggested in the valuable books by Leonard G. Ratner (*Classic Music*) and Wye Jamison Allanbrook (*Rhythmic Gesture in Mozart*). For the shaping of Mozart's style we must not forget the vocal realm and the powerful impressions he received in the opera house from, among others, dramatic accents and contrasts, the

74

*dolcezza* of Italian cantilenas, the humorous sparkle of buffo allegros, and many other forms.

**Dances as Tempo Guides.** In the music of the Baroque, and especially in that of Bach, the vast role of the dance offers important tempo leads that nevertheless must be used with circumspection. The dances themselves had, by their nature, standardized tempi that are fairly well known, at least for specific times and places. Many French and a number of German theorists have given us descriptions of the nature and forms of the various dances, including information about their meter signatures, number of beats, and "affects" (with their implications for tempo). With a few exceptions, these descriptions are notable for overall agreement.

Yet we must not mechanically apply a tempo to any piece that is related to that tempo's dance. Mattheson, for one, stresses on various occasions the difference between dance tunes for actual dancing and those for playing or for singing. One must add here such pieces of music that are not formally but spiritually akin to a specific dance. In all these cases the tempo will often deviate from that of the original model; but the model may still serve as an approximate guide.

**Metronome-Like Devices.** In addition to leaving such verbal explanations, several French authors, as well as Quantz, tried to establish the tempi with greater precision by means of metronome-like indications. For this purpose the French used various instruments based on a suspended pendulum, while Quantz, as mentioned before, used the much older procedure of referring to the pulse (at a rate of 80 beats per minute, which he considered the norm) as a point of reference.

Not long after Galileo discovered the physical laws that governed the pendulum's even swing regardless of amplitude, Marin Mersenne, in his *Harmonie universelle* of 1636, describes a pendulum clock that could divide hours into minutes and seconds. He saw many uses for it, such as measuring the pulse rate, but did not yet foresee an application to music (1:135–37). By way of contrast, Thomas Mace, in his *Musick's Monument* of 1676, describes a pendulum for the very purpose of keeping strict musical time. He suggests attaching a "bullet" of half a pound or a pound to a string suspended from a hook in the ceiling, then setting it in motion, whereupon it will swing with the exact same speed for about two hours. He also explains how to vary the speed by lengthening or shortening the string (80–81).

At the end of the century, Étienne Loulié, in his treatise of 1696, describes and illustrates a *chronomètre* (*Eléments ou principes de musique*, 81–88) that, though practical, found little acceptance. Joseph Sauveur, the founder of modern acoustics, describes in 1701 a device that could distinguish time lengths of ¹⁄₆₀ of a second, called *tierces*. In 1705 (beginning with the sixth edition of his well-known treatise of 1694), Michel

L'Affilard, the musical theorist, uses Sauveur's invention to provide the various songs and dances reprinted in the book with tempo markings. He did so by listing the number of *tierces* above the meter signature, referring to their basic beat (*Principes pour apprendre la musique* [1705], 9 and passim).

In 1732 the physicist-inventor Louis-Léon Pajot, also known as d'Onzembray, presents to the French Académie Royale des Sciences a new measuring instrument for musical tempo, the *métromètre*. With the help of this instrument, Pajot offers a listing of tempi for twenty-three specific dances and overtures from operas and ballets of the leading French composers from Lully to Destouches.[1]

In 1736, Jacques Alexandre de La Chapelle describes his *pendule* and with its help lists the tempi of fifteen dances by indicating the pendulum length in *pouces* (inches). His figures range from the fastest 4 for *tambourin* and 6 for *rigaudon* to the slowest 26 for *gaillarde* and 33 for the *passacaille* (*Les vrais principes*, 2:42–45).

In the same manner, Henri-Louis Choquel, in 1762, describes and illustrates his own pendulum device (which uses a 1 oz. weight) and lists the tempi of various dances in terms of pendulum length (*La musique rendue*, 115–55).

Table 8.1 transcribes the original data of these authors into metronome markings. For de La Chapelle and Choquel I am using the figures calculated by Eugène Borrel, for L'Affilard and Pajot the combined, near-identical figures of Eugène Borrel and Curt Sachs (regarding Borrel and Sachs, see note 1). These tabulations are fascinating but also bewildering because they show tempi that are on the whole faster, and in some cases considerably faster, than we would expect from the verbal descriptions or from what they have traditionally been assumed to be.

In an effort to adjust at least one set of tempo indications to our prevailing ideas on the matter, Erich Schwandt has tried to correct L'Affilard's figures by reducing them to one-half of their speed. His argument rested on the hypothesis that L'Affilard misunderstood and misapplied Sauveur, the inventor of the measuring device, and had meant by "one vibration" a complete movement of the pendulum back and forth ("L'Affilard," 389–400). L'Affilard's figures, however, agree surprisingly with those of the other writers mentioned in Table 8.1, some of whom arrived at their results with different means; among them is Choquel, who is very specific in counting as one beat the single pendulum move "from A to B" and not the complete cycle back to A. Finally, it is unrealistic to measure a ternary dance beaten in one, such as the minuet, with a double vibration of the pendulum. There is no getting around the fastness of the French dance tempi.

The overall agreement between the French sources is significant because their figures were arrived at independently and could hardly have involved plagiarism. Quantz was handicapped in his listings by his

TABLE 8.1  Tempi of French Dances*

| Pajot (1732) | meter | beats | MM | L'Affilard (1705) MM | La Chapelle (1737) MM | Choquel (1759) MM |
|---|---|---|---|---|---|---|
| Bourrée (Lully, *Phaéton*) | 2 | 2 | 112 | 120 | 120 | |
| Gavotte (Lully, *Roland*) | 2 | 2 | 97 | 120 | 152 | 126 |
| Passecaille (Lully, *Persée*) | 3 | 3 | 94 | | | |
| Chaconne (Lully, *Fêtes de Bacchus*) | 3 | 1 | 53 | ♩=156 | | |
| Gigue (Colasse, *Amadis*) | 6/4 | 2 | 112 | ♩.=116–20 | ♩=120 | |
| Loure (Colasse, *Thétis*) | 6/4 | 2 | 112 | | ♩.=120 | ♩.=120 |
| Ouverture (Colasse, *Thétis*–beginning) | 2 | 2 | 64 | | | |
| Passepied (Campra, *L'Europe galante*) | 3/8 | 1 | 100 | 84 | 136 | 92 |
| Rigaudon (Campra, *L'Europe galante*) | 2 | 2 | 116 | 120 | 152 | 126 |
| Menuet (Campra, *L'Europe galante*) | 3 | 1 | 70 | 72–76 | | 80 |
| Courante (Mato) | 3 | 3 | 84 | | | |
| Sarabande (Destouches, *Isée*) | 3/2 | 3 | 73 | 66–72–84 | 63 | |

*Original figures (*tierces* or pendulum swings) transcribed into MM by E. Borrel and C. Sachs. The specific pieces listed in the first column refer only to Pajot.

rigid basic speed of 80 beats per minute, so that his figures are either 80 or a multiple, which makes them at best crude approximations.

As to the French figures, their fastness may be at least in part due to a tendency to *think* a faster tempo than one would actually play or conduct. It is likely that even such figures as those of Pajot were recorded not during a performance but reconstructed from memory.

Yet even if we allow for the need for adjustments, the tabulations should dispose of the widely accepted idea that old music was played slowly. An earwitness, Antoine Bauderon de Sénecé (who was *l^er valet de chambre* to Marie-Thérèse, the wife of Louis XIV), reports with regard to the "Simphonie des champs Élisiens" in Lully's *Proserpine* that Lully beat time "with great impatience" (Lettre, 19–20). Similarly, we have a reliable report (from the obituary written by C. P. E. Bach and J. F. Agricola) that Bach took his tempi generally very lively. Quantz contributed to the belief in the early slow tempi by writing that fast music "was in previous times played twice as slowly as today." An allegro assai or presto furioso, he says, was played hardly faster than one plays the allegretto today (*Versuch einer Anweisung,* chap. 17, sec. 7, par. 50).

Besides the overall fastness of the tempi, the tabulations contain several individual points of interest. One is the liveliness of the chaconne, which reminds us that the French chaconne was on the whole faster than the Italian ciacona that served as the main model for the German masters of the Baroque. Often the French make a further distinction between the regular chaconne and an even livelier one, the *chaconne légère.*

The tempo of the courante refers to the slow French type in $\frac{3}{2}$ or $\frac{6}{4}$, not the fast Italian corrente in $\frac{3}{4}$ time.

Of special interest is Pajot's tempo of MM = 64 per half-note beat for the first part of Colasse's Overture to *Thétis et Pélée.* This relatively lively speed is sharply at odds with the prevalent ideas about the "majestic" pomp of French overtures.

The rather marked difference in the tempi for the gavotte reflects a variability in its character, which, according to several authorities, can be fast or moderate.

The allemande is missing in these listings (except for La Chapelle, who gives the surprisingly fast 120 for a quarter note), presumably because it had become at the time a pure instrumental piece, having become obsolete as a dance.

The figures of the French theorists may often be difficult to apply even to French dances around 1700 and may thus call for occasional adjustments. In the process of naturalization, the Germans and the English, who had adopted all of the French forms, also adapted them to their own collective and individual styles. Thus, if some of the figures of the tabulation may seem to be at the extreme range for the French, they are often beyond what is practicable and reasonable for, say, Bach and Handel, whose generally richer texture and polyphonic elaboration calls for a slowing of the beat.

*Character of the Dances.* What usually remains more or less unchanged is the character of the dance, which can well retain its identity even when the tempo adjusts to differences in texture. For these reasons today's performer will probably find more practical guidelines in the verbal descriptions of the character of the various dances by writers of various nationalities. A selected summary of such typologies is given in Table 8.2, which lists the Frenchmen Masson, Brossard, and J. J. Rousseau together with the Germans Mattheson and Quantz.

The courantes in this chart, too, are all of the French type. As mentioned before, the Italian corrente is strikingly different. The courante is slow, in $\frac{3}{2}$ or $\frac{6}{4}$ (often alternating the respective rhythmic dispositions), and usually contains dotted notes and varied rhythmic figures; the corrente, typically in $\frac{3}{4}$, is fast and characterized by (for the most part) evenly running eighth notes. Bach usually distinguished the two types in both style and nomenclature, but, except for the NBA, most editions, following the lead of the old Bach Gesellschaft edition, confuse the issue by using the term *courante* indiscriminately. Among his clavier suites, we find genuine—that is, French—courantes in all English suites, in the First and Third French suites, in the Second and Fourth partitas, and in the French Overture. All others are Italian correntes, mostly with running eighth notes. The correntes of the Third Partita and the Fifth and Sixth French suites have running sixteenth notes, which necessarily slow the beat. The corrente in the Sixth Partita is quite irregular in both style and form, but it leans to the Italian type.

The gigue in the charts is the French type with the prevailing rhythm of ♪.♫ . The Italian giga has no dotted notes but a series of even eighth notes: ♫♪ ♫♪ (Bach occasionally uses sixteenth notes, which again will slow the beat). Mattheson says it should be played with extreme speed ("äusserste Schnelligkeit"). The Italian giga is the dance rhythm most frequently found in Bach's vocal works.

Interesting are the conflicting views about the relative tempi of the chaconne and the passacaglia. To the Frenchmen Masson, Brossard, and J. J. Rousseau, the passacaglia is the slower of the two; to the Germans Mattheson and Quantz it is the opposite.

What shall we make of the information available about the dance tempi of the Baroque period? One thing we definitely must not do is to take any of the metronome figures and mechanically apply them to a specific dance or dance-derived piece. Being abstractions, these figures have to be adapted to individual situations while we keep in mind the verbal description of their characters.

TABLE 8.2   Character of French Dances

| | Masson 1699 | Brossard 1703 | Mattheson 1739 | Quantz 1752 | J. J. Rousseau 1768 |
|---|---|---|---|---|---|
| Allemande | | | serious | | *grave* |
| Bourrée | *vite* | | carefree, faster than gavotte | gay with short and light bowstrokes | *gay* |
| Canarie | somewhat faster than gigue | | a very fast gigue, somewhat naïve | short and sharp bowstrokes | |
| Chaconne | *léger* | sometimes gay, sometimes grave | slower than passacaglia | grand | *modéré* |
| Courante | *grave* | | | grand | *grave* |
| Gavotte | *léger* | gay, bouncing (*sautillant*) | joyful, sometimes fast, sometimes slow | like rigaudon but somewhat slower | *assez gay* |
| Gigue | same as bourrée and rigaudon | | fervent and hurried | short and light bowstrokes | |
| Loure | *lent* | | slow gigue, proud, pretentious | | |
| Menuet | *vite* | very gay and very fast | moderate gaiety | "*hebend*" (with bounce?); quarters marked with heavy but short bowstroke | elegant and noble simplicity, more moderate than fast |
| Passecaille | *grave* | more grave and tender than chaconne | faster than chaconne | like chaconne but somewhat faster | more gentle (*plus tendre*) and slower than chaconne |
| Passepied | *très vite* | | fast menuet, carefree, frivolous | lighter and faster than menuet | |
| Rigaudon | *vite* | | between gavotte and bourrée, playful, jocular | gay, short and light bowstrokes | *gay* |
| Sarabande | *grave* | a grave, slow, serious menuet | solemn, grave | grand but smoother than courante | *grave* |

One important lesson that must not be ignored is the liveliness of tempo for most of the dances. Exceptions are the sarabande, the passacaglia, the French courante, and, it would seem, the Italo-German ciacona. Yet even these "slow" dances must not be taken at a lethargic pace and certainly never so slow as to suggest the subdivision of the beat. For most of the other dances we should revise the widespread view of the sedateness of old music and experiment with faster tempi. The bourrée is very fast in two beats in binary meter. Very fast, too, are the gigue and passepied in $\frac{3}{8}$ (or its multiples). The gavotte (in binary meter in two beats) ranges from fast to unhurried; the French chaconne is moderately lively; the allemande moderate in $\frac{4}{4}$. The minuet is faster in $\frac{3}{8}$ than in $\frac{3}{4}$, the latter lively but not speeding and getting more leisurely in the symphonic and chamber music minuets of the Classical era. The proper tempo of these latter minuets has recently given rise to a lively controversy.[2]

Rameau writes in the preface to his *Nouvelles suites de pièces de clavecin* of ca. 1728: "The tempo of these pieces leans more toward fastness than slowness, except for the allemande, the sarabande, the *simple* of the gavotte [implying interestingly that the *doubles* were played faster!]." Then he adds that, generally speaking, too slow is better than too fast, but "once one has mastered a piece one grasps instinctively its character and senses its proper tempo" (quand on possède une pièce on en saisit insensiblement le goût et bientôt on en sent le vrai mouvement [2]).

This fundamental thought is echoed by J. J. Rousseau, who dismisses the metronome-type tools as useless for actual performance. "The only good *chronomètre* one can have is a capable musician with taste and judgment who has studied the music he is supposed to perform" (*Dictionnaire*, s.v. "Chronomètre").

We find variations on the theme of this thought expressed for music of all kinds by many masters throughout the centuries. Praetorius and Frescobaldi were quoted above in the same sense; 250 years later Richard Wagner had become disenchanted with the metronome and began using only very general time words, now relying solely on the musical insight of the conductor. He mentions Bach's frequent failure to give any tempo indications at all: "He may have said to himself: whoever does not understand my themes and my figurations, who does not sense their character and expression, will not be helped by any Italian tempo words" ("Über das Dirigieren," 275; I owe this reference to Professor Robert Bailey).

In the final analysis, we probably do best to fall back on Rousseau's "capable musician with taste and judgment who has studied the music he is supposed to perform." We only need to add that he should also be stylistically knowledgeable. If such a musician gives full consideration to all the clues the composer has given, such as meter, tempo words, the prevalent and the fastest note values, the overall "affect," the relationship to specific dance rhythms, the lightness or thickness of texture, the prevailing "live" or "dry" acoustics, and the nature of the melodies, the result is more likely to be a more artistic and "authentic" choice than we could obtain by relying on figures in tables (of the kind shown), on rules, on would-be traditions, on 19th-century metronomizations, or on doctrines.

Tempo is, as was said at the beginning of this part of the book, both the most pivotal and the most elusive of all elements of performance. First, there is no one "authentic" tempo that fits all circumstances of performance for any piece of music. There is always a certain range, sometimes narrow, sometimes less narrow, within which we can speculate the composer may have been satisfied. To the extent that the preceding discussion may have helped in adumbrating these ranges, it is probably the best that could be expected in a matter of such extraordinary complexity.

# Part II

## Rhythm

# Rhythm and Meter

"Rhythm" is a word everybody knows and uses confidently, but when we try to define its meaning we meet with frustrating difficulties. And with "meter," which is not the household word that "rhythm" is, and particularly with its relationship to "rhythm," we enter a highly controversial territory. Many definitions of the two concepts have been essayed, and very few are in agreement. I make no attempt here to offer a new solution that would replace all the earlier ones. My purpose is simply to establish a working terminology that will serve our purpose at hand so that, for example, when I speak of a "metric" or an "arbitrary" accent the reader will know what I mean.

With regard to "rhythm" the task of clarification is difficult because the idea of musical rhythm is complex: it embodies several elements that in turn interact with one another and with other elements of music in often complicated relationships. First, there is the pulse, a regularly recurring beat—the one that we instinctively tap when we hear a march or a dance; the one also the conductor traces with his beat. We might call this the "rhythm of the beat." The pulse, which can be slow, medium or fast, sped up or slowed down, is thereby inseparable from tempo; it is indeed the rate of the pulse that sets the tempo of a piece. The pulse is also linked to the "meter" in a more complex relationship that will be discussed presently.

Second, there is the pattern of long and short notes as they follow each other in a melody, referring to the temporal distances between the starting points of the constituent notes; we might call this "the rhythm of the melody"—the one children would bring out when asked to clap the melody of, say, the "Star-Spangled Banner."

Third is the pattern of accented and unaccented notes. Here we must distinguish two very distinct kinds of accents; I shall refer to one as "metric" and to the other—for want of a better term—as "arbitrary."

*The Metric Accent.* The "metric" accent is inherent in the meter chosen by the composer as indicated by signatures such as $\frac{2}{4}$, $\frac{3}{4}$, $\frac{4}{4}$, $\frac{2}{2}$, $\frac{3}{8}$, $\frac{6}{8}$, and so on. Each of these meters summons a different pattern of heavy and light beats, of stresses and releases, of "theses" and "arses." Regardless of the meter chosen, there is always a metric accent on 1, the conductor's downbeat. The patterns themselves exist in the abstract, independent of the music. Just as verse forms, such as the hexameter, the Alexandrine, and the iambic pentameter, exist independent of the poetry as a kind of formal mold selected by the poet into which words are poured, a musical meter calls forth a specific structure of heavy and light beats, a structure that organizes and helps mold the flow of the music. Thus a given meter will create the presumption that its implied stress patterns were intended and will be audible. "Presumption," but not certainty:

the composer is free to countermand the metric pattern by prescribing accents on weak beats, or between beats, by omitting a note on a stressed beat or by other methods. But no composer would ever do these things systematically, because by annulling metrical stresses for any extended period, meters would become pointless and irrational.

The meter itself, with its periodicity of heavy and light beats, may have its roots in facts revealed by experimental psychology: we tend to perceive a regularly recurring event like the pulse or the ticking of a clock in patterns of stressed and unstressed beats. The reason may be that such stress–release patterns permeate vital rhythms of our being: the systole and diastole of the heart beat, breathing in and out, tension and release involved in any physical action such as walking, running, or dancing, with the setting of the foot as thesis, the lifting as arsis, and so on.

The metrical stress patterns can all be reduced to the two basic ones of the binary heavy–light ( - ◡ ) and the ternary heavy–light–light ( - ◡ ◡ ). It is important to realize that these stress patterns occur on several levels, both lower (faster) and higher (slower) than that of the beat. Figure II.1 shows levels in a binary (a) and in a ternary (b) pattern. In Fig. II.1a the simple meter of $\frac{2}{4}$ shows the beat represented by quarter notes in their strong–weak alternation. On the next lower level we see how the pattern descends to eighth notes and from there to sixteenth notes, where again any odd-numbered unit is strong and any even-numbered weak. From the beat level the pattern may ascend to the higher level of half notes. Such strong–weak alternation on the half-note level explains why in a composite meter like that of $\frac{4}{4}$ the second half of a measure is weaker than the first: though the third beat is strong, it is less strong that the first. The same applies to all composite meters such as $\frac{6}{8}$, which in slow tempo will have two ternary halves (  ♪♪♪ ♪♪♪  ), of which the second is weaker than the first, or, in fast tempo, one binary unit: ♩· ♩· .

Metrical stress patterns received considerable attention from theorists beginning with the late 17th century. They discussed the importance of these patterns for, among others, the proper setting of words, for melodic design, for dissonance treatment, and for thorough bass realization. To list just a few among these theorists, there were Johann Georg Ahle in 1695 (*Musikalisches Frühlings-Gespräche*, 36–38), Wolfgang Caspar Printz in 1696 (*Phrynis*, 18ff.), Sebastien de Brossard (*Diction-naire*, s.v. "Tempus"), Saint Lambert in 1707 (*Nouveau traité*, 121), Johann Gottfried Walther in 1708 (*Praecepta*, 23–24), Johann Mattheson, first in 1722 (*Critica musica*, 44) and then at some length in 1739 (*Vollkommene Capellmeister*, pt. 2, chap. 8, pars. 7–32), and a good many others. Some of them were explicit about the descent of the heavy–light pattern to lower levels, such as Johann Friedrich Agricola in 1757 (*Anleitung zur*

FIGURE II.1

a. Binary pattern

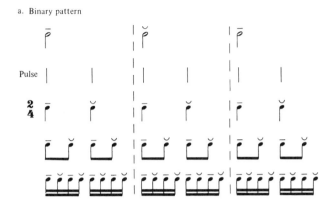

b. Ternary pattern

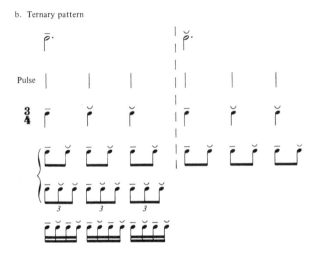

*Singkunst,* 73) and Johann Samuel Petri in 1782 (*Anleitung zur Musik,* 160–61). Some of the terms used by the theorists to designate this heavy–light design of notes, or rather of parts of the measure (since several notes can fall on a stressed or unstressed unit), were the following, with the common meaning of "good and bad notes": *note buone e cattive, notes de repos et de passage, gute und schlimme Tact-theile* (or *Tact-glieder), anschlagende und durchgehende Noten,* and *quantitate intrinseca* or *virtualiter* or *innerlich lange und kurtze Noten.* The latter of these, the adverbially qualified "long and short notes," are important because their infelicitous, ambiguous terms prompted some modern commentators to mistake what was heavy and light as genuinely long and short. More about this later.

The degree of the metric accent will vary, depending on style and texture of the work as a whole and of the specific situation. Generally, metric accents will be stronger in dances than in songs, stronger in homophonic than in polyphonic music, while in some works or passages they can fade to the point of near-disappearance. But they will always be implied and can never be ignored for the proper setting of a text or for the other mentioned musical associations.

*The Arbitrary Accent.* The other, "arbitrary" type of accentuation is independent of the meter, has no necessary regularity, and derives solely from the composer's specific ideas. By using accentual symbols the composer can place accents anywhere: on strong beats (reinforcing the metrical stress), on weak beats, or even between beats. In fact, their rhythmic effect will be the more striking the more they conflict with the metrical pattern. When not specified by symbols, "irregular" accents can be implied by the music: by a dissonance, an altered note, a striking clash of the melodic rhythm with the meter, a large leap, an unexpected articulation, and many more occurrences (see the discussion of various types of accents in chap. 14).

*Integration of Rhythm with Other Musical Elements.* Rhythm has a close link with tempo since, as mentioned before, the speed of the pulse, be it steady or changing, determines the tempo. A link with dynamics is established by both types of rhythmic accents. As to phrasing, I believe Grosvenor Cooper and Leonard B. Meyer, in their book *The Rhythmic Structure of Music,* go too far in nearly equating rhythm with phrasing by consistently analyzing rhythm as the agent that shapes melodies into groups on different structural levels. But there is no doubt that rhythmic designs of long and short notes with their accentuations and interspersed rests often determine proper phrasing and occasionally articulation as well. Rhythm's link with ornamentation is formed by the important implications an ornament's metrical position—before, on, after, or astride a beat or a barline—has for its function.

These are some, but by no means all, of the facets of rhythm, surely the oldest and arguably the most central of all musical elements. It is the one that invigorates, enlivens, and energizes the musical body just as the heartbeat, pumping blood through the organism, vitalizes the physical body. As I said before, these observations are not meant to offer a new definition of rhythm to replace all others attempted before but simply to show the complexity of an issue that defies a simple explanation and to point up the many ways in which the idea of rhythm is interwoven as if by nerve strands and blood vessels with all other parts of a musical organism.

Because of this interweaving, some aspects of rhythm have been or will be discussed in chapters on tempo, phrasing, articulation, dynamics, and ornamentation. The issues that form the focus of the following discussions have principally to do with length and shortness of notes and fall generally under the heading of what Arnold Dolmetsch called "rhythmic alterations." By this term he referred to cases where the proper rendition deviates from the arithmetic ratios of the notation. The main topics will be (1) "agogic accents"—that is, notes held longer than their nominal value for the sake of expression; (2) *rubato,* in the sense of rhythmic freedoms taken by the melody against the steady beat of the accompaniment as well as the slight freedoms and flexibilities that are inseparable from any artistic performance; (3) dotted notes that were meant to be rendered in other than a 3:1 ratio (either milder, for instance 2:1, or sharper, for instance 7:1 or 15:1); (4) evenly written notes that were meant to be rendered unevenly, be it long–short or short–long (including the French *notes inégales*); and (5) conflicts of binary and ternary rhythms in simultaneous voices and the question of whether they should clash by being rendered literally or should be assimilated in either direction.

# 9

# RHYTHMIC ALTERATIONS I: ARTISTIC LICENSE AND DEFECTS OF NOTATION

The symbols of rhythmic notation indicate definite mathematical ratios among the lengths of notes, as measured by the time span between their starting points. Performers will, however, often deviate from the implied ratios, either unintentionally or intentionally.

Unintentional deviations occur because human beings are not machines, and however good their sense of timing and muscular coordination, consistent mathematical precision is humanly unattainable. As long as such deviations remain insignificant they need not concern us, but where they become noticeable they reveal either a lack of rhythmic sense or a defective technique and call simply for remedial study.

Intentional deviations are of three principal kinds. The first results from a performer's striving for an artistically imaginative interpretation, leading to an exercise of "artistic license." The second has to do with imprecisions and even defects in the notation itself. The third springs from real or imagined historical conventions of performance.

# Artistic License

*Inflections and Nuances.* Small irregularities may result from an attempt to animate the dead letter of the score. No organic entity functions with mechanical precision, nor can a spontaneous performance be machine-like. Two notes of seemingly equal length, when touched with the breath of life, will not be exactly equal any more. Such slight irregularities, be they nuances of length, loudness, or coloring, are, and doubtless have always been, present in any artistic performance. They are not palpable enough to be considered "alterations" but are subtle inflections that many listeners might not even notice but would likely miss if they were absent. They have nothing to do with any "convention"; they are not subject to any "rules"—though to some extent they are governed by taste, thus historically variable. Basically they are simply manifestations of the artistic impulse.

*Agogic Accents.* The borderline is fluid between such inflections and the generally more sizable irregularity that occurs when a note, in a relatively fast sequence of pitches, is lengthened for the sake of emphasis. Such lengthening is now usually called an "agogic accent" (Hugo Riemann's term). It, too, responds primarily to the instinct, experience, and judgment of the performer, though several theorists, to be quoted presently, list circumstances where such agogic accents ought to be applied. In principle, such lengthening does not interfere with the steadiness of the pulse. Instead, the extra length is normally made up by a corresponding shortening of one or more of the following notes. Though used by all media, agogic accents are of particular importance for the harpsichord and the organ, which, owing to their lack of dynamic potential, depend on such slight lengthening as their only means of emphasis and often as the best means of clarifying the meter.

For media capable of dynamic nuances, an agogic accent will frequently be combined with a subtle dynamic emphasis. Quantz, speaking of the violin, writes that in order to render sixteenths of the kind shown in Ex. 9.1a beautifully in a slow tempo, the first note of each pair should be a little longer and a little heavier than the second, and the B (marked here by an asterisk) should be played *almost* as if it were followed by a dot (*Versuch einer Anweisung,* chap. 17, sec. 2, par. 12). Leopold Mozart writes that the first of two, three, or more slurred notes (see Exx. 9.1b and c) should be played a little louder and longer without in the least affecting the evenness of the meter ("dass der Tact auch nicht im geringsten aus seiner Gleichheit geräth"), implying the need for rhythmic compensation (*Versuch einer Violinschule,* chap. 7, sec. 2, par. 5). C. P. E. Bach describes the agogic accent for notes (as well as for rests) that for the sake of expression ("Affeckt") are held longer than their written value. He gives several illustrations, of which one is shown in Ex. 9.1d, where little crosses indicate such desirable lengthening (*Versuch über Art das Clavier* [1753], chap. 3, par. 28, and Tab. 6, fig. 13). When C. P. E. Bach writes earlier in the same chapter (par. 18) that the first note under a slur should be given a slightly stronger pressure, this directive spontaneously translates into a subtle agogic accent when applied to harpsichord or organ.

EXAMPLE 9.1

a. Quantz        b. L. Mozart        c. L. Mozart

d. C.P.E. Bach

Türk, in 1789, speaks of agogic accents ("the lingering on certain notes") as a means of emphasis that should be used with great care and more rarely than regular accents. Such lingering, he writes, should not exceed half the length of a note, and "as a matter of course" the following note has to lose what the first had gained (*Klavierschule,* chap. 6, sec. 2, pars. 17–18).

*Rubato.* The term *rubato* means robbed: the idea then is to rob some notes of part of their value and give it to others for the sake of enhanced expression. In this sense the agogic accent is the simplest form of rubato in that the accent usurps an extra increment of value that needs to be repaid by subsequent notes. Very often, however, not just one note but a series of notes is stretched out beyond their notational value and their expansion then made up by a corresponding contraction of notes that follow. Or, vice versa, an initial speeding up is balanced by a corresponding slowing down.

In most instances, such rhythmic play is a matter for a soloist and takes place against a steady beat in the accompaniment; also more often than not, the resolution of the imbalance takes place within a single measure. Resolution across the barline is perfectly possible, however, provided the bass remains steady and the resolution is not long delayed. We find a very early documentation for such rhythmic give-and-take in Sylvestro Ganassi's recorder treatise (*Opera intitulata Fontegara*) of 1535, where, among a huge mass of diminution patterns with added notes, there are scattered a few examples with pure rhythmic manipulation in a genuine rubato, as shown in Ex. 9.2. Here models a, b, c, d, taken from

"Regola seconda" of chapter 15, are followed by ornamented versions (a', b', c', d') in the form of simple rhythmic play. Ganassi achieves the suggestion of rubato freedom by the use of the $\frac{5}{4}$ ("sesquiquarta") proportion whereby the semibreve (whole note) is divided into five semiminims (quarter notes) in the manner of $\circ = \text{♩♩♩♩♩}$. On other occasions in the book Ganassi suggests rhythmic freedoms in the ornamented versions by, among other methods, even more complicated proportions such as $\frac{5}{8}$, $\frac{7}{4}$, $\frac{7}{5}$, $\frac{8}{7}$ (regarding proportions, see chap. 1 of this book).

EXAMPLE 9.2.   Ganassi (1535)

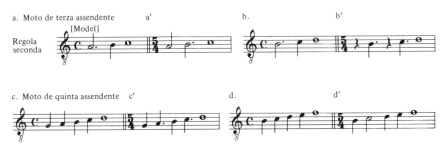

Like Ganassi, Zacconi in 1592 sees rhythmic play as a kind of ornamentation. He speaks of notes that "are attended by some *accenti* produced by the slowing down and sustaining of the voice and realized by taking a particle from one note and adding it to another one."[1]

Caccini, in the preface to his *Nuove musiche* of 1602, shows how to increase the affect of a passage by shortening or lengthening an individual note and compensating immediately such as in rendering evenly written notes as dotted ones or as a Lombard rhythm.[2]

When Christoph Bernhard, in the middle of the 17th century, shows a passage ornamented with the device of *anticipatione della nota* (Ex. 9.3) and ties the anticipation to the following note, as shown in the spot marked by an asterisk, the result is a rubato (*Tractatus compositionis*, chap. 22).

EXAMPLE 9.3.   Bernhard (ca. 1660)

Pierfrancesco Tosi, in 1723, lists as one of the important elements of artistic singing the "unexpected deceptive play with note values within the strict movement of the bass" (inaspettati inganni con rubamente di Tempo, e sul MOTO de' Bassi [*Opinioni de' cantori*, 82]). Strict adherence to the beat is for Tosi a paramount principle. He refers to it on various occasions and contrasts it with the metric arbitrariness that was practiced by "the oldest singers" until, over fifty years before (hence around 1675), such procedures began to be rejected by a number of leading artists. He names especially F. A. Pistocchi (1659–1726), "the most famous singer of all times," as the one who taught everyone how to apply all the adornments of the art without infringing the beat ("per aver insegnato a tutti le bellezze dell' Arte senza offendere le misure del Tempo" [65]).

C. P. E. Bach deals with *tempo rubato* in the third edition of the first volume of the *Versuch* (1787) in a lengthy addition to paragraph 28 of chapter 3. He describes the tempo rubato as playing either more or fewer than the normal number of notes within a metrical unit. "In so doing, one can, so to speak, deform [verziehen] a part of a measure, a whole measure, also several measures." It is well done when "one hand seems to play against the beat while the other sounds the beat with greatest precision." Slow notes and flattering and sad ideas are best suited for such treatment, dissonances better than consonances. Its good execution requires fine judgment and keen sensitivity and a freedom that tolerates not the slightest coercion. "In my clavier works are many examples [calling for] such treatment."

Mozart writes in a letter to his father of October 24, 1777: "All [listeners] are amazed that I always adhere strictly to the tempo. They cannot comprehend that in an adagio, in tempo rubato the left hand remains unaffected [die lincke hand nichts darum weiss]. With them the left hand always yields" (Schiedermair, *Die Briefe*, vol. 1, 96). This is the classic description of a rubato in its literal sense, artfully shifting the rhythm of a melody, yet coming out even after returning what has been "robbed."

Türk, in addition to the previously mentioned passage on agogic accents, also describes the rubato as shifting of the note values in either direction, as when in Ex. 9.4 the progression in (a) is played as written in (b) or in (c). Türk then blurs the concept of rubato by extending the term to the shifting of accents from the strong to the weak beats or to weak subdivisions of a beat, as for instance when of four eighth notes in $\frac{2}{4}$ meter the second and fourth are played strong, the first and third weak (*Klavierschule*, chap. 6, sec. 5, par. 72). In this he follows the lead of Petri, who in 1782 defined tempo rubato in this very manner—it is used, he says, to express a partly plaintive, partly stubborn and contrary affection (*Anleitung zur Musik* [1782], 164). In such purely accentual play the very essence of rubato—the speeding up and slowing down—is not involved, and the use of the term in this connection is not advisable.

EXAMPLE 9.4.  Türk (1789)

The rubato in the sense meant by Tosi and Mozart was unquestionably practiced by soloists in all media from at least the 16th century to the present, and it is an important means of enhancing expression in slow movements and is nearly indispensable for the dynamically inflexible organ and harpsichord.

***Tempo Rubato.*** The term *rubato* is occasionally used in the compound form of *tempo rubato* to designate tempo fluctuations in a wider sense. Here the term is not literal, because nothing is being "robbed" of something that needs to be restored; rather, the beat itself varies freely. We have testimonials about such variations at least from the 16th century on. They belong more properly under the heading of "tempo," which has been discussed in chapter 3.

## Defects and Imprecisions of Notation

*The Missing Symbol*. Certain defects or imprecisions of notation can lead to discrepancies between the desired execution and the literal meaning of rhythmic notation. Perhaps the most important of these defects was the absence of symbols for a 2:1 ratio within a binary rhythm: the modern C was not available until the mid-19th century, nor were its equivalents for shorter values such as. Since triplets had been known for a long time and were marked (at least in Italy and Germany) with the well-known little 3 on top—a spelling derived from mensural blackened notation—it seems surprising that it took so long, two and a half centuries in fact, for the spelling of to become widely used. In France the triplet notation with the little 3 was far less common; the French much preferred to write ternary rhythms in ternary meters such as $\frac{3}{8}$, $\frac{6}{8}$, etc. Within a binary meter they usually indicated triplets through beaming alone, mostly in the common three instead of two ratio: 2 ; once in a while with one beam more than we would expect: 2 = . It was not until the second half of the 18th century that the Italian triplet notation became common also in France.

As to the symbol, some masters such as Kuhnau used it once in a long while, as if by accident; so did Bach on at least two occasions (in the chorale of Cantata No. 105 and in the Organ Chorale "In dulci jubilo"), without apparently realizing that he had hit on a notational discovery. Had he realized it, one assumes that he would have kept using it. But he never did.

To fill the void opened by the missing symbol, the dotted note had in most cases to serve as a makeshift whereby its nominal 3:1 ratio had to yield to a 2:1 ratio. That means of course that the rhythm of the dotted note became ambiguous. The ambiguity becomes especially acute when the dotted note occurs opposite triplets in another voice or occurs in the same voice within a triplet environment. The opposition of dotted notes and triplets in another voice has given rise to differences of opinion in the 18th century as well as today. Quantz opposes synchronization and writes that the short note after the dot must not be played *with* the third triplet but *after* it. Otherwise it would sound as if written in a $\frac{6}{8}$ or $\frac{12}{8}$ meter (*Versuch einer Anweisung*, chap. 5, par. 22). C. P. E. Bach, in contrast, asks for synchronization. He wants to avoid the consecutive sounding ("der Nachschlag") that, he says, is often disagreeable and always difficult (*Versuch über Art das Clavier* [1753], chap. 3, par. 27). Interestingly, we have a testimonial that Johann Sebastian Bach in principle leaned to Quantz's solution. Johann Friedrich Agricola, who as a young man had studied with Bach, reviewed in 1769 a clavier treatise (by Löhlein) that advocated the synchronization of triplets with dotted notes. In answer to this principle Agricola writes: "Such synchronization takes place only in extreme speed. Barring this, the note after the dot must be played not with but *after* the last note of the triplet. Otherwise the difference between the binary measure, where such notes occur, and the $\frac{3}{8}$, $\frac{6}{8}$, $\frac{9}{8}$, $\frac{12}{8}$ meter would be obliterated. This is what J. S. Bach taught all his students and this is too what Quantz teaches in his treatise. Surely nobody will have reservations about the performing skill and artistic sensitivity of these two men" (Review of Löhlein's *Clavier-Schule*, 206).

Reading this passage, we might conclude that Bach desired literalness in most cases (excepting extreme speed) of binary–ternary clashes and, more generally, a literal interpretation of the dotted note. There is, however, much indisputable evidence that for Bach the tempo did not have to be extreme for dotted notes to be assimilated to triplets. We find such evidence, for instance, in calligraphic autographs in which the short note after the dot is precisely and consistently aligned with the third triplet. Still more strikingly, we find in these same autographs that in spots where the two notes are at the distance of a second, the short note is written inside of the triplet note, which would be unthinkable if a consecutive rather than synchronized sounding had been intended. We find such cases in the autograph score as well as in the autograph harpsichord part of the Fifth "Brandenburg" Concerto, as shown in Ex. 9.5a. The tempo here is rather lively and gigue-like, and clashes would sound awkward, rather like musical accidents.

When, on the other hand, the tempo is slow enough that a clash not only makes sense but adds interest to the passage, then literalness—and even slight overdotting in an occasional soloistic situation—could make good sense to clarify the intention of the clash. Such a solution might be appropriate in Ex. 9.5b, from Bach's Sonata in C Minor for Violin and Clavier. Here the violin part and the left hand of the harpsichord are in binary rhythm throughout, in contrast to the flowing triplet motion of the right hand. Both violin and bass part reinforce each other in their binary integrity—for instance, in measures 4, 8, 10–12, and many more times (not shown in the example); as a consequence it is highly probable that the dotted notes of the violin and the eighth notes of the bass line were meant to clash with the triplets. It is in situations similar to this that Bach's principle regarding the integrity of the binary rhythm vis-à-vis triplet motion was most fitting.

In a single voice a ternary interpretation of dotted notes will often be indicated when they are interspersed with triplets, as for instance in Ex. 9.5c, from Bach's Suite in D Minor for Solo Violin, or Ex. 9.5d, from Handel's Sonata in F for Violin.

EXAMPLE 9.5.

a. Bach, Fifth "Brandenburg" Concerto, BWV 1050/2

b. Bach, Sonata in C Minor for Violin and Clavier, BWV 1017/3

c. Bach, Suite in D Minor for Solo Violin, BWV 1004/2

d. Handel, Sonata in F for Violin, Op. 1, No. 12/4

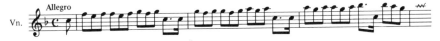

Bach used the dotted note so frequently in ternary meaning that on occasion he wrote it absent-mindedly within a triple meter in which he did not need a makeshift notation and in which the dotted note in fact made no sense. Thus, for instance, in the autograph of cantata No. 110/1, the middle section of this French overture in $\frac{9}{8}$ is filled with dotted eighth notes instead of the logical ♩♪, of which one instance is shown in Ex. 9.6a. In other cases when writing ternary rhythms, Bach seemingly forgot what kind of meter signature he had chosen. In Cantata No. 94/6, as shown in Ex. 9.6b, the continuo in the autograph score has a ternary notation in a binary meter, while the autograph organ part for the same spot has dotted notes in an (alternative) ternary meter. All this shows how readily the dotted note in a ternary surrounding assumed 2:1 meaning.

EXAMPLE 9.6.   Bach

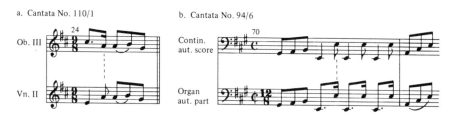

a. Cantata No. 110/1

b. Cantata No. 94/6

Whereas the dotted note is ambiguous, as a duplet can be, the *triplet is not ambiguous.* Here no notational deficiencies allow for different interpretations, and consequently we have no reason to assume that a triplet was ever meant to deviate from its literal meaning.

*The Missing Double Dot and the German Galant Mannerism of Overdotting.* Another notational deficiency was the unavailability, for a long time, of the double dot. As early as the mid-17th century, some Frenchmen hit on this ingenious device of indicating the lengthening of a note by three quarters. Among them were André Raison, in his *Livre d'orgue* of 1688 and his *Second livre d'orgue* of 1714. We find it also in the famous Bauyn Manuscript (an anthology of 17th-century French keyboard music at the Bibliothèque Nationale), in Louis Couperin, Chambonnières, and sporadically in Clérambault and Hotteterre. Lully did not use it, nor did François Couperin or Rameau, nor did, so it seems, any of the Italian or German masters. The double dot had to be reinvented. Friedrich Wilhelm Marpurg describes it in his *Anleitung zum Clavierspielen* of 1755 (p. 13 and Tab. 1, 21, c, and d); Leopold Mozart does the same in his *Versuch* of 1756 (chap. 1, sec. 3, par. 11) and half-apologetically mentions its unfamiliar appearance. Wolfgang used the double dot from his earliest youth (for instance, in the Symphony No. 8 in D Major K 48 of 1768).

Prior to this notational innovation (or its rediscovery), composers from the early 17th century on used and specified double-dotted rhythms with either the insertion of rests ( ♪⋅ ＂ ♪ ) or with the tie ( ♪⋅⌒♫ ). They had to do so for any ensemble music in which players or singers were expected to be faithful to the notation. Some composers sometimes failed to do so for the solo part, expecting the performer to read the single-dotted rhythm as a double-dotted one. In this they took a chance, since the performer may or may not have obliged them. At any rate, the difference between solo and ensemble playing was fundamental at the time. In a graphic metaphor, Quantz speaks of a soloist who finds himself playing an accompaniment as being transferred from freedom into slavery (*Versuch einer Anweisung,* chap. 17, sec. 7, par. 15). Soloists at the time were usually given a wide range of freedoms: they were permitted, often indeed expected, to add ornaments to the written notes; they had often to choose the tempo without the help of any tempo words; Bach's and Handel's keyboard players had to devise their own articulation, organists their registration; other lacunae of the notation, such as lack or scarcity of dynamic markings, opened wide fields to the judgment of the performer. We have also encountered the soloist's rhythmic freedoms in the agogic accent and the rubato. Robert Donington has a point when he speaks of a "performer-king" in the Baroque period (*Performer's Guide,* 32).

Given soloistic license and the basic flexibility of the dot, it was to be expected that some soloists would treat the dotted note arbitrarily; while shortening some dots, they lengthened others whenever they thought, rightly or wrongly, that such change would make a better effect. Out of such loose treatment of the dot emerged in northern Germany of the mid-18th century a spotty fashion of soloistic "overdotting"—that is, of strongly extending the value of certain dotted notes to the equivalent of double- or even triple-dotted notes. This mannerism was reflected in a few treatises by galant theorists, the first of whom was apparently Quantz—who in fact may have been the initiator of the fashion. In the first and most important of several passages devoted to this matter (*Versuch einer Anweisung,* chap. 5, pars. 20–21), Quantz *excludes the dotted quarter note from any extension* but asks for strong overdotting of dotted eighth, sixteenth, and thirty-second notes "because of the liveliness that these notes must express." Since dotted sixteenth notes leave hardly any space and dotted thirty-seconds no space at all for an extension of the dot, the practical meaning of the passage seems limited to dotted eighth notes, and even they allow such alteration only in a very slow tempo.

In another passage, devoted to orchestral playing of French ballet music, Quantz speaks of the dotted note in a paragraph that has been widely, and with momentous consequences, misinterpreted as a directive for strong overdotting. These comments will be discussed in the following chapter, which deals with the so-called French overture style.

Among German theorists who followed Quantz in discussing soloistic overdotting, the most important is C. P. E. Bach, who treats of the dotted note in two separate passages, the first in his book on the clavier soloist (*Versuch über Art das Clavier* [1753], chap. 2, sec. 3, par. 14), the second in his book on accompaniment (*Versuch über Art das Clavier* [1762], chap. 29, par. 15). The first of these is vaguely worded and in part obscure, but the lucid second one clarifies Bach's ideas on this subject. There he writes:

> The notation of the dotted note is often imprecise. Attempts were made to establish in this matter a principal rule which, however, suffers many exceptions. According to this rule the notes following the dot must be played very fast, and often this rule applies. However, it does not apply when the disposition of the notes in various voices requires their exact coordination; furthermore, a tender expression that does not tolerate the characteristic boldness [das Trotzige] of the dotted notes will cause us to shorten the length of the dot. In one stipulates one type of rendering these notes, one loses the other types.

The types he speaks of are (1) overdotting; (2) literalness; and (3) underdotting. In other words, he points to the flexibility of the dot and the need to adjust its length to the demands of the situation.

Johann Friedrich Agricola in 1757 essentially follows Quantz's lead when he writes:

> The short notes that follow a dot, especially sixteenth and thirty-seconds, and also the eighths in alla breve—be it in slow or fast tempo, be there one or more of these notes—will be rendered very short, at the extreme end of their value; the note before the dot will be correspondingly extended.

He illustrates this rule with a number of dotted eighths that are followed by one to four shorter values and their double dotting in execution (*Anleitung zur Singkunst*, 133–34).

Other German theorists explain soloistic overdotting in a similar vein, among them Löhlein in both his violin and clavier treatises, Tromlitz for the flute, and Türk for the clavier.

Leopold Mozart is often mentioned in this connection, but he does not truly belong in the company of the named theorists. The latter (with the exception of C. P. E. Bach) had in mind an obligatory overdotting of short note values (dotted eighths or shorter) in order to increase their liveliness; Leopold Mozart gives the directive that "in certain passages of slow movements" the dot should be "held a little longer [etwas länger gehalten]" to prevent too sleepy or lazy an impression (*Versuch einer Violinschule*, chap. 1, sec. 3, pars. 8–11). He formulates no rule and speaks only of an option for slow movements and one that can apply to values of any length.

We do not find similar principles of *strong* overdotting in Italy, France (the *notes inégales* led only to mild lengthening), or England. Yet even in Germany the manner was not uncontested. Quite apart from the strong qualifications of C. P. E. Bach, and the very limited range of Leopold Mozart's directive, we find eminent writers who strongly dissent. Friedrich Wilhelm Marpurg writes in 1755:

If ♩. ♪ is to be played as ♩ ♪♩ one also has to write it in this manner, or else like this: ♩.. ♪ . Unless this is done, nobody is under any obligation to divine the composer's thoughts, and since the latter has two methods at his disposal to clarify his intentions . . . I cannot see why one should write one way and want to have it performed in another way; i.e., why one puts only one dot and expects to have it read as one and a half. (*Anleitung zum Clavierspielen*, 13).

Georg Friedrich Wolf, in his clavier treatise of 1789, fully endorses Marpurg on this point and adds: "If a composer wants to avoid having his pieces spoiled by awkward performance, he must write the way he wants to have it performed and executed" (*Kurzer Unterricht*, 26). Johann Adam Hiller in 1774 uses bold type to lend emphasis to the rule: "a dot after a note **always stands for half of its value.** If the [tied] note, which is represented by a dot, already has a dot, one has to mark two dots, and the second has only half the value of the first" (*Anweisung zum musikalisch-richtigen Gesange*, 111). Johann Samuel Petri too, in 1767 and again in 1782, is very strict about the standard meaning of the dot (*Anleitung zur Musik* [1767], 21; [1782], 142). He, like Hiller, is obviously in accord with Marpurg and Wolf.

We see that the galant mannerism had only a spotty following in Germany, one that was limited to masters who did not yet use the double dot. Its importance has been vastly exaggerated by some scholars who read into the few overdotting directives the existence of an international convention of sharp rhythmic contractions and of what became widely known as the French overture style. The doctrine of this "style" will be the subject of the following chapter.

*The Flexible Dot.* The flexibility of the dot prior to Haydn and Mozart worked in both directions: the value of the dot could be extended, or it could be shortened. We encountered lengthening in the German soloistic overdotting, shortening in the cases of assimilation to a concurring triplet. In this latter case the dot lengthens the note by one-third of its value. A shortening of the dot to exactly one-fourth of the value of the preceding note occurred in the frequent notation of ♩. 𝅘𝅥𝅯𝅘𝅥𝅯𝅘𝅥𝅯 ,which often took the place of the more modern and explicit ♩ 𝅘𝅥𝅯𝅘𝅥𝅯𝅘𝅥𝅯 . To the end of his life Bach used both notational styles. Their synonymity was explained among others by Johann Peter Sperling in 1705 (*Principia musicae*, 55–56) and Simpertus Schmelz in 1752 (*Fundamenta musica*, 31–32). Their full equivalence for Bach is assured by numerous cases of clear external evidence. Apart from many instances of calligraphic vertical alignment, I shall mention here only the case of Cantata No. 110/1, where in measure 4 of the autograph score the identical figure is written in the bassoon and tympani with the quarter-value dot, in the continuo part with the tie. For Bach at least, this dotted pattern is unambiguous, and the three sixteenths that follow the dot must not be mistaken for triplets. Bach never failed to write a little 3 when he intended a triplet meaning. We find Bach using the dot elsewhere with quarter-value meaning in such rhythmic designs as 𝅘𝅥𝅯𝅘𝅥𝅯𝅘𝅥𝅯𝅘𝅥.𝅘𝅥 𝅘𝅥𝅯𝅘𝅥 in the allemande of the Partita in A Minor for Harpsichord, in measures 2, 3 (twice), and 11.

Notational irregularities that lengthen as well as shorten the dot are explained in manuscript fragments by the important French theorist Étienne Loulié. After giving the standard rule for the dot, he writes that it sometimes "augments the notes by ⅛, or ¼ , or ⅜ , or ½ , or ⅝ , or ¾ , or ⅞ . . . . In any given place, the time value of the dot is regulated by the notes that follow."[3] In other words, the dot simply fills the space unaccounted for by the measure's explicit note values; he offers the illustrations shown in Ex. 9.7. Of these patterns no. 4 presents the standard notation; no. 2, with the dot adding one-fourth of the value, is the design so frequently used by Bach and some of his contemporaries. The other forms are very rare in France as well as elsewhere, but some of them did occur from time to time. We must realize that, though these patterns illustrate the variability of the dot, they are not properly speaking cases of over- or underdotting. These terms are logically applicable only to dots that are written in standard fashion but performed with nonstandard values. This is no semantic hairsplitting, because an *irregular notation* that implies an exact nonstandard length of the dot, as in all these cases, does not admit the inference of an expected over- or underdotting for a dot written in standard notation. That is what is at issue when musicians or scholars speak of overdotting or the French overture style.

EXAMPLE 9.7.   Loulié

On the other hand, the dotted note in ternary meaning (in assimilation to a triplet) *is* a genuine underdotting—that is, a standard notation ( ♪♪ ) in which the dot lengthens the preceding note by only one-third instead of one-half. There are also occasional cases of analogous overdotting. Such overdotting occurs where musical common sense suggests or demands a synchronization of the small companion note, say, an eighth with a sixteenth, or a sixteenth with a thirty-second in another voice. Such a need will most likely occur in a homophonic setting where simultaneous harmonic progressions are more convincing than rhythmically disparate ones. Such adjustments will be easiest for keyboard players who see the whole score and can judge with a glance what makes and what does not make musical sense. An early theoretical mention of such synchronization is made by Nicholas Gigault, who writes in 1685: "Whenever a sixteenth note is placed on top of an eighth note they have to be played simultaneously" (*Livre de musique*, Preface). Such occurrences are, however, quite rare in that particular volume. We can find a better illustration for this idea in Jacques Boyvin's Trio from his *Second livre d'orgue* of 1700 (Ex. 9.8a), where the synchronization of the eighth-note g' with the sixteenth-note e" in this context of parallel sixths is virtually self-evident, the more so since Boyvin did not use the double dot. To play the eighth note here as written would not enrich the texture and would irritate listeners instead.

In the organ obbligato of Bach's Cantata No. 170/3, there is an obvious need to synchronize the last sixteenth note of the right hand with the thirty-second in the left (see Ex. 9.8b), and the autograph shows their clear vertical alignment. We see a similar alignment in the allemande of the Partita in A Minor (from the autograph in Anna Magdalena's notebook of 1725): here the sixteenth note in the middle voice is aligned with the thirty-second in the top voice (see Ex. 9.8c), suggesting synchronization—though here the latter is musically not a foregone conclusion. Such irregular notations usually result from a missing double dot. Although Bach could and often did use the alternate notations for the double-dotted rhythm—that is, the inserted rests or the tie—they were cumbersome; and he apparently felt, at least with keyboard players, that he could count on their musical judgment to do the logical thing.

Such synchronizations, sporadic in Bach and other polyphonic masters, became more frequent in the homophonic music of the galant era, where in purely harmonic progressions a rhythmic discrepancy would make little sense. C. P. E. Bach offers the illustration, shown in Ex. 9.8d, in which the clear vertical lineup clarifies such an intention (*Versuch über Art das Clavier* [1753], chap. 3, par. 23). Türk gives an almost identical example (*Klavierschule*, chap. 6, sec. 3, par. 48). The more the double dot became a standard device, the less we find these kinds of notational irregularities. They do not occur with a composer who, like Mozart, used the double dot methodically and consistently.

When such situations occur not for the keyboard but for an ensemble, the chances for their logical adjustment diminish; but the discrepancies were mostly readily absorbed by the greater tolerance level that existed at the time for flaws in ensemble precision. In the passage from section no. 22 of Handel's *Messiah,* shown in Ex. 9.8e, the eighth note at the end of measure 28 would most logically be synchronized with the sixteenth note of the sopranos. It is a minor matter, however, and whether or not the players made the adjustment probably made little difference at the time, nor does it make much difference today. Still, it might be advisable to change the eighth into a sixteenth.

EXAMPLE 9.8

a. Boyvin, *Second livre d'orgue* (1700)

c. Bach, Partita in A Minor, BWV 827

b. Bach, Cantata No. 170/3

Organ
(sounding a
whole tone higher)

d. C.P.E. Bach

e. Handel, *Messiah*, No. 22

Vn. I

Sop.

would that tak - eth a - way the sin of the world

At the opposite pole we find cases where a written synchronization was likely to be dissolved for better musical effect. These cases often occur when dots are followed by one or more pitches that are ornamental in character though written as regular notes. As ornaments they are not of melodic essence and have no vested interest in metrical coordination with another voice or voices but serve primarily to smooth the

transition to the following structural note. In such a situation the ornamental pitches can, and often should, be played more lightly and later
than their metrical face value indicates. For instance, in Ex. 9.9 from the
Prelude in A Flat Major from *WTC* I, the note after the cadential trill is
a *Nachschlag*. I believe that most experienced performers will find a delay
of this note corresponding roughly to a preceding double dot to be a
more satisfactory rendition than its exact coordination with the eighth
note in the bass. Similarly we find in Bach many a spot in which, for
instance, a trill ♪♩♪♪ will profit from being played as if it had been
written ♪♪ , hence with a lengthened dot—the more so since Bach
practically never used the two small, unmetrical notes to indicate a trill's
suffix.

EXAMPLE 9.9.   Bach, Prelude in A Flat Major, BWV 862

We find another type of imprecise notation in the frequent pattern
of ♪ 𝄾 ♩♩♩♪ , which sometimes may and other times may not have
stood for ♪ 𝄾 ♩♩♩♪ . Quantz, for one, sanctions this meaning for
dotted sixteenth notes that follow a rest on a heavy beat (*Versuch einer
Anweisung*, chap. 17, sec. 2, par. 16). For instrumentalists such adjustment of the first upbeat follows a natural impulse: an effort is necessary
to read it literally, especially when the patterns occur a few times in
succession. The tendency of orchestra players of the era to follow their
natural impulse may have prompted composers to choose what was also
simpler to write. When Bach writes a recurring string passage in the
duet of Cantata No. 91 𝄾 ♩♩♩♪♩♩♩♪ in its early version but
𝄾 𝄾 ♩♩♩♪ ♩♩♩♪ in the final version, this could have been a second
thought, but more likely it was a more precise spelling for the same
effect. If Bach's first version showed that he may have relied on the
players to take the easy way of assimilation, the final version shows that
he decided not to take any such chances.
     Today such assimilation by shortening the upbeat note is made with
greatest frequency, in the chorus "Surely, Surely" from Handel's *Messiah* (no. 24). This is done to avoid rhythmic discrepancies such as those
shown in Ex. 9.10a between the sixteenths in the bass and the middle

strings (the latter not shown here) and the thirty-second in the first violins. Furthermore, for the sake of synchronizing the pattern of Ex. 9.10b, the dotted note is usually double dotted. In the design of Ex. 9.10a and its many recurrences, assimilation makes good sense since we are dealing with near-identical figures in pure harmonic, parallel progressions, where no musical asset accrues from the rhythmic discrepancy. The case is different for the design of Ex. 9.10b. Here the parts are in a quasi-contrapuntal setting and gain in plasticity by the rhythmic conflict. Moreover, it is hard to believe that Handel would have expected his violinists to double dot where only a single dot was written. In addition, we have clear proof in measure 6 of the same chorus (Ex. 9.10c), as well as in the parallel measure 9, that in this pure harmonic context Handel explicitly called for a rhythmic clash that not even such an overenthusiastic synchronizer as Watkins Shaw (in his Novello edition) tried to assimilate.

EXAMPLE 9.10.    Handel, *Messiah*, No. 24

Whenever we encounter the fairly frequent rhythmic design of Ex. 9.10a, we cannot automatically assume that the upbeat was meant to be shortened. We have to look for clues that might divulge the composer's intention, and when in doubt it will be safer to follow the literal meaning of the notation, especially when the tempo is fairly slow or when we have dotted eighths rather than sixteenths. Here the tendency to assimilate mostly disappears. We have a striking illustration of the need for literalness in the third movement of Bach's Cantata No. 119, where at the place marked by an asterisk in Ex. 9.11 Bach had at first written a dotted pattern but then corrected it to even notes; the same correction appears at the parallel passage in measure 30.

Reviewing briefly the problems of imprecise and nonstandard notations, we see that the latter can be of several kinds. There are cases in

EXAMPLE 9.11.   Bach, Cantata No. 119/3

which a notation is nonstandard, yet exact, such as Bach's frequent
♩. ♫ = ♩ ♫♫ . There is no performance problem here if
one knows the meaning of this design and is therefore aware that the
dot has the length of only a sixteenth note and that the three notes
following the dot are not a triplet.

There are cases in which a precise notation was available but composers did not use it because it was time consuming and they relied on
the performer to guess their intention. Naturally they took a chance with
such reliance and may not have been served properly. In such cases
composers did not care enough about the exact execution to take the
trouble of being more specific. A typical case is the unavailable double
dot that could be indicated by either the tie ♩. ♫ or an inserted rest
♩. ♪ but that some German galant composers occasionally wrote as
single dot. The music involved in this type of imprecision occupies a
minor place in today's repertory and should not greatly concern us.
Unless circumstances make it clear that a double dot was meant when a
single one was written, we are, in general, on safe ground to follow the
literal meaning of the notation. Other cases in which imprecise notation
was not necessary—for instance, when an upbeat written as an eighth
note may or may not have been meant as a sixteenth note, or when a
simultaneous eighth and sixteenth note may or may not have been
intended to be synchronized—are of greater concern because they occur
with Bach, Handel, and their contemporaries.

Most important are the cases in which imprecision was unavoidable
and the ensuing ambiguities more troublesome, such as the uncertainty
whether a dotted note stood for a 3:1 or a 2:1 ratio; related to it are the
problems of the relationship between the dotted note and the triplet. In
some cases, as we have seen, the answer is fairly clear, in others it is not.
Where it is not, here as well as in the cases listed in the preceding
paragraph, we simply have to be aware of the options available and use
our musical intelligence to make the choice. Where such a choice is
difficult, because neither alternative seems to have a clear advantage,
both solutions are likely to be musically and historically justifiable.

# 10

# RHYTHMIC ALTERATIONS II: THE SO-CALLED FRENCH OVERTURE STYLE

One of the stranger chapters in the story of performance practice turns on a theory that modern research has proclaimed as one of the chief canons of proper Baroque performance. This theory claims the existence of a convention about the playing of certain rhythmic figures in a manner that involves three main elements: first, sharp overdotting, whereby ♩ ♪ is to be played ♩.. ♪ or ♩.. 𝄾 ♪ or sharper still; second, contraction of upbeat figures, whereby ♩ 𝄾 ♫ | ♩ is to be played ♩ 𝄿 𝄾 ♫ | ♩ or ♩ 𝄾• 𝄾 ♫ | ♩ ; and third, synchronization, whereby all rhythmic figures, regardless of what the notation says, adjust to the shortest notes written and move together "jerkily." The doctrine of this tripartite performance manner is today called the "French overture style." It is focused, as the name indicates, on the French overture (more specifically its slow introductory part) but ranges well beyond this central core. How far it ranges and how its three constituent elements are to function in a given case depend on who is interpreting the theory, be it with pen or with baton: all of its followers agree on the principle, but they disagree on its implementation. Before we discuss these differences of opinion it will be well to look into how these ideas came into being and have risen to near-universal acceptance. At the time of writing the doctrine still reigns nearly supreme in the performance of

French overtures, and it spills over into many other rhythmically related works.

Inasmuch as the validity of this theory may first have been questioned in several of my articles of the years 1965–81 (reprinted in *Essays 1982*, chaps. 5–9), which excited much opposition, this chapter will be unavoidably controversial. I shall state the case for the theory; but I shall also present the bases for my objections to it, arguing that the theory is built on misunderstandings and should be discarded from the set of principles governing historically appropriate performance.

## *Origins of the Theory*

The overdotting aspect of this performance manner emerged in England in connection with Handel's overtures. Its roots seem to reach back to the early 19th century with William Crotch's keyboard arrangements of these overtures, in which he replaced single dots by double dots. By that time, in the wake of mass performances of the *Messiah*, Handelian tempi had drastically slowed, and Crotch himself indicated with a metronome-like device truly funereal tempi for the overtures, which almost necessitated some rhythmic animation. Some other arrangers followed his example, and when in 1902 Ebenezer Prout published the *Messiah* for Novello, he double dotted the Sinfonia (a French overture) and several other numbers susceptible to such treatment. This seems to be the sum total of an alleged "Handel tradition" listed by some followers as powerful evidence for the existence of a French overture style: a performance manner initiated half a century after Handel's death in an effort to spruce up a much-too-sluggish tempo with a dose of rhythmic spice.

The decisive step in the elevation of the theory—with all its three elements—to the status of a requirement of Baroque performance was taken by Arnold Dolmetsch in his famous book of 1915 (*Interpretation of Music*, 53–65). He calls on Quantz as his principal witness. In Dolmetsch's first quotation from Quantz's chapter 5, paragraph 21 (reported above, in chap. 9, p. 99), Quantz urges the *soloist* to strongly overdot dotted eighth, sixteenth, and thirty-second notes because of the liveliness they are meant to express. He wished to intensify their liveliness; but at the same time he expressly *excluded* from this rule the dotted quarter note. This exclusion is logical since the dotted quarter note is hardly meant to express liveliness. Yet it is exactly this dotted quarter note that is—witness the *Messiah* Sinfonia—the rhythmical mainstay of most French overture introductions. As has already been mentioned, this was probably the first theoretical reflection of the spotty German galant mannerism of soloistic overdotting. It was not, as Dolmetsch believed, a late reflection of 17th-century and Bach-era practices.

In another passage quoted by Dolmetsch (*Interpretation of Music*, 58), Quantz listed as one way of expressing *das Prächtige*—"the splendorous," "the brilliant" (mistranslated by Dolmetsch and his followers as "the majestic")—the use of dotted notes, treated in the manner just described—that is, by overdotting the dotted eighth notes and shorter values (*Versuch einer Anweisung*, chap. 12, par. 24). Again he addressed the soloist.

Dolmetsch then presents Quantz's important passage from chapter 17, section 7, paragraph 58, which deals with a ballet orchestra's performance of French dances. The passage is important because it alone links the orchestra and the French style. In fact, the passage seems so far to be the *only* theoretical evidence that Dolmetsch—mistakenly—believed to describe *orchestral* overdotting; neither he nor anybody else has found convincing evidence from an earlier date. The key sentences of the passage in question are:

> In this **2** meter, as well as in the $\frac{3}{4}$ meter of the loure, sarabande, courante, or chaconne, the eighth notes following dotted quarter notes must be played not according to their literal value but *very short and sharp* [emphasis added]. The dotted note is emphasized and during the dot the bow is lifted.

> (In dieser Tactart sowohl, als im Dreyviertheiltacte, bei der Loure, Sarabande, Courante, und Chaconne, müssen die Achttheile, so auf punctirte Viertheile folgen, nicht nach ihrer eigentlichen Geltung, sondern sehr kurz und scharf gespielet werden. Die Note mit dem Puncte wird mit Nachdruck markiret, und unter dem Puncte der Bogen abgesetzet.)

To play a note "short and sharp" appears to mean to clip it drastically at the end and attack it with an accent; in other words, to play it not tenuto but with a brisk snappy staccato. It does *not* imply a delayed entry, which is what Dolmetsch and his followers hoped to read into the passage by interpreting "not according to their literal value" as taking value away from the start of the note rather than from its end. Now to take away from the end of a note is a normal procedure, followed routinely for *all* notes that are not slurred. Different here, and therefore in need of a specific directive, is the high degree of shortening. The explanation "not according to their literal value" simply means that the note is to be stopped long before the end of its "literal value." Several more times Quantz uses the phrase "short and sharp" with the identical meaning of acute staccato articulation (twice in the preceding par. 56; also chap. 17, sec. 2, par. 13).

In contrast to the habitual shortening of a note at its end, it is extremely unusual to take away from the beginning of a note and to delay its entry since doing so encroaches on the rhythm, which is determined by the *starting points* of the constituent pitches. Whenever such an unusual practice may be desired, it would have to be clearly specified with words such as "to be rendered at the end of its notated value." Not only is such clarification missing, but here, in fact, Quantz himself was to specify that his directive referred not to an altered rhythm but to the characteristic French *bowing style,* as opposed to the Italian and German one. From the time of Lully and well into the 18th century the French practiced an incisive and sharply clipped bowstroke, one that is "short and sharp" as opposed to the sustained and singing Italian one. Now in chapter 17, section 2, paragraph 26, after once more contrasting the French "short and articulated bowstroke" (kurzer und articulirter Bogenstrich) with the Italian "long and dragging stroke" (langer und schleppender Strich), Quantz adds that he will explain "the type of bowstroke used in French dance music" in chapter 17, section 7, paragraph 58, the *very paragraph that contains the two sentences in question.* We are thus explicitly told that the two sentences deal with "bowstroke," hence with articulation, not with rhythm, not with delayed entry.

Quantz actually deals with a rhythmic delay in the next sentence when he speaks of "three or more thirty-second or shorter notes that follow a dot or a rest [and] that are not always played with their literal value, especially in slow pieces, but at the extreme end of the time allotted to them and with the greatest possible speed." He speaks here of the *tirades,* fast scale passages that were a characteristic feature in many French overtures and *entrées.* Here rhythmic alteration is made explicit by the words "at the very end of their value"—the kind of explicitness that would have been indispensable in the previous sentence if Quantz had meant to convey an overdotting of the quarter note.

With the passage about the dotted quarter note eliminated as support for the French overture style, the latter has lost its principal theoretical mainstay—not to speak of the fact that, as we have seen, the dotted quarter note was specifically exempted even from soloistic overdotting.

In addition to Quantz, Dolmetsch called on C. P. E. Bach by quoting the first of two passages mentioned above (p. 100). This first passage (*Versuch über Art das Clavier,* [1753], chap. 3, par. 3) is poorly worded, contrary to Bach's habit, but not so poorly as to justify Dolmetsch's mistranslation (*Interpretation of Music,* 59), which, in order to make the point of unquestionable overdotting, mangled several sentences and added two sentences that Bach did not write.[1] Bach, too, like Quantz in his overdotting instructions, speaks of the soloist, not the orchestra, and not of the French style. Dolmetsch obviously was not aware of Bach's second passage in the treatise on accompaniment (*Versuch über Art das Clavier* [1762], chap. 29, par. 15), in which Bach formulates his ideas on the dotted note with exemplary clarity. There, as I pointed out in the preceding chapter, in addition to overdotting he lists literal exactness as well as underdotting as possible interpretations of the dotted note and thereby disqualifies himself as a useful witness for a performance style that admits no alternative to strong overdotting.

Inspired by Quantz's (soloistic) overdotting directives, while oblivious to their limitation to lively rhythms, and bolstered by the misunderstood paragraph from C. P. E. Bach, Dolmetsch gives an illustration

of the triple-dotted Sinfonia of the *Messiah,* changing ♩. ♪♩. ♪ to
♩. 𝄾·♪♩. 𝄾·♪ with a few upbeat figures similarly contracted and all parts
moving together "jerkily"—thus constructing the very paradigm of the
French overture style. Dolmetsch finds such rhythms "quite natural"
and extols their power to transform a ponderous movement to one of
"majestic beauty or thrilling energy." And since, he says, music of the
16th and 17th centuries "abounds in passages which demand it [i.e.,
such rhythmic treatment] we can but feel justified in *treating all the old
music alike in this respect*" (emphasis added). Dolmetsch further illustrates
his principle with examples from the *WTC* and lists several more numbers from the *Messiah,* as well as several numbers from the St. Matthew
Passion, as candidates for drastic rhythmic sharpening (*Interpretation of
Music,* 62–65).

Whether such intensely sharpened rhythms are more "natural"
than milder ones is of course highly debatable. Equally unconvincing
and even more dangerous is the argument of "majestic beauty and
thrilling energy" since—even if we agree with such aesthetic judgment
—we cannot take it for granted that this was the effect invariably intended by the composer. We could with no less logic argue that *forte* is
more exciting than *piano,* fastness more thrilling than slowness, and that
therefore all "old music" should be played loud and fast, which of
course would be absurd. When a performer consciously chooses an
interpretation that departs from the letter of the score and admits not to
care about the composer's intention, a case could be made for such an
attitude. But it is altogether different to argue, as Dolmetsch has done,
that he finds the drastic rhythmic contractions majestic and thrilling and
that therefore they must have been the composer's intent. Any such
argument that finds the key to historical correctness in a personal preference is vulnerable to the unanswerable riposte: "I disagree."

I have discussed Dolmetsch's theory in some detail because as the
fountainhead of the theory of the French overture style it has remained
enormously influential to the present day.[2]

After Dolmetsch, Thurston Dart became the chief interpreter and
propagator of the rhythmic contraction doctrine. He gave it more concrete shape, providing the first clear formulation of its three constituent
elements—overdotting, upbeat-figure contractions, and synchronization (with resulting "jerkiness"). It was he who singled out the French
overture as a particularly characteristic carrier for the doctrine, almost
certainly by taking a cue from Dolmetsch's illustration of the *Messiah*
Sinfonia. Apart from this illustration Dolmetsch himself had never mentioned the French overture, which to him was just one of a multitude of
genres subject, along with "all old music," to the rhythmic contraction
process, nor had he emphasized a particular link to the French style. Yet
Dart too saw an enormous field for the theory to which he refers as the

"conventional lengthening of the dotted note and shortening of the complementary note." Such overdotting, he wrote, "was in very widespread use over a very great length of time. . . . It is a fashion that lasted from the early years of the 17th century down to the last years of the 19th." Then he lists sample composers and works that were subject to the overdotting "convention," among them Monteverdi, Purcell, Handel, and Bach, overtures, marches, sicilianos, jigs, and andantes, "some" Gluck operas (which?) and those of Sarti (apparently all); the convention, he continues, is "implied" in Haydn, Mozart, and Beethoven (*Interpretation of Music*, 81–82). Dart is obviously satisfied with Dolmetsch's evidence and makes no attempt to find a firmer anchor in historical fact, other than by an oblique reference to the French *notes inégales*.

Robert Donington, a student of Dolmetsch and a highly respected voice in matters of historical performance, also focuses on the French overture; but, like Dart, he says that the influence of the "convention" was felt "much farther afield" and speaks of a "general baroque practice of rhythmic sharpening" (*Performer's Guide*, 297). Relying, like Dart, on Dolmetsch's arguments, he tries to bolster them with a reference to the would-be Handelian tradition that, as has been shown, originated in the 19th century.

## The Scholarly Debate

After I had questioned the legitimacy of this performance manner in the first of five articles I wrote on the subject, several scholars came to its defense, foremost among them David Fuller, Michael Collins, and John O'Donnell. Fuller, while first criticizing my arguments ("Dotting," 517–43; for my answer see *Essays 1982*, chap. 8), later disclaimed any intention "to preach the gospel of overdotting" (letter to EM [1979]; 279). Fuller also seems to agree with me that neither the *notes inégales* nor the galant German (soloistic) overdotting can be directly linked to this style of playing ("Dotting," 533–34).

Michael Collins and John O'Donnell tried to find a basis for overdotting in the French *notes inégales,* but for several reasons this avenue did not prove fruitful (as Fuller had already indicated).[3] For one thing, as will be presently shown, the French convention of unequal notes involved, by and large, only a mild lengthening of the first of a pair of evenly written notes, whereas a lengthening at a rate that would change a single dot into a double dot was so exceptional that no principle could be built on it. Second, the *notes inégales* were proper only in specific circumstances that were not necessarily present when overdotting was to apply. Third, there is no evidence that the convention of the *notes inégales* was known, let alone honored, in England, Germany, or Italy, outside of small circles of French musical influence or by French-trained performers. A Handelian orchestra cannot be assumed to have practiced the rather complex *notes inégales* convention, which, incidentally, would not have applied to the dotted quarter notes of Handel's overtures since most of the latter were written in C meter in which the eighth notes were not subject to *inégalité*.[4]

Collins also cites Sulzer's *Allgemeine Theorie der schönen Künste* of 1771–74. The article "Ouverture," written by J. A. P. Schulz, says that the dots are held longer than their value. This stipulated lengthening is very mild, as we can gather from the article "Punct, punctirte Note," in which the author specifies for the dotted note "a somewhat longer [than literal] rendition." This directive, which may perhaps be linked to French *inégalité* (Schulz heard French operas in Paris and subsequently wrote several French operas), would in its mildness nevertheless fall far short of supporting the sharp rhythmic contractions of the French overture style.

An exact contemporary of Schulz, Heinrich Christoph Koch, "the outstanding theorist-composer of his time" (*MGG*), included a chapter on the French overture in his *Versuch einer Anleitung zur Composition* (pt. 3, 283–301). He gives a detailed description of the overture's nature, supplemented by an illustration of its first part, that contains dotted quarter, eighth, and sixteenth notes and many *tirades* of thirty-second notes but makes no mention of any rhythmic alteration. Half a century earlier, when the overture was still in its heyday, Johann Adolf Scheibe, in a similar description of the overture in *Der critische Musicus* (667–70), was equally silent about any alterations. Such silences would be incomprehensible had the drastic alterations stipulated by 20th-century ideas been a historical fact.

## *The Impracticability of the Modern Doctrine*

In adopting this theory we have to assume that composers wrote differently from the way they wanted to be read. To write in a fashion that presents the performer with puzzles to be solved carries some risks for the composer who might not like the solution. But that was a risk that, in the era before the high Classical style, a composer frequently assumed when dealing with a *soloist*, whose considerable privileges were spelled out in the preceding chapter.

Matters were radically different for members of an orchestra or chorus. They were trained to play or sing the music as it was put before them. They may have been trained in a specific style of performance, as French violinists were trained to play detached notes with a sharp articulation (Quantz's "short and sharp"). The *notes inégales* were feasible in a French orchestra because every French musician was acquainted with its well-structured principles. Almost all French manuals, even elementary ones addressed to children, relayed the rules that included the "when" and the "how." All that was needed to make them work was the director's or concertmaster's indication of the desired long–short ratio. More about this in the next chapter.

For our purposes the distinction between solo and orchestral (or choral) performance is fundamental. Numerous theorists addressed this difference, and, while they did so usually in connection with improvised ornamentation, their discussions are invariably pertinent to the present issue since they all stress the necessity for orchestra players to follow strictly the letter of the score. We find many of these theorists listed and quoted in an essay by John Spitzer and Neal Zaslaw ("Improvised Ornamentation"). Among their number is Quantz, whose metaphor about the soloist who has to accept servitude when playing a ripieno part was quoted earlier. He enjoins the orchestra director to enforce ensemble discipline (*Versuch einer Anweisung*, chap. 17, sec. 1, pars. 5 and 14). The orchestra player, he says, "must pay the closest attention to the value of the notes. . . . For if he makes a mistake in this regard, he misleads all the others and produces confusion in the ensemble." It is thus no accident that all of Quantz's references to overdotting—that is, to a performance that differs from the text—refer exclusively to the soloist, and that the one directive in which he has been understood to speak of overdotting in the orchestral performance of French dances has, as explained above, been misinterpreted.

In his monograph of 1776 on the orchestral violinist, Johann Friedrich Reichardt devotes chapter 8 to the "exactness with which orchestra players must execute the notes in front of them. . . . The paramount duty of the ripienist, from which he must not deviate by a hairbreadth, is the greatest exactness in the execution. Not a note, not a staccato dash more or different from what is written" (*Über die Pflichten*, 79).[5] A year later, in an essay of 1777, reprinted by Neal Zaslaw ("The Compleat Orchestral Musician"), Robert Bremner, a student of Geminiani, emphasizes the sharp contrast between solo and orchestra performance. Whereas the soloist can modify the melody by embroidering or by simplifying it, the orchestra player has to abide strictly by the text.

Although a soloist, then, could interpret his written part with wide-ranging freedom, including willful rhythmic manipulations, the test for the practicability of the French overture style is the orchestra or chorus. Here the demands of this style, with its tripartite aspects of overdotting, upbeat contractions, and synchronization, present the orchestra player with insurmountable difficulties. He has to solve the puzzles posed by a notation that does not mean what it says. For modern performances in which such a rhythmic interpretation is routinely applied to certain works, these difficulties are solved by the editorial rewriting, the actual recomposing of the parts—the only way in which our overdotting-contracting-synchronizing conductors can safely operate. But if this performance manner had been a living historical convention, the performers would have had to divine on their own the hidden meaning of the composer's intentions. In trying to do so they would have been cast in the role of cryptographers who, faced with a coded message, had to decipher it. Such an enterprise meets at the very start with an awesome difficulty—the question of which music is written as intended and which is hiding its real meaning, which notation is "in the clear" and which is in code.

Just how formidable this hurdle is emerges from the inability of the modern advocates of this performance style to circumscribe clearly the range of its application. The advocates are extremely vague about this crucial question; and with all their vagueness, as was shown before, each opinion has differed from every other. Dolmetsch encompassed "all old music": one cannot get any more universal and nebulous than that. Dart focuses on the French overture but in a grand sweep takes in all kinds of musical genres and composer's names from Monteverdi to Mozart and Beethoven. Donington, less ambitiously, speaks of the "general baroque practice of rhythmic sharpening," being no less vague within a less grandiose range. Whatever "Baroque music" is, surely not all of it is considered appropriate for overdotting. Collins's grasp extends from Lully to Mozart, but he exempts "languid and expressive" works of the galant and Classical style.

If such were supposed to be the guidelines for deciding which music is in code and which is not, there seems no way in which they can be put to use. The very first hurdle of deciding which music was subject to this kind of performance was impossible for the individual orchestra member. Without knowing whether the music put before him means or does not mean what it says, a player cannot even begin to function. Here already the style becomes impracticable.

Yet even if the first hurdle could have been surmounted, the player would have been faced with a second one—the "how" of application. Here the dotted note would seem to be the simplest case: it is to be overdotted. But how much? Dolmetsch's examples range from double to quadruple dotting, with different ratios appearing side by side in the same piece. Dart has no precise answer either. For an illustration of a French overture he mixes double with triple dotting. Donington, too, is vague. For the "Baroque" he acknowledges a wide range for the dot, from underdotting, through literal value, to overdotting; for French overtures he wants the rhythm to be "as sharp as possible" (*Performer's Guide*, 281). Collins fails to commit himself to a specific ratio. O'Donnell is satisfied with double dotting for overtures because he wants them to be played faster than is commonly done. What matters to him is achievement of "jerkiness." David Fuller rejects sharp overdotting for overtures, but for what he calls "flagellation pieces" (whatever they are) the dotting "should be as savage as possible." Here, too, there is a bewildering variety of opinions even when we consider only the simple dotted note.

New complications arise in the many instances in which composers mix single- with double-dotted rhythms (written with the help of a tie or by insertion of rests), whether in melodic succession, as ♪·♪♪·♪ , or in simultaneous polyphonic interplay, such as ♪♪·♪ ♪♪·♪ . We find this kind of variety in the music of just about all composers from the early 17th century on. Handel is particularly fond of juxtaposing the two rhythmic modes. Yet the modern theory does not permit such variety either horizontally or vertically: horizontally the rhythms have to be homogenized to *at least* double dotting and to the sharpest common denominator; vertically any variety is banned by the principle of synchronization. Why then would composers have troubled to specify such variety if it was to be obliterated in performance? And since the written-out sharp rhythms were apparently meant to be taken at face value, whereas the milder ones had to match the sharper ones, the performer had constantly to leap from what looked like a message in the "clear" to one that was in code—a formidable complication to the already formidable challenge of decoding. Dolmetsch, Dart, and Donington were seemingly unaware of the problem posed by spelled-out rhythmic diversity and failed to address it. Collins does note Handel's mixing of 3:1 and 7:1 rhythms but tries to brush it off as a "vagary" since both notations in his opinion have the same 7:1 meaning; it seems that in his mind rhythmic variety was illegal and could not exist.

*The Upbeat Figures.* The second aspect of the theory, the contraction of the upbeat figures, adds a new dimension to the problem of deciphering. These upbeat figures come in all shapes, designs, and numbers. They can range from two to twenty or more notes, from scale fragments (*tirades*) to complex melodic designs, from eighth notes to sixty-fourth notes; they can start on, before, or after a beat, and after a dot, a rest, or a tie. The enormous, truly limitless diversity of these figures precludes the very idea of a conversion formula that would be fitting for all situations. Add to this the fact that figures in sixty-fourths are certainly in the "clear," those in thirty-seconds most likely so, whereas figures in eighths would certainly, and those in sixteenths possibly, look coded to the followers of the proposed style. Thus, not surprisingly, none of these proponents has attempted to provide guidance in this matter. Here, even more than with the dotted notes, recomposition and renotation are the only conceivable avenues to realizing the idea of this style. Without them, this aspect too is impracticable.

How did the idea of upbeat contractions originate? It, too, issued from Dolmetsch, who in turn seems to have derived it from Quantz's mentioned principle that upbeats of three or more thirty-second notes following a dot or a rest should—"time permitting"—be played as late as possible. Such note groups in thirty-seconds are practically always *tirades*—that is, fast scale passages with detached bowings—and as such purely ornamental figurations. As ornaments they neither have a vested interest in rhythmic literalness, nor are they in need of exact coordination with other voices. They simply aim at an orchestral effect that, surprisingly, is pleasing even if the individual instrumentalists do not play exactly together. It is not by chance that Quantz limited his principle to thirty-second notes. Figures in sixteenths, let alone in eighths (such as those, for instance, in Lully's Overture to *Proserpine* or in Dieupart's overtures), are, in a moderate tempo, almost always of structural importance. In contrast to the *tirades* they show varied melodic designs (occasionally very complex ones, as for instance the running sixteenths in Bach's Orchestral Overture in C Major). Those designs are far removed from a purely orchestral effect and do have a vested interest in melodic-rhythmic integrity. The efforts of many conductors to compress such melodic figures do violence to their very nature; and in the case of Bach's C-major overture, which even zealously overdotting conductors have usually found impervious to contraction, a few attempts to wring a measure of contraction from the recalcitrant design produced incongruous results that border on the musically absurd.

*Synchronization.* The third constituent of the style, synchronization, is hardly less of a problem for ensemble members than are the first two. The *occasional* need for synchronization, notably on the keyboard, was discussed above (Chap. 9, p. 103). A pervasive orchestral-choral principle to that effect is, however, unworkable. The individual performer cannot know what lines other parts will play or sing, and even if it were possible to know this, the performer would have to consider, for every note played, whether it needed to be synchronized and if so with whom and how: who is to be the synchronizer and who the synchronized? This seems to be an unworkable proposition.

Finally, we have to consider the further incongruity that, in the alleged performing style, composers from at least Lully on were not free to use the simple dotted rhythms (with a ratio of 3:1) that had been commonplace for centuries; for whenever this rhythm was put down on paper it was automatically transformed into the double-, triple-, or "ultra"-dotted "jerky pattern." Furthermore, composers would have been unable to mix milder and sharper rhythms, either horizontally or vertically: in sequence they were homogenized to the sharpest pattern, in simultaneity they were synchronized to eliminate rhythmic clashes. By such action any written counterpoint is in effect wiped out by synchronization. Moreover, composers were not at liberty to devise moderately paced upbeat figures since they too were altered by sharp contractions. These severe restrictions on the composer's freedom of invention seem to me to contradict all principles of musical aesthetics.

Thus we see that the totality of the French overture style is based on a long succession of assumptions and hypotheses, most of which are highly improbable; and on that basis alone this style cannot be considered a historical probability.

## *Summary*

The so-called French overture style involves sharp overdotting, upbeat contraction, and synchronization. Preceded by the practice of sporadic double dotting in keyboard arrangements (going back to ca. 1800) of Handel overtures, the much more comprehensive principles of the style were basically the brainchild of Arnold Dolmetsch (*Interpretation of Music,* 1915), who wanted them applied to "all old music." He derived the idea from misinterpreted passages in Quantz and C. P. E. Bach. In 1954 Thurston Dart adopted Dolmetsch's idea and formulated its principles with a focus on the French overture (hence its name) but ranging far and wide beyond this genre. Other scholars and editors followed this lead, and by today the style is widely practiced by "early music specialists."

In the 17th and 18th centuries, however, given the musical text, the application of this style would have been unworkable for orchestra or chorus. The question of *when* to apply it had no clear answer, nor had the question of *how* to apply it: how much to overdot, how to contract the upbeat figures, how to synchronize. Today this style of playing can be made to work only by recomposing and detailed editing, a resource clearly unavailable to 17th- or 18th-century directors. Add to this the associated inability of a composer to use a 3:1 rhythm or moderately paced upbeat figures, to introduce rhythmic variety, and to write polyphony that will not be obliterated by synchronization. Furthermore, if we consider the lack of any genuine historical evidence, it is time to recognize the style for what it is: a major historical misunderstanding.[6]

# 11

# RHYTHMIC ALTERATIONS III: THE *Notes Inégales*

## The Nature of the Convention

The *notes inégales* ("unequal notes") represent a special case of rhythmic alteration that differs from all other types in that it is regulated by a genuine, massively documented convention. This convention developed in France from unknown origins, revealed its presence in print perhaps first in the mid-16th century, assumed a clear outline in the mid-17th century, and crystallized by 1700 into a very distinctly structured system that remained basically unchanged until near the end of the 18th century.

It is necessary to discuss this convention at some length, in part because of its importance for the French music of the 17th and 18th centuries, and in part because influential modern writers and some well-known performers claim the convention for non-French music as well, in particular for Bach and Handel. This international application intensifies the need for a closer look.

The main features of the convention are these. Certain pairs of notes—pairs, never triplets or other ternary groups—though written evenly, were rendered unevenly, namely long–short. The notes in question had to be subdivisions of the beat, never the beat itself. Furthermore, there were exact rules that determined whether the notes eligible for inequality (hereafter, with regard to the French convention only, *inégalité*) were to be on the first level of subdivision of the beat, such as quarter notes in $\frac{3}{2}$ meter, eighth notes in **2**, **3**, or $\frac{6}{4}$ meter, or sixteenth notes in $\frac{3}{8}$, $\frac{6}{8}$, or $\frac{9}{8}$ meter; or whether they were to be on the second level of subdivision, such as sixteenth notes in $\mathbf{C}$ or $\frac{2}{4}$.[1] Finally, to be eligible, the notes had to move predominantly stepwise, whereas a series of leaps disqualified them.

*Inégalité* lengthened the first note and shortened the second in a ratio that for all practical purposes ranged from a barely perceptible 7:5 to about 2:1, hardly ever going beyond this limit. Whenever the conditions were right, *inégalité* was as good as mandatory unless the composer canceled it by placing dots or dashes above the notes or by using such words as *notes* (or *croches*) *égales, marqué,* or *détaché.*

The convention was explained in almost all French manuals from the late 17th to the late 18th century, even in those addressed to children. In my study of 1965 I listed and tabulated, without claiming completeness, thirty authors explaining the rules of *inégalité* ("The French *Inégales*," 322–23, or *Essays 1982*, 24–25). David Fuller has more recently given the number of French authors explaining the convention as over eighty-five (*New Harvard Dictionary*, s.v. "Notes Inégales," 549).

On first sight, the principles of the convention seem to be an arbitrary assembly of rules. Yet there is method in them, and once we discern it the system makes perfect sense, with all the details falling readily into place. The purpose of the convention was ornamental. It produced a rhythmic lilt that added grace and elegance to a musical line without impairing its structural guideposts. The limitation to subdivisions of the beat assures that the notes that do fall on the beat, and are thus most likely to be structural, may be lengthened, and thereby emphasized, but cannot be shortened, which would endanger their rhythmic integrity and proper weight. The rules about the meter/note-value relationship insure that only those notes that are likely to be the fastest in the piece, and therefore also likely to be ornamental in character, will be subject to rhythmic modulation. Thus, in meters that were beaten fast or fairly fast—such as, for instance, **3**, $\frac{3}{8}$, and $\frac{6}{8}$—the first level of subdivision of the beat was subject to *inégalité* because these could be and often were the fastest notes in the piece; but in a slow meter such as $\mathbf{C}$ or $\frac{2}{4}$, the eighth notes that made up the first subdivisions of the beat were leisurely enough to have structural meaning, so that the ornamental function devolved on the second subdivision, the sixteenth notes, which generally abound in this meter. The principle that *inégalité* was to be applied only to predominantly stepwise progression completes the picture: ornamental figurations tend to move by steps, whereas in an angular line the individual notes will tend to assume melodic-structural importance. Examining a melodic line from this vantage point we can usually make a reasonable judgment on whether the line is, or is not, conducive to *inégalité:* it need not proceed solely by steps but can

circumscribe a chord and can still be perceived as ornamental as long as
it has the character of an arpeggio; when, however, the single notes
assume melodic substance, then *inégalité* will be improper.

We see that the French convention was a unified system whose
parts fit together into an organic, logical whole. Logical, because in
terms of its function all its elements make perfect sense, and the individual principles complement each other. And this inner logic was the
cement that held this complex, sophisticated system together over a
period of a century and a half, during which the many writers of manuals agreed on all important points. The system must have grown spontaneously until it blossomed into a coherent form whose fitness for its
ornamental purpose permitted it to survive intact for a remarkable
length of time.

***An Early Document.*** A striking document from the mid-16th century
sheds some light on the otherwise obscure early stages of this evolution.
Loys Bourgeois in 1550 explains how to sing in the proper manner ("la
maniere de bien chanter") a series of semiminims (quarter notes) in the
signs 𝄴, 𝄵, o𝄵, o𝟮 , and c by grouping them in twos and somewhat
lengthening the first and shortening the second of each pair ("de deux
en deux, demourant quelque peu de temps dauantage sur la
premiere, que sur la seconde"). Analogous treatment is to be given a
sequence of fusae (eighth notes) when they occur under the signs
o , c, o𝟮, and c𝟮 (*Le droit chemin*, chap. 10). Bourgeois's illustrations
are shown in Exx. 11.1a and b.

EXAMPLE 11.1.   Loys Bourgeois (1550)

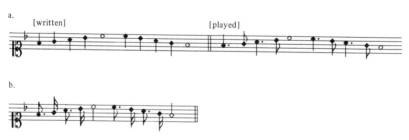

What is fascinating about this document is that it already contains
four and perhaps five ingredients of *inégalité*: the long–short sequence,
the mildness of *inégalité* ("quelque peu de temps dauantage"), *inégalité's*
dependence on the relationship of note value and meter, as well as the
reference to its ornamental function and the presumably implied stepwise progression. Bourgeois suggests the ornamental function by point-

ing to the first note as normally being a consonance, the second as being a dissonance ("un discord, ou [comme on dit] un faux accord" [*Le droit chemin*, chap. 10]). He thus implies that the second note is a passing note, hence ornamental in function, a suggestion confirmed by his examples, which show stepwise lines (both rising and falling) for both semiminims and fusae. Thus we see the main features of *inégalité* perhaps at or near its fountainhead.

Significant too is that the mild long–short *inégalité* spelled out in the text had to be shown as a series of dotted notes since a more fitting rhythmic notation was unavailable. Because of the continuing lack of a better graphic device, this same dualism of dotted-rhythm illustration and verbal indication of a ratio much milder than 3:1 runs like a red thread through the whole history of the convention.

The fully developed and integrated French system could work only in France, where every musician, from childhood training on, began absorbing these principles, as testified to by the huge number of French treatises that explain their rules, whereas French pedagogical tracts from the late 17th to the end of the 18th century that do *not* deal with it are rare exceptions. Thus the rules of *inégalité* became so much a part of every French musician's consciousness that *inégalité* could be practiced in an orchestra with the conductor or concertmaster merely indicating its ratio wherever applicable. Of course when Frenchmen traveled or worked abroad they carried this legacy with them. And wherever such French musicians taught students, they imparted these principles to some chosen individuals. Yet apart from a few such French-taught individuals, the rank and file of musicians outside of France apparently did not know the convention, so the evidence suggests. Whereas almost every French text explained the system, there is no known mention— with two interesting German exceptions—of a comparable explanation anywhere outside of France.

*Two German Followers.* Of the two German masters who endorsed the convention the first was Georg Muffat (1653–1704). For six years as an adolescent he had studied the Lullian style "under the best masters" in Paris. Then, in his maturity, he gave a detailed account of the Lullian performance manner—including *inégalité*—in the quadrilingual prefaces to his two *Florilegia* of 1695 and 1698 (especially the second one). The preface to the 1698 volume is introduced as "First observations of the author on the way of playing the *airs de ballet* in the French manner according to the method of the late M. de Lully" (Premières observations de l'Auteur sur la manière de jouer les airs de Ballet à la Françoise selon la méthode de feu Mons. de Lully). In this preface Muffat explains the long–short rendition, spells out the meter/note-value relationships in which *inégalité* applies, and, without specifying it in words, shows stepwise progression in all his examples. Clearly his intention was to acquaint his German compatriots with this performance manner, which he assumed was unknown to them along with other elements of the Lullian style such as bowing patterns, ornamentation, and other practices.

Half a century later Quantz described the principles of *inégalité* in his *Versuch einer Anweisung* of 1752 (chap. 11, par. 12). He did so in a paragraph that has become famous and has led to far-reaching claims about the international validity of the convention. Because of the large role it has played in the modern scholarly literature, the passage is given here almost in its entirety:

> I must make here a necessary remark that concerns the length of time each note is to be held. One must know how to distinguish in performance between, on the one side, *principal* notes, also called "on-beat" [anschlagende] or in Italian usage "good" notes, and, on the other side, *passing* notes, called by some foreigners "bad" notes. The principal notes must wherever possible be brought out more than the passing ones. According to this rule, the fastest notes in every piece in moderate tempo or in adagio must nevertheless be played a little unevenly [ein wenig ungleich gespielet], despite the fact that they are written even. Thus the "on-beat" notes of every group, namely, the first, third, fifth, and seventh, must be held somewhat longer than the "passing" ones, namely the second, fourth, sixth, and eighth. But this holding must not amount to as much as it would if there were dots after the notes. By the fastest notes I mean: quarters in $\frac{3}{2}$, eighths in $\frac{3}{4}$, sixteenths in $\frac{3}{8}$, eighths in alla breve, sixteenths or thirty-seconds in $\frac{2}{4}$ or $\mathbb{C}$. . . . Exempt from these rules are: first, passages in very fast tempo, where time does not allow an uneven rendition and where only the first of each four notes can be played longer and louder. Also exempt are all fast, unslurred passages for the singing voice. . . . Further exceptions occur: when notes have dashes or dots over them, or when there are several successive notes on the same pitch; also when there is a slur over more than two notes—that is, over four, six, and finally concerning all eighth notes in gigues. All these notes must be played even, that is, one as long as the other.

While he explains the basic principles of *inégalité,* including the required relationship of meter and note values, Quantz reveals a foreigner's incomplete understanding of the convention at the very start of his paragraph by relating *inégalité* to "good" and "bad" notes. To do so is a mistake that no Frenchman would have made. If *inégalité* were an outgrowth of the "good" and "bad" notes, it would make little sense to subject only the "fastest notes" to its principles. Whereas the first of the two notes lengthened by *inégalité* is normally a "good" note, there are innumerable "good" notes that are not subject to such lengthening, such as all the notes longer than the "fastest" ones, the odd-numbered half or quarter notes in **3** or **2** meter, or the half, quarter, or eighth notes in $\mathbb{C}$ meter, and so on.

The Quantz passage has created much excitement in the performance practice literature and has led, as has been mentioned, to far-reaching claims about the required application of *inégalité* to Bach, to Handel, and to all their contemporaries, their Baroque predecessors, and their galant followers. The scholars who arrived at such sweeping conclusions have, however, misunderstood and vastly overrated the scope of the passage, which has to be read against the background of Quantz's purpose.

That Quantz adopted the French manner is easy to understand. He not only had a French flute teacher (Buffardin) but was a self-confessed eclectic who prided himself on the fact that he was from personal experience acquainted with the various national styles. His proclaimed purpose was to help bring about a mixed style in both composition and performance, one that would combine the best features of what the French, the Italian, and the German manners had to offer. He greatly admired French performance practices; hence it is only natural that he would select one of their most characteristic features, the *notes inégales*, and recommend its use to his German readers. His passage—like Muffat's explanation of *inégalité*—did not report what was being done in Germany at the time but simply recommended the adoption of a French performance manner. A meaningful adoption in Germany, England, and Italy of the complicated and sophisticated convention, which even Quantz did not fully understand—as was just shown—would have required the kind of massive indoctrination that was so strikingly present in France and so strikingly absent in all other countries. And since there is no sign that Quantz's suggestion found an echo in any German or any other non-French texts, it is extremely unlikely that, outside of a few isolated islands of French musical influence, it could have been widely known and practiced in Germany.

The Quantz directive seems in fact to have been ignored by all his non-French contemporaries. It then lay dormant for a century and a half until it was rediscovered, possibly by Edward Dannreuther in 1893 (*Musical Ornamentation*, 1:54), who quoted it and saw in it, modestly if erroneously, along with Frescobaldi's famous preface to his *Toccate e partite* (1615–16), a confirmation of a general Baroque practice of rubato playing for certain preludes, toccatas, and the like. He did not realize its indebtedness to the *notes inégales*.

Dolmetsch, however, went much further; in 1915 he was the first to conclude that *inégalité* as described by Quantz should be applied to Bach, because Quantz, as he wrongly affirmed, belonged to Bach's school (*Interpretation of Music*, 78ff.). Sol Babitz, in 1952, saw in the passage a confirmation of his thesis that long–short or short–long (the latter not mentioned by Quantz) rendition of evenly written pairs of notes involves "nearly every measure of Baroque music," including of course that of Bach ("Problem of Rhythm," 533–65). Curt Sachs in 1953 and Alfred Dürr in 1955 also found in the passage proof that *inégalité* represented a general Baroque convention (Sachs, *Rhythm and Tempo*, 296ff.; Dürr, NBA II/3 [Magnificat], KB, 47ff.).

All these scholars have misread as a report on current international practices what was only a personal recommendation, one that to boot seems by and large to have fallen on deaf ears.

## Inequality Other Than Inégalité

There are many cases in the music of all times and all nations in which equally written notes have been and are still now being rendered unequally, mostly long–short but occasionally short–long. We must deal here with some of the better-known instances since several scholars have seen in them what they believed to be further evidence for the international validity of the *notes inégales*.

We have already encountered such cases in chapter 9 under the headings of "Inflections and Nuances," "Agogic Accents," and "Rubato." Considering that the more we go back in time the less precise notation becomes, and the more the solo performer was at liberty to deviate from the letter of the score, it is rather certain that rhythmic modulations were a commonplace occurrence. The few theoretical mentions of such freedoms can hardly be a true reflection of their indubitable omnipresence. Among theorists, Ganassi, Zacconi, Caccini, and Tosi have already been mentioned (in chap. 9).

Caccini in particular has been referred to by several scholars as directing rhythmic alteration allegedly related to *inégalité*. Yet Caccini's examples (those that show equally written notes manipulated in various manners while remaining within the beat) embody typical rubato freedoms arbitrarily chosen by artistic judgment. No regularity, no principle, no convention is involved here, and any resemblance to *inégalité* is coincidental and deceptive.

The Spaniard Tomás de Santa Maria is also frequently cited in this connection. His remarkable book on the clavichord (*Arte de tañer*, 1565) has a chapter on playing with grace ("con buen ayre") in which he recommends various kinds of rhythmic modulations. Evenly written quarter notes may be played dotted: ♩. ♪♩. ♪ ; even eighth notes may be played in three fashions: (1) dotted, ♫ ♫ , to be used in contrapuntal works and in ornamental variations ("glosas"); (2) in reverse dotting: ♫. ♫. ; and (3) by hurrying the first three of four notes and dwelling on the fourth. Then he cautions that in all these manners the alteration of the note values must be only mild, or else the result will be clumsiness and ugliness ("desgracia y fealdad"). His principles, in contrast to Caccini's, show a slight resemblance to the French convention by their regularity of alteration within a sequence of even notes, yet there is still a difference of kind. Basically his directives are an introduction to rubato playing: they list three different ways of manipulating eighth notes, to be chosen arbitrarily by the player. Such variety, which is obviously available only to the soloist, not to an ensemble, contrasts with the single mode of *inégalité;* moreover, there is no requirement, only a license, and no relationship between the measure sign and the note values, the relationship that, beginning with Bourgeois in 1550, is at the foundation of the French convention.

The same applies to the directive of Frescobaldi in his famous preface to the toccatas of 1615–16, in which he gives instructions about rubato freedoms in works that are improvisatory in character. One of these directives deals with sixteenth notes in one hand set against eighth notes in the other hand. In such a combination the sixteenths should be played with short–long unevenness ("e quella [mano] que sara le semicrome douerà farle alquanto puntato, cio è non la prima, ma la seconda sia con punto"). This unevenness is only mild, like Santa Maria's, since Frescobaldi speaks only of "alquanto puntato"—that is, slightly lengthened, not the snappy "Lombard" rhythm occasionally read into this passage. This is a very special case that depends on two different simultaneous rhythms, something totally foreign to the French convention. Basically, what Frescobaldi and others like Santa Maria or Caccini explain are the kinds of rubato freedoms that were within the soloist's license in the 16th, 17th, and early 18th centuries. The resemblance of these freedoms to the French convention is only superficial since none of them is part of a closed, integrated system, none can be used outside of a soloistic context, and none is de facto obligatory. It is misleading therefore to see in them sufficient cause for extending the roof of the *inégalité* convention over all of Europe.

*Dotted Notes Mistaken for* Notes Inégales. Several scholars, among them Robert Donington and David Fuller, have included notated dotted notes under the label of *notes inégales.* Of course, a dotted note and its companion, with their 3:1 ratio, are uneven quantities, but so are all notes of different denominations. To call them uneven notes or *notes inégales* is a tautology, and like every tautology it is true but pointless. If we insist on that statement we would inevitably have to conclude that, with insignificant exceptions, all music consists of *notes inégales.* That clearly makes no sense.

Certainly dotted notes bear a resemblance to *notes inégales,* and the idea of their overlapping or actual identity was encouraged by the way some theorists explained *inégalité* with dotted-note illustrations. These theorists could not help it: ♩♪ being unknown, the dotted note was at the time the *only* available graphic device to suggest *any* kind of long–short unevenness, even a very mild one. As we have seen, Bourgeois, Santa Maria, and Frescobaldi already used the dotted illustration for what they verbally described as mild unevenness. And later theorists who used this notation to illustrate *inégalité* (among them Muffat, Hotteterre, Montéclair, and La Chapelle) have misled some modern scholars into taking this rough approximation, this makeshift device, at its 3:1 face value and as a consequence believing in a "vigorous inequality" that exaggerated what was actually done (e.g., Donington, *Performer's Guide*, 259).

Another source for a similarly mistaken identity is the common use at the time of the term *pointer* for lengthening a note with an increment of undetermined and often minuscule size. Bénigne de Bacilly, previously mentioned author of a famous vocal treatise of 1668 (*Remarques curieuses*), in recommending *notes inégales* for improvised diminutions, speaks of *poincts alternatifs* but cautions that they be applied with such subtlety that the "dotting" is hardly noticeable ("notes pointées si finement que cela ne paroisse pas" [232]). Hotteterre defines *pointer* as making (in **C** meter) of two sixteenth notes one long and one short ("une longue et une brève" [*L'art de préluder*, 57]), which certainly falls short of suggesting a 3:1 ratio. Duval, concerned about the misleading use of the word *pointer*, says: "dotting is an improper term for *inégalité*" (Pointer se dit improprement pour faire les croches inégalles [*Méthode agréable*, 15]). Couperin directs in one of his pieces (the allemande "La Laborieuse"): "the sixteenth notes a little bit dotted" (les double croches un tant soit peu pointées [*Pieces de clavecin*]), and a half century earlier Nivers in his *Livre d'orgue* of 1665 spoke of "half dotting" (faire comme des demi-points) the first, third, fifth, and seventh of eight eighth notes in a measure by lengthening them "a little bit" (augmenter tant soit peu) and by proportionally shortening the companion notes. In other words, the term *pointer* can mean standard dotting but can also mean an undetermined lengthening, and where it is used to mean the latter it might be best to translate it with "lengthening" rather than "dotting."

This interpretation of the dotted illustrations and of the term *pointer* is confirmed by other important theorists who specify the mildness of *inégalité* and by that fact alone set it clearly apart from regular dotted notes. Loulié in 1696 makes this difference very clear when he distinguishes two types of unevenness. The first, contingent on stepwise motion—the proper setting for *inégalité*—he calls *lourer*, where the first of a pair of equal notes is held "a little longer"; the second type, in which the first note is "much longer than the second," he calls *pointer* or *piquer* but explains that this type has to be marked with a dot ("doit avoir un point" [*Éléments ou principes de musique*, 34–35]). The implication is clear: under the principles of *inégalité* the lengthening is only mild; any strong lengthening crosses over into the realm of standard dotted notes and has to be marked accordingly. To avoid the danger of exaggerating the ratio of *inégalité*, Loulié, in manuscript supplements to his treatise, indicates its mildness by the ingenious nonmetric design: ♩♩♩♩ .[2] Montéclair, in his *Nouvelle méthode* of 1709, also illustrates *inégalité* with dotted notes, saying that ♩ ♪♪♪♪ is "like" ♪.♪♪.♪ , while explaining that the first note should be held "a little longer" than the second ("un peu plus longue"), thus clearly belying a literal meaning of the dots. Other eminent theorists concurred in the mildness of *inégalité*. To list just a few among many, Villeneuve says in 1733: "one renders the second eighth note a little faster" (un peu plus vite [*Nouvelle méthode*, 4]); Choquel in 1762: "the first of two even notes that form a beat must be held a little longer than the second" (la première des deux qui forment un temps doit estre tenue un peu plus longtemps que la seconde [*La musique rendue*, 106]); Mercadier de Belesta in 1776: "the first a little longer than the second" (la première un peu plus longue que la seconde [*Nouveau système*, 67]); Jean Jacques Rousseau in 1768: "In French music . . . the eighth notes are equal only in ₵ meter; in all others one lengthens [literally, dots] them always a little" (on les pointe toujours un peu [*Dictionnaire*, s.v. "Pointer"]).

The mildness of *inégalité* is further confirmed by Père Engramelle both in his *Tonotechnie* of 1775 and in his essay on the mechanical organ for Bedos de Celle's *L'art du facteur d'orgues* vol. 4 of 1778. Though in theory he stakes out a range for *inégalité* from a barely noticeable 7:5 to a 3:1 ratio (the latter being reserved for marches), in practice, in the given examples—even in the "Marches du roy" Nos. 1 and 2 from the *Tonotechnie* and in the cylinder notations in *L'art*—the sharpest ratio to be found is 2:1. This extreme ratio is specified only in marches and in assimilation to triplets, whereas elsewhere the ratio is milder than 2:1. It will also be remembered that Quantz cautions against extending the unevenness to the length of a dot.

We can gather from this evidence derived from eminent contemporary authorities that the modern idea of a vigorous *inégalité* ranging from the equivalent of a dotted note to "extremely dotted" is a misunderstanding. It seems that, for instance, David Fuller's idea of such excessive inequality originated from a sentence in an *anonymous* 17th-century French manuscript treatise referring to *one* specific piece that is to be extremely dotted. Fuller quoted it in his article "Notes Inégales" (*Grove* 6) (a reprint of that treatise is now available in *L'Orgue* 152 [1974]: 107). An anonymous witness is always suspect, be it in the court of law or in historical research, and must be discounted when his testimony is at odds with statements by persons of recognized authority. There always have been and always will be performers who tend to eccentricity, but we need not concern ourselves about them: what matters is what was at the core and not at the fringe of the musical scene.

Actual dotted notes are a species altogether different from the *notes inégales*. They have occurred in the music of all times, of all Western nations, in all melodic contexts, with no immanent organic connection to ornamental function. We find them in ternary as well as in binary groupings and on all levels from the longest to the shortest note values; they are independent of meter/note-value relationships and are not limited to subdivisions of the beat. Because of their rhythmic angularity, dotted notes also favor the melodic angularity of large leaps, just as the rhythmic smoothness of the *notes inégales* favors, and is congenial to, melodic smoothness, the often-listed "stepwise progressions." All of which only reaffirms that there is a difference in kind between dotted notes and *inégalité*.

Yet we find Robert Donington equating dotted notes and *inégalité* when he prints (*Interpretation of Early Music*, 461) the opening measure of Handel's Sonata Op. 1, No. 1 "first in mainly equal notation, later [in m. 12] in unequal notation" (see Ex. 11.2a). "There can be," he continues, "no reason other than inadvertence." Though only the first half of measure 1 is—melodically—repeated with different articulation in measure 12, Donington sees in the rhythmic discrepancy between the two measures a proof that Handel practiced *inégalité* and that the whole movement should be played in "unequal rhythm." A more plausible reason for the discrepancy, however, is that, in addition to the melodic change in the second half of the measure, Handel wished to add a rhythmic variant to the quasi-repeat. The movement should most likely be played as written.

A similar caveat is in order for simultaneous undotted and dotted notation of melodically parallel voices and instruments. A frequently quoted case is the first movement of Bach's *Trauerode* (Cantata No. 198) where the voices are almost throughout written in even notes, the melodically parallel instruments in dotted ones. Several writers, among them Donington, call for rhythmic synchronization by dotting of the voice parts in the name of *inégalité*. Donington's illustration (*Performer's Guide*, 194) is given in Ex. 11.2b. Such discrepancies of rhythmic notation were frequent, however, because composers who knew how to write for the voice often adjusted the rhythms to the demands of the vocal idiom for less angularity, such as even notes for the voice and dotted for melodically unison instruments or single-dotted notes for the voice and double-dotted ones for the instruments. The resulting clashes may look surprising on paper, but in performance they are totally innocuous.

In a similar vein David Fuller, commenting on the question of whether Bach and other non-French composers used *notes inégales*, affirms that "countless scores show that they did" (*New Grove Dictionary of Musical Instruments*, 2:779). Since the indication *notes égales*, which by canceling *inégalité* implicitly proves its prevalence, has seemingly never been found in any non-French score, there appear to be only two ways in which these scores could conceivably show the use of *inégalité*, neither of which would be convincing. One would be the presence of dotted notes, the other that of dots over notes, which dots theoretically could

EXAMPLE 11.2

a. Handel, Sonata, Op. 1, No. 1

b. Bach, *Trauerode*, BWV 198/1

Lass noch ei - nen Strahl ——— aus Sa - lems Stern ——— gewöl - ben    schies-sen

cancel *inégalité*. As explained before, the mere presence of dotted notes, which are a common occurrence everywhere, provides no evidence for *inégalité*. The same is the case with dots over notes. Such dots over sixteenth notes in ¢ meter in the "Goldberg" Variation No. 16, measures 8–9, have been adduced—most recently by Paul Badura-Skoda (*Bach Interpretation*, 71)—as a case of canceled and therefore prevailing *iné-galité*. Yet Bach often writes dots over notes that (unlike the sixteenth notes of the "Goldberg" Variation) are *not* subject to *inégalité*: for a strik-ing case see the numerous dots over triplets in *Clavierübung III*, "Vater unser im Himmelreich." Since triplets are never subject to *inégalité*, the only conceivable meaning of these dots has to be staccato articulation— the likeliest meaning by far under any circumstances, for dots above or below notes. That was true also in France, where the dots canceled *inégalité* not simply by functioning as abstract symbols but—just like the words *détaché* or *marqué*—by denoting staccato, which was incompatible with the gentle lilt of *inégalité*.

**Strong and Weak Beats Equated with Notes Inégales.** A further source of misunderstanding lies in the belief that the metrical alternation of strong and weak beats was identical with the long–short alternation of the *notes inégales*. This belief, most emphatically proclaimed by Sol Babitz and endorsed by Curt Sachs and others, was fostered by 17th- and 18th-century German theorists who misleadingly referred to the metrical strong–weak alternation as "long" and "short," albeit invariably quali-fied by adverbial expressions such as "quantitate intrinseca" or "virtu-aliter" or "innerlich" (inwardly). This infelicitous terminology for "good" and "bad" parts of the measure was briefly mentioned in the Introduction to Part II.[3] *Inégalité* is an entirely different matter. The metrical alternation of strong–weak in binary meters, and of strong–weak–weak in ternary ones, has existed in Western music ever since metrical rhythm made its appearance, which may go back to the early Middle Ages; it persists even to the present day, when the barline still suggests patterns of recurrent heavy and light beats. This metric weight is primarily a matter of loud and soft, not of long and short. It applies to whole beats and occasionally even to whole measures, which alone shows the fundamental difference from *inégalité*.

**Limitation to French Music.** Regarding the claimed international validity of *inégalité*, we have several important French documents that stress the limitation of the convention to French music only. In the 1698 edition published in Amsterdam of his book of 1696, Loulié emphasizes in italics that *inégalité* does not apply to any non-French music. "In all kinds of foreign music one does not lengthen notes unless specifically notated [by added dots]" (dans toute sorte de musique étrangère ou l'on ne pointe jamais qu'il ne soit marqué [*Éléments ou principes de musique* (1698), 38]).

Michel Corrette writes in 1741 that *inégalité* does not apply to Italian music: "in any meter the eighth notes are played evenly in Italian music" (*Méthode pour le violoncelle*, 4).

With clear reference to *inégalité*, Couperin writes in 1716 that Frenchmen play foreign music better than foreigners play French music because foreign music is played as written whereas the French is not. He compares French musical notation to the nonphonetic spelling of the French language. The Italians, he writes, notate their music in their intended values, whereas "we dot [meaning inequalize] groups of eighth notes that move stepwise, yet we write them equal" (nous pointons plusieurs croches de suites par degrés-conjoints; Et cependant nous les marquons égales [*L'art*, 39–40]).

In a statement partially quoted before, J. J. Rousseau writes in 1768 that "in Italian music all eighth notes are always of equal length unless they are expressly marked as dotted. By way of contrast, in French music eighth notes are equal only in C meter" (dans la mesure à quatre temps [*Dictionnaire*, s.v. "Pointer"]).

Among modern writers Peter le Huray is one of very few who agree that the convention of *inégalité* is "exclusively French" (*Authenticity*, 53).

## *Summary and Conclusion:* Inégalité *for Bach?*

The important question of whether *inégalité* should be applied to Bach, to Handel, and to other non-French composers has no categorical answer: it can be neither proved nor disproved. In matters of style there never are Chinese walls around either nations or individuals, and there were musicians such as Quantz, Reicha, or Franz Benda who moved within the orbit of the French performance style (but whose works occupy only a negligible space in today's living repertory). Also there were in Germany some enclaves of French musical performance manner, such as Celle (the French Hofkapelle, 1666–1706) or the Dresden Hofkapelle under Volumier (until the latter's death in 1728). Certainly the French language held sway among high society, and many a socially ambitious individual put on French airs and affected French manners and mannerisms. Could Bach have been among them? It seems most doubtful. Unquestionably he learned a great deal from French composers, as he did from German and Italian ones. From the French he adopted the overture-suites and many of their ornaments. But what he adopted and how he did it can be compared to the way the English language had absorbed and amalgamated more than half the French vocabulary without therefore surrendering its native genius to either French grammar, syntax, or style.

If Bach had practiced *inégalité* we could expect it to have left ever so small a trace in the writings of his students or close associates, of Philipp Emanuel, Agricola, Kirnberger, or Walther, but it did not. If we add to this the absence, to the best of our knowledge, of *any* mention of *inégalité* outside of France, other than by the two devotees of French practices, Georg Muffat and Quantz; if we add further the practical impossibility of exporting the complex, highly integrated French convention without the benefit of the thorough conditioning practiced in France; the nonsuccess of scholarly attempts to link either dotted notes or the "good" and "bad" notes to *inégalité*; the failure to link arbitrary rubato-like inequalities that occur in any Western musical culture to the French convention; and finally the express statement by eminent Frenchmen about the nonvalidity of the convention beyond the French borders; then these considerations should permit the conclusion that a transplant of the convention to Bach, Handel, or Vivaldi is improbable to such a degree that we seem entitled to close the book on this issue.[4]

Thus, by and large, it will be advisable to limit the use of *inégalité* to French composers of the *ancien régime*. For them *inégalité* should be used for solo, for orchestra, and for chorus, whenever the rules of the convention call for it. It will be further advisable to be discreet, and stay well within the limit of a 2:1 ratio.

For just two illustrations where mild *inégalité* is indicated, see Rameau's *1er Rigaudon* from his *Pièces de clavecin* of 1724 (Ex. 11.3a) and Couperin's *La Bersan* from the 6th *Ordre* of his *Pièces de clavecin* (Ex. 11.3b).

EXAMPLE 11.3

a. Rameau, 1$^{er}$ Rigaudon

b. Couperin, *La Bersan*

# 12

# BINARY–TERNARY AND RELATED RHYTHMIC CONFLICTS

## *Rhythmic Counterpoint*

In defining polyphonic texture it is usual to point to the combination of independent voice parts, whose independence is manifested in both melody and rhythm. In contrast, definitions of homophonic textures point to a dominant melody voice while the others either accompany or move in harmony in identical rhythm. The borderline between polyphony and homophony is often blurred, but in genuinely polyphonic music such as a Bach fugue the rhythmic as well as the melodic independence of the voices is obvious. Although when speaking of counterpoint one often focuses on the combination of melodies, the rhythmic counterpoint (the combination of different rhythms) is of equal importance to the texture.

As long as the rhythms of the various voices are in the same meter, with the same subdivisions on all levels, they pose no specific performance problems. Problems arise, however, when the rhythmic counterpoint is complicated either by different meters for simultaneous parts or by different rhythmic designs that set, say, three equal notes or their subdivisions against two equal notes or their subdivisions, or four against three, five against two, and so on. This is the kind of rhythmic counterpoint that has given rise to much controversy in the scholarly literature and to divergent interpretations in performance.

The binary–ternary conflict has occupied the center of the controversy because it occurs so much more frequently than the other types. In general—and this applies to all types of rhythmic conflict—the controversy sets mathematical literalness, with resulting rhythmic clashes, against an assimilation of one mode to the other in order to avoid such clashes.

## *Binary–Ternary Conflicts: Why Are They a Problem?*

Binary rhythms such as ¢ ♩♪ ♩♪♪ ♩♪ ♩♪♪ and ternary rhythms such as ¢ ♩. ♩♪ ♩♪♪♪ or ⁹⁄₈ ♩ ♪ ♪♪♪ ♪ ♩ are defined by clear mathematical ratios. Deviations from these explicit relationships have two main sources: (1) defects in the system of notation, in which case the deviations from the notated values were intended; (2) inadequacies in the performer's skill, or inadvertence on his part, in which case the deviations were not intended.

The notational defect with the most serious consequences for our problem as mentioned in chapter 9, is the absence until the mid-19th century of the 2:1 symbol ♩.♪ within a binary meter.[1] In its stead composers were forced to make do with either the 3:1 dotted-note symbol: ♪♩ (=♩.♪) or, much less frequently, the 1:1 symbol of two equal notes: ♪♪ (=♩.♪) . As a result, both of these binary symbols occasionally became ambiguous, and their presumed meaning must be inferred from the context.

Inadvertence or technical shortcomings of an interpreter do not normally enter into the discussion of a desirable performance, but since some of these defects have given rise to questionable theories of interpretation, they need to be mentioned. At the root of these technical shortcomings is the fact that triplets can be difficult. While they are generally easy to render when strung out in a row (e.g., ¢ ♩ ♪♪♪ ♪♪♪ ♪♪♪ ), they can be more difficult when they occur alone in the middle of binary rhythms. Here we find a tendency (still operative today, even among highly skilled performers) to turn them into anapests; thus ¢ ♩. ♪♪♪ |♩ easily becomes ♩. ♪♪♪ |♩ . This tendency is strengthened when a triplet is preceded by binary rhythms such as ♩ ♪♪ ♪♪ ♪♪♪ . Conversely, binary rhythms can be troublesome when they follow a series of triplets. Here the binary notes will tend to adjust to the ternary swing: ¢ ♪♪♪ ♪♪♪ ♪♪ ♩ may become ♪♪♪ ♪♪♪ ♩. ♪ ♩ .

When, instead of following each other in sequence, these disparate rhythms occur simultaneously in two voices, the tendencies of assimilation are intensified. When one of these rhythmic modes is dominant, it will tend to pull the other into its orbit: thus a dominant binary rhythm can easily cause triplets to become binary: ♩ 𝄽 will tend to become ♩ . Similarly, a dominant ternary rhythm can easily cause duplets to become ternary: ♩ may become ♩ . The weaker the rhythmic skills of the performer, the stronger the tendency toward assimilation.

## Binary–Ternary Conflicts in Historical Perspective

Notated polyphony in Western music emerged around the 10th century and by the early 14th century developed into an art of extraordinary sophistication. By then, most notably in France, rhythmic along with melodic counterpoint reached a degree of complexity that was probably never surpassed and rarely matched again: there were combinations of different meters, cross-rhythms, syncopations, and written-out rubatos, with binary–ternary conflicts being among the least of the difficulties confronting the performers. Considering the great difficulty of the "mensural" notation (see chap. 1) and the absence of barlines, we can only marvel at the virtuosic skill the singers must have displayed in such enormously intricate settings. And their only chance of staying together and holding their own against disparate rhythms in other parts lay in punctilious exactness in the rendition of the symbols.

Music of considerable rhythmic complexity continued to be written until the age of Josquin around 1500. Binary–ternary conflicts occurred mostly in the form of different meters in different voice parts: binary in some, ternary in other parts. In its simplest form such confrontation was indicated by the signature of a binary measure such as $C$ or $\mathbb{C}$ in one voice opposed to a proportional sign such as $\frac{3}{2}$ (sesquialtera) in another voice. The symbol $\frac{3}{2}$ was a proportional sign indicating (as explained earlier) that three notes of a certain value, say, a minim (a modern half note) have now the value of two previous minims: $\mathbb{C}\,\uparrow\,\uparrow\,=\frac{3}{2}\,\uparrow\,\uparrow\,\uparrow$ . That is, under the ternary proportion each note loses one-third of its value. The result is a rhythmic clash that is relatively simple when we have notes of only one kind, such as minims, but can get more complicated when instead of a single larger denomination we have mixtures of smaller ones, quarter, eighth, and sixteenth notes (semiminims, fusae, and semifusae), in all kinds of combinations.

Although rhythms became simpler from roughly 1530 on, and the incidence of conflicting meters in simultaneous parts became rarer, it did not disappear altogether. Palestrina still used it, for instance, in his Mass

*L'homme armé;* a brief excerpt from the Kyrie of this Mass is given in Ex.
12.1 in modern transcription that preserves the original note values.

EXAMPLE 12.1.   Palestrina, Missa *L'homme armé* (Modern Transcription), Cantus
and Quintus Only

Conflicts continued for the rest of the 16th century, most often for
short stretches and in a different notational form. When only a few notes
or a few measures were set in ternary rhythms, composers often chose
to forego the writing of a ³⁄₂ symbol and resorted instead to "black notation" (see chap. 1), in which the normally white notes such as breves
( ⫟ ), semibreves ( ◊ ), and minims ( ↓ ) were blackened ( ▪ ◆↓ ). The
precise meaning of black notation is complicated and controversial. But
for our purposes it suffices to know that for relatively short groups of
notes the blackened notation indicated "hemiolia proportion," a relationship identical to the sesquialtera in that, by taking away one-third of
every note, it creates a ternary rhythm, analogous to the one produced
by modern triplets within a binary meter. When this hemiolia proportion occurred only in one of the voices, as was often the case, the result
was a binary–ternary clash. Such groups kept occurring well into the
17th century with the identical meaning. Most frequent was a group of
just three notes, either black semibreves ( ◆◆◆ ), black minims
( ↓↓↓ ), or their subdivisions (e.g., ♩.♪♩ ), over (or under) which the
composer placed as a precautionary sign a little **3**, creating a clear precursor of the modern triplet. Here, too, the frequent intention was a
clash with a simultaneous duplet. Had the composer had a dactyl or
anapest in mind, he would hardly have taken the trouble of resorting to
the black hemiolia notation.

Yet, in view of the difficulty of rendering an isolated triplet, it is
likely to the point of certainty that every so often singers followed the
line of least resistance—as do performers to the present day—and
squared these triplets by turning them into dactyls. That does not mean
that the composer intended it. But singers' skills, no longer honed by
the challenges of the earlier rhythmic complexities, may well have declined by the end of the 16th century so that they resorted to simplifi-

cation by squaring. When in 1619 Roland Lasso published one hundred Magnificat settings by his late father, he changed many of the blackened triplets into anapests. Whether in a time when mensural notation was in a state of dissolution Roland worried that performers might no longer understand blackened notation (and he had good reason for such assumption), or whether he wanted to facilitate the execution, is a moot question. At any rate, at the same time, early in the 17th century, a number of minor German theorists, some of whom mistook the blackened minims (half notes) for regular semiminims (quarter notes), in which case they failed to fill the measure, presented the anapest solution

for the triplet: ♪♪♪=♪ ♪ ♪ .

The single triplet and its careless assimilation may be a minor matter, but more serious are some modern theories that deny the existence of any kind of binary–ternary clashes. Such clashes, these theories hold, appear on paper only: in actual performance they were always resolved by assimilation. Although this was originally claimed to be true primarily of the 16th century, some scholars went further and extended the principle to the whole 17th century and at least the first half of the 18th, encompassing the music of both Bach and Handel. In the forefront of this school of thought is Michael Collins, who has developed his ideas in two major articles ("Performance of Sesquialtera"; "Performance of Triplets"). A careful scrutiny of the arguments supporting these tenets reveals, however, some logical flaws; moreover, a study of both theorists and musical evidence shows that there was actually no period that did not witness and approve of binary–ternary conflicts. (For more details see my "Conflicting Binary and Ternary Rhythms" or *Essays 1989*, chap. 3.) Here I shall first present some musical and theoretical evidence for the 17th and early 18th century for Italy, England, France, and Germany and then focus on the problem in Bach's music, which is typical of the period in including both cases—those in which rhythmic conflicts are to be resolved by assimilation and others in which the very conflict was intended.

## Binary–Ternary Clashes in the 17th Century

A few striking cases of binary–ternary conflict occur in the *Fitzwilliam Virginal Book*, dating from the early years of the 17th century. Perhaps the most remarkable passage is to be found in variation 14 of John Bull's "Gloria tibi trinitas."[2] In their notes to this passage, the 19th-century editors wrote that "the complicated cross-rhythms . . . are very carefully indicated in the MS where each triplet is preceded by '61' or '32,' sometimes by both together, and each pair of crotchets [quarter notes] by the sign ₵" (1:xxiv). They give additional information on this passage in their introduction (1:xv). Similar cross-rhythms may be found in variation 15 of John Bull's "Ut, re, mi, fa, sol, la" (No. 51, 1:186–87).

In the preface to Frescobaldi's *Primo libro delle canzoni* (1628), the publisher, Bartolomeo Grassi, discusses the "unusual meter symbols" (qualque tempo non solito). He tells us that these symbols, which indicate ternary meter ("tempo di proportione") in one part and common time ("tempo ordinario") in the other, are not mistakes but have been carefully thought out, and he writes that the exquisite care with which he (Grassi) has printed the notes to correspond to the exact disposition of their values ("que ogni una delle note porta il suo valore al debito luogo") has made them easy to play.

The Toccata No. 9 in Frescobaldi's *Secondo libro di toccate* (1637) also contains fascinating binary–ternary cross-rhythms in several episodes: the sesquialtera, expressed in one hand by $\frac{6}{4}$ and $\frac{12}{8}$ respectively, is set against the C signature in the other hand (see Ex. 12.2). At the end of the piece Frescobaldi himself comments on the problem of execution: "Not without exertion does one reach the end" (Non senza fatica si giunge al fine). If he had intended rhythmic assimilation rather than conflict, the performance of the piece would not have been troublesome. We find similar cross-rhythms in works of Caspar Kerll, Frescobaldi's student.[3]

EXAMPLE 12.2.   Frescobaldi, Toccata No. 9, *Secondo libro di toccate*

Theorists of the early 17th century continue to refer to binary–ternary conflicts and stress the need to conduct such clashing meters in equal beat. Long before them, Gioseffo Zarlino, the famous 16th-century theorist, had made that point in his treatise of 1558 (*Istitutioni harmoniche*, pt. 3, chap. 48, 208). There he said that when a sesquialtera ($\frac{3}{2}$) with its ternary measure occurs in all the parts, it is beaten (in three) with "unequal" beat, meaning one–two (down)–three (up); but when it is opposed in one or more voices by a binary meter, it is beaten (in two) with "equal" beat: one (down)–two (up). This is a common-sense directive. It is difficult to beat two and of course impossible to beat three different meters at the same time: hence today as well as four hundred years ago, the conductor usually beats the simplest of discrepant meters, while performers in the other meter(s) have to make the necessary adjustments. In a binary–ternary conflict the equal, binary beat is the simpler one.

In his monumental *Prattica di musica* of 1592, Lodovico Zacconi devotes a whole chapter to the question of binary–ternary clashes (bk. 3, chap. 73, fol. 183*v*). In it he writes: "If we consider the great potentialities of music and the vast jurisdiction of the composers in arranging and using the musical materials [Col considerare le facultà grande della Musica; e la spaciosa iurisdittione che hanno i Compositori nel disporre & adoperar le figure Musicali] . . . everybody can judge for himself, if he is not out of his mind [se non è privo di mente] that . . . in particular, hemiolia, sesquialtera, and tripla within a binary melody make no unpleasant effect but a very satisfactory one that gives great delight [non fanno effetto difforme; ma effetto competente, che rende assai dilettatione]." The whole chapter is in effect a eulogy of such polyrhythm. As an illustration, he presents an example by Senfl in which all parts except the tenor are in ternary meter, the tenor being in binary meter throughout ("secondo la misura binaria sino al fine").

Agostino Pisa, in his *Battuta della musica* of 1611, mentions Palestrina's Mass *L'homme armé*, where in the last Kyrie and the first Osanna, as shown above in Ex. 12.1, the quinta sings in tripla proportion, the other parts are alla breve, and the beat is that of the semibreve (meaning the complete beat, comprising down- and upbeat [128]). In 1609 Adriano Banchieri (like Tigrini before him in 1588) refers to the sesquialtera set against a binary meter as a "proportion of inequality" because, "singing the parts unequally, one singer sings two notes and the other three notes in the same time span" (*Conclusioni*, 31). If there were assimilation of the ternary rhythm, there would be no inequality. Earlier in the passage Banchieri confirms the interpretation of clashing rhythms by referring both to the difficulties singers experience in such cases for lack of practice and the reluctance of composers to risk embarrassment in public. Neither would be an issue in the case of assimilation.

Silvero Picerli, in 1630, restates the need for an equal beat in cases where a ternary meter applies to some but not all the parts, placing two of the (even) ternary notes within the first half of the measure and the third one within the second half "without changing the beat from its natural and even character" (dando similmente due note alla prima, & un'altr'alla seconda parte della battuta, senza mutarla dell'esser suo naturale, & uguale [*Specchio primo*, 26]). Although Collins quotes this passage ("Performance of Sesquialtera," 14) as a testimonial for the theory of binarization, the text does not warrant such interpretation. If one performs three notes against two even beats, the first two of the three notes do fall within the first half and the third within the second, just as Picerli wrote: ⌐——————¹——————⌐. He warns, moreover, against a tendency to change the beat (because the latter can easily be diverted by the ternary divisions). The warning would make no sense if all the rhythms were binary according to the assimilation doctrine.

The rhythmic conflict of two against three is suggestively evoked by several eminent theorists who emphasize the rhythmic clashes by the use of the word *contra*. Michael Praetorius suggests the use of blackened notation when the breve in tripla or the semibreve in sesquialtera are to be sung *against* the beat: "in sesquialtera proportione si quando *contra* tactum cantatur" (*Syntagma musicum,* 3:29). Adriano Banchieri describes such a conflict "when one or more voices sing three minims *against* others that sing only two" ('quand' una ò più voci cantano tre minime *contra* altri che ne cantano dui [*Cartella,* 31]).

These masters were preceded by such 16th-century theorists as Hermann Finck and Lucas Lossius, who in almost the same terms point to three identical notes in sesquialtera sung *against* two identical notes in the binary meter. By stressing the identity of the notes involved in each case, they exclude any rhythmic alteration (Finck, *Practica musica,* bk. 2; Lossius, *Erotemata,* chap. 12).

Whereas the modern assimilation school propounds the binarization of the blackened triplet (hemiolia) in, for instance, Fig. 12.1 (Collins, "Performance of Sesquialtera," 23), a number of important 17th-century theorists show the integrity of these triplets in clear graphic examples, among them Nicolaus Gengenbach in 1626 (*Musica nova,* 64–65), Daniel Friderici in 1619 (*Musica figuralis,* chap. 6, regula 3), Daniel Hitzler in 1623 (*Extract,* 52), Johann Crüger in 1630 (*Synopsis musica,* chap. 4, n. p.), Giacomo Carissimi in ca. 1640 (*Ars cantandi,* 11), Wolfgang Michael Mylius in 1685 (*Rudimenta musices,* chap. 4, n. p.), and Franz Xaver Anton Murschhauser in 1707 (*Fundamentalische,* n. p.), all of whom show the middle note of the blackened triplet straddling the beat in what is today still known as "hemiola." Here, for instance, is the last of these, by Murschhauser, showing the *hemiolia maior,* creating a ternary rhythm, with the second of three blackened breves split by the barline:

𝄴 ◼ ◆│◼ ◗ ◼│◼  (for the other writers see my "Binary–Ternary Conflicts," 103–5, or *Essays 1989,* 42–44).

FIGURE 12.1

That single triplets were occasionally squared in performance during the 17th century is certainly likely: as pointed out above, such carelessness is practiced to the present. Though a few minor writers sanctioned this procedure of "least resistance," important theorists, as we have seen, stressed the integrity of the ternary rhythm. To fit a ternary rhythm into a binary beat is only slightly troublesome; for a well-trained musician it is a routine task that looms larger in the proverbial armchair than in actual performance.

# Rhythmic Conflicts in the Early 18th Century

Italian composers of the first half of the 18th century seem to have had a special fondness for binary–ternary clashes. Such clashes abound in Vivaldi and are common as well in Bonporti, Dall'Abaco, Veracini, Tartini, and many others, in instances where an assimilation is either impossible or illogical. Only a few characteristic illustrations can be given here.

Example 12.3a is taken from Vivaldi's *L'incoronazione di Dario* (autograph, in Collection Giordano 38, BNT). A spot from Vivaldi's Violin Concerto in G, also autograph (Collection Foà 30, BNT), is shown in Ex. 12.3b, and a few measures from the same master's Violin Concerto in C (FI No. 169) are given in Ex. 12.3c. Finally, an excerpt from Bonporti's *Concertini, e Serenate . . . a violino, e violoncello o cembalo* (ca. 1715), showing a clash of three against four, is given in Ex. 12.3d.

EXAMPLE 12.3

a. Vivaldi, *L'incoronazione di Dario* (1717, aut.)  b. Vivaldi, Violin Concerto in G (aut.)

c. Vivaldi, Violin Concerto in C (FI No. 169)

d. Bonporti, *Concertini, e Serenate*, Op. 12, II Serenata (ca. 1715)

In France, too, we find many similar cases of conflicts that were not meant to be resolved. In Ex. 12.4a, from Clérambault's Cantata No. 2 (of his *Cantates françoises à I et II voix,* first book [1710]), on the words "let us sound the trumpets and drums," the bass imitates a binary trumpet–drum rhythm against triplets in the violins, later taken up by the voice.

Rameau was very fond of cross-rhythms, and his *Pièces de clavecin en concerts* of 1741 are a treasure trove of often unusual and sophisticated specimens. Of just two illustrations taken from this collection, the first, from "La Laborde," shows three against four (see Ex. 12.4b); the second, from "La timide," five against four (see Ex. 12.4c). Other striking examples may be seen in the same volume in "La pantomime," with seven against three (mm. 18–20), seven against four (mm. 23–25), and seven against two (mm. 39 and 43), and in "La Forqueray," where in a passage of two against three (mm. 48–51) the twos are divided among the two string parts using syncopations that could not possibly be assimilated to the triplets in the clavier. (*Notes inégales* are not applicable to any of these French examples.)

EXAMPLE 12.4

a. Clérambault, Cantata No. 2 (First Book, 1710)
  (Compressed score)

b. Rameau, "La Laborde"     c. Rameau, "La Timide"

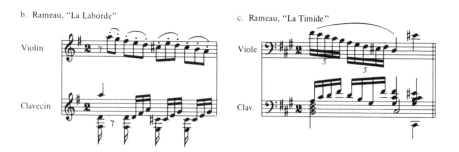

In all the examples given so far the conflicting rhythms were assigned to players of different parts, which facilitated the execution. In Ex. 12.5, taken from Johann Mattheson's *Der wohlklingenden Fingersprache,* part 2 (1737), the clash is between the two hands of the clavier player, its intention indicated by the graphic disposition of the parts: the second eighth falls clearly between the second and third notes of the triplet. We find the same careful graphic design in the second edition of the work by a different printer (1749).

EXAMPLE 12.5  Mattheson, *Der wohlklingenden Fingersprache*, part 2 (1737)

The examples shown here seem to leave no doubt that rhythmic clashes of all kinds, far from being prohibited, had international currency among the masters of the late Baroque.

## Rhythmic Conflict versus Assimilation in Bach

Turning now to the music of Bach and of his spiritual kinsmen, we find that many modern performers and editors share the belief that simultaneous binary and ternary divisions must be assimilated. Now while there are frequent cases in which assimilation was intended, in many others it was not, and in still others the solution is uncertain. In the following I shall try to sort out these alternatives.

One of the most striking passages in Bach's works where binary–ternary clashes form part of the structural essence is the chorale of Cantata No. 105 (see Ex. 12.6). Here the clashes are made explicit beyond any possible doubt. Against a steady **C** meter for voices and continuo with its many eighth notes, the continuous sixteenth notes of the upper strings change in the middle of measure 6 to eighth notes in $\frac{12}{8}$ meter (in genuine sesquialtera proportion), in contrast to the continuing **C** meter for all the other parts. In measure 12 the **C** meter is restored for the upper strings and the motion of the eighth notes correspondingly slowed. In measure 18 a tightly squeezed space did not allow Bach to insert another $\frac{12}{8}$ signature for the intended return of the sesquialtera. In its stead, Bach wrote, in one of only two cases known to me, the number 3 over each of four quarter-and-eighth-note pairs. This was the symbol that was to escape composers for another century and a half, but Bach used it in order to specify the intended ternary rhythm, here once more in conflict with other parts of the score. In the three last measures the movement slows further into regular quarter notes prior to the final fermata. The two episodes of ternary rhythms helped achieve a very gradual slowing down of the throbbing string motion from the agitated sixteenth notes at the outset to the quarter notes at the end; the rhythmic deceleration is a symbolic portrayal of the power of faith in calming a troubled conscience. This movement, shown here in a diplomatic transcription of the autograph score, is impervious to any rhythmic manipulations and is indeed a prime demonstration of the eloquence of binary–ternary clashes.

EXAMPLE 12.6.   Bach, Cantata No. 105/6

EXAMPLE 12.6. *continued*

dass auf die - ser son - dern e - wig le - ben will

For other instances of unquestionable clashes, see the Easter Oratorio, final chorus, measure 2, triplets in the oboes against eighths and sixteenth notes in the tympani; Cantata No. 75/12, bass aria, measure 1, binary trumpet rhythm against triplets in the violins; Concerto in E for Clavier (BWV 1053/3), measure 2, triplets in the clavier against sixteenth notes in the first violins; the First "Brandenburg" Concerto, first movement, measures 2 and 3, triplets in the horns against sixteenth notes and other binary rhythms in the rest of the orchestra. In this last case, the literal meaning of the triplets is clarified by the anapest that precedes the triplets in both the first and the second horns.

Less explicit in notation but equally convincing on musical grounds is the case of the final movement from the Sonata in E for Violin and Clavier, as illustrated in Ex. 12.7a–c. The first thirty-four measures are strictly binary and contain the thematically important rhythmic motive ♫♫ | ♪ (mm. 23–28; see Ex. 12.7b). Then measure 35 (Ex. 12.7c) initiates a long section of triplet figurations in the violin, interspersed in the clavier part with a series of quotations from the earlier binary section, that are consistently derived from the characteristic binary rhythmic motive of measures 23ff. The frequent assimilation in performance of the binary to the ternary rhythm—also suggested by the Bärenreiter edition of the work—is hard to justify. Here Bach's principle, as reported by Agricola (see above, chap. 9, p. 96), about the integrity of the binary rhythm in a clash seems particularly relevant.

Another controversial case is the Organ Chorale "In dulci jubilo" from the *Orgelbüchlein*, excerpts of which are shown in Ex. 12.8. Here

EXAMPLE 12.7.   Bach, Sonata in E for Violin and Clavier, BWV 1016/4

quarter notes are set against triplets that fill the space of a half note. Bach chose to write them beamed as eighth notes (in contrast to the quarter notes we would use today). This example not being a fair copy, the vertical alignments are on the whole inconclusive. Yet Bach usually arranged the horizontal spacing of notes according to their value, and we find that the repeated quarter notes in measures 3, 4, 7, and 8 are all written with great regularity, lined up like soldiers in a row. He would not have done so, not even in a sketch, had he had in mind the rhythmic spacing of 2:1:2:1, which is so frequently heard in this piece. (See Ex. 12.8a. For a reproduction of the autograph [which is available in a 1981 facsimile print by Bärenreiter], see my "Conflicting Binary and Ternary Rhythms," 120–21, or *Essays 1989*, 54–55.) Moreover, if—as seems prob-

Example 12.7. *continued*

able—the quarter notes on the repeated pitch are an imitative reflection of the chorale's opening, with its three half-note As and their canonic answer an octave lower in the second measure, then their evenness would be of the thematic essence.

In addition, there is the evidence of measures 25, 26, 28, and 30 (see Ex. 12.8b). In these measures, we find the other of the two instances known to me where Bach wrote a triplet quarter-plus-eighth-note symbol in order to insure synchronization with the triplets in the left hand. Particularly eloquent is measure 28, where the ternary figure of the first beat follows a whole measure of regular quarter notes. The difference in notation between measures 25, 26, and 28, on the one hand, where he specified ternary rhythms and synchronization, and measure 27, on the other, where he wrote six straight quarter notes, suggests the difference

EXAMPLE 12.8.    Bach, "In dulci jubilo," BWV 608

a.

b.

between synchronization and rhythmic clash. Needless to say, the poly-rhythms enrich the piece by adding depth to the intertwining parts.

Whereas there are many instances in which considerations such as those outlined for the preceding examples show the intention of rhyth-mic clashes, there are others in which an assimilation from binary to ternary rhythm was probably or even certainly intended. In the early Organ Chorale "Christ lag in Todesbanden," as shown in Ex. 12.9, we see how in a completely ternary passage the harmony often changes on the third triplet. The eighth-note iambic upbeats in the left hand have no motivic, only harmonic, significance, hence were most likely meant to be synchronized with the third triplet.

EXAMPLE 12.9.   Bach, "Christ lag in Todesbanden," BWV 7/8

Another case of ternarizing evenly written notes is shown in Ex. 12.10, from the Chorale "Herr Gott nun schleuss den Himmel auf" from the *Orgelbüchlein*. Here assimilation through a 2:1 adaptation of the eighth notes in the right hand is suggested internally by the resulting superior polyphonic combination with the running sixteenth notes of the left hand. Most convincingly, in measure 19 the B–B-flat progression in the alto, if played with rhythmic literalness, would clash intolerably with the C-sharp–B sixteenth notes in the tenor (Ex. 12.10a). The exter-nal evidence offers a measure of confirmation by the vertical alignment of the autograph, in spite of its noncalligraphic nature. As I have tried to show with broken lines that indicate the vertical alignment in the auto-graph, not all of these lineups are conclusive, except for two cases: the just-mentioned B flat in measure 19 and the F sharp in measure 22 (Ex. 12.10b) are clearly above the fifth sixteenth note. In two more cases (Ex. 12.10b and 12.10c) the second eighth note is definitely to the right of the fourth sixteenth note. The weird alignment in the last measure (Ex. 12.10c) was caused by great crowding.

The relationship between triplets and dotted notes in Bach was dis-cussed in chapter 9. There it was shown that Bach was flexible in this matter: on the one hand he insisted in principle on a rhythmic clash, as we are told by Agricola; on the other hand a great deal of external and musical evidence points to the frequent assimilation of the dotted note

EXAMPLE 12.10.   Bach, "Herr Gott nun Schleuss den Himmel auf," BWV 617

to the triplet whenever the tempo was not slow enough to make a clash sound purposeful. Unavoidably, there will remain an area of ambivalence where the tempo is not fast enough to call clearly for assimilation nor slow enough to call clearly for rhythmic independence. The choice of tempo will have a strong bearing on the performer's judgment regarding the two rhythmic alternatives.

A good illustration for such ambiguity is the *Tempo di Gavotta* from the Partita in E Minor for Clavier. It starts with a purely binary theme (Ex. 12.11a) in which the dotted notes would normally have literal meaning. When in the middle of the third measure the triplets begin to appear and continue in a seemingly endless row, the dotted notes in the other voice seem at least in part to be derived from the initial binary theme. A few times this theme even opposes the triplets with four sixteenth-note figures (Ex. 12.11b) that are not assimilable without actually distorting the notation. Thus it would seem that the binary rhythm—including that of the dotted notes—ought to assert its independence throughout. Yet in both the autograph of the early version in the notebook for Anna Magdalena and in the original print of the final version, the sixteenth note after the dot is consistently aligned with the third triplet. This evidence suggests that passages of rhythmic conflict were meant to alternate with passages of assimilation.

EXAMPLE 12.11.   Partita in E Minor for Clavier, BWV 830

# *Summary*

To sum up we can say that

1. there is no basis in the idea that binary–ternary clashes were forbidden in the 16th, the 17th, or the 18th century;

2. for Bach and his contemporaries, the uncertainty of synchronization versus polyrhythm very often arises from the lack of the ♪♪ sign for a 2:1 ratio in a binary meter;

3. dotted notes set against triplets should normally be synchronized in a lively tempo; they will tend to be differentiated in a slow tempo; in a moderate tempo much will depend on whether a pattern of dotted notes partakes of a characteristic binary theme or has other musical claims to independence;

4. when two even binary notes are set against triplets, there is reason to synchronize where the binary notes are only harmonic fillers or where contrapuntal or harmonic logic suggests such accommodation; where the binary notes are of motivic importance, they should be distinguished by rhythmic differentiation;

5. the triplet in Bach is always meant to remain a triplet; the fact that careless performers often square a single triplet does not mean that the composer intended it to be so rendered;

6. any assimilation occurs only by adjusting from binary rhythms to ternary ones, not from ternary to binary ones;

7. generally, literalness will be desirable when the resulting rhythmic clash sounds purposeful in clarifying thematic, or rhythmic, or contrapuntal relationships; it will not be desirable when it does none of these things and sounds like an unintentional imprecision.

There is no magic formula for solving all the problems we encounter. There are instances that clearly call for rhythmic independence; there are others that clearly call for synchronization; and in between there are still others in which after careful study of the context either option seems to make musical sense. In such ambiguous cases it will generally not matter greatly which alternative we select.

# Part III
# *Dynamics*

"Dynamics," the current designation for grades of loudness and softness in music, is not a felicitous linguistic choice since the term is properly associated with forces that generate, or are associated with, movement (as in thermodynamics, aerodynamics) or with patterns of change. But since its musical meaning is sanctioned by a long-standing use that goes back to the mid-19th century, we might as well accept it.

Loudness, softness, and all intermediate grades (as well as the gradual transition between them) must have played a role in music from times immemorial for the simple reason that such a range of intensities is a spontaneous manifestation of verbal communication. Volume varies from intimate contact to calls into the distance, from calm to excitement, from affection to hostility, from ease to fright. It stands to reason that these verbal dynamics have found their reflection in song, just as the underlying emotions must have found a similar reflection in dance, with a range from calm to frenzy.

It will be the purpose of the following two chapters to assess the role of dynamics for the performance of music in the period of our scrutiny. The first of these chapters will try to explain the two main types of dynamics—the one that is based on a steady sound (like that of the organ) and can increase or decrease only by leaps or "terraces," and the other that is based on a flexible sound (like the human voice) that is capable of gradual transitions—then to stake out the parts each of these two types played in the music of the period. The second chapter will discuss the ways in which dynamics have been indicated in notation.

# 13

# "TERRACED" AND TRANSITIONAL DYNAMICS

Dynamics is inherent in the very nature of music making and thus must have been a vital element of musical performance long before it showed in the score or was mentioned by theorists. During the period of our concern both of the mentioned types of dynamics, the "terraced" and the transitional, played an important role, and this chapter will attempt to assess and describe their respective shares.

Not so long ago a theory became part of conventional wisdom, and this theory was that the Baroque period had known only "terraced dynamics" without gradual transitions between the terraces. To cite only one of many scholar-musicians, Hermann Keller endorsed this belief by writing that only the passage from the late Baroque to the age of *Empfindsamkeit* and from there to the Viennese Classics brought about the change from terraced to transitional dynamics (*Klavierwerke Bachs,* 28). Although this theory in its sweeping generalization is hardly accepted anymore, it is important to realize that there was before the mid-18th century a large body of music that was linked exclusively or predominantly with terraced or quasi-terraced dynamics. There were several reasons for this fact.

First, in the polyphonic music of the late Baroque the role of dynamic gradation was small since each independent voice had its own internal dynamic leanings that would usually conflict with those of a simultaneous voice. Thus while polyphony admits, and favors, brief dynamic nuances that give plasticity to a phrase and make it stand out from the other voices, it is inconsonant with a simultaneous crescendo or decrescendo in all the parts. Also, contrapuntal music that provides enough musical interest with its complex interplay of voices, varied rhythms, and generally rich harmony has little or no need for the coloristic dimension that dynamics can provide.

Second, the lack, before the second half of the 18th century, of symbols for such gradations by itself severely restricted their use since it did not allow composers to convey any wishes along these lines and left performers in the dark about such intentions. While a soloist could use judgment and initiative in this respect, members of an orchestra or chorus were not free to do so and had to follow the notation that, if it listed dynamics at all, specified contrasting sections of *forte* and *piano* for the most part.

Third, there were important areas where terraced dynamics were built into the structure, and these areas were largely of two kinds. One was the juxtaposition of loud and soft in antiphonal or related effects of sudden contrasts; the other was due to the technical limitation of keyboard instruments.

The antiphonal effects presumably originated in large churches such as St. Mark's in Venice or St. Petronio in Bologna where choirs and their attendant instrumental ensembles were placed in two (or more) different parts of the edifice and their alternation produced pleasing dynamic contrasts with frequent tantalizing echo effects. A similar antiphonal effect is inherent in the alternation of solo singer(s) and chorus.

When instrumental ensembles began to come fully into their own around 1600, they set out to adopt similar antiphonal procedures. One of the first, if not the first, and certainly the most famous early specimen is Giovanni Gabrieli's Sonata pian' e forte from the end of the 16th century with its innovative specification of the instruments in the two bodies of players and the dynamic prescriptions of *piano* and *forte*.

The same antiphonal principle animated the concerto grosso when it emerged in the latter part of the 17th century. Here a small group of soloists, the "concertino"—in the Corellian form, two violins and a cello—were juxtaposed with a tutti ("grosso") group of all strings attended by a harpsichord (or organ). The quantitative difference between the two bodies created the dynamic antiphonal effect that was a hallmark of the form.

Related is the "trio" of 17th-century French dances, played between the first part of the dance, such as a minuet, and its da capo. In its Lullyan form it was typically assigned to two oboes and a bassoon, hence the name "trio." Although it was marked *doux*, in contrast to the marked or understood *fort* of the first section, it provided, like the concertino, a dynamic contrast by its scoring alone. As is well known, the name "trio" carried over to the minuets and scherzos of the Classical symphonies and quartets where it generally continued to contrast in character if not dynamics with the minuet's first part and its da capo.

With masters like Vivaldi, Bach, Handel, and Telemann we frequently encounter the juxtaposition of *forte* and *piano* in the same part upon the exact or approximate repetition of a motive or phrase. For characteristic samples see the alternations in the fourth movement of Bach's Sonata in A Minor for Violin Solo or in the Prelude of the Partita in E Major. There must be no gradualism in these transitions because they clearly derive from antiphonal procedures.

The dramatic potential of such antiphonal effects made them natural candidates for use in the theater, whence they were transferred in turn to the dramatically conceived Classical symphonies and sonatas. (See their characteristic use in Bartolo's aria [*Le nozze di Figaro*, Act I, Scene 4], with its quick alternations of sudden *fortes* and *pianos*, or in the start of the "Jupiter" Symphony.)

The second realm of terraced dynamics was due to the *idiomatic limitation* of the organ and the harpsichord. Both these instruments were incapable of dynamic shadings and had to make do with sudden changes from one keyboard to the next or from one registration to another. This incapacity was only slightly mitigated by the stopgap technique of thinning or thickening the texture. Composers and performers must have keenly felt this limitation. Bach's favorite keyboard instrument—so Johann Nicolaus Forkel reports in his pioneering biography of 1802—was the clavichord because the harpsichord "had not soul enough for him."[1] What determined his preference was obviously the possibility of shaping a phrase with dynamic nuances. Couperin explains how to compensate with rhythmic nuances for the tonal inflexibility of the harpsichord. Clearly, he too would have welcomed the potential for dynamic gradations.

Generally, then, we can circumscribe the theory regarding terraced dynamics by limiting it to (1) instruments incapable of graduated volume; (2) antiphonal or echo effects, including such built-in structural contrasts as produced by alternations of soloist and chorus or of concertino and concerto grosso; and (3) passages that, usually for dramatic effect, brusquely juxtapose the loud and the soft.

## Dynamic Gradations in Theory and Practice

In his recorder treatise of 1535 Sylvestro Ganassi devotes chapter 24 to the art of imitation. He explains how to imitate the human voice, which lets the breath swell and diminish in order to render the expression of the words. "In order to play a melody artistically you must imitate the human voice by varying the breath from tenderness to vivacity" (*Opera intitulata Fontegara*). Previously, in chapter 2, Ganassi had recommended using a breath of medium strength that makes it possible to swell and to taper the tone according to the needs of the situation. In his very first chapter Ganassi compares the shadings of the voice—his model for the flute—to the way a painter imitates shades of color in nature.

In Hermann Finck's treatise of 1556 we find a fascinating passage in which he recommends that in a "fuga" (at the time referring to any passage involving imitation) each imitative entrance has to be sung more loudly and distinctly than the rest in order to clarify form and texture.[2] Since the voices have to take turns in asserting themselves, they all have to blend in again with the rest; in contrapuntal textures such transition can hardly be other than gradual.

In the early 17th century, a period of passionate expression, singers in recitative and monody used dynamic devices of accentuation, of swelling and tapering on single pitches to respond to the emotions suggested by the words. That they occasionally used similar dynamic means over a whole phrase can be safely assumed when the text called for such intensification or for a gradual calming down. It was up to a soloist's own judgment and capability to enlist dynamic means for such expressive ends. The procedures themselves must have been as old as solo song. New was the way in which the monodists turned a previously spontaneous response into a method of sophisticated dynamic manipulations, as expounded above all by Giulio Caccini in the famous preface to his *Nuove musiche* of 1602.

Things were different for orchestra and chorus. Here, as noted before, the lack of notational means for the indication of dynamic gradations hindered their common use. Where a composer wished for a special swelling or tapering effect, he had to spell it out in so many words. Such occurrences were rare (see below for an instance in Stradella) and remained rare until the second half of the 18th century, when either symbols or words such as *crescendo* and *decrescendo* began to appear in scores.

Johann Friedrich Reichardt reports that Pisendel (1687–1755), the famous Dresden concertmaster, took "the almost incredible trouble" of marking all the parts not only with bowings but also with dynamic markings, including the crescendo and decrescendo fork symbols, which "Hasse and Graun have never used" (*Briefe*, 10–11). In a footnote Reichardt tells how in Jommelli's performances in Rome (presumably during the 1751–53 seasons) the audiences were moved by a crescendo to rise gradually in their seats, only to catch their breaths again on the decrescendo. Reichardt felt the same physical impulse on hearing the legendary crescendos of the Mannheim orchestra.

There were Roman precedents to Jommelli's famous crescendo effects, as we can tell from a report by Marchese Scipio Maffei (translated by Johann Mattheson in *Critica musica* 2:335–38) about "the great concerts in Rome" where the gradual swelling and tapering, occasionally mixed with sudden dynamic contrasts, gave "connoisseurs incredible and wondrous delight." In Rome too, as in Mannheim, there obviously was careful rehearsing, and there might have been editing of the parts à la Pisendel. The very wonderment of the reporters attests to the rarity of these accomplishments.

In contrast, Bach's vocal music had, with few exceptions, little to show in dynamic variety and gradation. His instrumental group may have never been rehearsed, or only rarely and minimally. In his cantatas he routinely wrote *piano* for the orchestra as soon as the voices entered, and *forte* for orchestral interludes; for the start, *forte* was understood unless otherwise marked. The result must have been extended orchestral *forte* or *piano* terraces, more by force of circumstances than by artistic choice. Intelligent soloists, be they singers or obbligato players, had of course the opportunity of introducing dynamic shadings in their parts.

Furthermore, stylistic-structural factors disfavored dynamic gradations that exceeded the length of single phrases. As noted before, the polyphonic textures of the middle and late Baroque were neither receptive to, nor in need of, long-breathed swellings and taperings. It was the homophony of the "modern" style galant, which coexisted from soon after 1700 until mid-century with the music of Bach, Handel, and their spiritual kinsmen, that favored and almost necessitated elaborate dynamic treatment in details of phrases and in extended stretches to add interest to a texture impoverished by commonplace rhythms and inconsistently inspired melodies. Pisendel's above-mentioned dynamic editing applied to music of this new style.

## The Rhetorical Principle

Baroque aesthetics inherited the 16th-century belief in a close link between music and rhetoric, a link that originated in the humanistic strivings of the Renaissance. Along with other subjects, the masters of classical rhetoric were avidly studied and formed a pillar of the school curriculum, where the subject was taught until the late 18th century and beyond. In view of the vast role of the word in the music of the era, overwhelming in the Renaissance, still powerful in the Baroque, the transfer of rhetorical principles to music was almost unavoidable. The rhetorical principles of affecting the listeners by stimulating their emotions and arousing their passions were to serve as models for the composer in inventing and shaping his works. Analogous ideas were applied to performance, and these ideas had an important bearing on dynamics. Ideal performance was likened to the effective delivery of a speech, and here the implications for dynamics were repeatedly formulated by contemporary writers.

From a passage by Praetorius of 1619 (*Syntagma musicum*, 3:229), quoted in the Introduction to this book, I repeat here an excerpt that deals with our immediate concern: the orator, he writes, has to deliver his speech in a way that arouses the motions "by raising the voice here, lowering it there, speaking alternately with powerful, with gentle, with full and resonant voice; so it is the duty of the musician not simply to sing but to sing with artistry and grace, so as to stir the heart of the listeners and move their emotions." The unmistakable implications for dynamic shadings encompassing whole phrases considerably transcend the range of the models from Caccini's *Nuove musiche* that are limited to single words.

Johann Andreas Herbst, in 1642 (*Practica musica,* 2), echoes Praetorius in pointing to the orator, who has to move the emotions ("Affecte moviren") by (gradually) raising or lowering the voice and by speaking here softly, there loudly, and in demanding that a singer follow this example.

Francesco Rognioni, in his diminution treatise of 1620, speaks of words that express grief, anxiety, pain, torments, or similar emotions; these words, he writes, must not be ornamented but instead be rendered with appropriate dynamic shadings "by diminishing the voice here, letting it grow there, with sweet and suave gestures, sometimes with sadness and grief in the voice, conforming to the meaning of the speech" (scemando hor la voce, hor accrescendola, con mouimenti dolci, e. soavi, & tal'hora con voce mesta, e dogliosa, conforme il senso dell'oratione [*Selva de passaggi,* pt. 1, 51]).

In France, Marin Mersenne, in his *Harmonie universelle* of 1636, elaborates on the link between music and rhetoric and, regarding dynamics, speaks of the numerous types of "accents," which he defines as inflections or modifications of the voice or the word in order to express different passions and affections. He illustrates the naturalness of their many shadings by pointing out that they are not limited to human beings: animals too make different sounds to show their joy or their sadness ("qui crient autrement pour monstrer leur ioye que pour monstrer leur tristesse" [*Harmonie universelle: Traitez des consonances,* 365–73]).

In a previous passage (359, incorrectly printed as 363) he writes of eight different degrees of loudness, ranging from the first for very weak echoes up to the eighth for the strongest possible exclamation, such as one of despair or great pain of body or soul. He regrets the lack of symbols for dynamic degrees.

Throughout the 17th and 18th centuries a number of eminent writer-musicians reaffirm the indebtedness of music in both composition and performance to the principles of rhetoric. Bach's deep involvement in rhetoric via Quintilian's *Institutio oratoria* was recently revealed in its full intensity in a brilliant study by Ursula Kirkendale ("The Source for Bach's *Musical Offering*"). An eloquent statement by Quantz about the orator's model, closely paralleling that of Praetorius with equally clear implications for dynamic shadings, was quoted above in the Introduction to this book. We find a similar passage in Johann Friedrich Agricola (*Anleitung zur Singkunst*, 139). Francesco Geminiani joins in the wide agreement that musical dynamics should be adapted from oratory. He writes under the heading "Of Piano and Forte": "They are both extremely necessary to express the Intention of the Melody; and as all good Musick should be composed in Imitation of a Discourse, these two Ornaments are designed to produce the same Effects that an Orator does by raising and falling his Voice" (*Treatise of Good Taste*, 3). As we have seen, the model of rhetoric opens a wide range for dynamic shadings, from what could be called "spot dynamics," the highlighting of single notes or small note groups, to what could be called "area dynamics," covering whole phrases or phrase groups.

A number of composers and writers explain dynamic shadings without mentioning the orator but, often in a related vein, by pointing to word meaning. Giulio Caccini, in the preface to his *Nuove musiche* of 1602, the chief manifesto of the new style of monody and recitative, describes a number of ways in which the voice can and should be dynamically modulated. He speaks of *esclamazione*, the swelling on a tone, its counterpart, the *esclamazione viva*, which begins loud and then tapers, then combinations of the two in the *messa di voce:* the soft start, followed by swelling and then tapering of the sound ( $\texttextless\!\!=\;\;=\!\!\textgreater$ ); the reverse of the pattern, starting loud, tapering, then swelling again ( $=\!\!\textgreater\;\;\textless\!\!=$ ); and finally the addition of a new swelling to the *messa di voce* ( $\textless\!\!=\;\;=\!\!\textgreater\;\;\textless\!\!=$ ).

In 1638, Domenico Mazzocchi may have been the first to introduce symbols for dynamic shadings of a tone: he used the letter "v" to signify a swelling on a tone ("sollevazione, ò . . . messa di voce") and the letter "c" for (what is the more common meaning of *messa di voce*) the gradual swelling then the very gradual diminishing "until the sound is reduced to nil" (*Madrigali*, Preface). Girolamo Fantini, in his trumpet school of 1638, also describes the swelling and tapering of the *messa di voce* that he says is necessary for lengthy notes—those that last for from one to four beats (*Modo per imparare*, Preface).

Christoph Bernhard, student of Schütz (whom we met briefly in chap. 9), wrote several tracts that report his teacher's ideas. Conserved only in manuscripts, the works are of uncertain date, but the vocal treatise originated presumably around 1650. Speaking of dynamics, he uses the symbols of *p* and *f* and explains the messa di voce for long notes, stressing the need for *gradual* swelling and tapering, or else, he says, what should be artistic would sound abominable ("recht abscheulich lauten"). He also gives an example in small note values where *forte* and *piano* alternate in a manner that clearly indicates loud starts and diminishing sounds for such phrases as: "Hic adest panis, hic adest panis, hic adest Christus" with *forte* on "hic" and *piano* on "panis," with a rest between phrases (*Von der Singe-Kunst*, 32–33).

Bernhard's student Wolfgang Michael Mylius follows his teacher's ideas. He lists the symbols of *p, pp,* and *ppp* for different shades of softness, *f* for *forte,* and cautions that the transitions from soft to loud and back to soft must be gradual, not sudden. His tract was widely used as a text (*Rudimenta musices,* chap. 5, n. p.). Georg Falck, who leans on Herbst, advises the singer to so modulate the voice that it can vary from strong to weak, from joyful to plaintive (*Idea boni cantoris,* 106).

In France, Marin Marais, the great gambist, introduced in 1711 new symbols, among them the letter "e" for signifying a crescendo. The "e" stands for *enfler le coup d'archet* (swell the bowstroke—i.e., a crescendo). This manner, he writes, brings soul to pieces that without it would be too monotonous ("trop uniformes" [*Troisième livre,* Preface]).

A year later, in 1712, the Italian violinist Giovanni Antonio Piani (des Planes in France) published in Paris his Violin Sonatas Op. 1. In the preface to this work he explains his use throughout the volume of the three modern (but blackened) wedge symbols for crescendo ( ◄█████ ), decrescendo ( ████► ), and *messa di voce* ( ◄██████► ). The idea apparently originated with Michel P. Montéclair, who reports that M. des Planes approached him for advice on how to mark these dynamic nuances and he, Montéclair, suggested the wedges. Having suggested them, he proceeded to use them in his own treatise to illustrate the *son enflé* with a fork over three successive whole notes in **C** meter; then similarly the *son diminué;* and finally, over six whole notes, the combination of swelling plus tapering (Montéclair, *Principes,* 88).

Michel Corrette, in his violin tutor of 1738, asks for a swelling of the sound on any note of one-quarter length or larger in sarabandes, adagios, and largos and a *messa di voce* on notes that end a phrase or a song (*L'école d'Orphée,* 34).

## Musical Evidence of Extended Gradations

In the absence of notational means for indicating extended dynamic gradations, we have few musical items of evidence for such happenings in the 17th century, but we do find some sporadic pieces of eloquent testimony. They come from various compositions from mainly the second half of the 17th century.

Matthew Locke, in the 1675 publication of his music to a revised version of Shakespeare's *The Tempest,* marked several numbers with such directives as "soft and slower by degrees," "lowder by degrees," and "violent."

The Biblioteca Estense in Modena has a contemporary (possibly autograph) manuscript of the cantata *L'accademia d'amore* for five voices by Alessandro Stradella from ca. 1670. Its opening Sinfonia starts with a series of long, held chords with the following directive: "One begins very softly; the viols are divided in three groups, entering one at a time and getting constantly stronger. With each beat one group enters almost unnoticeably after the other and growing from piano to fortissimo."[3]

Agostino Steffani used a wavy line to indicate either crescendo or decrescendo. A characteristic instance occurs in *Tassilone* of 1709. In no. 14, the aria of Gheroldi, there is a three-measure crescendo (mm. 43–45) on the word "lagrima" and a decrescendo (mm. 52–53) on "morir."

Rameau makes frequent and dramatically very effective use of crescendo and decrescendo devices. He had adopted the wedge symbol of Montéclair-Piani (without blackening it). For an illustration of its structural use, where the dynamics are part of the musical essence rather than an added touch of color or animation, see Ex. 13.1a, showing its role in the portrayal of thunder and storm from *Hippolite et Aricie* of 1733 (taken from a score that contains autograph additions in the library of the Paris Opera [Opéra A 128b]).

EXAMPLE 13.1.  Rameau

a. *Hippolite et Aricie* (Paris 1733)

Act I, Sc. 3  Tonnerre

b. *Zoroastre* (Paris 1749)

Act III, Sc. 3

\* les chiffres marqués aux violons, basse et bassons, signifient qu'ils entrent d'abord
  quatre, puis les 4 autres de deux en deux pour renforcer la gradation

In "Les paladins" there are (in the autograph at the BN [Rés Vm² 2120]) several spots, such as in Act II in the "Deuxième Menuet en Rondeau," where a long sustained note, written in four tied dotted half notes, has the caption: "avec violons très doux qui enflent insensiblement jusqu'au plus fort pour le da capo" (the violins [starting] very soft then growing imperceptibly up to greatest loudness for the da capo). For a similar crescendo on a long, held note from *Zoroastre* of 1749, the gradation of sound is reinforced by successive entries of divided violins reminiscent of Stradella's above-mentioned Sinfonia (see Ex. 13.1b; taken from a copy at the BN [Rés. 1693], part print, part MS.). An asterisk at the start of the passage refers to this explanation: "The numbers marked for the violins, basses, and bassoons indicate that at first only four enter, then the four others by twos and twos in order to reinforce the swelling." Interesting too in this example is the modern phrasing mark for a *Luftpause*—two oblique parallel dashes that separate the terminal *forte* from the following *piano*.

On other occasions Rameau combines the swelling of individual instruments with successive entrances and carefully calculated spacing of dynamic indications for the various parts. One such spot of unusual refinement and complexity in the manipulation of dynamics occurs in *Achante et Céphise* (1751), as culled from a copy at the BN (Rés A 174a) of printer's proofs with Rameau's autograph corrections and additions. Achante's ariette in Act III in **2** meter, marked *sans vitesse*, starts with half of the basses (and presumably cellos) *très doux* (i.e., *pp*); the second half enters in the second measure, *doux*; in measure 3 violins, *très doux*, and violas ("parties") *doux*⁴ join; in measure 5 violins and basses play *moins doux* and the bassoons enter; measure 6 has crescendo forks in violins and violas, the latter starting *à demi* (i.e., *mf*), with flutes entering *fort* on the second beat; in measure 7 a crescendo fork starts in the basses, and violins and violas reach *fort* on the second beat; on this beat the horns enter *doux* and grow to *fort* on the second beat of measure 8 along with the basses, ending the passage with full intensity. Rameau carefully proofread and corrected these measures, which attest to his unusually sophisticated handling of orchestral crescendos.

In the second half of the 18th century, following the lead of the Roman orchestras, of Jommelli, Rameau, Pisendel, and the Mannheim band, crescendos and decrescendos extending over whole phrases became generally familiar and their execution facilitated by the spread of both the fork symbols and the verbal indications of *crescendo* and *decrescendo*.

For a single illustration of a long-breathed crescendo that is a structural, not just coloristic, element of the musical idea, see the eight-measure melodic and dynamic ascent in the first movement of Mozart's Sinfonia Concertante for Violin and Viola K 320d (364) of 1779 (mm. 46–58). Starting *piano*, a mostly chromatically ascending series of trills rises over the range of two octaves to a *forte* climax; in measures 46–49 the melody alone starts its ascent; in measure 50 the volume is gradually increased by the entry of the horns on the first beat and the second violins on the third beat, and in measure 52 by the entrance of the oboes on the first beat; then in mid-measure 52, *crescendo* is marked for all the strings, in mid-measure 54 for oboes and horns, adding a powerful dynamic dimension to the broad sweep of the melodic rise, coming to a climax in measure 58.

As we have seen, the dynamic swell extending over many measures was known in the 17th century, where it was indicated by verbal directions, as witnessed by Stradella in Italy and by Locke in England. In the early 18th century, the startling crescendos of the Roman orchestras and the famous one of the Mannheim orchestra were presumably achieved through rehearsal procedures alone. Notational means to indicate such effects began to emerge in the early 18th century, first in the form of hairpins, later supplemented by the *crescendo* and *decrescendo* marks. They made slow, irregular progress but became well established by the Classical period. It was by such marks alone that the young Mozart indicated the just-quoted crescendo. A generation after Mozart, such dynamic groundswells became a favorite device of Rossini's, almost his trademark as the celebrated "Rossini crescendo."

# 14

# DYNAMICS IN NOTATION

## *Words and Symbols*

It is uncertain when the terms *piano* and *forte,* whether written in full or in abbreviation, were first used. We have seen Giovanni Gabrieli's use toward the end of the 16th century. Sweelinck around the same time wrote *f* and *p* for echo effects on the organ. The aging Schütz, in the famous "Saul, Saul, was verfolgst du mich" from the Symphoniae Sacrae No. 3 of 1650, makes remarkably frequent use of *f, mp,* and *pp.* His student Bernhard, as noted in chapter 13, explains the letter symbols and the gradual transitions between loud and soft. Johann Paul von Westhoff, famous 17th-century violinist, used *p, pp,* and *ppp* in his violin sonatas of 1694.

Vivaldi considerably enriched the repertory of dynamic indications, as reported by Walter Kolneder (*Aufführungspraxis bei Vivaldi,* 25). Besides the frequent *p, pp, f,* and *ff,* he uses *piano molto, piano assai, mezzo p, quasi piano, mezzo forte, un poco forte, f molto,* and *più f.* Kolneder also quotes a few sequences of *p–pp–pian^{mo}* and *p–un poco f–f;* in some of these passages only gradual change makes musical sense.

Bach limited himself in most cases to *piano* (mostly written *pia*) and *forte* (written *for* or *f*), but occasionally we find more specific markings. In the opening chorus of the St. Matthew Passion, there is the *mf* for the first orchestra in measure 42; *mf* again in measures 60 for both orchestras; the remarkable simultaneity in measures 63ff. of *forte* in the first orchestra with a *piano* in the second; and several more *mf*s between *f*s and *p*s. In the final chorus, we have the unusual sequence *p* (m. 76)–*più* *p* (m. 77)–*più p* (m. 78)–*pianissimo* (m. 79), indubitably a four-measure decrescendo, with the second *più piano* clearly a gradation of the first.

In Cantata No. 201/9 the figure of Ex. 14.1a calls for an obvious gradual swelling. In Ex. 14.1b from Cantata No. 202/5, measures 3–4, in the sequence *piano–piano–pianissimo,* repeated twice more in parallel spots, the second *piano* obviously means *più piano.* The meaning was probably that of a decrescendo, though terraced execution is feasible.

EXAMPLE 14.1. Bach

a. Cantata No. 201/9

b. Cantata No. 202/5

A few times in Cantata No. 63/3, Bach writes *poco forte,* which suggests that this may be the primary meaning of the abbreviation *pf,* occasionally found with him and other masters; *più forte* is another, though less likely, reading.

The wedge symbols, indicating swelling and tapering, preceded the use of the words *crescendo* and *decrescendo* (and their abbreviations), which seem to emerge around the middle of the 18th century. In Geminiani's Six Cello Sonatas Op. 5 (1747), transcribed by the composer for the violin, we find in Sonata No. 4, grave, the sequence *piano–crescendo–for[te].* The child Mozart used *cresc.* in measures 4 and 31 of the aria "Sol nascente" K 61c (70) of 1769. Throughout his life he preferred the terms *cresc.* and *decresc.* to the wedge symbols. He did use the symbols on occasion, for instance in the oracle scene of *Idomeneo,* in the *Maurerische Trauermusik,* in the adagio of the String Quintet in D Major, and here and there in other works. Once in a while he substitutes *calando* for *decrescendo.* In the 19th century, *calando* came to signify a slight retard, occasionally combined with a decrescendo. By contrast, the purely dynamic meaning of Mozart's *calando* emerges from several uses where a retard would be illogical; for instance, in the first movement of the String Quartet in D Major K 499, a *calando* in measure 130 is followed in measure 138 by *cresc.* and *forte* in measure 139; a *calando* at the end of this measure leads to a *piano* in measure 141 prior to the recapitulation in measure 142. This makes perfect sense in terms of dynamics but not of tempo: the double *calando* would slow the pulse to a musically unwarranted dragging pace that would require a *primo tempo* or an *a tempo* indication at the recapitulation. Furthermore, the second *calando* occurs in the violins half a measure before it is marked for the viola; it is not marked at all for the cello which enters only in measure 140 on a lower dynamic level with *mf*; again this makes sense only in terms of dynamics but not of tempo. For further confirmation, Koch explains the term as the equivalent of *diminuendo* (*Musikalisches Lexikon*, s.v. "Calando").

The Classical composers used a few other terms for dynamic directives, among them *sotto voce*, literally "under the voice," hence less than average loudness. The term is vague, but for Mozart it stands for a degree that is louder than *piano*, as can be gathered from several passages where the lead voice is marked *sotto voce* and accompanying parts with *piano*. See, for instance, the larghetto from the String Quartet in B Flat K 589, with its starting cello melody in *sotto voce*, the middle strings in *piano*, and then in measure 9 the entering melody in the first violin again marked *sotto voce*. Haydn used it with the same meaning, as revealed by similar external evidence, for instance a passage in the String Quartet Op. 20, No. 5 (Hob. III:35), first movement, measures 76ff., where *sotto voce* for the melody in the first violin is set off by *pp* for the other three instruments. Haydn more frequently specifies *mezza voce*, most likely with the identical meaning: since *mf* was a frequent symbol with him, both terms had to fit in the dynamic range between *piano* and *mezzoforte*. For Haydn as well as Mozart, the terms must have been the equivalent of *mp*, which was not yet known to them.

Composers of the galant style had, as attested by Quantz and discussed below, developed dynamic nuances of great, almost mannered refinement, but it took a while before new symbols that could at least roughly suggest such performance manners were developed. Important among these symbols are some that indicate emphases on single notes or brief note groups, such as *fp*, *mfp*, *rf* (or else *rinf.*), and *sf* (usually written *fz* by Haydn). The *fp* (i.e., *fortepiano*) and its gentler cousin, *mfp* (*mezzofortepiano*, frequent in Mozart), refer to single notes beginning loudly and immediately followed by *piano*. If this note is lengthy, the loudness is sudden but very brief. The *rinforzando* is an emphasis (within the given dynamic level) that will generally extend to the whole length of the marked note.

The *sforzando* is more complicated. According to Koch (*Musikalisches Lexikon*, s.v. "Sforzando"), the term calls for a note to be played with vehemence. He cautions not to confuse it with *rinforzando*, which implies only a gentle pressure ("gelinden Druck"). In Mozart's use the *sforzando* extends normally beyond a single note, unless it is a fairly long one, and calls for a forceful start, while dynamic intensity persists up to the succeeding *piano*. This *piano* can be several beats away, and, time permitting, just prior to the *piano* the sound tapers slightly. The degree of emphasis will vary in relation to the prevailing level: within a *forte* it will have Koch's vehemence; within a *piano* it will be proportionally milder and often not exceed a *mezzoforte* level. Such is probably the meaning in Ex. 14.2a, from the *Don Giovanni* Overture: a sharply articulated *mezzoforte* with a taper around the last sixteenth-note value in both violins; or in Ex. 14.2b, from the String Quartet in E Flat, a similar sharp stab introducing a *mezzoforte* that tapers on the last eighth note, whereas after the second *sforzando* the intensity generated by the accent persists to the high E flat, followed by a sudden *piano*. In Ex. 14.2c, from the Symphony No. 40 in G Minor, the *sforzandi* presumably must not be vehement, lest they mar the tenderness of the phrase. Occasionally, and especially against a *forte* background, the *sforzando* extends its meaning of forcefulness (Koch's "vehemence") over a fairly long stretch, as in Ex. 14.2d, from the first movement of the same symphony, where the dramatic intensity is maintained up to the *piano* five measures later.

EXAMPLE 14.2.   Mozart

a. *Don Giovanni* Overture, K 529

b.  String Quartet in E Flat, K 421 b (42 R)/2

EXAMPLE 14.2   *continued*

c. Symphony No. 40 in G Minor, K 550/2

d. Symphony No. 4 in G Minor, K 550/1

The modern accentual sign > was unknown to Mozart but makes its appearance in the late works of Haydn. For the frequent accentual meaning of dots and strokes from Bach and Handel to Mozart and Haydn, see chapter 16.

## *"Area Dynamics" When Unmarked*

The term "area dynamics," mentioned earlier, will refer to the dynamics of phrases or larger sections, as opposed to "spot dynamics," which will refer to that of single notes or brief note groups. To find the right volume for a passage, however short or long, can be a problem even when the composer has given us guidance by words or symbols. Not only are the meanings of these words or symbols imprecise (how loud is a *forte*, how soft a *piano*, how steep a *crescendo?*); other matters have to be considered: the size of the performance space, its acoustics when empty or full, the balance between the parts, the nature of the voices or the instruments, the character of the piece, of the passage, and so on.

The right choice is of course much harder when the composer has given us no or only insufficient guidance. In these cases we cannot look for rules but must rely on musical intelligence. C. P. E. Bach wisely says:

> It is not really possible to single out the cases where *forte* or *piano* are fitting, because even the best rules suffer exceptions as numerous as the cases which they regulate; the special effect of this shade and light depends on the ideas, or connection of ideas, and in general on the composer who can, with good cause, introduce a *forte* where on another occasion there was a *piano*, and who often marks a phrase [Gedancken], together with its consonances and dissonances, now *forte*, now *piano*. For that reason one likes to differentiate repeated phrases by *forte* and *piano* whether they reappear at the same pitch [in

eben derjenigen Modulation] or at another one, especially when accompanied by different harmonies. . . . An emphatic utterance [Ein
besonderer Schwung der Gedancken] meant to arouse a violent emotion must be powerfully expressed. (*Versuch über Art das Clavier* [1753],
chap. 3, par. 29)

Quantz limits himself to a few generalities regarding the broader
aspects of dynamic choices. He stresses the need for variety in a good
performance. Whoever plays with monotonous volume, he writes, who
cannot raise or lower the sound at the proper places, will hardly move
any listener. "It is necessary to observe a regular change of *forte* and
*piano*" (*Versuch einer Anleitung*, chap. 11, par. 14).

Elsewhere in his book (chap. 14, par. 25), Quantz amplifies the
thought by saying that a performer must proceed like a painter who
does not limit himself to light and dark but employs *mezze tinte,* the
intermediate colors where the dark and the light are imperceptibly combined. In musical performance one must similarly use diminishing softness, increasing loudness, as well as the intermediate sound levels.

In a brilliant article on performance, J. A. P. Schulz devotes a few
paragraphs to dynamics. The greatest perfection of performance requires, he writes, the correct disposition of loudness and softness, the
proper arrangement of light and shade. Principal notes, principal
phrases, and principal periods have to be placed in the light, the rest in
the shade. One can say nothing more specific than that; "one must hear,
feel and learn." In view of the importance of dynamic shadings, he
continues, instruments incapable of it are imperfect, and in particular
"the harpsichord is one of the most imperfect instruments" (in Sulzer,
*Allgemeine Theorie,* s.v. "Vortrag").

In the absence of any dynamic indications and in the absence of—to
use an expression of Türk's—a "ruling character" that summons either
forcefulness or gentleness from the music, today's performers generally
will do well to start playing a piece with a neutral volume or, on the
inflexible keyboard instruments, with a registration that permits
changes to louder and softer grades. In this manner the performer can
make adjustments in either direction when the work reveals more distinct clues either by symbols or by its character. This suggestion is in
accord with the timeless advice given by Ganassi in 1535, cited in chapter 13 ("Dynamic Gradations in Theory and Practice").

For the voice the appropriate dynamics (including gradations) were
often suggested by the affections expressed or implied by the words. In
instrumental music we have to judge the basic affection from the notes
and, if available, from the tempo words in order to divine whether the
music calls for robustness, vigor, gaiety, fervor, calm, tenderness, or
other emotions (*Leidenschaften,* as the old German theorists called them)
and adjust the loudness accordingly.

# Practical Applications

Since it is natural in speech to raise one's voice with growing tension and lower it with relaxation, it is also natural to get a sense of intensification from a rising melody and of relaxation from a falling one. In keeping with this tendency it has been an old cliché of teachers and editors to follow the line of the melody with appropriate dynamic nuance. Provided this is done with discretion, such a procedure will fairly often be appropriate. For an illustration, see Ex. 14.3a, from the Third "Brandenburg" Concerto, where a subtle dynamic shadowing of the melodic meanderings of violins and continuo can add clarity and plasticity to their contrary motions (as indicated in parentheses). Often, however, such automatism is misguided. When, for instance, a melody takes off from a strong downward pull and rises, it will tend to lighten in its ascent as if freeing itself from a gravitational force. For an illustration, see Ex. 14.3b, from Mozart's String Quartet in B Flat K 589, where the strongest dynamic weight seems to fall on the lowest point of the melody, the E flat" at the start of measure 87, for reasons of meter and dissonance that are confirmed by Mozart's *forte*, while the ascending scale in the next measure might best be rendered with a slight decrescendo. Conversely, there are melodies that descend as if pulled down toward a point of stronger attraction, in which cases a slight swelling rather than tapering is the more logical dynamic design. Such is likely to be the case when the descending line is either part of an ornamental figuration that leads into a pitch of structural importance (as shown in Ex. 14.3c, from Bach's Sonata in G Minor for Solo Violin) or when such descent moves to an accent that is either so marked by the composer or is a candidate for emphasis for various harmonic, melodic, or rhythmic reasons. For an illustration, see Ex. 14.3d, from the slow movement of Mozart's "Linz" Symphony, where the appoggiatura at the start of the second measure calls for an emphasis for reasons of meter and harmony. Consequently, so it seems, a slight swelling on the preceding measure's downward scale (as suggested in parentheses) might make for a better phrasing than would an attempt to match the descending melody with a similar dynamic gradation. Other typical cases are downrushing passages that seem to gather momentum as they fall. For an illustration, see Ex. 14.3e from Don Giovanni's reluctant challenge to the old Commendatore on the words "misero attendi." See also the start of the Count's aria in the third act of *La nozze di Figaro*.

When we approach works that have no dynamic markings (such as those by Bach or Handel), we can for flexible media derive comfort from knowing that polyphonic works have little need for dynamic variety. It is an interesting illustration of this fact that Haydn, who in his mature works scatters dynamic marks rather lavishly, has practically none in the three finale fugues of his string quartets of opus 20.

EXAMPLE 14.3

a. Bach, Third "Brandenburg" Concerto, BWV 1048/3

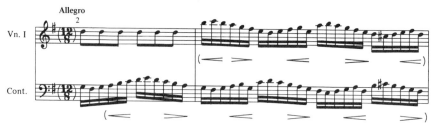

b. Mozart, String Quartet in B Flat, K 589/2

c. Bach, Sonata in G Minor for Solo Violin       d. Mozart, "Linz" Symphony, K 425/2

e. Mozart, *Don Giovanni*, K 529 I,1

## Spot Dynamics (Accents)

In the realm of spot dynamics, the emphasis by accent on single notes or brief note groups, we find quite a few discussions of contemporary theorists that refer to meter, to melody, to rhythm, and to harmony.

Koch, in his *Musikalisches Lexikon* of 1802 (s.v. "Accent") distinguishes three kinds of accents that, like certain emphasized syllables in the language, are rendered either louder or slightly longer (the "agogic accents"). The three types are: (1) grammatical; (2) oratorical; and (3) pathetic. The grammatical accent comprises three types of emphasis —on those notes that fall in the "good parts of the measure," on the first of several small notes of which the first starts a beat, or on the first of two slurred notes in an adagio. Koch cautions that the grammatical accent must be very subtle. The oratorical and pathetic accents, of which the second is only an intensified form of the first, are stronger than the grammatical and can fall on any part of the measure. They give, he says, a phrase its right meaning (Koch offers an illustration in col. 52) and bring to life the dead letter of the notes.

Overlapping with Koch's grammatical accent is the metrical accent, which was explained in the introduction to Part II. From the second half of the 17th century on, a number of theorists (most of them German) dealt with these accents, but their discussions tended to be clouded by an awkward terminology briefly discussed in chapter 11: they spoke not of loud and soft, which they meant, but of long and short, qualified by such expressions as "quantitate intrinseca" or "virtualiter" or "innerlich." These adverbial qualifiers did not refer to actual length, which would have been the "quantitas *extrinseca*," but to their inner nature as accents with their implications for rhythmic-metrical clarification, for setting a text with due consideration to prosody, to dissonance treatment, and to continuo realization. (On this topic see my *Essays 1982*, 34–42, or "French *Inégales*," 335–43; also Houle, *Meter in Music*, chaps. 4 and 6.)

As Koch wrote, the metrical accent must be subtle; yet it varies within a certain range according to musical type and texture. It will, as mentioned earlier, be strongest in dances and dance-derived music, weakest, often to the point of disappearance, in certain Baroque works where melodies are propelled across barlines by a strong linear impulse; it will be stronger in homophonic than in polyphonic music. Often the metrical accent is overridden by a melody's energy, its internal stresses and releases, its oratorical and pathetic accents (see the introduction to Part II and chap. 19).

What could be called a "harmonic accent" is the stress that is often appropriate for a dissonance that falls on a beat. The most typical and frequent case of an onbeat dissonance is an appoggiatura that should always be stressed and resolved with a taper to its principal note. The same is true of other dissonances, whether they enter freely or by suspension or are conventionally prepared.

In the above-quoted passage from C. P. E. Bach about dynamics and the impossibility of establishing principles about the proper use of *forte* and *piano* (except for a few directives such as the alternation of loud and soft on repeats of a phrase or motive), he adds that "dissonances are generally played louder and the consonances softer because the former arouse and accentuate the emotions while the latter calm them." He is, however, not rigid about this principle, which he qualifies and even contradicts in the further course of the paragraph (*Versuch über Art das Clavier*, [1753], chap. 3, par. 29).

Quantz writes at length about the accentuation of dissonances in connection with the realization of the continuo (*Versuch einer Anweisung,* chap. 17, sec. 6, pars. 9–18). His idea is that dissonances cause mental anguish ("erwecken im Gemüthe einen Verdruss") and that this unpleasantness is needed to prevent the music from being insipid and ennervatingly monotonous through an endless succession of consonances (par. 12). Dissonances, he continues, add the indispensable spice, and the stronger the dissonance the greater is the pleasure in its resolution. By playing the dissonance louder we further increase the delight of the following concord. There are different degrees of dissonances, and Quantz arranges them in three categories, from mild to strong, to which correspond the dynamic degrees of *mezzoforte, forte,* and *fortissimo,* while some dissonances are so mild that they require no special attention.Quantz finally qualifies his somewhat schoolmasterly rules about dissonance types and their corresponding loudness by saying that "judgment and sensitivity" (die gute Beurtheilungskraft, und eine feine Empfindung der Seele) have to play a large role in this matter (par. 14). He illustrates his ideas in an interesting example (Tab. 24) of an accompanied solo with ample markings of *pp, p, mf, f,* and *ff,* and we are gratified to see that on some occasion he lets "judgment and sensitivity" override his theoretical rules.

The practical execution of this kind of dynamically varied accompaniment is, of course, so Quantz notes, most convenient on the "Pianoforte," but for the one-keyboard harpsichord he gives very interesting advice on how to achieve different shades of volume. Playing *piano* requires a gentle touch and a thinning of the parts; *mezzoforte* requires doubling the bass; *forte* calls for the same procedure plus doubling in the left hand some of the consonant pitches; in *fortissimo* one adds a fast arpeggiation from below and a stronger and more vehement touch (par. 17). As we shall presently see, C. P. E. Bach supports the thinning and thickening of the texture as a means of dynamic shading, but he does not support Quantz's difference of touch.

Quantz's psychological explanation that the distress of dissonance needs to be increased by accentuation in order to augment the delight in the resolution seems somewhat overstated, though dissonances no doubt made a stronger impression on his contemporaries than on our jaded ears. What is at the heart of the matter is that dissonances create a tension that demands release and enforces movement toward resolution. Greater loudness strengthens this tension and clarifies, as under magnification, the involved energy play; since clarification of the music is a principal aim of performance, emphasis on dissonances will generally be desirable. Exceptions will apply to dissonances created *in transitu* between beats and sometimes on a weak beat and, in agreement with Quantz, to such technical dissonances that are so mild as to be hardly perceived as such. Incidentally, the question of what constitutes a consonance and a dissonance was highly controversial among theorists of the 17th and 18th centuries.[1]

One could call "melodic accents" those that are suggested by the kinetic energies inherent in a melodic sequence. Leopold Mozart obviously has such accents in mind when he writes that notes raised by a sharp or a natural sign as well as those lowered by a flat or a natural should be played somewhat louder (*Versuch einer Violinschule,* chap. 12, par. 8). Within a melodic sequence a raised note will most often reveal an upward-moving tendency, a lowered note will reveal a downward tendency. C. P. E. Bach writes in a similar vein that "notes of a melody that do not belong to the scale of its key like to be played loudly [gerne das Forte vertragen] regardless of whether they are consonances or dissonances" (*Versuch über Art das Clavier* [1753], chap. 3, par. 29). Bach's remark makes it clear that the forces at work here are of melodic, not harmonic, origin.

Quantz also mentions that lowered and raised notes deserve emphasis when he speaks of the cello (*Versuch einer Anweisung,* chap. 17, sec. 4, par. 7) and the accompaniment (chap. 17, sec. 6, par. 11). Generally, any note that for whatever reason is distinguished from its surroundings can be a candidate for such special treatment; among them are notes that make a wide leap, for which Leopold Mozart gives illustrations (*Versuch einer Violinschule,* chap. 12, pars. 13–14), or long notes that are mixed in with many short ones (see Quantz, *Versuch einer Anweisung,* chap. 17, sec. 6, par. 10).

Another species could be called "accents of articulation," which occur when the first note under a slur is given a slight emphasis. C. P. E. Bach, Quantz, and Leopold Mozart all discuss these cases. They will be dealt with in chapter 16.

One could call "rhythmic accents" those emphases that are desirable in order to place unusual rhythmic designs into clearer relief. The classic case is syncopations, where the rhythm of the melody clashes with the basic pulse of the meter. Here again, as with the nonstandard melodic progression, the unexpected character of the syncopation calls for emphasis. In general, the syncopation ought to be stronger when the clash is greater: stronger if the syncopation falls between rather than on beats, stronger if it crosses the barline, stronger if it is combined with a leap or with a dissonance.

In several paragraphs devoted to accentuation, Türk lists basically the same types of accents as the great mid-century writers (*Klavierschule,* chap. 6, sec. 2, pars. 14–18). Like Koch, he extends their theories by pointing to the lengthening of a note as a means of emphasis (par. 17). Lengthening was, incidentally, the only way in which organ or harpsichord could express emphases on single notes.

It is helpful to be aware of all these principles, but in the final analysis one cannot go by the book. One has to feel the phrase as a whole, sense its inner life, its energy flow—or, as Schulz says: "one must hear, feel, and learn"—and the proper distribution of stress and release is likely to fall spontaneously into place. This is the essence of the art of phrasing, and here the proverbial orator can truly serve as model, for in delivering a sentence, he aims to apportion its lights and shades in harmony with the meaning of the words.

## Gradation versus Sudden Contrasts

The conflict of terraced versus gradual dynamics, as played out on the large stage of stylistic principles, finds its small-scale reflection in countless cases where composers juxtapose a *forte* and a *piano* and where we have to guess from the circumstances whether a brusque contrast or a gradual transition was intended. The question presents itself many times in those cases before symbols or words for crescendo or decrescendo were in use, but, for those composers who use markings for swelling or taperings, we are inclined to assume that they will not leave us in doubt about their wishes. Unfortunately, this is a vain hope. The Classical composers who knew these markings were often sparing in their use and often relied on the instincts of their performers to divine the right solutions. Thus we have no right to interpret the absence of gradation marks as intention of a brusque change. Rules about the choice of sudden or gradual change are of course impossible to give, but guidelines that apply to the Baroque as well as to the Classical composers can be essayed.

Sudden change will likely be indicated for repeated passages, phrases, or motives, where the repeat need not be literal nor on the same pitch level; similarly, when the dynamic mark coincides with a motive that has an individuality of its own and that could be ever so slightly detached without hurting the continuity, sudden change will be the likely intention. By contrast, when the dynamic sign is placed in mid-phrase, gradual transition is the more likely solution. For an illustration, see Ex. 14.4a, from Mozart's Piano Sonata in D, K 205b (284); under the influence of Mannheim, this music is unusually rich in *piano–forte* contrasts. The first theme of the second movement shown in the example has different components or modules that in the first four measures are clearly set off by motivic contrasts, which in turn are reflected in dynamics. They are like two persons conversing, one assertively, the second timidly. (Their respective individualities are confirmed when on their recurrence in mm. 31–34 the dynamics are reversed.) It seems that they must not be mixed: their sharp differences would be blunted by either a tapering of the initial *forte* or a *crescendo* in the second (or fourth) measures. The fifth and sixth measures are different. Here the *forte* occurs in mid-phrase. If this were written for strings, there should prob-

EXAMPLE 14.4.  Mozart, Piano Sonata in D, K 205b (284)

a. Rondeau en Polonaise

b.

ably be a *crescendo* in the melody as well as in the accompaniment a beat later. On the piano, new or old, this is of course not feasible. In a later variant of these two measures, shown partially in Ex. 14.4b, a *crescendo* seems indicated on the turn (supported by the left hand) since a sudden *forte* on the sixteenth note following the turn would seem to be singularly incongruous.

A *crescendo* followed by a *piano* is almost always a case of intended brusqueness. Although we find this combination occasionally with Haydn, it is very frequent in Mozart, who favored the dramatic effect of the unexpected. As an indication of his partiality to this dynamic design, he uses it seven times in the slow movement of the String Quartet in B Flat Major ("Hunt"), six times in the slow movement of the String Quartet in E Flat, but most breathtakingly in the rising and falling scales in the final scene of *Don Giovanni,* as anticipated in the Overture. In all these cases it seems advisable not to blunt the edge of the contrast by smoothing the transition with a small taper prior to the *piano.*

Since Haydn and Mozart were sparing in dynamic extremes of *pianissimo* and *fortissimo,* we have to observe them conscientiously when they do occur. In a famous (undated) letter of 1768 that accompanied the score of the "Applausus" Cantata, Haydn writes: "the *fortes* and *pianos* are written correctly throughout, and should be observed exactly; for there is a very great difference between *piano* and *pianissimo, forte* and *fortissimo,* between *crescendo* and *forzando,* and so forth" (quoted in Landon, *Collected Correspondence,* 9).

# The Problem of Balance

The proper handling of dynamics for the sake of good balance between the various parts was stressed as early as 1558 by Zarlino in his famous *Istitutioni harmoniche,* where he writes: "one must sing with a moderate voice and adjust it to those of the other singers" (debbe cantare con voce moderata, & propotionarla con quelle degli altri cantori [204]). Richard Wagner once said that the job of the conductor was to find the melody. Here is the problem in a nutshell: to find what is important and to see to it that it is being heard by rendering the important part louder or the other parts softer or both. In modern music, where it is not always easy to find the melody, composers such as Schoenberg have taken to writing *hervortreten,* meaning "bring it out" (literally "step out in front"), or analogous instructions. The old masters had by and large to rely on the good judgment of their performers for emphasizing and deemphasizing the proper parts. Once in a while, though, we find them indicating balance by careful disposition of dynamic markings. Bach, in the "Brandenburg" Concertos, often uses very sophisticated mixtures of *forte, piano,* and *pianissimo* to insure the audibility of the principal parts. In the first movement of the third concerto (mm. 17 and 18), for instance, he protects the violas from being drowned out by writing *piano* in the three violins, and he does the same in analogous situations. The figurations of measures 47–49, which occur in various instruments in the course of the movement, are always similarly helped to "step out in front." Remarkable is the spot in measures 108–10 where single violins in *forte* play this figuration against *piano* in the accompaniment, but when the figuration is transferred to the darker-hued violas (mm. 111–13), the accompanying violins are marked *più piano* to compensate for their higher pitch and greater brightness. In the fifth concerto we find even more refined combinations of dynamic markings with a view to desirable balance.

Although Haydn and Mozart relied in most instances on the musicianship of their performers, they too resorted from time to time to similar methods. For a few illustrations, see how Haydn, in the first movement (m. 76) of his String Quartet Op. 20, No. 5 (Hob. IV:35), writes *sotto voce* for the first violin, *pp* for the other instruments; in Op. 20, No. 2, second movement (m. 34), he has *più forte* in first violin and viola, *piano* in the second violin and cello. In the third movement, the menuet, the cello carries the melody and is marked *p,* the rest *pp.* Mozart, in the andante variations of his String Quartet in A Major, has *mezzoforte* for the delightful drum rhythms of the cello versus *piano* in the other strings (mm. 126ff). For both Mozart and Haydn, see also the passages marked *sotto voce* versus *piano,* listed earlier in this chapter (p. 171).

Among theorists dealing with the question of balance, Quantz, as he does so often, imparts timeless wisdom. He does so mainly in connection with the accompaniment of a solo but branches out into more general observations (*Versuch einer Anweisung*, chap. 17, sec. 7, pars. 21–28). He mentions the need for musicians to adapt to the acoustical circumstances of the locale: whether the acoustics are live or dead, whether the listeners are close or distant, whether the solo medium is strong or weak, and whether the number of accompanying instruments is large, medium, or small. When accompanying a weak medium (such as a flute), one has to moderate the accompaniment and scale down both the *pianos* and the *fortes;* accompaniment should be weaker in allegro than in adagio; and accompanying violins should be weaker on the upper than on the lower strings. Then he sums up the art of balancing the accompaniment in what is the truly fundamental principle: what matters, he says, is "that the accompanist watches whether he himself can hear the solo." This is the key to achieving proper balance, not only in accompanying but in any ensemble, be it chamber music, orchestra, or opera: whenever a part does not have the melody, its performer must listen for the melody and adjust his own playing so that he can hear it. This is as valid today as it was hundreds of years ago.

Quantz has further valuable advice: since not all instruments (not even different violins) have the same power, the stronger one must adapt in *forte* to the weaker, and the weaker in *piano* to the stronger, lest the parts become uneven. Also, when a soloist in an adagio modulates his tone with greater or lesser strength, the accompanist will do well to follow the soloist's example and support his efforts of giving out light and shade.

C. P. E. Bach expresses similar concern for the balance of accompaniment and soloist (*Versuch über Art das Clavier* [1762], chap. 29, pars. 5–10). Among all continuo instruments, he says, the one-keyboard harpsichord causes the accompanist the greatest embarrassment. He must try to compensate for the limitations of the instrument by thickening or thinning the chords, although in thinning he must take care not to omit important harmony notes. Bach gives advice on how and when to double notes to achieve greater volume. The fortepiano and the clavichord, he says, are much superior to harpsichord and organ in matters of dynamic adaptability (par. 6), and the accompanist must be constantly alert to softnesses and strengths in the solo part and be careful not to overpower, say, the weak low register of a flute (par. 8).

All these concerns about balance are summed up in Quantz's single statement that the accompanist must at all times be able to hear the soloist.

## Summary

In trying to sum up the main problems of dynamics, let us address first the stylistic domain of what is commonly called the Baroque. Here the foremost need is to put the polarity of terraced and graduated dynamics in proper perspective. To do so we have to differentiate two things.

First, in some cases, terracing was the free artistic choice of the composer, as in antiphonal works such as polychoral compositions, in the contrast between grosso and concertino in concerti grossi, in echo effects (of which the period was so fond), and in abrupt contrasts for dramatic effect. In all these cases the terraced effect is integral to the musical thought.

Second, in many other cases, terracing was linked to the limitation of an instrument such as the harpsichord or the organ. In performing on modern instruments, we must take into consideration the fact that *some* of the music was written with the nature of the old instrument in mind and therefore to a certain extent adapted to its limitations. This means that, when performing such idiomatic works on a modern instrument, it seems best to avoid deviating *markedly* from the dynamic potential of the old instrument while allowing modest dynamic nuances to put phrases into clearer relief.

On the other hand, where the writing is not characteristically idiomatic, and where line is more important than color, as is so often the case with Bach's solo works for the keyboard, considerations of the original sound regarding dynamics can recede even further. But one should always keep in mind that in polyphonic textures dynamic gradations have to remain within modest limits: while perfectly legitimate when used to give life and plasticity to a phrase, they must not exceed this function and assume a role of structural significance.

For the masters of the galant style who did not make use of the symbols for extended gradations, we should feel free to insert some gradations where the music seems to favor them and where the homophonic texture seems to invite and need this kind of coloristic support.

The Classical masters have often given sufficient indications for area dynamics, but they were not consistent about it. As a consequence, a frequently encountered problem is the uncertainty about gradualism versus suddenness when a *piano* follows a *forte* or vice versa. Here, as a rule of thumb, gradualism is more likely when the contrasting dynamic marks occur in mid-phrase; suddenness is more likely when the marks are placed either at the seams of individual phrases or motives or on repeats of a melodic section, be they exact, in sequence, or approximate. Another problem is the correct differentiation of such marks as *fp*, *sf* (*fz*), and *rf* (*rinf*) as well as accentual dots and dashes; but probably the most important problem for music of all eras and styles is that of balance, of the correct level of volume for the various voices, and more particularly the concern that the melody or principal themes be clearly heard. We must be aware that in polyphony two or more melodies can be of equal importance, that subordinate parts must neither be obtrusive nor withdrawn but loud enough to provide sufficient support. Balance, in brief, means mutual adjustment for best clarification of the music.

# Part IV
## *Articulation*

# The Nature of Articulation

The musical term "articulation" comes originally from linguistics, where it refers to the ways in which various sounds of a language are enunciated, words are connected by fusion or separated by pauses, vowels started with or without distinct aspiration, various syllables of a word (and various words in a phrase) emphasized or deemphasized, and vowels and diphthongs rendered short or long—in short, to all the elements that combine to make for desirable diction in a specific language. Not surprisingly, the analogies to music are very close since the melodic elements of music that present the main articulation problems were born of song, and music's association with words, for many centuries paramount, never ceased to be a powerful influence.

The elements of linguistic articulation are almost literally applicable to music. In music, what is at stake is the way a tone is started, held, ended, and linked to the one that follows. The following four points are indeed the main aspects of musical articulation: (1) how to start a tone, whether smoothly, like an unaspirated vowel (as "aaa"), or sharply and percussively, as if with an explosive consonant (as "ta ta"), or in a way somewhere between the two extremes; (2) how to hold the tone, whether to sustain it for all or most of its written length or shorten it substantially, whether to keep the sound even or let it grow or taper; (3) how to end the tone, whether by simply discontinuing it or by abruptly terminating it with an accent-like inflection or by letting it come to an end with a finely sculpted taper; (4) how to connect it with the tone that follows, whether to link it smoothly and evenly without any interruption, or, at the other extreme, to separate it with a clear rest—or to connect it in any intermediate manner.

The fourth of these points suggests the central issue—namely, in what way does one connect two adjacent notes when there are seemingly countless choices ranging from legato, with its seamless blending, to staccato, with its clear and sharp separation? It is the issue that first comes to mind when we speak of articulation, but it behooves us to be aware of the other points as well and their potential to add to, or detract from, the rendering of a musical thought.

Only the voice and the strings have the full range of articulatory potential. Wind instruments follow in close order, but all the keyboard instruments have technical and idiomatic limitations of different types. The (Baroque) organ can sustain a tone but is incapable of accentuation and dynamic nuance. The harpsichord has the same dynamic limitations and in addition cannot sustain a tone. The clavichord cannot sustain a tone but has some dynamic flexibility within a rather narrow range. This flexibility is considerably increased for the fortepiano, which, however, like its modern descendant, can neither sustain a tone nor control its tapering.

Clearly, a perfect legato is not available to instruments that cannot sustain a tone. Here the aural imagination has to step in and substitute the missing continuity. Similar limitations beset all keyboard and plucked instruments with regard to the way a tone is started and ended: they are incapable both of a *pianissimo* start followed by a gradual swell and of the fully controlled *pianissimo* end to a tone, not to speak of the *portando la voce*—the singer's gentle glide into a pitch, which only strings can imitate. For such reasons of idiomatic limitations we find that for keyboard instruments the problems of articulation are by and large limited to legato—and quasi-legato for instruments other than the organ—and the various types of detachment.

All aspects of performance are interrelated, and elements of articulation are no exception. Some of these elements interrelate with phrasing, others, such as swelling and tapering, with dynamics, and accentuations affect both dynamics and rhythm, so that there is often an unavoidable arbitrariness in discussing certain matters under one or the other heading. With this proviso, the question of dynamic nuances in starting and ending a tone was dealt with in the chapters on dynamics. Accents in connection with staccato performance will be dealt with in this part, as far as they are linked to articulation symbols. Although phrasing and tempo, too, will have to be touched on from time to time, by and large Part IV will focus on the legato–staccato polarity: the idiomatic character of each for different performance media, their use in conformance with the evolving symbols of articulation, and their use in the absence of any directives from the composer. Before addressing the main subject, it will be well to have a look at the emphasis we ought to place on articulation in the scheme of historical performance.

## The Relative Importance of Articulation

Among the musical elements that combine to produce a historically valid performance, not all are of equal importance. How should we rank articulation in this context?

No simple answer can be given, since the importance of articulation ranges from essential to marginal. It is essential when it is an indispensable element of expression. If a phrase or section calls for smooth, singing legato, a sharp rendition is bound to change its character, often to the point of distortion. In the opposite case, where a notated staccato sequence is rendered legato, the effect may be less crass but is still bound to change the physiognomy of the phrase from the one intended. Hence, here too the basic articulation will be essential. The same can be said of a case in which a specific pattern of slurs, or of slurs combined with detached notes, is an integral part of the musical thought. Whether such is the case or not can often be recognized when the same pattern returns unchanged in all parallel spots, or when a change in the pattern will have a stronger than merely cosmetic impact.

Where on the other hand the composer betrays unconcern about the exact pattern by deviating from it in parallel spots, then articulation becomes a minor matter. What might be important in such cases is the use of *some* articulatory pattern, some mixture of linkage and detachment, even though the precise configuration may be of minor importance.

Georg von Dadelsen, in an article on Bach's articulation, distinguishes "essential" articulation, which is closely tied to the affect and is a matter of composition, from "accidental" articulation, which is tied to the instrumental technique and is a matter of performance. The first kind has to be scrupulously adhered to, the second is at the discretion of the performer ("Crux der Nebensache," 103).

In the allegro theme of Mozart's Symphony in E Flat K 543, the basic legato is of the essence, but the exact disposition of the slurs is a minor matter, as can be gathered from the recapitulation where the slur pattern is modified with no perceptible effect on expression or phrasing. The modification, moreover, is not noticeable enough to be an intentional variant, hence we are rather safe in concluding that here, within a legato frame, the specific pattern of bow change was to Mozart a matter of indifference.

With Bach we find cases of striking consistency, for instance in several homophonic movements of the Sonatas and Partitas for Solo Violin. These are "essential" articulations, integral to the musical thought. Among parallel spots we also find many cases of considerable inconsistency that may be due to haste, or, as in Mozart's case, to indifference. Since Bach, even in haste, never made mistakes with the actual pitches or their rhythm, the fact that he did vary the slur patterns does indicate that they were not of thematic significance. The same conclusion probably fits the many cases of inconsistencies in simultaneous statements of the same melody, typically involving voice and instruments (see John Butt, *Bach Interpretation*, 122–30, for several illustrations).

On the other side are cases in which consistency in the discrepancies among various parts points to intentional variety. In Cantata No. 84/1, for instance, a dotted rhythm is consistently articulated on the upbeat in the voice, on the downbeat in the instruments, both successively and simultaneously (see below, Ex. 16.8). Since the discrepancy is clearly intentional, attempts at assimilation would be misguided.

Then there are the innumerable works that have no articulation marks but that were written in a period when the slur and staccato symbols had long been in use. Typical are many of Bach's keyboard works that fall into this category. Though such wholesale omissions are rarely found with the Classical composers, Beethoven left unarticulated vast stretches of the solo violin part of his Violin Concerto of 1806, sections that could not possibly have been intended for unremitting detachment. Such failures to indicate the desired articulation—failures that have no counterpart in the notation of melody, harmony, or rhythm—would certainly seem to imply that the disposition of slurs and detached notes in those specific cases is relatively unimportant. It does not mean that anything goes; it does mean that, as with unmarked ornamentation, the composer counted on the performer's taste and imagination to devise the kind of articulation that would best fit a given situation.

The preceding paragraphs are not meant to belittle articulation, which is an important and often essential element of musical expression. They are meant rather to make the point that articulation has to be seen with a sense of proportion—that is, with a critical appraisal of where a specifically prescribed pattern of slurring and detachment is integral to a phrase and where it is not; where some articulation is needed when not prescribed; and where the specific pattern to be used is up to the performer's judgment. The role of articulation and its precise form when not marked will be of special importance to media with a meager capacity for articulation—the organ, for instance. Here the means of separation and linkage are often indispensable ways of clarifying phrasing, rhythm, and meter, since accents and other dynamic nuances used for such purposes in other media are not available.

The following chapters deal with the vocabulary of articulation available to the various performing media of the 17th and 18th centuries and the tendencies regarding their use; with the emergence of the various symbols and the questions concerning their meaning; with some more specialized questions such as the stroke-versus-dot controversy for Mozart and the problem of articulation unmarked by the composer (exemplified by Bach's keyboard music); and finally with the attempt by some scholars to use old keyboard fingerings as keys for deciphering a composer's intention with regard to articulatory and rhythmic nuances.

# 15

# VOCAL ARTICULATION

For the voice, the legato–staccato polarity is primarily a matter of continuous or interrupted tone. With continuous tone one can, in addition to a perfect legato, create patterns of articulation by more or less gentle emphases on successive pitches in a manner now referred to as *portato*.

Different effects ranging from gentle to violent are available by interruption of the breath. A gentle form of interruption results from the insertion of h's, frequently done in choral, very rarely in soloistic, singing, to achieve a clear definition of succeeding pitches. More marked interruptions ensue from other consonants, according to the degree of their hardness, as well as from vowels that are enunciated with a consonant-like explosive aspiration (a "glottal stroke") particularly characteristic of German in such words as *alt, aber, Achtung,* and others.

We have significant information on 15th-century German chorale practices from a tract by the Heidelberg professor Conrad von Zabern of 1474 (*De modo bene cantandi choralem cantum*) containing directives of what to do and not to do (quoted by Haas, *Aufführungspraxis der Musik*, 42). One of the things he cautions against is adding h's to vowels in words that do not contain any h. One must not, he writes, sing, as it is so frequently done, "Kyrie eleison" with "he-he-he." Obviously he refers to a melisma in "eleison," which in his mind ought to be sung with a perfect legato.

Two hundred years later, Demantius in 1656 finds fault with the same intrusion into a vocal legato when the fast notes of coloraturas are "quasi laughingly" torn apart in singing "canta-ha-ha-ha-ha-te" and "stu-hu-hu-hu-hu-hul-tus" (quoted by Haas, 47–48).

Yet it would be a mistake to assume that melismatic song always calls for a perfect legato. When the melismas are fast, as they are in virtuoso coloraturas, a full legato can blur the design; thus a compromise must be made, one that permits the clarity of the line to be perceived without its being "torn apart." With this in mind, Daniel Speer writes in 1697 that fast vocal passages "do not just require smooth continuous breath; each tone should be rendered through clear attacks of the breath" (geschwinde Läuffe . . . sollen nicht bloss durch des Athems hauchen / sondern durch deutlichers anschlagen dess Athems / soll jeder Note Thon exprimirt werden [*Grund-richtiger*, 30]).

Thirty years later, Tosi, the spokesman of the Italian bel canto school at perhaps its high point in the early years of the 18th century, wishes a total legato to be limited to stepwise rising or falling pitches, their sum not exceeding the range of a fourth. The *passaggi*—that is, the ornamental coloraturas—can be detached (*battuto*) or slurred (*strascino*). The slurred ones can be pleasing but must not be used too often, whereas the detached ones are more frequent. For these the voice must move with greatest facility; their notes should be articulated with great evenness and with a "moderate detachment" so that the *passaggio* is neither too legato nor too staccato.[1]

Tosi reemphasizes the predominance of the detached type when, summing up the issue, he says that "the whole beauty of the *passaggio* consists in its being perfectly in tune, detached, solid, equal, clearly articulated and fast" (Tutta la bellezza del Passaggio consiste nell' esser perfettamente intonato, battuto, granito, eguale, rotto, e veloce [*Opinioni de cantori*, 35]).

Johann Friedrich Agricola, Tosi's German translator, adds in his comments to this issue that, in order to achieve the semidetached articulation of *passaggi* one must gently repeat the vowel over which the coloratura is sung; for instance, one must pronounce as many a's as there are notes in the passage. Thus the breath "is divided in as many small fractions as there are notes, which thereby are articulated and clarified" (*Anleitung zur Singkunst*, 124). He then compares this articulation to that produced by many separate small bowstrokes on strings or by tonguing on the flute.

Tosi ridicules singers who wish to separate notes with such vigor ("con tal rinforzo di voce") that by singing a passage on "a" they seem to be singing "ga-ga-ga" (*Opinioni de cantori*, 34; the g's here are the equivalent for German or English sibilant h's, which do not exist in Italian diction). Agricola, in commenting on this passage, finds culprits in those German basses who aspire at fame in shouting rather than singing and who put an "h" before every note with such forcefulness ("mit solcher Gewalt") that they lose much breath in the process (*Anleitung zur Singkunst*, 132).

The strictures on the insertion of h's were not shared by everybody. Several theorists, old and new, point to such need. Johann Peter Sperling, in 1705, distinguishes contexts in which a slur linking repeated pitches sung with the same vowel indicates a *tremolando,* as in Ex. 15.1a, from those such as in Ex. 15.1b in which dots are placed over the notes, requiring the insertion of h's, so that the notes here are to be pronounced "mo ho ho ho ho ho ho ho tus" (*Porta musica,* 68–69). Agricola, after all, seemed to object mainly to the violence ("Gewalt") with which some singers pronounce it, and his directive of the repeated "a" with its explosive German start can be harder and sharper than the insertion of an "h."

EXAMPLE 15.1.   Sperling (1705)

Such insertion of h's in melismatic passages is still being used by choral directors who often consider it indispensable. It may not be relevant to 18th-century practices, but it is certainly interesting that in a number of instances Stravinsky does not take any chances with indistinct articulation and spells out the added h's in the text. He does so, for instance, in *Oedipus Rex,* when in the words "Theba peste moritur" (Thebes is dying of the plague) he uses the spelling "The-he-ba," or in the third movement of Symphony of Psalms, "laudate" becomes: "lau-(hau)-da-(ha)-te" (I owe this information to Professor James Erb).

It seems that the mid-18th century witnessed a certain change from a vocal style favoring detachment to one favoring legato. This change paralleled a similar change in instrumental style, to be discussed presently. In his comments on Tosi's nonlegato *passaggi,* Agricola testifies to this fashion swing when he writes that the mistake of slurring passages that should be detached has spread among singers coming from the latest schools (*Anleitung zur Singkunst,* 132). Ludger Lohmann, in his important book on keyboard articulation, believes that this tendency originated with the voice in Italy, then spread to all European countries and to the keyboard as well (*Studien zu Artikulationsproblemen,* 237).

J. A. Hiller writes in 1774 that "good vocal style requires that one tone should be linked to the next so precisely and smoothly [so genau und so sanft] that not the least pause can be heard between them and that all [tones] seem to form one extended breath [ein einziger langgedehnter Hauch]" (*Anweisung zum musikalisch-richtigen Gesange,* 74). He may have had relatively slow cantilenas in mind because in 1780 he prescribes detachment for lengthy passages (*Anweisung zum musikalisch-zierlichen Gesange,* 86).

It seems likely that in the many virtuoso coloraturas found in Mozart's opera and concert arias, ingredients of nonlegato had to be introduced to insure the desirable clarity of design.

The problem of legato versus nonlegato often centers on ornamental figurations that move fast in rounded, mostly stepwise, progression. In those cases in which the composer, often with a view to tone painting, notates staccato dots for the same vowel or inserts rests, a sharp separation, often with the help of h's or glottal strokes, is clearly indicated. For instance, in the second aria of the Queen of the Night (*Die Zauberflöte,* Act 2, Scene 8), Mozart juxtaposes legato (or near-legato) with staccato on the same vowel "a" in "Bande" (mm. 69–79).

When Tosi wrote about the limited role of the legato, he was speaking of ornamental passages, not of slow expressive cantilenas. For the latter, the vocal impulse will generally tend to favor legato. And even within the frame of coloraturas, Agricola points to the frequently broader use of a legato that extends over intervals wider than Tosi's fourth (*Anleitung zur Singkunst,* 128).

It would seem that the full range of articulatory possibilities of today's vocal art have been known and used over the centuries. They included a type that was favored in the 17th century but that has since become obsolete: the *trillo,* the fast regular tone repetition that was presumably done in either a quasi-legato manner without interruption of the breath, as a string of intensity fluctuations much like *portato,* or in a clearly separated staccato manner.

Apart from such a special case (which overlaps with the subject of ornamentation), other characteristics of vocal articulation must have mirrored the timeless ones that are rooted in the nature of the various languages, such as the importance of the glottal stroke on vowels or the aspiration after consonants such as "p," "t," and "k" in the Germanic, and the rarity of the glottal stroke and the absence of post-consonantal aspiration in the Romance languages. Concerning the legato–staccato polarity, the predominance of one or the other was subject to fashion swings such as the one noted by Lohmann of a tendency toward more legato, both vocal and instrumental, after the mid-18th century. But we must beware of too-sweeping generalizations. Scholars like to speak of a "common practice" because it simplifies their task of formulating rules. But there has never been a totally homogenized practice in any aspect of performance, not even within a single country, let alone all over Europe. There also were always strong individuals who did not abide by prevailing fashions and were a law unto themselves. Thus, while we should be aware of tendencies or fashions that favor one mode of articulation over another, we must not be too literal about them and must never fail to engage our own musical judgment, the more so the less we can be sure of what in a particular case was historically appropriate.

# Principles of Vocal Articulation

Finally, I would like to quote a set of principles of vocal articulation that the late Arthur Mendel has communicated to me. This eminent Bach scholar and fine choral conductor, who was my mentor and friend, considered these principles important and, in case I used them, asked me to state that he had learned them from the late Carl Deis.

The *vowel* always comes *on the beat*. Therefore, initial consonants must come before the beat—that is, at the end of the preceding beat.

*Unvoiced explosives* (hard "c," "k," "p," "q," "t") take so little time that they may be thought of as coming on the beat.

*Voiced explosives* (hard "g," "b," "d") must be prepared at the end of the preceding beat, "exploding" onto the vowel on the beat.

*Unvoiced sibilants* (soft "c," "f," "h," "s," hard "th"), since they take more time than the explosives, must be begun well before the beat, taking a perceptible fraction of the preceding beat.

All other consonants—that is, *voiced sibilants* (soft "g," "j," soft "s," soft "th," "v," "z"), *liquids* ("l," "r"), *semiliquids* ("m," "n"), and *consonantal vowels* ("u," "w," "y"), which have both a certain duration and a definite pitch, must be sounded

1. at the end of the previous beat; and
2. on the pitch of the previous beat, or at a "spoken" pitch, an indefinite distance below that of the vowel.

The more emphatic the expression, the greater the time devoted to initial consonants must be (that is, the longer in advance they must be prepared) and the more likely it is that they will be spoken at a pitch below that of the vowel.

*Final consonants* that are *voiced*, and so have a definite pitch, must ordinarily be sounded at the end of the beat to which they belong and not carried over onto the next beat.

*Final consonants* that are *unvoiced*, when followed by a rest, are pronounced *on the rest*. Otherwise, final unvoiced consonants are pronounced at the end of the beat to which they belong (or just enough before to make room for the initial consonant of the following word).

When there are several consonants, the combination must be begun early enough to get the last of them in at the moment indicated by these principles. But this remark does not apply to a final combination followed by a rest; in such a case, the first unvoiced consonant comes on the rest, and the others follow immediately.

In Ex. 15.2, an attempt has been made to indicate roughly where the consonants come (in pitch and rhythm) in slow, emphatic articulation.

Example 15.2

Written

Hear    me, O    Lord,    and    that    soon,

Sung

H-ea - r m- e, O — L - o - rd,    a - nd th-a - t s - oo - n

Written

and    that    soon,    for my    spir - it wax - eth    faint,    for...

Sung

a - nd th-a - t s - oo - n f - or my    spir - it wax - e - th f - ai — nt f - or...

Written

faint    Glo - ry    *etc.*

Sung

f - ai - n - t    Gl - o — ry

# *16*

# INSTRUMENTAL LEGATO

We find the gamut of articulation from legato to staccato, with its many transitional forms, duplicated in those instruments whose idioms permit the transfer of the various vocal styles. On winds, the technical execution of legato involves encompassing two or more pitches in an even, uninterrupted breath, for strings a similarly even, uninterrupted bow-stroke. On the keyboard it requires holding down one finger at least until the next is dropped.

## *Strings and Winds*

The voice is the fountainhead of legato articulation. Legato may have originated in folksong when a singer ornamented its melody with simple melismas. In the ecclesiastic chants of the Middle Ages, many parts had melismas, some of great floridity when destined for solo singing. Indicated by the "ligatures" of mensural notation, they were presumably rendered in smooth legato style.

The strings may have been the first instrumental media to adopt the legato mode from the voice. Their capacity to emulate a songful style led to the gradual emergence of melismatic legato playing in, presumably, the 16th century. When Samuel Scheidt, in the twelfth variation on "Wehe, Windgen, wehe" from his *Tabulatura nova* of 1624, refers to four notes under a slur as "Imitatio violistica," he seems to acknowledge that stringed instruments used and typified the legato mode before keyboards did. As stringed instruments began to employ legato, there arose the need for a notational symbol less cumbersome than the ligatures. The need was supplied in the form of the slur, which will be discussed presently in greater detail.

Christopher Simpson writes in 1667 that to such ornaments as the *messa di voce*, dynamic contrasts, or bow vibrato one can add "that of playing 2, 3 or more Notes with one Motion of the Bow, which would not have that Grace, or Ornament if they were Played severally" (*Division-violist* [1667], 10).

For the sister instrument, the lute, Thomas Mace in 1676 describes the legato also as an ornament, calling it the "Slur." Done on one string for several scalewise ascending notes, he marks it with a slur mark under the respective letters, such as "abd," and explains its execution as "only hitting the 1st and Falling the rest" (*Musick's Monument*, 108). In his examples the first note that is plucked by the right hand is always the open string ("a"), which is best suited for this articulation because it reverberates longer and thus more effectively supports the sound of the ascending pitches activated by the percussive falling of the left-hand fingers.

The French gambists used legato extensively, as we can gather best from works that, like those of Marin Marais, were carefully edited and showed numerous slur marks. German and Italian violinists of the 17th century in their written texts used legato in most cases for not more than three or four notes at a time, but they strung up many more notes in a bow for their improvised coloraturas or for similar ornamental figurations that happened to be written out.

In general, all ornaments, including the small ones such as the appoggiatura, slide, turn, and so forth, were slurred to their parent notes. Bach, who methodically wrote out his coloraturas, always encompassed them in long slurs, and for his structural notes he used a highly sophisticated mixture of legato and detachment that gave great plasticity to his phrases in both slow and fast movements.

Leopold Mozart extols the merit of the legato for the rendering of a songful theme. He warns against the interruption of the melody unless required by phrasing or special expression. He favors the legato mode in emulation of the voice that "spontaneously flows from one pitch to another" (Die menschliche Stimme ziehet sich ganz ungezwungen von einem Tone in den anderen). When, he continues, the nature of the melody does not call for a break in continuity, "one should not only keep the bow on the string and *when changing the stroke connect one tone smoothly with the next* but also try to fit many notes into the same bow-stroke" (Man bemühe sich also . . . nicht nur bei der Abänderung des Striches den Bogen auf der Violin zu lassen und folglich einen Strich mit dem andern wohl zu verbinden; sondern auch viele Noten in einem Bogenstrich . . . vorzutragen [*Versuch einer Violinschule*, chap. 5, par. 14; emphasis added]). This passage is of particular importance because it belies the persistent misinterpretation of another statement by Leopold Mozart about the mechanics of changing the stroke. This misinterpretation, perpetuated as recently as 1988 by both Rosenblum (*Performance*

*Practices,* 173) and Reidemeister (*Alte Musik,* 74), who ask for a distinct break in sound, has had undesirable consequences for many a would-be "historically informed" performance. More about this in the chapter on detachment.

In analogy to the voice, a legato on wind instruments results when two or more pitches are played with the same uninterrupted breath. It seems that Ganassi, in his tutor of 1535, may have described such legato articulation. After having discussed in Chapters 5–7 the various types of articulation produced with the help of syllables, from the hardest "teche, teche" (pronounced "te-ke") over the medium "tere, tere" to the softest "lere, lere," he describes in Chapter 8 a playing style that does not use any syllables and in which the breath is shaped by the lips and flows easily between them. This latter form seems to describe a legato.

More explicit is Hotteterre in his flute tract of 1707. He describes and illustrates the *coulez* as two or more notes that are played with a single tonguing and are marked by a slur. His examples show the syllable "tu" and up to seven pitches in one breath (*Principes de la flûte,* 27–28).

Bach wrote extensive legato passages for winds, such as the many long-breathed figurations for the first oboe in the adagio of the First "Brandenburg" Concerto or ornamental passages in the andante of the Fourth "Brandenburg" Concerto for the first recorder.

## *The Keyboard*

Of all the keyboard instruments, only the organ is capable of producing a perfect legato with an even, uninterrupted flow.

The legato on harpsichord, clavichord, and fortepiano is qualified by the fading of the sound from the moment the string is plucked or hit by the hammer or tangent. This technical shortcoming is a hindrance to the sustained rendering of a melody in which the pitches follow one another at a slow or leisurely pace. This weakness is mitigated, though, by the capacity of the ear to bridge the gap between the fading note and the subsequent sound by imagining continuity. The faster the sequence of notes, the less the demands on aural imagination and the closer we can come to a genuine legato. Generally, in order to come as close to a perfect legato as the idiom permits, the fingers on harpsichord and clavichord have to keep the key depressed until the next is played; on the fortepiano the same effect can be achieved if the instrument is equipped with a damper-lifting mechanism, activated by the knee, should the instrument not be equipped with pedals. (This damper-lifting mechanism was used before pedals were introduced for the same purpose.) On the organ it will occasionally be advisable to allow for a tiny space to compensate for lively acoustics in order to avoid overlapping the sounds of two neighbor pitches.

Like the organ, the harpsichord cannot accentuate single notes and is therefore not capable of adding plasticity to a legato sequence by a slight stress on the start of the slur. Here, too, a clearer detachment and a slight agogic accent will have to serve as substitutes where such effect is desired.

Girolamo Diruta in 1593 tells organists to depress the keys, not to hit them ("che le dita premano il tasto, e non lo battano" [*Transilvano*, fol. 4*v*]), to treat the keys as if to caress them, not to slap them in anger. By so treating the keys one can give continuity to the melody ("far l'armonia unita"), whereas by hitting them one disrupts it ("far disunita" [fol. 5*r*]). He demonstrates correct and incorrect execution in an illustration, shown in Ex. 16.1, that clearly implies legato playing (fol. 5*v*). (He uses the arc symbol only for ties, not yet for slurs.)

EXAMPLE 16.1.   Diruta (1593)

Diruta sees exceptions only for the performance of dances, but for them he considers the harpsichord to be better suited. The harpsichord, however, does not, he says, allow for continuity of tones, but this defect can be somewhat helped by trills and ornaments. Long values, he continues, have to be repeated several times to be kept alive (fol. 6*r*).

Seventy-five years later, Guillaume Nivers is less adverse to detached organ articulation. In his *Livre d'orgue* of 1665, he calls it a considerable musical asset "to detach all the notes clearly and to slur a few of them subtly, in accord with the principles of fine singing" (Preface). Slurs are especially important for the *ports de voix*, and one should, he says, always consult methods for singing because in such matters the organ must imitate the voice. Slurring, *le couler*, is halfway between clear separation and blurriness ("entre la distinction et la confusion"). What he calls the confusion of blurring is presumably caused by letting two successive notes overlap (the "superlegato," as I shall refer to it presently); it can also be the result of the kind of echo effect so often present in large churches.

In general, Nivers recommends an easy and comfortable touch on the organ, which can be achieved by placing the fingers gracefully with comfort and equality ("Pour toucher agréablement, il le faut faire facilement, pour toucher facilement, il le faut faire commodément, et pour cet effet disposer les doigts sur le clavier de bonne grace, avec convenance et égalité" [Preface]).

André Raison, in the preface to his *Livre d'orgue* of 1688, asks for the *grand plein jeu* to be done very legato.

In the late 17th century Jean Le Gallois reports in a small, interesting tract about the various styles of clavecin playing he has witnessed (*Lettre de M. le Gallois*, 69–77). He distinguishes in particular "le jeu brillant" from the "jeu coulant" (69). The "brillant" would seem to represent virtuosic playing with, presumably, detached articulation, whereas the "coulant" would stand for a calmer, slurred manner. Each style, he says, has its virtues and its vices when used exclusively and to an extreme. But Chambonnières, whom Le Gallois extols as the supreme artist on the clavecin, achieved an ideal mixture of the two manners that cannot be improved upon ("ménage l'un avec l'autre qu'il était impossible de mieux faire" [77]). When Le Gallois lists as one of the vices of "le jeu brillant" the practice of hitting the keys instead of slurring them ("[ils] frappent les touches au lieu de les couler" [77], we are reminded of Diruta's criticism of organists who are pounding the keys instead of caressing them. (David Fuller drew my attention to this source.)

Both F. Couperin and Rameau seem to have considered the legato as the basic touch for the harpsichord. In his *L'art de toucher le clavecin*, Couperin writes while speaking about harpsichord touch in general that one must maintain a perfect legato in what one plays ("Il faut conserver une liaison parfaite dans ce qu'on y èxècute" [61]). In the same work he presents a new fingering for scalewise thirds that can be given a legato rendition by alternating fingers (29–30). Couperin uses the arc symbol for ties and square brackets for slurred notes of different pitch, making lavish use of the brackets. His symbol of a dash connecting note heads will be discussed presently.

Rameau, too, seems to see in the legato the fundamental keyboard touch. In "De la méchanique des doigts sur le clavessin," published as introduction to his *Pièces de clavessin* of 1724, he writes: "Fingers must drop on the keys, not hit them; moreover, they must flow, so to speak, from one [key] to the next. . . . From the starting finger one moves to the next, and so from one to another: the lifting of one finger and the dropping of another must occur at the same moment" (Le lever d'un doigt et le toucher d'un autre doivent être exécutés dans le même moment" [4]). This is of course a clear description of legato playing. He also refers to the "superlegato"—to be discussed presently—when in his illustration of a *port de voix* he shows an overlapping of the slurred notes.

It is possible that the legato leanings of the eminent French composer-performers reflect an Italian influence that originated in the Italian emphasis on songfulness. The Italian Nicolo Pasquali, writing in England, emphasizes the legato touch on the harpsichord. In *The Art of Fingering the Harpsichord* of 1758 he writes: "The *Legato* is the Touch that this Treatise endeavors to teach, being a general Touch fit for almost all Kinds of Passages, and by which the Vibration[s] of the Strings are made perfect in every Note" (quoted by Richard Troeger, *Technique and Interpretation*, 228).

For the organ we have an interesting testimonial about J. S. Bach's predominant legato touch from the lexicographer Ernst Ludwig Gerber, son of Bach's devoted student Heinrich Nikolaus. Discussing the playing of the organist C. G. Schröter, Gerber writes: "whoever knows the superb legato manner [vortreffliche gebundene Manier] with which Bach treated the organ, cannot possibly like Schröter's way of playing in constant staccato fashion [durchaus staccato traktirte]" (quoted by Lohmann, *Studien zu Artikulationsproblemen*, 271).

Justin Heinrich Knecht, speaking in 1795 of the "natural sustained singing tone" of the organ, favors the legato as the basic touch and suggests that one lets the fingers "creep" (schleichen lassen) from one tone to the next so that the ear cannot perceive the slightest detachment of the tones (*Vollständige Orgelschule*, 1:53–54).

Georg Friedrich Wolf, in his clavier tract of 1789, asks, in the sense of Pasquali, for notes to be held for the exact duration of their value with the exception of special circumstances. They must not, he says, be held any longer, which, like a too-short rendition, would hinder good performance. He wants a legato as basic touch, not a superlegato, and detachment apparently only when especially called for (*Kurzer Unterricht*, 21).

J. F. Reichardt sees a particular technique as the premier means for furthering songfulness on the keyboard; this technique consists of holding down the key of the first note and thus preserving the sound until the next key is depressed. Mixing the sounds of the two pitches in this way, he says, emulates the effect that the singer achieves with the breath and the string player with the bow (cited by Lohmann, *Studien zu Artikulationsproblemen*, 250).

Hüllmandel, a student of C. P. E. Bach, writing in 1796 from England, considers one of the most essential rules to be holding down a key until the next is struck, except for an intended staccato (*Principles of Music*, 20).

Similarly, Milchmeyer in 1797 asks for the key to remain depressed until the end of its assigned value to avoid dryness of sound (*Die wahre Art*, 65).

Clementi, in his pianoforte tract of 1801, writes: "When the composer leaves the LEGATO, and STACCATO to the performer's taste; the best rule is, to adhere chiefly to the LEGATO; reserving the STACCATO to give SPIRIT occasionally to certain passages, and to set off the HIGHER BEAUTIES of the LEGATO" (*Introduction*, 9).

Legato on the keyboard was an omnipresence, dating presumably from the origins of the medium, and we have it documented by Diruta from the late 16th century. Also, fast passages are hardly playable other than with legato touch. Since such fast passages are mostly of ornamental nature, the legato naturally fits their ornamental character. The preference for legato over detachment (or vice versa) varied with individual tastes, fashions, media, and eras. The coming and going of such fashions is exemplified by the preference of Couperin and Rameau for the legato, by that of their successors—as will be shown in the next chapter—for detachment. With all due regard to individual differences, it can be said that a preference for the legato, evidenced by quotations from important masters, intensified in the latter part of the 18th century and lasted well into the 19th. We see this trend in the treatises and in reports about performers. Beethoven's intense partiality to the legato, visible in his scores by his lavish pedaling indications and his many long slurs, has been reported by many earwitnesses, notably by Czerny (see on this Newman, *Beethoven on Beethoven*, 78–79 and *passim;* Rosenblum, *Performance Practices,* 152). Beethoven's often-quoted, incomprehensibly disparaging remark about Mozart's "choppy" playing must not be taken at face value. Mozart used the legato frequently of course, as attested to by the many and often lengthy slur marks in his piano music. His great expressiveness was praised by many earwitnesses. After Mozart's famous competition with Clementi before the emperor Joseph in 1781 (when Mozart was twenty-five years old), Clementi wrote, "Until then I had never heard anyone perform with such spirit and grace. I was particularly astonished by an Adagio and some of his extemporized variations" (quoted in Plantinga, *Clementi,* 65). A "choppy" playing style would have hardly elicited such eulogy from a rival pianist-composer!

*Superlegato.* Another type of legato is idiomatic to the keyboard and could be called a "superlegato" when the successive tones overlap in a pedal effect. Troeger calls it "overlegato" (*Technique and Interpretation,* 85), Rosenblum "legatissimo" (*Performance Practices,* 152–53). Such an effect, occasionally the involuntary result of overlive acoustics, can be produced by holding a key down beyond the time that the next is touched. Safe to use when the melody circumscribes a chord, it can cause problems in other sequences, unless the time of overlap is brief.

In its basic form, it is frequently written out in notation, the classic case being the first prelude of *WTC I,* which consists of a series of arpeggiated chords, for which the held-over pedal effect is specified for the first and second notes.

Such sustaining in pedal fashion was often practiced, without being specified in notation, at the simple bidding of a slur mark. Saint Lambert, under the heading "Liaison," explains that the keys of notes under a slur should be held down up to the last note, then lifted simultaneously. His illustration, given in Ex. 16.2, shows a melody that moves within the G-major chord. By way of contrast, for a stepwise moving sequence (for which he gives an illustration), only the first and last notes are to be held (*Principes du clavecin,* 13). At the end of the book (62) he shows in an example how the simple slur mark, with its implied pedal

EXAMPLE 16.2.   Saint Lambert (1702)

effect, ought to replace the elaborate specification of held-out notes and corresponding rests in order to simplify notation and execution.

Ninety years later, in Germany, Türk reports on the custom of holding notes under a slur that break a chord in arpeggio fashion until the harmony changes. He advises, in contrast to Saint Lambert, not relying on such custom where holding out is intended but playing safe in specifying the desired length of the notes and pertaining rests (*Klavierschule*, chap. 6, sec. 3, par. 38).

Couperin frequently uses the symbol of a straight line that connects one note head to another: ♩——♩ (once in a long while it is written above rather than between the note heads). He nowhere explains this symbol, whose exact meaning is not entirely clear. In most cases it presumably stands for a superlegato of some overlapping, as for instance in Ex. 16.3a, from "Le rossignol en amour" (*Troisième livre de piéces*, ordre 14). This meaning is in most instances both possible and musically warranted. There are, however, several instances where this interpretation *appears* questionable because the notation would be redundant. Thus, in what may be the first occurrence of the symbol in "Les sylvains" from the Premier ordre, the superlegato is spelled out, as shown in Ex. 16.3b. For similar cases see "Les juméles" (ordre 12) or "Les tours de passe-passe" (ordre 22). Such redundancies do not necessarily invalidate the superlegato meaning: Couperin's notation contains frequent cases of capriciousness, such as extra beams not warranted by the meter (see on this my *Essays 1982*, 92–93, 131), and we must expect to find in it neither consistency nor strict logic.

EXAMPLE 16.3.   Couperin

a. "Le rossignol en amour"

b. "Les sylvains"

Also, the superlegato meaning is explicitly confirmed by other masters. Charles Dornel, for instance, in his *Pièces de clavecin* of 1731, explains the meaning of the dash symbols (above the notes), as given in
Ex. 16.4a, and writes that he uses these signs in order to simplify the
notation while preserving the harmony ("Pour la facilité de la tablature
et la Conservation de l'harmonie" [33]). Pierre Claude Foucquet, in his
"Méthode," published as preface to *Les caractères de la paix* of ca. 1749,
explains the dashes as partial overlapping, as shown in Ex. 16.4b.

EXAMPLE 16.4

a. Dornel (1731)

b. Foucquet (1749)

## Symbols and Their Implications

Lacking verbal clues, we are dependent for firm guidance on notational
signs. These signs, however, were late in emerging and slow in gaining
acceptance. The first symbol to appear, around 1600, was the arc-shaped
design for the tie and shortly thereafter for the slur. Praetorius writes in
1619 that he shares the opinion of Lippius (1585–1612), Hassler (1564–
1612), "and others" that one should abolish all complicated ligatures
and use in their place the sign ⌣ (*Syntagma musicum*, 3:29).[1] To indicate
legato linkage, the arc-shaped symbol was a logical choice for its graphic
suggestiveness, as was the square bracket, used by some composers.

The meaning of the symbol extended beyond legato articulation.
Between notes of the same pitch it could either mean a tie (i.e., an
uninterrupted addition of the denominations involved—in which meaning it served from the early 17th century to the present) or a tone repetition with only very gentle interruptions. This latter meaning is clear in
Ex. 16.5, from Johann Rudolf Ahle. He divides the notes into *simplices*
and *ligatas seu conjunctas*. Speaking of violin pieces, notes under the arc
symbol, he says, are to be slurred or taken in the same bowstroke (the
latter clearly referring to notes on the same pitch; *Kurze Anleitung* [1690],
10–11).

Bach used this instrumental design of a slur over repeated notes
frequently. For some examples from just the Mass in B Minor, see the

EXAMPLE 16.5.   J. R. Ahle

Crucifixus (throughout), Et incarnatus est (almost throughout), Et re-surrexit (mm. 10–13, 28–31, and parallel spots), and Cum sancto spiritu (mm. 25–30). Mozart and Haydn did not use the symbol in this mean-ing, but Beethoven did. The meaning of gentle separation is certain in the penultimate measure of the "Dankgesang" of the String Quartet in A Minor (Ex. 16.6) and possible throughout the first part of the "Grosse Fuge" for the countersubject (as introduced in mm. 26–30) and in similar occurrences in his late piano sonatas, as, for instance in the adagio of Op. 110. The meaning of these tie/slurs is controversial, however. William S. Newman believes they are essentially slurs but that they are to be performed with ever-so-subtle renewed articulation as an "audi-ble, but barely audible release" (*Beethoven on Beethoven*, 297). Newman quotes other authorities, among them Czerny, and Tovey in favor of audibility; Paul Badura-Skoda insists on a plain tie effect ("A Tie Is a Tie"). This manner may hark back to the *Bebung* effect of the clavichord, but whether or not this is the case is also a matter of controversy.[2] The tremolando meaning of slurs linking notes of the same pitch and value in vocal music has been mentioned in the previous chapter.

EXAMPLE 16.6.   Beethoven, String Quartet in A Minor, Op. 132/3

(Molto adagio)

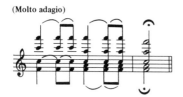

Far more important for articulation is the legato meaning of a slur that links notes of different pitches. In vocal music, a legato was gen-erally understood, without having to be specified, when the same syl-lable was set to two or more pitches. The need for the symbol was felt mainly when the text–music link was ambiguous and needed to be clarified. Such was very typically the case with anticipated *Vorschläge* or related ornaments—a ubiquitous design of the 17th century. Thus when Monteverdi writes as in Exx. 16.7a and 16.7b, he wanted to avoid the (simpler) substitution of 16.7c for 16.7a and Ex. 16.7d for 16.7b. Apart from such circumstances, slur symbols were rare in the vocal music of that era.

EXAMPLE 16.7.   Monteverdi, *Poppea*

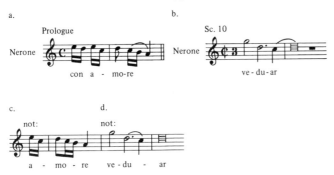

Among instruments (as mentioned above), strings seem to have been the first to adopt the slur as legato symbol. They were followed soon by the winds. By way of contrast, the keyboard instruments were much slower to do so, and here the tendency to trust the performer with the appropriate decisions persisted until Bach and beyond.

One of the reasons, perhaps the principal one, for the paucity of slur marks in keyboard music is the close link of the legato symbol with bowing and, for winds, with breathing. The earliest slur marks linked only a few notes, most frequently two, and rarely more than four or five. Gradually the range extended, but up to Haydn and Mozart a slur mark, even for the keyboard, hardly ever exceeded the limits of what can be comfortably played by a string player with one bowstroke, by a wind player with one breath. For all media, slurs often stopped with the barlines—though with Bach, for instance, we find many cases where in deference to the logic of phrasing the slur marks cross the barlines. But in the many instances where this is not the case, we meet an interpretive problem when two or more measure-length slurs follow one another. The question then arises whether each slur encompasses a musical entity by itself, as a unit of phrasing, or is simply a concession to the medium's limitations. If the slurs represent units of phrasing, then they should be distinctly separated by shortening the last note under the slur. If, on the other hand, they are technical concessions, then the seam should be deemphasized.

In dances, or in pieces inspired by the dance, the barline will usually signify a distinct accentuation, hence call for a clear separation of two slurred passages that meet at this point. The same will generally apply to music in the galant and Classical styles whenever a downbeat phrasing coincides with the metrical accent. In all these cases the slur implies a shortening of the last note.

Matters are different wherever the linear drive, so prominent in much Baroque music, carries its élan across barlines, impervious to the gravitational pull of the downbeat. The barline then ceases to be a metrical landmark and reverts to its earlier role as a simple means of measuring time units. For Bach we find such situations in many works of rich polyphonic texture, notably fugues, but also in keyboard music of a rhapsodic nature, such as toccatas or preludes. Thus, for instance, the first fourteen measures of the famous Toccata in C Major for Organ (BWV 564) have barlines, but they are there only to be seen for orientation, not to be heard. A legato articulation is implied, indeed necessitated, by the rapidity of the passages in thirty-second notes. The same is true of the Toccata in F-Sharp Minor for Harpsichord (BWV 910) and many other related works.

## The Accentual Principle for Slurs

Short slurs, those linking only a few notes, from two to perhaps six—to a number, at any rate, that can be comfortably accommodated in one bowstroke or breath—can also offer problems. Leopold Mozart formulated a principle that the first note under a slur should be slightly emphasized and lengthened (*Versuch einer Violinschule*, chap. 7, par. 20; chap. 12, par. 10). For the clavichord, C. P. E. Bach concurs by writing that the first note under a slur is to receive a small accent ("einen kleinen Druck"), whereas on the harpsichord, which does not allow accentuation, as well as on the clavichord, figures like ♩♩ are to be played ♩♩ (*Versuch über Art das Clavier* [1753], chap. 3, pars. 18, 21).

Türk agrees with the accentuation of the first note under a slur and points out that such emphasis is independent of the metrical placement, hence can fall on a "bad" as well as a "good" note (i.e., off as well as on a beat). He stresses the very gentle, "hardly noticeable" character of such accent ("sehr gelinde, kaum merklich" *Klavierschule*, chap. 6, sec. 3, par. 38).

If applied with discrimination, this principle will often make good sense, but to turn it into a universal law, as is often done, is dangerous. Its retrospective application to Bach is particularly questionable. We need only look at the numerous instances in which Bach's slurs for violins or woodwinds are at odds with the vocal articulation of the same melody as suggested by diction. Thus, for instance, in Ex. 16.8a, from Cantata No. 84, we find the melody articulated for oboes and violins throughout with downbeat slurs, whereas the vocal line is consistently articulated—and phrased—on the upbeats. In Ex. 16.8b we see this contrast in simultaneity resulting in a clash of articulation that is harmless and attractive, when the slurs follow one another without distinct accents. But where such accents are made according to Leopold Mozart's principle, the contrast in phrasing would be confusing in succession and

EXAMPLE 16.8.   Bach, Cantata No. 84

outright disturbing in simultaneity. Similar contrasts between instruments and voice are frequent in Bach. (See, for instance, in the last chorus of the St. Matthew Passion, the consistently repeated divergencies of mm. 18–19 or 22–23.)

When Bach writes for strings, the disposition of slurs is invariably geared to the idiomatic needs of comfortable bowing, with a strong tendency toward starting measures on the downbow (still following, so it seems, the Lullian downbow principle for strong beats). With few exceptions and minor adaptations, Bach's violin, cello, and gamba works will be found to be ideally bowed as written. We find a good illustration in the tenor aria of Cantata No. 107, where the first violins are throughout provided with slurs different from the unison flutes in a way ideally suited to the bowing demands (see Ex. 16.9). Here we see clearly that it would be wrong to apply the galant principle of accentuation since a clash of articulation between flutes and violins could hardly have been intended. For another illustration, see the slurs for oboe and violins respectively in the chorus movement of Cantata No. 31, in the allegro section following the adagio interlude.

EXAMPLE 16.9.   Bach, Cantata No. 107/6

In his vocal works such divergencies may be on occasion due to the fact that Bach often entered articulation marks when he either wrote or edited the performance parts without being concerned about coordinating such, to his mind, apparently minor details. But there are countless other illustrations of Bach's limited concern with the disposition of slurs, illustrations for which such mechanical explanation is not available. See, for instance, the slow movement of the Fifth "Brandenburg" Concerto, where the recurring motive in harpsichord, flute, and violin is indiscriminately marked ♪ 𝄢 𝄢𝄢 or ♪ 𝄢 𝄢𝄢 without any apparent cause for the differences. It seems reasonable to conclude that for Bach, and presumably for other masters of his stylistic affinity, it will be wise to be discreet about the treatment of slurs: for strings the sense of separation conveyed by bow change, for winds that of a soft tonguing, and for keyboards the equivalents of these techniques should generally be the first choices, and greater emphasis should be given only where the specifics of the context, such as the need for melodic, harmonic, or (on organ or harpsichord) rhythmic clarification, seem to call for it.

---

## Possible Applications

There are occasions in Mozart and Haydn where the accentual rule can be applied to advantage. For a few illustrations, see Ex. 16.10a, from Mozart's String Quartet in G, where subtle accents on the upbeats will add rhythmic piquancy and plasticity to the theme. The same might be advisable for Ex. 16.10b, the theme of the last movement of the Piano Concerto in C Minor, or Ex. 16.10c, the start of the "Hoffmeister" String Quartet.

A case where such upbeat accentuation seems almost provable is given in Ex. 16.10d from the minuet of the String Quintet in D Major. First, there is the written-out accentuation on the upbeats in measures 4 and 5 in phrases derived from measure 3; then, in measure 24, as shown in Ex. 16.10e, the theme in the first violin is followed at one beat's distance by a canon in the viola, where the upbeats have become downbeats. To give the canon its due, the two parts have to be articulated the same way, hence the slight metrical downbeat stress of the viola has to have its counterpart in a slight upbeat stress of the violin.

Mozart was fond of such upbeat accentuation and often specifies it with a *fp* or *sf*, as for instance in Ex. 16.11a, from the Violin Sonata in B Flat, or in Ex. 16.11b, from the Piano Sonata in the same key. This, of course, does not prove the case for the mild emphases suggested in the preceding paragraph, but it does show that such rhythmic-metric irregularity was stylistically not incongruous.

EXAMPLE 16.10.   Mozart

a. String Quartet in G, K 387/4

b. Piano Concerto in C Minor, K 491/3

c. "Hoffmeister" String Quartet, K 499/1

d. String Quintet in D Major, K 593/3

e. String Quintet in D Major, K 593/3

EXAMPLE 16.11.   Mozart

a. Violin Sonata in B Flat, K 454/1

b. Piano Sonata in B Flat, K 189 f(281)

Whenever such emphases are applied in connection with bow changes, the motto has to be great subtlety. Any obtrusiveness or, still worse, any tendency to let the principle degenerate into a mechanical mannerism wold be musically regrettable. Frequently, a bow change must not be emphasized at all but should be as unnoticeable as skill permits. Leopold Mozart, whose authority is always invoked for the slur–emphasis link, himself warns against the interruption of a melody unless required by phrasing or special expression (*Versuch einer Violinschule,* chap. 5, par. 14). As mentioned earlier in this chapter, he favors as a principle the legato mode in emulation of the voice that "spontaneously flows from one pitch into another." Where, he continues, the nature of the melody does not call for a break in continuity, "one should not only keep the bow on the string and *when changing the stroke connect one tone smoothly with the next* but also try to fit many notes into the same bow stroke [emphasis added]."

It would be better if accentuation were not applied when a slur starts a pure introductory upbeat figure that leads to a heavy downbeat, as for instance in Ex. 16.12a, the start of the solo of Mozart's Piano Concerto in D Minor, or in Ex. 16.12b, the start of the finale of the "Great" G-minor Symphony; nor does it seem fitting when it leads to a written or implied *crescendo,* be it ever so mild, as in Ex. 16.12c, from the minuet of the String Quartet in C ("dissonance").

EXAMPLE 16.12.   Mozart

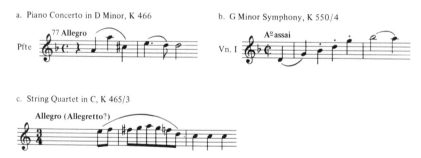

a. Piano Concerto in D Minor, K 466

b. G Minor Symphony, K 550/4

c. String Quartet in C, K 465/3

Because it can be difficult to differentiate Leopold Mozart's principle of emphasis from the stress due a metrical accent or an appoggiatura, the application of the principle will probably appear in its purest form when the slurs start off rather than on the beat, as in the cases shown above. A slight lengthening of the first note under a slur (i.e., an agogic accent in addition to the dynamic one) will generally be appropriate only in soloistic situations and more fitting in slow rather than in fast movements. For an illustration, see Ex. 16.13a, from the slow movement of the String Quintet in C, where the first four sixteenth notes are not an

EXAMPLE 16.13.   Mozart, String Quintet in C, K 515

anacrusic figure, in spite of their placement before the barline, but are integral to the melody; hence the first note C could be subtly length-ened—a freedom that should not be repeated when the figure returns two measures later. In the first movement of the same work (Ex. 16.13b), the first eighth note in measure 32 could be ever so slightly emphasized. Here as anywhere else, artistic instinct must have the final word in all such matters.

# 17

# INSTRUMENTAL
# DETACHMENT

The essence of detachment is the separation of two pitches by a break in sound. The nature of such detachment will depend mainly on the length of the break and on the way the first pitch is ended and the second started; whether the first is ended gently or brusquely and whether the second starts with or without an accent.

One of the earliest known descriptions of such detachment deals with the brusque category and comes from Mace in his lute tract from 1676. He treats the detachment as a grace and calls it onomatopoetically "Tut." It is done "in such a manner, as it will seem to cry *Tut;* and is very *Pretty,* and *Easily done. Thus.*" You pluck the tone that is to be detached and immediately "clap on your next striking Finger, upon the String which you struck; in which doing, you suddenly take away the Sound of the Letter, which is that, we call the *Tut*" (*Musick's Monument,* 109).

## Detachment on Strings

For strings (including the viol family), detachment can be achieved either with a bow change or by repeated articulations within the same bow stroke. With a bow change, detachment can run the gamut from gentle and barely noticeable to abrupt and energetic. Almost the same range of expression is available for detachment within the same bow-stroke.

*Change of Bow on the String.* A unique and very important kind of detachment is native to the strings alone. It is the separation that results simply from the change of the bowstroke without an attempt at interruption. With some technical skill in a sustained stroke, the sound of the change can be minimized but not eliminated. For that reason it probably deserves to be classed among detachments.

The same applies more definitely to another, frequent type of uninterrupted detachment by bow change (usually referred to, then as now, by the French term *détaché*) in which short and fast strokes follow one another while the pressure remains constant. Its most characteristic use is for a sequence of notes of the same denomination, such as ♩♩♩♩ ♩♩♩♩ . The separation between the individual tones is made audible by a slight noise somewhat reminiscent of a consonant between vowels. Its origin resides in the fact that the string, as activated by the bow—any bow of any period—does not vibrate vertically but obliquely, leaning toward the direction of the bow's pull. By changing the bowstroke from up to down, the string is forced from one vibrating pattern to the opposite one.[1] The noise, but not the sound, of separation can be nearly eliminated when the pressure is released for each bow change. In a fairly fast sequence of notes, the result will be one of a series of swells and tapers, resulting in a portato-like articulation: ♩♩♩♩ .

In the progression from gentle to abrupt detachment, the next type calls for a somewhat slower tempo and results from slightly accentuating each note by either a speedier start followed by a slowing down, or a quick vertical pressure impulse on the bow for the start of the pitch, or a combination of the two.

The sharpest detachment, while keeping the bow on the string, is produced by the sequence pressure–release–pressure. The first pressure produces a sharp consonant-like articulation; the release at the moment of moving the bow is needed to prevent the sound from being crushed, and the second pressure stops the sound abruptly with another consonant-like noise, like Mace's "Tut." This is perhaps the only one among on-the-string types of detachment that deserves the term *staccato* (in the early 18th century also spelled *stoccato*). It has the modern term of *martelé* (i.e., the hammered stroke) and is often believed to be practicable only on the modern bow. This is at best a half-truth. The Tourte-type bow (François Tourte was the master who around 1780 created the modern bow) can produce this type of staccato by and large with a sharper "bite" and can do it well in all parts of the bow; the pre-Tourte bow can do it almost as well in the lower and middle part of the bow but less effectively near the point.

**Leopold Mozart on the Change of Bow.** In connection with the change of bow there is a passage by Leopold Mozart that has given rise to questionable theories about contemporary articulation. Because these theories have been widely accepted, it is necessary to take a closer look. Mozart writes: "Every tone, even the strongest one, is preceded by a small, hardly noticeable softness: else it would not be a tone but a disagreeable and unintelligible sound. The same softness occurs at the end of the tone" (*Versuch einer Violinschule,* chap. 5, par. 3). The passage has been misinterpreted by some as proclaiming a definite crescendo and decrescendo effect (a *messa di voce*) as characteristic of the basic bowstroke of the age—or even the century. David Boyden associates the passage with what he calls the "Corelli-Tartini model" bow, whose "yielding bowhair" requires a small "take-up" or "give" before the tone emerges. Boyden credits the "yielding hair" together with the light head of the bow for a "brilliantly clear articulation of individual notes" ("Violin Bow," 203). This, however, seems to involve a contradiction since clear articulation calls for a crisp start of each note and not for the kind of loose "take-up" allegedly associated with those bows.

What Leopold describes in that paragraph deals neither with the playing qualities of certain bows in use at the time nor with a historically based articulation. What he does write about is a highly perceptive analysis of how to change the bow with minimal conspicuousness by near-elimination of the noise factor. The principle is timeless, as valid today with the finest modern bows as it was then. Since, as explained above, the strings vibrate obliquely in the direction of the bowstroke, the only way to change the vibrations from one oblique angle to the other with a minimum of conspicuousness is by releasing the pressure on the string for a tiny stretch of the bow while easing it into the opposite direction. Without this slight softness, the change of a sustained bow-stroke, most especially in forte, is bound to produce the kind of scratching sound that Mozart refers to as disagreeable and unintelligible noise.

That this is what he had in mind is confirmed in Chapter 5, Paragraph 10. There he writes that by the bow change the string is forced from the original vibration into a new one ("aus der vorigen Erzitterung in eine neue . . . gesetzet wird"), "hence it is necessary to start each bowing gently with a certain moderation, in such a manner that even the strongest bowstroke can coax the already vibrating string unnoticeably from the actual into the opposite direction. This is what I understood to be the softness I had mentioned in the previous par. 3."[2] No modern violin school has, to my knowledge, matched Leopold Mozart's penetrating analysis of a smooth bow change, regardless of what kind of bow or violin is being used. It follows that Mozart's analysis of this point cannot be used as the basis for a theory of historical articulation, least of all one that involves a *messa di voce* on every sustained note, since it deals simply with a matter of technical execution still valid today. The pervasive use of *messa di voce* by several early music specialists seems to have its origin in this misinterpreted Mozart passage, since I am not aware of any other historical source—with the exception of the trumpet school of Fantini of 1638 (see p. 00)—that would seem to encourage such *routine* practice in instrumental music. What we do find are scattered references to the occasional use of the *messa di voce*. We must supplement these Mozart quotations with the one cited in the previous chapter in which he extols the beauties of the legato and of the smooth, barely perceptible bow change.

*Bow Change and the Nature of the Old Bow.* Boyden's reference to the yielding hair in support of the *messa di voce* is not convincing either. Even today, it is impossible to generalize about the qualities of the modern bow, though at least its shape and, more or less its weight, are standardized. But there are such enormous differences in quality of wood and workmanship that some bows with a soft stick will have yielding hair, others will be hard and stiff. It is far harder still to generalize about the "Baroque" or "pre-Classical" pre-Tourte bow of Mozart's time. Neither length nor weight nor curvature were standardized: most were convex (as viewed from above, hence arched outward), but some were concave. French bows were generally shorter, Italian ones longer, but there were exceptions even here.

Professor Steven Hefling, who has extensively experimented with old bows, writes in a personal communication that among the few generalizations that can be made for nearly all old bows is that "the tip end seems lighter and the frog end heavier than with a good modern stick." Also, the nature of the stick's curvature—"either straight or bowed slightly convex [curving out] when the hair is tightened—tends to make a kind of gentle *sautillé* [a slightly bouncing] stroke happen quite readily in the middle of the bow." This type of bowing occurs with such spontaneity that "this semi-*sautillé* characteristic of old bows is, in my opinion, responsible for much of the articulate clarity that people talk about." Thus, though certain bowings and articulations come more, others less easily, on the old than on the new bow, as Professor Hefling also points out, in the last analysis everything depends far more on the player than on the equipment.

It would seem that on the grounds of the bow's nature alone, it is not possible to arrive at a principle of a basic detached articulation, let alone of an unremitting *messa di voce* for the Baroque or the early Classical era, as practiced by several specialists in this field. Stylistic considerations and national, regional, and personal preferences will have played a larger role. Thus we hear that the French preferred a "short and [sharply] articulated bowstroke" (kurtzer und articulirter Bogenstrich), and the Italians a "long and dragging stroke" (langer und schleppender Strich; Quantz, *Versuch einer Anweisung*, chap. 17, sec. 2, par. 26). These matters were dictated by style, not by the nature of the bows: the French emphasized the dance with its incisive rhythms, the Italians reveled in songfulness and the beauty of vocal melody. These differences did not derive from the respective nature of the bows. Rather, the bows were built in a manner that favored the preferred style.

A fascinating document reveals that the Italian predilection for the sustained, singing bowstroke goes back at least to the early 17th century. Heinrich Schütz, speaking in the preface to his Symphoniae Sacrae Book 2 (1643) of "modern," meaning Italian, music, extols the "steady, sustained musical bowstroke on the violin" (der stäte ausgedehnte musicalische Strich auff dem Violin), which, he says, is neither known nor practiced in Germany. Schütz therefore recommends instruction from a knowledgeable teacher and private practice before performing his Symphoniae.

As always, generalizations are dangerous. Depending on the character of a piece, Frenchmen must have used a connective style for songful works, just as Italians must have used sharp articulations in their proper places. We have a revealing Italian document about such staccato playing in a fast sequence of notes in a famous letter by Tartini to Signora Maddalena Lombardini.[3] In it Tartini passes along instructions on many things, but in particular he advises his student-friend to practice the three Corelli Allegros in perpetual motion style from Op. 5. He illustrates the start of the first one in D, and advises her to play the notes staccato—that is, clearly detached ("con l'arco distaccato, cioè granite") with space between them.

*Detachment in a Continuous Stroke.* Several kinds of detachments are possible within a single bowstroke that does not leave the string. The gentlest one is a hybrid whose nature is between legato and detachment, leaning more to the former than the latter. It is done by drawing the bow without interruption while emphasizing individual pitches with a wave-like series of mild pressures and releases that make each pitch stand out in a *portato* manner (the detachment factor) yet connect them in a continuous sound (the legato factor): ᴡᴡᴡ .

When instead of producing an uninterrupted stroke one stops the bow for each pitch, one achieves a clear detachment that can range from fairly mild to the very sharp "Tut" quality of the "hammered" stroke. Interestingly, this kind of hard and energetic staccato can be done at much faster speeds on a single stroke than the one with alternating bowstrokes (described above).

*Detachment by Bouncing the Bow.* Another type of detachment is native to the strings and in general more congenial to the violin than to the viol family because of the latter's underhanded bow grip. It consists of bouncing the bow: playing "*off* the string" rather than "*on* the string." At moderate speeds the bow is purposefully thrown on the string, whence it rebounds. It is then repeated in the opposite direction. In speeds too fast for individual impulses it is the elasticity of the stick that makes the bow bounce in the manner mentioned above in Professor Hefling's letter. The character of detachment can range from mild to sharp. The famous 19th-century violinist Joseph Joachim ingeniously characterized the different types of bounced detachment as "snow, rain, and hail." "Hail" is more effectively produced with a modern bow, but in a less extreme form it is feasible on a good old one too.

Bouncing detachment is feasible also with a continuous bowstroke in a manner now called a "flying staccato." It was practiced and described in the 17th century, as will be presently documented.

## Detachment on Wind Instruments

For wind instruments, the counterpart to string articulation through bowing is what is called "tonguing." Sylvestro Ganassi, in his recorder treatise of 1535, expounds a highly refined and sophisticated theory of articulation (see chap. 16). Beginning with three basic ways of starting a note—hard, with "teche [te-ke], teche, teche"; medium, "tere, tere, tere"; and soft, "lere, lere, lere"—he points to limitless variations in combinations of vowels and consonants and discusses the various ways of tonguing: breaking the breath with the throat or tongue or, in what must be a perfect legato, forming the breath with the lips and letting it "flow through them" (*Opera intitulata Fontegara*, chaps. 5–8, n.p.).

Over a century and a half later, Jacques Hotteterre ("le Romain"), in his 1707 treatise on the transverse flute, explains the use of the syllables "tu" and "ru" as the two "articulations principales" (*Principes de la flûte*, chap. 8). Of these two, which are often intermingled, the "tu" is the more important: being harder, it tends to fall on the beat, while the softer "ru" falls generally on the unstressed note. Among Hotteterre's examples are sequences of eighth notes that use "tu" exclusively, but none that use only "ru." Hotteterre gives a number of illustrations that show the use of these syllables with their regularities and exceptions.

In 1752 Quantz devotes Chapter 6 in his *Versuch* to the use of the tongue on the flute for separating sounds. One does so, he writes, with the use of several very short syllables. First there is "ti" or "di," then "tiri," which is, of course, not one syllable but a compound of two that are often used individually, often mixed, depending on the rhythm patterns, such as "ti, ti, ri, ti, ti, ti, ri," and so on. Finally, there is "didd'l," the "double tongue" used for fast sequences but also often interspersed, especially on leaps, with "ti" and "di." Quantz's rules are rather complicated, but the use of the syllables is well illustrated by many examples in Tables 3 and 4. (In Edward Reilly's translation the examples are inserted in the text.) In an Appendix to Chapter 6, Quantz explains the use of these syllables for oboe and bassoon and the necessary adjustments for the different embouchures.

In 1791 Johann Georg Tromlitz presents a very detailed discussion of flute articulation, using Quantz's syllables with slight modifications: "ta," "da," "tara," and "dadd'l" (*Ausführlicher Unterricht*, 154–237). By this substitution Tromlitz hopes to achieve a "fuller, rounder, and brighter tone" (158).

Techniques for detachment vary from one wind instrument to another, but they have one technique in common: the breath may be stopped suddenly from the diaphragm after a quick expulsion of air, as in "hu, hu, hu." Occasionally the stopping is done with the lip, which can be very clean, but this method gives a consonant-like brusque ending that may or may not be desirable.

## Detachment on the Keyboard

The possibilities for keyboard detachment are rather limited when compared to melody instruments, especially strings.

On the organ there is only one method of detachment, that of lifting the finger from the key. One can play staccato by depressing the key only very briefly; one can separate held notes by any kind of rest, from long to very short. But what is paramount for the organ, more than for any other instrument, is the prevailing acoustics. Many large churches have extremely resonant, echo-like acoustics, and if one were to play in such places with legato technique, the result would be a blur. A measure of detachment that has to be adjusted to the circumstances will then be necessary to achieve a clean legato effect. And where a small detachment is desired, a commensurately larger one will have to be played. By way of contrast, in a dry acoustical environment, frequent detachment can endanger the coherence of phrases. One needs to distinguish "finger detachment" from "ear detachment" and invariably defer to the ear.

The clavichord has a very small sound but has the precious ability for dynamic shading. The sound is so small that the instrument has no damping mechanism; as a result, the tone practically stops the moment the finger is lifted from the key. A staccato is effective, and so can relatively small detachments, while larger ones have to be used with great caution lest they disrupt the continuity.

The harpsichord has a brilliant and, compared to the clavichord, a large sound. It has a damping mechanism that stops the sound as soon as the finger is lifted from the key, hence it can command detachments from a short staccato to longer interruptions. It has no ability for dynamic shadings, hence no means of intensifying detachment by accents.

The pianoforte, like its descendent, the modern piano, has both a damping mechanism and a damper-lifting one. Its sound is smaller and decays faster than that of the modern piano. With dampers down, detachment is again nearly instantaneous with the lifting of the finger.

In much of the German and Italian keyboard music before 1750, composers wrote few articulation marks, while the French, and notably Couperin, used many more slurs as well as staccato (*aspiration*) marks. Absence of articulation marks either means that the composer delegated choice to the performer or indicates the neutral mode, which at the time meant an ever-so-short detachment.

Delegation generally implies that articulation was not of the musical essence. As mentioned, such delegation was much more common for the keyboard than for melody instruments, and even on the keyboard it became less common with the advent of the galant style. When we find neither slur marks nor staccato marks in page after page in a series of pieces or movements, we can assume that not all was intended to be done monotonously with short detachment and that slurs were meant to be added judiciously. When, on the other hand, the composer seems to have been explicit in his markings, then we are on firmer ground in interpreting a lack of marks as a sign of nonlegato intention.

That this mode was often understood can be inferred after the middle of the 18th century from the use of the mark *ten.* (*tenuto*) over notes that should be held out for their full, or nearly full, value, implying that notes not so marked were meant to be clipped at the end. We also have some theoretical confirmation.

Santa Maria, speaking in 1565 of the clavichord, seems to call for a small separation. For the sake of playing clearly and nobly ("con limpieça y distinction"), he asks that one should lift a finger before the next one descends to avoid getting the fingers entangled, which would result in impurities of sound (*Arte de tañer*, fol. 36v). Reidemeister speculates that this ruling has to do with the fretting of the strings, a mechanical feature that was common for older clavichords whereby each string produced several—up to four—pitches activated by the tangents and complicated legato playing (*Alte Musik*, 72–73; see also Troeger, *Technique and Interpretation*, 11–12). Thus it may well be that Santa Maria's ruling was based on technical considerations rather than on an aesthetic preference for detachment.

Heinichen, speaking in 1728 of thorough bass accompaniment, calls for detachment for the sake of its brilliant effect ("grosse Brilliant"); all passages should be played "clearly and distinctly without slurring" (ohne schleiffigtes Wesen [*Generalbass*, 552]). Accompaniment often favored a greater measure of detachment than soloistic playing. We find on this matter a number of historical quotes. Among them is Rellstab (1789) who in an adagio asks for quarter and longer notes to be held for their full value, then adds that in accompaniment they are to be held for only half of their value (*Über die Bemerkungen*, xii). Similarly, Knecht, whose legato preference for organ melodies was quoted before, says that accompaniment is mostly done with short detached notes (*Vollständige Orgelschule* 1:75). Even for solo harpsichord playing Richard Troeger makes in this connection an interesting comment by pointing out that a somewhat detached accompaniment of a melody is often useful in balancing sonorities when the middle and low ranges of the instrument tend to overwhelm the treble (*Technique and Interpretation,* 78).

Hartong (first name unknown, publishing under the pseudonym of P. C. Humanus) writes in 1749 that one should lift a finger before dropping the next one (*Musicus theoretico-practicus,* 8). Hartong's tract is mentioned several times by Adlung and praised by him (*Anleitung,* especially 246, n. k).

C. P. E. Bach writes in 1753 that "some people play stickily [klebericht], as if they had glue between the fingers. Their touch is too long in holding the notes beyond their values. Others want to do better and play too short, as if the keys were on fire; that too is bad. The middle way is the best. . . . All sorts of touch are good in their proper time" (*Versuch über Art das Clavier* [1753], chap. 3, par. 6).

Later in the chapter Bach writes that notes such as eighths, and quarter notes in moderate or slow tempo, that are neither slurred nor staccato nor marked *ten.* should be held for half their value. This is in contrast to notes marked with dots or strokes that are to be held less than half their value regardless of tempo or dynamics (chap. 3, pars. 17, 22).

Marpurg, who came under the influence of C. P. E. Bach, sees the standard touch on the keyboard ("das ordentliche Fortgehen") in a technique that inserts a minuscule rest between notes by lifting one finger very quickly from the key before touching with the next (*Anleitung zum Clavierspielen,* 29). The resulting articulation is what Richard Troeger calls a "structured legato" (*Technique and Interpretation,* 66–67). This, Marpurg writes, is the touch to be used generally whenever there are no articulation marks prescribed. A slur mark calls for a full legato, dots or vertical strokes stand for various degrees of detachment; the combination of dots and slurs in the same symbol ⌒ꞏꞏꞏꞏ⌐ calls for slight emphasis on each note, a *portamento* ("das Tragen der Töne") that, Marpurg adds, is possible only on the clavichord (*Anleitung zum Clavierspielen,* 28–29).

J. S. Petri in 1782 stresses the importance of teaching a student to lift a finger before the next one falls and thus wean him from the widespread bad habit of keeping the fingers down. If he learns to lift well he will have no problem learning to play legato, but if he persists in keeping the fingers down he will have difficulties with detachment (*Anleitung zur praktischen Musik* [1782], 334).

In 1789 Türk reminds the reader that detachment ("Stossen oder Absetzen") is indicated by dots or vertical strokes, and notes so marked should be held almost half of the regular time. How long, he says, depends on the character of the piece; longer in serious, tender, sad pieces, shorter in gay and lively pieces (*Klavierschule,* chap. 6, sec. 3, par.

36). When a slur is prescribed, the fingers must stay down for the full duration to avoid even the slightest separation (par. 28). Notes that are neither intended to be fully detached nor slurred are to be done in the *standard* manner ("gewöhnliche Art") of being ever so slightly separated: ♩ ♩ ♩ is to be done ♪. 𝄾 ♪. 𝄾 ♪. 𝄾 or ♪.. 𝄾♪.. 𝄾♪.. 𝄾 . Türk then takes issue with C. P. E. Bach's principle of a standard execution that takes away half of the note's value. In this manner, Türk says, the difference between the standard manner and a prescribed detachment would be almost obliterated and the performance become too choppy ("hackend" [par. 39]).

It seems that later keyboard treatises fail to mention detachment as something like the "standard" or "natural" touch and lean toward legato as the principal form of articulation. Some of these treatises were quoted in the previous chapter. Such a shift in emphasis might support the idea that around the end of the 18th century a trend, spearheaded perhaps by Beethoven, from more detachment to more legato playing might have made itself felt.

In France, the emphasis placed on legato playing by such masters as Couperin and Rameau seems to have yielded by the middle of the 18th century to a new fashion of sharply clipped articulation on both clavecin and organ. The fashion *may* have been inspired by the "short and sharp" bowstrokes of the French orchestral playing style. A book by Louis Bollioud de Mermet of 1746, while testifying to the emergence of the new fashion, shows at the same time that this new style was not universally admired. The author wonders what Couperin would say if he were to return and hear the "childish antics" of today's (i.e., mid-18th century) performers. "Our great [clavecin] masters tried to slur their playing [Nos grands Maîtres s'attachoient à lier leur jeu], but our new ones have no other thought than to detach the notes and as a consequence render their performances dry, on an instrument, to boot, that suffers from these very debilities to begin with" (*De la corruption*, 35). This new trend finds in 1775 a reflection in a book by Père Engramelle on the mechanical organ and in his chapter on this subject written for Dom Bedos de Celles's monumental study on organ building. Engramelle collaborated on his principles of sharp articulation with Bénigne Balbastre, an organist-composer of some eminence. Engramelle develops an elaborate system of articulation according to the degree to which notes are shortened. He distinguishes *tenues*—notes that are held for the greater part of their nominal value—and *tactées*, which are held only very briefly (as if to mark the tact only, hence the name). He calls the space between notes the "silence d'articulation" and distinguishes no less than five different types of such *silences*. When two equal notes such as quarters or eighths follow one another, the first is generally a *tenue*, the second a *tactée* (*Tonotechnie*, 18–27 and *passim*; Bedos de Celles, *L'art du facteur d'orgues*, vol. 4: chap. 4, sec. 2).

# The Notation of Detachment

**Short Notes Followed By Rests.** So far we have dealt with various types of detachment that were not indicated in the score. As to explicit directives, the simplest and most precise way of indicating detachment, the use of exact note values followed by rests, was late in forming. We do find some very early chance appearances, for instance in Sylvestro Ganassi's treatise of 1535 (*Opera intitulata Fontegara*, Regola prima). But more than two hundred years were to elapse before, in the galant style, this method became widely used. Bach only rarely resorted to this notation: among the few cases where he did, see the start of Cantata No. 26, the start of the Partita No. 5 for Harpsichord, and the first three notes of the Concerto in D for Harpsichord (BWV 1054), a transcription of the Violin Concerto in E, where the corresponding notes are written as plain quarters.

In the Classical era this notation became quite common, most typically in the form of eighth notes followed by eighth rests. For a few among countless examples, see the beginning of Mozart's Piano Concerto in C, K 467; the Romance of the Concerto in D Minor, measure 3 and parallel spots; the orchestral start of the Violin Concerto in A; and Don Ottavio's aria "Il mio tesoro," measure 2, in *Don Giovanni*.

**Symbols of Detachment: The Dot, the Stroke, the Slur-Dots Combination.** Dots and strokes above (or below) the notes are the most common staccato symbols. When, where, or by whom these signs were introduced is at present unknown. It seems, though, that the legato slur preceded the staccato symbols by about half a century. It is also likely that dots and strokes originated with the string instruments, where the differences between legato, nonlegato (*détaché*), and staccato are, even in the outward physical appearance of their execution, far more pronounced than they are for all other media. German violinists used dots at least in the mid-17th century; Italian ones may have preceded them. Among others, Johann Heinrich Schmelzer, the famous Austrian violinist, used dots in a sonata of 1664, as printed in the DTÖ XCVIII. The sonata is called "La gallina" (the hen), and the repeated staccato notes imitate cackling sounds.

Another symbol often mentioned in this connection is the wedge ( ▾ ), yet it seems that it is only a printer's version of the vertical stroke. A genuinely different symbol is the combination of dots or strokes (but mostly of dots) with the slur: ⌢⌢ . or ⌢ . Various problems are connected with these symbols. Generally, all indicated a shortening of the note to which they were attached or, rather, a stronger shortening than might have been expected in unmarked nonlegato. This is as much as can be said in a general way. Even today with our much more sophisticated and more precise notation where new symbols of detachment have emerged—notably the horizontal dash (–) and the dash-dot combination (÷)—the meaning of dots and of dots under a slur is still far from certain: a staccato dot does not tell us how much the written note should be shortened, whether slightly or substantially. Nor does it tell us, when strings are involved, how the staccato is to be executed, whether on or off the string, whether rendered with sharpness or mildness.

Though the difference between these types is substantial indeed, the notation does not tell the story. The uncertainties are even greater for pre-1800 music, when dots and strokes coexisted and had often, but not always, a different meaning. Furthermore, both dots and (more often) strokes were symbols for accents. (See below under "Accentual Meaning.") A further overlapping is to be found with the French *notes inégales,* where dots indicate cancellation of the *notes inégales,* presumably because *inégalité* was decisively congenial to a legato context.

*The Slur-Dot Combination.* In discussing the various symbols in some detail it might be best to start with the third one, the combination of dots (or more rarely strokes) with a slur, because it has generally a more clearly circumscribed meaning. For voice, keyboard, and winds, its meaning is overwhelmingly that of a gentle detachment, in accord with its graphic symbolism as a combination of legato and staccato, standing halfway between the two. Often the manner is referred to as portamento or portato; Germans referred to it often as *das Tragen der Töne,* which is a close equivalent of portato. It has in this most common meaning its modern equivalent in 𝄐 𝄐 𝄐 𝄐 or 𝄐 𝄐 𝄐 𝄐 .

For strings the slur-dot combination harbors an ambiguity. Though it can and often does have the same gentle portato meaning, it can also refer to a specific bowing technique rather than to a specific articulatory effect. As a bowing directive it calls for playing a series of clearly detached notes in one bowstroke with an often sharper articulation than that of the portato usually associated with the symbol; it so happens that here the articulation by technical necessity becomes sharper the shorter the note values are. There are two main methods of execution: either solidly on the string with sharp, short, and fast thrusts of the bow, or the "flying" type, by bouncing the bow while keeping the strokes in the same direction. In either case the slur mark is not a softening agent but simply the sign for maintaining this direction. Both types of the one-bowstroke staccato, unless they involve only few notes, actually produce a sharp articulation, the firm one being more vigorous, the flying one more graceful. But, from the 17th century to the present, the notation does not indicate which type is desired.

In the late 17th century we find this one-bowstroke staccato among others in Biber's sonatas of 1681 and in J. J. Walther's *Hortulus chelicus* of

1688, where there are so many short notes in one bowstroke that for the mentioned technical reasons their meaning has to be that of the sharp-edged one-bowstroke staccato, either flying or firm.

Georg Muffat describes the flying type of staccato in the preface to his *Florilegium secundum* of 1698, calling it *pétillement* (which is characterized by "letting the notes crackle" [faisant craqueter] with the same bowstroke), and specifies the bouncing style "mit hüpfender Bewegung" in the German version of the quadrilingual preface. Leopold Mozart in 1756 also describes the one-bowstroke flying staccato (*Versuch einer Violinschule*, chap. 7, sec. 1, par. 17). So does Johann Adam Hiller ("mit hüpfendem Bogen") at the end of the 18th century, though he marks it only with dots and no slur. Surprisingly, he calls it "punto d'arco," and for the soloist only, playing in a faster tempo, he calls it "Pikiren," for which he gives the example of a descending scale of fourteen thirty-second notes in one bowstroke (*Anweisung zum Violinspielen*, 41–42).

Marin Marais, in his *Second livre de pièces de viole* of 1701, refers probably to the firm type when saying that the slur over dots means the articulation of several notes under the same bowstroke, but "as if they were played with different bowstrokes" (Preface). For a specimen from Bach that may have been intended as a "firm" violin staccato, see the Mass in B Minor, no. 14, "Et in unum" (mm. 21–22). Michel Corrette, in his cello tutor of 1741, seems to have a firm staccato in mind when he explains the symbol as meaning that one must articulate the notes well and detach them in the same bow stroke (*Méthode pour le violoncelle*, 36).

Whenever there are fewer and slower notes involved, then, for strings as well as for other media, the slur-with-dots symbol is more likely to signify the gentle *portato* detachment than a sharp staccato.

*Dots and Strokes.* The most common symbols for staccato articulation are dots and strokes placed above or below the notes. They are, as mentioned above, imprecise symbols that fail to indicate the degree to which notes are to be shortened at their end and the manner in which they should be shortened, whether mildly or sharply. Here again the performer has to decide on the basis of the character of the passage. The mechanics of staccato rendition for various media have been discussed on the previous pages.

Two other issues concerning dots and strokes need to be addressed: one is their not infrequent accentual meaning, the other is the controversy about identity or difference between the two symbols.

*The Accentual Meaning.* The modern accentual sign > was unknown before the end of the 18th century. Before that, the use of staccato symbols for accentuation makes good sense since a sharply attacked single note spontaneously produces an accent. It is presumably from such experiences that composers used the staccato signs for accentuation even in spots where a staccato is out of the question (such as notes followed by a slur or a tie or notes under a fermata).

In Bach we find a few spots in which the dot stands for an accent, as in Ex. 17.1a, from the autograph basso part of Cantata No. 47 (BB St 104/16), in which accents punctuate the syllable "flu" from "verfluchen" (to curse) in the bass aria. The old Bach Gesellschaft edition, puzzled by this unusual notation, changed Bach's clear notation to that of Ex. 17.1b. Later in the same aria we find another intriguing accentual use of dots to add pungency to the word "Hochmut" (arrogance; Ex. 17.1c).

EXAMPLE 17.1.  Bach, Cantata No. 47/4

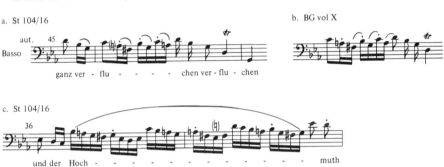

Strokes are more frequent than dots as accentual signs with Bach as well as with Handel and other masters of the period. In Ex. 17.2a, from the Christmas Oratorio, the accents stand again as symbols of arrogance ("Wenn die stolzen Feinde schnauben [when the arrogant enemies snort]"); they recur many times in the movement for trumpets as well as for strings and continuo in analogous contexts that exclude staccato meaning.

Handel's similar use is shown in Ex. 17.2b, taken from the autograph of the Concerto Op. 6, No. 6 (BL, RM 20 g.11). (Incidentally, Handel's clear markings, as reproduced here, are incorrectly rendered in the edition of the Handelgesellschaft.) Note especially the fermata-stroke combination. For another illustration, see Ex. 17.2c, from the autograph of *Serse* (RM 20 c.7).

In his *Singe- Spiel- und Generalbass-Übungen*, Telemann explains the accentual meaning of the strokes in his comments to the Lied No. 14, where they appear on a series of tied half notes in the bass: ![notation] . "The strokes under the tied notes indicate that the violoncello should make a gentle push with the bow" (mit dem Bogen einen gelinden Ruck tun sollte [n.p.]).

We find the same in Rameau. In a manuscript of "Les paladins" with autograph corrections and additions (*Opéra: Rés* A 201), we find on

EXAMPLE 17.2

a. Bach, Christmas Oratorio, BWV 248/VI/54

Vns. I, II
Va.

b. Handel, Concerto Op. 6, No. 6/1 aut.

Largo e affetuoso

Vn. solo

c. Handel, *Serse*, III, Sc. 9

aut.
Vn. I

page 40 this bassoon passage: **3** 𝄞| 𝅘𝅥| 𝅘𝅥 |𝅘𝅥 |𝅘𝅥 𝄀| 𝅘𝅥| 𝅘𝅥   with the following aucoup
                                                           de
                                                          vent
tograph annotation: "The dot or this stroke ❘ above a note indicates a
breath stroke without interrupting the exhalation, in the manner of a
bow that marks a sound without stopping its movement up or down"
(Le point audessus d'une notte ou bien ce trait, ❘, marque un coup de
vent sans reprendre haleine de même que l'archet continue de pousser
ou de tirer, en marquant un nouveau coup). On the next page
an analogous pattern occurs for the violins: **3** 𝅘𝅥|𝅘𝅥|𝅘𝅥|𝅘𝅥   with the
directive: "Mark [literally: repeat] the bow[stroke] at each measure while
continuing to draw it either up or down" (Répétez l'Archet à chaque
mesure toujours en tirant ou toujours en poussant).

Quantz writes that strokes over several notes mean staccato, but
when a stroke is placed over only one note that is followed by smaller
values, then the note is not only shortened by one-half but also accented
(*Versuch einer Anweisung*, chap. 17, sec. 2, par. 27).

The accentual meaning carries over to the Classical era. For characteristic illustrations from Mozart, see Ex. 17.3a, from the "Haffner" Symphony, where the accentual meaning of the third stroke is obvious, but
where the first two would seem to call for similar emphasis. In Ex. 17.3b,
from the minuet (trio) of the "Jupiter" Symphony, the strokes clearly
denote emphasis, not staccato articulation. See also the accentual
strokes over three half notes, of which the third is extended by a tie, in

EXAMPLE 17.3. Mozart

a. "Haffner" Symphony, K 385

b. "Jupiter" Symphony, K 551/3, Trio

measures 98–100 in the finale of the same symphony; and in measures 86–93 in the same movement, see the strokes over the first of two tied whole notes in the basses, four times repeated. In *Don Giovanni*, see Act I, Scene 6, Masetto's aria (mm. 77–79); also Act I, Scene 1, Introduction (mm. 75–76, 80–81), where the strokes are supported by *fp*s. There are innumerable other cases. (Mozart's use of dots and strokes will be discussed at some length in the next chapter.)

In addition to instances such as those shown, where a stroke (or dot) can have only accentual meaning, there are many others in which the exact meaning is uncertain, where either accentuation or shortening or both were intended. For some such occurrences, see the Fourth "Brandenburg" Concerto, in the first movement, measures 78–81, and its many parallel spots, or, near the end of the last movement, see the dots over the second of two half notes in measures 229, 231, and 233.

***Dots versus Strokes: Identity or Difference?*** The two symbols have identical meaning for some, different meanings for other masters. Some, like

Reinhard Keiser, use only strokes, never dots, and do so even under a slur. For those composers who use both, we face the question about their presumable differences.

Theorists who see no difference between the two include C. P. E. Bach (*Versuch über Art das Clavier* [1753], chap. 3, par. 17), Marpurg (*Anleitung zum Clavierspielen*, 28 and Tab. 2, fig. 8), Johann Samuel Petri (*Anleitung zur Musik* [1782], 147), and G. Wolf (*Kurzer Unterricht*, 36). In his flute tutor, Corrette says specifically that dots and strokes are the same. When either appears under a slur, then the individual notes are to be articulated with the same breath (*Méthode pour la flûte traversière*, 21).

To indicate staccato, Leopold Mozart lists only the strokes (*Versuch einer Violinschule*, chap. 1, sec. 3, par. 20). He distinguishes between dots and strokes only when they are placed under a slur, in which case the dots stand for a gentle portato, the strokes for clear separation under the same bowstroke. It may be no coincidence that two other important violin tutors, that of Geminiani (*Art of Playing Violin*, 1751) and that of L'Abbé le Fils (*Principes de violon*, 1761), show an identical pattern: strokes only for regular staccato and dots only for the combination with slurs. Türk equates dots and strokes but adds that "some [writers]" (Einige) wish to indicate a sharper staccato for the strokes than for the dots (*Klavierschule*, chap. 6, sec. 3, par. 36). Among the writers that Türk seems to have in mind is undoubtedly Quantz, who makes a clear distinction: notes with a stroke are to be fully detached, those with a dot by contrast played with short but sustained bowstrokes. The same difference (of greater or lesser detachment) obtains when strokes or dots are under a slur (*Versuch einer Anweisung*, chap. 7, sec. 2, par. 12).

Tromlitz, in his flute tutor of 1791, stresses the importance of differentiating dots and strokes, but his interpretation of the two signs is unusual. The strokes, he says, indicate that all notes so marked get special emphasis ("besonders markiert"), are articulated with "ta," and rendered not short but *long*: "ta, ta, ta [tā, tā, tā]." By contrast, dots above the notes mean that they are to be shortly clipped ♪ ♪ ♪ with the tongue kept tight ("gespannt gehalten") until the next *a* is pronounced. In other words, the stroke is an accentual, the dot a staccato sign (*Ausführlicher Unterricht*, 162).

Johann Adam Hiller also makes a clear distinction, but not in the sense of either Quantz or Tromlitz. Speaking of the violin, Hiller says that the strokes do signify staccato while the dots stand for *punto d'arco*. The latter means that several notes are to be taken with the same bowstroke but leaping off the string, whereas the addition of a slur to the dots calls for playing with a firm bow (i.e., on the string) and a series of gentle pressures (*Anweisung zum Violinspielen*, 41–42). Hiller's distinction is also found in Durieu, where strokes mean detachment with separate bowstrokes, dots (without a slur) mean playing on the same bow and always the upbow (*Méthode de violon*, 11).

For the pianoforte Muzio Clementi lists both strokes and dots to denote staccato and adds that composers "who are exact in their writing" signify "less staccato" for the dots than the strokes and "still less" when the dots are placed under a slur (*Introduction*, 5). Clementi's "exact" version is confirmed by Beethoven, who wrote in an undated letter in 1825 to Carl Holz: "where [a dot] is over the note, there must be no [stroke] or vice versa! ♪ ♪ ♪ and ♪ ♪ ♪ are not the same thing."

Bach used both dots and strokes but did so sparingly. For the simple staccato meaning, he seemed to have preferred the dot, while, as shown before, he used either dot or stroke as accentual sign.

---

## Practical Illustrations

In all cases in which detachment is spelled out with notes followed by rests, it is probably advisable to play the notes at or near their notated value. One should be especially careful not to follow a widespread fashion of rendering Mozart's detached or staccato notes too sharply. The danger of so doing is greatest in slow pieces, and the consequences are generally most questionable in works of tender expression. Thus one hears all too often the eighth notes in the romance of the Concerto in D Minor played very sharply as thirty-second notes that break the enchantment when—in Diruta's words—they are slapped instead of caressed. The same treatment is often meted out to the eighth notes in Don Ottavio's aria "Il mio tesoro" and in countless analogous situations. The tradition of overpointed articulation might go back to the 19th-century image of Mozart as a composer whose rococo daintiness evokes graceful porcelain figurines. The same comment is fitting also in comparable cases in which the detachment is not spelled out with rests but indicated by symbols.

At the opposite pole we find a tendency of more recent vintage, that of overarticulating notes and especially chords of power and energy with the more laudable aim of emphasizing Mozart's dramatic genius. Chords that should be festive, or powerful, or joyful are played like whiplashes conveying an energy more neurotic than dramatic. The whiplash school of interpretation may have been inaugurated by Arturo Toscanini's muscular and incisive manner in the rendition of Classical music. His clarity and transparency were always admirable, but his cutting edge was often too sharp for stylistic congruity.

Concerning the slur-dots combination and its basically gentle portato meaning, a passage that is often misinterpreted as regular staccato is shown in Ex. 17.4a, from Pamina's aria "Ach ich fühl's" from *Die Zauberflöte*. Here the four notes with dots under a slur call for an expression evoking tears, not sparkling stones. For a clavier passage, see Ex. 17.4b, from the Sonata for Violin and Piano K 454; for a flute melody, see Haydn's Symphony No. 104 in D, second movement, measure 115; for a violin passage, see the solo in Bach's Cantata No. 30/5, measures 4–7.

EXAMPLE 7.4.   Mozart

a. *Die Zauberflöte*, "Ach ich fühls," K 620 II

b. Sonata for Violin and Piano, K 454/2

The violinistic symbol of many dots under a slur that was and often had to be done in sharp staccato manner does not seem to have been used by Haydn and Mozart. In their works the symbol is likely to have the same portato meaning for the violin that it has for voice, keyboard, or winds. For an illustration, the descending scales in the first movement of Mozart's String Quartet in D, K 575 (mm. 66–74) should probably be softly rather than sharply articulated, as should also several passages in the adagio of Haydn's String Quartet in C Op. 54, No. 2 (mm. 10–12, 15, and parallel spots) or in the adagio of his String Quartet in B Flat Op. 64, No. 3 (mm. 52–56).

# 18

# SPECIAL ARTICULATION PROBLEMS

## Dots and Strokes in Mozart

Mozart's usage with regard to dots and strokes has given rise to much debate. The old Gesamtausgabe (1877–1910) used only dots, and so did all the numerous editions derived from it. A number of scholars up to the present hold that Mozart intended no difference in meaning between the two symbols. The most distinguished among them is Alfred Einstein, editor of the third edition of the Köchel catalog who believed that the dots were simply strokes that were shrunken due to haste. Paul Mies, in an article of 1958 ("Artikulationszeichen"), similarly ascribed the differences between the two signs to the "Schreibfaktor" (the writing factor). He argued that either symbol was used whenever it fell most easily into the hand. Thus, for instance, for single notes or chords, the stroke was easier to write; for a series of notes in a row, the dots were easier. Mies saw no intended musical difference and therefore suggested that editors use only dots. The latest follower of this school of thought is Robert D. Riggs, who, in his Harvard dissertation of 1987 ("Articulation in Mozart's and Beethoven's Sonatas"), tried to dispose once and for all of what he calls the "dualism" (a term he adopted from Mies)—that is, the belief in an intended difference between the two signs.

In 1954 the Gesellschaft für Musikforschung invited a competition on the question: "What is the meaning of the signs ▾ (wedge), ❘ (stroke), and • (dot) in Mozart's autographs and first editions; did Mozart intend a differentiation, and how should the signs be reproduced in new editions?" Of the five answers published by Bärenreiter in 1957 (under the title *Die Bedeutung der Zeichen*), four scholars, Hermann Keller, Hubert Unverricht, Oswald Jonas, and Alfred Kreutz, pointed to distinct differences between stroke and dot (all were agreed that the wedge is simply a printer's equivalent for the stroke). Only one, Ewald Zimmermann, saw no intended difference between the two signs.

The NMA came out on the side of "dualism" and has systematically tried to reproduce as faithfully as possible the two distinct signs, while various of its editors explained the rationale for this editorial policy (for instance, Rudolf Elvers in NMA IV/13/1, p. x). But since the controversy is still very much alive, it seems advisable to take a new look.

Mozart's autographs reveal his use of clear strokes and clear dots. Neither Einstein, nor Mies, nor Riggs denied this fact; these scholars simply denied any musical significance for the graphic difference. It is, however, not possible to accept this judgment in view of the consistency with which either sign appears in very specific musical contexts. The true facts of the matter have been beclouded by many cases in which the exact nature of the staccato did not greatly matter and consequently Mozart made no deliberate effort to distinguish the two types. The result of this casualness is a gray area where the two signs are not clearly differentiated graphically and can in fact become synonymous.

But outside of that gray area, Mozart used strokes and dots deliberately for different purposes, and we can group those different purposes into several categories: three for the stroke, two for the dot, and one in between these two groups—the "gray area" of casualness. For the discussion of these categories it will be helpful to borrow the very clever metaphors, mentioned in the previous chapter, with which Joseph Joachim characterized the types of staccato as snow, rain, and hail. Though focused on the bouncing bow of the violin, these types can, with some caution, be transferred to other media as well.

Turning first to the stroke, Mozart used it deliberately in the following three ways: (1) to indicate an accent without a staccato; (2) to indicate a staccato with special emphasis of either accent or sharpness, ranging from hail to heavy rain; (3) to mark a staccato, usually without special emphasis, that serves to separate clearly a single note from a group of slurred notes.

As to the first category, the modern accentual sign >, as mentioned above, was not available to Mozart, but the stroke as accentual sign had already been used by older composers, as was shown in the preceding chapter.

Example 17.3a, taken from the "Haffner" Symphony, shows two emphasized heavy-rain staccato notes followed by a third, tied to its neighbor, where the stroke can only have accentual meaning. The same is true of Ex. 17.3b, from the minuet (trio) of the "Jupiter" Symphony. For related cases see Exx. 18.1a and 18.1b, both from the finale of the

EXAMPLE 18.1.   Mozart, "Jupiter" Symphony, K 551/4, finale

a. K 551/4

Vn. I

b. K 551/4

Basses

same symphony, since a note has to be reasonably short for the stroke to be perceived as a staccato sign, shorter certainly than a dotted half note in allegretto or a whole note—let alone a tied whole note—in any tempo.

As to the second category, Exx. 18.2a and 18.2b, from the minuet of the String Quartet in D, K 575, show an interesting juxtaposition of dots and strokes. First we see, in *piano*, unmistakable dots over the quarter notes in all instruments followed by dots over a similarly gentle descending passage in the first violin. That the dots were purposeful, not due to Mies's "writing factor," becomes clear at the start of the second section (Ex. 18.2b), where the theme returns in *forte:* here we see clear strokes to indicate emphatic forcefulness.

In Ex. 18.2c, from Don Giovanni's duel with the Commendatore, the strokes call for power and sharpness to evoke the violence of sword thrusts. We find the same clear strokes in the imitative response of the basses. It is unthinkable that in this passage Mozart would have written dots instead.

Example 18.2d (like Ex. 18.2g) was copied from the autograph, which was not accessible for reproduction. It is from the third movement of the "Luetzow" Piano Concerto K 246 and shows accentual emphasis put into sharp focus by a clear stroke over the first and dots over the following eighth notes—a pattern repeated a number of times in exactly the same manner.

Word meaning often calls for more emphatic articulation, which is evoked in notation by clear strokes. See, for instance, Ex. 18.2e from the first quintet of *Die Zauberflöte*, where the forceful words "Hass, Verleumdung, schwarzer Galle" (hatred, calumny, black gall) are reflected by a similarly forceful hail-like articulation that is indicated by clear strokes for the violins. In this sequence of eighth notes the "writing factor" would have called for dots! Related is the case with Sarastro's stern announcement "wenn ich dich ihren Händen liesse" ([you would be deprived of happiness] were I to leave you in her hands): here, as shown

EXAMPLE 18.2.   Mozart

a.  String Quartet in D, K 575/3

b.  String Quartet in D, K 575/3

EXAMPLE 18.2. *continued*

c. *Don Giovanni*, K 529 I, 1

Vn. I

d. "Luetzow" Piano Concerto, K 246/3

Vn. I

e. *Die Zauberflöte*, K 620 I, 5

f. *Die Zauberflöte*, K 620 I Finale

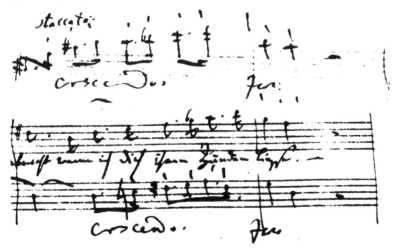

g. *Così fan tutte*, K 588 I, 4

Vn. I

staccato

in Ex. 18.2f, Mozart underlines an emphatic crescendo to the climax of the phrase with the word *staccato* (in the upper left corner) and decisive strokes in violins and basses.

Example 18.2g shows a similar case in which Mozart combines the spelled-out *staccato* with clear strokes. It is a passage in *Così fan tutte* set to Dorabella's words: "See the fire in his eyes that seem to shoot off flames and darts." The strokes are also consistent throughout two measures of accompanying sixteenth notes in the violas and basses. The staccato should be of the "hail" type.

Turning to the third category, strokes that clearly separate a single note from a group of slurred notes that either precede or follow, we could call them "separation strokes." We find strokes in such patterns as shown in Ex. 18.3a so overwhelmingly that we can identify sporadic dots as shrunken strokes. Illustrations are given in Ex. 18.3b, from the String Quartet in D Minor (for an upbeat) and Ex. 18.3c, from *Die Zauberflöte* (for a downbeat). Though once in a while such separation strokes may have slight accentual implication—as perhaps in Ex. 18.3c—in the majority of cases they don't. Their purpose seems to be simply that of differentiating a clear staccato separation from the very mild nonlegato

EXAMPLE 18.3

a.

b. Mozart, String Quartet in D Minor, K 421 (417b)/2

EXAMPLE 18.3 *continued*

c. Mozart, *Die Zauberflöte*, K 620 I, 6

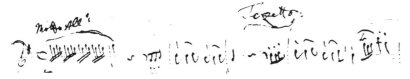

d. Mozart, "Hunt" Quartet, K 458/1

e. Mozart, String Quartet in A, K 464/1

separation in such places as those of Ex. 18.3d, from the start of the "Hunt" Quartet K 458, or Ex. 18.3e, from the start of the String Quartet in A, K 464. In the "Hunt" Quartet the single upbeat note, in the many appearances of the theme throughout the movement, has never a dot or a stroke. In the String quartet in A, among twenty-odd entrances of the complete theme (with the upbeat), Mozart wrote a stroke only two times: at the start of the development for the first violin and four measures later for the imitative entrance of the cello, but not for the similar entrance, in between, of the middle strings. On the basis of these two instances, the NMA placed editorial strokes over every single upbeat. I believe this to be a mistake: in view of the gross statistical disparity, the two instances are more likely to be an oversight, or an isolated directive, rather than an indication of an articulatory intention that is to be spread over the whole movement.[1]

Adjoining the third category of purposeful strokes, the "gray area" follows as fourth category. This is the ordinary, all-purpose staccato with no implication of accent, emphasis, or special sharpness. Here the staccato ranges presumably from "snow" to "rain" but hardly to "hail." It is here where, given the speed of Mozart's writing, the exact character of the staccato was not important enough for him to make a conscious effort at graphic differentiation and where, as a consequence, dots and strokes have the same meaning. For two illustrations, see Ex. 18.4a, from the Overture to *Don Giovanni*, where the two violins have a mixture of strokes, dots, and no marks, without any apparent rationale; and Ex. 18.4b, from the Sonata in B Flat for Violin and Piano K 454, where, in the violin and the piano right hand, dots and strokes are haphazardly mixed. It is this gray area that has engendered much of the confusion that beclouds the issue. The confusion yields when we realize that we are dealing with a *limited* area, however large, and that the "unionists," if I may use this term, made the mistake of extrapolating the ambiguity and interchangeability within this limited area to the whole scope of Mozart's staccato notation.

The fifth category concerns the purposeful use of the dot. In view of the "gray area," it is not always easy to identify dots as being purposeful. We can do so confidently in cases such as those of Exx. 18.2a or

EXAMPLE 18.4.    Mozart

a. *Don Giovanni*, K 529, Overture

b. Sonata in B Flat for Violin and Piano, K 454/3

18.3c, where the dots are written in clear contrast to strokes. We find similar striking juxtapositions in the finale of the "Jupiter" Symphony, where the contrast between the signs helps set off two of the five main motives of the movement (see Fig. 18.1). The angular four-note motive,

FIGURE 18.1.   Mozart, "Jupiter" Symphony, K 551/4, Finale

with its downward leaps of a fifth and a seventh, is marked by strokes, and the linear, stepwise ascending six-note motive is marked by dots. On five occasions, where the two themes happen to be joined, the consistently repeated patterns of strokes for the four-note and dots for the six-note theme prove a purposeful differentiation (the NMA missed this differentiation in all five cases): in Ex. 18.5a, the first violins with this theme combination; in Ex. 18.5b, the first oboe in a parallel spot; in Ex. 18.5c, the celli (on the upper stave in tenor clef), first with the twice-repeated dotted linear theme, then the angular four-note theme, marked with strokes, joining the basses in measure 401 (now in the bass clef) in a third of the five themes; again in Ex. 18.5c, the basses announcing the angular theme, with strokes, followed by a dotted fragment of the linear theme (in support of the celli) leading into the third theme, with its signal-like opening and descending eighth-note passagework. In a fifth instance, given in Ex. 18.5d, the celli, again in tenor clef, have the combined angular and linear theme, the first with strokes, the second with dots, while in measure 383 the basses give out the fourth of the five themes, with strokes in pure accentual meaning, as proved by the third half note, which is tied to its neighbor. I believe these examples offer eloquent testimony against the "unionists' " theories. At the same time this differentiation acts as an agent of effective phrasing by tellingly setting off the two heterogeneous themes from one another—provided the director is aware of Mozart's signs and interprets them correctly— with greater sharpness for the strokes.

Other than in such cases of clear juxtaposition, dots can be assumed to be purposeful when there is graphic consistency and especially when such consistency is combined with gentle expression. For an illustration, see Ex. 18.5e, from Zerlina's second act aria, where she caressingly comforts the battered Masetto. Passages with presumably purposeful dots should be rendered gracefully, without sharpness, from "snow" to light "rain."

The sixth category is the very frequent combination of slurs and dots (never strokes). It indicates the gentlest form of detachment. See, for an illustration, Ex. 18.6, from Donna Anna's first accompanied recitative.

EXAMPLE 18.5.    Mozart

a. "Jupiter" Symphony, K 551/4, Finale

Vn. I

b. "Jupiter" Symphony, K 551/4, Finale

Ob. I

c. "Jupiter" Symphony, K 551/4, Finale

Celli

Basses

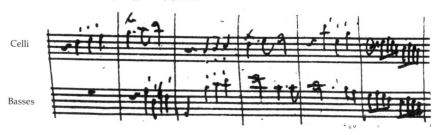

d. "Jupiter" Symphony, K 551/4, Finale

Celli

Basses

This use of dots with slurs is so consistent that I have not found a single instance where in this combination the dots were not clearly identifiable as such. Even Riggs confirms the total consistency of this usage. In accord with its graphic image, the desired detachment stands halfway between a mild staccato and a legato. The effect is more a portato than a staccato. In modern notation it would be marked with horizontal dashes under a slur.

Further evidence about the intended difference between the two signs is shown in Ex. 18.7. In the first finale of *Die Zauberflöte* (Scene 19),

EXAMPLE 18.5. *continued*

e. *Don Giovanni*, K 529 II, 12

EXAMPLE 18.6.   Mozart, *Don Giovanni*, K 529 I, 2

Mozart revised the staccato signs. What happened here was apparently the attempt to change strokes into dots; and it is dots he wrote for the immediate repeat of the theme. Although in the further course of the scene Mozart made no determined effort to use clear dots for parallel spots, the fact of an intended correction is significant in itself.

EXAMPLE 18.7.   Mozart, *Die Zauberflöte*, K 620 I, Finale

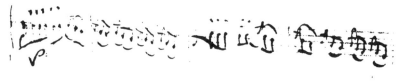

Briefly summing up, there seems to be little doubt that Mozart distinguished dots and strokes, and while he was nonchalant about the graphic shapes where it mattered little, he distinguished the signs with deliberation where it did matter. And by so doing he gave us priceless cues for a richer, more colorful, and sometimes more dramatic range of expression than the score could suggest without the eloquence of the two signs.

## The Problems of Bach's Keyboard Articulation

If the articulation signs offer problems of interpretation, the problems are magnified when the composer fails to use the available symbols. A notorious case is the paucity of articulation marks in Bach's keyboard music. Those among these works that were transcribed from the violin (or oboe), such as the clavier concertos, or that had their origin in string works, such as—undoubtedly—the organ sonatas, mostly have ample articulation marks that were apparently literally transferred from the originals (as we can judge from a few cases where the original survived along with the transcription).

If we look for guidance to theorists, we find, understandably, only generalities. C. P. E. Bach, for instance, has this to say: "The liveliness of the allegro calls *generally* for detached notes, the tenderness of the adagio for sustained and slurred ones" (*Versuch über Art das Clavier* [1753], chap. 3, par. 5 [emphasis in original]). The reservation implied by "generally" makes it clear that he saw many exceptions to this principle. In a similar vein, Quantz connects slurring and close intervals with tenderness and sadness, staccato and intervallic leaps with gaiety and boldness (*Versuch einer Anweisung*, chap. 11, par. 16). Both statements have an aura of timelessness, but their principles are too vague to be of practical use since both fast and slow movements will mostly call for a mixture of both styles.

*The Approach of Modern Scholars.* In order to get more specific guidance for the articulation of unmarked works, it seems reasonable to look to the many works for melody instruments that were carefully, often lavishly, equipped with articulation marks. Though some of these marks were rooted in idiomatic concerns, the vast majority is based on the character of the melody. Furthermore, since Bach himself transferred his articulation marks automatically from one medium to another, we certainly have ample justification to try to explore the well-marked works for clues to what Bach did and what he did not do for specific melodic-rhythmic patterns. If we succeed in finding certain regularities that would uncover leanings toward what is likely and not likely, we would accomplish more than has so far been done.

Albert Schweitzer, in his well-known biography of 1905, may have been the first to point to the orchestral and chamber music parts, notably the "Brandenburg" Concertos, as models for the missing keyboard articulation. His own illustrations, however, are strongly influenced by Hugo Riemann's principle of upbeat phrasing (on this, see chap. 19) and are consequently often rather one-sided in following this orientation (*J. S. Bach* [1908], 272–78, 319–92, 699–716).

Hermann Keller, who wrote in 1925 the first monograph on phrasing and articulation, points out that harpsichord, clavichord, and modern piano all call for different styles of articulation and that therefore one cannot formulate rules that are valid for all three instruments: one can derive only general principles that are deduced from the music itself. He also points to the special role of articulation on the organ, where articulation alone can suggest accents and the location of the beat (*Phrasierung* [1955], 68–69, 71).

Keller does give specific advice on the articulation of Bach's keyboard works in his monograph (55–74) and in his two books on Bach's clavier and organ works (*Die Klavierwerke Bachs, passim; Die Orgelwerke Bachs, passim*). He favors legato for stepwise progressions and detachments for leaps, and other than that he seems to prefer downbeat to upbeat phrasing; hence his suggestions deviate, often dramatically, from those by Schweitzer. Keller recognized that his solutions can well be replaced by others of equal merit.

In contrast to Keller, Ludger Lohmann, in his important study of 1982, considers the basic principles of articulation to be the same for all keyboard instruments and consequently makes no effort to distinguish between the media with regard to the legato–staccato polarity. There seems to be merit in this stance since desirable articulation is inherent in the nature of the melody and this nature is not affected by the change from one keyboard instrument to the other. "Rules" for proper articulation cannot be formulated to begin with; tendencies are the best we can hope to uncover.

When we look at the efforts of many editors of the keyboard works, beginning with Czerny, we find the greatest variety with very few common denominators. This fact prompted Erwin Bodky to undertake a thorough study of all the autograph articulation materials he was able to inspect. He was disappointed by the results of his labors. He found that cases of parallelism that would permit a direct transfer from marked to unmarked music are "infinitely less frequent than anticipated" (*Interpretation of Bach's Keyboard Works*, 214). Bodky illustrates his frustration with an interesting articulation table (382–98, not always from autograph sources and on occasions unreliable), where among other examples he includes differently articulated versions of identical melodic patterns. Bodky in the end resigned himself to the generalizations of C. P. E. Bach and Quantz that fast movements lean to staccato, slow ones to legato. For moderato, Bodky adds that small intervals are slurred, large ones (larger than thirds) are detached. That is a meager result of much research, but it may not need to be so.

John Butt's recent book *Bach Interpretation: Articulation Marks in the Primary Sources of J. S. Bach* is the first comprehensive study of the subject in English. It embodies a remarkable feat of research and presents wide-ranging data that will prove invaluable to future investigations. Butt does not make any suggestions for the articulation of specific passages. Instead, he does show a multitude of slurring patterns found in

Bach's vocal works. They are presented, in the abstract, for even (eighth) notes that are all classified and labeled. They almost overwhelm by their mass. (Presently I shall try to show similar samples, far less complete, but I think more manageable.) Butt's book has great strengths, notably in its massive documentation, but has a few weaknesses that need to be mentioned because they affect interpretation.

For one, Butt does not consider the accentual meaning of some of Bach's dots or strokes, and this failure leads to doubtful conclusions. Thus, for instance, he speculates that the dots in Ex. 17.1a suggest a Lombard rhythm, or those in Ex. 17.2c a phrasing break, when in either case accents that heighten the strong affect of the words "verfluchen" (to curse) or "Hochmut" (arrogance) seem to make the best sense. The same is the case with dots under slurs in other examples (e.g., Butt's Ex. 44).

In speaking of strings, and the violin in particular, Butt downgrades the principle of the downbow on the downbeat. Yet in countless cases the intention to favor the downbow is so obvious (to a string player) that its importance cannot be discounted. In fact it is this partiality for the downbow that often provides the best explanation for slurring discrepancies between strings and woodwinds. In Ex. 16.9 above, for instance, we see, as was explained on the occasion, a clear case in which the violin bowings are dictated by the tendency to the downbow on every single beat. The flute, by way of contrast, can easily slur by four; furthermore, in the second measure of the example, the flute has no reason to slur the eighth note to the following sixteenth (on the third beat), whereas the violins must slur them to insure a downbow on the next beat. By ignoring the downbow principle, Butt has to resort to a complex theory to account for the discrepancies. The case is analogous with Butt's example from the Easter Oratorio, given here in Ex. 18.8, for which he again essays an involved explanation when the simple clue is the downbow principle.

EXAMPLE 18.8.   Bach, Easter Oratorio, BWV 249/11 (St 353)

In the fairly frequent differences between simultaneous instrumental and vocal articulation (for which Butt gives many interesting examples on pages 123–29), the reason is sometimes simply indifference toward a "minor matter" (von Dadelsen's "Nebensache"), and there is no need for the complex explanations offered.

I have some reservations also about Butt's summarizing statement that "slurs relate to accentuation, voice-leading and general coloring of the line" (209). If the "accentuation" refers to the start of a slur, the application of this galant principle seems questionable for those many unison passages with discrepant slurs where, as pointed out in chapter 16, such accentuation would create confusion.

All in all, Butt's book is a remarkable scholarly achievement, but it must to be used with care as a guide to performance.

**Tendencies and Disinclinations.** On the basis of fairly wide-ranging but far from all-embracing research into Bach's articulation of strings and winds, it is possible to formulate certain tendencies, both positive and negative, that can be useful as guidelines. Certain tendencies are related to rhythm patterns, others to melodic patterns.

*Rhythm patterns.* Among the few certainties is the two-by-two slurring of all Lombard rhythms ⌐♪· ⌐♪· and by analogy the three-by-three slurring of the closely related patterns ⌐♪♪· ⌐♪♪· .

I am aware of the often-quoted slurring pattern ♪·♪· in the Clavier Concerto in D Major, slow movement (m. 23), but this seeming exception disappears on inspection of the autograph (P 271). We see that Bach had at first written even sixteenth notes ♪♪♪♪ in accord with the rhythm in the original Violin Concerto in E major, then on second thought, ostensibly to compensate for the lack of dynamic nuance available to the harpsichord, added the rhythmic modulation. This second thought occurred to him when he finished writing measure 23: from measure 24 on we find not only the two-by-two slurring but also the proper horizontal spacing of the note heads in accord with their time values.

Nearly as certain is a negative: it is extremely rare that two slurred and two detached notes occur in a group of four equal notes, or similarly two slurred and four detached notes in a group of six equal notes (Fig. 18.2). Bodky's Ex. 10 (*Interpretation of Bach's Keyboard Works*, 394), which seems to contradict this statement, is incorrect, but once in a long while we do find exceptions. For instance, the first pattern in Fig. 18.2a, ♪♪♪♪ , occurs in the double of the Bourrée of the Suite in B Minor for Solo Violin (mm. 42–43), and the third pattern, ♪♪♪♪ , occurs in the Gavotte en Rondeau of the Suite in E Major (mm. 26–27 and parallel spots). The reason for this surprising abstention, prevalent also, so it seems, in other masters such as Handel or Vivaldi (in sharp contrast to the ubiquitous use of all these patterns in the Classical era), *may* derive from the violin and the preference of composers to start strong beats with the downbow as well as to start a repeated pattern with the same rather than the opposite bow stroke. Admittedly, this is speculation, but whatever the reason, the aversion is indubitable and it will be well to respect it.

FIGURE 18.2

a.

Hardly ever found:

b.

For four and for six equal notes, we find the patterns shown in Fig. 18.3, in the approximate order of their frequency.

FIGURE 18.3

a.

Found:

b.

The dactylic pattern 𝄞 and the anapestic pattern 𝄞 occur in most combinations, of which those found in Fig. 18.4 are some examples.

The dotted note occurs with about equal frequency slurred by twos 𝄞 or detached 𝄞 . For strings the detached manner was most probably made idiomatic by shortening the dotted note: 𝄞 (rather than by doing it in the modern manner: 𝄞 ). The form 𝄞 , very rare for instruments (but see the second movement of the Clavier Concerto in E Major, mm. 8 and 20), occurs occasionally for the voice (such as in Cantata No. 84/1, "Ich bin vergnügt"), as mentioned earlier in connection with Ex. 16.3.

FIGURE 18.4

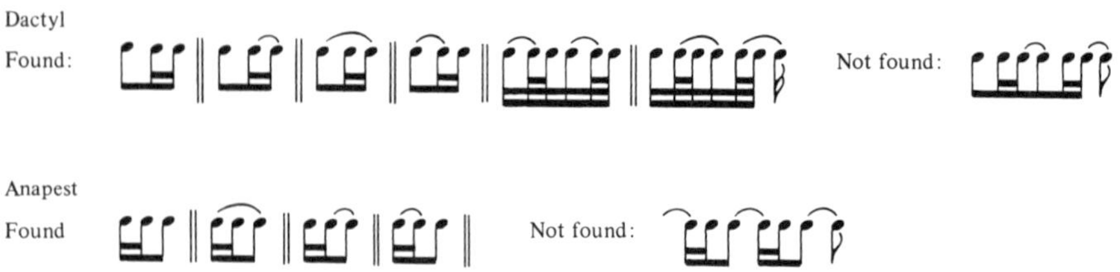

Dactyl

Found:

Not found:

Anapest

Found

Not found:

Triplets, as well as their ternary counterparts in meters such as $^6_8$, $^9_8$, and so forth, are adaptable to most slurring patterns. They can all be slurred by threes or in larger groups; they can all be detached; or they can be shaped in a two-to-one pattern, with ⌐⌐⌐ the most frequent, ⌐⌐⌐ less so, and ⌐⌐⌐⌐⌐ quite rare.

The dotted ternary figure of the siciliano rhythm will either be all detached or have the first two notes slurred: ⌐⌐ . Slurring all three notes is rare, but tying the third note over does occur: ⌐⌐ ⌐⌐ .

Passages in thirty-second notes are mostly of an ornamental character and generally ought to be slurred.

*Melodic design.* Here one absolute rule is the slurring of an appoggiatura to its parent note, regardless of whether the appoggiatura is written in regular notes or as an ornamental symbol (a half circle or a small unmetrical note). This is true also of other *Vorschläge*, such as an unaccented, rhythmically anticipated grace, or a slide, or a turn, or a related ornament.

Apart from these certainties we can speak only in general terms. Generally, then, scalewise movements favor slurs, leaps favor detachment. In Ex. 18.9a, from the Sonata in G Minor for Solo Violin, we see two slurs of three and two of five notes, comprising exactly those pitches that move stepwise. This is simply a tendency, by no means a rule. Many scale passages are detached, and often large leaps are encompassed in a slur (see Ex. 18.10). Among the leaps that tend to be slurred are upward or downward leaps involving pitches from a chord, as shown in Ex. 18.9b, from the Corrente of the Suite in B Minor for Solo Violin; as quasi-arpeggios they are more of harmonic than melodic nature. Pitches that alternate with a changing tone either above or below are also candidates for slurring, as shown in Ex. 18.9c, from the Third "Brandenburg" Concerto. The same tendency applies with a figure on the upbeat, as for instance in the Violin Concerto in A Minor (Ex. 18.9d) and parallel spots.

An upbeat of one or more notes tends to be detached from the following downbeat unless it is purely ornamental, such as a written-out anticipated slide or *Vorschlag*. This is generally of special importance for

EXAMPLE 18.9.   Bach

a. Sonata in G Minor for Solo Violin, BWV 1001/4

b. Suite in B Minor for Solo Violin, BWV 1002/3

c. Third "Brandenburg" Concerto, BWV 1048/1

d. Violin Concerto in A Minor, BWV 1041/1

organ or harpsichord, where such detachment is often needed to clarify the meter.

As a final thought, we should be aware that long slurs, other than for ornamental figurations in thirty-second notes or for fast-moving passages in even values, are generally out of place. For any theme or phrase of some length, especially if it is made up of different note values, it behooves us to search for its subunits and clarify the latter through the combination of slurring and detachment.

Limitation of space does not permit more examples and the illustration of other, probably less distinct tendencies. Though all these tendencies have to yield to Bach's limitless imagination also in matters of articulation, an awareness of those mentioned may be of some help and encourage further, perhaps computerized, research.

*Additional comment.* Considering how hard it is to find the right articulation for works that are not marked, it is unfortunate that modern editors will revise, often drastically, authentic autograph markings. A case in point concerns the solo violin sonatas and suites. Their articulation is a feat of genius not alone from the musical but also from the violinistic-technical point of view. Except for a few spots where, unquestionably due to oversight, minor adjustments are called for, all the pieces can be played as written to the best musical effect and greatest bowing comfort. To tamper with Bach's articulation without good cause is unconscionable. For one illustration out of many, see Ex. 18.10, from the Sonata in A Minor, where Bach's clear markings are written below the notes and those of a number of modern editors above the notes (in the manner mostly heard on disks and in concert these days). No technical necessity caused this change that so drastically alters the character of the passage, turning it from one expressing anger or stubbornness to one of shallow frivolity. This distortion of the musical affection illustrates well the occasional power of articulation to shape and to misshape.

EXAMPLE 18.10.   Bach, Sonata in A Minor, BWV 1003/4

modern editions:

Bach:

## *Keyboard Fingerings and Articulation*

Up to the early 18th century, keyboard players used the thumb only sparingly, and in particular the most common fingering pattern for scales was one that alternated two fingers—for example, 3, 4, 3, 4, 3, 4 for the ascending right or the descending left hand, or 2, 3, 2, 3, 2, 3 and occasionally 1, 2, 1, 2, 1, 2 for the rising left and the falling right hand. Other fingerings must have been in use to accommodate different rhythms and keys as well as personal preferences. As early as 1565, Tomás de Santa Maria, in his remarkable clavichord treatise *Arte de tañer fantasia*, presented fingerings with many modern features, including the frequent use of the thumb in sequences such as 1, 2, 3, 1, 2, 3 or 1, 2, 3, 4, 1, 2, 3, 4 (1 standing for the thumb) as well as adjustments for various keys and scale fragments of different lengths. Michael Praetorius had in 1619 expressed his contempt for the pedantic authors of fingering patterns by saying that all that matters in a passage is that it be played agreeably and precisely, even if one has to use one's nose to do so (*Syntagma musicum*, 2:44). It is naive to assume that everybody used only the textbook formulas.

What concerns us here is that a number of modern scholars and historically oriented performers (notably organists) have derived from the two-finger textbook patterns theories about intended two-by-two articulation and two-by-two rhythmic unevenness. Yet both these theories rest on very weak foundations.

The rhythmic thesis is flawed by assuming an "involuntary uneven-ness" when crossing fingers, such as the third above the fourth; this unevenness is in turn to be proof of a composer's wish to that effect. As I have discussed at some length in my earlier (1965) study ("French *Inégales*," 345–52), involuntary unevenness is due to technical defect (like out-of-tune playing on string instruments) and as such cannot be proof of the composer's intention, since the latter has a right to expect technical competence from performers. *Every* fingering is uneven and has built-in tendencies to unevenness because the hand is asymmetrical and the fingers differ in their length, strength, and degree of mobility and independence. Such tendencies show up in rhythmic irregularities during the early stages of technical study, and the success of the latter can be measured in the way in which the natural tendencies are over-come. Thus a fingering can tell us something about how a beginner on that instrument sounded but nothing more than that. In the evolution of keyboard playing, the prevalent fingerings reflected simply the current state of technology, as did comparable procedures in the fields of man-ufacturing and transportation: these fields were trying to find the most efficient ways to solve technical problems. In that sense a better, more "modern" fingering is comparable to the invention of the stirrup, a better mousetrap, or a jet engine to replace the propeller. The old fin-gerings were not ideal vehicles for the rendition of intended rhythmic and articulatory nuances; they were simply the best available, the state of the art, for rendering a sequence with regularity and precision. The idea of a built-in *intentional* unevenness can be easily led *ad absurdum* if instead of evenly written scale-like sequences we deal with rhythmic variants: with triplets, dactyls, anapests, and other rhythmic patterns for which a would-be two-by-two unevenness would create havoc.

Similar is the case with articulation. It is true that the use of the old alternating fingering practically enforces a two-by-two articulation *if one uses the modern hand position* and holds one's hands more or less parallel to the keyboard or, for ascending scales, leans the right hand to the left to allow the thumb to move easily under the other fingers. The old alternating fingering required a different hand position: for a rising scale the right hand was turned to the right to permit a "walking" action with the third finger easily climbing over the fourth, and similarly turned to the left for descending scales (see Santa Maria, *Arte de tañer*, fol. 38*v*). By keeping the hand soft and flexible ("like cats' paws," in Santa Maria's graphic simile), any scale passage could then be executed with perfect evenness and in any desired articulation, including the smooth legato linking any number of notes. We ought therefore to discount all theories regarding fingerings that dictate two-by-two slurring sequences or rhythm patterns of long–short or short–long. Peter le Huray agrees that "it is incorrect to argue . . . that paired fingerings have any influence on phrasing or articulation" (*Authenticity*, 58).

It is true, though, that certain fingerings do have interpretive impli-cations, but they are far more frequent on the violin than on the key-board. On the violin specific fingerings can change the timbre (use of different strings), strengthen a tone (use of a stronger finger), produce a portamento, or else avoid one, use harmonics, and so on; but if so intended they have to be written in by the composer at the very spot in the music where such effect is desired. They will never show up in a scale exercise that by definition is not meant to produce a special ex-pressive effect but is meant to sharpen one's technical skill. In order not to confuse abstract technical skill and the use of fingerings for special effects, it is important to keep in mind that there are two types of fingerings that must be kept apart. French violinists referred to them as *doigté du mécanisme* and *doigté de l'expression*. Of these two the "mechan-ical" fingering showed the easiest manner (known to the author) of negotiating a sequence of notes with accuracy and at the required speed. The "expressive" fingering sacrifices ease for a certain more desirable result. A scale fingering in a textbook is the classic example of a "me-chanical" fingering that can give us no clue to any intended expressive result. On the keyboard, "expressive" fingerings are far rarer, and even where we have surviving original fingerings for actual works, they can tell us something about this or that master's technical vocabulary but very little, if anything about his musical intentions.

## *Summary*

Summarizing briefly the preceding four chapters, it can be said that the role of articulation in performance can range from essential to marginal. The role is essential (1) where a pattern of slurring and detachment is revealed as integral to the musical thought by remaining the same on each occurrence; (2) where such a pattern is a needed means of proper phrasing in clarifying melodic units and subunits in both their inner coherence and their relationship to what precedes and follows; (3) where the expression of a passage or phrase calls for either the smooth-ness of legato or the clarity and brilliance of staccato.

In other musical situations where the composer indicates a pattern of articulation but is inconsistent about it on repeats or in parallel spots, the important matter may be the overall character, such as basically legato, basically staccato, basically a mixture of slurring and detach-ment, while in each instance the exact disposition of the slurs, the de-gree of detachment, and the precise mixture of the two styles may be of minor importance.

Where the composer failed to indicate the desired articulation—the keyboard works of Bach and of many of his Italian and German con-temporaries are prime examples—the very neglect to specify patterns of slurring and detachment marks articulation to be a minor concern. Here the performer has to supply some design of articulation with a view to supporting the expression of the work and its phrasing. For Bach, for instance, it will be wise to derive guidelines from the study of his many fully articulated works for melody instruments, from which we can extract certain leanings both positive and negative. But we must beware of turning these leanings into rules to be mechanically applied, such as slurring all stepwise progressions and detaching all leaps; the results of such procedure could be deplorable. By and large we should be aware of the leanings but must not be afraid to follow our own musical instincts, inasmuch as the composer, through a *laissez faire* attitude, placed himself, in full awareness of what he was doing, into the hands of the performers' judgment.

For the Classical era, where the masters generally provided explicit markings, the main problems probably center on the greater or lesser sharpness of staccato; on the difference between dots and strokes; and on the question of emphasis on the first note under a slur. Furthermore—and this applies as well to the masters of the late Baroque—we have to be alert to the frequent accentual meaning of strokes, where this articulation symbol takes the place of the modern accentual sign $>$, which was not available before the last years of the 18th century.

The widely held idea that the basic bowstroke of the era involved swelling and tapering similar to the *messa di voce* is probably based largely on the misinterpretation of a passage in Leopold Mozart.

Other fashionable theories about old keyboard fingerings and their implications of two-by-two articulation and rhythmic unevenness also are better discounted.

# Part V

## *Phrasing*

# 19

# THEORY OF PHRASING

Phrasing consists of identifying the internal organization of a musical work and clarifying it in performance. All elements of music enter into this organization: melody, rhythm, harmony, counterpoint, dynamics, articulation. They are often so closely interwoven that for simplicity's sake I shall in the following refer mainly to melody, which, with its inherent rhythm, is the dominant structural factor. I shall do so in full awareness that harmony, with its cadences and half cadences, is often an equal component in shaping and articulating the internal organization of a musical work.

There are two main aspects to melodic structure. The first is the segmentation of melody in distinct units, whereby larger ones may be composed of smaller ones, which in turn can contain subunits in an often complex hierarchic pattern. This aspect will be referred to as the "anatomy" of phrasing. The second aspect refers to the way in which the single pitches of a melody, meaningless by themselves, generate through their interaction an energy flow between levels of lower and higher intensity—for instance, from impulse over climax to repose. This aspect will be referred to as the "physiology" of phrasing.

The principal, though not the sole, means of clarifying melodic units is the caesura. The principal means of clarifying energy flow is dynamic shading, occasionally supplemented by rhythmic nuances of *rubato, accelerando, ritardando.*

## The Linguistic Analogy

"Phrase" is a linguistic term, and the concept of phrasing, like that of articulation, is derived from language. Whereas articulation has its analogy in diction, the linguistic parallel to musical phrasing is the way a piece of prose, a poem, or a speech is organized in a hierarchy of units of different structural levels, from chapters, to paragraphs, to sentences, to clauses (or, in poetry, from a poem, to stanzas, to verses, to word groups). All of these units form a unity of meaning. Within paragraphs or stanzas the demarcation of the units is externalized by punctuation marks that range from periods for a self-sufficient unit, to colons and semicolons, to commas indicating groupings with increasing degrees of incompleteness. Energy flow within a musical unit has its linguistic parallel in the way words create patterns of emphasis and deemphasis whose inner dynamics in a speech or recitation is reflected in speeding up, slowing down, lowering or raising the voice.

*Words and Music.* The analogy with language has been emphasized in all essays on musical phrasing, historical as well as modern ones. The similarities are indeed striking, and whenever music is linked to words we usually find a measure of coordination between linguistic and musical structure—a coordination that can range from very close to very loose. It is closest in recitative, in which musical declamation is fully adapted to the rhythms and inflections of the words. It is loose when, in arias or choruses, words or whole sentences are repeated and syllables extended in rich melismatic figurations. The closer the link the more guidance we gain from the text for the proper phrasing of the music.

In a closed number, such as an aria, the link can still be quite close when the words are by and large set syllabically. For an example, see Ex. 19.1, from the duettino "La ci darem la mano" from *Don Giovanni* (Act I, Scene 7). Here we see how closely the musical organization follows the textual one, how clearly the demarcation of the textual units—their hierarchy as marked by commas, semicolon, and period—are reflected in both melody and harmony. The semicolon has its perfect realization in the half cadence, the period in the full cadence, and the various commas marking the subunits will suggest corresponding musical dividing lines—quite clearly after "mano" and "lontano," ever so subtly for the others. Where, in contrast to this example, the composer introduces lengthy florid passages, the word–music link is loosened and the linguistic guidance to musical phrasing diminished.

For instrumental music we have to extract the internal structure from musical considerations alone, and here we encounter the problem of phrasing in its most challenging form. Through analysis we have to try to discover both the organization of units and the fluctuations in intensity. For instrumental music of some complexity, there is often

EXAMPLE 19.1.   Mozart, *Don Giovanni,* K 529 I,7

more than one reasonable solution; hence the results of our analysis may well be challenged by others. It will help us in our endeavor to know how the task was approached by contemporary theorists as well as by a few later ones that may still have some pertinence. But before we survey their opinions, it will be well to look at, and try to sort out, the terminological confusion that has bedeviled the discussion of phrasing ever since it began.

***Problems of Terminology.*** The first theorists who addressed the question of phrasing in the early part of the 18th century did so from the vantage point of composition by discussing how to write good melodies and how to fit them best to a given text. For this reason they were mainly concerned with the sectional aspect of the melody. They had to invent a new terminology for this purpose, and the terms they used were predictably taken from grammar and rhetoric, terms such as "paragraph," "period," *Abschnitt, Einschnitt, rhythmus, caesura,* or the French *incise.* Problems arose from the frequent double meaning of these terms, many of which can stand either for a melodic unit or for the break that separates units.

The confusion in the meanings of these terms goes back all the way to Latin. There *incisio* meant basically "cutting into," and hence "incision"; but in classical rhetoric the word had the double meaning of a caesura (the verbal counterpart to "incision") and of a speech segment such as a clause. The French grammatical term *incise* stands for a small subphrase, but, as in Latin, has been used in music with the double meaning of both the cut that separates and the segment that has been separated by the cut. Such equivocation is unnecessary since there are two distinct French words for the two concepts: *incision* for the cut, *incise* for the segment. A similar equivocation has created confusion in German. The language has two perfectly good terms, *Einschnitt* and *Abschnitt*, the first of which denotes an incision, the second a segment separated by an incision. Yet the German theorists in the 18th century used both terms indiscriminately in both meanings. Similarly perplexing is the double use by some old writers (Kirnberger among them) of *caesura* both as a small unit of melody and (in the meaning used exclusively today) as a break between two distinct melodic units. The resulting confusion prompted Kirnberger's lament (in Sulzer, *Allgemeine Theorie*, s.v. "Einschnitt") that one speaks of *Perioden, Abschnitte, Einschnitte, Rhythmen,* and *Caesuren* in ways that show that the same word sometimes has two meanings and two different words have the same meaning.[1]

The confusion does not end here. Besides the equivocations, there are, as Kirnberger has noted, the synonyms that clutter the discussions with a bewildering multitude of terms. Among them is the term *rhythmus* for a relatively small melodic section. It is presumably derived from the poetic feet and their musical counterpart of "sound feet" (*Klangfüsse*), both of which offer a vocabulary of rhythmic patterns for melodic modules. *Rhythmopoeia* is the term used by a number of theorists for this system of "sound feet." Marpurg used the term *Rhythmus* in the sense of a small melodic section in 1758 (*Anleitung zur Singcomposition*, 51) and defines it as a few poetic feet—no more than four, he adds—that can be sung in one breath. Kirnberger uses the term in a similar sense (in Sulzer, *Allgemeine Theorie*, s.v. "Einschnitt"), as does Schulz (in Sulzer, *Allgemeine Theorie*, s.v. "Vortrag"), and it is adopted as well by Türk in his *Klavierschule* of 1789. A hundred years later, Mathis Lussy uses the French term *rythme* as the musical counterpart of an alexandrine (twelve-foot) line (*Traité de l'expression musicale*, 54). It would be advisable not to translate these German and French words as "rhythm" but as "phrase," "melodic unit," or "subphrase," as the case may be, to avoid confusion with the modern English meaning of "rhythm." Yet this modern meaning was also known in the 18th century: Mattheson defines the term *rhythmus* in the modern sense of patterns of accented and unaccented, long and short notes (*Vollkommene Capellmeister*, pt. 2, chap. 5, par. 1).

It is advisable not to perpetuate the confusion created by the double meanings and the terminological redundancies. We cannot undo ambiguous usage by the old theorists; but when we coin new terms, we should do so with a view to clarifying matters, not to preserving a chaotic state, however venerable its family tree. In the interest of clarity, whatever terms we choose, we must leave no possible doubt whether we speak of a melodic unit or of the point of separation between two neighboring units. For this reason the anglicization of "incise" is not, to my mind, a happy move, and its spreading use is inauspicious. It is not an English term that would be readily understood, and its double meaning is confusing. For the notion of a subphrase, we might use this very word or speak of "subunit," "subsection," "fraction," or some such term that implies a melodic entity.

In *modern* discussions of phrasing, regardless of period, we also meet with terminological difficulties that are due to the nature of the subject rather than to semantic infelicities. In view of the vagueness of musical "meaning" and the abstract nature of pitch combinations, such familiar terms as "motive," "theme," "phrase," and "period" are bound to be imprecise. Different analysts vary in the use of these terms, so that even in seemingly clear-cut cases there will hardly ever be agreement. Taking the relatively simple case of the opening of Mozart's Symphony in G Minor (Ex. 19.2), the term "motive" might be given to section a, or else to section b. To others, section b would be a "phrase," in which case c would become a "period." Yet others will call c a "phrase" and d a "period," in which case b would be a "subphrase," a "clause," an "incise," a "rhythm," or one of many other terms used to designate an incomplete melodic unit; and any or all of these terms could just as well be applied to the "motive" of section a.

EXAMPLE 19.2.    Mozart, Symphony in G Minor, K 550/1

It is not possible to resolve this particular muddle since there is no compelling reason, whether musical, logical, or semantic, for preferring one over the other term, other than that "phrase" or "period," in keeping with linguistic use, should stand for a unit that has a greater sense of completeness than a subphrase or motive and ends with a full or at least half cadence. One simply has to agree on the terms on a case-by-case basis.

## Phrasing in Notation

Singers and players of wind and brass instruments have to breathe. Whenever possible they should do so where a caesura is in order—that is, between melodic units, not in the midst of one. Since an untimely breath can be disturbing, it is understandable that some composers introduced breathing signs to avoid such a musical mishap. It is hardly a coincidence that what seem to be the first such signs turned up in 1600, when solo song began to blossom in recitative and monody. Cavalieri placed in several of his works the breathing sign ⅋ above the last note of a melodic unit. In Ex. 19.3a we see the sign for voice as well as for flutes in his "Aria cantata e sonata, al modo antico" of 1600. Schütz, in the *Psalmen Davids* of 1628, and in later works, used a vertical stroke ❙ at the point of the caesura and did so predictably at the end of each verse.

Le Bègue, in his *Troisième livre d'orgue* of ca. 1700, used a vertical stroke between notes especially where phrases are irregular and their endings not obvious. The German Johann Peter Sperling explained in 1705 the vertical stroke as "a sign that right there the text ['text' standing here not for words but for a melodic unit that may or may not be set to words] in some fashion ends: it is called *comma* or *virgula*. Such a sign is also found at the end of an affect which was marked with a musical term (such as *piano, presto, tardo*) and generally a different affect begins right there."[2]

We find some masters using letters in addition to the vertical stroke: L'Affilard, in his treatise of 1694, used the letter c as breathing sign, as shown in Ex. 19.3b (*Principes pour apprendre la musique*, 45; [1697], 57–58). The flutist Michel Blavet, in his sonatas of 1728 and 1731, used the letter h (standing probably for *haleine*) and placed it in accord with modern expectations.

EXAMPLE 19.3

a. Cavalieri (1600)

b. L'Affilard (1694, 1697)

François Couperin, in the first volumes of his two sets of clavecin pieces of 1713 and 1716–17, occasionally indicated the demarcation of melodic units by beaming eighth notes and shorter values, as shown in Ex. 19.4a. In his third book of *Pièces de clavecin* of 1722, he introduced the

EXAMPLE 19.4.  Couperin

a. V. La Bandoline
Rondeau
Légèrement, sans vitesse

b. XIV. Le Rossignol vainqueur
Tres légèrement

c. XIV. Les Fauvètes Plaintives
Tres tendrement

d. XVI. La Létiville

e. XVI. le Drôle de corps

sign of a large comma ❩, the meaning of which he explains in the preface: it serves "to indicate the end of a melody or of harmonic [polyphonic?] groups [la terminaison du chant, ou de nos phrases harmoniques] and to convey the need to separate the end of one melody before moving to the next. Though in general [the separation will be] hardly perceptible, persons of taste will sense that there is something amiss in the performance if one does not observe this little silence. . . . These silences must be inserted without affecting the beat [Ces silences se doivent faire sentir sans altérer la mesure] [Preface])."

Couperin's placement of this caesura sign conforms in most cases with our present-day sensibilities: we find it often at cadences, both masculine and feminine, each of which is illustrated in Ex. 19.4b, from the quatorzième *ordre*. Occasionally we meet with surprises, as in Ex. 19.4c, from the same *ordre*, where the unexpected caesura finds its explanation in the left hand part with its quick upbeats. On other occasions the sign will demarcate not phrases but subphrases, as in Ex. 19.4d, from the seizième *ordre*, and sometimes even smaller segments, as in Ex. 19.4e, from the same *ordre*.

## *18th-Century Theorists on Phrasing*

In matters of phrasing, as so often happens in other matters, theory lags behind practice. Few references have so far surfaced from 17th-century theorists. One of these is a brief passage in Thomas Mace's *Musick's Monument* of 1676 about the caesura, a passage of some interest. At the end of his Chapter 23, which deals with graces, he speaks of "the Pause." Though not a grace properly speaking, "yet the performance of It, (in proper Places) adds much *Grace:* And the thing to be done, is but only to make a kind of *Cessation, or standing still*, sometimes *Longer* and sometimes *shorter* according to the *Nature*, or *Requiring* of the *Humour* of the *Musick*" (109–10).

Johann Mattheson seems to have been the first theorist who dealt thoroughly with the sectional organization of melody, and he himself claims his priority in this "most important" matter. We find his detailed analysis of the segments of musical discourse and their borderlines in *Der vollkommene Capellmeister* of 1739 in a chapter entitled "Von den Ab- und Einschnitten der Klang-Rede" (pt. 2, chap. 9).[3] He instructs the composer how to write a good melody and in particular how to fit a melody to a given text. His long, rambling disquisition does not address the performer, but its historical importance calls for a brief report. Mattheson stresses the analogy of poetic and musical rhetoric and the ensuing need to parallel the punctuation in poetry with an appropriate segmentation of the melody. A section ended by a comma is compared to a joint of the body (an *articulus*, par. 39); a section ended by a colon is compared to a whole member (*membrum*); and a part ended by a semicolon lies in between, as a half member. The period ends a *periodus*, which contains a full, self-sufficient meaning. The punctuation is underlined in music by cadences, with a perfect cadence for the period, half cadences for the semicolon. A colon does not call for a full cadence, only for a "delay," a calming of the melody (par. 54: "einen Aufschub, eine verlangende Ruhe, *clausulam desiderantem*"). Though in the chapter heading he lists both *Abschnitte* and *Einschnitte*, in the text itself he speaks only of *Einschnitte*; by using this term in the double meaning of segment and caesura, he may have been responsible for the long-lasting confusion of the German terms discussed above.

Quantz, in his *Versuch einer Anweisung* of 1752, more than once mentions the need to clarify borderlines between phrases. He does so most succinctly in Chapter 11, Paragraph 10, where he writes: "Ideas that belong together must not be separated; but one must make a separation where one musical idea ends and a new one starts without a [notated] break or rest; especially when the last note of the preceding and the first note of the following idea are of the same pitch."

More important than these statements is Quantz's example of a whole adagio movement with detailed indications about its phrasing through very sophisticated nuances of dynamics.[4] The illustration was meant to demonstrate the free embellishment of an austerely notated adagio, and the important lesson it provides about phrasing was a by-product of the primary goal. The notational resources of the time did not allow the indications of the highly refined, almost mannered shaping of the individual phrases that Quantz tried to convey. Consequently, he had to explain his ideas verbally and did so in numerous paragraphs of such forbidding dryness that they must have deterred readers than as well as now. In *OrnB* (568–69), I have given an excerpt of this embellished adagio with Quantz's verbal directives transcribed into modern dynamic marks, and I reproduce it here in Ex. 19.5. Quantz specifies "strong," "stronger," "weak," "very weak," "waxing," "waning," "flattering," and so on. The dynamic marks, though by necessity only approximations, get the basic idea across and provide us with a remarkably vivid demonstration of Quantz's refined playing style and of phrasing ideals in the galant style (see also Ex. 33.4 for another transcribed segment of the same movement).

Joseph Riepel, like Mattheson, deals with phrasing in 1752 and 1755 from the vantage point of the composer. He is a pioneer in stressing the importance of symmetry and melodic consistency between units of phrasing. He speaks of "Zweyer," "Dreyer," "Vierer," and "Fünfer," whereby a "Zweyer" is defined as two measures that resemble the next two in their melodic design ("2 Tacte, die den nächsten 2 Tacten der Bewegung nach ähnlich sind" [Anfangsgründe, 2:2]). Interesting and important is his reliance on feeling and intuition rather than on abstract principles. He may also have been the first to have recognized the confusion between the terms *Abschnitt* and *Einschnitt*.

C. R. Brijon writes in his violin treatise of 1763: "It is certain that song is, or should be, the foundation of all music. . . . Every instrument, and in particular the violin, must follow this law. But in order to do so it is absolutely necessary to phrase what one plays [il est absolument nécessaire de phraser ce que l'on exécute]; this means to observe the periods, the commas, the breathing [des aspirations] just as in vocal music" (*Reflexions sur la musique*, 11). Later, in Article 4, "Des phrases & des repos," after comparing musical phrases to phrases that in a speech must comprise a complete meaning, he writes: "One must observe a

EXAMPLE 19.5.    Quantz, Adagio movement

(Dynamic marks added according
to Quantz's verbal directives)

small pause [un petit intervalle] between the note that ends a phrase and the one that starts the next one, without disturbing the meter [sans que cela préjudicie à la mesure]" (17).

Jean Jacques Rousseau, in his *Dictionnaire* of 1768, treats of phrasing in the articles "Ponctuer" and "Phrase." The short entry under "Ponctuer" addresses the composer. The other article has some interest for the performer. In it he defines a phrase as an uninterrupted sequence of pitches or harmonies that form a more or less complete meaning and that come to a rest point with a more or less perfect cadence. A singer who grasps the meaning of the phrase and conveys it well, he writes, is a man of taste. He who only renders the pitches, the intervals, and the rhythm, however exactly, without grasping the significance ("le sens") of the phrases, is only a bungler.

Johann Philipp Kirnberger's lament about the confusion of terms has been quoted above. He, too, points to the parallel between musical phrasing and the versification of a poem or the sections of a speech.[5] In speech, he says, one grasps the meaning of a sentence only at its end, and the same is true of music. When after a series of connected pitches there occurs a noticeable easing that gives the ear a sense of rest and concludes the meaning of the phrase, the ear combines these pitches into an intelligible unit ("einen faßlichen Satz"). Such an ending may be either a complete cadence or simply a melodic formula ("melodische Klausel") with a calming harmony (*Kunst des reinen Satzes,* 2:138). In his terminology the largest unit is the *Abschnitt,* or *Periode,* which corresponds to a sentence ending with a period. A good melody should consist of several *Abschnitte;* and each *Abschnitt* consists of several *Einschnitte* or *Rhythmen,* which together form a meaning but require more to make complete sense. The best *Einschnitte* have four measures, but other lengths are also frequent. The *Einschnitte,* in turn, often have smaller subunits, the *Caesuren.* We see how the terminological confusion thickens: whereas others, following Mattheson's example, use *Abschnitt* and *Einschnitt* indiscriminately, for Kirnberger, *Einschnitt* is a synonym for *Rhythmus* as a smaller subunit; and his *Caesur* is a further subsegment, not a brief silence.

Some German theorists writing later in the century deal systematically with the performer's problems of proper phrasing. The first of these may have been J. A. P. Schulz in his article "Vortrag" in Sulzer's *Allgemeine Theorie.*[6] As others had before him, Schulz compares a performance with an oration. Every piece of music, he says, has its phrases, periods, and accents, just as a speech has. Schulz uses the term *Phrase* in the widest sense of designating any melodic unit, from periods to small segments. He stresses the need of making clear the caesuras, which he refers to as the "commata of song." One marks caesuras either by slightly shortening the last note of a phrase and starting the first note of the next phrase with firmness or by letting the sound taper at the end

of a phrase and swell for the start of the new one. When the composer
has written a rest, there is no problem in finding the demarcation. Without a written rest, however, the seam is harder to detect. Singers usually
find the answers in the words, but instrumentalists have to discover
them by other means. Schulz advises the performer to examine the start
of a piece to determine whether it starts on the beat or with one, two,
three, or more notes before the barline or with a characteristic pattern
such as four notes slurred by twos. Then, if the piece has a regular
construction, the next phrase will most likely start in the same fashion.
Some of Schulz's illustrations are given in Ex. 19.6a (with a beginning on
the beat), 19.6b (with an upbeat of one note), 19.6c (with three notes),
19.6d (with five notes), and 19.6e (with a pattern of four notes slurred
two by two). He marks the phrase ending with a circle ( o ) and the start
of a phrase with a cross ( + ).

EXAMPLE 19.6.    Schulz

Schulz's principle works very well on many occasions, though more
so with galant and Classical than with Baroque works, whose melodies
tend to have irregular shapes. It is surprising, though, how often his
principle can be of help for the proper phrasing of, say, Bach's works, as
will be presently shown. Schulz himself was wise to make "regular
construction" a condition for the successful application of his rule. Yet
while a rule may be very logical, the great masters were no pedants who
went by the book. Often they avoided the obvious by indicating through
articulation marks a felicitous inconsistency of phrasing. For instance, in
his Rondo in A Minor K 511, as shown in Ex. 19.7, Mozart had at the
sign of the asterisk at first slurred only the first two notes, allowing for
the identical upbeat phrasing for the repeat of the theme; then on second thought he crossed out this slur with five strokes and replaced it,

EXAMPLE 19.7. Mozart, Rondo in A Minor, K 511

Stems, beams, and cancellation of slur according to autograph.

above the notes, with another slur that encompassed the following would-be upbeat note E, adding a delightful touch of the unexpected.

Schulz advises composers to indicate the meeting places of two phrases by interrupting the beams—in the manner of Couperin. For the longer note values that have no beams, Schulz advises a staccato stroke ("Strichlein") over the note preceding the caesura.

Türk, in his *Klavierschule* of 1789, summarizes the problem of phrasing in the two questions: (1) how to execute a musical thought coherently while separating two phrases (*Perioden*) without interrupting the meter; and (2) how to recognize the points of repose (*Ruhestellen*) in a composition. He answers the first question by advising the performer to stress the continuity of a line, without the insertion of rests, until the thought is completed; as a means to separate the phrases one shortens and lightens the last note, then starts the next phrase with a stronger touch (340–41). He answers the second question by adopting Schulz's principle about the guidance gained from the way a piece starts (343–47).

Heinrich Christoph Koch, in his *Versuch einer Anleitung zur Composition*, addresses primarily composers but offers important insights to performers as well. In his discussion of phrase divisions in the second volume of his treatise (1787), he—like all other writers—refers to language but notes that the units of musical thought are not as precise as those of speech and lack clear grammatical and syntactical relationships such as that of subject and predicate. Thus while music, like speech, poetry, and rhetoric, is in need of resting points ("Ruhepuncte des Geistes"), only *feeling* can determine their location and nature (2:356). These resting points can be more or less distinct, a quality that depends on the completeness or incompleteness of the preceding phrase or segment. A phrase ("ein Satz") is complete when it can be understood as a self-sufficient section of the whole; it is not complete when we expect one or more phrases still to follow. Furthermore, Koch continues, there are also resting points *within* a "Satz," and again only our feeling can persuade us. They are the subphrases, which he calls "Einschnitte."[7]

Phrases can be of different lengths, among which Koch prefers those of four measures ("Vierer"). They can be shortened ("enger"), extended ("erweitert"), and compounded ("zusammengeschoben"). The "compound phrases," where two or more phrases are connected, can originate in various ways. Most common is what he calls "Tacterstickung" or

"Tactunderdrückung" (metrical stifling or elision), where the caesura note of the first phrase is the initial tone of the second one. Kirnberger had also mentioned such occasional overlappings in his article "Einschnitt."

For the issue of performance, Koch's most important contribution may well be the idea that our "feelings"—that is, our musical instincts— rather than any mechanical rules of grammar or syntax, must detect the nature and location of endings and beginnings of phrases and subphrases. It will be well to recall this idea when dealing with later, more sophisticated theories of melodic structure that rely too much on rigid principles.

During the 18th century, theoretical concern focused on what I have called the first aspect of phrasing: identifying phrase beginnings and endings and then differentiating those melodic units that in the invariable analogies to language ended with the counterpart of a comma from those that ended with a semicolon, a colon, or a period. Contemporary theorists did not systematically explore the second aspect of phrasing: the energy flow created by the interaction of the single pitches of a melody. It is this dynamic flux that determines which notes should be stronger, which weaker, which closely linked, and which detached and which ones lead to a climax and which to a repose. We do find in treatises of the time scattered hints about some of these requirements, notably the need to emphasize certain pitches for their importance *within* a musical unit. Quantz's, C. P. E. Bach's, and Leopold Mozart's discussions of this point were reported in chapter 14.

Prior to these three famous mid-century theorists, Mattheson had been a pioneer also in the matter of phrasing by having investigated the question of emphasis and its relation to accentuation (*Vollkommene Capellmeister*, pt. 3, chap. 8). He proceeds predictably from language, defining accent as the stress on a syllable as dictated by pronunciation. As such it is immutable and inhabits every word of two or more syllables. Emphasis, by contrast, is the stress on a whole word, not owing to its usual sound but reflecting its weight within the thought expressed ("nicht nach dem Klange desselben, sondern nach dem darin enthaltenen Bilde des Verstandes" [par. 8]).

Mattheson then demonstrates how vocal music has to mirror both accents and emphases of the text. In that sense, musical accents are stresses dictated by their metrical placement on strong beats or by their length; emphasis is stress expressing the importance of a pitch or group of pitches within the musical unit. Thus accent is a matter of rhythm and meter, emphasis a matter of phrasing, of the internal energy flux.

Mattheson also alludes briefly to the notions of arsis and thesis as two complementary elements, derived from the poetic feet, the musical equivalent of which he refers to as sound-feet ("Klangfüsse" [pt. 2, chap. 7, pars. 10–13]).

*Momigny.* At the end of the 18th century the Frenchman Jérôme-Joseph Momigny started opening new perspectives for the discussion of phrasing. He did so perhaps for the first time in the *Encyclopédie méthodique, musique* (1798), of which he was the coeditor with Framery and Ginguené. In his article "Ponctuer" for that publication, Momigny formulates two basic principles of phrasing, which he was to elaborate in later works. The first is the tenet that music moves from upbeat to downbeat ("la musique marche . . . du levé au frappé") and never in the reverse direction; the second is the precept that proper phrasing in performance involves "stressing the first note of each phrase that requires separation from the preceding one; reinforcing those notes in the body of the phrase that call for emphasis; and making clear which is the note that ends the phrase not only by a rest that follows but also by a fitting inflection that differs from the [initial] stress" (Ponctuer: . . . c'est attaquer la première note de chaque sens qui demande à être séparée de celui qui le précède; c'est renforcer les sons du corps de la phrase qui exigent de l'emphase, & faire sentir quelle est la note qui termine le sens, non seulement par le silence qui la suit, mais encore par l'inflexion convenable, & qui diffère de l'attaque).

He later developed these ideas more fully, mainly in the second of the three volumes of his *Cours complet d'harmonie et de composition* of 1806 as well as in several other publications.[8] Like others before him, Momigny bases his ideas about musical phrasing on the analogy with speech and poetry. He breaks new ground, however, when he sets out to explore systematically the forces that shape and hold together the melodic units on different structural levels and the ways these levels interact with one another.

He sees the smallest unit in the succession of two "members," to which he refers to variously—and in apparent synonymity—as "levé" and "frappé," "antécédent" and "conséquent," arsis and thesis, and action and rest ("action–repos"). These terms always occur in this order, never reversed. He calls the pair *levé* and *frappé* a *cadence*, which consists of either two or three notes forming a binary (masculine) *cadence*, ♩ | ♩ , or a ternary (feminine) *cadence*, ♩ | ♩ or ♩ | ♩♩ . This *cadence* is the fundamental metric-rhythmic unit, the "logical measure," the "proposition musicale." Momigny compares it to the subject–attribute relationship and to the inseparable link between lifting and setting a foot in walking, breathing in and out. A barline that is placed between the *levé* and the *frappé* is not a sign of separation but rather one of close union: a hyphen, not a partition.

Several *cadences* in a series combine to form larger units when linked by the same meaning. Momigny compares these larger units, again in analogy to language, in ascending order from a hemistich (half an alexandrine line), which can contain seven, eight, or more *cadences;* a line

(Momigny uses the French word "vers"), consisting of two hemistiches; a strophe, a combination of several lines; and a stanza, which is a group of strophes. The line seems to correspond roughly to what today is often called a "phrase" when Momigny says that "modern music" (that of the Classical masters) has mostly lines of two, four, or eight measures. Momigny also refers to a group of *cadences* sometimes as "période" and sometimes as "phrase," and the exact relationship of all these terms is never clarified; the casualness with which he uses them is shown in his changing use from one case to another. Thus, in a different context (186), Momigny gives the following different hierarchy: *cadence, phrases, périodes, hémistiche, vers, distique, quatrain, couplet, reprise,* a poem or a whole musical work. Beyond *cadence,* we must not expect consistency of terms.

But what matters is not the precision of terms but the fact that there *is* a hierarchy among the units of "meaning," and here Momigny has taken a significant step in pointing to the various structural levels of melodic units, from the *cadence* upward, and to their interaction: units on each of these levels have their own arsis and thesis, he writes, and in case of conflict the higher one prevails over the lower one. In that sense he sees phrasing as the art of subordinating the subunits one to another in their proper relationships so as to fit them into the higher unit of the total period ("le phrasé est l'art de subordonner, l'une à l'autre toutes les propositions qui forment un même sens, de manière à ce qu'elles ne fassent qu'un tout" [185]). And the performer has the duty to clarify ("faire sentir") the periods with its constituent parts in their mutual relationship.

Interesting and surprising is Momigny's principle that in the *cadence* the *antécédent* is to be accented ("accentué," "forcé," "attaqué"). It is also to be sustained in order to achieve a more intense connection with the *conséquent.* Sometimes this accentuation pattern will coincide with the stress patterns of the meter, in which case they reinforce each other. But where the two are in conflict, the accent on the arsis prevails over the metrical stress, in a hierarchy similar to the mentioned dynamic priorities of higher over lower structural units.

Interesting too is Momigny's theory of the rest points ("points de repos"), the caesuras. They occur at the end of a *cadence,* of a unit of meaning ("la fin d'un sens"), of a *période* or a *hémistiche,* of a phrase or a line, or a large section ("reprise" [195]). The weight of the rest point is proportional to the length of the phrasing unit: after a single *cadence* it is very small; when two or more *cadences* follow one another forming a unit of meaning, the rest point is stronger for the last of these, and the same is true also of rest points after hemistiches or larger units.

Momigny's theories are arresting, but some of them are open to question. Apart from some overwrought cerebrations that were not reported here because they have no bearing on actual music making, there are some less esoteric principles that can be questioned. For instance, the irreversible arsis–thesis sequence does not fit the many phrases that start on the downbeat. Momigny tries to bypass this difficulty by explaining the missing arsis as an "ellipsis" (an omission [169]) and by imagining a phantom arsis that precedes the downbeat. This seems an artificial expedient that raises the question whether such an ellipsis does not in fact invalidate the principle of an immutable arsis–thesis sequence.

Another reservation concerns such firm principles as the accented upbeat and, as a consequence, a masculine cadence that moves from strong to weak: Such sweeping rules are dangerous. There is an infinite variety of melodic designs, and an attempt to press them all into a rigid mold can lead in many cases to unmusical results. Consider Ex. 19.2, from Mozart's Symphony in G Minor. Each of the first three sections is certainly what Momigny calls a *cadence,* yet an attempt to play them according to his rules ( ) on every one of the numerous appearances of this first brief module would be musically questionable. Similarly, the principle that every phrase of any extent is to start with an accent would often produce undesirable results. Schulz's mentioned alternative of either starting a new phrase with firmness or, when the last phrase has ended with a taper, to let the new one grow again seems more to the point by allowing adjustments to meet the needs of individual situations.

These reservations must not obscure the importance of Momigny's pioneering contribution: the extension of the notion of phrasing beyond the demarcation of units to include the consideration of the inner forces that form and hold together melodic units, and the exploration of how these units interact at different structural levels. The results of these explorations may have yielded some wrong answers, but having raised these questions and pointed up these problems, of which nobody seems to have been aware before, was a pathbreaking achievement. It was for these innovative thoughts that Hugo Riemann called Momigny "the father of phrasing."

## Later Theorists

In concluding this section, a few words seem in order about two later theorists, Lussy and Riemann. Though certainly not even near contemporaries of the era under examination, they both addressed phrasing problems of the 18th as well as of the 19th century. And they both unintentionally illuminate from different vantage points the pitfalls of an attempt to regulate phrasing with binding rules.

***Lussy.*** The Swiss pedagogue Mathis Lussy published in 1874 his *Traité de l'expression musicale,* whose many editions—eight by 1904—attested to its success and influence. Lussy adopted several ideas from Momigny, though not the latter's central thesis of the fixed *levé–frappé* sequence. Lussy did agree with the supremacy of the *accent rhythmique* (in the sense of an expressive emphasis) over the *accent métrique*,[9] and he did echo Momigny's rule that the first note of each phrasing unit is to be rendered strong and the last one weak [1904] 89). Lussy sees one of the main difficulties of phrasing in the uncertainty over whether a note is the final feminine one of the preceding phrase or the first note of the next ([1904] 70). If final, it has to be weak and tapering; if initial, it has to be strong. He does allow for the possibility of overlap ("l'ellipse"), in which the same note is the end of one and the start of another phrase ([1904] 43).

Whereas, Lussy says, phrases are easy to identify in vocal music, he gives guidelines for their recognition in instrumental music. Among others he points to analogy, symmetry, and the harmony of the accompaniment (i.e., the cadence); but what decides the phrase ending is common sense, logic, context (of melody, harmony, and accompaniment), and above all the sense of rest as perceived by the ear ("le repos que [la note] apporte à l'oreille" [(1904) 71]).

Lussy realized that there is no sensible way of forcing the infinite variety of melodic, harmonic, and rhythmic designs that occur in the music of the 18th and 19th centuries into the frame of a grammar and syntax akin to those of language. Instead, he emphasizes the guidance that common sense and the judgment of the ear can provide. Rather than starting with a theory, then trying to make the facts of musical examples fit its principles, Lussy, with inductive reasoning, proceeded in the opposite direction by first listing and analyzing many examples from the Classical and Romantic masters, then trying to extract principles from these analyses, only to find that he had to adjust these principles to make them fit other cases. His solutions make very good musical sense, but his procedure yielded such a multitude of rules and exceptions that would surely overwhelm anybody's memory. Yet by saying that feeling must be the principal guide, he cuts through the maze of ever so many rules and echoes what Koch had said one hundred years earlier and what, with some qualifications, seems to remain valid to the present. The qualifications are that "feeling" has to have an underpinning of rational analysis and stylistic awareness. Thus fortified, artistic intuition could well be the most practical way of dealing with the problem posed by the great variety of phrase designs—a variety considerable for any one of the Classical masters but rising in, say, the music of Bach to a degree of complexity that defies any attempt to fit the designs into normative patterns.

**Riemann.** The last attempt at a unified theory of phrasing was undertaken by the great German scholar Hugo Riemann, who focused distinctly on the Classical masters. He first published his theory in several monographs beginning in 1886, of which the most important is the

*Vademecum der Phrasierung* (1900). He elaborated his ideas further in various editions of his famous *Musik Lexicon*.

Inspired by Momigny's *levé–frappé* model, Riemann formulated a pervasive upbeat principle whereby all musical figuration leads from an upbeat to the next center of gravity. He also advanced a model of phrase structure that he believed to inhere in all Classical music. According to this model the basic building blocks are *Taktmotive*—musical segments that contain only one strong beat (for instance, one measure) that may be preceded or followed by weaker beats; *Taktgruppe*—segments consisting of two *Taktmotiven* combined into a unit whereby the center of gravity is the second measure; *Halbsätze* (half phrases)—segments consisting of four measures, with the center of gravity the fourth measure; and *Perioden*—segments combining a "Vordersatz" (antecedent phrase) and a "Nachsatz" (consequent phrase) and forming a unit of eight strong beats, resulting in his famous eight-measure (or, rather, twice four-measure) unit that was supposed to be the universal model of musical organization. The inflexibility of this square design was incapable of accommodating the many cases of phrases containing an odd number of measures, frequent even in the Classical repertoire, not to speak of the pervasive irregularity of Baroque melodic designs. This alone was sufficient to put the theory into question and subject it to severe criticism. Added to it, the rigid upbeat theory presented a formidable difficulty with how to account for the countless cases of seemingly obvious downbeat starts. In order to fit such phrases into the procrustean bed of this theory, he resorted to such farfetched devices as chopping off the first downbeat note, pretending it to be the last note of an imaginary preceding phrase, and starting the phrase with the following note, creating an arbitrary upbeat. (Momigny may have inspired this idea.) The artificiality of this procedure and the violence it inflicted on many a melody compounded the problems raised by his rigid, square, phrase model. Together the two difficulties spelled the doom of the theory. Though the latter is today rejected by most scholars, the influence of the upbeat doctrine was profound, and its repercussions are still being felt today in many performances and performing editions. To list just one example out of many: in Mandyczewsky's edition of Haydn's *The Creation* (1922), which is widely used to the present day, the editor has shifted the start of many of Haydn's slurs from the downbeat to the next note in order to change a downbeat phrasing into an upbeat phrasing.

# 20

## PRACTICE OF PHRASING

I have reported on the way the musical thinkers of the 17th and 18th centuries visualized the problem of phrasing and mapped out approaches to its solution. The present chapter will attempt to analyze a few concrete cases.

As some of the theorists have shown us, there are elements of phrasing that lend themselves in part to objective analysis, notably those that deal with the demarcation of units. There are others for which, *pace* Momigny and Riemann, there are no hard and fast rules, notably those that have to do with the energy flow within a phrase. Hence the suggestions proposed here for the phrasing of several individual works had to have in large part recourse to musical judgment and instinct—in other words, to Koch's "feelings." As a result this chapter contains many subjective elements that put it into the category of personal evaluation. It was written with the intention of showing how a solution to phrasing problems can be approached and not necessarily how it can be accomplished. It is meant to encourage critical response and individual explorations of the same or similar problems.

Concerning the first, the "anatomic" aspect of phrasing, the demarcation of units and subunits, its difficulties vary with the style and texture of the music involved. The difficulties for the second, the "physiological" aspect, the energy flow within a melodic sequence, are considerable regardless of style.

In Baroque music—and more specifically in Bach—phrasing on the "anatomic" level is complicated first by the prevalent polyphony, where each voice has to be phrased individually, second by the frequent irregularity of phrase structure, and third by the spinning out of many melodies into extended designs of considerable complexity. In cases of free melodic unfolding, though, we often get some help when we encounter parallelisms such as sequential repetitions of motives, which provide clues to the identification of subunits. We get further help from articulation markings, notably slurs, which are so conspicuously rare, indeed nearly absent, in Bach's keyboard works (other than those transcribed from melody instruments) but often abound in music for strings and winds. The markings themselves have been explained in detail in the chapters on articulation. What matters for us here is that the notes encompassed by a slur are to be sung with an uninterrupted breath and played on strings with an uninterrupted bowstroke and on the keyboard with as close a linkage as feasible in the particular medium. The resulting seamless junction does not allow the ever-so-slight separation of sounds, the caesura, that is needed to clarify the borderline between phrase units or between subunits. For this reason a slur mark will almost always be an indication that the notes under a slur were meant to be part of the same phrase unit or subunit; there are cases where an overlap of units does not allow for a caesura and where a slur might hide a meeting of units; there are others, such as the one shown in Ex. 19.7, where the composer wishes to disguise the seam between phrases and give the impression of an overlap. But these are infrequent happenings; by and large the slur will indicate an absence of demarcation lines and therefore shed light upon the phrase structure, especially with regard to its downbeat or upbeat character.

Dances, which play such a large role in the music of the era, as well as many dance-derived works that have symmetrical designs, often of eight-measure groups, offer generally a smaller problem for the analysis of their phrase structures than the long, irregular, spun-out melodies carried forward by a powerful horizontal impulse. These latter melodies are the ones that confront us with the knottiest challenges for analyzing the "anatomy" and the "physiology" of their phrasing.

For an illustration of such challenge and of the clues that articulation can provide see the start of the Third "Brandenburg" Concerto, given in Ex. 20.1. (The illustrations in this chapter are given in a conventional manner that is accessible to all readers.) Here we have a melody whose propulsive power carries it aloft through eight long measures before its élan is exhausted and it comes to rest with a perfect cadence. In performance it would seem that the dominant interpretive need is to convey the sense of one grand, monolithic arc that represents the melodic unit on the highest structural level. Yet with all its powerful cohesion, this unit is not homogeneous but has distinct subunits that need to be clarified. Thus on a second, intermediary structural level, there are at least four large sections, marked here by brackets, and numbered with Roman numerals. At the juncture of I and II the segments overlap by having one note in common. At the juncture of II and III it is possible to argue that the two should overlap on the first note of the measure;

EXAMPLE 20.1.   Bach, Third "Brandenburg" Concerto, BWV 1048

however, the anapestic character of the elements of section I would suggest a similar anapestic rather than downbeat character for the elements of section III, as marked in the example. The same reasoning would seem to apply to section IV.

On the lowest structural level, that of poetic feet or of motives, we find small units that, like the anapests of section I, are indicated by subdivisions of the brackets. These anapests are typically Momigny-style *cadences* with a *levé* on the upbeat, the *frappé* on the downbeat. The same anapestic module is repeated several times. In Section II the units are larger and fall on the beat. Again we have three quasi-sequential units. Here the downbeat phrasing is clarified by the articulation slurs for the first three sixteenth notes. In section III the upbeat mode is resumed with sequential anapests that on the third occurrence are extended into a longer module that is repeated sequentially and further extended into a scale-like figuration. The anatomy of section III is, however, ambiguous: by starting the section *on* rather than *after* the beat, the repeated motives *could* be interpreted as (downbeat) dactyls. In section IV the three subunits seem definitely upbeat-impelled.

We see that the melody in its totality has a complex structure that is irregular in its change from upbeat to downbeat orientation, from symmetry—in terms of melodic-rhythmic similarity and length of units—to asymmetry and in the varying length of its subunits. In view of this complexity, and lacking the guidance of words, there is nothing inevitable about the analysis attempted here, and it is certainly possible to arrive at different solutions.

The inner structure of such a melody ought to be clarified in performance through a combination of articulation, accents, and dynamic shadings. The anapests at the start should be brought out by shortening the time the eighth notes are held and inserting corresponding rests. I believe it is not advisable to apply Momigny's principle of moving from an accented upbeat to the weak downbeat, in which case the listener would more likely than not perceive the upbeats as downbeats and hear a distorted metric-rhythmic structure. Definite metrical accents on the beats would seem to do better justice to the motoric drive underlying the whole phrase. In section II the change to downbeat phrasing might be underlined by a slight emphasis on the first note under each slur. In section III the actual sound of the eighth notes needs again to be shortened; the ascending scale line from the end of measure 5 through measure 6 should be rendered with a vocal sense of melody and an ever-so-subtle crescendo to prevent it from becoming machine-like. The end of section IV calls for authority and emphasis on its final cadence.

The two next examples are taken from Bach's violin sonatas and partitas, which are, among other things, remarkable for the wealth of slur marks, as preserved in a superb autograph fair copy (P 967; facs. ed. [Kassel, 1950]). The examples are meant to show both new challenges of phrasing and the clues we can derive from carefully placed slurs.

The Allemande from the Suite in D Minor for Solo Violin has the usual two parts, here of sixteen measures each. It is built from a melodic impulse that is spun out, mostly in sixteenth-note figuration, until it reaches a full cadence on the dominant in measure 16. The second, symmetrical part is analogous, but it moves from the dominant to the final cadence in the tonic. Thus on the highest structural level there are only two large units, phrases, or "periods" or whatever one chooses to call them. Together they form, on this level, an arsis and thesis. Again, as in the preceding example, these two long, seemingly uninterrupted melodic units have subunits that need to be suggested in performance, and these subunits are further articulated by smaller groups on the lowest structural level. The exact demarcation of the subdivisions and their components is not obvious, and the ones I shall propose for the beginning measures of the piece (Ex. 20.2) may well be challenged. With only about one-half of the first part given in the example, the brackets indicate the (sub-) units on the intermediate structural level, and the notches within the brackets indicate their smaller components, (sub-) subunits on the lowest level. While the piece does not seem particularly evocative of a dance (the allemande as a dance had been obsolete for over a century), its dance roots manifest themselves in a good measure of regularity and symmetry between the melodic units.

The typical allemande opening—a short one-note upbeat—introduces a subphrase (marked "I") that seems to come to an end on the third beat of the second measure on the low A with a half cadence on the dominant. This unit in turn seems to be subtly subdivided at the upbeat to the second measure into two small groups, marked a1 and a2, the reason being that the upbeat start of the piece seems to suggest a similar

EXAMPLE 20.2.   Bach, Suite in D Minor for Solo Violin, BWV 1004/1

upbeat character for the sixteenth note at the end of the first measure. This note strives for connection with the following downbeat F, to which it is "hyphenated" in the sense of Momigny (as described in the preceding chapter), whereas its link to the preceding note is less firm. If, as here suggested, section I ends on the low A, section II overlaps on this pivot note, starting with three upbeat notes (the arpeggiated A-major triad) and comes to an apparent end at the start of the fourth measure. The section easily divides into three symmetrical, quasi-sequential subunits, each a half measure in length and upbeat-impelled (here marked b1, b2, b3). So does section III, which ends in mid-fifth measure and, like section II, contains three symmetrical subunits of eight notes each (marked c1, c2, c3). They are united again through a quasi-sequential melody and a parallel articulation of three upbeat detached and three downbeat slurred notes; the slurred notes ascend stepwise on pitches 1–2–3 and 3–4–5 of their respective underlying harmony. At first glance one might be inclined to extend this section to the rest of measure 5 and the first three notes of measure 6 with its half cadence on the relative major. But a closer look reveals that a start of a new section IV, as labeled in the example, seems indicated inasmuch as it starts with a group (marked d1) that is followed by two other groups (d2 and d3) that again are in a similar symmetrical relationship with each other as well as with the three groups of section III. Here, too, each group culminates in three downbeat slurred stepwise pitches that descend in inversion: 3–2–1 of the underlying harmony. Whereas large leaps are often indicative of a seam between melodic units, the leaps in this section are deceptive in that they bespeak a hidden counterpoint (so often found in Bach's single melodic lines) that might, for measures 6 and 7, be sketched as shown in Ex. 20.3.

EXAMPLE 20.3.   Bach, Suite in D Minor for Solo Violin

The likelihood for the proposed upbeat phrasing for sections II–IV in Ex. 20.2 emerges when we try, from group b1 on, to start the units one note earlier, on the beat, and realize how the melody becomes plodding and static. The upbeat phrasing does not persist, however: those three downbeat slurred pitches in the middle of each of the c and d groups prepare a turn to downbeat phrasing. At the start of measure 8 the last of these three-note groups of section IV overlaps with the start of section V, whose consistent downbeat phrasing is clarified by its slurs. We have the interesting situation of an overlap not just of a single note but of three notes that had assumed considerable motivic importance. There are many further challenges in the remainder of the piece, with its content of sequential downbeat motives, downbeat subphrases, and mixtures of up and downbeat units.

Here and in all other cases involving complex Baroque figurations, one cannot stress enough how important it is to proceed with the utmost subtlety in trying to clarify the internal structure. Any overphrasing, any attempt to magnify caesuras for fear they might be missed, will only destroy the musical line. Usually it will be sufficient to be aware of the seams and let one's instinct take over in letting them be felt through near-imperceptible nuances of articulation and dynamics.

For a case of unquestionable downbeat phrasing, see Ex. 20.4, from the Sonata in A Minor for Solo Violin. Here the start on the downbeat and the repeat of the half-measure motives with sharply defined echo effects leaves no doubt about the proper shape of the initial phrase. In the further course of the piece, downbeat phrasing seems to predominate, as often made clear by many carefully marked slurs; but as was to be expected in view of Bach's enormous richness of melodic shapes, we encounter upbeat forms as well. (See chap. 16 about the frequent misrepresentation by editors and performers of articulatory and phrasing patterns in this piece.)

In Bach's keyboard music we hardly ever have slur marks to provide clues to desirable rhythmic groupings. In those works or sections of works that are marked by regularity of melodic design, we can derive

EXAMPLE 20.4. Bach, Sonata in A Minor for Solo Violin, BWV 1003/4

BWV 1003/4

guidelines from Schulz's principle, explained above, whereby the start of the piece will tend to illuminate the desirable groupings of related, symmetrical units. Several of the preludes of *WTC* fall into this category. The most obvious case is the Prelude in C Major, *WTC I*, which consists of a series of arpeggiated chords. The Prelude in C Minor of *WTC I* is almost as obvious: the first twenty-four measures are built entirely on a four-note design with the melodic first note followed by a harmonic second note that alternates with its lower neighbor (see Ex. 20.5a), the alternation being doubled in either sixths or thirds in the left hand. The start offers the key to downbeat phrasing. On the harpsichord the only available nuance would seem to be a minuscule agogic lengthening of the first note whenever it changes pitch and thereby marks a melodic progression. (For agogic accents on the harpsichord, see C. P. E. Bach's *Versuch über Art das Clavier* [1753], chap. 3, par. 28, as quoted above in chap. 9, p. 91.) On clavichord and modern piano these melodic keynotes might be played ever so slightly stronger than the rest. In measure 28 the tempo changes to presto, and the figures start on the upbeat (Ex. 20.5b). The following six measures, then, prior to the rhapsodic adagio ending, should probably be conceived as upbeat-oriented.

EXAMPLE 20.5. Bach, Prelude in C Minor, *WTC I*, BWV 847/1

We find many instances where the melodic-rhythmic design of a passage offers clues to its most appropriate grouping. For example, a series of stepwise moves will tend to belong together, while a large leap might suggest a seam; so might a reversal of melodic motion, a change in rhythmic values from smaller to larger denominations, a striking change of harmony, a rest written out in mid-melody (for instance in the theme of the Fugue in B-Flat Minor of *WTC I*), or the symmetrical recurrence of a melodic figure.

In Ex. 20.6a, from the Fugue in D Minor, *WTC II*, the seam after the first eighth note is suggested by the combination of rhythmic change, a leap (admittedly modest) interrupting the otherwise consistent stepwise motion, and a reversal of melodic direction. In Ex. 20.6b, from the Prelude in D Minor, *WTC I*, the symmetry of the six-note modules suggests almost imperceptible seams, while the two leaps in measure 2, preceding symmetrical twelve-note figures, call for a more noticeable separation.

EXAMPLE 20.6.  Bach

a. Fugue in D Minor, *WTC II*, BWV 875/2

b. Prelude in D Minor, *WTC I*, BWV 851/1

In counterpoint, as has been mentioned, each voice has to be phrased independently. For an illustration of a simple two-part passage, see Ex. 20.7, from the Prelude in A Flat, of *WTC I*. The bass line is a series of sequential motives whose phrasing seems unequivocal. The groupings of the soprano part are almost as clear inasmuch as in the third and fourth measure of the example we find a sequential "rhyme" to the motive of the first and second measures. Only in the fifth measure the suggested grouping might be challenged by an overlap on the first note of the measure and subsequent downbeat phrasing. In a performance on the harpsichord, the seams can be clarified by shortening the last note of each group and inserting corresponding rests; on clavichord or modern piano this procedure can be supplemented or replaced by an ever-so-subtle accent on the first note of each group.

In the music of the galant style, the structure of melody became much simpler in that Koch's favorite four-measure phrases predominated and polyphony yielded to homophony. After this wide swing of

EXAMPLE 20.7.   Bach, Prelude in A Flat, *WTC I*, BWV 862/1

BWV 862/1

the pendulum the advent of the high Classical style brought a partial reversal. At the hand of Haydn, notably in his string quartets, a new kind of free-spirited, unrestrictive polyphony returned, and melodic designs became more varied and freer in form. It is indeed this reappearance of polyphony in a new form, this synthesis of Baroque textural elements with galant melodic forms, that is one of the main features separating the high Classical from the pre-Classical, galant style.

For the *Classical composers* as well, it is generally less difficult to identify the boundaries of phrases, whether they connect or overlap. But the greater simplicity of melody, harmony, and texture can conceal ambiguities even for the "anatomy" of the music. The problems of energy flow and dynamic direction, on the other hand, will be omnipresent and represent at least as hard a phrasing challenge for the Classical era as they did for the music of the Baroque masters.

In a specimen like that of Ex. 20.8a, from Haydn's String Quartet Op. 74, No. 2 in F, the phrase is extended over twelve measures, reminiscent in its long arc of spun-out Baroque melodies. It could perhaps be grouped into a section of nine measures whose inner forces seemingly strive—apart from the obvious emphases on the three *sforzati*—toward the cadence on the dominant at the start of measure 9 (17). Here the end of this nine-measure unit overlaps with the start of a subphrase of four measures, which, prolonging the dominant chord, tapers off to its end.

On a lower structural level the nine-measure phrase is composed of motives of about one measure's length. These motives, I believe, overlap on each downbeat, as indicated in Ex. 20.8b by phrasing notches

EXAMPLE 20.8. Haydn, String Quartet Op. 74, No. 2 in F

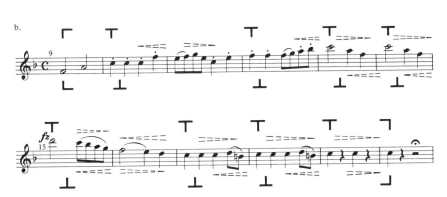

*above* the notes in what would amount to a downbeat phrasing mode. (The dotted hairpin signs here and elsewhere are my suggested nuances.) Analysts favoring upbeat phrasing might argue not for overlap but for seams after the first note of each measure, as indicated *below* the notes.

As to the energy flow, the first small emphasis seems to occur at the start of measure 11 on the dissonance (dominant seventh against organ point on tonic), stronger emphases on the notated *sforzandi* at the start of measures 13, 14, and 15. In these measures the flux will differ according to the diagnosed "anatomy": if we opt for downbeat phrasing, there would be a tapering for each measure:

if we choose the upbeat solution, a caesura would follow the *sforzandi;* the two quarter notes would start *piano subito* and lead with a subtle crescendo to the next accented half note: . The four-measure consequent subphrase would then follow for its motives the same anatomic alternative of downbeat overlap (my preference) versus an upbeat design with a seam after the first quarter note. The two types would call for opposing dynamic flux: for the downbeat type, as indicated above the notes, a swell in the preceding measure 16, and slight accents on the following downbeats, followed by tapers. For the upbeat type, as shown below the notes, a taper in measure 16 might be proper, while in measures 17 and 18 each, a swell, starting from the seam, might be indicated. And for the last two measures a taper presumably would be indicated.

We see how even comparatively simple melodies can harbor problems for both the anatomy and the physiology of phrasing. These problems often have no clear-cut answer.

Let us take as another example the "subsidiary" theme from the *Figaro* Overture (Ex. 20.9). Here we have a melody of eight measures

EXAMPLE 20.9.   Mozart, *Le nozze di Figaro* Overture, K 492

that ends on a perfect cadence and is clearly divided in two subphrases, each starting on the downbeat. It would seem that in the first subphrase the energy flow is aimed at the start of measure 111, on the last of the five repeated quarter-note Es that intensify with each quarter until their tension is released in the feminine ending of measure 111. Similarly, the second subphrase, in spite of the high start and descending melodic line, might gain in eloquence if here, too, we aim the dynamic direction ever so slightly toward the start of measure 115 rather than mirror with dynamics the descent of the melodic line. It is as if the first three measures of each subphrase form an arsis, the fourth the thesis. In spite of Momigny's dictum, echoed by Lussy, that each subphrase should start with strength and then move to weakness, it would seem that for both subphrases an unemphasized start and a simple move toward a gentle climax at the start of the fourth measure will give more plasticity to the melody.

In analyzing the dynamic shadings of a phrase, we have to remember the discussion in the chapters on dynamics about emphasis on certain pitches, appoggiaturas, or chromatically altered, syncopated, or otherwise rhythmically prominent notes. In music with contrapuntal textures, each voice has to have its individual phrasing with the dynamic nuances that help to bring the independence of the parts into clear relief. In Ex. 20.10, from the Finale of Mozart's String Quartet in G Major K 387, the counterpoint of the second violin begins in measure 5 with a series of brief suspensions. It will, I believe, be better not to start each one with an accent but rather swell on the tie to clarify the appoggiatura character, then taper, as suggested in the example by the dotted slurs. (Such nuances would of course not be available to the keyboard.)

EXAMPLE 20.10.  Mozart, String Quartet in G Major, K 387/4

## Summary

The problem of phrasing has two main aspects, which have been referred to here as the "anatomy" and the "physiology" of phrasing. "Anatomy" is concerned with the external division of a melody into units and subunits and the way they are joined to the unit that follows. "Physiology" has to do with the currents of energy engendered by the interaction of a melody's notes with one another and by the ensuing forces that form attractions, tensions, and relaxations and to create momentum, climaxes, and points of rest. The demarcations can be made audible either by inserting a minuscule caesura, usually through short-ening the last note of a phrase, by briefly tapering the last note of a unit and swelling the first note of the next unit, by slightly emphasizing the first note, or by combinations of these. The sequence of tapering and swelling will be indicated also in some cases of an overlap on one or more pivot notes. The energy play is clarified through the combination of rhythmic-agogic and dynamic nuances.

If one thing has emerged from all the preceding discussions, it is the impossibility of providing secure guidelines, let alone rules, for either the anatomy or the physiology of phrasing. The infinite variety of me-lodic designs resists attempts at imposing rules from the outside. Yet some theorists have attempted to do just that. Their rules fit in some circumstances, but not in others. Riemann's upbeat-only principle was self-defeating because of the violence it inflicted on many a musical phrase. The same is true of a rule that every phrase or subphrase starts loud and ends soft, or that every masculine cadence goes from loud to soft. In matters of physiology we have to beware of the venerable old principle that a rising melody should swell, a falling one taper off. Oc-casionally such treatment is fitting, but often it is not, and the gravita-tional forces often work in the reverse. We simply have to study, ana-lyze, and feel in every individual instance. In the end, it is our feeling, supported ideally by stylistic literacy and sensitive musicianship, that will suggest to us an appropriate or, at the least, an acceptable phrasing for a given situation.

# Part VI

## *Ornamentation*

# 21

# PROBLEMS OF MUSICAL ORNAMENTATION

Ever since people have been singing, which means from time immemorial, there has been ornamentation. The urge to toy with musical materials, to manipulate a melody playfully by changing its inner rhythm or by substituting pitches or adding new ones must spring from a deep-seated human instinct because we find its manifestations in all ages and cultures. Today such impromptu embellishment may not be much in evidence in Western art music because it is repressed by our prevailing conventions of performance. But where the restrictions are lifted, as in jazz, the instinct manifests itself with undiminished vigor. Leopold Mozart spoke of a force of nature that compels us to ornament; even a peasant, he said, cannot help but adorn his peasant song with graces (*Versuch einer Violinschule,* chap. 9, par. 1). Musical ornamentation is only one aspect of a general urge to improve life's experience by embellishing the surroundings as well as oneself. There is ornamentation in the figurative arts, in architecture and landscaping, in fashion, jewelry, make-up, hair-do, perfume, even in rhetoric and of course in the decorative arts, all of which are dedicated to beautifying the environment.

The vast role of ornamentation in music of all times is not generally recognized. When we speak of musical ornamentation we think of the 17th and 18th centuries with their strange symbols, miniature notes, cadenzas, and coloraturas. The reason for this one-sided view resides in changed habits of notation and performance conventions: after 1800 improvisation practically disappeared (except for cadenzas) and symbols gradually vanished (except for trills and sporadic miniature notes), while ornamentation, its role hardly diminished, became fully absorbed into the written score. Because of these changes ornamentation is a far more serious performance problem in the 17th and 18th centuries than it became in the subsequent eras.

## The Nature of Ornamentation

Ornamentation, like rhythm, is a complex phenomenon and therefore difficult to define. In music, as well as in the visual arts, an ornament is generally conceived as an addition to structure, in the sense that structure embodies what is of the artistic essence while ornamentation serves to enhance the aesthetic appeal of the structural elements, most typically by adding elegance, grace, smoothness, or variety. Ornament and structure complement one another, and theoretically they can appear in their pure state: structure in no need of additions and ornaments as dispensable decoration. Practically, however, they will usually combine in mixtures that defy clear separation yet will mostly permit an estimate of either structural or ornamental preponderance.[1] The difference between the two contrasting prototypes has important implications for performance. The structural elements have greater specific weight, and in principle their rendition should reflect this fact by being unhurried, rhythmically disciplined, and solidly projected. Ornamentation, by contrast, because of its lighter specific weight, calls in general for a more flowing tempo, easier dynamics, and flexible rhythm. This is true in particular of all ornaments that fall between the beats, whether they consist of one, two, or many notes. By contrast, a brief ornament that is placed on the strong beat—for instance, an appoggiatura—is due by its placement alone a rhythmic-dynamic emphasis that can confer on it a quasi-structural status.

For the purpose of this study, ornamentation will be understood in the sense of pitches that are added to the structural frame. Not fitting this definition, but included nevertheless, will be the arpeggio and the vibrato because both of these, in the era under discussion, were viewed and treated as ornaments.

## Notation and the Problems of Performance

All the problems of performance practice have their roots in the deficiencies and ambiguities of notation. The ornaments are no exception. The score treated them in three different ways: they were either (1) written out in regular notes; (2) indicated by symbols (including the unmetrical miniature notes); or (3) not notated at all. Each of these three alternatives has its own performance problems for the modern interpreter.

For ornaments written out in regular notes, the problem is to identify notes, singly or in groups, as ornamental in order to render them accordingly. For ornaments indicated by symbols, the problem is their proper interpretation. For ornaments not written at all, the problem is the double one, first to determine where embellishment is desirable, second to devise an appropriate design.

*Spelled-Out Ornaments.* Of these three problem areas, the first is the least troublesome but is in need of a brief discussion because its very existence is not often recognized. As a consequence of such oversight, we meet with cases of ill-chosen interpretation when ornament is mistaken for structure. The problem can arise even for the briefest ornaments of one or two pitches but is more important for florid passages.

The ornamental nature of a single note can affect its proper rendition when, for instance, an appoggiatura calls for a different kind of emphasis than would be proper for the straight note;[2] also, as appoggiatura its rhythm can be more flexible and will on occasion benefit from being held slightly shorter or slightly longer than its literal value.

If, on the other hand, a note or small group of notes has the nature of a *Nachschlag*, such ornamental unit will often call for a softer, faster, delayed rendition. This point was discussed in chapter 9 and illustrated in Ex. 9.9

Important as these cases are, of more consequence are the instances of florid passages that disguise their ornamental nature with regular notation. They are the kinds of ornamental figurations that Italian composers and, following their example, many German and English masters of the 17th and 18th centuries did not write down at all. They notated in slow movements more or less only the structural skeleton of the melody and left its embroidery to the improvisatory skills of the performer. (These are the unwritten ornaments of the third category.) While some composers were rather consistent about the skeletal notation (among them Corelli or Purcell), others were variable in their practice, among them Vivaldi and Handel. While they used the austere notation preponderantly, on occasion they wrote out ornamental figures with different degrees of completeness. Bach, at the other extreme, practically always spelled out the *passaggi*, also called "coloraturas," in their definitive form. Therefore it is in his music more than anywhere else that we ought to be on the alert to examine passage work in slow movements as to its potentially ornamental nature with all that this implies for interpretation. In fact, whenever we encounter adagio passages in thirty-second notes either by Bach or by other composers, they will have a strong presumption of being ornamental, especially if they move predominantly by steps or outline chords. The same often applies to sixteenth notes in an andante, larghetto, or a comparable, more flowing tempo.

The interpretation problem of written-out ornaments has received little attention in the literature, partly because it has not been recognized as a problem, partly because it has been eclipsed by the admittedly far more complex difficulties of the symbolized and unwritten ornaments. But it needs to be brought to the attention of all performers because there are many cases of the kind mentioned here, where the identification of passages as ornamental will provide important clues for their interpretation, as will be presently discussed.

*Symbolized Ornaments and the Dangers of Ornament Tables.* Some small ornamental figures containing one to three or four pitches were used in certain characteristic combinations that allowed them to be grouped into formulas. These formulas in turn lent themselves to representation by the shorthand devices of symbols. When the symbols proliferated, first with the French lutenists and later with their heirs and followers, the French clavecinists, the growing number of symbols created problems for the performers who, unable to guess the meaning of various signs, needed an explanation. When a few composers provided such explanation, they produced the first ornament tables. Yet these ornaments were still descendants of improvisation and thus carried a strong genetic strand of freedom. Even when the ornaments were small enough to allow symbolization and a degree of standardization into formulas, they retained the measure of congenital liberty that is needed to fulfill the function of ornament within a musical work. This function is to provide variety, add grace and elegance, soften hardness, round angularity, and in general smooth and liquefy.

By its nature, then, an ornament has no rigid shape but is in constant flux. Standard notation cannot do justice to the innate flexibility of a given ornament because notation is too rigid with its fixed mathematical ratios. (This is the reason that ornaments written out in regular notes present the interpretation problems discussed above.) A symbol, on the other hand, is not only a convenient shorthand device but is actually a superior form of notation because it does not bind the ornament to exact ratios but rather allows it to assume, however subtly, ever differing shapes. But the only way by which the symbol can be explained in writing to the uninitiated is by offering an abstraction of the design, a reduction to its conceptual essence, its Platonic idea, as it were, even though the symbol has countless differing manifestations in reality. The intelligent music student of those bygone days who had heard such differing manifestations had no difficulty in distinguishing what in the model was of the conceptual essence and what was not. There was thus little danger that he might mistake the model for a pattern to be reproduced literally. The idea that ornaments are too free to be regimented into regularity and that they cannot be taught by book but only by demonstration (*viva voce*) goes like a red thread through the literature of two centuries.[3]

Because modern performers are separated by centuries from the experience of those times and have only the ornament tables to turn to, they have sometimes misunderstood the abstract nature of these models.[4] Ornament tables, which were often written by eminent musicians, are an indispensable means of explaining the *basic* design of an ornament; but their abstractions must be adapted in each case to an ever-changing musical environment while permitting the ornament to live, breathe, and change. Those all-too-many performers who routinely take the models of a table on their exact face value, subvert the very nature of ornaments by creating monotony instead of variety and by rigidifying the texture instead of loosening it. It is also essential to realize that ornament tables by one composer cannot be unthinkingly applied to another who may be separated by time, style, region, and nationality. Even Bach's own brief ornament table, written as a child's introduction for the nine-year-old Wilhelm Friedemann, offers only a pale reflection of the richness of his ornamental designs.

*The Unwritten Ornaments.* As to the third problem, that of unwritten, hence totally improvised ornaments, its difficulties are of an entirely different kind. For the 17th century and for about two-thirds of the 18th, many composers expected the solo performer to embellish slow movements or arias. Some notated only the bare structural skeleton of the melody, others (or the same ones on different occasions) added a degree of embellishment to the notation but expected further embroidery on the part of the performer. Only once in a while did a composer write out all the ornamentation he had in mind, leaving no room for further additions. The performers, in turn, be they star singers or instrumental virtuosi, expected to be given the opportunity for displaying their skill in improvised ornamentation. Such additions were often obligatory, but often optional, and sometimes unwelcome. The degree to which the score left room for such additions varied from nation to nation, from composer to composer, and often from work to work. There was far more room for improvisation in Italy than in France. Bach, as noted above, consistently wrote out practically all of his desired ornamentation. So did many Frenchmen, and so did Haydn and Mozart later in the century.

The modern performer must ask first whether a written melodic line is austere to a degree that embellishment seems to be a stylistic necessity or whether a modicum of written-out floridity is stylistically adequate without further embroidery. Whenever additions seem appropriate, the challenge is to determine where and how extensively they should be supplied and what form they should take. This challenge is among the most difficult problems the study of performance practice has to face. It is, moreover, a problem that by its nature can have no definite solutions. The best one can do is to show how to approach this difficulty. In the last chapters of Part VI an attempt will be made to sketch some guidelines.

---

## Practical Applications

In chapter 4, under "The Clue of Ornamentation," I dealt with florid ornamental passages that call for a faster tempo and lighter dynamics. Here I repeat in Ex. 21.1a one of the illustrations shown there (in Ex. 4.5), the beginning of the Sonata in G Minor for Unaccompanied Violin. Too often we hear it played at a dragging tempo with each of the thirty-second notes imbued with deep feeling. Such an approach is wrongly focused. We realize this when we recognize the passage as an ornament and search for its structural nucleus. We cannot do so with the mathematical accuracy of extracting a square root because ornamentation is not a precise science, but Ex. 21.1b (not previously given) shows approximately how an Italian master, or Handel, or Telemann might have written the same musical thought in near-skeletal form. "Near-skeletal" because the appoggiatura on the third beat of the first measure is theoretically an ornament, but its specific weight within the musical thought is such that it partakes of the structural essence. With this musical core in mind, the thirty-second notes change from a would-be profound melody to a lovely, elegant embroidery that winds around the pillars of a grand musical thought. The passage should be rendered accordingly. First, the tempo should be chosen so as to allow the pillars to be perceived without being obscured by a heavyhanded, obtrusive emphasis on the coloraturas. In chapter 4 it was suggested that the beat not be taken slower than ♩ = 36. Though this is a slow pulse, it would be advisable not to subdivide it into ♪ = 72 because the wider space between quarter note beats will encourage a desirable rubato-like rhythmic flexibility in the rendition of the coloraturas, whereas a count of eighth notes would be rhythmically more confining and would tend to produce undesirable accents on each beat besides.

EXAMPLE 21.1.    Bach, Sonata in G Minor for Unaccompanied Violin, BWV 1001

Examples 4.6, 4.7, and 4.8 show several other Bach passages for which pervasive ornamental figurations equally suggest a more flowing tempo than is frequently taken. Of the many more examples that could be listed, a few well-known ones include the Andante movement of the "Italian" Concerto; the Organ Fantasia (and Fugue) in G Minor BWV 542; the "Goldberg" Variations Nos. 13 and 25; the first movement of the Violin and Clavier Sonata in E Major; and the Prelude of the Sonata in A Minor for Violin Solo.

In the 19th century, composers often used the unmetrical miniature notes for ornamental melismas. Beethoven did so in the slow movement of his Violin Concerto and in many of his piano works, and Chopin of course made lavish use of this notation for his many exuberant coloraturas and cascading arabesques. This notation clarifies the need for a fleeting, light-weight rendition. Performers of 18th-century music will do well to treat passage work, once they have identified its ornamental character, in an analogous way by imagining that it was written with miniature rather than regular notes.

# 22

## ONE-NOTE GRACES I: FRANCE

### *Nature, Types, and Working Terminology*

Ornaments that consist of a single tone only will be referred to here as one-note graces. Like all ornaments, they are linked to a principal or parent note that they are meant to embellish. This can be either the note that precedes the grace or the one that follows it. The grace can also link—like a hyphen—the preceding and the following notes, thus serving two equal parents.

The grace is always slurred to its single parent, with which, in vocal music, it shares the same syllable. The "hyphenating" grace is included within a slur linking both its equal parent notes and shares with them the same syllable. These slurs are understood wherever the composer omitted to specify them.

A one-note grace that precedes its parent note, ♪ , will be called by the German generic term *Vorschlag* (literally "forenote"; plural: *Vorschläge*). This term has seemed preferable to the commonly used "appoggiatura" because it is neutral with regard to rhythmic, melodic, and dynamic design. A grace that follows its parent, ♪ , will be called *Nachschlag* (literally "afternote"), another German term but one that has been in use for some time. Finally, a grace that connects two equal parent notes, ♪♪ , and that has the double function of a *Nachschlag* for the preceding note and a *Vorschlag* for the following one, will be called *Zwischenschlag* (literally "between-note"; a term introduced by Leopold Mozart), again one that has no satisfactory English equivalent.

The *Nachschlag* is the least problematical member of this family of graces; it connects its parents with, but is not slurred to, whatever follows it. In this linking function it always takes its value from its preceding parent note.

The *Zwischenschlag* is also a purely connective ornament that graces the transition from one structural note to another. It belongs to both, as a *Nachschlag* to the preceding and as a *Vorschlag* to the following parent note. In this subservient function it ought generally not to interfere with the starting points of its parent notes, hence not affect rhythm, harmony, or counterpoint. Whenever the two parents fall on separate beats, the *Zwischenschlag*, like the *Nachschlag*, will usually tend to take its place between beats within the time of the preceding note. When both parent notes fall within the same beat, $\frac{2}{4}$ ♩♩ , with only a subdivision of the beat separating them, the exact rhythmic disposition of the grace can become unimportant. Both the *Zwischenschlag* and the *Nachschlag* will as a rule be short and light.

The truly problematic member of the family of one-note graces is the *Vorschlag*, which can run the whole gamut of rhythmic-dynamic designs. The *Vorschlag* can be rendered before the metrical pulse, or prominently on the beat, or it can straddle the beat in a variety of syncopated designs; it can be short or long, soft, swelled or stressed, and can have consequently the most varied effect on melody, harmony, or counterpoint.

Its two most important designs are the polar opposites of a brief and soft prebeat *Vorschlag*, which in the following will be called a "grace note," and the onbeat *Vorschlag*, which alone, regardless of its length, will be referred to as "appoggiatura."

A number of ornament tables from the late 17th through the 18th century, most importantly those of d'Anglebert and C. P. E. Bach, follow a nearly consistent pattern of beginning ornaments on the beat. On the basis of these tables, scholars of performance practice concluded that during these two centuries all ornaments must start on the beat and hence be rendered within the time of the following note. Perhaps because the *Vorschlag* is so ubiquitous, it has been the most widely interpreted by modern performers in accordance with this conclusion. But the *Vorschlag* was far from being petrified as an immutable onbeat appoggiatura: during these two hundred years it assumed many different shapes, as the following chapters should help to show.

## One-Note Graces in France

*Agréments* is the French generic term for ornaments small enough to be expressed by symbols. Nivers, in his organ book of 1665, used the term to signify one specific mordent-like grace. But beginning at the latest with Chambonnières in 1670, the term assumed its generic meaning.

Since French terminology regarding one-note graces is not overly consistent, the terms that will be used in the following are those that have been the most common ones. They fall into four groups: the *port de voix* and the *coulé*, both of which are *Vorschläge*, and the *accent* and *chûte*, both of which are *Nachschläge*. Of these four graces, we shall first address the two *Vorschlag* types, which are by far the most important ones.

**Port de voix and coulé.** The *port de voix* is a *Vorschlag* that ascends to its parent note: ♪ . The term is the equivalent of the Italian *portamento di voce*. The *coulé* is a *Vorschlag* that descends to its parent note: ♪ . The term makes sense since *couler* means "to flow," and water flows downward.

The symbols for these two graces display considerable variety. By 1600 the lutenists had already developed various symbols whose forms were for the most part highly individual and varied from master to master. There were dots and commas before or after the tablature letter, hooks below the letter, and various combinations of these signs (for more details, see *OrnB*, 66–67). Symbols for other media emerged in the later part of the 17th century. By then the small ornamental notes had come into use, and they served all one-note graces for all media and became the dominant symbols by the second half of the 18th century. Among other signs there was the horizontal dash between notes (Fig. 22.1a), the caret between notes (Fig. 22.1b), and a V-like inverted caret above the note head (Fig. 22.1c). For the keyboard only, a frequent symbol for the *coulé* and the *port de voix* is the hook before the note head (Fig. 22.1d). It is identical for both graces: it signifies a *port de voix* when the melody line rises, a *coulé* when it falls. (Bach, who adopted the keyboard symbol, places it on the line or space where the grace is to be played.) Since the corresponding symbol for the mordent is a hook *after* the note head (Fig. 22.1e), the combination of the two hooks stands for the very frequent composite grace of a *port de voix* followed by a mordent (Fig. 22.1f), called the *port de voix et pincé* ( ).

Figure 22.1

a. *port de voix*   b. *port de voix*   c. *port de voix*   d.   e. mordent (*pincé*)   f. *port de voix*
               or *coulé*                                                 et pincé

Before the advent of the symbols (Lully did not use them yet, and those that appear in posthumous scores were editorial accretions), their judicious improvised addition was expected. Bénigne de Bacilly, in his famous vocal treatise of 1668, gives guidelines for such practices, occasionally suggesting a beat-straddling execution (*Remarques curieuses*, 141–43). Jean Rousseau, at a time when symbols were already current, did not use any in either of his two treatises of 1683 and 1687 but explains the circumstances that favor, or indeed demand, their addition.

**Rhythmic Design.** Both the *port de voix* and *coulé* can assume any rhythmic shape, from full anticipation to straddling to full onbeat placement. The *port de voix* was followed very frequently, almost routinely, by a mordent in the mentioned combination called *port de voix et pincé:* .Whenever the *port de voix* takes (or straddles) the beat in this combination, the *pincé* sequel follows off the beat, lightly and fleetingly: . In a special case, where the onbeat *port de voix* is long sustained and resolves into its parent note at the very end of the latter's value, the *pincé* embellishes the resolution with a tiny curl, as shown below in Ex. 22.6c, from Jean Jacques Rousseau's *Dictionnaire*. He calls it *port de voix jetté*, but the more common term for this design is *port de voix feint*.

When the *port de voix* is fully anticipated, the *pincé* suffix may either still fall into the space before the beat, , or be rendered accented on the beat, . During most of the 17th century, anticipation was by far the preponderant design for both *port de voix* and *coulé*, as we can gather from countless pieces of both theoretical and musical evidence.

For a few examples, Marin Mersenne's explanation of the *port de voix* of 1636 is given in Ex. 22.1a (*Harmonie universelle: Traitez des consonances*, 2:355–56). In addition to showing the anticipation for this type of grace, the example shows the repeat of the preceding note that is characteristic of stepwise ascent. In the *airs de cour* of that era, singers were expected to embellish the second couplets with elegant melismas that included many *coulés* and *ports de voix*. Fortunately, we have many examples of such written-out embellishments, and they invariably show a vast preponderance of anticipation for both *port de voix* and *coulé* (see Ex. 32.1 and *OrnB*, Exx. 5.1 and 5.2). Near the end of the century, Jean Rousseau, the famous gambist, wrote a treatise for the voice and one for the gamba (*Méthode claire* and *Traité de la viole*, respectively). The vocal treatise shows anticipation for the most part (Ex. 22.1b), then demonstrates the onbeat type of *port de voix*, which he says is fitting when ascending from a short note to one at least twice as long (Ex. 22.1c, *Méthode*, 51). In the

EXAMPLE 22.1

a. Mersenne (1636)

b. Jean Rousseau (1683)

c. Jean Rousseau (1683)

viol treatise of 1687, however, all *coulés* and *ports de voix* without exception are shown in anticipation (*Traité de la viole*, chap. 6; see also *OrnB*, Exx. 9.13 and 9.14). Rousseau, as mentioned before, does not use any symbols but explains the circumstances in which impromptu addition of the two graces is fitting. Danoville, his fellow student of the legendary gambist Sainte Colombe, shows in his treatise of 1687 the small notes as symbol for the *port de voix* and explains it in full anticipation: the *port de voix*, he says, "is done by halving the note which precedes the one to which the grace is applied and by slurring the second half to the following note" (*L'art de toucher*, 42). Pierre Berthet, in his vocal treatise of 1695, gives only one illustration, using the "V" symbol above the note for the *port de voix* and showing it in full anticipation (*Leçons de musique*, 47). (See also *OrnB*, Exx. 9.9 and 9.15.)

In his *Éléments ou principes de musique* of 1696, Étienne Loulié speaks of small ornaments (*agréments du chant*) of one, two, or more "little tones" (*petits sons*) that, he says, are weaker and shorter than the "regular" ones and are sounded sometimes before and sometimes on the beat (66). He shows both types for the *port de voix* (Ex. 22.2a); but his illustration of the *coulé*, which gives ten patterns, includes only prebeat designs (three of which are given in Ex. 22.2b).

Michel L'Affilard, whose *Principes* of 1694 Rameau recommended (along with Loulié's treatise) for elementary instruction, shows in his ornament table an anticipated *port de voix* with a written-out mordent annex that was presumably intended to fall on the beat (Ex. 22.2c). He also shows, incidentally, while illustrating other ornaments, three more pre-barline *ports de voix* as well as a premeasure *coulé* as the anticipated auxiliary of a trill (20–21).

EXAMPLE 22.2

a. Loulié (1696)

b. Loulié (1696)

c. L'Affilard (1694)

d. Montéclair (1736)

e. Montéclair (1736)

Michel Pignolet de Montéclair, successful composer and well-known theorist, points to the need to add unmarked, and presumably prebeat, *coulés* to descending steps, thirds, or larger leaps in the melody. He gives several illustrations of a pre-barline *port de voix*, such as the ones shown in Ex. 22.2d, as well as one other in a paragraph dealing with the *pincé* and shown in Ex. 22.2e, in which an onbeat rendition followed by an offbeat *pincé* seems indicated (*Principes*, 78–79, 84, 92).

In his *Pièces pour la flûte traversière* of 1703, De La Barre clarifies the anticipation for both graces by invariably writing their small-note symbols before the barline whenever they belong to the first note in a measure.

When the French lute school lost prominence after the mid-17th century, its rich ornamental vocabulary was adopted by the upcoming school of clavecinists. Champion de Chambonnières set a pattern that was to be followed by many later clavecinists when in his brief ornament table of 1670 (in *Les pièces de clavessin*) he showed the *port de voix* starting on the beat. In 1689, Jean Henri d'Anglebert, in the richest ornament table up to that time, printed in the preface of his *Pièces de clavecin*, showed both the *coulé* and the *port de voix*, along with practically all other ornaments, on the beat (Ex. 22.3a). That he was not, however, doctrinaire about this design is evident from various musical passages (in the same book) in which the two graces are written out in anticipation (Ex. 22.3b). Gaspard Le Roux, in his *Pièces de clavessin* of 1705, adopted d'Anglebert's onbeat models but, in addition to using the latter's hook symbol before the note head (and the one after the note head for the *pincé*), Le Roux often used small notes for both the *port de voix* and the *coulé* with an apparent prebeat meaning. For one illustration out of many, see the *coulé* in Ex. 22.3c; this *coulé* would create objectionable parallels if taken on the beat. Charles Dieupart, too, in his *Six suittes de clavessin* of ca. 1702, copied his onbeat models for the two graces from d'Anglebert, and he also occasionally uses small notes that seem to call for prebeat execution.

In contrast, several keyboard players showed in their tables exclusively the prebeat pattern for these graces. Prominent among them are several organists, among them Guillaume-Gabriel Nivers in his *Livre d'orgue* of 1665; André Raison in his *Livre d'orgue* of 1688, and Lambert Chaumont in his *Pièces d'orgues sur les 8 tons* of 1696. Also, the organist Nicolas Gigault presents an instructional piece in each of two organ books of 1682 (*Livre de musique dédié à la très Ste. Vierge*) and 1685 (*Livre de musique pour l'orgue*), both of which show the use of the two graces in an invariably prebeat design (for the illustrations, see *OrnB*, Exs. 10.6–10.9).

Michel de Saint Lambert, in his *Principes du clavecin* of 1702 (the first French clavecin tutor), uses d'Anglebert's hook symbols but gives only the prebeat design for both graces. He reproduces d'Anglebert's onbeat

Example 22.3

a. d'Anglebert (1689)

*Cheute ou port
de voix en montant*   *en descendant*   *Cheute et pincé*

b. d'Anglebert (1689)

*Tombeau de
Mr. de Chambonnieres*   *Suite de la Passacaille*, p. 53

c. Le Roux (1705)

VII, *Pièce sans titre*

design and comments that it may often be fitting for the voice but that anticipation is much more appropriate ("beaucoup plus convenable") for instrumental works (49).

François Couperin writes in his *L'art de toucher le clavecin* that "the little note of a *coulé* or *port de voix* must strike with the harmony in the time of the following note" (22). This sentence has carried great weight in support of the modern ideas regarding obligatory onbeat .start of all *Vorschläge;* yet—as so often with rules in treatises—the principle seems to have applied often but by no means always. There is substantial musical evidence that on many occasions, when the logic of melody, harmony, rhythm, notation, or technical feasibility argues against downbeat execution, the small note of both graces was to be anticipated. There is space here only for two illustrations (Exx. 22.4a and b) of places where an onbeat rendition of *coulés* would produce highly offensive parallels of a kind that Couperin, who was scrupulous about his voice leading, would surely never have tolerated (for many other illustrations see *Essays 1982*, chap. 14, as well as *OrnB*, chap. 11).

The situation is similar with Rameau. His ornament tables of 1706 (*Premier livre de pièces de clavecin*) and of 1724 (*Pièces de clavecin avec une*

EXAMPLE 22.4.   Couperin (1716)

méthode) show both the *coulé* and the *port de voix* on the downbeat. (In keyboard music he uses d'Anglebert's hook symbol for either grace, whereas he uses small notes for both voice and melody instruments.) Yet in his music, though less frequently than with Couperin, we find occasional spots where a downbeat execution makes for unmusical results and where anticipation seems to be the logical solution. An interesting piece of direct evidence to this effect can be found in "L'Agaçante" from the Deuxième Concert where Rameau writes a *coulé* for the violin with the little note symbol, whereas in the keyboard transcription of the same piece (in *Cinq pièces*) he writes it out in full anticipation (see Ex. 22.5).

EXAMPLE 22.5.   Rameau

Nicolas Siret, organist of the Troyes Cathedral, provides evidence for anticipation of the *port de voix* in his two books (*Pièces de clavecin* of ca. 1710 and *Second livre de pièces de clavecin* of 1719) by writing on repeated occasions the small note of the grace before the barline and slurring it to the downbeat principal note with the mordent sign ( ⤴ ) or by spelling out the anticipation in regular notes ( ⤴ ) .

François David, in his *Méthode nouvelle* of 1737, shows the *port de voix* on the beat, written out in regular notes, while the *coulé*, indicated with rhythmically ambiguous small notes, may have been intended either for the beat or for anticipation (135–36).

Alexandre de Villeneuve, in his treatise of 1733 (reprinted in 1756) adopts L'Affilard's explanation of ornaments and with it the repeated pre-barline notation of both the *port de voix* and the *coulé* (*Nouvelle méthode*, 38) (see *OrnB*, Ex. 12.10).

Jacques Alexandre de La Chapelle demonstrates in 1737 the anticipation of both the *coulé* and the *port de voix* by first spelling out the prebeat design, then showing its symbolized notation (*Les vrais principes*, 2:14). In 1761 L'Abbé le Fils shows the *port de voix* on the beat, the *coulé* in both forms: sustained on the beat when followed by a weak sound ("suivi d'un son feint") and before the beat when the main note is emphasized ("suivi d'un son soûtenu") (*Principes du violon*, 15–16).

Jean Jacques Rousseau, in his *Dictionnaire* of 1768, shows the *coulé* in anticipation, the *port de voix* on the beat, as given in Ex. 22.6. As mentioned before, what he calls the *port de voix jetté*, a long, sustained onbeat grace, followed at its end by a lightly rendered mordent, is better known as *port de voix feint* (Planche B, fig. 13).

EXAMPLE 22.6.  Jean Jacques Rousseau (1768)

In 1775 Duval (first name unknown) shows both graces on the beat (*Méthode*, 11), whereas Antonio Borghese in 1786 describes the *port de voix* exclusively in terms of anticipation (*L'art*, 80).

It is also significant that Quantz, who had a French teacher and spent six months studying in Paris, refers to the anticipation of the *coulé* as the typically French manner of execution. In his famous treatise on the flute, Quantz points to the first of the two models shown in Ex. 22.7 and tells us that especially in slow tempos their small notes must *not* be played on the beat. To do so "would not only be contrary to the intention of the composer but also to the French manner of execution from which these *Vorschläge* originate. For the small notes belong in the time of the preceding note and must not, as shown in the second example [Ex. 22.7b], be played in the time of the following note" (*Versuch einer Anweisung*, chap. 17, sec. 2, par. 20).

Summarizing briefly, the *coulé* and *port de voix* occurred in all rhythmic shapes, from full anticipation through partial anticipation through a short downbeat to a lengthy downbeat design (the latter more common with the *port de voix* than with the *coulé*). The *port de voix* was frequently, almost routinely, followed by a mordent annex as *port de voix et pincé*. The prebeat type for both graces was predominant in the 17th century,

EXAMPLE 22.7.   Quantz (1752)

while the downbeat type, a distinct minority option in the 17th century, strongly asserted itself in the course of the 18th. This was true more for the *port de voix* than for the *coulé*, more for the keyboard than for voice and melody instruments. Yet during the whole 18th century, anticipation never ceased to coexist in appropriate contexts, of which the *tierces coulées*, the interbeat filling in of descending thirds, is the most typical but by no means only one. (For more detailed documentation on the *port de voix* and *coulé*, see OrnB, chaps. 8–12.)

*Accent and Chûte.* Compared with the *coulé* and the *port de voix*, the two French *Nachschlag* graces play only a minor role. The *accent* is a small, brief sound slurred delicately to the very end of the tone to which it belongs. The borrowed note is most often the diatonic upper neighbor; the melodic line then usually either returns to the pitch of the parent or descends to a lower one. Although there are other designs as well, the *accent* typically entails a change of melodic direction. Some writers called it *aspiration*, some *plainte*, but *accent* was the most common term. This latter term must not be confused with the Italian *accento* or the German *Accent*, which are both *Vorschläge*.

The most frequent symbol used is the little unmetrical note, but among abstract signs we find the vertical stroke above the parent note ( ᵖ ), not to be taken for a staccato sign, or the upright caret placed between parent and following note ( ᵖ^ᵖ ). Often it was not marked at all and left to improvised addition by a solo singer or player. A few specimens are shown in Ex. 22.8: an improvised one by Jean Rousseau (*aspiration*) of 1687 in Ex. 22.8a (*Traité*, 90–93); specimens symbolized with the vertical stroke by L'Affilard in 1694 in Ex. 22.8b (*Principes*, 20–21) and Loulié in 1696 in Ex. 22.8c (*Éléments*, 68–69); marked with the caret by Saint Lambert in 1702 in Ex. 22.8d (*Principes*, 80); marked with small notes by Hotteterre in 1707 in Ex. 22.8e (*Principes*, 29); and unmarked, hence improvised, by Choquel in 1762 in Ex. 22.8f (*La musique*, 65).

The *accent* is a typically French grace that is not often found abroad. Among Germans, Stierlein shows it in his treatise of 1691 (*Trifolium*, 16); J. G. Walther liked it and, marked by small notes, used it frequently. Bach practically never used it (a rare instance occurs in the Canonic Variations, Var. 3, m. 2). Quantz mentions it as a desirable impromptu addition when two notes in slow tempo move stepwise up or down

EXAMPLE 22.8

(*Versuch einer Anweisung,* chap. 13, par. 34) and illustrates it in his Table 15, Fig. 20, h and i).

The *chûte* is a *Nachschlag* that typically descends (*chûte* means "fall") to the level of the following note, ![musical example], thus anticipating its pitch. As such, it is the counterpart to what the Italians called the *anticipazione della nota.* (We must not be confused by d'Anglebert's infelicitous use of the term *cheute* to designate a rising (!) *port de voix.* The little note was the most common symbol, but here too improvised use must have exceeded its prescription in the score.

It seems that the heyday of these two *Nachschlag*-type graces was the era around 1700. After that their popularity waned, and they have become great rarities in the scores of Couperin and Rameau, as contrasted with the ubiquitous *ports de voix* and *coulés.* It is, however, likely that their extempore use continued, as we can gather from the listed examples of Choquel and of Quantz, who was strongly indebted to French practices.

# 23

# ONE-NOTE GRACES II:
# ITALY AND ENGLAND

## One-Note Graces in Italy

Italian ornamentation of the 16th century, whether consisting of single notes or of lengthy passages (referred to as *passaggi*), served to fill in the space between the structural pillars of a line. We have a number of treatises from this period that provided instruction in the art of *diminution*—that is, the breaking up of a few slow notes into many faster ones. These models show the one-note graces as well as the *passaggi* consistently between beats. We find these prebeat one-note graces from Sylvestro Ganassi in 1535 to Girolamo Diruta in 1609 and Francesco Rognioni in 1620—after which date Italian ornamentation theory fell silent for roughly a century.

It was apparently Giovanni Battista Bovicelli who in his diminution treatise of 1594 pioneered, or more probably merely recorded, a new design: for the progression of Ex. 23.1a he gives two possible diminutions—first the prebeat model of Ex. 23.1b but then the downbeat model of 22.1c (*Regole,* 17, 18). He uses this pattern in his diminution examples for a number of cadences, always in stepwise ascent. The vivid dissonance of this downbeat pattern was congenial to the nascent Baroque style with its striving for emotional expression.

EXAMPLE 23.1.   Bovicelli (1594)

For *musical* evidence concerning one-note graces, we must turn to specimens written out in regular notation, because symbols were not yet in use in Italy. Fortunately, Italian vocal composers wrote out the *Vorschlag* innumerable times, and the record thus created from the start of the 17th to the early years of the 18th century points to a predominantly prebeat usage. Examples 23.2a–23.2c show a few characteristic specimens spanning a century, from Peri to Alessandro Scarlatti.

When we find the onbeat pattern on accented syllables, it occurs—in contrast to Bovicelli's examples—more often with a descending than with an ascending line, as shown in Ex. 23.2d, with two such descending specimens in a single phrase from Monteverdi's *Poppea*.

EXAMPLE 23.2

a. Peri, *Flora*, II

b. Monteverdi, *Poppea*, I, 4

c. Scarlatti (ca. 1700), *Concerti sacri*

d. Monteverdi, *Poppea*, I, 1

It was only after 1710 that Italian composers began to adopt the French unmetrical little notes to indicate one-note graces, slides, and turns. Their denominations varied from composer to composer but were not meant to be taken literally, as was to be the case later with some composers of northen Germany. The little notes were ambiguous in that, as in France, they could stand either for prebeat *Vorschläge* (grace notes) or for onbeat *Vorschläge* (appoggiaturas) of various lengths. In Italian vocal music of the 18th century, the onbeat meaning predominated, whereas in instrumental works a prebeat execution seems often to have been intended.

Musical evidence for a prebeat interpretation can be found, for instance, in passages in which onbeat execution would be either impractical, because the principal note is too short to support an appoggiatura, or illogical, because the composer presumably intended something different when he wrote ⌐⌐ rather than the very common ⌐⌐

The difference between these two resides less in the exact location of the beat than in its accentuation. In all cases of the first sort, the accent seems intended to fall on the principal note, not the *Vorschlag*. Such is the case in spots such as in Ex. 23.3a, from Vinci, and Ex. 23.3b, from Pergolesi.

EXAMPLE 23.3

a. Vinci, *Artaserse*, II, 1

non sen- ti pie- tà

b. Pergolesi, *L'Olimpiade*, aria Aristea

Andante

Vlns.

Perhaps the most characteristic case of anticipation before short notes is the typically Italian form of the mordent preceded by a grace note. Although the Italians had no symbol for the mordent, the formula

⌐⌐ occurs with such regularity and frequency in the Italian music of the 18th century that it assumes the character of a standard ornament. In this formula the dynamic stress seems to be always placed on the principal note, a presumption underlined by Tartini's later explanation that, whenever tempo and time permit, the emphasis is strengthened by the addition of a trill ( ⌐⌐ ; *Regole,* 7). Onbeat emphasis on the little note would produce not a mordent but a turn. An intended turn, however, was written by the Italians as ⌐⌐ . For two illustrations of what could be called the "Italian mordent," see Exx. 23.4a and 23.4b.

EXAMPLE 23.4

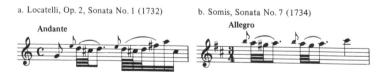

a. Locatelli, Op. 2, Sonata No. 1 (1732)

Andante

b. Somis, Sonata No. 7 (1734)

Allegro

Anticipation is often indicated when onbeat execution would create offensive parallels of the kind the composer would never have written in regular notes. In Ex. 23.5, from two sonatas by Domenico Scarlatti, the thin texture would make the parallel octaves and fifths resulting from an onbeat *Vorschlag* especially prominent. A study of Scarlatti's work from this point of view suggests that his little *Vorschlag* notes were most often intended for prebeat rendition. For a variety of musical reasons the same seems to be the case for the instrumental works of Vivaldi and other Italian composers in the first half of the 18th century. (For more details, see *OrnB*, 166–73).

EXAMPLE 23.5.   D. Scarlatti

a. Sonata K 420

b. Sonata K 169

## 18th-Century Theorists

In his famous tract of 1723, Pierfrancesco Tosi devotes a chapter to the appoggiatura but has little to say that is enlightening. The grace, he writes, is easy to learn and easy to teach. He believes only in its impro-vised use and fulminates against the "foreign puerility" of indicating it in the score (with the recently introduced small notes, no doubt). He considers this an encroachment on the singer's traditional privilege (*Opinioni*, 19–23).

Francesco Geminiani, distinguished violinist-composer, describes the long, descending appoggiatura thus: it "is supposed to express love, affection, pleasure, etc. It should be made pretty long, giving it more than half the length of the note it belongs to, observing to swell the Sound by Degrees, and toward the End to force the Bow a little. If it be made short, it will lose much of the aforesaid Qualities; but will always have a pleasing Effect, and it may be added to any Note you will." The ascending appoggiatura, he continues, has the same qualities, but its use is limited to places where the melody rises one or two steps. Furthermore, it should always be followed by a mordent (the French *port de voix et pincé*; Prefaces to *The Art* and *Treatise*).

Geminiani's instructions about the short *Vorschlag* are rather vague. Yet when he says that it loses much of its expressive potential but will be pleasing and can be added to any note, this characterization fits the prebeat type more than the onbeat type. The reason for the better fit is that the prebeat type has a neutral, unobtrusive nature that does not affect harmony and counterpoint and can therefore be unconcernedly "added to any note you will," whereas the onbeat type has to be handled with far greater circumspection because of its much stronger flavor and its impact on harmony and counterpoint. It can by no means be "added to any note you will." This assumption finds confirmation in musical evidence as well as in Tartini's explicit directives.

In his *Regole* from ca. 1750, Giuseppe Tartini distinguishes two main kinds of *Vorschläge:* the long and sustained one (*appoggiatura lunga ossia sostentata*) and the short or passing one (*appoggiatura breve ossia di passaggio*). The long appoggiatura, Tartini says, takes half the value of the principal (binary) note and two-thirds of the value of a dotted note, as shown in Ex. 23.6a. (This rule was to be repeated many times by later theorists.) Composers, he continues, use the small-note symbol to indicate long appoggiaturas because as ornamental notes they call for special treatment. As a regular note the first eighth note of the example would carry the normal metrical accent and be in need of a trill to further underline it; as an appoggiatura it should start softly, then swell and diminish before it falls onto the main note. Geminiani, as reported above, gave a similar description, as did Quantz and Leopold Mozart.

Tartini places considerable limits on the use of the long appoggiatura. It belongs only to the strong beat, he says, and is generally proper only for pieces in a slow tempo; the long species would dim the brilliance of faster pieces and weaken their liveliness. Tartini sees the natural location of long appoggiaturas among notes of unequal length when the note carrying the grace is longer than the one that follows, as seen in Ex. 23.6a.

Particularly significant is Tartini's principle that the long appoggiatura is out of place within a setting of equal notes because, he says, it would then prejudice the intended effect of evenness. This principle is to apply to any note value in any tempo. In Ex. 23.6b we see Tartini's illustration of such even notes preceded by *Vorschläge* that explicitly spell out their full anticipation (*Regole*, 7). It seems most probable, therefore, that in a passage such as the one shown in Ex. 23.6c, from a Tartini sonata, all the *Vorschläge* before the triplets were meant to be played as grace notes.

EXAMPLE 23.6. Tartini

a.

"Equivalent"

b.

"rendered thus"

c. Sonata No. 32

Like Geminiani, Tartini places no restrictions on the grace notes, the *appoggiature di passaggio*, and actually demands their use when the symbol occurs in a setting of even notes. It is also significant that Tartini, like Geminiani, presents only the two contrasting types, the long appoggiatura and the short grace note, omitting any mention of a short accented onbeat *Vorschlag*.

The dual nature of the *Vorschlag*—admitting both onbeat and prebeat execution—which is so clearly laid out by Tartini, persisted in Italy throughout the 18th century. At century's end, in 1800, Carlo Gervasoni seems to favor an onbeat style for the *Vorschlag*, which he illustrates in his musical examples. In the text, however, he offers the choice of rendering the short *Vorschlag* either in the time of the preceding note or in the time of the following one, according to the "just expression" (*La scuola della musica*, 1:184).

## One-Note Graces in England

The ornamentation of the English virginalists of the late 16th and early 17th centuries has puzzled many a scholar and performer. The main symbols used were the single and the double stroke across the stem or—in the case of a stemless one—simply written below or above: 

The meaning of these strokes is uncertain: they may not have stood for any specific ornaments but may only have indicated the need for some ornamental figure, in which case it would seem likely that the single stroke stood for a simpler, shorter ornament and the double stroke for a longer one, whether florid or percussive. The most likely solutions for at least some of the double strokes are trills or mordents. The single stroke may well have occasionally stood for a one-note grace, but so far we have no hard evidence and can only resort to speculation.

In the mid-17th century Christopher Simpson, in his *Division-Violist*, uses an upward-slanted stroke between notes to signify a rising *Vorschlag*, which he calls "beat" (see Ex. 23.7a). It corresponds to a French onbeat *port de voix* (as shown in Ex. 22.2a as the second and fourth pattern from Loulié's illustration). A similar stroke *above* the note denotes a rising *Nachschlag* of the French *accent* type; it is called "springer" (Ex. 23.7b). (It compares with Ex. 22.8c from Loulié.) A downward-slanted stroke between notes stands for a falling *Nachschlag* of the French *chûte* type and is called a "cadent" (Ex. 23.7c). A comma before the note indicates a descending onbeat *Vorschlag;* called a "backfall" (Ex. 23.7d), it compares with the second of d'Anglebert's models as given in Ex. 22.3a (*Division-Violist* [1667], 12).

EXAMPLE 23.7.   Christopher Simpson

Simpson's ornament table was taken over verbatim by John Playford in his extraordinarily successful *Introduction to the Skill of Musick*, which went through nineteen editions from 1654 to 1730. The twelfth edition is labeled "corrected and amended by Mr. H. Purcell," which gave great prestige to all its contents, including Simpson's adopted ornament table.

In these tables we find the *Vorschläge* placed on the beat, the *Nachschläge*, true to their nature, before the beat. That does not mean that all the *Vorschläge* in England were rendered on the beat. Here too, as we had previous occasion to observe, ornament table theory seems to have deviated from practice, and the tables have to be qualified in the light of musical evidence. As to Purcell, for instance, he wrote out many cases of prebeat *Vorschläge* of the kind shown in Ex. 23.8, from an autograph of the trio "When on My Sickbed I Languish" (BL add. MS. 30930). We see in it an upbeat phrasing, first on the unstressed syllable of "a-men" (Ex. 23.8a); then later in the piece (Ex. 23.8b), an upbeat phrasing even on the first stressed syllable as well as on the second unstressed one. Certainly the downbeat style played a large role, but as we can gather from much musical evidence of the kind just shown, the upbeat style too was omnipresent.

EXAMPLE 23.8.   Purcell, "When on My Sickbed I Languish"

In 1676, Thomas Mace, a late English representative of the French lute school (which by that time was virtually extinct), wrote the most thorough treatise on the instrument. In it he deals with ornaments in considerable detail (*Musick's Monument*, chap. 22). He describes both the descending *Vorschlag* ("backfall") and the ascending one ("half-fall") as very short graces. Their shortness was dictated largely by the technical execution, since only the grace is plucked by the right hand, whereas the principal note is sounded by a left-hand pizzicato following the descending "backfall" and by a vigorous drop of the finger after the ascending "half-fall." The conclusion drawn by some modern writers that all lute graces must fall on the beat because they alone were plucked and therefore had the natural dynamic accent that seeks the beat is not necessarily justified. Not only was the precise location of the beat often vague in the extremely flexible rhythm of the *style luthé*, but the dynamics of the two pitches involved can by clever handling be manipulated in any desired fashion.

## Handel

It is difficult to pigeonhole Handel as to his musical nationality. Born in Germany, naturalized in England, he was deeply indebted to the Italian style, with some later admixtures of English ingredients. His ornamentation overwhelmingly follows Italian models (with a few exceptions in some harpsichord works that show French influence). It seems appropriate, therefore, to deal with him in the frame of Italian and English performance manners. As to the *Vorschlag*, the long appoggiatura is occasionally written out, especially in the cadential appoggiatura–trill combination, but often left to the discretion of the performer. Often a little note will denote a long appoggiatura; not infrequently, however, the little note stands for a very brief grace.

In Handel's operas and oratorios the little ornamental notes are very rare. They are less rare in his instrumental music but cannot compare in frequency with Bach's lavish use of them. Their occasional appoggiatura meaning was mentioned; their occasional grace-note meaning reveals itself in passages such as the one shown in Ex. 23.9, from *Arianna*, where the little note is systematically juxtaposed with written-out Lombard rhythms. The very consistency in the notational difference in this example points to a different rhythmic intent, and there seems to be no reasonable alternative to grace-note meaning.

EXAMPLE 23.9.   Handel, *Arianna*, I, 1

Examples like these along, with a good deal of other musical evidence, permit us to say that whenever a short interbeat rendition of a little note seems to make musical sense in Handel's works, it is likely to have been thus intended. Here too context, "affect," or, as Gervasoni had put it, the "just expression" will give us clues whether an appoggiatura or a grace note is more appropriate for a given situation.

# 24

# ONE-NOTE GRACES III: GERMANY

## The Pre-Bach Period in Germany

To generalize is dangerous, and therefore it is possible to make wide-ranging statements only by adding the qualifier "by and large." By and large, then, German ornamentation of the 17th century was patterned on Italian models. While Italian influence was strongest in the Catholic south, it extended well into the Protestant north, where such eminent Protestant masters as Praetorius, Schütz, Schein, Kittel, and many others became ardent advocates and efficient propagators of the Italian singing style, including its ornamental practices. For that reason the practices current in Germany of that age can sensibly be referred to as "Italo-German." They represent one of the two great influences that shaped the ornamental situation in the Germany of Bach's time. The other, which joined with it later, but with telling impact, was French.

The third volume of Michael Praetorius's *Syntagma musicum* deals with the new type of Italian ornamentation, for which he names Caccini and Bovicelli as his chief sources (chap. 9). As to one-note graces, Praetorius shows, with several variants, Bovicelli's prebeat and onbeat patterns of *Vorschläge* (given in Ex. 23.1a) as well as *Nachschläge* under the collective name of *accenti.* Two specimens are given in Ex. 24.1 (*Syntagma musicum*, 3:233). Since symbols did not yet exist, all these models instruct about improvisatory practices.

Johann Andreas Herbst (1588–1666), in his *Musica practica* of 1642 (and again in 1650 and 1658), follows Praetorius quite literally in matters of *Vorschläge* and *accenti* (4).

EXAMPLE 24.1. Praetorius (1619); also Herbst (1642, 1658)

Johann Crüger (1598–1662), in his *Synopsis musica* of 1654, also follows a similar line by displaying both the prebeat and onbeat types of
*Vorschläge,* as well as different kinds of *Nachschläge* (191–93). (For more
details, see *OrnB,* 103–4.)

Christoph Bernhard (1628–1692), a student of Schütz and highly
esteemed by him (as previously mentioned in chapters 9 and 13), wrote
three treatises that are considered to be a faithful reflection of Schütz's
own ideas. At the time they circulated widely in manuscript copies but
were not printed until 1926. The first of these tracts, *Von der Singe-Kunst
oder Manier,* deals exclusively with vocal ornamentation and reflects
Bernhard's firsthand knowledge of Italian mid-century practices, for
which it is the most important source.

Concerning one-note graces, Bernhard describes four categories that
however overlap in part: the *accento, anticipatione della syllaba, anticipatione della nota,* and *cercar della nota. All* of these are interbeat designs.
The *accento* is a *Nachschlag,* related to the French *accent,* an added tone a
step above the principal note. The *anticipatione della syllaba* is a prebeat
*Vorschlag* defined as ''a grace which assigns to the preceding note a part
of the syllable that belongs to the following one,'' and illustrated as
shown in Ex. 24.2a and b.

EXAMPLE 24.2. Bernhard, *anticipatione della syllaba*

The *cercar della nota,* which means ''to search for the note,'' partially
overlaps syllabic anticipation but extends well beyond it, always approaching the following tone stepwise from either below or above and
always before the beat. Three illustrations from Bernhard's *Von der
Singe-Kunst* are given in Ex. 24.3a ([1963], 33–35).

Bernhard describes the *anticipatione della nota* as a grace having "the first note divided and its latter part drawn to the pitch of the following one. A sample is given in Ex. 24.3b ([1963], 33–35).

EXAMPLE 24.3.   Bernhard

a. *cercar della nota*

b. *anticipatione della nota*

It is remarkable that among the many illustrations in the tract, Bernhard does not list a single onbeat pattern. Though this does not prove an aversion to these patterns, it nevertheless suggests that they could have played at best a minor role. We can find here important support for the idea that the strong preponderance of the prebeat over the onbeat *Vorschläge*, found in the notated ornaments of 17th-century Italian and German music, must have had its counterpart in the field of improvisation because it is the latter that Bernhard is writing about.

Wolfgang Mylius (1636–1712), a student of Bernhard's, published his *Rudimenta musices* in 1685. The book was widely disseminated and remained popular well past the mid-18th century. Mylius declares that his discussion of ornaments is based on his teacher's principles and describes accordingly the same four one-note graces. Three of these four, the *anticipatione della syllaba*, the *anticipatione della nota*, and the *cercar della nota* are identical with Bernhard's and show consistent antici-pation of the beat. For the fourth one there is a difference: whereas Bernhard's *accento* was a *Nachschlag,* for Mylius it is a *Vorschlag* that can either anticipate the beat or coincide with it (chap. 5, n. p.).

In Johann Christoph Stierlein's (d. 1693) *Trifolium* of 1691, the term *Accent* is used to signify both a *Nachschlag* and either a prebeat or an onbeat *Vorschlag* (16). In contrast, Moritz Feyertag, who published his *Syntaxis* in 1695, shows only the prebeat style of the *Vorschlag* (205, 211), as Bernhard had done before. Johann Samuel Beyer, in his *Primae lineae* of 1703, shows the more common alternative of prebeat or (short) onbeat *Vorschlag* ([1730], 32–33). In Martin Heinrich Fuhrmann (1669–1745) we meet an interesting individual whom the *MGG* declared to be closer to the world of Bach than either of the two antagonists Mattheson and Buttstedt. Fuhrmann, an important theorist, was one of the first admir-ers of Bach's music, not just of his organ virtuosity. In his two treatises, *Musicalischer Trichter* (1706, 24) and *Musica vocalis* (ca. 1715, 46), he pre-sents the persistent rhythmic alternative between prebeat and onbeat one-note graces and, like Beyer, shows the shortness of the grace when it does occur on the beat. For illustrations of Mylius, Stierlein, Feyertag, Beyer, and Fuhrmann, see *OrnB,* Exx. 15.8–15.12, 15.15–15.20, and 15.23.

With Johann Gottfried Walther (1684–1748) we move even closer to Bach. Walther was a close relative of Bach's, and at least during the years of Bach's second stay in Weimar (1708–1717) the two were closely associated in many musical pursuits.

Walther wrote two important treatises. The first, *Praecepta der musi-calischen Composition* (1708) remained in manuscript until it was pub-lished in 1955; the second, the famous *Musicalisches Lexicon,* was pub-lished in 1732. The first of these is of special interest because it reflects Walther's ideas at the very start of his ten-year association with Bach.

In his tract of 1708 Walther illustrates the *accentus* as prebeat *Vor-schlag* (see Ex. 24.4), revealing at the same time the anticipatory nature of his symbols ( ╱ or ⌒ for the ascending, ╲ or ⌣ for the descend-ing type). Yet he also reproduces fragments of two examples by Mylius that combine two onbeat with six prebeat *Vorschläge,* thereby showing

EXAMPLE 24.4.   Walther (1708)

the onbeat potential of the grace. In accord with Mylius, on whom he relies strongly, he also lists the anticipatory *cercar della nota,* the *antici- patione della syllabe,* and the *anticipatione della nota* ([1708], 38–39).

The twenty-four years that separated his early manuscript from the publication of the *Lexicon* witnessed two developments. One was the influx into Germany of French ornamental practices, the other was the growing popularity of the onbeat *Vorschlag.* Reflecting this trend in the *Lexicon,* Walther writes in the article "Accento" that a long note following an *accento* loses only a little, whereas short notes may lose as much as half of their value. This implies an onbeat design but ex- cludes any extended appoggiaturas on long notes. His models for three kinds of symbols and their execution are shown in Ex. 24.5. They follow d'Anglebert's patterns.

EXAMPLE 24.5. Walther (1732)

a. [*Accentus*] *descendens, minor, simplex*     b. *Ascendens, major, simplex*

The article on the *accento* has often been quoted in support of the idea that onbeat rendition of every *Vorschlag* was the rule for Bach and his contemporaries. Such a conclusion is misleading. Like Walther's early *Praecepta,* the *Lexicon* itself contains many more references to one- note graces, under headings such as *anticipatione della syllaba* or *anticipa- tione della nota, aspiration, cercar della nota, coulé, port de voix,* and *super- jectio,* some familiar from the *Praecepta* and every one describing either exclusively or partially an interbeat placement. There are, moreover, many pieces of external evidence from Walther's works, in which, as shown in Ex. 24.6, the prebar placement of little *Vorschlag* notes proves their anticipation.

EXAMPLE 24.6. Walther

a. Chorale Prelude, No. 84, Verse 2     b. Chorale Prelude, No. 47, Verse 2

The picture gained from the sum of Walther's theoretical writings and from the evidence of his own music reflects the continuing ambiv- alence, the "Janus face," of the *Vorschläge* and related graces. The onbeat design has made headway, but the interbeat designs of both *Nachschläge* and anticipated *Vorschläge* are still very much alive.

## *J. S. Bach*

Bach developed his ornamental style early in his career, and by the years 1710 to 1715 he had settled on procedures of notation and rendition that to judge from all available musical evidence showed no marked changes for the rest of his life. For the understanding of this style we therefore have to look for models in the time of his youth, roughly from 1700 to 1710, if not before, and certainly no later than 1715. We must not, as is all too commonly done, look for answers to the galant mid-century treatises, notably those of C. P. E. Bach, Quantz, Marpurg, and Agricola. To do so may be convenient because they give so many detailed answers, but it is historically wrong. These writings reflect a style that Bach chose to ignore along with the style's new ornamental procedures. In particular it is misleading to "apply" the ornamental rules of Philipp Emanuel to his father when countless items of musical evidence show that such a transplant is inappropriate.

Yet the models of Bach's youth, the necessary starting point for our enquiry, are not in themselves sufficient to enlighten us on Bach's practices. In order to find out what Bach decided to select and what he did with it afterwards, we must look for answers in Bach's music itself. For, unfortunately, we cannot find the answers in Bach's own ornamentation table, the "Explication" from the *Clavierbüchlein vor Wilhelm Friedemann Bach*, a resource that has been much overrated and misinterpreted.

Even the rather cursory sketch in the preceding pages of one-note graces in France, Italy, and Germany during Bach's youthful years showed in all three countries a widespread use of *Nachschläge* and *Zwischenschläge*, together with a variety of *Vorschläge* of both prebeat and onbeat design. Given this situation and Bach's inveterate eagerness to learn from worthy models, we might speculate that he would have adopted many of the designs he came across in his younger years. A study of his music confirms this speculation and reveals that he did use some of these designs throughout his lifetime.

As far as the problematic *Vorschläge* are concerned, his use appears to have ranged approximately as indicated in the tabulation of Ex. 24.7—that is, from the anticipated grace note to an appoggiatura that can take up to about half the value from *short* binary notes (eighth notes and, less frequently, quarter notes) and up to about one-third of the value from ternary notes. The designs labeled in the tabulation as "overlong," such as one-half of a long binary note (half note or longer) or two-thirds of a ternary note, were generally not intended. Exceptions always occur, but they seem to have been very rare. The "overlong" interpretations were for the most part later developments brought to the fore by the galant

EXAMPLE 24.7.   Bach, Ornament Table

style. Musical evidence repeatedly confirms their inappropriateness for Bach's music.

Bach certainly used appoggiaturas of all lengths; but when they exceeded the common range of his symbols, he had to write them out in regular notes. Appoggiaturas predominated in his vocal music, while *Nachschläge* and grace notes occurred less often. In instrumental music, on the other hand, grace notes are very frequent indeed. There are no rules that can give us ready solutions, and we must analyze musical evidence in order to gain a measure of guidance.

*The "Explication."* Bach's above-mentioned ornament table has contributed mightily to the rigidification of his ornaments by modern performers who, in awe of its autograph authenticity, take the models strictly at face value whenever the respective symbols appear in the score. To do so is in principle inadmissible (as has been pointed out previously) but is still more improper for the "Explication." Written as a first introduction for a child, it called more than any other table for oversimplification, and as such it is totally inadequate for Bach's own, exceptionally complex melodic-ornamental requirements. The table tells us that the graces *may* have the shapes indicated, but not that they *must* have them. With this caveat the various models will be shown in the appropriate chapters. There are just two models for the *Vorschlag*, which Bach calls *accent*, both given in Ex. 24.8; they show only the hook symbol, not the little unmetrical note.

*The Relative Shortness of Bach's Appoggiaturas.* The "overlong" types of *Vorschläge* listed in the above tabulation of Bach's presumable usage became widely known through the mid-18th century galant treatises that called for them. These treatises, as mentioned above, have been

Example 24.8.   Bach, "Explication"

widely applied to Bach in the mistaken belief that their principles, notably those of C. P. E. Bach, are pertinent to Johann Sebastian as well.
This reasoning rests on shaky ground. The long types were appropriate
for the new style, which was basically homophonic, with slow harmonic
rhythm and by and large not very intricate melodies. In fact in this new
music the long species was needed, as Quantz himself admits when he
explains in the first paragraph of his chapter 8 (*Versuch einer Anweisung*)
that the enrichment of the harmony (by long appoggiaturas) is a "necessary thing" to prevent a melody from sounding "meager and simple-
minded" (sehr mager und einfältig) and to relieve the monotony of too
many consonances, which are, he says, usually associated with a galant
air. Nobody would argue that J. S. Bach's music needed long appoggiaturas to relieve the monotony of consonances and lend a helping hand
to meager and simple-minded melodies.

By way of contrast, it stands to reason that in Bach's linear music the
execution of an ornament ought not to interfere with the basic relationships of the voices. Hence the degree of freedom with which a *Vorschlag*
can be manipulated—especially with regard to its length—will depend
on the complexity of the texture and on the speed of the harmonic and
melodic rhythm. What matters for the melodic rhythm is the sequence
of structural linear impulses, not the succession of pitches that may
simply break a chord in arpeggio fashion or may be purely ornamental.
A long *Vorschlag* that would outlast two or more linear impulses in
another voice would affect the desired polyphonic relationships; in this
case, *only shortness of the grace* can prevent such interference. A long
appoggiatura may be possible on the last note of a piece or on a fermata
where all the voices have come to rest. Appoggiaturas of any length are
of course often integrated into a contrapuntal texture but must in that
case be written out in regular notes.

How long is "long" and how short is "short"? That depends on the
circumstances, especially on the density of the texture. As a rule of
thumb, eighth-note length will be frequent (as shown in the "Explication"); it is "long" in the sense of the above tabulation but "short" in the
frame of the galant writer-composers. Quarter-note length will be extremely rare, other than on fermatas and final chords.

Even the eighth notes of the "Explication" are often too long, as can be seen from a mass of examples of which only two can be shown here: one (Ex. 24.9a) from Cantata No. 97/7 and a double one (Ex. 24.9b) from Cantata No. 201/9. In each case the *Vorschlag* has to be much shorter than an eighth note to avoid blatant parallel fifths.

EXAMPLE 24.9.    Bach

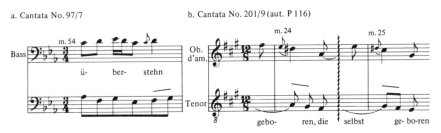

There is further important evidence against Bach's use of *Vorschläge* of the long galant types or in fact any that would exceed the approximate length of an eighth note. Whereas many or even most of Bach's written-out *Vorschläge* are reflected in his bass figures, none of those indicated by symbol ever are (any exceptions must be extremely rare). This contrast is so striking that it can hardly be explained other than by the basic shortness of Bach's symbolized appoggiaturas.

*The Anticipated Design ("grace note").* The prebeat *Vorschlag* of the type called *anticipatione della syllaba* was, as will be remembered, lavishly used by the Italians and Germans throughout the 17th century and was described by many German theorists from Bernhard to Walther. Bach's continued use of such an anticipation is attested to by a number of cases in which he writes it out in regular notes (for illustrations, see *OrnB*, Ex. 16.10).

Furthermore, there are many cases in which onbeat rendition would produce parallels of such obtrusiveness that Bach would surely not have tolerated them. In most of these cases anticipation is the only reasonable alternative. Of a multitude of instances that could be cited, perhaps the most eloquent is the one shown in Ex. 24.10a, from the *Art of Fugue*, the "Canon per augmentationem in contrario motu," in which onbeat rendition of the *Vorschläge* would result in a series of egregiously offensive hidden octaves. Here several reasons combine to make anticipation imperative: (1) we are dealing here with the supreme manifesto of voice leading; (2) this is a two-part setting, which is the most sensitive to faulty counterpoint; (3) the repeated sounding of the open octave is singularly offensive; (4) we are dealing with *Vorschläge* before written-out appoggiaturas, the very case for which Quantz, with timeless musical logic and common sense, requires anticipation (*Versuch einer Anweisung*, chap. 8, par. 6); (5) the *Vorschläge* are disregarded in the augmentation (mm. 48–51 and parallel spots), which proves that they are inconsequential to the melodic profile, hence have to be unobtrusive in the metrical shade of the measure, and cannot be emphasized as they would be if placed on the beat. Thus, despite Bach's onbeat model shown in the "Explication" for the young Friedemann, his music reveals a more flexible and diversified practice. It is therefore a mistake to infer from the "Explication" a downbeat-only rule for Bach's *Vorschläge*. Of many other examples only three can be shown here: two (Exx. 24.10b and 24.10c), from the Canonic Variations, the first with open octaves, the second with open fifths, and one (Ex. 24.10d), from the "Goldberg" Variations with open octaves to be avoided.

EXAMPLE 24.10.   Bach

a. Canon per Augmentationem in contrario motu, BWV 1080, 14 (aut. P 200)

Canonic Variations, BWV 769, Variation 3

b.                                          c.

d. "Goldberg" Variations, BWV 988, Variation 13

In addition to such contrapuntal logic, harmonic logic sometimes suggests the anticipation of a *Vorschlag*. In some cases, the principal note needs to strike on the beat in order to clarify a characteristic harmonic progression such as a suspension-dissonance in another voice; in other cases the onbeat rendition of a *Vorschlag* would impoverish the harmony by, say, turning a dissonance into a consonance, even though enrichment of the harmony is the alleged main purpose of the downbeat principle.

Rhythmic logic will often favor anticipation when onbeat rendition of one or more *Vorschläge* would disturb a characteristic rhythm pattern. Tartini, as noted above in connection with Exx. 23.6b and 23.6c), had expressed this idea with regard to a series of even notes whose evenness must not be compromised by onbeat execution of *Vorschläge*. This principle applies not just to such even notes but to any recurring rhythm pattern with a claim to integrity. Before a short staccato note, furthermore, a *Vorschlag* will tend toward anticipation when a downbeat rendition would blunt the desired sharpness of articulation.

In addition to such musical reasons we have some interesting external evidence about the intended anticipation of Bach's *Vorschläge*. One type of such evidence can be found in a number of manuscript copies from Bach's closest associates: every so often the hook symbol, and once in a whole even the small note, is written before the barline, even though there was plenty of space available after the barline. (For specimens see *OrnB*, Ex. 16.11.)

Another type of external evidence can be found when the same or parallel passages show a symbol in one writing and a written-out anticipation in another, with no apparent reason for an intended difference of execution. Here I have space for only one double example, taken from the Two-Part Invention in D Major as written in two autographs of 1720 (Friedemann's *Clavierbüchlein*) and 1723, respectively. In Ex. 24.11a we see the B in measure 46 written out in 1720 as an interbeat *tierce coulée*, but it is indicated by a hook in the parallel spot of measure 4. In Ex. 24.11b we see measure 46 written in 1723 with a hook and the parallel spot of measure 4 with a little note. Since there is little reason to assume a different intent, we must conclude that in these spots at least both the hook symbol and the little note were meant to be anticipated. Among modern writers, Paul Badura-Skoda, standing apart from the conventional view, agrees with me in assigning to the grace note a sizable role in Bach (*Bach Interpretation, passim*).

In other passages the same symbols before an eighth note can have appoggiatura meaning of circa sixteenth-note length, for which, too, we have similar external evidence from parallel spots, as shown in Ex. 24.11c, from Cantata No. 54.

Within the frame of Bach's ornamental flexibility, we can assume that he used on proper occasions a very short onbeat *Vorschlag* that, too short for a distinct harmonic effect, had an invigorating impact on rhythm. It can be expected to find a sympathetic context in energetic, brilliant pieces that have a pronounced metrical beat. Example 24.11d offers an illustration from the Fourth Partita, where the descending *Vorschlag* might be played very short on the beat and accented on the fortepiano.

EXAMPLE 24.11.   Bach

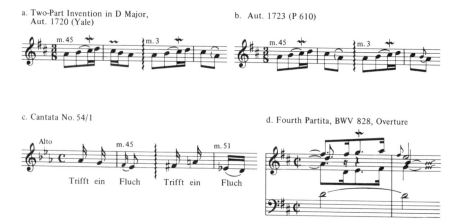

a. Two-Part Invention in D Major, Aut. 1720 (Yale)

b. Aut. 1723 (P 610)

c. Cantata No. 54/1

d. Fourth Partita, BWV 828, Overture

**Summary.** Contrary to conventional opinion, it is impossible to give rules for Bach's one-note graces, and it is especially misleading to follow automatically the "Explication" or to "apply" to his music the principles of the mid-century galant treatises. In particular it can be said with some assurance that long onbeat interpretations lasting for a quarter note or more are generally out of place. But within the range of the tabulation of Ex. 24.7, any of the solutions are possible, and it is the performer's difficult responsibility to make the proper choices. To provide at least some measure of orientation, the following tentative guidelines will be essayed.

The harmony-enhancing appoggiatura will usually be called for in vocal music before an accented syllable of an eighth or longer that occurs on a strong beat; in instrumental music it will be favored on principal beats where for notes of an eighth or longer it strengthens the harmony by changing a consonance into a dissonance or a mild dissonance into a stronger one; it will be required in recitatives, before a final note and before a hold.

Anticipation is more likely when the *Vorschlag* symbol, be it hook or small note, is placed *before* the following kinds of notes: a short note such as a sixteenth or smaller; a written-out appoggiatura or another kind of dissonance on a strong beat; a group of even notes (Tartini's principle), especially triplets; a rhythmic pattern that is characteristic for the piece and whose integrity ought to be preserved; an unaccented syllable on a weak beat or between beats; a short note with a staccato dot or dash. Furthermore, a *Vorschlag* will tend to anticipation whenever its onbeat placement would occasion obtrusive parallels, be they open or hidden, or when it is included within a slur or tie linking two neighbor notes (as *Zwischenschlag*). In a few of these contexts anticipation alone will be indicated; in others a short, onbeat rendition, accented or unaccented—depending on circumstances—may be a reasonable alternative.

## The Galant Period

The galant style, with its ingratiating, regular melodies, simple homophonic texture, and slow harmonic rhythm, emerged in Italy in the first decades of the 18th century. It immediately invaded Germany, where it grew into a powerful movement that belligerently set out to do away with contrapuntal complexities in favor of a music that appealed not to the brain but to the heart. The new, "modern" style coexisted for several decades with such representatives of the "old" school as Bach and a few other conservative holdovers who had not succumbed to the lure of *galanterie*.

The stylistic revolution strongly influenced ornamentation. With respect to one-note graces, the main change concerned the frequency and length of the appoggiatura. Its long and "overlong" forms, which were incompatible with the contrapuntal music of the Baroque, were now not only free to proliferate but were, in the words of Quantz quoted above, frequently needed to enrich the "simple-minded" galant melodies and to relieve the tedium of too much consonance.

Theophil (Gottlieb) Muffat (1690–1770), the son of Georg, published in 1736 a detailed ornament table that, like d'Anglebert's, shows all *Vorschläge* on the beat, with durations up to the length of a quarter note, but no "overlong" patterns (*Componimenti*, Appendix). As with d'Anglebert, we find in Muffat's music external evidence for prebeat performance of *Vorschläge* (such as *Vorschlag* symbols written before the barline). Nevertheless, his table is an important precursor to C. P. E. Bach's later exclusive downbeat designs.

C. P. E. Bach published his celebrated essay on the art of clavier playing in two parts, of which the first deals with solo performance, the second with accompaniment. His famous onbeat rule is formulated in the first part (chap. 2, sec. 1, par. 23), where he categorically states that all ornaments indicated by small notes belong to the following note, "consequently the value of the preceding notes must never be diminished; the value of the small notes has to be subtracted from the following note." He admits that this rule is frequently ignored: "this remark is all the more necessary, the more it is disregarded."

C. P. E. Bach distinguishes two types of *Vorschläge*: the variable and the invariable ones. Variable *Vorschläge* can range from slightly long to very long; the invariable ones are always very short. He then makes the significant statement that because of the variable length of some *Vorschläge*, "one has *not so long ago* started to indicate the *Vorschläge* according to their true value, instead of marking all of them with eighth notes. *Before that, Vorschläge of such variable length were not yet introduced. In* today's style, however, unable to rely on rules about their length, we cannot do without such exact indication, since all kinds [of lengths] occur with all kinds of notes" (par. 14; italics added).

This paragraph is extremely revealing. In it Philipp Emanuel contrasts "today's" (i.e., the galant) style, into which the new symbolism was introduced "not so long ago," with the older style, where the eighth note was adequate because *Vorschläge* of such varying length did not yet exist. Since J. S. Bach did not belong to "today's style" but represented what was practiced "before," we have here a clear statement by Philipp Emanuel himself that *his rules do not apply to the music of his father*. It further confirms what has been inferred above that Johann Sebastian's *Vorschläge* were basically short since only short ones cannot substantially vary in length; and that the "overlong" formulas of the galant theorists were inappropriate for his music.

These are C. P. E. Bach's general principles regarding the "variable" *Vorschläge*: they take half the value of binary notes (Ex. 24.12a) and two-thirds that of ternary notes (Ex. 24.12b); they take the *full* value of a note extended by a tie, be it binary (Ex. 24.12c) or ternary (Ex. 24.12d), or of one followed by a rest (Ex. 24.12e). These latter two cases of *Vorschläge* followed by ties or rests are, even by galant terminology, the "overlong" patterns. (The term "overlong" is relative and was used in the tabulation of Ex. 24.7 for durations that were standard for Philipp Emanuel but presumably beyond the range of Johann Sebastian's usage.) Whereas the principle regarding the binary and ternary notes had been previously formulated by Tartini (see chap. 23), and was to be repeated many times again by German and some foreign theorists, the "overlong" patterns are not mentioned by French or Italian writers and

EXAMPLE 24.12.    C. P. E. Bach

seem to be perhaps exclusively German galant designs. For C. P. E. Bach and his followers, the denomination of the small note symbol indicates the desired length of the *Vorschlag* note.

C. P. E. Bach's "invariable" *Vorschlag*, although performed on the beat, is to be so short that the loss of value to the following note is "barely noticeable" (par. 14). He recommends its use for weak beats, before triplets, for filling descending thirds, for consonances before dissonances. There are some of the contexts that were listed above as presumably favoring grace-note use for Johann Sebastian.

Friedrich Wilhelm Marpurg (1718–95), after early French leanings in matters of ornamentation, came under the powerful influence of C. P. E. Bach and from then on followed him quite faithfully (*Anleitung zum Clavierspielen*, 48). In matters of one-note graces he deviates from him in admitting *Nachschläge*, which Bach had banned for being "ugly" and above all for being at odds with the onbeat-only principle. Marpurg devised a special symbol of a little note with reversed flag ( ♪ ), which can stand for either a *Nachschlag* or an anticipated *Vorschlag* (50).

Johann Friedrich Agricola (1720–74), who in his youth had been Johann Sebastian's student, presented his ideas in extensive annotations to his German translation (1757) of Pierfrancesco Tosi's above-cited treatise of 1723 (*Opinioni*). Agricola too had by now adopted almost all of C. P. E. Bach's ideas on ornaments. Like Marpurg, he deviates from his mentor in two matters. He mentions that "several famous performers" play *Vorschläge* between descending thirds in the French manner—that is, in anticipation. Second, he emphasizes the frequent need for *Nachschläge* to connect and fill in the melody (*Anleitung zur Singkunst*, 68, 81).

In 1752 Johann Joachim Quantz (1697–1773) published his justly famous *Versuch einer Anweisung die Flöte traversiere zu spielen*, which, in spite of its title, deals with questions of performance that are of universal interest. In matters of the *Vorschlag* his ideas coincide in part with those of C. P. E. Bach. Thus he adheres to the principle that the long appoggiatura lasts for half of a binary and two-thirds of a ternary note, and he agrees as well with the "overlong" solution of *Vorschläge* that are followed by rests or extended by a tie (chap. 8, pars. 7–11). Earlier in the present chapter, in discussing J. S. Bach, I quoted Quantz's remarkable statement that long appoggiaturas are necessary to enrich melody and harmony of "meager and simple-minded" galant airs. This observation supports C. P. E. Bach's statement that the long appoggiaturas were a recent development ("not so long ago") and indicates that these appoggiaturas were clearly associated with the new galant style.

On the other hand, Quantz disagrees with C. P. E. Bach on several important matters. He does not mention the "invariable" (short) appoggiaturas; instead he divides the *Vorschläge*—as Tartini had done about the same time—into onbeat ("anschlagende") and prebeat ("durchgehende") types (chap. 8, par. 5). They share the little eighth-note symbol, which can stand for anything from an anticipated *Vorschlag* to the longest appoggiatura. The only other symbol he uses, the small sixteenth note, is reserved for very short *Vorschläge*. Whether the latter include both onbeat and prebeat ornaments (i.e., appoggiaturas and grace notes) is uncertain but likely.

In several cases, however, Quantz explicitly calls for prebeat execution. I have already quoted a passage (chap. 22, p. 309 above) in which Quantz specifies prebeat interpretations not only for *tierces coulées* but also in the pattern of ♪ ♫, which for the Classical era we now, rightly or wrongly, almost routinely resolve into four equal sixteenth notes. Elsewhere (*Versuch einer Anweisung*, chap. 8, par. 6) Quantz offers the illustration of Ex. 24.13, where the *Vorschläge* must be played neither as short nor as long appoggiaturas but as grace notes because the expression here calls not for boldness and vivacity but for caressing smoothness ("einen schmeichelnden Ausdruck"). Although he refers to the design as *tierces coulées,* two of the five *Vorschläge* do not actually fill in descending thirds. Particularly important is Quantz's use of the grace note in the case of a *Vorschlag* that precedes a written-out appoggiatura. His illustration is given in Ex. 24.14 (par. 6). There is timeless wisdom in this principle: an appoggiatura is meant to enrich the harmony, but a second appoggiatura placed on top of the first will weaken if not annul this enrichment and usually create an awkward melodic-rhythmic design as well. That J. S. Bach used Quantz's solution was shown above in Ex. 24.10a.

EXAMPLE 24.13.   Quantz

EXAMPLE 24.14.   Quantz

In 1756, the year of Wolfgang's birth, Leopold Mozart published his important violin treatise *Versuch einer gründlichen Violinschule*. It shows his acquaintance with the tracts of Quantz, Philipp Emanuel Bach, and Tartini. In matters of ornamentation he is closer to Quantz and Tartini than to Philipp Emanuel.

Leopold discusses *Vorschläge* in chapter 9 (to which all references will be made). Like Quantz, Leopold distinguishes between appoggiaturas ("anschlagend") and grace notes ("durchgehend"). He calls appoggiaturas "long" when they take one-half of the principal note's value, even if the latter is as short as a sixteenth note (par. 3). His illustration is shown in Ex. 24.15. The appoggiatura is "longer" when it

EXAMPLE 24.15.   L. Mozart (1756)

takes more than half of the principal note's value, be it two-thirds, three-quarters, or all of it. The two-thirds solution applies mainly to dotted (thus ternary) notes. If this dotted note is followed by its (short) companion, the characteristic dotted rhythm of 3:1, which is disturbed by the long appoggiatura, is restored by halving the value of the companion note, as shown in Ex. 24.16a (par. 4). A *Vorschlag* before a half note can under circumstances extend to three-fourths of the latter (Ex. 24.16b).

Just like Philipp Emanuel Bach and Quantz, Leopold Mozart explains and illustrates also the "overlong" type that takes the whole value of the note when it is extended by a tie or followed by a rest (see Exx. 24.16c and 24.16d). He cautions, however, that this pattern should be used mainly for soloistic playing: when other parts are involved, such extension could interfere with a middle or lower voice in a way the composer had not intended (par. 5).

Leopold's presentation of the grace notes is blurred by inconsistencies of both outline and terminology. He speaks both of "short" and of "passing" (durchgehende) *Vorschläge,* and what he says about them points to their identity. In his explanation of the "short" descending *Vorschlag* (par. 9), he writes: "There are also short *Vorschläge* where the accent falls not on the *Vorschlag* but on the principal note. The short *Vorschlag* is done as fast as possible and touched not strongly but very weakly." This is of course the exact opposite of C. P. E. Bach's short

EXAMPLE 24.16.   L. Mozart (1756)

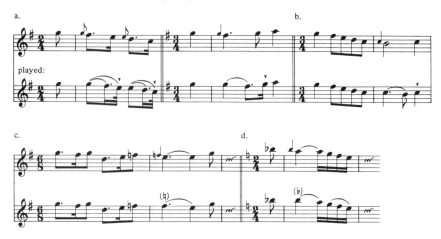

"invariable *Vorschlag*" with its sharp accent. Yet some scholars, be-holden to the downbeat dogma, believe that Leopold Mozart's "short" *Vorschlag* must take the beat. Yet he says nothing to that effect; and such an interpretation makes little musical sense since the accent on the principal note is spontaneously attracted to the beat. If one fought this spontaneous impulse and played the soft, fast "short *Vorschlag*" on the beat, the effect would be still that of a grace note, agogically delayed, not that of an appoggiatura. As an occasional execution it might have its charm; as a routine it would become an unpleasant mannerism.

That Leopold Mozart's passing *Vorschläge* are anticipated would be clear from the very term, even if he did not declare (par. 17) that they belong in the time of the preceding note. It is revealing that the two terms are defined nearly identically: the chief criterion of the "short" *Vorschlag,* namely the fact that the accent falls on the principal note, is also the distinguishing characteristic of the passing ones. "Now we come to speak of the passing *Vorschläge, Zwischenschläge,* and other re-lated graces that have the accent fall on the principal note and that are rarely or not at all indicated by the composer"; the violinist, he says, has to supply them in the right places according to "sound judgment" (par. 16). With this statement Mozart opens the door to their widest use. He illustrates their unspecified as well as symbolized notation and execu-tion, as shown in Ex. 24.17. It is significant that the passing and the short *Vorschläge* share not only the accentual pattern but also such pre-ferred contexts as descending thirds and scale passages, giving a further indication of their basic identity.

Leopold Mozart's ideas cannot of course be taken as an indication of his son's practice; they are important, however, because they do show

EXAMPLE 24.17.   L. Mozart (1756), "passing *Vorschläge*"

what kind of ornamental style Wolfgang was exposed to in his child-hood years.

Georg Simon Löhlein (1725–81) was an influential theorist whose Clavier-Schule of 1765 saw four editions up to 1782 and whose *Anwei-sung zum Violinspielen* of 1774 was reedited by Reichardt eleven years after Löhlein's death. In matters of the appoggiatura he follows the common galant principles of taking one-half of a binary note, two-thirds of a ternary one, and the whole value of a parent note extended by a tie. In his piano treatise he indicated grace-note use for *Vorschläge* before eighth and sixteenth notes in a fast tempo. In his violin treatise he is much more specific: "There are also *fast* types of *Vorschläge* that are irrelevant to the measure. They either take the upper neighbor or they repeat the preceding note or fill the empty space between two notes. They are slurred very fast to the following note" (*Anweisung zum Vio-linspielen*, 44). His illustration of such *Vorschläge* (Ex. 24.18) confirms their anticipation.

EXAMPLE 24.18.   Löhlein

Johann Friedrich Reichardt (1752–1814) gives in his treatise of 1774 on ripieno playing the usual rules for the long appoggiatura and then adds that "there are also very short *Vorschläge* attached to notes that do not seem to lose anything of their value" (Über die Pflichten, 41). Only unaccented brevity, in other words de facto grace notes, would seem to give the impression he describes.

Johann Christian Bach (1735–82), the youngest son of Johann Sebastian and mentor of the boy Mozart during the latter's London sojourns, wrote with F. Pasquale Ricci a treatise for the Naples Conservatory that was later published in Paris in 1786. In it the authors say that *Vorschläge*, as well as other ornaments consisting of more than one note that are written as small notes, take their value *either* from the preceding *or* the following note (*Méthode*, 5). *Vorschläge*, then, can be rendered either on or before the beat.

## Late-18th-Century Theorists

In 1778 the important theorist Georg Joseph Vogler (1749–1814), teacher of Weber and Meyerbeer, describes and illustrates "grosse Vorschläge" (appoggiaturas), "kleine Vorschläge" (grace notes), "Zwischenklänge" (*Zwischenschläge*), and *Nachschläge*. The appoggiaturas follow the usual rules, while *kleine Vorschläge* are grace notes that "do not lessen the value of the following note" (*Kuhrpfälzische Tonschule*, 21).

Johann Adam Hiller, in both of his major treatises of 1774 (*Anweisung zum musikalisch-richtigen Gesange*, 165ff.) and 1780 (*Anweisung zum musikalisch-zierlichen Gesange*, 40ff.), follows C. P. E. Bach's *Vorschlag* rules very closely, except that, like Marpurg and Agricola, he does admit *Nachschläge*.

Daniel Gottlob Türk (1750–1813), in his *Klavierschule* of 1789, devotes his entire third chapter to *Vorschläge* and *Nachschläge*. (References in the following are to this chapter.) He also follows C. P. E. Bach faithfully in matters of the long appoggiatura but deviates from his teaching on two points: he admits *Nachschläge*, and he disagrees about the accentuation of the short, "invariable" *Vorschlag*. Since, he says, these *Vorschläge* are mostly passing ("durchgehend") and often even appear before a written-out appoggiatura, he prefers to play them gently, "flatteringly," leaving the emphasis on the following note (par. 19). As was pointed out on various occasions, this dynamic pattern instinctively produces anticipation. It seems hardly a coincidence that the term "flatteringly" was also Quantz's characterization for the prebeat *durchgehende Vorschläge*. Thus, in principle Türk insists on the downbeat rendition, both in 1789 and in his second edition of 1802, but in practice his principle was bound to be frustrated.

Of special significance is the testimony of Johann Peter Milchmeyer (1750–1813) in his treatise of 1797 (*Die wahre Art das Pianoforte zu spielen*). An extended stay in France may account for his immunity to the powerful influence of C. P. E. Bach, whose ideas had strongly affected many north German musicians and writers for decades after his books had come out in mid-century. Milchmeyer is flexible about the length of appoggiaturas, which he says depends on the expression. His short *Vorschläge* are grace notes, "rendered as if they still belonged to the preceding measure" (37–38). Anticipation is explicitly shown by juxtaposing notation and execution, of which Ex. 24.19 gives a few striking specimens. It so happens that all of these shown here fall into Tartini's category of *Vorschläge* before even notes, which, he said, call for anticipation. Since Türk, in his 1802 edition, takes two writers to task for such unorthodox views but identifies only Milchmeyer, there must have been at least one more German theorist who was equally explicit about anticipation.

EXAMPLE 24.19.   Milchmeyer

Heinrich Christoph Koch, the eminent theorist, describes the very short *Vorschläge* as being "slurred so fast to the principal note that the latter seems to lose nothing of its value (*Journal,* 185–87). The accent, he specifies, falls on the principal note, not on the *Vorschlag.* Though his illustrations show downbeat placement of the *Vorschlag,* here too the combination of unnoticeable loss and reverse dynamics is bound in the vast majority of cases to result in anticipation.

## The Classical Composers

*Haydn.* The music of Haydn and Mozart has time and again been interpreted in terms of C. P. E. Bach's rule that all ornaments—including of course the *Vorschläge*—should be rendered on the beat. Haydn in particular has been singled out for alignment with Bach's rules because he is known to have studied Bach's treatise and to have held his music in high esteem. Therefore, so it has been argued, Haydn can be expected to have adopted Bach's teachings. The inference is deceptive: respect or even admiration for a teacher or artist does not imply necessary endorsement of every word he spoke or wrote. An automatic "application" of C. P. E. Bach's rules to Haydn's music is the more questionable since Haydn grew up in a musical environment that was oriented toward Italy, not northern Germany; and of course the Italian Nicola Porpora was his personal teacher. Moreover, a great deal of musical evidence points to the extension of Haydn's compositional originality and independence to matters of ornamentation.

The controversy centers primarily on the legitimacy of the grace note. Here the reader will remember that several important theorists called for this ornament explicitly, others did so implicitly when stressing the unaccented shortness of the grace and the placement of the accent on the principal note.

The question of Haydn's ornamental style is as complex as is that of his overall style, which in a gratifyingly long career encompassed significant changes. In his early years Haydn was fully committed to the galant style; but he himself then became a prime agent in transforming it into the high Classical style through his procedures of thematic development and polyphonic enrichment and through an aesthetic reorientation from pure entertainment to expressiveness and edification. This transformation was bound to affect ornamentation.

Like all of Haydn's ornaments, *Vorschläge* have various functions, and one rigid principle cannot do justice to all of them. In Haydn's early years the harmony-enriching, dissonance-producing long appoggiatura was very much in evidence, while the grace note entered where its specific virtues were called for. In Haydn's mature works, with their fuller, more complex texture, the length of the appoggiaturas is generally diminished, with quarter notes and longer values less in evidence and grace notes more frequent. The latter are generally indicated when the function of the *Vorschlag* is to add luster and emphasis to the parent note, or to smooth its transition to the following pitch, or to fill the space between notes more engagingly and gracefully while doing any of these things *without obtruding* on the prevailing rhythmic and melodic profile as a *Vorschlag* placed on the beat would do.

In a much-quoted letter, Haydn offered advice on the performance of the *Vorschläge* in his "Applausus" Cantata of 1768. He deals here only with the appoggiatura in recitatives (a limitation that has been overlooked by some scholars). In the recitative, Haydn writes, the form written as Ex. 24.20a is to be rendered as in Ex. 24.20b and not as in Ex. 24.20c; that is, he wishes the traditional prosodic appoggiatura for feminine endings to take the full value of the first note.

Haydn used various denominations for his *Vorschlag* symbols, from the rare half-note to the thirty-second note. The long values from a quarter note and longer will almost always indicate an appoggiatura and will often suggest its approximate length. In particular the frequent

EXAMPLE 24.20.   Haydn, "Applausus" Cantata (1768)

will most often mean ♪♪ —not always. In Ex. 24.21, from the Benedictus of the Theresienmesse of 1799, we gather from the accompanying violins that the quarter-note soprano appoggiatura was more likely intended as an approximate eighth note.

EXAMPLE 24.21.   Haydn, Theresienmesse (1799)

Benedictus

As to the "overlong" design (outside of recitatives), where the *Vorschlag* takes the full value of the parent note, Haydn may have used it once in a while, probably more often in his earlier than in his later years. But such a usage is not provable, and great caution is advised in its use.

The design will frequently, perhaps most often, stand for , but there are cases where it may signify a grace note. In the double fugue from the String Quartet in F Minor Op. 20, No. 5 (Hob. III:35), the second subject is announced in the viola as in Ex. 24.22a, its answer in the second violin as in Ex. 24.22b. The answer sounds exact, as it must, only if the *Vorschlag* is rendered as a grace note. If rendered as an appoggiatura the answer would be improper for a fugue. The subject occurs over and over again, in the majority of cases written with a *Vorschlag,* but many times—and in all instrumental parts—written simply as in the first statement (see, for instance, Ex. 24.22c, from the first violin part). Grace-note rendition would seem to be the logical solution.

The shorter denominations are more ambiguous still. Eighth and sixteenth notes can often denote an appoggiatura and sometimes one of longer duration than their written value. Sixteenth notes will generally

have  appoggiatura  meaning  in  the  frequent  designs

and . Whereas Quantz, as will be remembered (p. 309), asked

EXAMPLE 24.22.   Haydn, String Quartet in F Minor, Op. 20, No. 5/4 (Hob. III:35)

for grace-note use in this design, it seems to have turned with the Classical composers into an appoggiatura formula that we now resolve, almost routinely and probably correctly, into four roughly equal notes, while on occasion the appoggiatura might call for a subtle dynamic-agogic emphasis.

On the other hand, the smaller denominations from the eighth note down will often stand for a grace note. Haydn's use of the little *Vorschlag* note in anticipation of the principal note is clearly shown in Ex. 24.23, from *L'Anima del filosofo*, in which the equivalence of the little note and its written-out counterpart in the next measure should be obvious. For the most part, however, only musical instinct and intelligence can tell us, as they had also to tell contemporary performers, when an appoggiatura and when a grace note was appropriate.

EXAMPLE 24.23.   Haydn, *L'Anima del filosofo*, ouverture

It is particularly helpful to remember that several important instrumental ornaments are direct descendants of the vocal portamento, probably the oldest and most frequent of ornaments—one that is invariably done before the beat. The short, ascending *Vorschlag*, especially the upward-leaping one, the slide, and the arpeggio are stylized forms of the vocal portamento and as such retain its innate tendency to anticipation. A striking illustration of this parallelism is shown in Ex. 24.24a, from the String Quartet Op. 64, No. 2 (Hob. III:64), where Haydn's original fingerings specify his wish for an audible portamento in as exact an imitation as any instrument is capable of making of its vocal model. Here, too, the glissando (the violinistic term for the portamento), and hence the grace note, must anticipate the beat so that it can reach the principal note exactly on its proper time. Similar are cases such as those of Exx. 24.24b and 24.24c, from Symphony No. 101, in which the upward-leaping *Vorschläge* are portamento-related and the strokes over the parent notes have accentual as well as staccato implication. Both staccato and accent are emasculated when the *Vorschlag* displaces the parent note from the beat.

EXAMPLE 24.24.   Haydn

a. String Quartet, Op. 64, No. 2/3 (Hob. III: 64)

Symphony No. 101/2 (Hob. I: 101)

There are also other reasons for musical logic that can militate against downbeat placement of a *Vorschlag*. Among them are the frequent cases where the downbeat would infringe on a characteristic rhythmic design (such as a pattern of even notes, of dotted rhythms, or syncopation) that under the circumstances are of structural importance and have a claim to integrity. For a good illustration, see Ex. 24.25, from the String Quartet Op. 77, No. 1 (Hob. III:81). This dotted march-like rhythm pervades the better part of the movement, thereby achieving structural importance and a claim to integrity. Although at least one Haydn scholar believes that virtually all of Haydn's *Vorschläge,* including

EXAMPLE 24.25.   Haydn, String Quartet, Op. 77, No. 1/1 (Hob. III:81)

those in this movement, should on principle be played on the beat, to do so here alters not only the rhythm but also the profile of the melody, destroys the unity of the pattern throughout the movement, and impairs its spirit of sparkling briskness.[1] The grace note, which leaves the rhythm intact while adding to the sparkle, is on these grounds the indicated solution.

Yet within Haydn's enormous wealth of melodic-rhythmic designs, it is impossible to formulate anything resembling a rule about when a grace note is appropriate and when not. Apart from the circumstances discussed above, I shall simply list in Fig. 24.1, with no claim to completeness, a few rhythmic-notational patterns that favor a prebeat interpretation. (The eighth-note and sixteenth-note symbols are often interchangeable.) Moreover, the illustrations shown below in Exx. 24.27 and 24.28 for Mozart's use of the grace note can all be said to have equal relevance for the mature Haydn.

FIGURE 24.1

*Mozart.* Leopold's treatise, as has been pointed out, provides useful background information on young Wolfgang's musical environment; but we must beware of seeing in the treatise more than that. It is certainly not a rule book for the performance of the son's music. Wolfgang emancipated himself from paternal tutelage musically much earlier than personally. It is likely, though, that Leopold's endorsement of both prebeat and onbeat interpretations of *Vorschläge* helped to shape Wolfgang's parallel usage. But as for the length of appoggiaturas, Leopold's traditional rule of two-thirds of a ternary note, as well as his "overlong" rule of taking the whole value of the note before a tie or a rest, do not apply to Wolfgang except perhaps on occasions so rare that they can be disregarded. We can gather that much from numerous passages in which a vocal appoggiatura is marked by symbol, with a doubling or parallel instrument, usually the violins, written out in regular notes. Whereas there are a great many cases where such juxtaposition points to a length one-third of a ternary note (or shorter), as for instance in Ex. 24.26a, a diligent search has not revealed a single one that showed the intention of a length of two-thirds. This is true even in many a passage that would seem to invite "overlong" treatment but in which Mozart invariably opted for a shorter value. Example 24.26 shows two characteristic specimens, one for the appoggiatura before a tied note (Ex. 24.26b) and one before a rest (Ex. 24.26c).

Appoggiaturas before binary notes may take one-half of a relatively short note—that is, a quarter note or shorter. Before a half note the duration of the appoggiatura will be rarely as much as a quarter note and

EXAMPLE 24.26. Mozart

a. K 527, II, 21b

b. K 623, 2

c. K 492, II, 10

usually much less. The shorter the value of the principal note, the more likely will the half-a-binary-note principle apply.

Although the denominations of the *Vorschlag* symbols have some meaning, taking them at face value invites misunderstanding. In his younger years Mozart occasionally used half-note denominations for the *Vorschlag* symbol, with usually half-note meaning, but he stopped doing so after about 1778. Until the end of his life he used quarter-note symbols interchangeably with eighth-note symbols. Both forms more often had approximate eighth-note rather than quarter-note value. Whereas the quarter-note symbol stood always for an appoggiatura, the eighth-note symbol was ambiguous: though mostly, especially in vocal music, it signified an appoggiatura of roughly eighth-note length, in instrumental music it could once in a while indicate a grace note. Sixteenth-note symbols, as in Haydn, tend to be appoggiaturas in the formulas of ♪ ♫ . In slow movements they may be appoggiaturas of approximately sixteenth-note to eighth-note length; in fast movements, especially when preceding a parent of a quarter note or longer, they will often be grace notes.

The medium is also important: in vocal music, although occasional grace notes occur, appoggiaturas are much more frequent because of their greater singability. In instrumental music, on the other hand, the snappy briskness of the grace note plays a large role, notably in fast movements, in which the added brilliance or elegance achieved without interfering with the structural rhythm is of special importance.

The circumstances that favor or even call for the grace note seem parallel to those listed for Haydn. Some of these are *Vorschläge* that precede: (1) a written-out appoggiatura (see Ex. 24.27a, from the Trio for Clarinet, Viola, and Piano); (2) a characteristic rhythm pattern such as triplets (Ex. 24.27b, from *Don Giovanni*); (3) groups of even binary notes (Ex. 24.27c, from the "Linz" Symphony); (4) groups of dotted notes (Ex. 24.27d, from the Violin Sonata in C); (5) syncopations (Ex. 24.27e, from the Violin Concerto in A); (6) notes with a staccato mark (Ex. 24.27f, from *Die Zauberflöte*); (7) notes that carry a *sforzando* sign (Ex. 24.27g, from the Symphony No. 29 in A); (8) groups of even sixteenth or thirty-second notes (Ex. 24.27h, from the "Hoffmeister" String Quartet); (9) single notes followed by rests (Ex. 24.27i, from the Violin Concerto No. 4); (10) an upward leap (Ex. 24.27j, from the Piano Concerto in C Minor).

EXAMPLE 24.27.   Mozart

a. Trio for Clarinet, Viola, and Piano, K 498/3

b. *Don Giovanni*, K 527, I, 5

c. "Linz" Symphony, K 425/5

EXAMPLE 24.27   *continued*

d. Violin Sonata in C, K 296/1

e. Violin Concerto in A, K 219/2

f. *Die Zauberflöte*, K 620, II, Finale

g. Symphony No. 29 in A, K 186a (201)

h. "Hoffmeister" String Quartet, K 499/3

i. Violin Concerto No. 4, K 218/3

EXAMPLE 24.27    *continued*

j. Piano Concerto in C Minor, K 491/1

This is of course not an exhaustive listing. In general, grace notes will be indicated when for whatever reason the musical priorities call for the principal note to sound on the beat. For just one illustration, see Ex. 24.28, from the Finale of the "Haffner" Symphony: only grace notes will permit the chromatically ascending melody to be properly perceived, whereas the addition of appoggiaturas would distort the melody. There are countless other cases in which for musical reasons the *Vorschlag* has to be anticipated. (For a detailed discussion, see chap. 4 of *OrnM*.)

EXAMPLE 24.28.    Mozart, "Haffner" Symphony, Finale, K 385/4

K 385/4

Above all, it is imperative for the enlightened performer to know that there are no easy automatic rules, that he has to figure out every case on its merits, realizing that the worst thing, then as now, is any sense of rigidity and formulaic stereotype.

# 25

# TWO-NOTE GRACES: THE SLIDE

Graces that consist of two ornamental notes, like the one-note graces, can have the character of a *Vorschlag*, a *Zwischenschlag*, or a *Nachschlag*.

Within the *Nachschlag* category, the most common species is the suffix to a trill:  ♪♪ . This pattern can of course be used without a trill and can be inverted. It is generally recognized that such *Nachschläge* should be rendered within the time of the preceding parent note.

When the two little notes are assigned *Zwischenschlag* function, either by a slur encompassing the ornament together with the principal notes before and after, ♪♪♪ , or by the logic of the context, interbeat rendition will almost always be in order. Such a rendition was stipulated by Leopold Mozart, who coined the term *Zwischenschlag* with such two-note graces in mind (*Versuch einer Violinschule*, chap. 9, pars. 19–20). This type of grace, like the two-note *Nachschlag*, presents few difficulties of interpretation.

The chief interpretive problems are rather centered once again on the patterns related to the *Vorschlag*. A few of these have become standardized within larger ornamental families. Thus the design ♪♪ , called the *Schneller*, is a miniature trill; its mirror image, ♪♪ , is a one-alternation mordent. Both of these will be discussed together with their respective families. A third one, the *Anschlag*, ♪♪ , which is of much lesser importance, will be briefly touched upon at the end of this chapter. The only remaining two-note grace of the *Vorschlag* type that played a prominent part in our period and beyond is the slide, which will be the main subject of this chapter.

The term "slide" (French: *port de voix double* or *doublé*; German: *Schleifer;* no Italian term) refers most commonly to a two-note grace whose pitches rise in diatonic steps to the principal note and are slurred to it ♪ . Less frequent are the descending type ♪ and a type that consists of three notes ♪ . When four or more notes are included in a scale-like design of this sort, it is called *tirata* by the Italians, *tirade* or *coulade* by the French, *Pfeil* by the Germans, and belongs more properly to the diminutions.

The slide is amenable to various rhythmic dispositions, which can be designated as shown in Ex. 25.1 as anapestic (Ex. 25.1a), Lombard (Ex. 25.1b), or dactylic (Exx. 25.1c and 25.1d). For all three types the third pitch is the principal note. The usual dynamic treatment for the anapestic pattern will be softness of the grace and accentuation of the principal note; for the Lombard type, a distinct accent on the first note of the grace; and for the dactyl, a gentle emphasis on the first note.

EXAMPLE 25.1

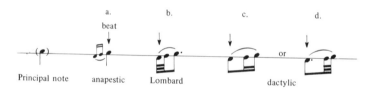

In contrast to its effect on the one-vote *Vorschlag*, onbeat rendition of the slide cannot enrich the harmony. The first note of an onbeat slide will normally have to be consonant since as dissonance it would have no proper resolution.

## The French Slide

French composers started to indicate the slide by symbol in the last quarter of the 17th century. Little notes slurred to their parent were the most frequent symbol, although a few composers of the early period used a slanted dash before the principal note: /♪ .

D'Anglebert may have been the first to explain the slide, in his extensive ornament table of 1689 (*Pièces de clavecin*). Using a crescent-shaped symbol that starts on the line or space of the slide's start, he presents three types (Ex. 25.2), of which the first and third start on the beat, the second before the beat. The two onbeat models may appear, however, to be the only French reference to such design: all other

EXAMPLE 25.2.   d'Anglebert (1689)

French sources that could be found either specify or imply prebeat rendition, as does a great deal of musical evidence. Even d'Anglebert used
his own slide symbol only a very few times, and nobody else seems to
have adopted it. Bach, who copied the table, never used the slide symbol, which seems to have existed in a near-vacuum.

L'Affilard, in his treatise of 1694, called the slide *port de voix doublé*
and indicates it with a slanted dash symbol that, though written *after* the
barline, is clearly spelled out in anticipation (*Principes pour apprendre la
musique* [1694; 1697], 20–21; [1705], 26–27; see Ex. 25.3).

EXAMPLE 25.3.   L'Affilard (1694), *Port de voix doublé*

In his treatise of 1733 and 1756, Villeneuve copied L'Affilard's model
(adding to the dash symbol an inverted caret above the note head) with
the same explicit prebarline execution (*Nouvelle méthode*, 38).

In 1696 Loulié used no symbol but illustrates the slide both rising
and falling under the term of *coulade* in a series of patterns from two to
six ornamental notes that are slurred either to the preceding or the
following note (*Éléments ou principes de musique*, 74). A few are given
in Ex. 25.4a. The slurring to the preceding note reveals the interbeat
nature of the grace, something already implied in the term *coulade*,
which, like its Italian counterpart, the *tirata*, is always rendered in interbeat space. In further confirming this interpretation, Loulié, in a syn-
optic tabulation of all ornaments at the end of the treatise, shows as the
sole representative of the *coulade* the pattern given in Ex. 25.4b with its
telltale slur to the preceding note. It seems that Loulié's slide, like L'Affilard's, was basically of the anapestic, prebeat type.

In 1736 Montéclair, following the lead of Loulié, explained and illustrated the slide as a *coulade*, with its usual implication of interbeat

EXAMPLE 25.4.   Loulié (1696)

a. *Coulade* (rising)

*Coulade* (falling)

b. *Coulade* (synopsis)

rendition (*Principes de musique*, 87). La Chapelle in 1737 explains the *port de voix double*, as shown in Ex. 25.5a, in a "demonstration how to under-stand the execution [of various ornaments]." The prebeat meaning of the symbol in the third measure is clear from the spelled-out anticipation in measures one and two (*Vrais principes*, 2:14).

Denis invites the same interpretation by the prebarline notation of the second slide in Ex. 25.5b (*Nouveau système*, 45; *Nouvelle méthode*, 44).

EXAMPLE 25.5

a. La Chapelle (1737)

b. Denis (1747, c. 1762)

**Musical Evidence.** Nicolas de Grigny's anticipated slides are of special interest because both Bach and Walther copied out the Frenchman's first organ book (*Premier livre d'orgue*, 1699) with meticulous care, including his prebarline spelling of numerous slides, both rising and falling. Many times he writes the slide before the barline, as for instance in Ex. 25.6a. In other, rarer, spots where the slide symbol is written after the barline, we find several instances, like the one given in Ex. 25.6b, in which onbeat performance would produce offensive parallels.

EXAMPLE 25.6.   Grigny

a. 1st *Sanctus*, p. 31

b. *Dialogue*, p. 18

In Couperin's works many passages point similarly to prebarline execution. In Ex. 25.7a (from the Treizième ordre of the *Pièces de clavecin*), for instance, the G sharp of the slide could not be taken on a beat preempted by the G natural of the second voice; in Ex. 25.7b, from the Douzième ordre (and representative of several others), onbeat playing in this transparent two-part writing would result in impossible parallel octaves.

Nicolas Siret, organist of Troyes, has the slide written before the barline a few times in his *Pièces de clavecin* of circa 1716, as shown in Ex. 25.7c. Example 25.7d shows yet another prebarline notation by d'Agincour (*Pièces de clavecin*, Première ordre), Ex. 25.7e one of several by Luc Marchand (*Pièces de clavecin avec accompagnement*, 5), and Ex. 25.7f one by Azaïs in a didactic composition included in his treatise as well as one in which onbeat rendition is disqualified by impossible open octaves (*Méthode de musique*, 63).

Should there be any evidence for onbeat interpretation after d'Anglebert, it has escaped my search. The French slide, then, as symbolized by two little notes, seems to have been predominantly, maybe systematically, rendered in anticipation of the following principal note.

A related ornament, which was usually marked with an oblique dash between thirds, ⨍ , was often taken on the beat; it will be discussed in connection with the arpeggio.

EXAMPLE 25.7

a. Couperin, XIII, *Les Folies Françoises*, 11th couplet

b. Couperin, XII, *L'Intîme*

c. Siret (1716), Courante

d. d'Agincour, *La pressante Angélique*

e. Luc Marchand (1748), *Carillon du Parnasse*

f. Azaïs (1776)

# The Italian Slide

Slides or slide-like patterns were common in improvised diminutions, and we find many of them in diminution treatises beginning with Ganassi (1535) and Ortiz (1553) and ending with Francesco Rognioni in 1620 (the last Italian ornamentation tract of the 17th century).

Richardo Rogniono (the father of Francesco, with a different final vowel) includes a plethora of slide designs, both rising and falling, in his treatise of 1592 (*Passaggi per potersi*, pt. 2, 7, 11, 25, 26, 29, 30). *All* of them, of which just two specimens are given in Ex. 25.8a, are rendered before the beat.

Bovicelli in 1594 fills the interval of a rising fourth with both a prebeat and an onbeat slide, whereas for the descending leap both examples show the prebeat style (Ex. 25.8b). For starting a piece, his favorite design was an (onbeat) dactylic slide starting—on a consonance—a third below the written note (ex. 25.8c), a design also given in Francesco Rognioni (*Selva,* 1:1). Caccini did not like this pattern and preferred to start with the written note (*Nuove musiche,* 3).

For the keyboard, Diruta in 1609 has a dotted, dactylic, hence onbeat pattern that he calls *Clamatione,* shown in Ex. 25.8d (*Transilvano* pt. 2, bk. 1, 13).

In addition to the onbeat, dactylic opening pattern, Francesco Rognioni shows a connective design of prebeat slides ornamenting a rising scale, identical with his father's pattern of Ex. 25.8a (*Selva* 1:11, No. 2).

For the remainder of the 17th century the slide was a frequent improvised addition in no doubt both the prebeat and the onbeat designs. As the century neared its end, the slide was more and more frequently spelled out in regular notes, now notably in the newly emerging fashion of the Lombard design ⟨music symbol⟩ , which (along with the plain two-note Lombard rhythm ⟨music symbol⟩ ) became around the turn of the century a favorite formula in Italy; the prebeat slide was left to the realm of improvisation.

A change came with the introduction in Italy after circa 1720 of the French small unmetrical notes. While the Lombard slide continued to be written out in regular notes, the prebeat slide was now more and more specified by the small notes ⟨music symbol⟩ . There is truly rich musical evidence that those small notes were usually, maybe always, meant to be rendered in anticipation of the beat. The evidence is of two kinds. First are the many cases in which onbeat rendition is rhythmically incongruous or musically nonsensical because lack of time would either not permit it or lead to absurd overcrowding, as for instance in Exx. 25.9a–25.9b, from Geminiani and Locatelli. Second are the multitude of cases where an onbeat execution would produce unacceptable parallels. From a vast

EXAMPLE 25.8

a. R. Rogniono (1592)

b. Bovicelli (1594)

c. Bovicelli (Palestrina, *Io son ferito*), p. 38

d. Diruta (1609)

number only four illustrations are given in Exx. 25.9c–25.9f, from Locatelli, Padre Martini, Tartini, and Giustini (for many more, see *OrnB*, chap. 22). From such evidence it appears most probable that the Italian slide, when indicated by two even little notes, was basically anticipated.

The situation is quite different, however, for the occasional small dotted note pair that was unknown to the French and that was later adopted by the Germans of the galant period. It apparently indicates the onbeat dactylic slide shown in Ex. 25.10a, from Porpora, and Ex. 25.10b, from Geminiani. The design may possibly go back to the early dotted slide patterns of Bovicelli, Diruta, and Francesco Rognioni.

EXAMPLE 25.9

a. Geminiani (1739),
   Op. 1, Sonata No. 2

b. Locatelli (1746),
   Op. 6, Sonata No. 2

c. Locatelli (1732), Op. 2, No. 2

d. G. B. Martini, Cantata (aut. 1745)

e. Tartini, Sinfonia à violino solo (aut.)

f. Giustini (1732), Sonata No. 3

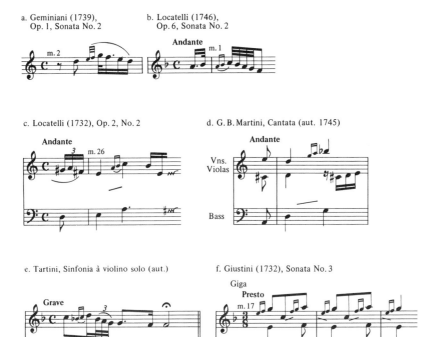

EXAMPLE 25.10

a. Porpora (1735), Cantata 8

b. Geminiani (1743)

[t'ascon-] de i- rai    quan-    ta pie- tà

To summarize, then, in the 17th century the Italian slide was improvised in its varied shapes; in the 18th century—notably after circa 1725—the two little notes signified mostly the anapestic slide, the little dotted pair the dactylic one, while the Lombard was written out in regular notes.

## *The English Slide*

In the *Fitzwilliam Virginal Book* we find here and there some slide-like figurations such as, for instance, the anapestic passage of Ex. 25.11a, from John Bull's "Quadran Pavan" (1:XXXI, var. 4), or the more clearly ornamental four-note *tirate* of Ex. 25.11b, from John Bull's "Pavana" (1:XXXIV, m. 17).

EXAMPLE 25.11.   John Bull

a. "Quadran Pavan" ( 1: XXXI, var. 4)

b. "Pavana" ( 1: XXXIV, m. 17)

Theoretical documentation on the English slide is rather meager. Christopher Simpson in 1667 includes in his ornament table a model of both a rising slide, the "elevation," which is marked by a cross above the note, and a falling one, the "double backfall," marked by two crescents or commas. Both are performed on the beat, as given in Ex. 25.12a (*Division-Violist* [1667], 12). Example 25.12b is taken from the section on "divisions," in which Simpson illustrates how to embroider an austere melody with improvised diminutions ("divisions"), which in this case show a series of prebeat slides ([1667], 47). John Playford, in his *Introduction to the Skill of Musick,* adopted Simpson's models of the slide along with his complete ornament table ([1674], 116); in the twelfth edition of 1694, which was revised by his friend Purcell, we find the French symbol of Ex. 25.12c for what is called a "slur."

Thomas Mace, in his lute treatise of 1676, calls the rising slide a "Whole-fall" and says that it is "much out of use, in These our Days," but can give delight when properly applied (*Musick's Monument,* 105). Although his description of its execution on the lute is usually transcribed as an onbeat, Lombard type, such an interpretation is not a foregone conclusion. The first note is plucked by the right hand, the second and the third, the principal note, are sounded by vigorously dropping the fingers of the left hand. He writes that "you must take *Care,* that you strike not the first *so Loud,* as that the *strength* of the *finger,* is not sufficient to cause the other 2 *Following Letters* [i.e., pitches] *to Sound as Loud, as the first, which was struck.*" He aims to equalize the sounds and to avoid an accent on the first note—which would not be out

EXAMPLE 25.12

a. Simpson (1667)

Elevation            (played)            Double Backfall     (played)

b. Simpson, "divisions" (1667)

c. Purcell (1694)

"slur"

of place for a Lombard type. If we view this aim in connection with the rhythmic flexibility and frequent vagueness of the beat in the "style luthé," the rhythmic design of the slide is at best ambiguous.

## The German Slide

German ornamentation during most of the 17th century was, as mentioned before, so closely patterned after Italian models that we are entitled to speak of an "Italo-German" style. Praetorius in 1619 reproduced Bovicelli's designs (see Ex. 25.8b) of both prebeat and onbeat slides for the interval of a rising fourth, but the prebeat type only for the falling fourth (*Syntagma musicum,* 3:234). With only insignificant variants, Crüger in 1654 (*Synopsis musica,* 193) and Herbst in 1658 follow Praetorius faithfully. Herbst also reproduces Francesco Rognioni's prebeat slides, which are identical with those of his father, shown in Ex. 25.8a (*Musica practica,* 4, 20, 23, 25, 28–29). Falck in 1688 shows among his diminution patterns only the prebeat type (*Idea boni cantoris,* 94); the same is true of Stierlein in 1691 (*Trifolium,* 19).

Johann Kuhnau may have been the first to use the custos symbol ( ~ for the rising, ~ for the falling slide). Slides, he says, are "drawn into the following note from either the third below or the third above" (*Clavier-Übung erster Theil,* Preface). His reference to a specific example in his music is unfortunately ambiguous. The musical evidence from his keyboard works is also ambiguous and seems to point sometimes to the anapestic, sometimes to the Lombard design.

The slides in Reinhard Keiser's autographs, mostly written with two little notes, seem frequently to lean toward anticipation, especially in their frequent mixture with written-out Lombard types (BB, Mus. mss. autogr. Keiser 1 [*Circe*] [1702]; Keiser 5, *Arsinoë* [1710]; Keiser 6, Massaniello Furioso [1706]).

Thomas Balthasar Janowka illustrates in 1701 a combination of slide and turn that is entirely before the beat (*Clavis ad thesaurum*, s.v. "Circuitus"). Interestingly, he declares this anticipatory principle to be the same that underlies the meaning of all the French little notes, therewith providing further testimony about their frequent prebeat nature.

In 1708 Johann Gottfried Walther illustrates the slide fully before the beat, as shown in Ex. 25.13a (*Praecepta*, 37).

In the *Andreas Bach Buch*, an important manuscript from the inner Bach circle, the scribe of three Kuhnau sonatas places the custos symbol very frequently before the barline, as shown in Ex. 25.13b. Since there is no lack of space that can explain this notation, the prebeat implication seems clear.

EXAMPLE 25.13

a. Walther (1708)

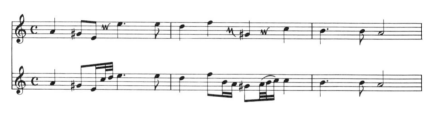

b. Kuhnau, 2nd Sonata          Kuhnau, 5th Sonata

*J. S. Bach.* Bach's slide, like several others of his ornaments, has multinational roots. He uses all three types: the predominantly French prebeat anapest, the Italo-German Lombard, the predominantly Italian—always onbeat—dactyl. For symbols, Bach uses for all media both Kuhnau's strictly German custos (only its ascending type ⌣ ) and the French little notes. All three slide designs are also often written out in regular notes. We find the written-out Lombard type characteristically on the strong beat in affect-filled adagios.[1] It is significant that in none of the cases where the Lombard slide is part of a recurring theme is the full notation ever replaced by either of the symbols. If, as has often been assumed, both symbols stood only for this very Lombard type and never had any other meanings, the consistent avoidance of the symbols in such situations would be hard to explain.

The dactylic pattern, derived from the Italians, was one of Bach's favorite melodic figures and appears countless times in regular notes, most characteristically in moderate tempo and on unaccented beats or their subdivisions.[2] The fairly frequently written-out anapestic slide shows no preference of tempo or placement within the measure.[3]

Either of the two slide symbols, the custos or the little notes, could stand for the onbeat Lombard design or the prebeat anapestic one. But only the custos, not the little notes, could also stand for the dactylic design.

Given the two alternatives for the little notes, the three for the custos, what can be the criteria for our choices? As to the Lombard interpretation of either symbol, this is what traditional opinion has so far considered to be the standard execution for Bach. Yet there is actually no clear evidence available that calls for it: neither is there musical evidence of the kind mentioned above, where a Lombard slide is written out in regular notes, then indicated by symbol on a parallel spot; nor does there seem to be a theoretical model before Theophil Muffat in 1736—a late date for Bach, not to speak of the even later galant theorists of mid-century.[4] Yet in view of the design being spelled out so often in Bach's music, we can speculate that the Lombard interpretation can be justified whenever the context seems favorable: favorable may be lively pieces of rhythmic incisiveness; whereas in the mentioned sorrowful moods, Bach was likely to spell out the Lombard slides in regular notes.

The dactylic interpretation is authenticated by several instances in which in either a parallel spot, a simultaneous unison part, or a later version of the same piece the custos is replaced by the written-out dactyl. One such case is given in Ex. 25.14, from the Organ Chorale Fantasia "Super Schmücke dich" in its early Weimar version with the custos and the late Leipzig version with the spelled-out dactyl. There is also theoretical evidence going back as far as Bovicelli, Diruta, and their German 17th-century followers Praetorius, Crüger, Herbst, and Falck.[5] Bach did not use a dotted little note pair as symbol for the dactylic slide, as some Italians had done before 1750 and as C. P. E. Bach and other *galant*

EXAMPLE 25.14.   Bach, Organ Chorale Fantasia, "Super Schmücke dich"

a. BWV 654a                         b. BWV 654

composers would do after 1750. Besides, J. S. Bach's dactylic slide, as we can gather from the many written-out specimens, tended to the design of Ex. 25.1c rather than that of Ex. 25.1d.

Received opinion generally rejects the anapest, yet there is solid musical evidence for its having been frequently intended. Apart from Bach's painstakingly copied instances of premeasure slide notations in Grigny's *Livre d'orgue*, which alone might suggest adoption on Bach's part, there are a fair number of cases where a Lombard interpretation would produce parallels of forbidding offensiveness. Such is especially frequent in cases where either of the slide symbols occurs following an upbeat that leaps upward, often to a siciliano rhythm,  , or to a related setting. The dactyl would only make matters worse by dwelling on the faulty progression, and consequently many of these cases would seem to admit only the anapestic solution. For one characteristic illustration, see Ex. 25.15a, from Cantata No. 140.[6] We find a number of similar cases in keyboard works in which parallels are even more obtrusive. One specimen is shown in Ex. 25.15b, from the Sixth Organ Sonata, in which the octaves, though hidden, would be greatly disturbing in transparent two-part writing.

EXAMPLE 25.15.   Bach

a. Cantata No. 140/3, BWV 140, 3 (Thomana)      b. Organ Sonata No. 6, BWV 530, 2

There is again no rule that can provide an "authentic" solution. The French little notes will probably most often stand for the anapest, which ought to be the first choice, but perhaps occasionally for the Lombard; the custos can in addition stand for the dactyl. As a rather rough guide, an incisively rhythmical phrase might favor the Lombard; a gentle phrase the dactyl; a neutral one, the anapest. The anapest fits anywhere in the measure, the dactyl is more proper for weak, the Lombard for strong beats. Aware of the options, musical intelligence has to make the choice.

***Contemporaries and Followers.*** Among Bach's galant-leaning contemporaries and followers, we find all three types of the slide represented.

There was clearly no unified practice, and although C. P. E. Bach and his adherents favored the Lombard and dactyl for their onbeat style, they could not, even in north Germany, claim a monopoly for their preference.

Johann David Heinichen, who was strongly influenced by Italian practices and was an ardent advocate of galant orientation, demonstrated in both 1711 and in 1728 only the dactylic slide in its dotted rhythm of Ex. 25.1d above (*Neu erfundene Anweisung*, 174; *Generalbass*, 528). Theophil Muffat, on the other hand, displayed in his ornament table of circa 1736 only the Lombard design. And yet a third German of that generation, the eminent flutist Johann Christian Schickhardt (1680–1762), in a treatise written between 1720 and 1730, used the French little notes and, as shown in Ex. 25.16, placed them systematically before the barline whenever they ornament the downbeat (*Principes de la flûte*, 3). In 1753 Carl August Thielo, Walther's student, also implies the anapestic design in his explanation of a slide leading to G: one strikes E, F, G, quickly he said, "but in such a manner that the G sounds strongest at the end" (*Grund-Regeln*, 52).

EXAMPLE 25.16.   Schickhardt (ca. 1720–1730)

C. P. E. Bach, in accordance with his preference for onbeat ornaments, as mentioned, recognizes only the Lombard and dactyl. For the Lombard he uses either the little notes or the custos; for the dactyl, the Italian symbol of a little dotted note pair, , in which the dotted note can be of such varying length that it can lead to extreme disproportion between the first note and the following ones, as shown in Ex. 25.17.

EXAMPLE 25.17.   C. P. E. Bach

Marpurg, in his table of 1755, showed three symbols, the little notes, the custos, and a dash connecting two note heads, all signifying a Lombard pattern (*Anleitung zum Clavierspielen*, 153).

Johann Friedrich Agricola voices an interesting dissent from his two Berlin colleagues. In matters of the dactyl with the dotted symbol, he follows C. P. E. Bach closely. But he deviates in discussing the "even" or "fast" slide. The latter, he says, can precede either a strong or weak *Tactglied* (i.e., a beat or subdivision of a beat). When preceding such a strong part of the measure, it is often written out in regular notes, as shown in his illustration of Ex. 25.18a. In this case "the two short [ornamental] notes are rendered very loudly: whereas a slide which fills in a leap and falls truly within the weak part of the measure [Tactglied] will be performed softer" (*Anleitung zur Singkunst*, 88). This passage has bewildered those readers who assumed that a slide had to be accented and begin on the beat. The passage can only be understood in the sense that a slide that fills in a leap is placed not *on* but *before* a strong part of the measure, hence within the preceding weak part: in other words, it is rendered without accent before the beat. It is not surprising that Agricola, who was a singer, should have made this statement: a slide filling in a leap is a surrogate for a vocal portamento that is never accented and invariably done before the beat.

EXAMPLE 25.18

a. Agricola

b. Quantz

Quantz lists the dactyl, with its dotted symbol and double-dotted execution, as well as the fast Lombard type and illustrates them in a table (*Versuch einer Anweisung*, chap. 17, sec. 2, par. 21; Table 22, fig. 40). Then he offers another of his object lessons about not taking ornament tables literally. In discussing improvised ornamentation he shows how leaps may be filled in with the scale notes that lie between (chap. 13, par. 42). In an illustration reproduced in Ex. 25.18b, he first shows ascending structural melodic leaps, then on the next line adds both full-sized quarter notes, to complete broken chords, and small ornamental note symbols, to fill in a stepwise ascent; finally on the third line he spells out the completed meaning in regular notation. In this case we see how both *Vorschlag* and slide symbols are rendered in anticipation of onbeat principal notes.

Leopold Mozart has little to say about the slide. He mentions only in passing the dactylic variety, which he sees as a variant of the long *Vorschlag* (*Versuch einer Violinschule*, chap. 9, par. 11).

Türk, like C. P. E. Bach, explains the Lombard and the dactylic slide. He points to the *Nachschlag* potential of the grace, especially in the absence of a slur. Thus  can mean          or (*Klavierschule*, chap. 4, sec. 2, pars. 18–23).

In the keyboard method, published circa 1786 under the names of J. C. Bach and F. Pasquale Ricci, the only illustration of the grace shows the two-note slide symbol placed before the barline (*Méthode pour le forte-piano*, 17).[7]

Heinrich Christoph Koch stipulates for the two- or three-note slide that the accent be placed on the principal note. This suggests anapestic rendition (*Musikalisches Lexicon*, s.v. "Vorschlag").

**Haydn and Mozart.** In the music of Haydn and Mozart the two *even* little notes are the only slide symbol used; we find neither the custos nor the galant dotted little-note symbol of the dactyl. The Lombard style was frequent but probably mostly spelled out in regular notes—more often by Mozart than by Haydn—as shown in Exx. 25.19a and 25.19b, from the *Figaro* Overture and Haydn's String Quartet in F, Op. 74, No. 2, respectively.

EXAMPLE 25.19

a. Mozart, *Le nozze di Figaro*, K 492, Overture

b. Haydn, String Quartet in F, Op. 74, No. 2

As to the little-note symbol, both masters often emphasize accentuation of the principal note with a *sforzando* sign placed strictly under or above its note head (as shown in Ex. 25.20a for Haydn, in Ex. 25.21a for Mozart) in a notation that strongly suggests prebeat execution of the ornamental notes. Apart from such external evidence, there is a great deal of internal evidence that points to a far-reaching anapestic execution of the slide. Many are cases in which a Lombard interpretation would produce parallels of an offensiveness that could not have been intended. For two illustrations from Haydn, the first is from Symphony No. 103 (Ex. 25.20a). Here a Lombard rendition would result in unlikely parallel unisons with the second violins, while the anapest is further suggested by the *sforzando* sign clearly written in the autograph under the principal note head. (The unisons here have nothing to do with doublings between the two violin parts: such doublings between the violins occur in Haydn occasionally, if rarely, in octaves, probably never in unisons; also the violin parts in this minuet are throughout completely independent, hence the unison *would* be offensive.) In the second example, from the Symphony No. 99 (Ex. 25.20b), only anticipation can avoid the ungainly parallel octaves between the outer voices.

There are many cases in which the purely connective function of a slide suggests anticipation, such as in Ex. 25.20c, from Haydn's Symphony No. 95, where the first two slides fill in a leap. To do so is a strictly subservient, portamento-like function that calls for unobtrusiveness, not accentual emphasis. Anticipation here incidentally conforms to Agricola's model of the ornamental slide notes that fill in a leap and should be rendered softly in the weak part of the measure.

Example 25.20.   Haydn

a. Symphony No. 103/3 (Hob. I:103)

b. Symphony No. 99/2 (Hob. I:99)

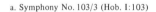
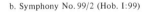

c. Symphony No. 95/2 (Hob. I:95)

Mozart's placement of a *sforzato* sign under a principal note preceded by a slide is shown in Ex. 25.21a, from the String Quartet in D
Minor. Here the desirability of anticipation is further underscored by the
need to maintain the integrity of the distinctive siciliano rhythm; it is the
same principle whose relevance to the *Vorschlag* was discussed above.
As first probably formulated by Tartini, a grace note should replace an
appoggiatura that would infringe a characteristic rhythm.

Every so often Mozart places a slide before the first most prominent
note of a phrase that descends stepwise or by triads, such as shown
in Ex. 25.21b, from the Violin Sonata in F, in Ex. 25.21c, from the
"Posthorn" Serenade, Ex. 25.21d, from *Don Giovanni.* In all these cases
the slide serves to highlight the top note and can do so only in anticipation, whereas a Lombard style would obscure that very note. For the
specimen from *Don Giovanni,* we have significant proof in a parallel spot
(Ex. 25.21e), where the anticipation is spelled out. In all these cases,
integrity of the structural rhythm is another important consideration.

EXAMPLE 25.21.   Mozart

a. String Quartet in D Minor, K 417b (421)/4

b. Violin Sonata in F, K 374e (377)

c. "Posthorn" Serenade, K 320/7

d. *Don Giovanni*, K 527, II, 20 (aut.)          e. *Don Giovanni*, K 527, II, 20

The slide, like the previously discussed upward-leaping *Vorschlag,* often functions as stylized vocal portamento, which—in one of the few certainties in the field of ornamentation—is always anticipated; see, for instance, Ex. 25.22a, from the first aria of the Queen of the Night, where the slide suggests a sigh-like expression of grief. In a striking instrumental counterpart to just such a vocal portamento, the slide in Ex. 25.22b, from Zerlina's "Vedrai carino," seems intended as an inflection of tenderness that would be adulterated by Lombard accentuation.

EXAMPLE 25.22.   Mozart

a. *Die Zauberflöte*, K 620, I, 4

b. *Don Giovanni*, K 527, II, 18

Moreover, related to the *sforzando* sign, a staccato mark over the principal note will usually invite the anapest lest the sharpness of articulation be blunted by a Lombard-type slide.

In trying to evaluate the proper interpretation of the slide symbols, it is helpful to know that in the many cases where a Lombard slide is written out in regular notes—just as was the case with J. S. Bach—not one instance has yet come to light for either Haydn or Mozart in which such a spelled-out slide is replaced on later recurrence by the symbol. This circumstance would be hard indeed to understand if the symbol had, as is maintained by many, primarily Lombard meaning. If we add to this fact the decided prebeat predominance of this symbol in France and Italy, and the many instances in which musical evidence, both external and internal, strongly favors anticipation, it does not seem unreasonable to suggest that for the little-note symbol in both Haydn and Mozart the first choice should be the anapest.

## *Appendix: The* Anschlag

The *Anschlag* (also: *Doppelvorschlag*) is a grace of the German galant style that has no contemporary French or Italian equivalents of any consequence. It consists of two notes that precede and melodically straddle the principal note, most commonly in the sequence lower neighbor–upper neighbor–principal note, ♪ , though the first ornamental note may leap up from a lower pitch.

With regard to rhythm, there is the usual alternative of prebeat and onbeat with the concomitant mixtures of straddling designs. There is also a dactylic pattern, marked with a dotted small-note pair that will normally fall on the beat:  . The only symbol is that of the small even notes or, for the dactyl, dotted.

Before the galant era we find the grace in chance occurrences only. Quantz may have been the first to have acknowledged and described the *Anschlag* under this term (*Versuch einer Anweisung,* chap. 13, par. 41). He limits the grace to the lower–upper neighbor design and illustrates its application for all intervallic progressions, of which two are shown in Ex. 25.23. Singers, he says, use the grace for large leaps in order to hit high pitches more securely. The grace, he instructs, must be tied *very fast but weak* to the principal note, which is a little stronger. This directive, plus the ornament's subservient role as an aid to vocal marksmanship, would seem to favor prebeat character.

EXAMPLE 25.23.   Quantz

C. P. E. Bach devotes considerable space to the *Anschlag* (*Versuch über Art das Clavier* [1753], chap. 2, sec. 6, pars. 1–11) and shows next to Quantz's spread of a third a model with a wider interval as well as the dactylic form with the dotted symbol (see Ex. 25.24). Like Quantz, he wants the two little notes to be "always played softer than the principal note" (par. 3), but, true to his own principles, he places them on the beat, as shown in his examples. Dynamics are different for the dactyl, which he says is proper for expressive ("affectuösen") passages in slow pieces. Here the first, dotted, note is loud, the second and the principal notes are soft, and all three are slurred.

EXAMPLE 25.24.   C. P. E. Bach (1753)

(played)

In 1755 Marpurg calls the grace *Doppelvorschlag* and follows C. P. E. Bach in his three designs (*Anleitung zum Clavierspielen,* 51). Johann Friedrich Agricola in 1757 explains the *Anschlag* as a combination of a

*Vorschlag* from below and a *Nachschlag* one step above the principal note while adopting C. P. E. Bach's models (*Anleitung zur Singkunst*, 85–87). Löhlein in 1765 shows both the even design (with the spread of a third only) and the dotted one (*Clavier-Schule*, 15).

Leopold Mozart shows the design of the *Anschlag* as a form of the "Mordant" (see Ex. 25.25), and his Mordant, like Tartini's *mordente*, is a prebeat grace, as will be discussed in the chapter on the mordent.

EXAMPLE 25.25.   L. Mozart

("Mordant")

Türk, near the end of the century, follows C. P. E. Bach, as usual, but seems to sense an inconsistency in the soft onbeat start of the grace as contrasted with the *Vorschlag* that, short or long, is always to be louder than the principal note. He tries to resolve the contradiction by suggesting that the short *Vorschlag* too may be played softly (*Klavier-schule*, chap. 4, sec. 2, pars. 12–17). In the majority of cases in actual practice, this dynamic pattern would, for both graces, spontaneously lead to prebeat execution.

Haydn used the grace a few times in his younger years. Mozart may have never used it as a symbolized ornament. As a structural figure, its melodic (anticipated) design pervades Don Giovanni's aria "Metà di voi" with unforgettable wit.

# 26

# THE TRILL I: FRANCE

## Designs and Terms

*Nature of the Trill.* The trill is an age-old grace whose Western ancestry can be traced to the early Middle Ages. Its basic idea is the rapid, regular alternation of a tone with its upper neighbor. Though this idea seems simple enough, it lends itself to a surprising variety of designs. Apart from the interval involved, whether half tone or whole tone, this variety can have to do with the way the trill starts, proceeds, and ends.

The trill can start with either the "main" note (the term to be used in the following for the pitch that is to be ornamented) or the upper note (the "auxiliary"). The starting pitch may occur on the beat (i.e., the starting time of the written note) or precede this beat; in fact, several or even all alternations may precede this beat in partial or full anticipation of the trill. The alternations can also be preceded by either a turn or a slide ( ) involving a third pitch, the lower neighbor of the main note. These combination forms will be discussed in chapter 29.

As to the way the trill proceeds, the alternations may begin immediately or may be delayed, while the initial pitch is sustained; once they start, their speed may range from fast to moderately fast, and on long trills the speed of the oscillations may gradually increase or decrease; the alternations may last for the full duration of the main note or come to an earlier stop. While they last, metrical emphasis may be placed on one of the two pitches or be neutrally divided between them.

The trill always ends, in what may be the only invariable element of this grace, on the main note. But once ended, it is often followed by a suffix of mostly two notes involving again the third pitch: ; the suffix will occasionally consist of one note only to permit a smoother transition to the following pitch, as for instance in

***One-Sided Beliefs.*** In the two hundred years of our period the trill encompassed a far wider variety of shapes than has most often been recognized. In fact, there is good reason to assume that every mentioned trill type had found its niche somewhere, sometime, within the space and time under consideration. This statement is in stark contrast to the widespread belief that in the era studied the trill, as far as its start is concerned, centered on one design only, the one that begins with the accented upper note on the beat. To quote just one recent characteristic expression of this belief, David Fuller writes in the *New Harvard Dictionary of Music* (s.v. "Trill"): "The upper-note, on-beat start was clearly normal for trills from the late 17th to the early 19th century, in all countries and all media." This belief, which will be revealed as grossly one-sided, may have come into existence as a reaction against a similarly one-sided belief, current in the 19th and early 20th century, that all trills, regardless of style, ought to start with the main note. Though there are other notable aspects of the trill, its start is the most important one because of its potential impact on both melody and harmony. For this reason a good deal of the following discussions will aim at restoring a more balanced picture of this issue—one that will do justice to the wide variety of trill starts as well as of overall trill designs that were in use by various composers in various countries, periods, and media.

In order to facilitate the discussion of the varied designs from different countries over two hundred years, and to serve as ready reference, the following tabulation shows the principal trill shapes along with the working terminology adopted for our purposes. Such working terminology is needed to help us cope with the chaos of symbols and terms that is even more confusing for the trill than for any other ornament.

***Schematic Tabulation of Trill Designs and Terms.*** The trill that starts with the main note will be called a "main-note trill." Figure 26.1a shows it with both pitches on an equal footing; Fig. 26.1b shows it with the main note metrically favored ("anchored"). Figure 26.1c shows a miniature main-note trill with only one alternation that will be called a

FIGURE 26.1.   Main-note Trill

*Schneller*, a term coined by C. P. E. Bach. A trill that starts with the upper note, on the beat, will be called an "appoggiatura trill" because a distinct onbeat entrance with the upper note has the effect of a short appoggiatura, as shown in Fig. 26.2a in a "neutral" mode and Fig. 26.2b with metrical emphasis on the upper note. A miniature appoggiatura trill with only two alternations is sometimes called a "prall trill" (also a coinage of C. P. E. Bach), though the term is used by some also to signify the *Schneller* with or without a two-note suffix.

FIGURE 26.2. Appoggiatura Trill

The lengthening of the first note of the trill, be it the main or the upper note, will be called "support" and a trill thus started a "supported trill." A supported main-note trill is shown in Fig. 26.3a, a supported appoggiatura trill in Fig. 26.3b, which is the equivalent of a long appoggiatura whose resolution is ornamented by the trill.

FIGURE 26.3

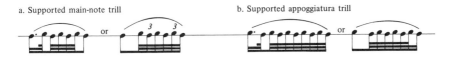

A trill with the auxiliary before the beat and the main note on it (Fig. 26.4a) will be called a "grace-note trill" because the anticipated auxiliary will have the function of a grace note. In an occasional variant of this type, the trill dwells, after the prebeat auxiliary, on the main note before starting the alternations, as shown in Fig. 26.4b.

FIGURE 26.4. Grace-note Trill

If the alternations take place entirely in the time of the preceding note, we shall speak of an "anticipated trill" (Fig. 26.5a–26.5c). The trill will be called "straddling" when the alternations are divided between the preceding and the principal note (Fig. 26.5d–26.5e).

FIGURE 26.5.    Anticipated and Straddling Trills

When a trill of some length stops its alternations before the end of the trilled note (Fig. 26.6), such stopping will be referred to as a "rest point" (Couperin's *point d'arrêt*).

FIGURE 26.6.    Trill with Rest Point

Although only certain composers seem to have actually used all these designs, by and large there was in use a far wider range of designs than modern research has tended to acknowledge. While the typical modern belief in the monopoly of the appoggiatura trill entails a rejection of the main-note trill as unhistorical, grace-note and anticipated trills are not even rejected, just ignored. In my earlier work, particularly in *OrnB*, *OrnM*, and *Essays 1989* (chap. 9), I have documented the inadequacy of these ideas; here I can offer only a relatively small sampling.

## The French Trill

If prevalent scholarly opinion holds that, in the words of David Fuller, the appoggiatura trill was "clearly normal . . . for all countries and all media," it is more extreme and more adamant still about the French trill, for which the belief in the inevitability of the upper-note onbeat start has become a generally accepted article of faith. It is necessary to point to a large mass of evidence to the contrary. By so doing I hope not to be suspected of painting a lopsided picture: I wish simply to restore a measure of balance to a severely unbalanced assessment.

**Voice and Melody Instruments.** In his *Harmonie universelle* of 1636, Marin Mersenne illustrates the trill with the auxiliary on the beat (see Ex. 26.1a; (*Harmonie universelle: Traitez des consonances*, 355). The trill he has in mind is improvised since he does not yet use a symbol. By way of contrast, in the same work, an illustration of diminutions (also improvised) has many trills written out, and almost all of them start not with the auxiliary but with main-note support on the beat, as shown in a brief excerpt in Ex. 26.1b (*Harmonie universelle: Traité des instrumens à chordes*, 186, 188).

EXAMPLE 26.1.   Mersenne (1636)

a.

b.

Jean Millet in 1666 hesitates to offer an illustration for the trill (*tremblement*), which he says defies description and can be truly learned only by imitation. Although his reluctantly produced model is rather complicated, since it contains tone repetitions in addition to alternations, two features stand out: a start with the anticipated auxiliary and an end leading with an anticipated *port de voix* to the following note one step above (*La belle méthode*, 10). In his illustrations of embellished cadences (37–46) he indicates the trill with the (multiplication) cross "×," which seems to have been used interchangeably with the (addition) cross "+" by French composers and theorists of the 17th and 18th centuries. In the embellished cadences here and in songs at the end of the book, we find quite a few supported appoggiatura trills, some grace-note trills, and others that are ambiguous because the spelling of the embellishments is (intentionally) unmetrical.

Lully marked trills either with the Italian *t* or the French cross: +. We find many cases where such trills have a written-out appoggiatura support, as shown in Ex. 26.2a (and presumably sung as in Ex. 26.2b) and many a written-out main note support, as shown in Ex. 26.2c (and presumably sung as in Ex. 26.2d).

In the *airs de cour* of Michel Lambert (1666), Bénigne de Bacilly (1668), and Honoré d'Ambruis (1685), all of whom wrote out ornamented second couplets, the largest number of trills start with the

EXAMPLE 26.2

a. Lully, *Armide* (1686), Prologue   b.

la    gloi  -  re.

c. Lully, *Armide* (1686)   d.
Prologue

la    gloi  -  re

e. D'Ambruis, *Livre d'airs* (1685)
p. 5

de trou-ver____   du sou-la - ge-ment____   du sou - la    -    ge-ment____

f. Lambert (1666)
p. 42

C'est _ es    -    tre

g. Bacilly
p. 15

veux ____ rien ____ di  -  re

anticipated auxiliary (grace-note trills), others again have the anticipated auxiliary followed by the lengthened main note leading to the alternations. We find also, as in Lully, quite a few main note supported trills and—though far less frequently and mostly limited to final cadences—supported appoggiatura trills. For just one characteristic illustration each for these main types, see Ex. 26.2e, with three grace-note trills in three measures; Ex. 26.2f, for a main-note supported trill preceded by a grace note; Ex. 26.2g, for two supported appoggiatura trills (d'Ambruis, *Livre d'airs;* Lambert, *Les airs de M. Lambert;* Bacilly, *Les trois livres d'airs: Second livre d'airs*).

Bénigne de Bacilly, in his important vocal treatise *Remarques curieuses* of 1668 (which unfortunately has no illustrations), distinguishes various trill types. His term is either *tremblement* or *cadence.* His basic form has a preparation on the auxiliary pitch, then the actual alternations (beginning with the main note), and finally a *liaison,* a delicate *Nachschlag.* In his own and in his fellow songmasters' music the spelled-out preparation occurs either before or on the beat, though much more frequently the former. Often, however, as Bacilly tells us, this preparation is very fittingly omitted. He excoriates pedants who insist on strict observance of rules, who "would not for anything in the world omit that preparation of the trill . . . as if it were of its essence. . . . There are even cases of cadential trills where the preparation is inappropriate and where one plunges immediately into the alternations *from low to high* [Il y a mesme des Cadences finales, ou cette preparation sied mal, & dans lesquelles on se jette d'abord sur les Tremblemens de bas en haut] . . . and after these observations it would be naïve to try establishing rules where such [preparation] fits and where it does not fit: good taste alone has to be the judge" (167, 178–79 [emphasis added]).

The passage is significant for its clear formulation of main-note trills, occasionally even on final cadences; for the eloquent attack on the tyranny of rules; and for the enthronement of *bon goût* as sovereign authority in matters of performance—a principle that will recur like a leitmotiv for the next 150 years of French musical interpretation.

Jean Rousseau, in two treatises, the one of 1683 for the voice (*Méthode,* 54–55), the other of 1687 for the gamba (*Traité de la viole,* 76–84), distinguishes trills "with preparation [by the auxiliary]" and those "without preparation." A preparation can be either anticipated ("by anticipation of note value and sound") or done on the beat ("by anticipation of sound only"). The unprepared trill, which he calls the *cadence simple,* is a main-note trill, done "on the natural tone of the note simply by agitation of the voice," its main-note start confirmed in the gamba treatise by the instruction that this trill type be done like the prepared ones, "with the preparation cut off" (en retranchant l'appuy). In a fourth type of trill, proper for certain long notes such as whole notes in common time, the written note is held for the first half while the second half is trilled; in other words, a main-note supported trill with a long support.

Briefly, Rousseau's four trill types are the grace-note trill, the supported appoggiatura trill, the main-note trill, and the supported main-note trill. His grace-note trill is shown in Ex. 26.3a, his appoggiatura trill in Ex. 26.3b.

EXAMPLE 26.3.   J. Rousseau (1683, 1691)

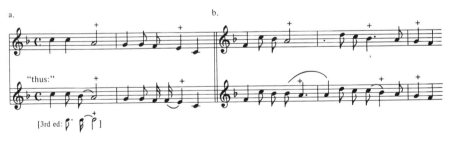

Sainte Colombe, Rousseau's teacher and a gambist of legendary fame, displays in a volume of compositions unmetrically written-out trills that start with either the main note or the upper note. The unusual notation of crisscrossing stems and flags does not show their rhythmic disposition. He also specifies in metrical notation many grace-note trills.

For a symbol he uses the lutenists' comma after the note head $\curvearrowright$ (*Concerts à deux violes*). (For illustrations see *OrnB* Ex. 24.11.)

Marin Marais, also a student of Sainte Colombe, uses a similar comma-like hook after the note as trill symbol. He does not explain the nature of the trill in his various informative prefaces but just takes it for granted. Musical evidence points to a variety of designs including appoggiatura-supported, main-note supported, and plain main-note trills. For a supported appoggiatura trill, see Ex. 26.4a; Ex. 26.4b shows a supported main-note trill (as described by Rousseau); and Ex. 26.4c (from the *Deuxiéme livre de pièces de viole* of 1701) reveals one of many indubitable main-note trills since the V-shaped symbol between the A and the A sharp indicates a gentle sliding of the second finger to achieve a glissando effect that makes the main-note start of the trill a necessity. A truly striking illustration of a main-note trill (from Marais's opera *Semelé*) is reproduced in Ex. 26.4d, where the trill is written out in order to insure coordination of the two flutes.[1]

EXAMPLE 26.4.    Marais

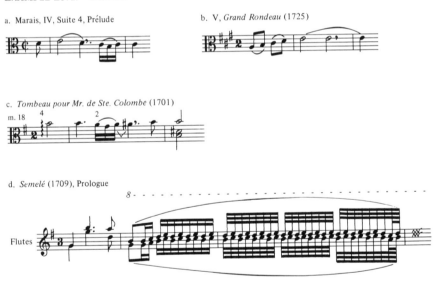

a. Marais, IV, Suite 4, Prélude

b. V, *Grand Rondeau* (1725)

c. *Tombeau pour Mr. de Ste. Colombe* (1701)

d. *Semelé* (1709), Prologue

Among more general theorists, Loulié in 1696 explains the trill as "a twice or more times repeated *coulé* that moves from a small sound to a regular sound one step below" (*Éléments ou principes de musique*, 70). He had, as noted before, defined the *coulé* as "an inflection of the voice from a small, or weak, or short tone to a lower and stronger one" and had illustrated it in full anticipation, as was shown in Ex. 22.2b. A series of such iambic *coulés* will make for a trill with emphasis on the main note and an anticipated auxiliary. Hence Loulié's basic trill design would seem to lean to the grace-note type.

As a second type, Loulié lists the *tremblement appuyé*, in which the voice dwells on the first *coulé*. While this seems to be a trill with appoggiatura support, only the first of two illustrations (Ex. 26.5a) appears to bear this out, while the second one (Ex. 26.5b) shows the support (*appuy*) in full anticipation.

EXAMPLE 26.5

a. Loulié          b.

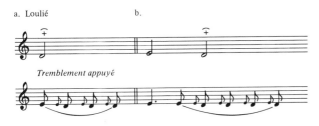

*Tremblement appuyé*

c. L'Affilard (1694, 1697), *Cadence coupée avec une Note, martellement avec deux Notes*

[sung]

In 1694 (and later editions) L'Affilard presents, as shown in Ex. 26.5c, a supported appoggiatura trill followed in the next measure by a grace-note trill (*Principes pour apprendre le musique*, 20–21).

Montéclair follows Loulié in explaining the trill as a series of *coulés;* and since to him too the *coulé* implies descent from a weak to a strong note, his basic trill design may well also have been the iambic grace-note type. This is the type he most likely had in mind for the *tremblement subit*, which is done without *appuy* and is marked by the symbol +. The *tremblement appuyé*, on the other hand, has the symbol *t* and starts with a long appoggiatura support (*Principes*, 80–83).

**The Keyboard.** Nivers, in the preface to his *Livre d'orgue* of 1665, distinguishes the simple trill (*cadence*) and the trill with two-note suffix (*double cadence*), but in his models he writes the alternations with unmetrical little notes that do not divulge their rhythmic design. He may have left the latter intentionally vague to allow for flexibility.

Four years later Chambonnières gives the metrical model of Ex. 26.6a in his *Pièces de clavessin* of 1670. It shows the auxiliary starting on the beat and retaining its metrically strong placement. For the basic trill pattern, be it called *tremblement* or *cadence,* this model was from then on repeated many times in keyboard ornamentation tables. We find it among others with Le Bègue (1677), Raison (1688), d'Anglebert (1689), Chaumont (1696), Saint Lambert (1702), Dieupart (ca. 1702), Le Roux (1705), Rameau (1706, 1724), and Dandrieu (1724).

D'Anglebert lists in addition to the simple trill a *tremblement appuyé* (Ex. 26.6b), which was repeated in near-identical form by Le Roux, Rameau, and Dandrieu.

EXAMPLE 26.6

a. Chambonnières (1670), *Cadence*

b. d'Anglebert

*Tremblement appuyé*

These wide-ranging agreements are certainly impressive, but we must keep in mind that they were for all practical purposes limited to the keyboard, and even there they were by no means total, as will be presently seen. It may also be well to remember that a generation before Chambonnières, Mersenne had presented a similar appoggiatura-trill model but then revealed how he himself deviated from it. There is also considerable evidence pointing to the need for flexibility and variability in the interpretation of these standardized models (not to speak of the imprudence of taking ornament tables at face value). There are, for instance, innumerable cases in which the trilled note coincides with a second voice that has a claim to rhythmic integrity, as in the typical illustrations of Ex. 26.7a, from Le Bègue, or Ex. 26.7b, from d'Anglebert (in whose works a second voice descending from a trill is almost a stereotype). In such cases a pedantic insistence on appoggiatura start of the trill would obscure the second voice, occasionally to the point of obliteration. To avoid such an outcome, the performer has three possibilities: a main-note trill, a grace-note trill, or a fully anticipated trill.

EXAMPLE 26.7

a. Le Bègue, 2nd Organ Book, *Agnus Dei*

b. d'Anglebert, *Pieces de clavecin,* Allemande, p. 4

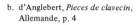

There is direct evidence for grace-note trills also on the keyboard. Lambert Chaumont's clear prebeat illustration of the *Vorschlag* (symbolized by a caret:  ) in the preface to his *Pièces d'orgue* was mentioned in chapter 22. Throughout the work the caret symbol occurs numerous times in front of the trill symbol, as shown in Ex. 26.8a, from the fourth piece of the book, where a grace-note trill meaning seems hardly questionable. In Grigny's *Premier livre d'orgue* of 1699 we find other clear cases of grace-note trills as shown in Ex. 26.8b (along with all details of the book, this prebeat notation of the little *Vorschlag* note was copied by Bach with scrupulous precision). A similar specimen of a grace-note trill by Jean Baptiste (John) Loeillet from his *Lessons for the Harpsichord or Spinet* of ca. 1710 is given in Ex. 26.8c.

EXAMPLE 26.8

a. Chaumont (1696)

Duo

b. Grigny (1699), *Premier livre d'orgue*
*Ave Maris Stella*, p. 58

c. J.B. Loeillet
(1709–1715)

*Couperin's Trill.* Like all other French keyboard players, Couperin says that every trill starts with the upper note (*L'art*, 23). Yet he neither says that this start should fall on the beat nor does he adopt the Chambonnières-d'Anglebert metrical appoggiatura trill design. This is no coincidence since at least one of Couperin's basic trill types seems to lean toward the grace-note trill, in the sense of Loulié's and Montéclair's series of iambic *coulés*. This pattern is explicit in Ex. 26.9 (from the

EXAMPLE 26.9.   Couperin (1722), XIV, *Le Rossignol-en-Amour*

quatorzième ordre of *Pièces de clavecin*), where a lengthy trill, consisting of just such a series of iambic *coulés*, is written out in order to clarify the degree of its intended acceleration. But above all, the start with the anticipated auxiliary is strongly suggested in Couperin's ornament table (*Pièces de clavecin*, premier livre, 47), where he illustrates the *tremblement continu* along with the *pincé continu*, as given in Ex. 26.10. Though this trill starts with the upper note, the second and third measures reveal unmistakably the metrical emphasis on the main note. We see the trill as

EXAMPLE 26.10.   Couperin (1713)

a.

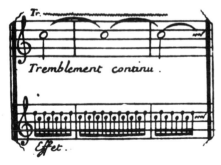

b.

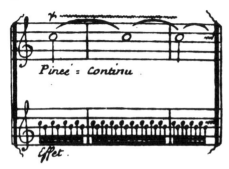

the mirror image of the mordent, both anchored on the main note but alternating in opposite directions. The only deviation from the mirror image is the first note of the trill, a surplus sixteenth for the time of a half note, the only note that does not fit into the otherwise exact metrical pattern. It would seem that the only logical solution is to play the first note *before* the beat ♪♫♫♫♫ rather than to try to force it unto the beat ♫♫♫♫♫ , thus beginning the metric trill with a disturbingly irregular motion.

We find a striking confirmation of this idea in a passage given in Ex. 26.11, from the Sarabande "La majestueuse" from the premier ordre of clavecin pieces. The last phrase of this piece is repeated in a *petite reprise* in which a few new ornaments are added. Thus the passage given in Ex. 26.11a appears in the reprise as Ex. 26.11b. If we compare the *three* small notes in the bass at the end of the first measure in Ex. 26.11a with the *two* small notes in Ex. 26.11b, it becomes obvious that the missing third note is the *anticipated auxiliary* of the newly added *tremblement continu*.

The appoggiatura enters for the supported trill. In his treatise, Couperin describes this design for trills of a certain length as consisting of

EXAMPLE 26.11.   Couperin (1713), I, "La majesteuse," Sarabande

three parts: first the *appuy*—that is, the long appoggiatura—then the shake proper (*les batements*), and finally a *point d'arrest*, a rest on the main note, as shown in Ex. 26.12a. "Other trills are arbitrary," Couperin continues; "some have an *appuy*, others are so short that they have neither *appuy* nor *point d'arrest*" (*L'art*, 24).

EXAMPLE 26.12.   Couperin

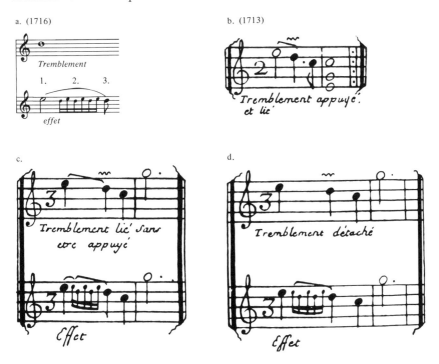

In Couperin's ornament table we find also the interesting patterns of Exx. 26.12b–26.12d. It is important to note that the quarter notes in Exx. 26.12c–26.12d are precisely lined up and that the notes in small print, representing the trill proper, are clearly placed between the first and the

second quarter notes. The graphic design speaks eloquently for anticipation of the trill proper inasmuch as the exact alignment of the quarter
notes points to their identical start. Furthermore, Couperin's phrase
"sans être appuyé" would make no sense if, as some scholars contend,
the first note were to be held for its full value plus the increment of the
tie: it would in fact be more *appuyé* than the *tremblement appuyé* of Ex.
26.12b. In order to justify the designation as "not supported," the alternations ought to start with only the smallest delay after the preceding
note is sounded.

These two patterns, with the apparent full anticipation of the trills,
recur in Père Engramelle's chapter on the mechanical organ in Bedos de
Celles's four-volume work *L'art du facteur d'orgues* of 1778. There we find
the designs of Exx. 26.13a and 26.13b (4: Plates 106 and 107). Although
the terms are different, the patterns are closely related to Couperin's
patterns in Exx. 26.12c and 26.12d, and the anticipation is metrically
spelled out.

EXAMPLE 26.13.    Engramelle (Bedos de Celles) (1778)

Many are the cases in which only a main-note trill makes musical
sense. We find such cases often when the trill is approached in a fast
movement from the upper neighbor, especially, but not solely, when
the two notes are slurred, as for instance in Ex. 26.14a, from the
vingtième ordre. Other cases are those in which a trill, regardless of
tempo, is preceded by a mordent one step higher, as in Ex. 26.14b, from
the sixième ordre.

EXAMPLE 26.14.    Couperin

Finally, it should be mentioned that Couperin marked the suffix of
the trill quite meticulously with two little notes of either eighth- or

sixteenth-note denomination. His fairly frequent symbol $\overset{\text{♯♯}}{\text{ρ}}$ , which combines the trill with a turn, is not explained in either treatise or ornament table. It is invariably followed by a stepwise rise. In its execution the trill comes first, the turn second, often separated by a rest point, as verified by both musical and theoretical evidence.[2]

In Couperin, then, we have encountered trills with appoggiatura support, grace-note trills, main-note trills, and fully anticipated trills. This variety is in keeping with his quoted statement that "other trills are arbitrary." Couperin truly exploited the potential of the trill idea in all dimensions.

*After Couperin.* After the tables of Rameau and Dandrieu, who still present for the keyboard the much-repeated model of the auxiliary on the beat, this pattern seems gradually to vanish from French theoretical documents. One of the few remaining followers is Corrette in his keyboard treatise of ca. 1749 (*Les amusements du Parnasse*, p. g). The pattern was taken up, after mid-century, however, by several north German theorists.

Just as Couperin deviated from the standard trill model, so did a few other keyboard players. In a model called *tremblement lié,* François Dandrieu introduces a special symbol to indicate the start of the trill with the main note on the beat, as shown in Ex. 26.15a.[3] It applies, as the check mark in the model indicates, in cases where the trill is preceded by its upper neighbor. For typical instances in Dandrieu's music, see Exx. 26.15b and 26.15c.

EXAMPLE 26.15

a. Dandrieu (1724, 1739);
also Fiocco (1730)
and Van Helmont (1737)

*Tremblement lié*

b. Dandrieu, 1st Organ Book, *Offertoire*

c. Dandrieu, Harpsichord pieces, *Le Carillon*

EXAMPLE 26.15.   *continued*

d. Van Helmont *Fuga prima*

Version with spelled-out ornaments:

e. Rameau (1724)

Dandrieu's symbol and usage were adopted by the Brussels composers Joseph-Hector Fiocco (*Pièces de clavecin*) and Charles-Joseph van
Helmont (*Pièces de clavecin*), the latter of whom added to his Fuga Prima
a version with written-out ornaments. Its many trills start throughout
with the supported main note, as shown in Ex. 26.15d.

In his ornament table of 1724, Rameau includes a model (Ex. 26.15e)
that is related to Dandrieu's *tremblement lié* by starting the alternations
with the main note on the beat. It is the logical outcome of his accompanying statement that "the note that is slurred to a trill or a mordent
serves as a beginning to each of these ornaments." There seems little
doubt that, in accord with this principle, Couperin had a similar design
in mind with his *Tremblement appuyé et lié* of Ex. 26.12b, for which he
gave no solution. He would have given one, had he had in mind the
more complex tying over the beat of the auxiliary in the manner of
C. P. E. Bach and his followers, who insisted on such a tie in order to
abide by the auxiliary-on-the-beat rule.

***Voice and Melody Instruments.*** For voice and melody instruments the
start with the main note was much more common than in keyboard
music. There was already a difference in the symbol: the waggles (*chevron*) ∿ were a keyboard symbol, whereas the cross, either standing (+)
or lying (×) was the most frequent symbol for voice and melody instruments. Rameau made it clear in his *Pièces de clavecin en concerts* (1741) for
clavier, violin, and gamba that the different symbols had different meanings. When the keyboard has a common trill with one or both of the
strings, he routinely adds a little *coulé* note to the string symbol to insure
its identity with the plain *chevron* for the keyboard, as shown in Ex.
26.16. This is a clear sign that the string symbol, unlike the *chevron*, did
not imply the start with the upper note.

EXAMPLE 26.16.   Rameau, II$^e$ Concert, 1$^{er}$ Menuet

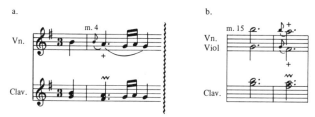

For the nonkeyboard media we find a great deal of evidence for the large role of the main-note trill. For the plain trill (i.e., one without support by either pitch), we encounter outside of the keyboard a number of terms, such as *cadence jetée, subite, précipitée, coupée*, and so on, all of which indicate that the alternations begin immediately. In many cases the terms stand for main-note trills, though the meaning of the terms varied somewhat from one writer to another. Here are some theoretical statements specifying the main-note start of the trill.

Buterne in 1752 defines the *cadence subite* as one "that starts with the note that occasions [the trill]" (*Méthode pour apprendre la musique*, 15), as apposed to the *appuyé*, in which the *son supérieur* forms the *appuy*.

Bérard in 1755 and Blanchet in 1756, in identical words, give in their vocal treatises an analogous directive for the *cadence précipitée*: "Throw the first alternation on the note on which the trill is to be made" (Jettez le premier martellement sur la notte où l'on doit battre cette cadence).[4]

Choquel in 1759 describes the *martellement* as "a very short trill that is made after sustaining the sound of a tone," and he uses the symbol ⚬⚬⚬ for this supported main-note trill (*La musique rendue*, 173).

L'abbé Duval in 1764 defines the *cadence subite* as one "that is never preceded by the sound of the upper note."[5]

Lacassagne in 1766 illustrates in his important vocal treatise the *cadence jetée* only as a main-note type, as given in Exs. 26.17a–26.17c (*Traité general du chant*, 47–48). His *cadence préparée* is "prepared" by either a long main-note or a long upper-note support.

Jean Jacques Rousseau in 1768 uses the term *battement* to designate a main-note trill. He explains the trill as "a French vocal ornament, which consists in shaking a trill upward from the note which one has started plain. The *cadence* and the *battement* differ in that the *cadence* starts with the note above the one on which it is marked; whereupon one shakes alternatingly the upper and the true [véritable] note: by contrast the *battement* starts with the very note that is marked: whereupon one shakes alternately this note with the one above" (*Dictionnaire*, s.v. "Battement").

Théodore-Jean Tarade, in his violin treatise of ca. 1774, gives examples of trills in thirds starting either with their main notes or their upper notes. But he sees the upper-note start as going out of fashion: "The

EXAMPLE 26.17

a. Lacassagne (1766)

*Cadence jetée*

b. Lacassagne (1766)

c. Lacassagne (1766)

d. Durieu (1793)

e. Durieu (1793)

f. Durieu (1793)

g. L'Abbé le Fils (1761) Cadence appuyée

h. J.J. Rousseau (1768)

French always prepare their trills; though these old preparations are still used in operas and old songs, they are not done any more in modern music, and still less by other nations. . . . Today one does not even prepare final cadences." Since he sets his term *préparer* distinctly apart from *appuyer*, the former almost certainly refers to the simple upper-note start (*Traité du violon*, 45, 47–48).

Mercadier de Belesta in 1776 distinguishes the *cadence pleine* and the *cadence brisée*. "The former starts the shake with the written note, the latter starts with the upper note." He too, like Lacassagne, describes two types of prepared trills. The first sustains the upper note and is close to the *tremblement feint*;[6] the other, for which he uses Rousseau's term *battement,* is prepared by the sustained main note (*Nouveau système,* 214).

Brijon in 1780 graphically expresses his agreement with Lacassagne's main-note style by adopting the latter's models for the *cadences jettées.* Brijon's *cadence pleine* is identical with Lacassagne's *cadence préparée* but is limited to main-note support (*L'Apollon,* 50–52).

Durieu in 1793 shows the main-note pattern as the basic trill type (Ex. 26.17d). His *cadence subite* is shown with either a main-note start written in regular notes (Ex. 26.17e) or with an upper-note start written with little notes (Ex. 26.17f) that are rhythmically ambiguous and could possibly suggest full or partial anticipation of the trill (*Nouvelle méthode,* 61–62).

Concerning the *tremblement lié,* the trill slurred to its preceding upper neighbor, be it an appoggiatura or not, we have seen important documents about its main-note start for the keyboard. It will hardly be a surprise that we find similar documents about the nonkeyboard media. Here is space for only two illustrations. The first, Ex. 26.17g, is from L'Abbé le Fils (1761), who indicates by the heavily inked note head the main-note start on the beat (*Principes du violon,* 14). The second is Jean Jacques Rousseau's hardly less eloquent illustration in Ex. 26.17h (*Dictionnaire,* Planche B).

The preceding documentation should suffice to make the point that even in France, the chief domicile of the trill that starts with the auxiliary, a strong undercurrent of main-note trills continued to flow throughout the 17th and 18th centuries. The current was strongest for voice and melody instruments, but the keyboard was by no means immune to its intrusion. In all media, furthermore, the beginning auxiliary, though frequent on the beat, often took instead the form of anticipation, resulting in a grace-note trill. A few words still need to be said about this important yet widely unrecognized design.

We have seen musical evidence for this design from the *airs de cour* and from Millet, Ste. Colombe, Chaumont, Grigny, J. B. Loeillet, together with theoretical support from Jean Rousseau, L'Affilard, Loulié, and Montéclair, and above all we have seen that Couperin's basic type for the unprepared trill was that very grace-note trill, with the auxiliary anticipated and the rhythmic emphasis on the main note. We find further confirmation in Foucquet's ornament table of ca. 1750, with its clear indebtedness to Couperin in terms, symbols, and designs. When Foucquet describes the *effet* of the trills with the little notes as part of the resolution (Ex. 26.18a), the interpretation as anticipated *coulé* is the most likely one, given the notational precision of the regular notes. Also, the interpretation of the little notes as *appuy* would make little sense in the delayed version of Ex. 26.18b, or the shortened one of Ex. 26.18c (both delay and shortening indicated with Couperin's symbols to that effect).

EXAMPLE 26.18

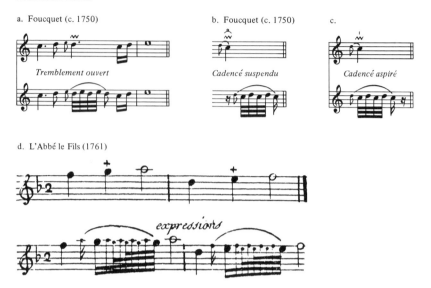

a. Foucquet (c. 1750)

*Tremblement ouvert*

b. Foucquet (c. 1750)

*Cadencé suspendu*

c.

*Cadencé aspiré*

d. L'Abbé le Fils (1761)

*expressions*

L'Abbé le Fils offers revealing information on the grace-note trill in his violin treatise of 1761 by illustrating the *cadence subit, ou jettée* as shown in Ex. 26.18d. The implication of the heavily inked notes is again unmistakable: the main note has the stress of the metrical accent, and the auxiliary is anticipated.

Lécuyer, in his vocal treatise of 1769, gives an unusual illustration of the *cadence parfaite,* shown in Ex. 26.19a, that reveals anticipation of the auxiliary as well as the partial anticipation of the trill itself.

Jean-Joseph Rodolphe, opera composer and eminent horn virtuoso, in his treatise of ca. 1784, illustrates the *cadence préparée* as shown in Ex. 26.19b. It strongly suggests anticipation of the little note, especially when compared with the *cadence brisée* of Ex. 26.19c, which shows an appoggiatura trill in its obvious notation, and with the *cadence sans pré- paration* of Ex. 26.19d.

An interesting document is contained in the *Encyclopédie méthodique, musique* of 1798. A table belonging to the article "Agréments du chant" begins with several *agréments* labeled as "obsolete." Among them is the *cadence brisée* given in Ex. 26.19e, a classic grace-note trill. "Obsolete" by the end of the century presumably meant "current" a generation earlier.

It is time to recognize not just the existence of the grace-note trill but the important role it played in French practices of the 17th and 18th centuries.

Finally, a few words on anticipation of the whole trill. We have seen its documentation for Couperin's trill that is slurred to its preceding note as well as to one that is detached from it, and we have seen the spelled- out confirmation by Père Engramelle (see Exx. 26.12 and 26.13). Apart

EXAMPLE 26.19

a. Lécuyer (1769)

*Cadence parfaite*

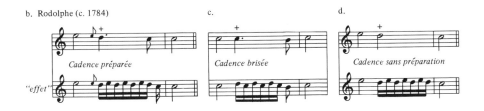

b. Rodolphe (c. 1784)                    c.                                      d.

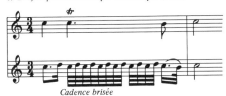

*Cadence préparée*          *Cadence brisée*              *Cadence sans préparation*

"effet"

e. *Encyclopédie méthodique . . . Musique* (1798)

*Cadence brisée*

from the attractiveness of the design, which alone suggests the likelihood of its frequent undocumented use, there are yet a few more theoretical references to it. In autograph additions to his woodwind treatise of ca. 1772, Francoeur ("neveu") gives the illustration of a *cadence brise* [sic] *ou f[e]inte* given in Ex. 26.20a, with the spelled-out anticipation of the trill (the additions BN, MS 1843–1844).

Durieu, in the vocal treatise of 1793 mentioned above, lists a *cadence feinte* as given in Ex. 26.20b and says that "one puts two little notes between the trilled note and the one that precedes it." This would seem to be a rather clear description of an anticipated miniature trill of the *Schneller* type (*Nouvelle méthode*, 62).

EXAMPLE 26.20

a. Francoeur ("neveu") (1772)                              b. Durieu (1793)

*Signe*

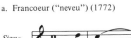

*Cadence brise ou finte* [sic]

*effet:*

*Cadence feinte*

*Effets*

# Conclusion

The widely held view of a rigidly uniform French trill that starts with the auxiliary on the beat and was valid for all media throughout the 17th and 18th centuries must be recognized as a myth. The picture was far more complicated and, happily, far more varied. The start with the auxiliary was strongly favored by keyboard players, but every so often this start occurred unaccented before the beat. Furthermore, main-note trills occurred on the keyboard on short notes that were slurred to the preceding pitch, as did full anticipation of the whole trill in certain favorable contexts. Outside of the keyboard the preference for the upper-note start was far less pronounced. Singers and players of melody instruments ranged freely over the whole range of the trill's potential, which included—in addition to the appoggiatura trill—the main-note trill, either supported or not supported, the grace-note trill, and the fully or partially anticipated trill.

# *27*

# THE TRILL II: ITALY AND ENGLAND

## *The Italian Trill*

Toward the end of the 16th century a number of Italian theorists discussed, illustrated, and named various trill species. The most common terms for the regular trill were *tremolo* and *trillo,* with *tremoletto* signifying a miniature trill of one or two alternations. The term *tremolo* had throughout the 17th and the better part of the 18th century a double meaning of *di sopra,* the regular trill, and its inversion, *di sotto,* which is a multiple mordent (i.e., an alternation with the lower neighbor).

A complication set in early in the 17th century, when the term *trillo* was used by (among others) Caccini and Monteverdi for a new species of oscillation, in which a single pitch was repeated. Caccini illustrates this grace with acceleration: ♩ ♩ ♫♫ ♬♬ . Its performance seems to have ranged from a clear, sharp, staccato-style execution to a more legato-style rendition that smoothly connects dynamic stresses without a break of the breath.

The symbols *t* or *tr* were used for both species, the *tremolo* (in both directions) and the tone repetitions or *trillo.* When the symbol was written not on top of a note but *between* two notes of the same pitch, ⌐⌐ , it always stood for tone repetition.

The terms *gruppo* or *groppo* (or their derivatives) generally designated a trill-related grace with slower and more sharply articulated alternations that ended with a turn of four notes.

The trill models of both Diruta (1593) and of Cavalieri (1600) start with the main note (see Exx. 27.1a and 27.1b), as do the *groppo* models (with a lengthy main-note support) of Conforto (1593 or 1603) and Caccini (1602). Diruta shows in addition a fully anticipated four-note *tremoletto*, given in Ex. 27.1c.

EXAMPLE 27.1

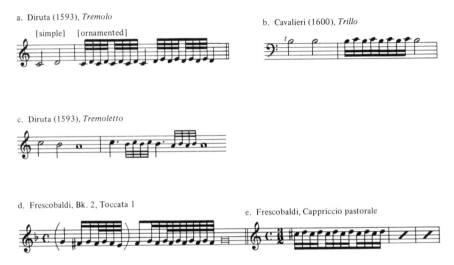

a. Diruta (1593), *Tremolo*

[simple]   [ornamented]

b. Cavalieri (1600), *Trillo*

c. Diruta (1593), *Tremoletto*

d. Frescobaldi, Bk. 2, Toccata 1

e. Frescobaldi, Cappriccio pastorale

Frescobaldi used the *t* symbol for a fairly short (main-note) trill but writes out in regular notes trills of some duration to insure their proper length. In the famous preface to book I of his *Toccate e partite* of 1615–16 (cited in chap. 2), he makes it clear that such written-out trills must not be played at their face value but faster and freer, coming to a rest on the final note. The overwhelming majority of these trills start with the main note, including even cadential trills such as the one given in Ex. 27.1d. We also find trills lasting for several measures, such as the one of Ex. 27.1e.

Michelangelo Rossi, Frescobaldi's student, follows closely in his master's footsteps with an equally decided preference for main-note trills. Tarquinio Merula uses various designs, including both the upper-note and the main-note type. Bernardo Storace, an important keyboard master of the post-Frescobaldi era, consistently prefers the main-note trill (*Selva di varie compositioni, passim*). In the second half of the 17th century, several keyboard composers, among them Lorenzo Penna in 1672, Gregorio Strozzi in 1687, and Giovanni Salvatore (d. 1688), liked to insert patterns of tone repetition into their written-out trill designs.

For the voice, the trillo's original medium, the use of tone repetition seems to have gradually declined, yet there are indications that it survived sporadically well into the 18th century. The famous Faustina, Hasse's wife, was a master of its execution and Handel wrote for her in his opera *Alessandro* passages of written-out *trilli* such as in Act II, Scene 4, measures 34–36.[1] Also, his accelerating tone repetitions in the first movement of the Organ Concerto in A No. 14 (mm. 24–25, 38–39, and 46–49) would seem to be, like Strozzi's and Salvatore's designs, keyboard adaptations of the vocal style that are hardly idiomatic for the organ.

Pierfrancesco Tosi, whom we met before in connection with rubato singing (chap. 9) and with the appoggiatura (chap. 23), was in the prime of his life a celebrated castrato singer. In his old age, in 1723, he wrote the treatise *Opinioni . . . sopra il canto figurato,* which became famous as the authoritative discourse on the most admired vocal style of the period. It was translated into many languages, among others into English by J. E. Galliard in 1742 (*Observations*), and into German (with extensive commentary) by J. F. Agricola in 1758 (the previously quoted *Anleitung*). Tosi's book has the drawback of lacking music examples, but his text makes it clear that his trill emphasizes the main note and starts with the latter for all unprepared trills. The main note, he writes, "is the master tone because it occupies with greater forcefulness the site of the note that is to be trilled" (merita il nome di principale, perchè occupa con più padronanza il sito della nota, che lo chiede [*Opinioni de' cantori antichi,* 25]). Later in the chapter, speaking of the trill with a semitone, he points to the corresponding weakness of the auxiliary ("[la] poca forza che ha l'ausiliario per farsi sentire" [26]). Tosi's trills must often be prepared with a presumably lengthy appoggiatura. Such preparation is needed in most final cadences and analogous locations; it is not always required, however, "because every so often time or taste would not permit it" (28). Whenever prepared, the alternations, in accord with Tosi's description of the trill, are bound to emphasize the main note both rhythmically and dynamically.

Galliard and Agricola, the English and German translators, have misrepresented Tosi's trill by illustrations that run counter to the latter's verbal directives: under the influence of their allegiance to modern English and German fashions, both writers show in their inserted illustrations exclusively the appoggiatura-trill pattern with pervasive upper-note emphasis—the opposite of what Tosi had unequivocally described (Tosi, *Observations* [1742], Plate 4; Agricola, *Anleitung zur Singkunst,* 95).

The degree of misrepresentation by Galliard is nowhere more blatant than in his illustration of the *trillo cresciuto* and *trillo calato,* which are trilled glissandi (one rising, the other falling). Tosi's explanation of "raising the voice imperceptibly while trilling from comma to comma so that the rise is not noticeable" (*Opinioni de' cantori antichi,* 28) is translated into an example in which Galliard's insistence on starting each trill with the upper note produces leaps of a third that are very noticeable indeed; and for the descending type, moreover, every other trill starts with the note *above* the auxiliary in order to avoid tone repetition (see Ex. 27.2). The result is totally at odds with Tosi's directives and musically incongruous to boot.

EXAMPLE 27.2.   Galliard

**Domenico Scarlatti.** Scarlatti's trills (which he symbolizes with *tr* and ✳ interchangeably) appear to have followed the by then century-old Italian tradition of favoring the main-note type. This statement is born out by plentiful musical evidence.

For characteristic instances of the many cases in which an onbeat auxiliary cannot have been intended, see Ex. 27.3a, where open fifths in two-part writing would result and practically enforce a main-note start; or Ex. 27.3b, where a downrushing scale hits bottom on the main note

EXAMPLE 27.3.   D. Scarlatti

a. Sonata K 308

b. Sonata K 119

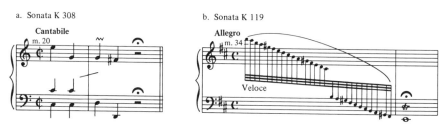

c. Sonata K 105

d. Sonata K 17

of a trill and where the insertion of an appoggiatura would be unthink-able. Similar musical sense requires main-note start in Ex. 27.3c, where the theme fragment of three successive As (indicated in the example by a bracket) is played four times, landing the last time on the trill, which logically has to start with the main note.

That an upper-note start was not understood is further witnessed by the many cases in which a *Vorschlag* symbol—often written in small thirty-second notes—precedes a trill in places where a support is out of the question for lack of time and where even a plain upper-note start would create faulty voice leading, as for instance in Ex. 27.3d. The meaning of such a *Vorschlag* note is mostly, perhaps always, that of a grace note.

In his early sonatas Scarlatti occasionally writes *tremulo di sopra,* meaning an extended main-note trill. Much more frequently we encoun-ter simply *tremulo,* which usually stands for a multiple mordent. I be-lieve I have established that fact (in *OrnB,* 354) with, among others, a striking passage from Sonata K 175, measures 25–32, where Scarlatti systematically alternates trill symbols with the term *tremulo.* In these measures, which are filled with Scarlatti's famous dissonant tone clus-ters (like those shown in Ex. 31.25), the chords under the trills are densely clustered, whereas those under *tremulo,* in contrast, always pro-vide sufficient space for the mordent. Often he indicates the pitch for the mordent alternations with a *Vorschlag* from below, as shown in Ex. 27.4a. In accord with the long-standing Italian mirror-image duality of *di sopra* and *di sotto,* it is quite certain that even the simple trill symbol can stand for a mordent when the latter makes better musical sense; such is notably true in cases in which the trill symbol is preceded by a *Vorschlag* from below, as shown in Ex. 27.4b.[2] The Italians had no symbol for the mordent, other than Scarlatti's *tremulo,* which however indicated a mul-tiple mordent. For a brief mordent, the trill symbol had to do double duty. In spots such as the one shown in Ex. 27.4b, Thomas Roseingrave, Scarlatti's friend and admirer, used the French mordent symbol in his 1739 edition of forty-two of Scarlatti's sonatas.[3]

EXAMPLE 27.4. D. Scarlatti

a. Sonata K 115

b. Sonata K 105

*Vivaldi.*  There is plenty of musical evidence for the primarily main-note character of Vivaldi's trills as well. A typical illustration appears in Ex. 27.5a, taken from the Violin Concerto del Guardellino (F XII No. 9), where Vivaldi has written out (as well as notation permits it) an acceleration pattern for a main-note trill (two more related passages occur in the same concerto, third movement, mm. 166–67 and 250–52, the latter with anticipated auxiliary). The passage given in Ex. 27.5b, from the Concerto in A Minor for Bassoon (F VIII, No. 2) is hardly less eloquent.

EXAMPLE 27.5.   Vivaldi

a. Violin Concerto del Gardellino (F XII, No. 9)

b. Concerto in A Minor for Bassoon (F VIII, No. 2/1)

*Padre Martini.*  The works of Padre Martini (1706–84), who was revered for his teaching and especially for his mastery of traditional counterpoint, are filled with examples that are incompatible both with the trill beginning with the auxiliary on the beat and with the long appoggiatura meaning of the *Vorschlag* symbol before a trilled note. Just two small samples from the organ sonatas of 1730 and 1742 (Exx. 27.6a and 27.6b, respectively), show trills in sensitive two-part writing, where the auxiliary on the beat would produce unacceptable fifths. In Ex. 27.6c, from 1742, an interpretation of the *Vorschlag* note as an appoggiatura would also be disqualified by the resulting open fifths, and giving it eighth-note length according to the "rules" would immediately thereafter produce another open fifth with the middle voice. Only a grace-note rendition can avoid these pitfalls. From these and many other analogous examples, we can conclude that Padre Martini's basic trill type started with the main note unless a little *Vorschlag* symbol signaled a grace-note start.

EXAMPLE 27.6.   G. B. Martini

a. Organ Sonata (c. 1730)

b. Organ Sonata No. 2 (1742)

c. Sonata No. 1 (1742)

**Mid-Century Violinists.** Often the grace-note execution of the *Vorschlag* note before a trill is necessary when the trilled note is too short to accommodate an appoggiatura without crowding. Such is the case with the trilled thirty-seconds in Ex. 27.7a, from the third, fast movement of Locatelli's Concerto for Four Solo Violins No. 12. This is a favorite Italian melodic-ornamental formula for both voices and instruments to which I referred in chapter 23 as "Italian mordent"; the fairly obvious anticipation of the *Vorschlag* in this formula is confirmed by Tartini, as will be presently shown.

EXAMPLE 27.7

a. Locatelli, Concerto for Four Solo Violins No. 12 (1735)        b. Geminiani, Violin Sonata Op. 4, No. 1

    Veracini often writes out a lengthy appoggiatura support of a trill in regular notes. On other occasions he indicates such support with a little *Vorschlag* note whose long appoggiatura meaning is revealed by the bass figures. Often long appoggiatura preparation was understood, notably on cadential trills, even without the prompt of a *Vorschlag* symbol. Frequently the *Vorschlag* symbol is not reflected in the bass figures, suggesting either brevity or anticipation. As did most Italians, Veracini too often uses the "Italian mordent" with or without a trill with grace-note start in either case.

    In his treatises Geminiani illustrates the *trillo semplice* as starting with the auxiliary on the beat, while his *trattenimento sopra la nota* ("holding a note") starts with the supported main note. Both types can have a turned ending. A supported appoggiatura trill is indicated by the symbol of the little *Vorschlag* note (*Treatise of Good Taste,* 2 [text], 1 [music]). Yet this little note can also have grace-note meaning. In Ex. 27.7b we see the explicit notation of a grace-note trill (on F sharp) from his Violin Sonata Op. 4, No. 1.

    Geminiani's model of an appoggiatura trill, perhaps the first such theoretical design by an Italian, *may* have been influenced by the prevailing fashion in England, where Geminiani lived and where his treatises were published in English. Musical evidence points to a range of trill designs that transcends the mentioned patterns and includes the regular main note, in addition to the supported *trattenimento,* and the grace-note type; of this latter we have just seen a spelled-out specimen, not to speak of the "Italian mordent" with added trill, also frequent in his works.

Tartini made brilliant use of the trill in his works, and his treatise reflects the importance he attached to the grace. His regular trill patterns show the start with the upper note on the beat (*Regole*, 10–15), yet further theoretical and musical evidence proves great flexibility in his use of many different trill types. Thus, in a famous letter to Signora Maddalena Lombardini, he discusses the trill, advises its practice in acceleration, and illustrates it with main-note start and continuing metric emphasis on the main note. The main-note trill is furthermore inherent in the execution of trill chains, as explained by Tartini: derived from the *portamento* of the voice—and reminiscent of Tosi's trill on a glissando—they are performed by gliding up the second finger and trilling as it moves (12). Such trills are feasible on the violin only with a main-note start. A supported main-note trill results when a trill on dotted notes starts only on the dot, as shown in Ex. 27.8a (14). He also demonstrates the grace-note trill when in his discussion on the anticipated *Vorschlag* (*appoggiatura breve ossia di passaggio*), as reported above in chapter 23, he first explains that appoggiaturas are out of place in a setting of even notes because they would destroy the sense of evenness, whereupon he spells out grace-note anticipation in such a setting, as was shown in Ex. 23.6b. He then illustrates how in a sequence of such grace notes before even quarter notes or even eighth notes it is advisable to add trills, as reproduced in Ex. 27.8b. These are inescapably grace-note trills that incidentally provide additional proof for the grace-note nature of the *Vorschläge* in the "Italian mordent" as encountered before without trill (in Exx. 23.4a and 23.4b) and with trill (in Ex. 27.7a).

There are also many passages in Tartini's works where an auxiliary-on-the-beat start is disqualified by ensuing offensive parallels such as shown in Exx. 27.8c for unaccompanied open octaves and 27.8d for open fifths.

We see that the evidence from Tartini's theory and practice points to a rich variety of his trill types including at least appoggiatura, main-note, main-note supported, and grace-note trills. Trills with appoggiatura support, though not listed here, are certain to have occurred in cadences and similar spots.

**Later Theorists.** Luigi Antonio Sabbatini, a student of Padre Martini's and an important theorist in his own right, describes in 1789 the trill exclusively in its main-note form and, speaking of final cadences, he explains their execution as first settling the voice on the note to be trilled ("Fissata la voce su della *nota* che il Cantante vorrà trillare"), then quickly alternating with the auxiliary (*Elementi teorici*, 12).

The theorists Carlo Testori in 1767, Vincenzo Manfredini in 1775, Vincenzo Panerai in ca. 1775, and Antonio D. R. Borghese in 1786 show only a main-note pattern for the trill.[4] The Italian P. Signoretti, writing in French, follows Geminiani in showing the plain trill starting with the

EXAMPLE 27.8.   Tartini

auxiliary on the beat and the *tenue* starting with main-note support (*Méthode de la musique et du violon*, 3:10–11 and plate of illustrations).

At the end of the century we have two witnesses to the continuing vitality of the centuries-old Italian inversion-pairing of main-note trill and multiple mordent (with the half tone below) as well as a persistence of the double meaning of the trill symbols for both graces. Giuseppe Liverziani expounds on this double meaning of the symbol in his treatise of 1797 (*Grammatica della musica*, 23), and Carlo Gervasoni in 1800 gives illustrations of the identical trill symbol, calling for either a main-note trill or for a multiple mordent with the half tone below (*La scuola della musica*, 1:183).

In summary, Italian practice ranged over the whole spectrum of the trill, but the center of gravity for the regular, the unprepared, trill rested on the main-note type. We can gather that much in theory over a span of two hundred years from Diruta and Cavalieri to Liverziani and Sabbatini; in practice from Caccini and Frescobaldi to D. Scarlatti and Padre Martini (Mozart's mentor). Exceptions such as Tartini's and Geminiani's appoggiatura-trill models are in part contradicted by opposite theoretical statements, in part qualified by the proof of discrepant practices. The long appoggiatura preparation was used in many but not all cadences as well as in other spots where expression favored it. The grace-note trill flourished simultaneously, as revealed by both musical and theoretical evidence. In the absence of a mordent symbol and in view of the lasting Italian inversion-pairing of the (main-note) trill and the multiple mordent as manifestations of the same ornament, the trill symbol could for many composers (among others for D. Scarlatti) signify the mordent as well as the trill.

The powerful Italian main-note tradition has been overlooked by most scholars who have been engrossed by (incompletely understood) French *keyboard* designs and the rigid patterns of C. P. E. Bach and his north German followers. Yet it is this very Italian tradition that helps explain the predominance of main-note trills (to be discussed later) in Haydn and Mozart as well as their strong presence in Bach, via late 17th century Italian-influenced practices in Germany.

## The English Trill

The meaning of the stroke or double stroke above or below the notes, which are the only ornamental markings in the *Fitzwilliam Virginal Book*, have not yet been elucidated. It is very likely that one or the other could often stand for a trill or a trill-like grace; but nothing more can be said.

From later theorists we receive mixed signals. From the first important sources in mid-17th century to about the mid-18th century the upper-note-on-the-beat trill seems to predominate, though not without dissent. In the second half of the 18th century a number of theorists favor the main-note type, but the relative paucity of substantial tracts makes it difficult to trace a definite trend if one should have prevailed. It is more likely, though, that here, as elsewhere, differing styles coexisted.

Christopher Simpson, in his *Division-Violist* of 1659, shows the appoggiatura trill as given in Ex. 27.9a, using the comma before the note as a symbol ([1667], 12). With it he antedates Chambonnières's identical design of 1660, but not his symbol. As has already been mentioned, John Playford, in his popular *Introduction to the Skill of Musick*, adopted most of Simpson's ornament models, among them the plain trill, which he lists as "backfall shaked" ("backfall" being a falling appoggiatura), using Simpson's comma symbol. Under the term "double relish," however, with a symbol of a seven-dot cluster, he shows first the main-note supported trill of Ex. 27.9b, then the upper-note version of Ex. 27.9c as alternative ([1674], 116).

Henry Purcell, in his *Choice Collection of Lessons*, published posthumously in 1696, also gives the appoggiatura model with the symbol of a double stroke (Ex. 27.9d). He writes: "Observe that you always shake from the note above & beat ['beat' is a mordent] from the note or half note below, according to the key you play in. . . . If it be a note without

EXAMPLE 27.9

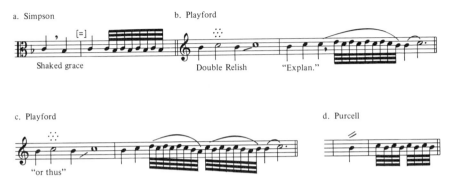

a. Simpson     b. Playford

Shaked grace     Double Relish     "Explan."

c. Playford     d. Purcell

"or thus"

a point you are to hold half the quantity of it plain, & that upon the note above that which is marked and shake the other half, but if it be a note with a point to it you are to hold all the note plain and shake only the point" (n. p.). So it appears that a trill on a binary note of—presumably—some length is preceded by a long appoggiatura support (half the length of the principal note), whereas a trill on a dotted note starts with main-note support for the length of the note head, followed by a trill on the dot.

Thomas Mace, in his lute treatise of 1676, explains the simple shake as a main-note trill. "If you Shake any String Open, you must first strike it with some Right Hand Finger, and then be ready with the Fore-finger, of the Left Hand to pick it up, with the very Tip of your Finger; and so, by often, and quick picking it up in that manner . . . you will have performed it." He distinguishes two types of shakes, hard and soft: they vary in sharpness of articulation but not in design (the "hard" uses left-hand pizzicato, the "soft" one a simple hard striking of the string without plucking it). He confirms the main-note start when he explains the trill on stopped notes (*Musick's Monument,* 103). Later he also explains the appoggiatura trill as a species of a "backfall" that is "shaked." Here the upper note gets plucked by the right hand, whereupon the trill has to be started with a plucking motion of the stopping finger followed by either the "hard" or the "soft" shake (104).

For about the next one hundred years there seems to be no substantial English source on ornamentation. Theorists of the later part of the 18th century are divided regarding the trill's design, but there seems to emerge a penchant for the main-note start.

John Danby, composer and organist, writes in his *Guida della musica instrumentale* of ca. 1790: "The Trill as written *tr* is performed by a quick and regular motion with that note over which it is placed and the Note above it" and illustrates the execution as shown in Ex. 27.10a (9). In his *Guida alla musica vocale* of ca. 1785, he gives the model of Ex. 27.10b (14).

The prolific composer James Hook offers two designs in his brief booklet *Guida di musica* of ca. 1785: for the "shake" he offers the appoggiatura-trill pattern of Ex. 27.10c, for the "trill" the *Schneller*-like renditions of Ex. 27.10d–27.10e.

Similarly, John W. Calcott in 1793 shows the "turned shake" with upper-note start of Ex. 27.10f, the "transient shake" as the *Schneller* type of Ex. 27.10g (*Explanation*, 20).

EXAMPLE 27.10

a. Danby          b. Danby

"as written" "as played"          as written

c. Hook          d. Hook          e. Hook

A shake  Explained          A trill  Explained

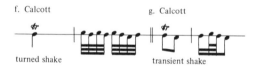

f. Calcott          g. Calcott

turned shake          transient shake

h. Corfe

J. N. Hüllmandel (a German student of C. P. E. Bach), who lived in England and published his *Principles of Music* in 1795 in London, will be quoted among the German theorists in the following chapter. He was a composer esteemed by Mozart, and his ideas about the trill may be briefly outlined here for their possible relevance to English practices. The trill, he writes, may be indifferently started with either the main note or the note above or the note below (*Principles of Music*, 16ff.).

Finally, in his *Treatise on Singing* of ca. 1800, Joseph Corfe, organist at the Salisbury Cathedral, gives exclusively the main-note model of Ex. 27.10h.

The English trill seems to have moved from a basic, though not unanimous, preference for the upper-note start in the 17th century to a more varied practice by the end of the 18th century with strong ingredients of the main-note type—and probably, though not verifiably, of the grace-note type as well. It is very possible that Handel's very flexible, totally undogmatic practices with regard to the trill played a part in this transformation since it is much more likely that Handel influenced English practices than the other way around.

*Handel.* The multinational Handel, as has been said before, is hard to classify; a discussion of him in the wake of both the Italian and the English schools is somewhat of a practical compromise that seems justified by his predominantly Italianate ornamentation on the one hand, by the enormous impact he made on 18th-century English music on the other hand.

Much musical evidence points to the prevalence of the main-note style of Handel's basic trill. Considering his strong indebtedness to Italian practice, such a tendency could be expected. In the third movement of the *Water Music* (in the traditional sequence), for instance, the trills of the oboes (Ex. 27.11a) and later of the violins assume in their enforced simplification for the less agile horns the shape of *Schneller,* written out as seen in Ex. 27.11b. Example 27.11c, from the Organ Concerto Op. 7, No. 1, shows a main-note trill that had to be written out to indicate its approximate acceleration.

Many are the trills in which an auxiliary on the beat is disqualified because of faulty voice leading. There are cases in which the notation calls for an upper-note start but not necessarily on the beat. In a spot such as the one shown in Ex. 27.11d, the two little notes seem intended to slide into the trill via the auxiliary. In this connective function, the auxiliary could not easily be placed on the beat. In his own copy of Handel's suites, in which he added his own ornamental interpretations and additions, Theophil Muffat in 1736 spells out the prebeat insertion of the auxiliary as part of the slide (Ex. 27.11e).[5] This is the same musician who is known for the seemingly uncompromising onbeat style in his extensive ornament table of the very same year, 1736 (regarding this table, see chap. 24 above).

For cadential trills Handel often writes out an appoggiatura support in regular notes and often omits the trill symbol. When not so specified, an appoggiatura support was often intended to be improvised, but not necessarily always. He rarely indicated the suffix after the trill, which needs to be added for most trills of any length. Here too as elsewhere,

EXAMPLE 27.11.   Handel

a. *Water Music* / 3

b. *Water Music* / 3

c. Organ Concerto, Op. 7, No. 1

(Pedale)

d.  Suite No. 2

e.  Suite No. 2, Theo. Muffat's version

Handel, in true Italian manner, showed his indifference to matters of detail by delegating much of the executive authority to the performer.

Adolf Beyschlag, in his remarkable book *Die Ornamentik der Musik* of 1908, had already inferred from the study of Handel's music that the latter's trills seem for the most part to have started with the main note (108). It is regrettable that most of today's "early music specialists" seem to have forgotten such insights and, by surrendering to the problematic upper-note-on-the-beat imperative, rigidify Handel's trills (and other ornaments) along with Bach's, Haydn's, and Mozart's.

# 28

# THE TRILL III: GERMANY

## The German Trill in the 17th Century

Praetorius, writing in 1619 about the trill, continues to use Italian models and sounds the leitmotiv for the century by showing a main-note model for the trill (*tremulus ascendens*) side by side with its inversion, the multiple mordent (*tremulus descendens*), as given in Ex. 28.1a.

Under the term *tremoletti* Praetorius introduces miniature trills with one or two alternations (i.e., *Schneller* and short main-note trills), shown in Ex. 28.1b as embellishments of a plain melody. Under the term *gruppo* or *groppo*, Praetorius gives a main-note supported trill-like design with a turned ending, as shown in Ex. 28.1c. He says it is used in cadences and related clauses and ought to be rendered with greater sharpness than the *tremoli* ("müssen scherffer alss die *Tremoli* angeschlagen werden"). He also reports on and illustrates the *trillo* with its accelerating tone repetition, as given in Ex. 28.1d (*Syntagma musicum*, 3:235–37).

Many of the German *tremuli* in the early 17th century were improvised, but following the Italian lead, the symbols *t* and *tr* were beginning to be used to signify the pair of *tremuli* and occasionally the tone repetition *trillo*.

Johann Andreas Herbst in 1642 and 1658, as well as Johann Crüger in 1654 and 1660, follow Praetorius very closely and help transmit his Italian models to later German generations (Herbst, *Musica practica* [1642], 7ff.; Crüger, *Synopsis musica* [1654], 197ff., and *Musicae practicae*, 27ff.). Wolfgang Michael Mylius, in 1685, follows in the same line with the mirror-image *tremulus*, the *tremoletti*, and analogous remarks about

*409*

EXAMPLE 28.1.    Praetorius (1619)

a.

the *groppo*. He may have been one of the first to show the use of the *tr* symbol for both the main-note trill or the multiple mordent (*Rudimenta musices*, chap. 5, n. p.). Georg Falck in 1688 is another representative of the same tradition with his *tremulus ascendens* and *descendens,* his *groppo,* and the tone repetition *trillo in unisono* straight out of Praetorius's book. We find, with some unimportant variants of terminology, the same designs of mirror-image *tremuli* and tone repetition *trilli* with Moritz Feyertag in 1695 (*Syntaxis,* 220–21) and with Johann Samuel Beyer in 1703 (*Primae lineae,* 57ff.). Wolfgang Caspar Printz, in various treatises covering a span of thirty-five years (1678–1714) varies the terms but shows consistently the same ascending and descending tremolo as well as a *groppo* with main-note support. (For illustrations regarding this paragraph, see *OrnB,* chap. 28.)

The dual nature of the tremolo fully clarifies a passage by the famous Johann Adam Reincken in 1687, which some have considered obscure. He wrote (in Latin): "Should anyone be unaware of what is meant by the simple [symbol] ×, he may know that it stands for a *tremulus* that touches the note below: whereas the two dashes ‖ indicate a *tremulus* that touches the note above" (*Hortus musicus,* Preface). Clearly the two types are inversions of one another—namely multiple mordent and main-note trill.

F. X. A. Murschhauser in 1703 gives the patterns of Ex. 28.2a. He no longer shows a single ornament in two guises but gives the main-note trill and the mordent as two distinct ornaments, one the inversion of the other (*Prototypon,* 1: Preface).

EXAMPLE 28.2

a. Murschhauser (1703)

b. Fuhrmann (1706, 1715)

*Trillo* (1706)

c. Fuhrmann (1706, 1715)

*Tremoletto*

Martin Heinrich Fuhrmann, in his two treatises from 1706 and 1715, shows the trill solely in its main-note form (Ex. 28.2b), the mordent in its usual form with the half step below; and the tone repetition in its apparently sharply articulated form, as given in Ex. 28.2c.[1]

The theoretical documents thus point to a de facto monopoly of the main-note trill for 17th-century Germany. With Fuhrmann and Printz this current can be traced to 1715. These documents are tellingly supported by musical evidence. Following the lead of Italian keyboard players, the Germans Froberger and Kerll, both students of Frescobaldi, follow their master's manner of writing out in regular notes those trills of substantial duration. Other German keyboard composers, among them Lübeck, Pachelbel, and Buxtehude, followed the same procedure. Its purpose was to insure proper design and length, not metric regularity. These written-out trills are overwhelmingly of the main-note type, such as shown in Ex. 28.3a, from Froberger, and Ex. 28.3b, from Kerll, with only very sporadic appoggiatura-type trills.

In Buxtehude, we again find frequent instances of written-out main-note trills as well as the near absence of the appoggiatura variety. For just one illustration, see Ex. 28.3c, from a Fugue in E (BB Mus. MS 2681/1) that is of special interest because the caption *trillo longo* (repeated later in the piece) offers clear proof that the written-out trill alternations were not meant to be taken at metrical face value.

The basic main-note character of his trills is further suggested by numerous instances of trills marked by symbol (on the organ the French *chevron* is most commonly used) the placement of the auxiliary on the beat is excluded by offensive parallels such as the fifths among the outer voices in transparent setting in Ex. 28.3d, similar fifths again in Ex. 28.3e, or the octaves among the outer voices in Ex. 28.3f. Grace-note trills would be an option for the unlikely case that, along with the French symbol, Buxtehude might have on occasion followed the French manner of starting the trill with the auxiliary. For more illustrations of written-out and of parallel-engendering trills, see *OrnB*, Exx. 28.20–28.22.

EXAMPLE 28.3

a. Froberger (c. 1645–1650)

Canzona 6

b. Kerll (1627–1693)

Toccata (Hintze, MS)

c. Buxtehude

Fugue in E

"trillo longo"

d. Buxtehude, *Vater Unser*    e. Buxtehude, *Der Tag*    f. Buxtehude, *Der Tag*

The first German theoretical document that directly presents the appoggiatura trill is probably Johann Caspar Fischer's ornament table of 1696 (*Musicalisches Blumenbüschlein*). In it the French-oriented Fischer uses the French symbols and with them the trill model of Chambonnières and his followers, as shown in Ex. 28.4a. Johann Gottfried Walther in 1708, also under French influence, presents the same trill patterns, for which he gives the symbols *t, tr,* and the *chevron,* as shown in Ex. 28.4b.

In the early 18th century, French influence—as witnessed by Fischer and Walther—began gradually to make itself felt in the practice of German musicians. It coexisted with the continuing strong presence of Italian-derived styles with their main-note–multiple mordent pair. A number of noted composers, among them the brothers Graun, Graupner, and Mattheson, remained committed to Italian ways, and so did (in

EXAMPLE 28.4

a. Fischer (1696)      b. Walther (1708)

principle) Handel in England. With Bach both the Italian and the French traditions merged in a very flexible and far from unified mixture. It is a misconception that Bach was totally committed to the French keyboard style.

## J. S. Bach's Trill

Bach's trills must be viewed against the background of the practices he encountered in Germany in the early years of the 18th century. Characteristic of these practices was a coexistence and interpenetration of the old but very vigorous Italo-German main-note tradition with the whole spectrum of the newly introduced French models. The latter included the full range of upper-note trills—from appoggiatura types through the grace-note design to full anticipation—as well as an element of main-note trills, primarily from the media of the voice and melody instruments.

In view of this situation alone, the common modern assumptions that limits Bach's trills to the appoggiatura species, usually to one with continued upper-note emphasis, becomes highly suspect. Here too, as in the cases of *Vorschläge* and slides, it seems unrealistic to assume that Bach, in an environment offering the richness of a wide choice, would have confined himself to the poverty of a single design that is utterly inadequate for the needs of his infinitely varied musical contexts.

Yet this single principle has been endorsed by many twentieth-century scholars (among them Arnold Dolmetsch, Robert Donington, Putnam Aldrich, Karl Hochreither, and Hans Klotz) and by many of today's "early music specialists." Other scholars, while considering the upper-note-on-the-beat style to be the basic principle valid for "the vast majority" of Bach's trills, admit occasional exceptions to avoid unmusical results. Among them are Walter Emery, Hermann Keller, Erwin Bodky, and Alfred Kreutz. Paul Badura-Skoda, in his important new book *Bach Interpretation*, follows the latter line, albeit with greater flexibility. While acknowledging that the "old-German" 17th century trill practice (meaning the main-note start) was in the first two decades of the

18th century still traceable in several of Bach's works, Badura-Skoda believes there is "good reason" to assume that the "standard form" of Bach's trills was the French pattern (meaning the appoggiatura type), the main-note start being an exception (*Bach Interpretation*, 379). As examples of such reasons he lists, as others before him, the "Explication" and the models of Philipp Emanuel and other Bach students. I have already explained before why Bach's own small ornament table has to be viewed with greatest reserve, and why Philipp Emanuel cannot be considered an authority on his father's ornamentation. What is really necessary here is a close analysis of Bach's own use of trills and their function in specific settings. For an illustration of such an analysis, we might look at just one example from Badura-Skoda's book where the "standard" solution could be questioned.

For the trill in measure 13 of the chromatic (Fantasy and) Fugue, given in Ex. 28.5a, Badura-Skoda offers the solution of Ex. 28.5b (*Bach Interpretation*, 382). Several reasons argue against this execution. This trill is a purely melodic ornament with the function of keeping the sound of the G sharp alive until its resolution to the A, from leading tone to temporary tonic in A minor. For this progression to be clarified, the sound of the G sharp has to be distinctly heard. Whereas a main-note trill will sharply profile this progression, the appoggiatura trill with continuing upper-note emphasis would severely blur it. Moreover, the G sharp forms a dissonance that intensifies the tension inherent in the leading tone. The proposed solution diminishes this tension while impoverishing the harmony. A main-note trill, preferably with a subtle support, seems the better solution here.[2]

EXAMPLE 28.5.   Bach, Fugue, BWV 903

a.

b. Execution (Badura-Skoda)

Except for one or two instances in very early organ works, Bach does not write out extended trills in regular notes in the manner of Froberger, Kerll, Buxtehude, and other 17th-century organists. There are a few exceptions, such as in the case shown in Ex. 28.6a, from the Violin Sonata in E Minor, where he wished to underline the leading-tone–temporary tonic progression by a slight main-note support, or where he tried to indicate with inadequate notational means a slow start and gradual acceleration of a main-note trill from the Dorian toccata (Ex. 28.6b) or of a grace-note trill from the *Praeludium & fuga pedaliter* (Ex. 28.6c).

EXAMPLE 28.6.  Bach

a. Violin Sonata in E Minor, BWV 1023, Allemande

b. Dorian toccata, BWV 538, 2

c. Praeludium and fuga pedaliter, BWV 531, 2

*Symbols.* In Bach's "Explication" we find the following trill symbols, as shown in Ex. 28.7: Ex. 28.7a, the two-waggle *chevron* for the plain trill; Ex. 28.7b, the combination of *chevron* and mordent for the trill with a suffix; Ex. 28.7c, the combination of hook and *chevron* for the supported appoggiatura trill, and a synonymous symbol (Ex. 28.7d) in which the *chevron* is started by a longer vertical stroke. These are all strictly keyboard symbols of French origin that Bach used for other media only on extremely rare occasions, apparently by oversight. When he intentionally used a wavy line for voice or a melody instrument, it indicated not a trill but a vibrato. In addition, Bach used for all media, including the

EXAMPLE 28.7.  Bach, "Explication"

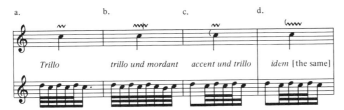

keyboard, the letter *t*, either by itself or with an added stroke, a fragmentary *r*: *t̄* . Bach never indicated chromatic alterations of the auxiliary and relied on the performer's judgment to make the right choice.

*Multiple Designs.* As was briefly pointed out at the start of this section, the idea that the appoggiatura type of the "Explication" is the basic, let alone the sole, trill type for Bach is unrealistic. Countless are the instances in which an initial emphasis on the auxiliary simply does not fit. Such an instance has been shown in Ex. 28.5, where a start with the auxiliary on the beat and its continuing emphasis would impair both melody and harmony (as pointed out in note 2); a similar case is shown in Ex. 28.12. There are many other circumstances that disfavor the orthodox solution and many passages where such a solution would be outright objectionable. Among the latter are the numerous instances in which truly offensive parallels would result. Only four specimens can be shown here (for twenty-two others, see *OrnB*, Exx. 28.7–28.13).

The passages given in Ex. 28.8a–28.8c are from the Two-Part Inventions, and Ex. 28.8d is from the Canonic Variations. By applying the rule we would produce octaves in Ex. 28.8a, unisons in Ex. 28.8b, and fifths in Ex. 28.8c, errors aggravated in all instances by the transparency of two-part writing. This solution is also harmonically illogical. All these trills are applied to written-out appoggiaturas; the "rule" would place a second appoggiatura on top of the first, which would be thereby emasculated. It will be remembered how Quantz in an analogous case spelled out the need for grace-note anticipation (see Ex. 24.14). Example 28.8d is especially eloquent because two trills, both set to written-out appoggiaturas, follow one another in close sequence; appoggiatura trills would form parallel octaves first with the middle voice, and then with the bass.

In all these instances the main note of the trill—that is, the appoggiatura itself—must sound on the beat. For this to happen there are three possible solutions: (1) main-note trill; (2) grace-note trill; and (3) fully anticipated trill. In Ex. 28.9 these three alternatives are sketched for Ex. 28.8a.

*Main-Note Start.* A main-note start is frequently either specified or implied or is suggested for musical or technical considerations. The notation, first of all, often indicates clearly that the main note should be sustained before the start of the alternations. Ties frequently serve this purpose when the trill symbol is placed only on the second of two tied notes, as for instance in Ex. 28.10a, from Cantata No. 42. There are also cases of dotted notes where Bach has written the symbol over the dot, which in turn he placed at a purposeful distance from the principal note, as shown in Ex. 28.10b, from the Mass in A Major. Here this notational pattern is repeated for several similar entrances of the theme in both tutti and solo passages.

EXAMPLE 28.8.   Bach

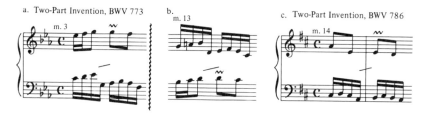

a. Two-Part Invention, BWV 773
b. m. 13
c. Two-Part Invention, BWV 786

d. Canonic Variations, BWV 769

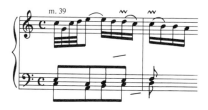

EXAMPLE 28.9.   Bach, Two-Part Invention, BWV 773

a.                          b.                          c.

EXAMPLE 28.10.   Bach

a. Cantata No. 42/1 (aut. P 55)

Ob. I

(incompl. score)

Cont.

b. Mass in A Major. BWV 234, 6 (aut. Darmstadt)

in glo - ri- a De - i

Musical logic will call for main-note start and continuing main-note emphasis whenever the trill is a purely melodic embellishment serving merely to give the written pitch more brilliance or to keep it from decaying on the harpsichord. Whenever the trill serves such a function, an emphasis on the auxiliary would make no sense because the resulting appoggiatura effect would distort both melody and harmony. In Ex. 28.5

we have seen the case of a trill with the melodic function of underlining the leading-tone–tonic progression, and, with a view to this function, main-note start and continued main-note emphasis seemed to suggest themselves. Where in addition there is the need to sustain a short-lived keyboard sound, main-note emphasis becomes imperative. We find a characteristic case in the Prelude in G Minor of *WTC I*, in the long trills in measures 1, 3, 7, and 9 (Ex. 28.11a). For a sustained tonic note at the very beginning of a piece there seems to be no musical justification for an appoggiatura start.[3] Cogent melodic reasons call for a main-note start as well for the second trill in measure 3. The second measure introduces

an important four-note motive, a kind of prebeat turn ![motive] di-

rected toward the fourth, onbeat, note that pervades a good part of the prelude (see Ex. 28.11b). Musical logic demands that on its fourth appearance in the measure this figure maintain its motivic-rhythmic integrity by ending on the downbeat with the G (i.e., with the main note of the trill), as shown in Ex. 28.11c.

EXAMPLE 28.11.   Bach, Prelude in G Minor, *WTC I*, BWV 861

Bach's fugue themes are paragons of linearity whose horizontal impulse creates the momentum that carries the fugues forward. A "harmonic" trill is therefore misplaced in a fugue theme, where on its initial announcement there is no harmony to be enriched, while in the answer and all later appearances there is counterpoint to be disturbed by emphasis on a note that is not part of the linear design.

A good example is the theme of the Fugue in F Sharp (*WTC II*), which starts with a trill on the leading tone (Ex. 28.12a). To start with the tonic as appoggiatura would deprive the leading tone of the potential energy deriving from its inherent suspense and impulse toward the tonic. Moreover, in measures 20 and 70 (Exx. 28.12b and 28.12c) we encounter a stylized written-out form of this trill that clarifies the main-note start and emphasis on the leading tone.

Linear primacy is also logical when trills occur in a chromatic melody, whether singly or in chains. The sharply defined contour of a chromatic progression has a claim to melodic integrity; hence any trill within such a progression should start on the main note and preferably linger slightly on the latter to underscore the melodic line.

EXAMPLE 28.12.   Bach, Fugue in F-Sharp, *WTC II*, BWV 882/2

Many are the cases in which the trill follows its upper neighbor under a slur. When this upper neighbor is very brief and unaccented, a repetition of the preceding note would be musically incongruous and in addition break the intended slur. For an illustration, see Ex. 28.13a, from the Sonata in G Minor for Solo Violin. In those of Bach's keyboard works that are almost entirely devoid of articulation marks, similar contexts will call for a main-note start whenever a slur seems to be indicated, as for example in Ex. 28.13b, from the Third Partita.[4]

EXAMPLE 28.13.   Bach

a. Sonata in G Minor for Solo Violin,
   BWV 1001/1

b. Third Keyboard Partita, BWV 827, Allemande

***Schneller and Pralltriller.***  As explained in chapter 26, the terms *Schneller* and *Pralltriller* were coined by C. P. E. Bach, but their designs had been used long before. The *Schneller* [♪] is a miniature main-note trill, the *Pralltriller* (hereafter "prall trill") is often a miniature upper-note trill [♪] , but many writers, old and modern, use this term as a synonym for the *Schneller* with or without a two-note suffix.

Whenever a main-note trill is appropriate and there is neither time nor need for more than one alternation, the *Schneller* can be used. By the same token, an onbeat four-note prall trill can take the place of an appoggiatura trill, and a grace-note propelled *Schneller* [♪] that of a grace-note trill. For Bach it does not seem necessary to make a categorical distinction between *Schneller* and prall trill on one side and the regular trill on the other side. For J. S. Bach the difference between them is by all indications only in size, not in kind, just as there is no categorical difference between the one-stroke mordent and the two- or multiple stroke one. There is, on the other hand, reason to differentiate for Philipp Emanuel and his followers, as will be discussed below.

Paul Badura-Skoda lavishes unusual attention on the prall trill in J. S. Bach, and I am not sure that such emphasis is warranted. Bach gave no hint—as for instance by a distinctive symbol—that he considered the miniature trill an ornament in its own right. By considering and treating the one- or two-alternation trill simply as a short version of the regular trill, we simplify the trill problem in Bach without, I trust, cutting any corners.

A good illustration of the use of the *Schneller* is given in Ex. 28.14a, from the Organ Chorale "Christ lag in Todesbanden." Here the trills and mordents are used in the Italian tradition of counterparts, as inversions of each other, the mordent for an approach from below, the trill for an approach from the same pitch or from above. In this role the trill has to start with the main note; and owing to the lack of time both graces have to be of the one-stroke variety—that is, *Schneller* and simple mordent.[5] Were the note values doubled, the corresponding ornament pairs would be two- or three-alternation trills and mordents. They would still be the same ornaments, only longer.

EXAMPLE 28.14.   Bach, Organ Chorale, "Christ lag in Todesbanden," BWV 718

The preceding passage is a good example for indicated anticipation. If performed on the beat, the graces would obscure the rhythm since the organ cannot accent the beats to counteract the weight that the graces lend to the offbeats. The ear would perceive [music], whereas the anticipated rendition suggested in Ex. 28.14b will both clarify the rhythmic design and easily absorb the multitude of graces without a feeling of congestion.

*Anticipated Alternations.* Such anticipation of trills (or mordents), as suggested in Ex. 28.14b, will find many other applications. Generally, whenever the start of the alternations *on* the beat sounds ungraceful or stiff, anticipation should be considered.[6] A favorable context for anticipation is provided by supported appoggiatura trills for which Bach wrote out the appoggiatura in regular notes, [symbol], rather than by symbol, [symbol]. Whether the slur is marked or implied, appoggiatura and trill belong together as *one* single ornament. Because of this ornamental unity, the metrical notation is only approximate: there is no mathematical division between the two components, and the alternations will often to good advantage begin before, once in a while after, the notational dividing line, and often they will best be completely anticipated. Take the case of Ex. 28.15a, from the Fourth Organ Sonata. Delay is favored here by those who insist that the auxiliary must sound on the beat, as shown in Ex. 28.15b. Yet here this solution makes little sense, because in the absence of a clarifying beat a delay confuses the rhythmic perception. To start the trill *on* the beat is better but not good: the trill will act as accent on the appoggiatura's resolution when the latter ought to taper off. Anticipation (Ex. 28.15c) seems preferable because it clarifies the rhythm, does justice to the trill, and gives no false emphasis.

EXAMPLE 28.15.   Bach, Fourth Organ Sonata, BWV 528/4

***The Grace-Note Trill.*** Modern scholars have so far overlooked the grace-note trill as an important element in Bach performance, neither acknowledging that Couperin's *tremblement continu* was of the grace-note variety (as were presumably many of his shorter trills as well) nor recognizing that to start a trill "with the upper note" does not always mean "on the beat." We have seen in Ex. 28.5c Bach's written-out grace-note start of a long trill with implied acceleration. In the Organ Chorale "Nun komm, der Heiden Heiland," Bach offers further evidence. Bach wrote measure 5 as shown in Ex. 28.16a and measure 28 as given in Ex. 28.16b. The unquestionable grace note in measure 5 clarifies its analogous use with the trill in measure 29.

There are many cases in which an upper-note start seems desirable but in which an appoggiatura seems improper. A frequent context are trills preceded by their tied main note, as for instance in Ex. 28.17, from the Third Organ Sonata. A start with the auxiliary on the beat is here

EXAMPLE 28.16.   Bach, Organ Chorale, "Nun komm, der Heiden Heiland,"
BWV 659

doubly undesirable: first because of the offensive open octaves, second,
because an appoggiatura in the middle of a tie makes little sense. There
are three possible solutions: grace-note start, full anticipation, or delayed start. Delay is possible here because the beat is articulated in the
bass, thus preventing a rhythmic ambiguity. Yet in this spot the grace-
note alternative might be the best choice. In many similar situations the
grace-note solution will serve well though the two other alternatives
deserve consideration.

EXAMPLE 28.17.   Bach, Third Organ Sonata, BWV 527/1

***The Appoggiatura Trill.***  Many scholars and many "early music specialists" consider the appoggiatura trill to be the only legitimate design for
Bach's trills. They base their belief mainly on the autograph authority of
the trill model in the "Explication" and in the second place on French
ornament tables while claiming that Bach's ornamentation was entirely
French-oriented. The severe limitations of Bach's models were discussed
at some length in chapter 24, and the arguments of the present chapter
should suffice to question the idea of Bach's exclusive French orientation. As to those who invoke Philipp Emanuel's prescriptions, it should
not be necessary to restate the pitfalls of applying the son's principles to
the father's music. Yet it is quite certain that the appoggiatura trill in
both its simple and supported forms did occupy an important place in
Bach's music. The question is when and where it was used. No clear and
authoritative answer is possible; but it seems most probable that the
simple form was likely to be used whenever a very brief appoggiatura
could be substituted for the trill. Frequent among such contexts are
cadential trills on notes of relatively short duration, such as for instance
the trill in Ex. 28.18a, from the Fifth English Suite, and innumerable

similar cases. Whenever two trills follow one another in a cadence, it may sometimes be advisable to vary their style. In Ex. 28.18b, from the Two-Part Invention No. 7, the first of the trills, on a dissonant main note, may be better if played as a main-note or grace-note type in order to preserve the dissonance, and only the second one as an appoggiatura trill. By analogy, the supported appoggiatura trill was likely to be used whenever a slightly longer appoggiatura could be substituted for the trill.

EXAMPLE 28.18.　Bach

a. Fifth English Suite, BWV 810　　　b. Two-Part Invention, No. 7, BWV 778

As to the supported appoggiatura trill, Bach wrote out innumerable occurrences in regular notes, which were necessary whenever the desired appoggiatura was too long to be understood by a symbol. See, for instance, Ex. 28.19, from the Fugue in B Flat Minor of *WTC II*. The half-note appoggiatura had to be spelled out since none of Bach's symbols could be so interpreted. Here, incidentally, there are various ways to render the trill. It could start on the beat with its main note, it could be fully or partially anticipated, or it could enter with delay since the beat is articulated by other voices. Bach also wrote out many much shorter appoggiaturas, often, so it seems, to safeguard his melodic and polyphonic intentions.

EXAMPLE 28.19.　Bach, Fugue in B Flat Minor, *WTC II*, BWV 891/2

In the "Explication" Bach had two synonymous keyboard symbols for the supported appoggiatura trill (see Ex. 28.7c and 28.7d), which he called *accent und trillo*. The first, with the hook symbol before the note head, is rare in his autographs; the second, with the vertical stroke at the start of the *chevron,* is less rare but still infrequent. In accord with the basic shortness of Bach's symbolized appoggiaturas, the support indicated by the two signs is never long, as is confirmed by musical evidence in many of their occurrences. Some of these cases suggest that the symbols stood not necessarily for an appoggiatura start but rather for a start with the upper note whereby the latter could be, and often was, an appoggiatura in accord with Bach's model but could also be a grace note if the circumstances favored such interpretation. For a characteristic illustration, see Ex. 28.20a, from Prelude No. 4 of *WTC I,* where the *Vorschlag,* if done on the beat as an appoggiatura, has to be shorter than an eighth note in order not to interfere with the fast-moving polyphonic rhythm of the bass. Anticipation is a distinct possibility here since it would help to clarify the harmonic progression against the tie in the bass. Anticipation is advisable in Ex. 28.20b, from the Organ Chorale "Allein Gott" to avoid open fifths. In Ex. 28.20c, from the Aria of the "Goldberg" Variations, the rather conservative Walter Emery finds it "not impossible" that both the little *Vorschlag* note and the *Vorschlag* opening of the trill called for by the sign should be played as grace notes ("Nachschläge" in his terminology), and he also questions, I believe with good reason, the "awkwardness" of the "orthodox" supported appoggiatura interpretation of the same *accent und trillo* symbol in Ex. 20.28d from the Organ Chorale "Komm heiliger Geist" (BWV 652, mm. 15–18; *Bach's Ornaments,* 60–61).

EXAMPLE 28.20.   Bach

a. Prelude No. 4, *WTC I,* BWV 849 (aut. P 415)

b. Organ Chorale "Allein Gott," BWV 663 (aut. P 271)

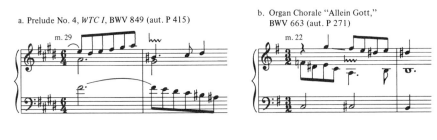

c. "Goldberg" Variations, BWV 988

d. Organ Chorale "Komm heilger Geist," BWV 652

A third, and much more frequent, symbol that is used for all media to indicate the start of the trill with the upper note, but not listed in the "Explication," is the trill sign preceded by the little *Vorschlag* note: . It too can cover the range from short appoggiatura to grace note.

For the latter we find graphic confirmation in a spot from the Christmas Oratorio, given in Ex. 28.21a, where in a unison passage of oboe and violins, a *Vorschlag* before a trill is written by symbol for the violins and written out in anticipation for the oboe.

EXAMPLE 28.21.   Bach

a. Christmas Oratorio, BWV 248/42

b. Concerto in D Minor for Two Violins, BWV 1043/3

A grace-note interpretation also seems indicated in the passage of Ex. 28.21b, from the Concerto in D Minor for Two Violins. An appoggiatura interpretation would weaken the melody: its bold ascent and dissonant leap into the leading tone would be transformed into a plain broken triad, the leading tone deprived of its tension, and its resolution anticlimactically anticipated. By contrast, the grace note, with its unaccented little snap, highlights the pungency of the accented leading tone.

**Unwritten Trills.** Bach's habit of writing out embellishments that other composers left to the discretion of the performer often did not extend to the cadential trill. The latter was such a standard procedure that Bach failed in many instances to mark a symbol, taking the addition of a trill for granted. This trill was presumably often an appoggiatura trill but did not have to be. There is no genuine evidence for the modern idea that appoggiatura trills are indispensable for Bach's cadences.

**The Suffix.** Many of Bach's trills end with a suffix of one or two notes. Although often notated, often it should or may be added without specification. In keyboard music only, Bach uses from time to time the symbol ∿, called in the "Explication" *trillo und mordant* (see above Ex. 28.7b), hence a trill with a suffix of two notes. For all media Bach often writes out the suffix in regular notes and practically never with the two little unmetrical notes of Couperin.

Even when not marked, an added suffix seems desirable when the straight trill would sound too angular or too bare with no apparent reason that such an effect was intended. The decision must be one of personal judgment. Bach's failure to indicate a suffix must not be interpreted as a rejection of this often desirable, sometimes indispensable ornament.

*The Alternations.* The speed of the alternations should vary according to the character of the piece, the pitch (slower for lower pitches), and the acoustics (slower in a live room). They need not last for the whole length of the note but may often stop for a rest point, even when followed by a suffix. For longer trills a slightly slower start and gradual acceleration will often be pleasing, provided this device does not congeal into a mechanical formula.

To summarize the preceding points, it is mistaken to believe that all of Bach's trills have to start with the upper note, let alone on the beat. A powerful and long-standing Italo-German tradition, together with much musical evidence, make it probable that Bach's trills frequently started on the main note. It is possible—though absolutely unprovable—that the greater part of Bach's keyboard trills started with the upper note; but it is likely that a large percentage of these trills were not of the appoggiatura but of the grace-note type. The trills preceded by one of the three *Vorschlag* symbols are the only ones for which the start with the upper note is obligatory. It is incorrect to assume that these symbols always stood for a supported appoggiatura trill and that the support had to be "overlong" according to Berlin formulas.

The main problem centers on the proper starting style. Although no rules can be given, the following procedure is recommended. Leave out the trill and consider whether a *Vorschlag* could be properly added to the naked note, and if so what kind of *Vorschlag*. If an appoggiatura of moderate length would be fitting—of a kind that could be understood by Bach's *Vorschlag* symbols—so also would a corresponding appoggiatura support of the trill; if a short appoggiatura is appropriate, a plain appoggiatura trill without support or with a short one will suggest itself; where a grace note seems best, a grace-note trill will be the preferred choice. Where no *Vorschlag* will fit, a main-note trill will be in order; if starting the alternations on the beat seems constrained or angular, anticipation of part or all the alternations should be considered. When test results overlap, more than one choice will be fitting. But in the end, musical intelligence and judgment cannot abdicate their responsibility here or elsewhere in the field of performance.

## The German Trill in the 18th Century

The Baroque–galant stylistic schism that divided Germany in the Bach era was paralleled by analogous contrasts in ornamental practice, to which the trill was no exception. Simultaneously with the freedom claimed for this grace by Bach and many other German masters of the older school, as well as by Italians and Italianate Germans, we find the emergence of new galant fashions that narrowed the scope of this ornament and prepared its hardening by the Berlin disciplinarians.

Theophil Muffat, Georg's son, showed the new trend in his extensive table of 1736 (see above, p. 333), in which all ornaments start on the beat and all trills start with the upper note. At just the same time, however, many composers of the older school, among them the brothers Graun and Christoph Graupner, followed an Italianate style and showed no indication of having adopted the new French-derived ornamental fashions. Telemann, who was more cosmopolitan and—not unlike Bach—had absorbed both Italian and French influences, showed in his demonstration of plain and ornamented melodies on various occasions embellishments in the form of main-note supported trills.[7]

Mattheson too, in 1739, did not seem to adopt French keyboard patterns for the trill. He defines the trill as the very fast, sharp, and clear alternation of two neighbor tones but seems unconcerned about its start. French singers, he tells us, prefer a rather slow trill, whereas the Italians render their regular trills (*gemeine Triller*) very fast, strong, and short, except when they first hold either of the two tones. He refers here clearly to either main-note or appoggiatura support. His explanation and illustration of the *ribattuta*, a dotted pattern that gradually accelerates and "finally ends in a regular trill," identifies the latter as a main-note trill. Moreover, his explanation of trill chains is compatible only with main-note types (*Vollkommene Capellmeister*, pt. 2, chap. 3, pars. 27–37).

Hartong (whose first name is unknown) published in 1749 under the pseudonym "Humanus" a treatise that won high praise from the two eminent contemporary critics Adlung and Hiller. He explains the trill solely as main-note type with main-note emphasis (*Musicus theoretico-practicus*, 26). We can gather from the above that the French keyboard pattern, however strong its inroads, has by mid-century not yet swept the country.

***C. P. E. Bach.*** The trills, C. P. E. Bach says, "animate the melody and are therefore indispensable" (*Versuch über Art das Clavier* [1753], chap. 2, sec. 3); he does not mention enrichment of the harmony. The trill has to start with the auxiliary on the beat and for the regular type is to be sustained for the whole length of the note (in contrast to Couperin's and J. S.

Bach's *point d'arrêt*). The regular trill is marked for the keyboard with a three-waggle *chevron*, as shown in Ex. 28.22a with its realization. A *Vorschlag* symbol before the trill (Ex. 28.22b) indicates an appoggiatura support. It is not necessary for the regular, unsupported trill, where the upper-note start is understood.

Philipp Emanuel uses the two-waggle *chevron* to indicate a very short, very sharp, and fast trill, which he calls *Prall-Triller*, as shown in Ex. 28.22c (according to the revised explanation of the second edition). Its only context is said to be stepwise slurred descent. (The delay of the alternations by means of the tie serves to insure the upper-note-on-the-

Example 28.22.   C. P. E. Bach (1753)

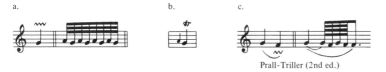

Prall-Triller (2nd ed.)

beat start of the trill proper.) It must be rendered vigorously and with such extraordinary speed that one has difficulty perceiving all the individual pitches ("dass man Mühe hat, alle Noten in diesem Triller zu hören"). It must truly crackle ("prallen"—hence the name). Philipp Emanuel considers this *Prall-Triller* to be "the most indispensable, most agreeable, but also the most difficult of all ornaments, one that adds vivacity and brilliance to the performance" ([1753], chap. 2, sec. 3, pars. 30–36).

Philipp Emanuel discusses the *Schneller* in chapter 2, section 8, where he explains this miniature main-note trill as an inverted simple mordent and marks it ♫♪ . He wrongly believed himself to be the first to describe this grace, though he did invent the term. He sees its main use for short staccato notes where it fulfills the function of a trill without its suffix; it never occurs within a slur.

As to the trill's suffix, it should be rendered as fast as the trill itself and connected to the following note with the greatest speed. When not marked it should be added whenever the ear judges it to be needed ([1753] chap. 2, sec. 3, par. 17).

*Marpurg.* Marpurg's trill too starts on the beat with the auxiliary (*Anleitung zum Clavierspielen*, 53–58). His is the often-cited statement that a trill is a series of "extremely fast repeated falling appoggiaturas" (53). He mildly deviates from C. P. E. Bach by stopping on a rest point; besides, he sees no reason in differentiating a two-waggle from a three-waggle symbol and uses both as synonyms. A brief trill slurred to its preceding note (C. P. E. Bach's *Prall-Triller*) can, so Marpurg says, often shed its first note (the tied one) and start "against the rule" with the main note (see Ex. 28.23a), thus forming the miniature main-note trill design of a *Schneller*. As we see from his illustration given in Ex. 28.23b, the same can be done when there is no slur from the preceding note. Marpurg also refers to C. P. E. Bach's description of the *Schneller* but shows it in a nonstaccato setting. From these illustrations it appears that in many circumstances C. P. E. Bach's *Prall-Triller* and *Schneller* merged for Marpurg into the identical design of the three-note miniature main-note trill, independent of articulation or a specific linkage to the preceding note.

EXAMPLE 28.23.   Marpurg (1755)

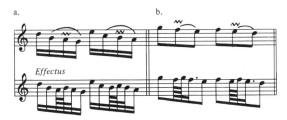

*Agricola.* The singer Agricola was another member of the Berlin school that was closely linked with C. P. E. Bach. As was pointed out before, he had translated Tosi's treatise with extensive comments and misinterpreted the latter's trill. In his, for mid-18th century Berlin, fashionable trill design with the auxiliary on the beat and continuing emphasis throughout the trill, he followed not what Tosi wrote but what C. P. E. Bach had to say (*Anleitung zur Singkunst*, 92–122). Like Bach, Agricola calls for the trill to be shaken for the whole length of the note, especially at cadences. As to an appoggiatura support, he says with good logic that such a support should be made only when, if there were no trill, an appoggiatura could be added to the naked note (109). He also reiterates the principle that one appoggiatura must not be superimposed on another one.

Interesting is his advice to singers on how to practice a trill because it seems to contradict the emphasis on the upper note. Agricola suggests the technique of the *ribattuta,* starting with slurred dotted pairs of notes (as illustrated in Ex. 28.24 [97–98]) and then gradually accelerating, whereupon both the dot and the two-by-two slurs disappear. A trill practiced by this method will emphasize the main note and unless prepared by an appoggiatura support is likely to place the main note on the beat.

EXAMPLE 28.24.   Agricola (1757)

EXAMPLE 28.25.    Quantz (1752)

*Quantz.* Quantz devotes the whole ninth chapter of his *Versuch einer Anweisung* to the trill. His basic trill model (Ex. 28.25), given in his Table 7.1, shows both a main-note rhythmic emphasis and a main-note start of the alternations. He does say that each trill starts with a *Vorschlag* from either above or below, while referring to the treatment of the *Vorschlag* in the preceding chapter of his treatise. There, as reported above, the *Vorschläge* were divided into *anschlagende* and *durchgehende*—that is, appoggiaturas and grace notes. Either of these *Vorschlag* types can introduce a trill; and many are the spots in Quantz's compositions where his principle that a *Vorschlag* before a written-out appoggiatura has to be anticipated leads to a grace-note trill. This trill type is also confirmed in several of his diminution tables, where detailed verbal directives about their dynamic treatment clarifies the grace-note character of several trills, notably those in *tierces coulées* contexts.

Elsewhere in the book (chap. 17, sec. 2, par. 24) he speaks of trills written over several fast notes, where "on account of the shortness of time, *Vor-* and *Nachschlag* are not always done." A Quantzian trill without a *Vorschlag* is a main-note type. Interestingly, the one trill design for which no record can be found in Quantz's discussions is the one considered by many to be the fundamental trill pattern of the century, the series of descending appoggiaturas.

*Leopold Mozart.* The tenth chapter of Leopold Mozart's *Versuch einer Violinschule* deals with the trill and is heavily indebted to Tartini. Although Mozart mentions no rule about an upper-note start, he shows Tartini's pattern of the start and continuing emphasis on the auxiliary (see Ex. 28.26a), understandably unaware of Tartini's main-note design in the letter to Signora Lombardini. Leopold does say that "all short trills are played with a fast *Vorschlag* and *Nachschlag*" (par. 6) as illustrated in Ex. 28.26b. Since his regular trill pattern starts with the upper note as a brief appoggiatura, the "fast" *Vorschlag* is probably identical with the "short" *Vorschlag*, which is defined as a grace note (chap. 9, par. 9) and will produce grace-note trills in such context.

Following Tartini, Leopold Mozart explains that a trill on a dotted note can be made on the dot, after sustaining the note proper (chap. 10, par. 19). The result is a main-note support. Main-note trills are furthermore implied in the explication of trill chains (par. 22) and most convincingly in their chromatic version (par. 24). Here Leopold's comment

EXAMPLE 28.26. L. Mozart

that the first and second fingers in moving up as well as down have to make the change imperceptibly, while the shaking finger must continue without interruption, makes technical sense only with a main-note start.

*Other Theorists.* After mid-century many German theorists followed the leadership of C. P. E. Bach, though their agreement is not always total. Most faithful among the followers were Adam Hiller in his three major treatises and Türk in his *Klavierschule*. The latter goes so far in extolling the dominant role of the auxiliary that he proposes to change the term "main note" (*Hauptnote*) to "written note" (chap. 4, sec. 3, par. 27). He also chides Marpurg for rejecting C. P. E. Bach's differentiation of the two- and three-waggle *chevron* and for his main-note interpretation of the *Pralltriller* (par. 55).[8]

Georg Simon Löhlein, in both his clavier treatise of 1765 and his violin treatise of 1774, gives the usual upper-note basic trill model but like Marpurg shows the *Pralltriller* (or, for the violin, *halber Triller*) in the form of the main-note *Schneller*.[9]

Interesting are the efforts of some writers to get away from metrical definition. Johann Samuel Petri, who had offered the traditional model of Ex. 28.27a in the first edition of his treatise (1767), changed to the unmetrical little notes of Ex. 28.27b in the second edition (1782). The little notes suggest a rhythmic flexibility that might include anticipation of one or more notes (*Anleitung zur Musik* [1767], 31; [1782], 154).

Johann Franz Peter Deysinger in both 1763 and 1788 shows the unmistakable grace-note trill by saying that the two notes of Ex. 28.27c "must be played or sung" as given in Ex. 28.27d (*Compendium musicum* [1763], 11; [1788], 11).

J. A. P. Schulz, whom we have met as the author of a brilliant article on performance ("Vortrag") in Sulzer's *Theorie der schönen Künste*, gives in an ornament table of his Clavier Sonata Op. 2 of ca. 1778 the main note model for both the short and the regular trill, as shown in Ex. 28.27e (cited by Rosenblum, *Performance Practices*, 243).

Among other writers who show the main-note pattern is Abbé Georg Joseph Vogler ("a key figure in music history" [*MGG*]), who illustrates in 1778 under the term of *Schnelzer* a brief, two-alternation main-note trill with suffix, and as *Triller* a lengthy main-note anchored trill prepared on the beat by an appoggiatura from below (*Kurpfälzische Tonschule*, Table 6).

EXAMPLE 28.27

a. Petri (1767)          b. Petri (1782)

c. Deysinger (1763, 1788) d.

e. Schulz (c. 1778)

C. F. W. Nopitsch, music director in Nördlingen, gives in 1784 a straight main-note design for a cadential trill while adding in the text that the auxiliary has the "privilege" of starting the trill (*Versuch der Singkunst*, 33).

The German Schwartzendorf, writing in France ca. 1791 under the name of Martini, shows, even for cadences, only the main-note trill (*Mélopée moderne*, 23ff.).

J. N. Hüllmandel, a student of C. P. E. Bach and a composer of note, writing in England ca. 1795, observes that "the shake begins indiscriminately with either of the two Shaken Notes, or sometimes by a Note under those of the Shake," and shows corresponding models (*Principles of Music*, 16ff.).

Similarly, the eminent theorist Heinrich Christoph Koch reports in 1802 on the disagreement about the main-note or upper-note start of the trill and expresses no preference. For the soloist, he says, it makes no difference; only in ensemble where trills occur in thirds and sixths does one have to agree on the way to start and on the speed. In keeping with this idea he shows a miniature trill, which he calls *Pralltriller* (without reference to C. P. E. Bach's definition), starting with either note (*Musikalisches Lexikon*, s.v. "Triller").

In 1791 Johann George Tromlitz devotes the whole eleventh chapter of his substantial flute treatise to the trill. His basic trill pattern is identical with Quantz's main-note design (see Ex. 28.25). Tromlitz makes a difference between a trill in mid-melody and one at its start. In mid-melody a trill is always preceded by a *Vorschlag* from either above or below—appoggiaturas according to his illustrations; but a preceding note that is slurred to the trill takes the place of the *Vorschlag* (*Ausführlicher Unterricht,* 269–70). (This statement is reminiscent of Rameau's explanation that a note—any note, so it seems—that is slurred to a trill serves as its preparation [ornament table to *Pièces de clavessin* of 1724].) A trill at the start of a phrase, Tromlitz continues, may receive a very short *Vorschlag* or may be made without one. A trill without a *Vorschlag* in Tromlitz's as well as in Quantz's sense is a main-note trill. And a "very short" *Vorschlag* before Tromlitz's main-note emphasizing trill is likely to be a grace note.

Very significant is Tromlitz's violent diatribe against the emphasis on the upper note, as explicitly demanded by Türk and implied by C. P. E. Bach, Marpurg, and their disciples. Tromlitz, mentioning Marpurg's "series of descending appoggiaturas" declares such emphasis to be unnatural because the main note has to be heard the same as if there were no trill; when instead we emphasize the upper note, the real melody note is "displaced and obliterated, the sequence of the melody torn, the proper melody defaced" (wird die Hauptnote verdränget und vertilget, die Folge des guten Gesanges zerrissen, und der eigentliche Gesang unkenntlich gemacht [272–73]). While the trill may be preceded by an appoggiatura from above, the alternations proper have to emphasize the main note.

Johann Georg Albrechtsberger (1736–1809), who was a teacher of Beethoven, in an undated autograph treatise shows the trill only in its main-note form (Ex. 28.28a).

Johann Peter Milchmeyer writes in 1797: "There are trills that start with the main note, but mostly they start with the note above the one written, except the embellished [verzierten] trills, many of which start with the written note." Ex. 28.28b shows a model for the appoggiatura trill, Ex. 28.28c one for the main note trill. "Embellished" are sustained trills set against a moving part in another voice (*Die wahre Art,* 42–43).

Justin Heinrich Knecht, in his time a "much-esteemed music director" (*MGG*), illustrates in 1800 first the "usual trill" in the standard upper-note-on-the-beat form, but for the "long trill" at final cadences he gives the main-note design of Ex. 28.28d, and for practicing the trill he proposes a slowly accelerating main-note pattern (*Kleine theoretische Klavierschule,* 60).

Andreas Dauscher, in a flute treatise of 1801, first offers Quantz's and Tromlitz's main-note model and then, like Deysinger before him, shows a grace-note trill with suffix, as given in Ex. 28.28e (*Kleines Handbuch,* 107–9).

Before turning to the Classical composers, let us briefly pause for a short overview of what we have learned so far from musical and theoretical evidence. We have seen on one side the strict principles of appoggiatura start and continuing upper-note emphasis, as formulated by C. P. E. Bach, Marpurg, Agricola (the "Berlin school") in mid-century, preceded by Theophil Muffat and followed by other north German

EXAMPLE 28.28

a. Albrechtsberger

b. Milchmeyer (1797)

c. Milchmeyer (1797)

d. Knecht (1800)

e. Dauscher (1801)

disciples, and most emphatically proclaimed by Türk near the end of the century. At the other pole we have seen a number of theorists, with some eminent names in their middle, who called for main-note start. Among them were Hartong ("Humanus"), Albrechtsberger, Abbé Vogler, J. A. P. Schulz, Nopitsch, Schwarzendorf ("Martini"). Two theorists, Dauscher and Deysinger, showed only the grace-note trill. A number of important writers are ambivalent and admit more than one trill design, including the main note start, among them Quantz, Leopold Mozart, Tromlitz, Hüllmandel, Koch, and Knecht. If we add, as Tromlitz has so eloquently pointed out, that the continuing emphasis on the upper note is unnatural for its melodic illogic, and if we further consider that the long-standing Italian tradition of the main-note trill–multiple mordent pairing was still very much alive, we must realize the need to revise drastically our still overwhelming reliance on C. P. E. Bach's and his disciples' rules for the whole 18th century, from J. S. Bach to Mozart. If we look for reasons for our inordinate overestimation of C. P. E. Bach's rules, we can probably find them partly in the importance of his treatise, partly in his considerable repute as a composer, partly in his being the son of his father, and, perhaps not least in the great convenience of having a simple hard-and-fast rule that can be applied mechanically to the music of a whole century (once I referred to this convenience as "instant authenticity"). Awareness of these circumstances should help us approach Haydn and Mozart with a more open ear and mind.

*Haydn's Trill.* Haydn's trills too are widely believed to have to start always with the auxiliary on the beat.[10] But there are countless spots in Haydn's music where a standard appoggiatura trill start makes little musical sense. For just one typical illustration, see Ex. 28.29, from the String Quartet in F, Op. 74, No. 2. Here the addition of brief appoggiaturas to the unison descending scale of the lower three instruments over the interval of an eleventh would make no melodic sense, and, consequently, appoggiatura-propelled trills would not either. Besides they would clash irrationally with the first violin's figurations that are anchored in the key unison notes.

EXAMPLE 28.29.   Haydn, String Quartet, Op. 74, No. 2/1 (Hob. III:73)

In addition to abundant musical evidence of this kind, there is evidence of a more direct nature. We are in possession of three surviving musical clocks for whose builder Haydn wrote, after 1790, a series of charming original pieces as well as a few arrangements of his earlier compositions. The recipient was Joseph Niemecz, a master builder of musical clocks who was librarian at Esterháza during Haydn's tenure there and who was most probably his composition student as well. Two of the three clocks were made in 1792 and 1793 respectively, hence during Haydn's absence in Vienna and London. The third clock is undated, but, since it contains a piece from 1796, it must have been made after that date. Volume 21 of the new *Joseph Haydn: Werke* (Munich, 1984) contains a collection of *Flötenuhrstücke*, edited by Sonja Gerlach and George R. Hill. The edition presents for these pieces both the original score and, above it, a transcription of the way the Niemecz clocks interpret it.[11]

By the time the undated clock was built, Haydn had returned to Vienna, where Niemecz had moved too in 1795 after Esterháza was abandoned. Under the circumstances it is hardly daring to speculate that the master craftsman solicited Haydn's advice for the making of the undated clock. Supporting this theory is the Fugue (No. II.7 in the Henle edition), as shown in Ex. 28.30a. The clock of 1793 misinterprets a clear directive by Haydn in his autograph, whereas the undated clock rectifies the mistake.[12] The probability is strong that the undated clock with its main-note trills and its anticipated turns and mordents is a truly authoritative document.

Observe that on both clocks all the trills in the fugue start with the main note, even though they occur after a falling third—that is, in a context conducive to the insertion of a connective pitch, hence favoring an upper-note start of the trill. Such a start, however, would have blurred the sharp contour of the fugue theme. (All the trills match those shown here in mm. 2 and 4.)

In the minuet numbered I.4 we see trills that on the clock of 1792 start with the auxiliary, on the undated, most likely more authoritative clock, on the main note (Ex. 28.30b, mm. 4, 6, and parallel spots). A long, sustained trill (mm. 9ff.) starts on both clocks with the main note and emphasizes the latter by its rhythmic disposition. This is only logical since the function of this trill is simply to sustain the pitch, not to strengthen the harmony.

From a thousand spots, such as the one shown in Ex. 28.29, where musical logic calls for main-note start, as well as from the testimony of the clocks made by a close associate of Haydn's—and most likely with the latter's collaboration—we are entitled to infer that many, perhaps most, of Haydn's trills were of the main-note type. In deciding an individual case it is advisable to look for guidance not to would-be rules but to musical sense.

*Mozart's Trill.* What has just been said about Haydn's trills applies with equal force to Mozart. There is no trill type that was out of bounds to him. It is a mistake with Mozart too to try to confine him to the upper-

EXAMPLE 28.30.   Haydn

a. Fugue (Henle II.7)

b. Piece (Henle I.4)

note-on-the-beat design, the "appoggiatura trill," let alone to the "series of descending appoggiaturas." That he used the appoggiatura trill is quite certain—but as one among various types, and probably far less often than is frequently assumed. The overview of theoretical thought given above should excuse us from the need for authorization when we try to explore different trill designs for their fitness in varied circumstances.

The start with the upper note on the beat, be it as brief as a single alternation or extended as "appoggiatura support," is certainly one of the options. Often Mozart specified the appoggiatura support and did so in his early years, until roughly 1778, with little notes, as in Ex. 28.31a, from the Violin Sonata in E Minor. In his later years his notation became more precise, and he preferred to write out the support in regular notes, as in Ex. 28.31b, from the Sonata for Two Pianos.

EXAMPLE 28.31.   Mozart

a.  Violin Sonata in E Minor, K 300c (304)/2     b.  Sonata for Two Pianos, K 375a (448)/2

c.  Piano Concerto in G, K 453/2                  d.              e.

f.  String Quartet in E Flat, K 421b (438)

There are no doubt many instances in which a supported or unsupported appoggiatura trill has a place without being specified. In order to identify them it is well to use the test (described in connection with Bach's trills) of leaving out the trill and considering whether or not the addition of a *Vorschlag* is desirable, and if so of what kind. The test will often favor, notably in slow movements, such an appoggiatura support, for instance in Ex. 28.31c, from the Piano concerto in G, as sketched in Ex. 28.31d. But another option, here and in many other similar cases, would be to start with the inverted turn of Ex. 28.31e, one of Mozart's favorite formulas, here played on, before, or astride the beat. A plain, unsupported appoggiatura trill might often be fitting in an allegro movement on cadences, as in Ex. 28.31f, from the String Quartet in E Flat. In this frequent cadential formula even a slight support would seem to be proper.

Whereas the appoggiatura trill in both the supported and unsupported style will find more than a few legitimate applications, and be more effective for not occurring too frequently, it quite certainly must not be used routinely. Rather, it is the main-note design that will turn out to be the most important one for Mozart's usage. Here we have by luck a demonstration by Mozart himself. In *Così fan tutte*, Guglielmo, in the aria "Rivolgete a lui lo sguardo" (later replaced by "Non siate ritrosi"), demonstrates on the words "se cantano con trillo" the *ribattuta*-introduced main-note trill of Ex. 28.32a. Apart from this lesson "from the horse's mouth," Mozart has given us many other demonstrations of passages in which only a main-note start makes musical sense. None is perhaps as forceful and incontrovertible as the one from the Concerto for Two Pianos shown in Ex. 28.32b, where a start with the auxiliary is out of the question.

EXAMPLE 28.32.   Mozart

a. *Così fan tutte*, "Rivolgete a lui lo sguardo"

b. Concerto for Two Pianos, K 316a (365)/2

This illustration is given by the Badura-Skodas in their book on Mozart interpretation to demonstrate an exception from upper-note start in Mozart (*Interpreting Mozart,* 115). By viewing it as an exception, the authors indicate that they consider the upper-note start to be the rule, the basic pattern for Mozart. They make it clear, however, that in "many passages . . . one can only begin a trill on the main note" (110), and they proceed to formulate a number of principles for identifying such cases. Among them are trills that are preceded by the slurred upper neighbor, trills on dissonant notes, in the bass, or at the end of rising scales, trills after a sharply attacked anacrusis on the same pitch, trills in chains, and, finally, trills in various special circumstances that are hard to classify. It is to this latter category that they assign example 28.31b (111–15).

Valuable as is this list of contexts favoring the main-note trill, my suggested test for identifying the best trill type is, I believe, more practical and more reliable. It is more practical because it does not require memorizing a list that must be passed in review in each case, and more reliable because it takes all possible starting styles into consideration, including the main-note, grace-note, and compound trill; moreover, by growing out of the individual situation it also points up those cases that admit more than one solution.

Paul Badura-Skoda then published an important essay on Mozart's trills in which he basically reaffirms the findings of the earlier book, but he expands, with many convincing examples, the role of the main-note trill and the *Schneller* while recognizing the grace-note trill as an "authentic" option in certain contexts.[13]

At the beginning of a piece or a section, an appoggiatura is normally out of place and even a grace-note not often fitting: hence a trill on the first note should usually be of the main-note type, as in Ex. 28.33a, from the Piano Sonata in B Flat. The same is true of many trills that start *ex abrupto* after a rest, as in Ex. 28.33b, from the Piano Sonata in D ("Dürnitz").

EXAMPLE 28.33.   Mozart

a.  Piano Sonata in B Flat, K 189 f (281)    b.  Piano Sonata in D, "Durnitz," K 205 b (284)/3

When trills are placed on a sharply profiled, angular theme, appoggiaturas are out of place since they would impair the intended profile, as for instance in Ex. 28.34a, from the Piano Sonata in A Minor. Often a triadic formula will be of the thematic essence and have a claim to melodic integrity. Such is the case with Ex. 28.34b, from the festive opening of the Sonata for Two Pianos. Where pitch repetition is clearly thematic, there is no place for an appoggiatura and often not even for the much less obtrusive grace note. Such is the case with Ex. 28.34c, from the Piano Concerto in E Flat, with its military, signal-like theme, or in Ex. 28.34d, from the Piano Sonata in D, K 284.

EXAMPLE 28.34. Mozart

a. Piano Sonata in A Minor, K 300d (310)

b. Sonata for Two Pianos, K 375a (448)/1

c. Piano Concerto in E Flat, K 482/1

d. Piano Sonata in D, K 205b (284)  Rondeau en Polonaise

e. *Die Zauberflöte*, K 620, I, 1

f. Piano Sonata in B Flat, K 189f (281)/3

g. Piano Sonata in F, K 189c (280)/1

A scalewise moving melody carrying trills offers a similarly characteristic profile that is sensitive to interference. In the passage of Ex. 28.34e, from *Die Zauberflöte*, appoggiaturas would weaken the sense of urgency conveyed by the chromatic ascent with its steep crescendo. A melody moving in a diatonic scale pattern will mostly be equally resistant to linear disturbance, as shown in Ex. 28.34f, from the Piano Sonata in B Flat K 281. It is for the very same reason that trills in chains (one of the items in the Badura-Skoda list) should be of the main-note type.

A trill on a leading tone, as we had observed on several occasions, will usually have to start with the main note to bring out the tension

inherent in its pull toward resolution. Occasionally, on notes of sufficient length, a grace note might still permit such sense of direction to be
felt, but an appoggiatura would break the tension by preempting the
pitch of the resolution. For shorter note values, such as those in Ex.
28.34g, from the Piano Sonata in F, K 280, a main-note start is as good
as mandatory.

The widely held conviction that at least a cadential trill has to be of
the appoggiatura type is contradicted by numerous items of musical
evidence. The final cadential trill of the Capriccio for Piano K 395 is given
in Ex. 28.35a. Here the lower neighbor is anticipated and the main note
falls on the beat in starting the trill, which in turn necessitates main-note
start of the trill on the leading tone in the left hand—an execution suggested to begin with by the leading tone–tonic sequence. In a number of
other cases the final trill is reached as the culmination of a rising scale,
be it chromatic, diatonic, or in broken thirds, all of which can logically
land only on the main note. Just one specimen is given here from the
Piano Concerto in E Flat K 482 in Ex. 28.35b (for more samples see
*OrnM*, Exs. 9.19–9.20). If we add to the evidence of these scale passages
the frequent cases of turn and slide prefixes, we cannot help speculating
that even Mozart's cadential trills may have been not very often of the
appoggiatura type.

EXAMPLE 28.35.   Mozart

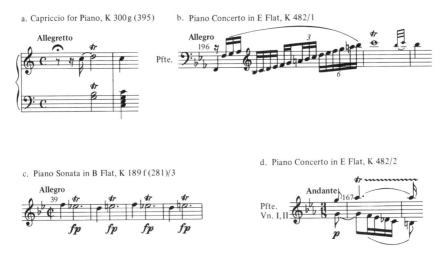

a. Capriccio for Piano, K 300g (395)     b. Piano Concerto in E Flat, K 482/1

c. Piano Sonata in B Flat, K 189 f (281)/3

d. Piano Concerto in E Flat, K 482/2

Dynamic markings can clearly suggest a main-note start. In Ex.
28.35c, from the Piano Sonata in B Flat K 281, the *fp* marks can refer only
to the main notes, admitting not even a grace note. An example of the
trill on a dissonance is shown in Ex. 28.35d, taken from the Piano Con-

certo in E Flat K 482; as the Badura-Skodas comment in connection with the same example: "the friction of the A flat with the suspended G must, of course, be preserved" (*Interpreting Mozart*, 133).

There are many additional contexts in which musical logic calls for a main-note start. These instances cannot be dealt with here for lack of space, but the interested reader can find a discussion of them in chapter 9 of *OrnM*. Considering the number, range, and variety of these contexts, and considering further that no instance seems yet to have been found in which musical reasons demand an upper-note-on-the-beat start that is not specified by the notation, we are entitled to the hypothesis that *main-note start was not an exception but the rule,* the basic pattern for Mozart. And whenever the start with the auxiliary seems desirable within a particular musical context, often the grace-note rather than the appoggiatura start is likely to be the preferred choice.

The use of this grace-note trill long before Mozart was documented in *OrnB*. In view of its attractive unobtrusiveness in many musical situations in which a start with the upper note is welcome but an appoggiatura out of place, its frequent presence in Mozart should come as no surprise. Although some sensitive performers have used it all along in appropriate places, modern scholarship has practically ignored it for Mozart as it did for Bach. The grace-note type will be generally advisable where upper-note start is either prescribed by symbol, as in Ex. 28.36a, from the Violin Sonata in B Flat, or in a context that favors the insertion of a grace, as in Ex. 28.36b, from the String Quartet in D Minor, where an appoggiatura is musically unwarranted. We also find a few spots where a grace-note trill seems almost mandatory, as in the case shown in Exx. 28.36c and 28.36d, from the Serenade in D, K 204. In Ex. 28.36c there is an inserted *Vorschlag* for which the NMA with good reason suggests a grace note; this grace note will then naturally transfer to the trill of Ex. 28.36d. By and large, grace-note trills are rarely indispensable but often desirable whenever our test either suggests or admits them.

In Mozart's trills too, as elsewhere, it is imperative to go by the music and not "by the book."

EXAMPLE 28.36.    Mozart

a. Violin Sonata in E Flat, K 317d (378)/3

EXAMPLE 28.36    *continued*

b. String Quartet in D Minor, K 417b(421)/4

c. Serenade in D, K 213a(204)/3                    d.

**Summary.** During the 17th century, German musicians followed the Italian lead with its main-note trill/multiple mordent duality. The north German organists, including Reincken and Buxtehude, were, so it seems, still under its influence. Around the turn of the 18th century the French upper-note keyboard designs began to spread into Germany and gradually gain ground. But for the early decades of the century the Italo-German main-note trill was still the leading model. In the ensuing mixture of two traditions through mid-century and beyond, one can roughly distinguish two main streams of development. One was linked to galant stylistic tendencies and favored both a start and continuing emphasis on the auxiliary, in a trend that led from French models and Theophil Muffat to C. P. E. Bach, Marpurg, and Türk. The other, older stream, generally linked to the Baroque tradition, issued from 17th-century Italo-German sources that retained their vital force in spite of having later absorbed French admixtures of varying strength. The followers of this stream, among them Bach and Handel, ranged freely over the field of the combined practices. Some of these freedoms survived the demise of the Baroque style among musicians who had a more cosmopolitan outlook. Quantz, whose trill emphasized the main note, used in addition the appoggiatura support, the grace-note trill, the preparation with a rising *Vorschlag,* and the main-note trill. Other musicians, among them J. A. P. Schulz, Abbé Vogler, Hüllmandel, Nopitsch, Martini, Tromlitz, Koch, and others, confirmed the continuing use of the main-note trill. When Haydn and Mozart used predominantly the main-note trill, they did so not as pioneers of 19th-century practices but as followers of the old stream of the Italo-German tradition, which never ceased to flow during the whole of the 17th and 18th centuries.

# 29

# THE COMPOUND TRILL

A grace can be joined to many another one to form a new combination. Some of these pairings have produced such felicitous designs that they have led to semipermanent unions. Among such unions we have already encountered the appoggiatura (or grace note) and trill, the rising *Vorschlag* and mordent (*port de voix et pincé*), and the trill and suffix. Three more mergers need to be discussed at this point because they play an important role in the music of important composers throughout the 18th century. They are the combinations of turn and trill (  ) , slide and trill ( ) , and mordent and trill ( ) . Under the collective term of "compound trills," these combinations shall be referred to as "turn-trill," "slide-trill," and "mordent-trill" respectively. The melodic shapes of these graces are sketched in Fig. 29.1.

FIGURE 29.1

a.  Turn-trill           b.  Slide-trill           c.  Mordent-trill

The performance problems of these trills center on the rhythmic shape of their start. The turn-trill can begin on the beat or have three, four, or even five pitches placed before the beat. The slide-trill too can either take the beat or precede it by one, two, or three of its initial pitches. The mordent-trill is the least problematic because it is usually written out in metrical notation and is practically always anticipated.

# *The French Compound Trill*

Although the slide trill may have made its first appearance in England, where in 1659 Christopher Simpson explained a grace called "cadent," shown in Ex. 29.1a, the compound trill in its various shapes is mainly of French origin, and it was d'Anglebert's models that Bach adopted and introduced to Germany. D'Anglebert, in his table of 1689, presents the patterns of Ex. 29.1b. He calls them *cadence* and places their start on the beat.

EXAMPLE 29.1

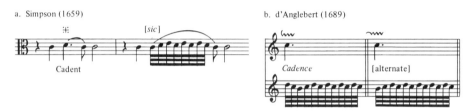

a. Simpson (1659)                          b. d'Anglebert (1689)

D'Anglebert's onbeat models were, as far as has been possible to ascertain, the first and the only ones of their kind in France. All the remaining French evidence points to anticipated designs.

In his gamba works, Marin Marais indicated the turn-trill with four little notes preceding the trill symbol (a hook after the note), as shown in Ex. 29.2a, and the slide-trill with two little notes as shown in Ex. 29.2b. Two or more little notes invariably had interbeat meaning in Marais, as proved in numerous instances in which, as in Ex. 29.2b, the downbeat rendition of the four little notes would make no musical sense; moreover, there are cases in which the four "unmetrical" little notes are nevertheless metrically divided into the measure explicitly showing their anticipation, as in the passage shown in Ex. 29.2c, from Bk. 4, No. 73, Caprice (the *e* indicates a swell, the vertical wavy line a one-finger, the horizontal wavy line a two-finger vibrato). Marais writes the mordent-trill usually in regular notes, always in anticipation.

In 1689 Boyvin (*Premier livre*) shows in regular notation the prebeat turn-trill of Ex. 29.3a; Grigny, in the book of 1699 (*Premier livre*) that Bach copied, gives the similar pattern of Ex. 29.3b; and Le Roux follows the same model in 1705, as shown in Ex. 29.3c (*Pièces de clavessin*). De la Barre, in Ex. 29.3d, from 1703 (*Pièces pour la flûte*), clarifies the anticipation of the little notes of the turn-trill in the first measure by their metrical notation, and of the slide-trill in the second measure by the premeasure placement of the two little notes.

EXAMPLE 29.2.  Marais (1686–1717)

a. II, *Folies*, Variation 21

b. I, Fantaisie, p. 11

c. IV, 73 Caprice

EXAMPLE 29.3

a. Boyvin (1689),
   *Dessus de Tierce*

b. Grigny (1699), Trio

c. Le Roux (1705), Prelude

d. De la Barre (1703), Prelude

Once in a while Couperin writes out in regular notes a prebeat turn before a trill (e.g., in the bass of the Gigue [*Pièces de clavecin*, bk. 2, *Huitième ordre*] m. 37); but much more frequently he writes the turn with four little notes whose prebeat meaning seems clear simply from their graphical image but is further confirmed in a number of passages such as the one of Ex. 29.4. This example is particularly instructive because it proves the need for full *five*-note anticipation including the trill's auxiliary along with the turn. In the sequence shown, the left-hand part alternates two mordent-trills with two turn-trills. In both turn-trills (mm. 19 and 21) an onbeat rendition of the turn, as well as of the auxiliary, would produce unacceptable fifths with the upper line. For the same reason, the trill on the second eighth of measure 17 has to be a grace-note trill (a main-note trill would be the only other, but less likely, alternative), providing along with measures 19 and 21 further evidence for Couperin's use of the trill with the anticipated auxiliary.

EXAMPLE 29.4.   Couperin, XXI, *La Reine des Coeurs*

Since Couperin's slides, as demonstrated before (chap. 26), were played in anticipation, it would be expected that this design would apply as well to his slide-trills written with two little notes (e.g., in bk. 2, *Septième ordre*, "Les délices," m. 15, or bk. 3, *Treizième ordre*, "L'enga-geante," m. 32). This execution is confirmed both by Nicolas Siret, who belonged to Couperin's circle, and by François d'Agincour, who prided himself on not having deviated from the manner of playing that Couperin had "so well defined and characterized" (si bien désignée et ca-ractérisée). Siret writes the two little notes of the slide-trill in several instances before the barline (Ex. 29.5a) and the turn-trill with written-out anticipation of the turn (Ex. 29.5b; *Pièces de clavecin* [ca. 1716]). D'Agin-cour too writes the slide notes before the barline, as shown in Exx. 29.5c and 29.5d (*Pièces de clavecin*, Premier livre [1733]).

Rameau most probably fell into the same pattern, as suggested by Ex. 29.5e, where onbeat rendition of the slide notes would produce unlikely fifths. As to Rameau's turn-trill, the two examples 29.5f and 29.5g show the anticipation of the turn, the first with regular notes, the second with a turn symbol.

In perhaps the first theoretical discussion of the turn-trill after d'An-glebert's table, La Chapelle shows in his treatise of 1736 the two-mea-sure passage of Ex. 29.6 in three versions (a, b, and c). First each note is treated as a structural unit and independently syllabified (a); second, the three eighth notes of the first measure and the four sixteenth notes of the second measure (the turn) are viewed as ornamental and pro-nounced with a single syllable (b); third, the melismas are written as ornamental small notes. The prebeat position of the symbolized turn can be inferred from the apparent acoustical identity of the three versions. I found not a single instance in French theory or practice that matched d'Anglebert's downbeat models. It is possible that in performance d'An-glebert himself deviated from his models, as he was shown to deviate from his onbeat model of the *port de voix*.

EXAMPLE 29.5

a. Siret, Sarabande grave

b. Siret, 1ᵉ Courante

c. D'Agincour, II, *Le Précieux*

d. D'Agincour, IV, *Les Violettes fleuries*

e. Rameau, *L'Entretien des muses* (1724)

f. Rameau, *Pièces de clavessin,* Allemande

g. Rameau, *Nouvelles suites,* Allemande

EXAMPLE 29.6.   La Chapelle (1736)

Sol sol fa sol  ut ut si la si si      Sol  sol        ut ut        si        Sol  sol        ut ut        si

## Bach's Compound Trill

The compound trill came to Germany with the influx of French ornamental fashions in the early years of the 18th century. Bach was if not
the first then certainly among the first German composers to use these
French graces systematically. He became acquainted with them through
d'Anglebert's table, which he copied at an early stage of his career. In
his "Explication" he reproduced d'Anglebert's models of the slide-trill
and the turn-trill under the collective term of *Doppelt-cadence* (Ex. 29.7).

These are again strictly keyboard symbols. For melody instruments

Bach writes the turn-trill always in regular notes  .

EXAMPLE 29.7.   Bach, "Explication"

He sometimes writes the slide-trill in regular notes

as well, but more frequently he uses either little notes [image] or the slide symbol [image] . Only a small sampling of written-out turn- or slide-trills can be given here (for many more specimens, see *OrnB*, chap. 33). Examples 29.8a and 29.8b show turn-trills from the Sonata in G for Gamba and Clavier and *The Musical Offering* respectively. Slide-trills with two written-out notes—where the auxiliary may or may not have been placed on the beat—are given from the Christmas Oratorio (Ex. 29.8c) and from the First "Brandenburg" Concerto (Ex. 29.8d). Slide-trills written out with three notes, including the anticipated auxiliary, are shown from Cantata No. 47 (Ex. 29.8e) and Cantata No. 63 (Ex. 29.8f).

EXAMPLE 29.8.   Bach

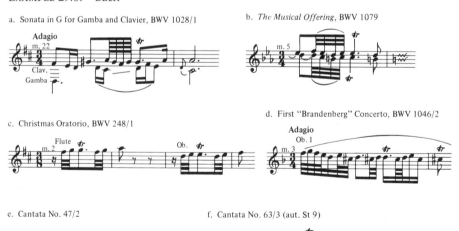

a. Sonata in G for Gamba and Clavier, BWV 1028/1

b. *The Musical Offering*, BWV 1079

c. Christmas Oratorio, BWV 248/1

d. First "Brandenberg" Concerto, BWV 1046/2

e. Cantata No. 47/2

f. Cantata No. 63/3 (aut. St 9)

It is significant that seemingly all the turn-trills as well as all those slide-trills written in regular notes show the turn or the slide in anticipation. *Not one instance was found in which Bach writes out a pattern resembling his models from the "Explication."* From that evidence alone it seems safe to infer (1) that the slides in the slide-trills notated with the *custos* symbol were also most often anticipated and (2) that even on the keyboard the *doppelt-cadence* should be rendered with much greater flexibility than is commonly done. With this kind of flexibility one or more or even all the notes of the prefix plus the auxiliary (à la Couperin) could then move across the beat.

The need for such partial or total anticipation can be seen in Ex. 29.9, from the trio sonata of *The Musical Offering,* where three out of four slide-trills, written with little, hence metrically ambiguous notes, would produce offensive parallel fifths if played on the beat (two are shown here, the third is in m. 26).

EXAMPLE 29.9. Bach, *The Musical Offering*, trio sonata, BWV 1079/8

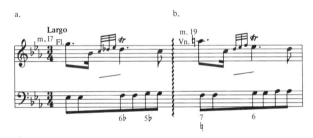

Often purely musical considerations will call for similar adjustments. In measure 3 of the Aria of the "Goldberg" Variations (Ex. 29.10a), the conventional rendition of the turn-trill, as indicated in Ex. 29.10b, obscures the thematically essential tone repetition and invests the second tone with an appoggiatura quality where an appoggiatura is out of place. Three-note anticipation, as suggested in Ex. 29.10c, offers a solution that graces the melody without impinging on its essence. It must be clear that for the rendition of Bach's compound trills, too, our guides must be imagination and musical judgment, not pedantic adherence to the book models.

**The Italians and Handel.** In Italy the compound trill was not a standard ornament. We do find sporadic traces of the anticipated slide-trill in Geminiani and Tartini but seemingly no turn-trill, the most typically French member of the family.

Handel, following Italian procedures, rarely uses any compound trills, and it is not surprising that the few we do find are in his French-oriented harpsichord pieces. In the first movement of his second Harpsichord Suite, we find slide-trills written out in regular notes in both the

EXAMPLE 29.10.　Bach, "Goldberg" Variations, BWV 988, Aria

a.

b.

c.

prebeat style (Ex. 29.11a) and the onbeat style (Ex. 29.11b). We find the same two styles represented also in the Air from the third suite. Clearly, Handel, like Bach, did not limit himself to only one design.

EXAMPLE 29.11.　Handel, Harpsichord Suite, No. 2/1

***The German Compound Trill.*** Theophil Muffat included in his extensive table of ca. 1736 only the slide-trill, which he presents in onbeat style, in keeping with the rest of his models.

C. P. E. Bach's models for the compound trill, shown in Ex. 29.12a and 29.12b, are practically the same as his father's (except for being slightly unmetrical). As usual, the symbols are only for the keyboard. For other media these designs have to be indicated with the help of little notes. To Philipp Emanuel the models mean literally what they say, as can be seen from his comments on Ex. 29.12c: he points out that only a turn-trill or a regular trill should be used, and not a slide-trill, because the latter would cause forbidden parallels (*Versuch über Art das Clavier* [1753], chap. 2, sec. 3, pars. 22–29). Anticipation, which would avoid such parallels, was obviously unacceptable.

EXAMPLE 29.12.   C. P. E. Bach (1753)

Marpurg's models of the compound trill underwent an interesting change. In a table of 1749 he gave four types under the term *Der gezogene oder geschleifte Triller,* all responding to the same symbol ⌒ (the one used by d'Anglebert and Bach only for the slide-trill). Among them are the slide-trill and the turn-trill, shown in Ex. 29.13a and 29.13b. The two others are of nonstandard and rather awkward designs. Significant is Marpurg's specified anticipation of the little notes; he explains these ornaments as types "where, *before the beat starts,* a few neighboring notes are quickly touched" (*Des critischen Musicus,* 1:58ff. and Tab. 2, Fig. 7).

EXAMPLE 29.13.   Marpurg (1749), *Critischer Musicus,* Table 2

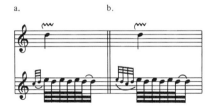

Six years later, however, in his clavier treatise of 1755, when Marpurg had come under the influence of C. P. E. Bach, his new models of turn- and slide-trill now fully agree with the latter's downbeat-only principles (*Anleitung zum Clavierspielen,* 57 and Tab. 5, Figs. 9 and 10).

In 1757 Agricola gives the same onbeat models as C. P. E. Bach but he says they are very rare in the vocal medium (*Anleitung zur Singkunst,* 101–2, 112–13). Löhlein, in four editions of his clavier treatise (1765–82), shows both a slide-trill with unmistakable anticipation of the prefix (Ex. 29.14a) and an onbeat turn-trill, mistakenly spelled out one step too high (Ex. 29.14b). He repeats only the slide-trill pattern in his violin treatise of 1774 (*Clavier-Schule,* pt. 1, chap. 6, par. 4; *Anweisung zum Violinspielen,* 46).

Petri, in the second edition (1782) of his general treatise, speaks only of the slide-trill and gives a design (Ex. 29.14c) that with its unmetrical little notes and its graphic disposition in groups of two-four-two, set apart by the alternating direction of the stems, strongly suggests the anticipation of the prefix and the *Nachschlag* treatment of the suffix (*An-leitung zur Musik* [1782], 155).

A few years later, in 1789, Türk once again follows C. P. E. Bach, except for one significant prebeat model (Ex. 29.14d), which he says is "not unusual," even if less "correct" (*Klavierschule*, chap. 4, sec. 3, par. 52).

EXAMPLE 29.14

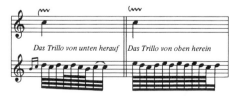

a. Löhlein, *Clavier-Schule*   b.
   (1765–1782)

*Das Trillo von unten herauf* | *Das Trillo von oben herein*

c. Petri (1782)

"is thus executed"

d. Türk (1789)

"not unusual:"   "instead of the more correct:"

*Haydn and Mozart.* It would seem that Haydn used compound trills only sporadically. In his early keyboard works he still used once in a while the Bachian slide-trill symbol, as shown in Ex. 29.15a, from the first movement of the Piano Sonata No. 3 in F. Its interpretation would seem to be amenable to various rhythmic options of downbeat or one- or three-note anticipation. More ambiguous is the use of the symbol in the slow movement of the same sonata (Ex. 29.15b), where in the second measure either the symbol or the *Vorschlag* from below would seem to be redundant. More frequent is the notation with the regular trill combined with a *Vorschlag* from below:  . We find it, for instance, in the slow movement, measure 51, of the Sonata in A Flat (Hob. XVI: 46) and frequently also in nonkeyboard works.

Mozart writes the compound trill fairly frequently in the forms of  for the slide-trill and for the turn-trill. He does so more

EXAMPLE 29.15. Haydn, Piano Sonata No. 3 in F (Hob. XVI: 23)

often for the keyboard than for other media. There are certainly some cases in which an onbeat rendition seems desirable, but there are numerous instances in which Mozart clarifies his preference for anticipation for these designs. Such anticipation is written out in regular notes in the cadenza to the Concerto in B Flat K 456 (Ex. 29.16a) and in the cadenza to the third movement of the Concerto in B Flat K 450 (Ex. 29.16b) for the turn-trill. Similarly, we find at the end of the cadenza for the Concerto in F K 459 the written-out anticipation of the turn-trill, as given in Ex. 29.16c. Commenting on such trills with prefixes of three notes, either small or large, Paul Badura-Skoda writes with good reason: "To begin the trills on the upper note, as unfortunately often happens, is a mistake" ("Mozart's Trills," 9–10).

In the Piano Sonata in D, K 205b (284), the unmistakable autograph alignment of the *f* sign with the trilled note in two successive measures, as given in Ex. 29.16d, signifies the trill's placement on the beat and hence anticipation of the prefix. An analogous alignment in Ex. 29.16e, from the "Hunt" Quartet, reveals the same dynamic-rhythmic disposition.

EXAMPLE 29.16. Mozart

a. Piano Concerto in B Flat, K 456, Cadenza    b. Piano Concerto in B Flat, K 450, Cadenza    c. Piano Concerto in F, K 459, Cadenza

d. Piano Sonata in D, K 205 b (284)/2

e. "Hunt" Quartet, K 485/1

Summarizing briefly, in France, d'Anglebert seems to stand alone with his downbeat models of the compound trill. It is symptomatic of his isolation that neither his patterns nor his symbols seem to have been taken up by any other French composer. Except for d'Anglebert, there is an apparent unanimity of all other French masters in favor of the prebeat rendition for all compound trills.

Bach adopted d'Anglebert's symbols for the keyboard and in theory also his models, giving them a new lease on life in Germany. In practice, there is good reason to assume that he treated the designs with great flexibility inasmuch as he wrote out the designs in regular notes for all other media and did so invariably in anticipation.

Handel, true to his Italian leanings, hardly ever used these designs. They seem to occur only sporadically in his French-oriented keyboard works. In them we find, written out, both the prebeat and the onbeat forms of the slide-trill as well as the prebeat form only of the turn-trill.

C. P. E. Bach was predictably uncompromising about the downbeat and influenced many subsequent writers, the last of whom was Türk, who, however, qualified this stance with a significant prebeat model of the turn-trill. Other theoretical prebeat patterns are still found in Marpurg in 1749, for the slide-trill in Löhlein, and quite certainly also in Petri in 1782. Mozart used both types of trills, and his written-out designs disclosed a distinct preference for anticipation.

# 30

# THE MORDENT

The mordent, or "the biter" (Fr. *pincé*, It. *mordente*, Ger. *Mordent*) in its usual meaning is an oscillation of the principal note with its lower neighbor; it starts and ends with the principal note. Its most common type has only one oscillation, but two or more are frequent variants.

The basic one-alternation mordent will often strike on the beat and follow with a fast alternation that produces a sharp "biting" accentual effect. Often, however, the simple mordent does not "bite" but has a melodic-connective rather than rhythmic-accentual function. This is mostly the case when it occurs between the beats or on a weak beat that the composer has not singled out notationally for special emphasis. Such a connective mordent will be unaccented and will tend to precede or follow the beat. A typical unaccented mordent is the one so frequently appended to a rising appoggiatura—the French *port de voix et pincé,* when ⌐♩⌐ may signify approximately ⌐♩♩♩⌐ , though many other rhythmic designs occur for this combination.

Not every grace called *mordent* or *mordente* belongs to the category dealt with in this chapter. The Italians in particular used the term *mordente* rather loosely and applied it to various graces that can produce a "biting" effect.

## The French Mordent

Nivers, in 1665, describes a grace that he simply calls *agrément*. His illustration (Ex. 30.1a), which shows at the same time the symbol and its realization, reveals a "prepared" mordent—that is, one preceded by its auxiliary (*Livre d'orgue,* Preface). Its rhythmic design is ambiguous.

Chambonnières sets a pattern by showing the mordent (*pincement*) with a single alternation on the beat, as given in Ex. 30.1b (*Pièces de clavessin*). Le Bègue gives the identical model in 1677 and Raison an analogous one pitched one step higher, showing his preference for a half-tone oscillation by sharping the auxiliary. D'Anglebert in 1689 presents both a simple and a double mordent (*pincé*) with the symbol of a hook after the note (Ex. 30.1c). His *cheute* (*port de voix*) *et pincé* has a long onbeat *port de voix* followed by an unaccented mordent, as shown in Ex. 30.1d (*Pièces de clavecin*). Dieupart in ca. 1702 (*Six Suittes*) and Le Roux in 1705 (*Pièces de clavessin*) give the same models.

EXAMPLE 30.1

a. Nivers (1665), *Agrément*

b. Chambonnières (1670),
   Le Bègue (1677)

*Pincement*

c. d'Anglebert (1689)

*Pincé*

d. d'Anglebert (1689)

*Cheute et pincé*

The mordent of the gambists is marked by a greater than usual confusion of terms and symbols. Some of the terms used were *batement* (Marais), *martellement* (Demachy), and *pincé* (Danoville); but these terms had different meanings for other writers. Among various symbols the more common ones were the plain or the slanted cross *before* the note: ₊♩ or ₓ♩. Generally, the French gambists favored a double or multiple mordent, rendered with great speed, faster than a trill.

Jean Rousseau, who provides no symbols for mordents in his gamba treatise of 1687, gives instead directives about their improvised use. Among others he stresses the close connection with the *port de voix*, which he says "must always end with a mordent" (*Traité de la viole*, 87).

In Marais's gamba works we find mordents preceded by a *port de voix* but also many plain, unprepared ones, in almost every conceivable location, on both strong and weak beats and even on subdivisions of beats, showing the versatility of the grace. This versatility extends to its rhythmic shapes. In many cases in which the mordent is placed on a strong beat, as in Ex. 30.2a, the intended rhythmic intensification suggests precise onbeat placement. On the other hand, a mordent on a weak beat, preceded by and slurred to an accented note, as in Ex. 30.2b, favors anticipation inasmuch as such mordents are purely connective graces closely related to the mordent sequel of an accented *port de voix*. Onbeat placement in such a context would produce an emphasis that does not seem appropriate here. Such unstressed mordents were most likely of the one-stroke kind, whereas the stressed ones, time permitting, seem to have leaned to multiple strokes.

EXAMPLE 30.2.   Marais

a. V, 20, Gigue

b. IV, 4th Suite, Gavotte

Jean Pierre Freillon-Poncein, in his oboe treatise of 1700, calls for the mordent (*battement* or *pincé*) to be executed with suddenness and great speed. His only illustration shows three anticipated mordents of the kind:  (*La véritable manière*, 20–21).

L'Affilard, beginning with the 1705 edition of his treatise, illustrates a grace (*hélan*) that combines the *port de voix* (*et pincé*) and an *accent*; in this grace the whole *port de voix et pincé* is anticipated:  (*Principes pour apprendre la musique*, 26–27).

Loulié, in his treatise of 1696, explains the mordent (*martellement*) as "two small, very light [i.e., very soft] sounds in the manner of the *chute* [2 *petits Sons fort legers en maniere de Chute*], one a step below the other, which precedes the note on which the mordent [symbol ( V  for a single, W  for a double mordent)] is marked" (*Éléments ou principes de musique*, 72). The comparison with a *chute*, which is always anticipated, and the "very soft" sound suggest at the least an unaccented rendition, and probably an anticipated one.

In his ornament table of 1713, Couperin shows the three types of mordents given in Ex. 30.3: the simple, the multiple, and the continuous one (*Pièces de clavecin*, bk. 1).

In his treatise of 1716/17 he adds that "the alternations and the tone on which they end must be comprised in the value of the principal note" (*L'art*, 19). This statement implies a start with the main note on the beat. Most of Couperin's mordents undoubtedly followed this rule. We can, however, expect exceptions for single mordents that, as in Marais, occur

EXAMPLE 30.3.   Couperin

on a light beat or between beats. In the case of Ex. 30.4a, for instance, the mordent is slurred to the preceding accented note one step below and is thus related to the *port de voix et pincé* figure with the mordent as unaccented *Nachschlag*-type appendix. A perhaps still more striking case of the anticipation of the mordents is shown in Ex. 30.4b, from the "Double du Rossignol." In a comment to this piece that calls for exquisite tenderness (*très tendrement*), Couperin writes: "In this *Double* one must not observe the beat too precisely, everything must be sacrificed to the *goût* for the proper expression, and care be taken to mollify the inflections marked by the mordents" (il faut . . . bien atendrir les accens marqués par des pincés). If the mordents were played strictly on the beats, they would harden and stiffen rather than "mollify" the inflections.

EXAMPLE 30.4.   Couperin

a. XXVI, Gavotte

b. XIV, *Double du Rossignol*

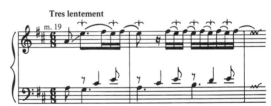

Rameau's ornament tables of 1706 and 1724 show the mordent only in its multiple form, as given in Ex. 30.5a (from 1724). For the *pincé et port de voix* he shows the emphasis on the *port de voix* and the unaccented mordent sequel. His symbol, for the keyboard only, is d'Anglebert's hook after the note.

For apparent deviations from these models, see for instance Ex. 30.5b, from the Fifth Concert (*Pièces de clavecin en concerts*; only the keyboard part is given). Here the *ports de voix et pincés* at numbers 1 and 3 coincide with plain mordents in the left hand, and some adjustment seems needed. Either the *port de voix* is anticipated and the mordents synchronized, or the whole combined grace is anticipated and the plain mordent done on the beat. At number 2 simultaneous mordents in parallel fifths were hardly intended. A possible solution would be anticipation of the mordent on the eighth note and onbeat execution of the left-hand mordent. For similar cases, see in the same volume "La La Poplinière," the mordents in measures 6, 8, 45, and 47.

EXAMPLE 30.5

a. Rameau (1706, 1724)

b. *La Marais* (1747)

*Pincé*      *Pincé et port de voix*

Dandrieu, in his tables of 1724 and 1739, shows a *pincé simple,* a multiple mordent (see Ex. 30.6a), and a *pincé et port de voix* with the latter apparently anticipated (Ex. 30.6b; *Premier livre de clavecin* [1724]; *Premier livre d'orgue* [1739]). David, in 1737, describes the mordent (*martellement*) as being *feint et précipité; feint* indicates great delicacy and thus suggests offbeat placement (*Méthode nouvelle,* 136).

Michel Corrette, in his flute treatise of 1735, mentions only the mordent (*martellement*) that is begun with a *port de voix.* Like Jean Rousseau before him, Corrette calls for the mordent to be executed with two or three little oscillations, "narrower and faster than those of a trill" (*Méthode pour la flûte,* 34–35).

Lacassagne, in his important vocal treatise of 1766, uses no symbol; his illustration, given in Ex. 30.6c, shows full anticipation of the double mordent (*martellement*) since the alternations belong to the quarter note D (the wavy line over the whole note stands for vibrato).

In his vocal treatise of 1775, Duval shows the grace (*martellement*) as a single alternation on the beat, yet by defining it as "a light inflection of the throat" (un léger coup de gosier) he suggests lack of emphasis.

EXAMPLE 30.6

a. Dandrieu (1724, 1739)      b.      c. Lacassagne (1766)

*Pincé simple*      *Pincé et port de voix*      *Martellement*

Explication

In France both keyboard players and gambists had a preference, time permitting, for the multiple onbeat mordent on strong beats. In contrast, on weak beats or between beats the mordent tended to be single and was presumably often anticipated to avoid an undesired emphasis. Whereas the keyboard players needed a sharply defined mordent on strong beats to clarify rhythm and meter on their accentless instruments, the same kind of crackling mordent is nonvocal, and the singers seemed more inclined to gentle inflections, which in turn favor unaccented placement in interbeat space.

## The Italian Mordent

For the Italian mordent of the 17th and the first half of the 18th centuries, we are dependent chiefly on what the German disciples of Italian practices have to tell us. Here we have many sources that will be presently reviewed. Their main feature is the pairing of *tremulo di sopra,* a main-note trill, and the *tremulo di sotto,* the multiple mordent. In Italy this parallelism survived until fairly late in the 18th century. For a long time the Italians lacked a specific symbol for the mordent, which was left to improvisation or played at the summons of a trill symbol.

After a long theoretical silence regarding the mordent, Geminiani in exact mid-18th century gives as a principal model a multiple mordent that he calls either *mordente* (*Art of Playing Violin,* 26) or "Beat" (*Treatise of Good Taste,* n.p.). As shown in Ex. 30.7, he uses an English symbol of two oblique strokes that was not adopted by his compatriots at home.

EXAMPLE 30.7.   Geminiani (1749, 1751)

Terminological confusion sets in when Tartini, ca. 1750, uses the term *mordente* for two different graces, namely the turn and the genuine mordent. What he says about the turn-*mordente* sheds light on the performance of the genuine mordent and needs to be reported here. He describes and shows the regular and the inverted turn as given in Exx. 30.8a and 30.8b. The three little notes, he says, have to be played with utmost speed, while the accent "does not fall on the three added notes but on the principal written note of the melody, so that the three added notes are sung or played *piano,* the principle note *forte*" (*Regole,* 17–19). These directives strongly suggest the anticipation of the little notes.

The second type of *mordente* is the regular mordent, which he shows with single and multiple alternations (Ex. 30.8c), while illustrating its use as shown in Exx. 30.8d and 30.8e, which reproduce Tartini's alignment. For its execution he gives the important directive that the grace is to be rendered "with the expression of the above mentioned [i.e., the turn-] *mordente.*" This means it is to be done *piano* with the utmost speed and with the accent falling on the principal note; in other words, it too will tend to be anticipated. Such anticipation in the case of Exx. 30.8d and 30.8e is fully in line with Tartini's previously reported principle (see above, p. 316) that genuine appoggiaturas are out of place in the context of evenly written notes, because they would prejudice the intended effect of evenness, and the *Vorschläge* in such settings have to be anticipated. In our two illustrations the evenness of the eighth notes (in terms of their starting points, of course) would be severely infringed by onbeat rendition of the double mordents.

EXAMPLE 30.8.   Tartini (c. 1750)

The old mirror-image pairing of main-note trill and mordent was still very much alive with Domenico Scarlatti. As discussed in chapter 27, his trill symbols ( ∿ or *tr* ) could stand for the mordent as well, and his term *tremulo* by itself, unless qualified by *di sopra*, was a multiple mordent.

We find this duality as late as 1775 with Manfredini's main-note trill, shown in Ex. 30.9a, and his corresponding mordent—using now the French symbol—in Ex. 30.9b (*Regole armoniche,* 26).

EXAMPLE 30.9.    Manfredini (1775)

a.

*Trillo*

b.

*Mordente*

In addition to these usually multiple mordent designs, the Italians developed a mordent pattern that is typically theirs, the one-stroke mordent preceded by a prebeat descending *Vorschlag:* ⟨symbol⟩ . This ornament, which I have called the "Italian mordent," has already been discussed in chapter 24, where it was mentioned in connection with the grace note, illustrated in Exx. 23.4a and 23.4b, and later with added trills in Exx. 27.5d and 27.6a.

## A Note on the English Mordent

Christopher Simpson, in his ornament table of 1659, shows a prepared multiple mordent that he calls the "shaked beat," as given in Ex. 30.10 (*Division-Violist*, 12). Playford then adopted the same model in his famous, much-reprinted *Introduction to the Skill of Musick* ([1674], 116).

EXAMPLE 30.10.    Simpson (1659)

shaked beat

Mace, in his lute treatise of 1676, describes a multiple mordent with a half step below and explains how the performer can lend it either a sharper or a softer articulation (*Musick's Monument*, 103).

## The German Mordent

Following closely their Italian models, the Germans continued, throughout the 17th century and even beyond, the complementary pairing of main-note trill and its inversion, the multiple mordent. They were considered the same ornament, the *tremulus:* the trill *ascendens,* the mordent *descendens.* Both start and end with the main note, the only difference being that the mordent had a distinct preference for half-tone oscillations.

Praetorius's model for the dual grace was shown in Ex. 28.1. The same or closely related models were given by Herbst in 1642 (*Musica practica,* 7, and again in 1650 and 1658), by Crüger in 1654 (*Synopsis musica,* 194), by Printz in 1678 (*Musica modulatoria,* 47), by Mylius in 1685, who used the *tr* symbol for the mordent as well as for the trill (*Rudimenta musices,* chap. 5, n.p.), by Falck in 1688 (*Idea boni cantoris* 100), by Beyer in 1703 (*Primae lineae,* 58), and in the same year by Murschhauser, whose model was given in Ex. 28.2a.

The sources so far quoted, which have all issued from the Italo-German tradition, all agree on multiple-alternation type in keeping with its trill counterpart. Then in 1696 Johann Caspar Fischer, in what may be the first French-oriented ornament table in Germany, showed Chambonnières's symbol ( ᪲ ) as well as his single-alternation model, as given in Ex. 30.11 (*Musicales Blumenbüschlein,* Preface). And twelve years later J. G. Walther showed in his early treatise of 1708 the same French symbol, which he used in all of his music.

EXAMPLE 30.11.   Fischer (1696)

*Bach's mordent.* Bach prescribed mordents only for the keyboard and used the French symbol ᪲ , which he transcribed in his "Explication," as shown in Ex. 30.12a; his model of the *port de voix et pincé* (*Accent und Mordant*) is shown in Ex. 30.12b. As with the trill, he does not mark chromatic alterations. In adding them the player has to be aware of the mordent's penchant to half-tone oscillations.

Although this single onbeat mordent may well be the design he most frequently used, here too Bach's mordent cannot be limited to the literal replica of the model. In view of Bach's Italo-German and French legacies, we have reason to assume that his mordent was changeable in both melodic and rhythmic design: that on longish notes or on very emphatic ones it could call for more than one alternation and that on occasion it could be anticipated. For instance, the starting notes of the Organ Toccata in D Minor, of the slow movement of the Italian

EXAMPLE 30.12.    Bach, "Explication"

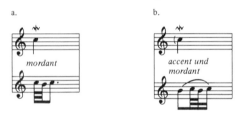

Concerto, and of the Organ Prelude in G Minor ("Fantasy" [BWV 542]), or the last note of the Organ Chorale "Komm, heiliger Geist" (BWV 652), might all benefit from double, perhaps even multiple alternations.

A long sustained mordent is actually required in the Gigue of the Sixth English Suite. Here the thematic material of the first part is exactly inverted in the second. As shown in Exx. 30.13a and 30.13b, the long sustained trills in the first part are logically inverted into similarly sustained mordents. This consistently literal inversion also establishes for the first part the main-note nature of the trill in the classic Italo-German complementary pairing of *tremulus ascendens* and *descendens*.[1] Another long mordent occurs at the start of the slow movement of the Clavier Concerto in D (a transcription of the Violin Concerto in E), where Bach's autograph, in the vein of Couperin's *pincé continu*, extends the mordent symbol with a wavy line for over two measures to emulate the long sustained note of the violin.

EXAMPLE 30.13.    Bach, Sixth English Suite, BWV 811, Gigue

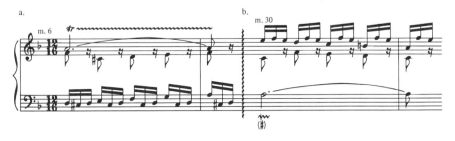

Concerning the rhythmic shape of the mordent, its onbeat design has no monopoly. Its offbeat potential has been revealed alone by the *Accent und Mordant* combination. As we have already noted, an onbeat mordent is unconvincing on light beats or on subdivisions of beats where its function is not accentual. A good illustration is the passage given in Ex. 28.14, from the Organ Chorale "Christ lag in Todesbanden," where miniature trills (*Schneller*) and one-stroke mordents alternate in their Italo-German inversion-pairings. In discussing this passage (p. 420), it was explained why it calls for anticipation of the graces, anticipation that both clarifies the meter and relieves the sense of stiffness that would ensue from onbeat rendition.

Another context frequently encountered in Bach's works in which anticipation of the mordent will usually be indicated is that of a genuine or a quasi-*port de voix et pincé* in which a long appoggiatura from below is written out in regular notes and followed by a mordent. In such cases the notation makes the mordent look like an independent ornament when in fact it is the junior partner in a combination grace, embodying the tapering resolution of the appoggiatura. Look, for instance, at Ex. 30.14a, from the Third Organ Sonata, where the rising appoggiatura resolves gently into a mordent. The mordent gracing the resolution will be better if done before rather than on the beat.[2]

Similar is the mordent in the first measure of the Aria from the "Goldberg" Variations (Ex. 30.14b). Though the second note g″, which is slurred to the following mordent, is not a genuine appoggiatura since it falls on a consonance, it is a heavy note, being the second beat of a Sarabande, leading to the lightest beat of the measure. We have here a quasi-*port de voix et pincé* where on the harpsichord an onbeat rendition of the mordent would impart undue weight to the third beat. Anticipation of the mordent, as sketched in Exx. 30.14c and 30.14d, would seem to be the preferable and more elegant solution.

EXAMPLE 30.14.   Bach

a. Third Organ Sonata, BWV 527/2

As to the *Accent und Mordant,* the above formula of the "Explication" (Ex. 30.12), which shows the appoggiatura on and the mordent off the beat, will be fitting mostly where there is enough space and where the combined grace does not collide with another moving part. For an illustration see Ex. 30.15a, from the Chorale Prelude "Wenn wir in höchsten Nöthen sein," with the suggested execution of Ex. 30.15b. Where, however, there is not enough space to accommodate the combined grace, as in Ex. 30.15c, from the same work, the *Vorschlag* has to be anticipated, as suggested in Ex. 30.15d.

EXAMPLE 30.15.  Bach, Chorale Prelude "Wenn wir in höchsten Nöthen sein," BWV 641

   Briefly, Bach's mordent, whether by itself or as sequel to the rising *Vorschlag*, had a wider range of rhythmic-melodic design than is usually assumed. The performer will have to decide whether a given phrase is best served by the intensifying effect of the onbeat or by the connective qualities of the prebeat or postbeat style; whether single or multiple alternations seem more fitting; and also whether there is reason for not raising the auxiliary to the half step below the main note.

***The Mordent After J. S. Bach.*** Theophil Muffat in ca. 1736 shows the single and double mordent as well as the mordent as sequel to an appoggiatura from below, the usual *port de voix et pincé* (*Componimenti*, Appendix). Mattheson in 1739 shows only the single mordent (with rhythmically ambiguous little notes) together with the *port de voix et pincé*, which he calls *Accent mit dem Mordanten* (*Vollkommene Capellmeister*, pt. 2, chap. 3, pars. 53–59).
   In 1753 C. P. E. Bach sees the main function of the mordent in connecting notes, in filling them out, and in rendering them brilliant. The mordent can be multiple with a three-waggle symbol or simple with the standard two-waggle symbol, shown in Exx. 30.16a and 30.16b. It is best

used, he says, in upward-stepping or leaping notes, but rarely on downward leaps, and it never occurs on descending seconds. A multiple mordent must come to a definite rest before the note is over. In a *port de voix et pincé* (*der Mordent nach einem Vorschlage*), as shown in Ex. 30.16c, the mordent is slurred softly to the preceding *Vorschlag* according to "the rules for the appoggiatura" (*Versuch über Art das Clavier* [1753], chap. 2, sec. 5).

EXAMPLE 30.16.   C. P. E. Bach (1753)

Marpurg in 1755 shows both one-stroke and two-stroke designs and differs from C. P. E. Bach only in using the two- and three-waggle symbol interchangeably (*Anleitung zum Clavierspielen*, Tab. 5, Fig. 11).

Quantz's remarks on the mordent are brief and somewhat confusing, partly because he treats mordent-related figures under two terms. He first illustrates what he calls the *pincé*, as given in Ex. 31.17a, showing it on an upbeat and seeming to suggest that the whole grace, including the *Vorschlag*, might be unaccented. Under the term *battemens* he shows the two patterns of Ex. 30.17b; their intended rhythmic design is uncertain.

EXAMPLE 30.17.   Quantz (1752)

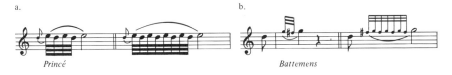

Leopold Mozart's discussion of the mordent is both interesting and important. Writing in the spirit of Tartini, he defines the mordent as two or three little notes "that very fast and softly grab hold, so to speak, of the principal note but disappear immediately so that the principal note alone is heard strongly" (*Versuch einer Violinschule*, chap. 11, par. 8). "Very fast and softly" are the key words. A few paragraphs later he reemphasizes the decisive dynamic design: "the loudness of the tone falls on the note itself: the mordent by contrast is slurred to the latter very softly and very fast [ganz schwach und recht geschwind] or else it would not be called a mordent" (par. 13). The dynamics favor anticipation of the little notes.

Leopold presents both types of Tartini's *mordente:* the regular mordent in both one-stroke and two-stroke style (Ex. 30.18a) and the three-note pattern of the prebeat turn from either above or below (Ex. 30.18b).[3] In addition, he shows a third type of *mordente* (Ex. 30.18c) that was often called an *Anschlag.* The unifying bond that justifies a single term of "mordent" for these three variegated formulas is their dynamic-rhythmic design of speeding softly into the accented main note, a design that by itself strongly suggests the anticipation of the graces.

EXAMPLE 30.18.   L. Mozart

a.                                          b.

Mordant

c.

After the famous mid-century treatises I have been able to find little of consequence in theoretical sources. Löhlein, in his violin treatise, shows the mordent only in its one-stroke onbeat style, except in its *port de voix et pincé* setting (*Anweisung zum Violinspielen,* 50). Türk distinguishes the short or "half" (halben) one-stroke mordent and the long or "whole" multistroke one. He stresses for the short one the need for utmost speed of the (onbeat) oscillations and implies its strong accentuation, whereas in the *port de voix et pincé* the mordent is rendered weak. The long mordent, which (following C. P. E. Bach) he marks with the three-waggle symbol ⁓⁓⁓ , may have many oscillations, but they must come to a stop before the end of the note (*Klavierschule,* chap. 4, sec. 3, pars. 60–65).

***Haydn's Mordent.*** Although Haydn used the French mordent symbol ⁓⁓ only rarely, the very frequent so-called Haydn ornament ⁓ had a very flexible meaning that for the keyboard included not just the turn and the trill but also the mordent.[4] For a characteristic case, see Exx. 30.19a and 30.19b, from the Piano Sonata in B Minor (Hob. XVI:32), where the mordents are first indicated with (rhythmically ambiguous) little notes, then replaced by the Haydn ornament. Mordent meaning is also very likely in such spots as the start of the slow movement of the Sonata in F (Hob. XVI:23; Ex. 30.19c).

EXAMPLE 30.19.   Haydn

a. Piano Sonata in B Minor, (Hob. XVI:32/1)     b.

c. Piano Sonata in F, (Hob. XVI:23/2)

Most important, Haydn himself, in the autograph of the fugue for a mechanical clock (discussed in chap. 28, pp. 436–67), wrote at the end of the musical text that every time the theme occurs the half note must receive the following "half mordent" (Halbe Mordent): . As I pointed out in that earlier discussion of the surviving clocks, the later of the two clocks, which was manufactured after Haydn's return from London, proved to be closer to his intentions by inserting the mordent as Haydn had directed, whereas the clock of 1793, made during Haydn's stay in England, failed to heed this directive. Significantly, following the editorial procedure of the transcription, an onbeat mordent would have been indicated not by small notes but by regular ones . The listing by small notes indicates that all the mordents at the start of the theme were *anticipated,* providing further proof for the anticipatory potential of the grace.

We can end the narrative of this chapter with Haydn. There is no mordent problem for Mozart, who used neither a symbol nor, as far as could be ascertained, little or regular notes to indicate this grace.

The mordent is usually viewed as an accented onbeat ornament par excellence. Yet there is the theoretical evidence all the way from Freillon-Poncein and L'Affilard to Tartini and Leopold Mozart, and graphic evidence from Haydn, that it might also be used in anticipation even on the strongest beats. Furthermore, musical logic points in the same direction whenever the mordent is used on a light beat in a purely connective function. However important the onbeat accentual function of the mordent, we must never lose sight of its alternative, regardless of its placement in the measure.

# 31

## OTHER ORNAMENTS

The *Vorschlag* and the trill in their various guises have been throughout our period the most frequent ornaments. They were also highly controversial. Next to these two ornaments there are a few others whose importance and incidence varies from one composer to the next and from one medium to another. They are the turn, the arpeggio, the acciaccatura, and the vibrato; they too have many problems, and they too are very controversial.

### The Turn

"Turn" is a collective name for a group of graces that center on a design in which three ornamental notes start on the upper neighbor of the parent note and move scalewise to the lower one. The turn either (1) precedes its parent note (━•━•━•━■) and will be called the "prenote turn" or (2) is embedded in its middle (━■━•━•━•━■) and will be called the "postnote turn." Once in a while the "pre-note turn" is inverted by starting from the lower neighbor note and rising to the upper one (━•━•━•━■).

The prenote turn has a basically intensifying function and can be accented or unaccented: if accented it normally coincides with the beat and adds emphasis to its parent note similar to that engendered by a brief trill; if unaccented it normally anticipates the beat and adds luster to the accented parent note.

***The Prenote Turn.*** When the most common turn symbol ∾, which is of French origin, is placed above or below the note head ($\overset{\infty}{\underset{\infty}{\rho}}$ ), it will

472

normally signify the prenote type, though there are exceptions. The rhythmic design of the accented prenote turn will vary according to the prevailing tempo. For an assumed quarter-note parent it may range from circa ♪♪♪♪ to ♪♪♪♪ . Once in a while when circumstances favor it, the turn can start with the main note, which as part of the ornament is rendered as fast as the three following ones ♪♪♪♪ . The unaccented prenote turn ♪♪ will always be rendered soft and fast.

*The Postnote Turn.* The second type, the embedded postnote turn, is a connective ornament that characteristically graces the transition to another pitch, often its upper neighbor. It is always indicated when the symbol is placed after the note head ♪∞♪ . Its rhythmic design lends itself to a variety of dispositions, depending on tempo and expression. To sketch just the most frequent shapes, such a turn after a binary note may take forms such as those shown in Fig. 31.1, and the turn after a dotted note (in a binary meter) such as those shown in Fig. 31.2. (A dotted note in a ternary meter, such as $\frac{6}{8}$ ♪·∞♪· , is a unit of the beat and as such is treated like the binary note in a binary meter.)

FIGURE 31.1

FIGURE 31.2

*The French Turn.* In France various terms were used to signify the turn, including *double cadence, double, doublé,* and, mainly for singers, *tour de gozier.* Although Chambonnières in 1670 was perhaps the first to introduce the standard wavy symbol, he gives a design for what he calls the *double cadence* (Ex. 31.1a) that deviates from the most common one by starting on the main note and moving first two pitches down and then back up (*Pièces de clavessin*). This design was adopted, along with the term *double cadence,* by only very few early clavecinists, among them by d'Anglebert in 1689, who simultaneously shows the standard form of the grace (*Pièces de clavecin*), by Saint Lambert in 1702 (*Principes de clave-cin*, 53), and by Dieupart in ca. 1702 (*Six suittes*, "Explication des marques"). It seems to disappear from all later sources. Le Roux in 1705 shows the standard design for the prenote turn (*double cadence sans trem-blement*), and so do Couperin in 1713 (*double*), as given in Ex. 31.1b (*Pièces de clavecin*, bk. 1), and Rameau in 1724 (*doublé; Pièces de clavecin*).

EXAMPLE 31.1

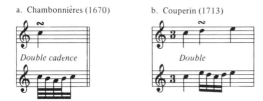

In Couperin we find both the prenote and the postnote types of the turn fairly frequently. He also uses the combination symbol ∾ to indi-cate the turn as a *sequel* to a trill (*not* as its start). (See also the various French turns—most of them prefixes to turn-trills—in examples 29.2a–29.2c; 19.4a–19.4d; 29.4; 29.5b, 29.5f–29.5g; and 29.6.)

An interesting model of an anticipated turn is given in Bedos de Celle's *L'art du facteur d'orgue* in the chapter on the mechanical organ that was written by Père Engramelle. There we are shown, without the use of a symbol, two forms of *doublés*, one on the beat with its first note lengthened (Ex. 31.2a), and the other with the turn anticipated (Ex. 31.2b; *L'art du facteur d'orgue*, 4: Planche 109).

EXAMPLE 31.2.    Engramelle (Bedos de Celles) (1778)

The French gambists had a special variant of the turn that looks on first glance like an appoggiatura trill with a turned ending, as shown in Ex. 31.3, from Marais (*Pièces de violes*, 1686). It is not a trill, however, as pointed out in chapter 26, n. 1, since these turn figures were quite certainly done with separate bowstrokes for every note. This bowed execution was specified by Jean Rousseau in his viol treatise of 1687 for what he called the *double cadence* (*Traité de la viole*, 97–100) and is confirmed by the consistency with which Marais never placed a slur mark over these figures in editions that are throughout painstakingly edited with slurs, fingerings, and other interpretive symbols.

EXAMPLE 31.3.  Marais, I, Double of Gigue, p. 22

*The Italo-German Turn.* In the Italo-German tradition of the 17th century, we find, quite apart from many turn- and turn-like patterns in diminution treatises, a design closely resembling that of the French gambists. Used primarily for final cadences, it starts with either the upper note or with the slightly sustained main note (in order to come out even): . Rendered more slowly and articulated more sharply than trills, the design was thought of as *groppo,* an elongated turn, not as a trill.

*J. S. Bach.* Bach used the turn symbol almost exclusively for the keyboard, and then only sparingly. There are thus relatively few problems; where there does seem to be one, it can usually be solved by flexibly adjusting the design and by considering what is going on at the same time in the other voices. One case only might be discussed here because it occurs in a much-loved piece, the Two-part Invention in D, and is very often misunderstood. In measure 11 (and in the parallel spot in m. 53) Bach added as a second thought a turn symbol that reads in the autograph as shown in Ex. 31.4a. In modern editions the obsolete dot across the barline is replaced by a tie (Ex. 31.4b). Normally this would be simply a matter of clearer notation, but here it makes the turn appear to be of the prenote type, placed as it is on top of the note head. Yet the very old-fashioned way of using the dot shows that the turn belongs not to the downbeat as an accentual grace but to the preceding parent note as a connective grace, a *postnote* turn. Two logical alternatives would be either to play the turn in anticipation (Ex. 31.4c) or, probably better, with a slight delay (Ex. 31.4d).

*Mid-Century Theorists.* The special importance of Tartini (and his disciple, Leopold Mozart) with regard to the turn has already been discussed in chapter 30, where Tartini's prebeat design for the turn (which he calls *mordente*) plus accentuation of the principal note served to shed light on the analogous prebeat patterns for the genuine mordent.

EXAMPLE 31.4.    Bach, Two-Part Invention in D, BWV 774 (aut. P 610)

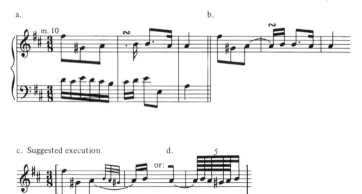

Leopold Mozart, as was also shown in the same section of the preceding chapter, sees in the turn a species of the mordent and, in full accord with Tartini's prebeat style, has it done soft and fast with the accent falling on the principal note (*Versuch einer Violinschule,* chap. 11, pars. 8–14).

C. P. E. Bach treats the turn (*Doppelschlag*) with great thoroughness and extols the versatility of this grace (*Versuch über Art das Clavier* [1753], chap. 2, sec. 4; the following references are to this section). As to the prenote turn, he stresses its usual fast execution and shows how its rhythmic design varies with the tempo (Ex. 31.5a). He also points to the turn's frequent function as a substitute for a trill with suffix (par. 9). Another very interesting trill substitute, this time for a main-note trill with suffix, is provided by what C. P. E. Bach calls the *geschnellter Doppelschlag,* which is a turn preceded by the principal note. He notates it by adding an unmetrical thirty-second *Vorschlag* note on the same pitch and transcribes it as shown in Ex. 31.5b. On fast notes, Bach says, this grace "is more convenient than the trill" (par. 34). Very interestingly, he does not limit the use of this main-note-propelled design to the cases specified by notation. On the keyboard, he says, the plain turn symbol (when placed above the note) may be rendered as *geschnellter Doppelschlag,* and on instruments other than the keyboard the trill sign may be given the same interpretation (par. 34). In other words, C. P. E. Bach makes it clear that ℘ may stand for ⌢♪♪♪♪⌣ (i.e., a *Schneller* plus suffix) and that any nonkeyboard trill symbol on short notes may be interpreted in the same manner.

C. P. E. Bach devotes only a brief mention to the postnote, "simple" turn (*einfacher Doppelschlag*), "which occurs after a note." It is met, he says, with slurred and sustained notes and starts "a good while after the note." Interesting about his illustration (given in Ex. 31.5c) is the gradation in the lengths of the four fast notes, which might serve to clarify the nature of the fourth note as extension of the parent (par. 36, Fig. 70).

In his section devoted to the slide (chap. 2, sec. 7), C. P. E. Bach describes in paragraph 5 the inverted turn under the name of "three-note slide" (*Schleiffer von dreyen Nötgen*) and claims to be the first to introduce the reversed turn symbol of Ex. 31.5d.

EXAMPLE 31.5.   C. P. E. Bach (1753)

Although Quantz does not formally deal with the turn, one of his tables demonstrating the practice of diminutions offers a strong hint that for the turn before the note he too agrees with the Tartini-Leopold Mozart manner of rendering the grace unaccented before the beat. Using the pattern of Ex. 31.6a as a basic motive, he lists the sequence of Ex. 31.6b as one among several forms of embellishment. In the verbal commentary on this example, he explains its rendition: "The thirty-seconds weak, the quarter notes C, C, C, growing" (*Versuch einer Anweisung*, Tab. 9, Fig. 1; commentary in Chap. 14, par. 26). Although, unlike Tartini and Leopold Mozart, he does not ask for accentuation of the principal note, his dynamic design with the swelling quarter notes is certainly far more compatible with anticipation of the grace than with its accented downbeat start.

EXAMPLE 31.6.   Quantz (1752)

**Later Treatises.** Among the well-known treatises written after Leopold Mozart, those of Agricola, Löhlein, Türk, and others all followed C. P. E. Bach's lead. Albrechtsberger and Clementi also show analogous onbeat patterns for the prenote turn, which is always the more problematical type (Albrechtsberger, *Anfangsgründe*, 4; Clementi, *Introduction*, 11).

In 1798 J. B. Lasser, in addition to showing the traditional three-note onbeat design (*Doppelschlag*), supplements it with some interesting variants. One of these, which he calls the *Zwicker*, embodies the pitches of the turn but is in fact a mordent preceded by a grace note (the anticipation that is obvious from the notation is also spelled out in the text). This is what I have referred to as the "Italian mordent," and Lasser marks it with the traditional mordent symbol, as shown in Ex. 31.7a. Somewhat confusingly, he refers to the common turn symbol above the note head as a *mordent*, which in "gay, sprightly" spots has the meaning of the four-note turn (C. P. E. Bach's *geschnellter Doppelschlag*) of Ex. 31.7b, whereas in "expressive" spots it takes the form of the postnote turn with the first note lengthened (Ex. 31.7c; *Vollständige Anleitung*, 135–38).

Lasser is not alone in treating the "Italian mordent" as a form of the turn. J. F. Schubert shows, in ca. 1804, under the usual term of *Doppelschlag*, the same design as an alternative solution for the turn symbol above the note head, as given in Ex. 31.7d. This illustration, along with Lasser's *Zwicker*, provides some possibly important theoretical support for a number of spots in Mozart where this design appears to be a felicitous interpretation of the turn symbol written above the note. Also interesting is Schubert's further option "in slow tempo" of an embedded, postnote execution for the symbol written above the note (Ex. 31.7e; *Neue Singe-Schule*, 67).

In 1786 J. C. Bach and F. P. Ricci illustrate only the inverted turn and show it, in the spirit of Tartini and Leopold Mozart, in anticipation, as given in Ex. 31.7f (*Méthode pour le forte-piano*, 17). J. P. Milchmeyer, in 1797, shows the identical prebeat design in his illustration of Ex. 31.7g (*Die wahre Art*, 38). Koch, in 1795, implies the same, and when speaking of the turn and such related figures as the *Anschlag* (both given in Ex. 31.7h) says they should be "fleetingly and roundly [flüchtig und rund] slurred to the following notes." This suggests speed and lightness, hence presumable anticipation (*Journal der Tonkunst*, 1 [1795]: 188).[1]

In the music of Haydn and Mozart the turn offers problems that call for a more detailed accounting.

**Haydn's Turn.** Haydn used the turn with remarkable frequency, more than any other great master. He marks the turn in both its prenote and postnote types, either with three little thirty-second notes, ⨾ , or with the traditional symbol ∾ , or with the "Haydn ornament" ⤶ . The

EXAMPLE 31.7

a. Lasser (1798)

*Zwicker*

Ac-cel-le- rar-

b. Lasser (1798)

Mordent

bril- lar il cor mi sen-to

c. Lasser (1798)

Die Lie - be

d. J.F. Schubert (1804)

e. J.F. Schubert (1804)

f. J.C. Bach and Ricci (1786)

g. Milchmeyer (1797)

h. Koch (1795)

casual way in which he often substitutes in parallel spots one symbol for the other can give valuable clues to their interpretation.

Much evidence points to his frequent use of the Tartini-Leopold Mozart *mordente* type of fast anticipation and accentuation on the parent note. This design—as briefly mentioned in the Introduction to this book—is indicated in Ex. 31.8, from the autograph of the Symphony No.

90, where the turn for the identical motive is at first written with the little notes, as in Ex. 31.8a. Then in Exx. 31.8b, 31.8c, and 31.8f the slur to the preceding note establishes *Nachschlag* character, hence placement before the beat. The same rhythmic design is unquestionable when the motive recurs in the other parallel spots, such as in Exx. 31.8d, 31.8e, and 31.8g; and when in Ex. 31.8h Haydn substitutes the Haydn ornament, we can be sure that it too was to be rendered in anticipation.

EXAMPLE 31.8.    Haydn, Symphony No. 90/1 (Hob. I:90)

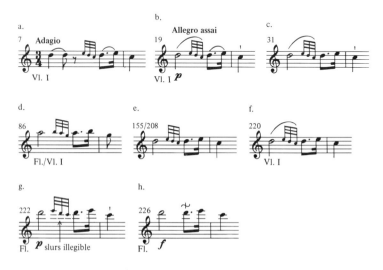

The same rendition suggests itself in Ex. 31.9a, from the Piano Sonata in D, where the *sforzando* marks force the parent note on the beat, the turn into anticipation. In Ex. 31.9b, from the String Quartet Op. 64, No. 1, the staccato marks call for anticipation of the turn, both to maintain the rhythmic integrity of the six even eighth notes and to allow for the staccato rendition of the note following the turn. In Ex. 31.9c, from the Piano Trio in E Flat, the autograph *crescendo-decrescendo* fork peaking at the note following the four-note turn makes musical sense only when the latter is anticipated.

Moreover, we have evidence from the "undated" musical clock, which, for reasons given earlier, we can take to be closer to Haydn's intention than the other two surviving clocks from 1792 and 1793 that were built during Haydn's absence in England (see chap. 28, p. 436, and n. 12). In two of the pieces that Haydn wrote for these clocks we find turns, written by three little notes, that are played by the clock of 1793 on the beat but by the undated one in anticipation, as shown in Ex. 31.9d for the piece No. II, 1 (in the Henle edition).[2]

EXAMPLE 31.9.  Haydn

a.  Piano Sonata in D Major (Hob. XVI:42), m. 87

b.  String Quartet, Op. 64, no. 1/4
    (Hob. III:65), m. 31

c.  Piano Trio in E Flat (Hob. XV:29/2)

d.

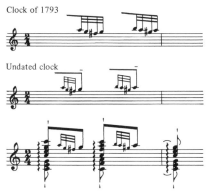

Text of Haydn autograph

Undoubtedly, many turns indicated by one of the two abstract symbols, and maybe some written with little notes, were intended to fall in the beat. But, just as undoubtedly, the anticipated turn occupied a far more important place in Haydn's music than has been generally believed to be the case, and the performer will do well to keep that important alternative always in mind.

*Mozart's turn.* Mozart notates the turn either with the wavy symbol ∾ that always stands for the descending kind or with three little thirty-second notes that can go in either direction. The symbol, when placed above the note head, practically always signifies the prenote turn and often suggests its standard three-note form, starting on the beat: . Often, but not always. Many are the cases in which musical reasons call for other options. Among these are the approximate variants shown in Fig. 31.3, all of which, as we have seen, found their reflection in various treatises of the time.

FIGURE 31.3

The standard interpretation should always be considered but not automatically applied. When, for instance, the turn is written over a note on a strong beat and the pitch of this note is of thematic importance, say for reasons of motivic pitch repetition, then one of the three listed variants is likely to fit better than the standard design. In Ex. 31.10a, from the Piano Trio in G, K 496, pitch repetition is clearly thematic and therefore any of the three variants of Exx. 31.10b–31.10d (of which the first, Ex. 31.10b, was suggested by the Badura-Skodas) is preferable to the standard solution of Ex. 31.10e, where an accented auxiliary would blur the thematic contour. Or take the allegro theme of the Violin Sonata in G. of Ex. 31.10f. Here the threateningly hammered-out main notes of the turns transmit the awesome energy of the theme. The standard solution of Ex. 31.10g, with an onbeat accented auxiliary would blunt the sharp edges of the motive, and here any of the three variants, shown as Ex. 31.10h–31.10j, will offer a better solution.

The three variants are not equivalent, however, and many are the situations in which only one or the other will be the indicated choice. In a case such as the passage from the Piano Sonata in A Minor, its initial appearance (Ex. 31.10k) shows how the subsequent ornamented version (Ex. 31.10l) has to be done: it is clear that the *sforzandi* refer to the main notes and that the turns need to start with the stressed main notes as indicated in Ex. 31.10m.

The standard textbook solution will have numerous applications as well, especially when the turn occurs on light beats or between beats, as for instance in Ex. 31.10n, from the Piano Sonata in C Minor, which seems best rendered as shown in Ex. 31.10o.

For the postnote "embedded" turn, marked by the wave symbol to the right of the note head, all that can be said in a general way is that, time permitting, the pitch of the parent note should be more or less sustained before the onset of the turn. There are, however, important differences between a turn after a binary note and one after a dotted one (in binary meter). After a binary note the three inserted notes plus the repeated principal note will lead directly without stopping into the fol-

lowing pitch, as for example ♩ (the internal rhythm

EXAMPLE 31.10. Mozart

a. Piano Trio in G, K 496/3

b.                    c.        d.        e.

Badura-Skoda

f. Violin Sonata in G, K 373a (379)

g.           h.        i.        j.

k. Piano Sonata in A Minor,          l.                              m.
   K 300 d (310)

Andante cantabile con espressione

n. Piano Sonata in C Minor,          o.
   K 457/2

Adagio

varying with the tempo). We find this design, which differs from C. P. E. Bach's, in every one of the numerous cases in which Mozart writes out such a turn in regular notes.

The turn symbol after a dotted note (in a binary meter) permits a wider range of solutions. The most common one, found in many treatises, ⟨music example⟩, can be applied in most cases where the dotted note falls on a strong beat. But adjustments will often be advisable, especially when the dotted note is followed not by one but by two or more shorter companion notes. A lengthening of the parent note, and the rendering of the turn plus the repeated pitch of the parent note at the end of the latter's value, will often be musically attractive. For an illustration, see Ex. 31.11a, from the Piano Concerto in D Minor: here the rendition of Ex. 31.11b, which is close to the conventional one, is acceptable, but the version of Ex. 31.11c seems more graceful.

EXAMPLE 31.11.   Mozart, Piano Concerto in D Minor, K 466/2 (Romance)

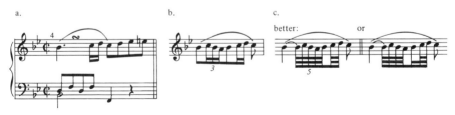

Mozart frequently wrote the turn with small notes, using three for the prenote and four for the postnote type. For the prenote turn we find both the design ![turn] or its inversion ![inverted turn] . The postnote "embedded" turn, written with four little notes, occurs only in the standard design from above ![turn design] .

The descending three-note design for the prenote turn will often be synonymous with the wave symbol, but not always: unlike the little notes, the wave symbol *may* start with the main note; on the other hand, the little notes are more likely than the symbol to have prebeat meaning. (The latter meaning, as was shown, is associated with the little notes in a number of treatises from Tartini, Leopold Mozart, and Quantz to Milchmeyer, Koch, and J. C. Bach and Ricci.)

Certainly the little notes can have onbeat meaning, notably before a final note or a fermata or in a similar context, as in Ex. 31.12a, from the Sonata for Four Hands in F, which might perhaps be rendered as in Ex. 31.12b. But seemingly more often they suggest anticipation, as for instance in Ex. 31.12c, from the Piano Concerto K 449, corresponding to a manner so frequently used by Haydn; or in Ex. 31.12d, from the Piano Sonata in D, K 284c (311), in order to insure the integrity of the octave doubling; or in Ex. 31.12e, from the Piano Trio in C, to allow for the (accented) staccato rendition of the downbeat; or in Ex. 31.12f, from the Piano Sonata in C, K 189d (279), which in the autograph has an *f* (in *sforzando* meaning) aligned each time with the principal note.

For the postnote turn, as already mentioned, Mozart often uses four little notes, ![postnote turn] , in which the fourth note stands for the tail end of the parent note. This notation, which is adequate for binary notes, can be confusing for turns after dotted notes, where the end of the principal

EXAMPLE 31.12. Mozart

a. Sonata for Four Hands in F, K 497/1    b.

c. Piano Concerto, K 449/2    d. Piano Sonata in D, K 284c (311)/3

e. Piano Trio in C, K 548/3    f. Piano Sonata in C, K 189d (279)/2

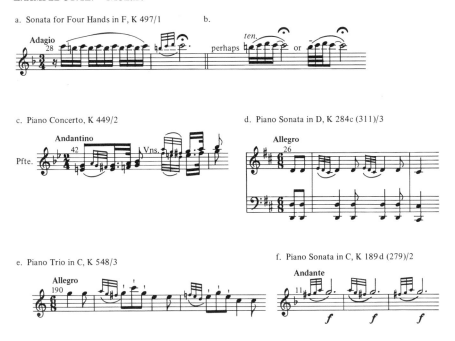

note usually needs to be longer than the three ornamental ones. Thus a phrase such as the one of Ex. 31.13a, from the String Quartet in G, K 387, was most likely intended to be played as given in Ex. 31.13b. Though there are some cases in which, following dotted notes, the turn plus the terminal pitch of the parent note can be rendered convincingly in even values, more often a lengthening of the terminal pitch is advisable.

EXAMPLE 31.13.    Mozart, String Quartet in G, K 387/3

a.                                        b.

In summing up, what is considered to be the "standard" interpretation for the prenote turn—that is, its starting on the beat with the upper note—must not be considered to be the "rule" from which other designs are only occasional "exceptions." Instead, for Mozart as well as for Haydn and other composers, there were several manifestations of the turn, each to be used when its specific qualities were best fitting. They were generally on an equal footing except that anticipation is often favored when the turn is notated with little notes.

The postnote turn has few problems that good musical instinct cannot solve. But for Mozart's notation with four equal little notes we must, for dotted notes, be alert to the frequent need to deviate from the graphic design by lengthening the fourth note, which represents the end of the parent note.

## The Arpeggio

The essence of the arpeggio is the successive sounding of the pitches that form a chord. The idea finds its realization in two different ways that will be referred to as the "chordal" and the "linear" arpeggio. In the chordal arpeggio the pitches are announced in very close succession, *without* any specified rhythm, and are sustained to form the sound of the full chord. In the linear arpeggio the pitches are strung up melodically in a *definite* rhythm, without being sustained (though not excluding on the keyboard occasional pedal-like effects by keeping the keys depressed beyond the written value of some of the notes).

*The Chordal Arpeggio.* The chordal arpeggio is limited to a few media only: besides the harp, which gave it its name, mainly to the lute, the harpsichord, pianoforte, and clavichord, with only negligible significance for the organ. It is also important for the strings, though often as a technical makeshift for chords that cannot be sustained in their entirety.

The chordal arpeggio falls into two distinct types: the plain, and the figurate. In the plain type the pitches of the chord are "broken," usually upward, but very occasionally downward, as shown in Exx. 31.14a and 31.14b. In the figurate arpeggio, nonchordal pitches are inserted in the manner of *Zwischenshläge* but not sustained (Ex. 31.14c).

Example 31.14

a.       b.      c.

Although modern theory and practice generally extend the downbeat rule to the chordal arpeggio, no explicit formulation of such a rule has so far been found in any historical documents. Not even C. P. E. Bach's authority can be invoked, since he limited his sweeping onbeat rule to "those graces that are indicated by little notes" (*Versuch über Art*

*das Clavier* [1753], chap. 2, sec. 1, par. 23). The only rationale for encompassing the arpeggio in the onbeat rule is the literal interpretation of certain ornament tables. The pitfalls of such a procedure have been outlined in chapter 21. Its dangers are raised to another power when applied to the arpeggio, as will be presently seen.

There are situations in which an onbeat start is fitting: when the lowest note of an upward arpeggio is part of the main melody (see for instance the Sarabande from Bach's Fourth French Suite, mm. 3–4); in an accompaniment when—as often happens—the bass-note pitch and rhythm are more important than what happens at the end of the arpeggiated chord; or, in the absence of any distinct melody, when the musical essence of a passage resides in a succession of chords, where an onbeat start can often be a valid alternative to a prebeat or straddling one.

But whenever the arpeggio, as it does most often, serves to highlight a note in the melody by ending on it, the function of the arpeggio resembles that of the anapestic slide or of Tartini's and Leopold Mozart's *mordente*, which add brilliance to the parent note by their fast, soft, prebeat renditions. Example 31.15a, from Mozart's Violin Sonata in G, K 373a (379), might serve as an illustration. The melody of the introductory solemn adagio is accompanied by majestic chords, arpeggiated as on a big lute. By starting the arpeggios on the beat, the melody would be impaired, almost caricatured to the point of sputtering, if instead of sounding like Ex. 31.15b it were to sound like Ex. 31.15c. The arpeggios have to be anticipated.

EXAMPLE 31.15.   Mozart, Violin Sonata in G, K 373a (379)

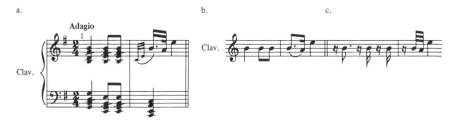

Deviating from modern onbeat theory while speaking of Bach, Paul Badura-Skoda admits anticipation of lengthy arpeggios that start with the lowest note (*Bach Interpretation,* 410–11).[3]

Early documents about the arpeggio come chiefly from France, where lutenists in the early 17th century indicated it by various symbols. Most common was the oblique stroke between the vertically aligned letters of a chord: ⸝⁄ₐ.

The French clavecinists, beginning with Chambonnières, both used and explained arpeggio symbols, which were mostly of two kinds. One is the vertical wavy line ⁚❙ that is still used today; the other is the lutenist's oblique stroke, applied in standard notation through the stem of the note ♪ . Most of the documentation comes from ornament tables; two important instances, which seem to indicate an onbeat start, are given in Ex. 31.16a, from Chambonnières in 1670 (*Pièces de clavessin*), and Ex. 31.16b, from d'Anglebert in 1689 (*Pièces de clavecin*). We find closely related illustrations in Le Bègue from 1677 (*Pièces de clavessin*), Raison from 1687 (*Livre d'orgue*), Dieupart from ca. 1702 (*Six suittes*), and Rameau from 1724 (*Pièces de clavessin*).

EXAMPLE 31.16

a. Chambonnières (1670)          b. d'Anglebert (1689) and Le Roux (1705)

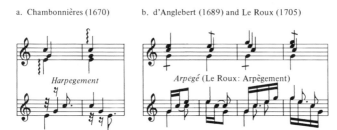

These models aim simply at conveying in the abstract the idea of "breaking" a chord note by note. None shows the arpeggio in its most frequent setting, in which it serves as the pedestal that places a melody note into brighter light. Like the pedestal, the arpeggio is not of the artistic essence and must not be rendered as if it were. It is a surface adornment of minor importance that must not draw attention to itself at the expense of the melody; it must remain in the rhythmic shade. We need only look at the four-note model of d'Anglebert to realize that it could not possibly be used in support of an upper-voice melody note that starts on the beat. The authors of these models, as of so many others, did not have to explain the details of their rhythmic adjustments to changing musical needs: to their musical contemporaries such adjustment was a matter of course.[4]

Some 18th-century authors saw the potential for confusion in these metrical models and devised better ways to convey the arpeggio idea. Among them were Saint Lambert in 1702 and Couperin in 1713. Saint Lambert's models for the plain arpeggio, as shown in Ex. 31.17a, are rhythmically noncommittal in using the ingenious graphic device of a slight shift to the right, which suggests successiveness without any metrical commitment (*Principes de clavecin,* chap. 26). Couperin, a decade later, illustrates in his table of 1713 the arpeggio (both upward and downward) with comparable rhythmic vagueness, as shown in Ex. 31.17b (*Pièces de clavecin,* bk. 1).

EXAMPLE 31.17

a. Saint Lambert (1702), *Harpegé simple*

"on two notes"    "on three notes"

b. Couperin (1713)

*Arpègement en montant*    *Arpègement en descendant*

In Germany the oblique dash predated the vertical wavy line as an arpeggio symbol. J. S. Bach may have been one of the first Germans to adopt the vertical wavy line; to judge from his usage it most probably stood always for an upward arpeggiation. In the few instances in which Bach uses oblique dashes between note heads, they signify a figurate insert within an arpeggiated chord. This will be discussed presently.

Marpurg in 1749 and 1755 uses the slanted stroke and adopts Rameau's onbeat model, which is practically identical with d'Anglebert's (see Ex. 31.16b). His terms for arpeggiation are *Griffbrechen* or *Zergliederung* (*Des critischen Musicus*, 68; *Anleitung zum Clavierspielen*, 59–60).

C. P. E. Bach does not include the arpeggio among the ornaments and mentions it only briefly in his chapter on performance. Calling it "broken harmony" (gebrochene Harmonie), he offers the models of Ex. 31.18, which show the wavy line for the rising arpeggio only. He adds a new symbol, a straight vertical line with a small horizontal bend at the bottom for the rising arpeggio and at the top for the descending one. A connection may possibly exist between the exclusively ascending meaning of the wavy line for C. P. E. Bach and the—presumably—identical meaning for his father.

While German keyboard tutors after Marpurg generally continued to show the latter's and C. P. E. Bach's downbeat patterns, in 1797 Milchmeyer deviated, like Saint Lambert and Couperin before him, from the usual routine of staying within the metrical space of the chord and

EXAMPLE 31.18.   C. P. E. Bach (1753)

EXAMPLE 31.19.   Milchmeyer (1797)

spelled out the anticipation of the arpeggio, as shown in Ex. 31.19 (*Die wahre Art*, 38).

Türk, as was to be expected, shows the downbeat start of the arpeggio in his first edition (*Klavierschule*, chap. 4, sec. 4, pars. 89–90), and in his revised edition of 1802 (271 n.*) he criticizes Milchmeyer for his prebeat design, which, Türk says, leads to "hardening" (Härten), yet the illustrations that were to show such "hardening" fail to convince (for more on this see *OrnM*, 166–67).

Haydn often spells out the anticipated arpeggio in regular notes, as for instance in the first two measures of the adagio from the Piano Sonata in E Flat (Hob. XVI:38) or in the first movement of the Piano Sonata in F (Hob. XVI:29, m. 15). Once in a while in his keyboard music he, like Mozart in Ex. 31.15a, indicates an arpeggio by a single slanted stroke between note heads (in modern editions replaced by the vertical wavy line). Here, as so often, we have to be aware of a confusing symbol that can mean different things: for several French clavecinists and some of their German disciples the single oblique stroke across the *stem* indicates a regular arpeggio. For the same masters, single or multiple oblique strokes *between note heads* indicate "figurate" inserts of nonchordal tones (to be discussed presently). Bach used this sign once in a while (see for instance Ex. 31.23, where the wavy line and the oblique stroke are combined: the wavy line indicates the arpeggio, the stroke the figurate insert).

Returning to Haydn and Mozart, they both use the little notes more often than the oblique strokes and do so always in nonkeyboard music. And they both appear to have intended these arpeggiated little notes most often, if not always, for prebeat rendition. Especially when they serve a melody note, as in the second measure of Ex. 31.15a, the arpeggios are only the "pedestals" whose place is below, not on top of, statues if they are to fulfill their helpmate function.

Take for instance the illustration of Ex. 31.20, from Haydn's Piano Trio in C (Hob. XV:27). It shows a series of arpeggios ascending along the same dominant seventh chord. Their anticipation is urged by the staccato marks on their parent notes, marks that confer accents on them along with sharpness of articulation. Surely the melody that is intended to come out is F–B–D–F, not G–D–F–B. An onbeat rendition of the arpeggios would not only produce wrong melodic emphases but also interfere with the accentuation and staccato rendition of the parent notes.

EXAMPLE 31.20.   Haydn, Piano Trio in C (Hob. XV:27/1, m. 3)

Many are the passages in Haydn as well as in Mozart in which a *sforzando* sign is written in the autographs directly below a parent note that is preceded by an arpeggio. Even more than the staccato mark, such as *sforzando* in order to be effective relegates the arpeggio into prebeat space.[5]

The same considerations that favor anticipation of the arpeggio in Haydn when it precedes a melody note apply equally to Mozart. For his music too, this function of adding brilliance to a melody note by the preparatory arpeggio gesture is by far the most frequent. We have encountered and discussed one such instance in Ex. 31.15. For just two more characteristic passages, let us look first at Ex. 31.21a, from the coda of the *alla Turca* finale of the Piano Sonata in A Major. Whether the not infrequent notation of the right hand with a longer value for the top note indicates a partially sustained arpeggio, as some editors believe, is not certain but possible. In the left hand the percussive rhythm of relentless eighth notes is of the rhythmic essence, and nothing must interfere with their evenness: the arpeggios must be anticipated.

In Ex. 31.21b, from the finale of the Piano Concerto in C Minor, we see the insistently pressing chromatic ascent to the high F (the highest note on Mozart's fortepiano). Then, after the dramatic pause, the held F is pronounced again as the brilliant climax of the build-up, sounding assertively, triumphantly on the beat, its luster enhanced by the "pedestal" of the anticipated arpeggio. If, as so often heard, the arpeggio is

placed on the beat, even if unaccented, it weakens the power and brilliance of the high F by substituting for it a much lower note of melodic
irrelevance.

EXAMPLE 31.21.   Mozart

a. Piano Sonata in A Major, K 300i (331)/3

b. Piano Concerto in C Minor, K 491/3

For an interesting case, in which the melodic-rhythmic logic of the
melody demands anticipation of a five-note arpeggio but where the
space needed for it is unavailable and has to be inserted (in the vein of
a caesura), see *OrnM*, 166–67.

*The Figurate Arpeggio (Arpégé figuré).* In the figurate arpeggio, pitches
alien to the chord are inserted between two or more of the chordal notes.
They are quickly touched but not sustained, as shown in Ex. 31.14c. The
simplest form is the arpeggiated interval of a third with the middle note
momentarily sounded. Chambonnières shows in 1670 the ascending
type in his brief table. He calls it *coulé* and marks it with an oblique
stroke between the note heads, as given in Ex. 31.22a (*Pièces de clavessin*).
Raison in 1687 shows the same model (*Livre d'orgue*). D'Anglebert in
1689 gives the same resolution while using as symbol a crescent before
the affected notes: (♪ (*Pièces de clavecin*). Couperin uses the oblique
stroke but gives the rhythmically ambiguous model of Ex. 31.22b for
what he calls *tierce coulée* (*Pièces de clavecin*, bk. 1).

For figurate inserts into larger chords, French composers used either
of these symbols. Saint Lambert, using the crescent symbol in 1702,
again gives an ingenious model that allows for rhythmic choice (Ex.
31.22c; *Principes du clavecin* 55).

In Germany, Bach indicates the figurate arpeggio with Chambonnières's oblique stroke symbol between those note heads where the

EXAMPLE 31.22

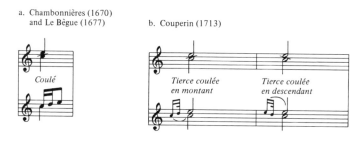

a. Chambonnières (1670)
   and Le Bègue (1677)

b. Couperin (1713)

*Coulé*

*Tierce coulée
en montant*

*Tierce coulée
en descendant*

c. Saint Lambert (1702)

*Harpegé figuré*

"with two borrowed notes"

insert is to be made. Although the grace is rather rare in his keyboard scores, there are several occurrences in the English Suites as well as in some partitas in their early autograph version in Anna Magdalena's note book (but not in the later engraved edition). An example from the Sarabande of the English Suite in A Major is given in Ex. 31.23a, with its suggested execution in Ex. 31.23b. Anticipation seems indicated to safeguard the rhythm of the melody.

EXAMPLE 31.23.  Bach, English Suite in A Major, BWV 806 (P1072), Sarabande

a.

b. Suggested execution

After Bach the grace seems to have gone out of fashion, though it is still recorded in a few treatises. It receives a one-sentence mention in C. P. E. Bach (*Versuch über Art das Clavier* [1753], chap. 3, par. 26) and is listed by Marpurg in 1755 (*Anleitung zum Clavierspielen,* 60), by Löhlein in 1765 (*Clavier-Schule,* pt. 1, chap. 9, par. 92), and by Türk in 1789 (*Klavierschule,* chap. 4, sec. 4, par. 92).

**The Linear Arpeggio.** In the linear arpeggio the chord loses its vertical substance and is dissolved into continuous movement. The chordal tones are strung up, one by one, usually throughout the whole time span allotted to the harmony. Here the arpeggio often embodies the musical essence of a passage, though on occasions thematic ideas may be interwoven with the chordal tapestry.

For shorter chords each pitch may be sounded only once; for longer ones they may be restrung twice or more times, moving up and down in either the order of the pitches or in all manners of irregular patterns. As long as such arpeggios are written out they present no problem. Problems start when the composer uses an abbreviated notation to signify or imply his wish for arpeggiation but leaves it to the performer to choose both design and articulation. Bach usually provided a pattern, especially for strings, but also in some keyboard music, as in measure 27 of the Chromatic Fantasy (and Fugue). Another problem arises when a model given at the outset of a lengthy arpeggio passage ceases to fit later chords—as is the case with the Chromatic Fantasy. In such cases the performer has to use his imagination unless he wishes to follow the modern editor's suggestions. Whenever we have no guidance from the composer, it will generally be advisable to aim at simple, not fancy, solutions.

Summing up briefly, the widely accepted idea that the chordal arpeggio should always start on the beat has no historical justification. No rule to such effect is known to have been formulated by any theoretical source, and those ornament tables that showed the execution within the metrical value of the parent note demonstrated the "breaking" of the chord in simple abstraction with no reference to any concrete musical situation. There are a few cases in which an onbeat start is fitting, but there are many more where it is *not* because it would turn musical priorities upside down. Where, as is mostly the case, an arpeggio is to grace a melody note, the latter has the decisive claim to rhythmic integrity; hence the arpeggio has to be anticipated. It makes no sense that a device meant to embellish a melody should be used in a way that cripples it instead.

## The Acciaccatura

The acciaccatura is an elusive ornament. Its nature is difficult to define, as the few writers who describe it are far from clear. Even the term is ambiguous: several authors, among them Marpurg and C. P. E. Bach, use it to denote the inserts in a figurate arpeggio.

The acciaccatura, as understood in the following discussion, is basically a clash created by the simultaneous sounding of a chord with one or more added unharmonic tones that are neither prepared nor resolved. It was predominantly an Italian grace used mostly in recitative accompaniment. Unknown in France, it had, however, a few followers in Germany.

The best-known discussion is contained in Francesco Gasparini's treatise of 1708 on the thorough bass (*L'armonico pratico al cimbalo*). In the recitative, he says, one arpeggiates the chords and can insert two kinds of graces. One he calls *mordente,* always a half step below a chordal tone, striking it "adroitly together with . . . or rather slightly before the principal note" (toccandole con certa destrezza nel medemo tempo . . . anzi un poco prima) and then immediately releasing it (91). If struck before its parent and released before clashing, the *mordente* would be simply a figurate insert in the arpeggiated chord. But Gasparini's comparison of its effect with the bite of a little animal that immediately lets go again and does not hurt might indicate at least a very brief clash, or else there would be no perception of a "bite," however painless.

As to the second kind of insert, Gasparini calls it *acciaccatura* and explains it as a dissonance, created by two, three, or four (added) notes combined one next to the other, that makes a "wonderful effect" ("Si usa alcune volte qualche falsa, che sarà con acciaccatura di due, tre, o quattro tasti uno appresso l'altro" [93]). It is often, so it seems, placed at a whole-tone distance from its parent note, but not always, especially when two or more added pitches are involved. Unfortunately, Gasparini's illustrations are more confusing than illuminating and fail to reveal how the acciaccatura was rendered. They show the pitches of the chords plus the *mordenti* and acciaccaturas involved strung up one after the other. The graphic design clearly suggests arpeggiation but fails to reveal any vertical element; yet from the explanation as dissonance the acciaccatura must have been either struck simultaneously with its parent or, if sounded earlier, sustained to form a clash. And such a clash is also confirmed when Gasparini writes that occasionally one has to strike two notes with the same finger (94).

We get a much better idea about the Italian acciaccatura practice from Ex. 31.24. It gives a few measures from a manuscript treatise (by an anonymous author in the Biblioteca Corsini in Rome) that deals with the role of the *mordente* and the acciaccatura in accompaniment in a manner related to Gasparini.[6] We find in this illustration many dissonant pitches that are written in shorter note values followed by corresponding rests but many that are written out in the full values of the principal chordal notes. Since the author differentiates in the text between *mordente* and acciaccatura (using for the *mordente* Gasparini's simile of a little animal's bite), we seem entitled to assume that the shorter note values indicate *mordenti* that are touched and immediately released, whereas the held-out ones are the genuine acciaccaturas. But then the author significantly adds, speaking of the *mordenti:* "should anyone prefer to hold rather than to release the dissonances, he may follow his judgment" (Landshoff, 207)—in other words, he may use sharply clashing acciaccaturas throughout.

EXAMPLE 31.24.  Anon. (c. 1700)

In his *Treatise of Good Taste* of 1749, Geminiani discusses thorough bass accompaniment and follows Gasparini quite faithfully in distinguishing two types of inserted notes. He needed to change Gasparini's term *mordente* (which he used elsewhere in its common meaning) and calls it instead *tatto* (sometimes *tacto*); but the meaning has not changed: it is "performed by touching the Key lightly, and quitting it with such a Spring as if it was Fire." The other grace, the acciaccatura, "is a Composition of such Chords as are dissonant with Respect to the fundamental Laws of Harmony; and yet when disposed in their proper Place produce that very effect it might be expected they would destroy" (Preface and examples on first [unnumbered] page of music). It has been used, he adds, for over a hundred years. His examples, patterned after Gasparini, are similarly ambiguous.

It is possible that the acciaccaturas of Italian thorough bass practice with their astringent sounds may have been the fertile soil from which sprouted Domenico Scarlatti's daring harmonic visions. Their thoroughly modern, Stravinskian tone clusters, such as those shown in Ex. 31.25, can be said to contain several acciaccaturas.

EXAMPLE 31.25.   D. Scarlatti, Sonata K 119

In Germany, Heinichen in 1728 reports Gasparini's principles at some length "because especially on the harpsichord his manner is highly effective" (*Generalbass*, 534–42). But he seems to misrepresent him by explaining the rendition of both *mordente* and acciaccatura in the same manner: as a "mild arpeggio" with an immediate release of the "false" pitches. Heinichen seems to see as the only difference between these two ornamental inserts the half-tone distance of the *mordente* and the whole-tone distance of the acciaccatura. Yet while Gasparini specified the half-tone distance for the *mordente*, he did not specify the distance for the acciaccatura and shows in his examples an occasional half-tone distance for the latter. Also, his mention of striking two notes with one finger, which caused Heinichen some discomfort, and the clustering of two or more acciaccaturas for the same chordal note, make it clear that there was indeed a difference in kind between the two types of inserts.

Walther, in 1732, gives as an example of an acciaccatura a G-major triad where, together with B, G, and D, the F sharp is also sounded (*Musicalisches Lexicon*, s.v. "Acciaccatura"). In 1739 Mattheson mentions the acciaccatura, on which he says Gasparini and Heinichen have bestowed more attention than it is worth. Exclusively used in heavily set thorough bass accompaniments, this grace, he says, causes much impurity of harmony (*Vollkommene Capellmeister*, pt. 2, chap. 3, pars. 57–60).

C. P. E. Bach describes an acciaccatura-like clash as a subspecies of the mordent, to be used where a very fast mordent is needed, and illustrates it as shown in Ex. 31.26a. Both notes, he says, are struck simultaneously, but the grace is lifted almost immediately. It occurs only "ex abrupto," not in connective situations, and should be used less often than the regular mordent (*Versuch über Art das Clavier* [1753], chap. 2, sec. 5, pars. 3–4).

Marpurg in 1755 follows C. P. E. Bach and gives the identical illustration (*Anleitung zum Clavierspielen,* 58–59). Moreover, in his chapter on the arpeggio, he lists as a subspecies of the figurate arpeggio a genuine acciaccatura: instead of inserting notes alien to the chord in the manner of *Zwischenschläge* during arpeggiation, they may be struck simultaneously with the unbroken chord and then quickly released, as shown in Ex. 31.26b.

Example 31.26

a. C.P.E. Bach
   (1753)

b. Marpurg
   (1755)

Though Türk still mentions the acciaccatura briefly in 1789 as a "not very well-known ornament," the grace seems to have gone out of fashion in the latter part of the 18th century (*Klavierschule,* chap. 4, pars. 66–67). Gasparini's *mordente* was basically a figurate insert in an arpeggiated chord. As such it was of international currency and not limited to accompaniment. In contrast, the acciaccatura with its sharp dissonant clash was an essentially Italian manner in thorough bass realization. It seems to have made only small inroads into the German practice of accompaniment yet left some traces in soloistic keyboard performance as an occasional substitute for a quick mordent, for a short *Vorschlag,* or for a figurate arpeggio.

## *The Vibrato*

The term "vibrato" is of modern, perhaps 20th-century, vintage. In the era of our concern there were a variety of terms in use, among them the French *flattement, balancement, plainte,* or *battement,* the German *Bebung, Schwebung, Tremulo,* or *Tremulant,* the English "close shake," the Italian *tremolo* (overlapping with the meaning of a trill) or *ondeggiamento,* as well as a number of others.

The vibrato is a means of enriching the musical tone by fast, regular fluctuations of pitch, or of loudness, or of timbre, or by some combination of them. Of these three types of oscillations those of pitch are by far the most important ones for voice and strings. Pitch oscillations can occur by themselves, as for instance in the two-finger vibrato of the gambists produced by trilling at the distance of a microtone. Intensity oscillations can also occur by themselves, most notably in the tremulant stop of the organ where oscillations are caused by the intermittent interruptions of the air supply. Another pure intensity vibrato is the one produced on strings by pressure pulsations of a bow that is drawn across the string without interruption, or on winds by similar pulsations of the breath. By way of contrast, the oscillations of timbre do not seem to occur by themselves but materialize often as a by-product of intensity and pitch pulsations, particularly with strings.[7] They are frequent too with the voice, where they show up in electronic diagrams, but their workings, along with the functioning of the whole vocal vibrato apparatus, is so far still shrouded in mystery. String vibrato, though complex with its frequent mixture of the three types of oscillations, is somewhat less elusive than its vocal counterpart because it is in the open and visible and hence more accessible to analysis. It has nevertheless been often misunderstood.

The effect of the pitch vibrato rests on the physio-psychological phenomenon of what has been referred to as "sonance": the vibrato oscillations above a certain threshold of speed (ca. 6.5–7 cycles per second) are fused into the sensation of a richer tone as the perception of the oscillations diminishes, often to the point of near-disappearance. The mysterious action of the brain involved in this phenomenon is closely akin to the one resulting in the stereophonic merger of slightly different sound impressions into a single one with added depth, as well as to the one involved in the stereoscopic merger of slightly different photographs into the perception of three-dimensionality.

The remarkable transformation that occurs on crossing the critical threshold of pitch pulsations is comparable to the way in which a rotating disk with the rainbow colors turns pure white when the speed of rotation crosses a similar critical threshold. The eye is deceived in failing to see the rainbow colors, just as the ear is deceived in failing to hear the often substantial deviations of the pitch oscillations. The failure to understand this remarkable, mysterious phenomenon has led some writers to vilify the vibrato and condemn its use. They have charged it with the "impurities" of pitch deviations, not realizing that in a well-produced vibrato these "impurities" become inaudible. We shall return to this matter in connection with the vibrato controversy.

Vocal vibrato must be ageless, because in many, or even most, mature voices the throat produces oscillations spontaneously. Mozart wrote in a letter, to be quoted later *in extenso*, "the human voice vibrates by itself," and nobody better understood the human voice than he. On strings or winds, by way of contrast, the oscillations are artificially superimposed on the bland tone by a technique that has to be consciously acquired. Yet even instrumental vibrato might be as old as many instruments themselves. Haas speaks of a vibrato effect in classical Greece through the use of a plectron in kithara playing. He mentions as well the use in the Middle Ages of specific ornamental neumes, the *bistropha* and *tristropha*, which prescribed a pulsation of the voice (*Aufführungspraxis,* 25, 42). From this we can gather that the attempt to enliven and color the straight, "white" musical tone with some kind of oscillations may respond to a deep-seated human impulse.

Today, "mainstream" performances use the vibrato extensively, often pervasively, while many performances that aspire to the epithet of being "historically informed" use it not at all or restrict it severely, even for the voice. For the reason of that discrepancy alone, the degree of its use in the 17th and 18th centuries has become an important issue. Yet, today's extensive use of the vibrato is not, as many believe, a modern phenomenon to be contrasted with abstinence or very sparing use in earlier periods. To think so is at best an oversimplification. At various times and places in the past the use of the vibrato ranged from persistent to selective, depending on fashions that came and went.

**France.** In France, Basset (first name unknown), writing about lute playing in Mersenne's *Harmonie universelle* of 1636, describes the violent shaking of the hand without allowing the finger to leave the string but then adds the interesting remark that at the time of his writing this vibrato (he calls it strangely *verre cassé* [broken glass]) was used infrequently, in a reaction to its overuse by the older generation. Here we have testimony of a fashion swing. Basset himself considers both extremes deplorable and recommends a golden mean (Mersenne, *Harmonie universelle: Traité des instrumens a chordes,* 3: 80–81).

Thomas Mace, the English exponent of the French lute school, confirms in 1676 a similar fashion swing. He calls the vibrato "sting," using the symbol of a horizontal wavy line, and describes its execution. He says it is "pretty and neat but not modish in these days." Nevertheless, he finds it "very excellent for certain Humours" (*Musick's Monument,* 109).

Toward the end of the 17th century we have ample documentation about the French gambists' use of the vibrato. They knew two distinct types. The one they originally preferred was done with two fingers: the lower-numbered finger was firmly placed on the string and the upper finger was pressed tightly against the lower one; a shaking of the hand brought the upper finger into gentle repercussive contact with the string. The result was a trill-like oscillation with a microtone (Jean Rousseau, *Traité de la viole,* 100; Danoville, *L'art de basse de violle,* 40).

Such a trill-type technique was possible only with the three fingers closest to the thumb, the lower-numbered ones. When the little finger was on the string, the gambists had to resort to the shaking of the stopping finger instead (in the manner described in n. 7). After about 1700, Marais and other players, realizing the wider color potential of the one-finger vibrato (with its intensity and timbre ingredients), extended its use to the other fingers as well, but without abandoning the two-finger type.

Danoville (first name unknown) in 1687 writes that the vibrato ("battement") "has tenderness and fills the ear with sad and languishing sweetness" (*L'art de basse de violle*, 41). In the same year, Jean Rousseau writes that one uses the vibrato ("batement" for the two-finger, "langueur" for the one-finger type) any place ("en toutes rencontres") where the length of the note permits it and that it is done for the full extent of the tone (*Traité de la viole*, 100–101).

An interesting analogy to the gambists' two-finger vibrato can be found with the French flutists. When Jacques Hotteterre speaks in 1707 of a *flattement* or *tremblement mineur*—both are terms for the vibrato—he says that it is done with the technique of the trill but that only the edge of the hole is struck. Thus, instead of the higher microtone of the gambists, the flute's vibrato is done with the lower one: striking the edge of an open hole lowers the pitch ever so slightly, and Hotteterre explicitly confirms that "it [the *flattement*] partakes of the lower tone, which is the opposite of the trill." When all holes are held and this technique is impossible, then Hotteterre says, one should *shake the flute* in order to imitate the effect of the ordinary *flattement* (*Principes de la flûte*, 29–30).

In his first book of flute pieces of 1708, Hotteterre says that the vibrato should be done on almost all long notes and that, like the trills and (multiple) mordents, one must do it slower or faster according to the tempo and character of the piece (*Premier livre*, Preface).

The general theorists have mainly the voice in mind when they speak of a *balancement*, which to them appeared to be a wavering of the voice on a single pitch. For a symbol the French used the horizontal wavy line, as shown in Ex. 31.27, from Montéclair (*Principes*, 85). This wavy line must not be mistaken for a trill symbol; it had trill meaning only for the keyboard.

EXAMPLE 31.27.  Montéclair (1736)

mo - - ta        est        ter - - - ra

Sébastien de Brossard, in his lexicon of 1703, describes the tremolo for stings as an intensity vibrato, produced by pulsations of the *bow*, playing several notes on the same pitch with one stroke "as if to imitate the *tremblant* of the organ" (*Dictionnaire*, s.v. "Tremolo"). The same grace, he says, is also often marked *trem.* for the voice; as an example for both voice and instrument, he cites the *trembleurs* from Lully's opera, *Isis*. François Joseph Gossec, in his *Messe des morts* of 1760, lavishly used the bow undulations on repeated notes, probably with a concomitant left-hand vibrato.

Charles de Lusse, in his flute treatise of 1760, describes three kinds of vibrato. One, in the *tremblement flexible*, is done by rotating the flute with the left thumb around its axis without losing the embouchure. After listing the various affections it can evoke in combination with dynamic shadings, de Lusse praises its capacity, when used on short notes, "to render the melody more agreeable and tender. One should use it as often as possible" (On doit le mettre en usage le plus souvent qu'il est possible). A second kind of vibrato, also under the heading of *tremblement flexible*, is done with the breath by blowing the syllables "hou, hou, hou, hou" (rough English equivalent: u, u, u), which "adds a great deal to the melody when properly used." A third kind, the *martellement*, is Hotteterre's trilling on the border of the hole, "which produces approximately the same effect as does [the vibrato] on the violin" (*L'art de la flûte*, 9–10). Here we have one of the few references to the violin vibrato in France, yet sporadic mention does not imply only sporadic use. After all, Mersenne, speaking of the violin in his *Harmonie universelle* of 1636, had referred in matters of ornamentation to the lute, indicating that the same graces, including therefore the left-hand vibrato, were to be practiced on the violin as well (*Traité des instrumens à chordes*, 3:182). Moreover, since the vibrato was much used by the gambists, we can reasonably assume that violinists would have followed their example. After de Lusse we have, in 1777, another clear reference for the violin by P. (first name unknown) Signoretti. Speaking of *le balancé*, he gives the symbol of the wavy line and adds that it is done "by the movement of the wrist while firmly pressing the finger on the string." He also gives an ingenious graphic design that shows a kind of vibrato-*messa di voce* where on a whole note the oscillations start small, get larger to the middle, then decline again: ⁎⁎⁎ (*Méthode de la musique et du violon*, 11).

*Italy.* An early reference to the string vibrato in Italy is the following interesting passage from Sylvestro Ganassi's viol treatise of 1543: "At times one trembles with the bow arm and with the fingers of the hand around the neck in order to achieve an expression appropriate for sad and aggrieved music" (*Regola rubertina* pt. 1, chap. 2). He speaks here clearly of a combination of left-hand (pitch) and right-hand (intensity) vibrato. Lodovico Zacconi in 1592 sees in the vocal vibrato ("il tremolo, cioè la voce tremante") "the entrance door to the *passaggi*. . . . This tremolo must be succinct and attractive [succinto & vago]; when overdone and forced it becomes tedious and annoying; its nature is such that when used, it must be used always" (*Prattica di musica*, fol. 60r). Thirty years later, Carlo Farina, a pioneer of virtuoso violin playing, explains in the preface to his *Capriccio stravagante* of 1627 the tremolo as being done "by pulsating the hand that carries the bow in the manner of the tremulant of the organ." Antonio Cesti uses this bow vibrato in his operas, for instance in *Il pomo d'oro* of 1666, to express Athena's trembling rage at being slighted. He marks it (in perhaps the earliest use of the symbol) with the wavy line above repeated pitches.[8]

In the early 18th century Vivaldi indicates the same effect with slur marks over repeated pitches. Yet in mid-18th century we find composers such as Padre Martini or Veracini returning to the wavy line symbol.

In Italy the vibrato picture is complicated by the vocal grace of the *trillo,* the fast tone repetition that ranged from a clear staccato articulation to a legato-style rendition of fast emphases without interruption of the breath. It is the latter type that produces a vibrato-like effect, as a true counterpart to the bow pulsations of string instruments. This consciously and artfully contrived effect must not, however, be confused with the innate, spontaneous (predominantly pitch-) vibration of the human voice. The *trillo* was unknown in France, certainly in its staccato mode, though the French vocal manipulations of the *balancement* had a probable kinship with its legato mode. The *trillo* in both of its manifestations found disciples in Germany.

Tartini devotes in his ornamentation treatise of ca. 1750 a whole chapter to the tremolo, referring now solely to the left-hand vibrato. He shows how the speed of the vibrato can be varied, being even, slow, fast, or accelerating according to the needs of the "affect" (*Regole*, 15–16). Tartini reserved the vibrato for special occasions, treating it as a genuine ornament, but gave no symbol for it.

At nearly the same time, however, Geminiani advocates a much wider use of what he calls the "close shake." He lists the various affects the vibrato can help produce on long and medium-length notes, depending on the dynamic shadings of the bowstroke. On short notes, it simply "makes their sound more agreeable and for this reason it should be made use of as often as possible" (*Art of Playing Violin,* Preface). Greta Moens-Haenen, who, in her voluminous monograph on the vibrato, tries to establish the latter's very limited use in the 17th and 18th centuries, misinterprets Geminiani's presentation: her claims that Geminiani "rejects a continuous vibrato" and that he "greatly restricts" its use ("sehr eingeschränkt") have no basis in the text. As to his advice of using the vibrato on short notes "as often as possible," Moens-Haenen argues remarkably that to vibrate "on any note" does not imply "on every note" (*Das Vibrato*, 174). Geminiani, however, did not write "on any note" but "as often as possible," and that hardly sounds "greatly restrictive." There is no denying Geminiani's preference for generous vibrato use, and, as we have seen, he is by no means alone in this partiality.

As to the voice, the famous soprano Francesca Cuzzoni (ca. 1698–1770), according to Burney, had a "natural warble" and a "nest of night-ingales in her belly," referring no doubt to her fine vibrato (quoted by Ellen Harris, "Voices"). J. A. Hiller reports in 1780 that the castrato Carestini used the vibrato "frequently and with very fine effect" (quoted in Moens-Haenen, *Das Vibrato*, 214).

*England.* Christopher Simpson in 1659 calls the vibrato a "close shake" and cleverly indicates its nature by means of a trill design that remains within the confines of one space on the staff, as shown in Ex. 31.28 (*Division-Violist* [1659], 9; [1667], 12). John Playford adopted this model for his *Introduction to the Skill of Musick* ([1674], bk. 1, 116). Simpson lists the vibrato as a "feminine" grace that is used to express love, sorrow, or compassion (*Division-Violist* [1659], 9; [1667], 12). His vibrato was most likely of the one-finger shaking type inasmuch as the more sophisticated two-finger technique would seem to have called for a special explanation and perhaps a special term and symbol.

EXAMPLE 31.28.   Simpson (1659)

In addition Simpson also describes the bow vibrato and warns against its overuse: "Some also affect a Shake or Tremble with the bow, like a Shaking Stop of an Organ, but the frequent use thereof is not (in my opinion) much commendable" ([1667], 9). Purcell, in *King Arthur,* Act III, Scene 2, uses the wavy line to indicate first bow oscillations, then the shivering of the voice at the rise of the "Cold Genius."

*Germany.* In Germany, an early mention of the left-hand vibrato is made in the mid-16th century by Martin Agricola, who, speaking of Polish violins (*Polische Geigen*), tells in poetic form how the "free [loose?] trembling" sweetens the melody ("Auch schafft man mit dem zittern frey / Das süsser laut die melodey"; *Musica instrumentalis deudsch* [1545], fol. 42).

Toward the end of the century, in 1598, Georg Quitschreiber asks for a fluctuating voice: "Tremula voce optime canitur" (one sings best with a quivering voice; quoted in Moens-Haenen, *Das Vibrato*, 158).

In the 17th century the *trillo* in both its forms became familiar in Germany along with other Italian ornamental practices. As was mentioned above, its legato mode, with its consciously produced series of fast intensity pulsations, is related to the vibrato. Praetorius, through his presentation in the *Syntagma musicum* of 1619, may have been the chief conduit for the German adoption of the *trillo* with its two modes.

Very important for us, and for the issue at hand, Praetorius expresses the opinion that the spontaneous vibrato—as contrasted with the artifact of the *trillo*—is an innate component of the human voice and a requisite for artistic singing. Speaking of boys to be instructed in the Italian manner of singing, he writes that they have to have a good voice to begin with, and as the first of three requirements he lists the possession of a vibrato: "that a singer possess a beautiful, lovely, trembling and wavering voice" (eine schöne liebliche zittern- und bebende Stimme). Earlier in the chapter, Praetorius anticipated this statement when he criticized singers, who, "gifted by God and nature with a singularly lovely, trembling, and fluctuating or wavering voice," indulge in excesses of embellishments that obscure the text (*Syntagma musicum*, 3:229–31).

A century and a half later we find this statement confirmed by another unimpeachable authority. Mozart, in a letter to his father from Paris of June 12, 1778, had this to say:

> Meissner, as you know, has the bad habit of purposefully pulsating the voice, marking on a long-held note all the quarters and sometimes even the eighths—and that manner of his I have never been able to tolerate. It is truly abominable and such singing runs counter to nature. The human voice vibrates by itself, but in a way and to a degree that is beautiful—this is the nature of the voice, and one imitates it not only on wind instruments, but also on strings, and even on the clavichord but as soon as one carries it too far, it ceases to be beautiful, because it is unnatural.

This passage is remarkable on several counts. It confirms the presence of vibrato as being in "the nature of the voice," and it stresses its beauty, which prompted an imitation on string and wind instruments that Mozart clearly approved of; it characterizes the vibrato as a natural, spontaneous component of the voice, setting it apart from the willful, pulsating manipulations of the voice that Mozart found objectionable and outright "abominable" when done in the bad taste of Meissner's (slow) rhythmic emphases. One thing emerges clearly: Mozart desired the vocal vibrato as well as its discreet instrumental imitation.

During the 150 years that separated the strikingly similar documents of Praetorius and Mozart, German writers continued to remark on the vibrato. Beginning with the enlarged 1624 edition of his *Musica figuralis*, Daniel Friderici echoes Praetorius's admonition that boys should learn from the beginning to form the voice naturally and if possible in a delicately wavering, fluctuating, quivering manner ("fein zitternd / schwebend oder bebend"; chap. 7, regula 2).

Also following Praetorius's lead, a number of writers showed models of the *trillo*, among them Herbst, Crüger, Printz, Mylius, Feyertag, Beyer, and Fuhrmann. Some of these, for instance Printz, made a clear distinction between the staccato and legato modes as *trillo* and *trilletto* respectively (*Compendium*, chap. 5, par. 22), as did Feyertag with the same two terms (*Syntaxis*, 220–21). Fuhrmann in 1706 illustrates his *tremoletto* with staccato dots over a series of notes on the same pitch but explains the grace in unmistakable vibrato terms by a reference to the violin left-hand vibrato (*Musikalischer Trichter*, 66; *Musica vocalis*, 45), thus seemingly forming a bridge between *trillo* and the standard pitch vibrato.

Johann Crüger in 1654, while criticizing the abuse of *passaggi*, writes: "It would be more praiseworthy and more agreeable to the listener if on the violin [instead of coloraturas] they would make use of a steady, sustained, long bowstroke together with a fine vibrato [mit feinem Tremulanten]" (*Synopsis musica*, 189). His reference to a steady, sustained bowstroke makes it clear that he is speaking not of a right-hand but of a left-hand pitch vibrato.

Sperling in 1708 writes that a slur over several notes of the same pitch indicates that they are to be sung with a *Tremulant*. On a later page he describes a tremolo or *tremolante* as a "half trill" in which the upper note is only barely "half-touched" (*Porta musica*, 68, 84).

Walther in 1732 applies the term *tremolo* for string instruments primarily to bow pulsations (*Musicalisches Lexicon*, s.v. "Tremolo"). Mattheson in 1739 explains the term *Tremolo* (or *Beben*) for lute and violin as pitch vibrato, then adds that such pulsations can be produced on the violin with the *bow alone*, without any change of pitch (*Vollkommene Capellmeister*, pt. 2, chap. 3, pars. 27–29). We need not be surprised to find the bow oscillations cropping up here and there in Bach's music.

J. S. Bach uses the wavy-line symbol with unquestionable vibrato meaning a few times for the voice and for melody instruments. We have to remember that for him too the symbol has extended trill (or mordent) meaning only for the keyboard. The symbol occurs invariably in a chromatic progression that by itself is affect-colored and for the voice always in connection with words that express a strong emotion such as fear or sorrow. Two characteristic vocal phrases are given in Ex. 31.29a and 31.29b, from the autographs of Cantatas No. 66 and 116 respectively; Exx. 31.29c and 31.29d show two instrumental phrases, from the autographs of the Fifth "Brandenburg" Concerto and from the Sonata in A Minor for Violin Solo respectively.[9] The vocal phrases are presumably to be done with a tremor of the voice, as if evoked by grief or fear. The instrumental ones—usually misinterpreted as trills—ought presumably to be done for the violin with a bow undulation, as sketched in Ex. 31.29e, probably meant to be supplemented by a left-hand pitch vibrato, and for the flute in a similar manner. (For more illustrations, see *OrnB*, Ex. 45.8.)

EXAMPLE 31.29.   Bach

a. Cantata No. 66/1 (aut. P 73)

Trau - - - ren

b. Cantata No. 116/2 (aut. BN)

Angst - - - -

c. Fifth "Brandenburg" Concerto, BWV 1050, 1

d. Sonata in A Minor for Solo Violin, BWV 1003 (aut. P 967)    e. Suggested execution

Several authors mention the vibrato on the clavichord, for instance C. P. E. Bach, who calls it *Bebung* and uses the following symbol: ⌢⌢·⌢. (*Versuch über Art das Clavier* [1753], chap. 3, par. 20). Marpurg uses the same term and symbol but finds that only a few clavichords permit its tolerable rendition (*Anleitung zum Clavierspielen,* 46). Türk follows in the same pattern (*Klavierschule,* chap. 4, par. 88).[10]

Quantz recommends the (left-hand) vibrato on the violin in order to cover up a slight rise in pitch that results when on a long-held note the tone is swelled and a concomitant growth of the finger pressure slightly sharpens the pitch (as was explained above in n. 7; *Versuch einer Anweisung,* chap. 17, sec. 2, par. 32). It will be well to keep in mind Quantz's use of the vibrato to *improve* intonation when we shall presently hear the charge by some that vibrato impairs it.

Leopold Mozart's discussion of the violin vibrato is derived from Tartini, whose examples he takes over bodily (*Versuch einer Violinschule,* chap. 11, pars. 1–7). Leopold does, however, preface his discussion by saying that the vibrato originates in nature itself and can be used on long notes with graceful effect ("zierlich kann angebracht werden") by good instrumentalists and skillful singers (par. 1). "Nature" in this context is the wavering sound of a struck bell. On the negative side he adds that there are players who "tremble constantly on every note, as if they had the permanent fever" (par. 3). The remark shows two things; that some players used the incessant vibrato and that he, in agreement with Tartini, favored instead its selective use.[11]

Johann Georg Tromlitz, in his flute treatise of 1791, discusses the vibrato (*Bebung*) and prefers its execution with the fingers rather than with the breath. The finger technique is similar to Hotteterres trilling by covering only a fraction of the next open hole. He does admit the breath only as subsidiary technique to reinforce the finger action. He advises restraint in its use and lists long notes, fermatas, and the note before a cadence as good candidates for its application (*Ausführlicher Unterricht,* 239–40).

---

## The Vibrato Controversy

The main issue (regarding vibrato) for historical performance is the degree to which it is to be used for both voices and instruments in whatever might be understood as "early music." The issue is important because of the strong effect that vibrato (or its absence) exerts on any performance.

As to the voice, we have the testimonials of Praetorius and Mozart to the effect that the vibrato is a natural component of a desirable voice. Consider a singer who is blessed with a voice that, in Mozart's terms, "vibrates by itself" yet who wants to eliminate this vibrato as supposedly unhistorical. To do so, a singer must make a special effort to suppress it, and this effort involves a build-up of muscular tension that is both tiring and in the long run believed to be harmful to the voice.

To my knowledge nobody has so far produced genuine evidence that singers before 1800 were expected to sing without vibrato. Sporadic attempts to unearth such evidence have not been convincing.[12]

Neil Zaslaw has argued, however, with respect to Mozart and strings: "There is good historical evidence to suggest that [vibrato was] used sparingly by soloists and generally eschewed by well-disciplined orchestra players" (*Mozart's Symphonies,* 481). We need to inquire into the "good historical evidence" that would ban vibrato from orchestral playing and severely restrict it for soloistic performance.

Zaslaw quotes the same passage from Mozart's letter that has been presented above (p. 505) about Meissner's deplorable habit of constant rhythmic emphases, but he interprets it in conjunction with a few other quotations as a decisively negative verdict on vocal vibrato. One of these supporting passages is from another letter (April 4, 1787) by Mozart in which he complains about the oboist Johann Christian Fischer, who "plays like a bad beginner" and has a nasal, tremulous tone. This is, however, an indictment of Mr. Fischer's defective technique, not a rejection of a well-executed vibrato.

As one of his main witnesses, Zaslaw quotes Robert Bremner, a pupil of Geminiani. Bremner disagreed with his teacher's idea of using the vibrato as often as possible. Vibrato reminds him of "the voice of one who is paralytic." Nevertheless he conceded that—in solo playing—the vibrato "may . . . be admitted, at times, on a long note in simple melody; yet, if it be introduced into harmony . . . it becomes hurtful. The proper stop is a fixed point, from which the least deviation is erroneous: consequently the *tremolo,* which is a departure from this point, will not only confuse the harmony . . . but also enfeeble it" (quoted in Zaslaw, *Mozart's Symphonies,* 479). Thus while Bremner allows the use of vibrato by a soloist on long notes, he wants to ban it completely for orchestral playing. On the other hand, as Zaslaw reports, Carl Friedrich Cramer (Bremner's German translator), writing in the 1780s, found Bremner "entirely too much prejudiced against the vibrato" and argued for its instrumental use "with discretion and upon reflection" (479).

Zaslaw then quotes Leopold Mozart, whose dislike of a pervasive vibrato has been mentioned above (p. 507), and who gave as his reason the fact that the tremolo is not pure on one pitch but sounds undulating (Zaslaw, *Mozart's Symphonies,* 480). Yet Leopold did, like Tartini, recommend the vibrato for long notes where it can be used "with graceful effect."

Zaslaw's last and severest witness is Francesco Galeazzi, who wrote: "[Vibrato] consists in pressing the finger well on the string . . . and then, marking with the hand a certain paralytic and trembling motion . . . resulting in a vacillating pitch and a certain continual trembling . . .; but these are most genuine discords which . . . should be entirely banned from music by anybody equipped with good taste" (480). Galeazzi's aversion, unlike Bremner's, is unconditional. It would seem that both Bremner and Galeazzi failed to recognize the aural delusion of "sonance" in a well-produced vibrato.[13]

In summarizing the evidence, Zaslaw emphasizes the negative aspects, notably the alleged impurities of intonation, and the claim that "Mozart writes three times 'contrary to nature' " (481). This last reference, however, is misleading: what Mozart found to be "contrary to nature" was not the vibrato but Meissner's periodic emphases on quarters and eighths.

As Zaslaw has shown in his résumé, several writers opposed vibrato in varying degrees. But we must put those statements within the larger context of the impressive array of positive comments by writers from France, Italy, England, and Germany who in a steady stream, beginning in the mid-16th century, extolled the values and virtues of good vibrato. And above all, we must always recall Mozart's own words, which bear repetition: "The human voice vibrates by itself, but in a way that is beautiful—this is in the nature of the voice, and one imitates it not only on wind instruments, but also on strings, and even on the clavichord."

All in all, the historical evidence might be read to favor moderation in the use of the vibrato, be it vocal or instrumental, but cannot be read to call for its drastic restriction, let alone for its total elimination, be it for solo or ensemble performance.

# 32

# IMPROVISATION I: FRANCE AND ITALY

The small graces prescribed by symbol that have so far occupied our attention represent only one wing of the ornamental structure for the era of our concern. The other consists of ornaments not marked in the score but added on the performer's initiative. Whether improvised or prepared in advance, such additions were often expected, in which case the failure to provide them would present the composition in an unfinished form not desired by the composer. These supplements can range from the briefest one-note graces to fanciful flourishes or even lengthy cadenzas.

Understandably, the main problems of improvisation concern first the question of when additions should, may, or should not be made and, second, the question of their desirable form and design. For help in trying to answer these questions we can turn to a number of theoretical primary sources as well as to many cases in which noted composers have written out ornamental figurations that others would have left unwritten.

In what follows, the terms "improvisation" and "free ornamentation" will be used interchangeably. Other terms have more specific meanings: "diminutions" (the old English "divisions") are embellishments in which the written notes are broken up into smaller denominations; *passaggio* (pl: *-ggi*), *coloratura* (*-ure*), and *fioritura* (*-ure*) are Italian synonyms for a florid ornamental figuration; their French equivalent is *passage*, also *roulade*, the German approximate equivalent is *willkürliche Manier*. While diminutions are always based on a melodic progression spelled out in the score, *passaggi* and its equivalents may refer not only to the embroidery of a written melody but also to an added transition between phrases or to the embellishment of fermatas.

## French Practices

In France the first two-thirds of the 17th century saw the blossoming of the *airs de cour* (court airs), secular songs set most often to love lyrics. They typically had two couplets (and sometimes more), of which the first was sung with only small ornamental additions at the most, whereas the second was floridly embellished. We have many illustrations of such embellishments as spelled out by the composer or by well-known singers. Example 32.1 gives a sample excerpt from a late stage of this genre, in which the embellishments have achieved a high degree of refinement. Michel Lambert, the composer, was the most famous singer of his time and the father-in-law of Lully. Lully himself was opposed to the practice of improvised ornamentation and was said to have tolerated in his operas only very occasional second couplet embellishments, and then only those that were prepared by Lambert.

The style of these *air de cour* embellishments shows a significant predominance of the prebeat *Vorschlag*-type graces of the *ports de voix* and *coulés*. In the brief but thoroughly typical ten-measure excerpt in Ex. 32.1, there are no less than nine anticipated *ports de voix* and *coulés* and not one unambiguous appoggiatura.[1]

Lully's rejection of florid improvised embellishments, which he called nonsensical, was rooted in his ideal of truthful dramatic declamation. His opposition was directed against elaborate, coloratura-type embroideries, not against the small graces such as the *port de voix* or the slide. Additions of the latter were expected and needed to alleviate the stark austerity of Lully's written text, where the only symbols for ornaments are those for trills since others were not yet in use.[2]

Lully's aversion against florid embellishments was certainly a weighty factor in the subsequent decline of this style in France, but it was not the only factor. Powerful as he was, Lully could not have single-handedly brought about such profound change in ornamental practices had he not been backed in his attitude by the growing wave of rationalism that had begun to sweep the nation. This rationalism not only favored the word in its conflict with music but went so far as to find the ultimate justification of music in its literary or pictorial associations. Dominance of the word in turn implied opposition to fanciful musical embroidery.

The gradual atrophy of the French coloraturas is reflected in the works of important theorists. Bacilly, along with Lambert one of the most accomplished practitioners of vocal improvisation, devotes the thirteenth chapter of his famous treatise of 1668 (*Remarques curieuses*) to

EXAMPLE 32.1.    Lambert, *Air de cour* (*Les airs de M. Lambert*, Paris, 1666) with 2nd couplet diminutions

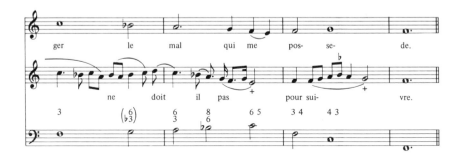

"Passages et diminutions." The better part of this chapter is concerned with a defense of the coloraturas against a rising wave of criticism. Bacilly speaks of "extremely influential" critics who charge the coloraturas with irrationality and accuse them of destroying true expression and obscuring both melody and words. Bacilly responds by asserting that only poorly placed or poorly invented diminutions have the deplorable effect the critics try to pin unjustly on all of them. Well-invented and correctly placed diminutions, so Bacilly holds, will add beauty and expression at no cost whatever to music and poetry. He was, however, fighting a losing battle, and soon after vocal diminutions had reached their highest point of refinement around the 1660s, they began a rapid descent. As a consequence, by the end of the 17th century vocal diminutions were drastically reduced in size. We can gather that much from Loulié's treatise of 1696, where he illustrates *passages* and *diminutions* as given in Exx. 32.2a and 32.2b respectively (*Éléments ou principes de musique*, 74ff.). L'Affilard in 1694 (and thereafter) makes no mention of improvisation of any kind. Montéclair in 1736 gives several illustrations of modest embroidery, of which one is shown in Ex. 32.2c. Such *passages* are arbitrary, and everyone, he says, can make them according to their own taste and disposition. But he was adamantly opposed to any more lavish embroidery, "which is practiced less in vocal than in instrumental music, especially now when the instrumentalist, wishing to imitate the Italian style, disfigures with frequently ridiculous variations the nobility of simple melodies." He then goes on to confirm in a memorable passage Lully's aversion to diminutions: "the incomparable Lully, this superior genius . . . has preferred the melody, beautiful modulation, pleasing harmony, truthfulness of expression, naturalness, noble simplicity to the ridiculousness of the *doubles* and heteroclite strains, whose merit consists only in deviancy, in twisted modulations, in the harshness of chords, in noise, and in confusion. All this deceptive luster reveals the aridity of the author's talent yet never fails to impress ignorant ears" (*Principes*, 86–87).

EXAMPLE 32.2

a. Loulié (1696), *Passages*

b. Loulié (1696), *Diminutions*

c. Montéclair (1736)

While improvised diminutions and *passaggi* did not disappear entirely, by the start of the 18th century they had become a marginal
phenomenon on the French musical scene. Even on the violin, where
Italian influence was greatest, the vogue of florid embellishments was
also fast receding. The early masters of the sonata, like Aubert, Senallié,
or Francoeur "aîné," who looked to Corelli as their master, only rarely
wrote adagios that were so bare that they craved diminutions, though
some additions often seemed desirable. Leclaire, in the preface to his
fourth book of violin sonatas of 1738, demands that his performers refrain from adding to songful and expressive pieces "that confusion of
notes which serves only to disfigure" (*Quatrième livre de sonates à violon
seul avec la basse continue*).

In mid-18th century we get further confirmation of the absence of
improvised diminutions in France from Quantz, who had a French flute
teacher, played under a French director in Dresden, and visited Paris for
half a year to study French practices. Pieces in the French style, he says,
are written in such a way "that hardly anything else can be added to
what the composer has written," in contrast to works in the Italian style,
where "much is left to the willfulness and ability of the player." He
confirms this statement in a later paragraph by declaring that the French
style "suffers no extended *passages*" (*Versuch einer Anweisung*, chap. 14,
pars. 2 and 4).

The void left by the demise of the diminutions was filled by a multitude of small graces, the *agréments*. The lutenists first developed them
around 1600, and when in the second half of the 17th century lute
playing went out of fashion, the rising school of clavecinists adopted
and further evolved and refined them. The now widespread use of
symbols did not spell the end of improvisatory embellishments. Composers differed greatly in the degree to which they prescribed the desirable graces. Some tried to keep a tight rein on the performer, while
others gave more latitude. Couperin bitterly complained about those
performers who did not honor all of his detailed ornamental instructions
and demanded that no ornaments he marked be left out and that none
be added (*Pièces de clavecin*, bk. 3, Preface). Other composers were far
less explicit and relied on improvisatory additions by the performer.

The right of the performer to use his judgment in matters of the
*agréments* had an eloquent advocate in Saint Lambert, whose important
clavecin treatise of 1702 has been repeatedly referred to in previous
chapters. In sharp contrast to Couperin, he stresses the complete freedom of the small ornaments and claims for the performer the right not
only to add new ones but to leave out those that are prescribed and to
substitute others in their stead (*Principes de clavecin*, 57). In consequence
of this unsettled state of affairs, we find many late 18th-century treatises
still preoccupied not only with explaining the ornamental designs of the
*agréments* but also with explaining the contexts in which a certain ornament could, should, or should not be used.

In briefest summary, we may discreetly add a few *agréments* of the *port de voix* and slide variety to Lully's airs to alleviate the austerity of the vocal line, inasmuch as these graces were not included in his ban on diminutions. Diminutions are possibly appropriate only in *airs de cour* and in certain violin sonatas or concertos with adagios written in semi-skeletal style. For the clavecin, the gamba, the flute, and other wind instruments, no additions should be made whenever composers (such as Couperin or Marais) gave copious ornamental prescriptions. Where such prescriptions are relatively sparse, a few careful additions may be made but will rarely be indispensable.

## Italian Practices

By the end of the 16th century the Italians had developed the practice of diminutions to a high degree of refinement and complexity, as we can gather from a number of pedagogical works that discuss the procedures involved and demonstrate their application to contemporary music such as motets and madrigals.[3] For a characteristic illustration of these procedures, Ex. 32.3 shows excerpts from Bovicelli's embellishments of 1594 of the Palestrina motet "Ave verum." The embellishments start with moderate simplicity, then wax more florid and end with an expansive coloratura. The ornamentation often emancipates itself from the basic melody, but whenever it fails to coincide with the model on the beats it strikes a pitch from the harmony of the chord.[4]

Around the same time, shortly before 1600, momentous happenings, foremost among them the invention of the recitative and monody and the birth of opera, ushered in what has sometimes been called the "Baroque revolution." The upheaval centered on the relationship of words to music, or rather on the primacy of one or the other. In the perennial tug-of-war between words and music the "Baroque revolution" constituted a pendulum swing of unprecedented scope in favor of the word. In the dramatic recitative, the focal center of the new style, music was assigned the relatively subservient role of enhancing rhetorical declamation and of deepening the "affect" of the words by melodic inflection and chordal coloring. It was a natural consequence of this new orientation that vocal polyphony was rejected and florid ornamentation severely restricted. The reformers were animated by the same ideal of truthful declamation that sixty years later prompted Lully to reject *passages* and diminutions. Cavalieri, one of the pioneers of the new style, banned *passaggi* outright in his *Rappresentatione di anima e di corpo* of 1600. Caccini, in his *Nuove musiche* of 1602, the chief manifesto of the new style, reaffirms the ban against extensive diminutions, but being a virtuoso singer himself, he is less strict and admits brief *passaggi* up to half of a beat in length; and to judge from many examples in his music, he exempts final cadences from any restrictions.

EXAMPLE 32.3.    Bovicelli (1594) (Palestrina, "Ave verum")

When composers in the new style asked in their prefaces that nothing be added to the written score, they meant *passaggi* but *not* small graces, then often referred to as *accenti e trilli*. *Accenti* were small melodic graces of up to about four or five notes, and *trilli* small repercussive graces of the trill, *trillo*, or mordent types. Their extempore addition in appropriate places was always welcome. In addition, rhythmic manipulations of the rubato type and dynamic nuances of the *messa di voce* or *esclamazione* species were recommended to increase the affective power of certain melodic figures and provide another enlivening compensation for the absence of lengthy *passaggi*.

What was actually done we cannot know since genuine improvisations do not leave any traces. Furthermore, Italian theory on matters of performance fell silent for a hundred years after Francesco Rognioni in

1620, and Francesco himself, in spite of some modern traits such as the *trillo* or lively Lombard rhythms, may have reflected his father Richardo's 16th-century vein more than the new style. The void of Italian theory is to a certain (minor) extent filled by German writers (to be discussed in the following chapter) who report on Italian practices as models for their readers.

There seems little doubt, however, that in monody and early opera, extensive vocal *passaggi* were restricted, more by some composers than by others. Monteverdi, in reporting on singers, judged them on their ability to sing *gorgie* (i.e., *passaggi*) and *trilli*.[5] He himself, who had embraced the new style (the *seconda prattica*, as he called it), wrote out on infrequent occasions some very rich *passaggi* such as the one shown in Ex. 32.4. This example is especially interesting for the way it integrates scale passages, broken chords, the *trillo*, the regular (main-note) trill, the prebeat *Vorschlag*, the *Nachschlag*, and the slide into the coloraturas. Such written-out specimens of *passaggi* by important masters offer us the best possible insight into the contemporary style of desirable improvisations.

Instruments are not involved in the word–music antagonism, and Caccini is only being consistent when he writes that "diminutions are more appropriate for winds and strings than for the voices" (*Nuove musiche,* Preface). The keyboard as a solo instrument was farthest removed from the stylistic break. Frescobaldi's music developed in an unbroken line from his 16th-century predecessors and displayed a continuity of polyphonic writing in an era that often turned its back on it. His toccatas, however, with their rhythmic freedom and declamatory character, had a distinct kinship to the recitative. Ornamental figurations are spelled out in regular notes, and there seems to be no place for the addition of *passaggi,* though *accenti* and *trilli* might occasionally be introduced in slow-moving sections of, for instance, a canzona. This is true also of Frescobaldi's students, Michelangelo Rossi, Froberger, and Kerll, and of such later Italian masters as Strozzi and Starace.

The most vexing problem of instrumental improvisation refers to ensembles, church music, and opera. Here we have very little solid information and must often have recourse to pure speculation. Schütz, in the preface to his Resurrection Oratorio of 1634, encourages one solo viola to play diminutions in the recitatives of the Evangelist but apparently nowhere else. Though the Italians were probably less reserved than their northern disciples, it is questionable whether they went as far as Robert Donington seems to imply when he speaks of collective improvisation by the "ornament instruments" (i.e., high melody instruments) in those places where only a bass line survives, or even no instrumental part at all (*Interpretation of Early Music,* 171–72, 606–9). Perhaps, as Gloria Rose surmises, material was handed out that did not survive ("Agazzari and the Improvising Orchestra"); more likely such

EXAMPLE 32.4.   Monteverdi (1629), *Exulta filia Sion*

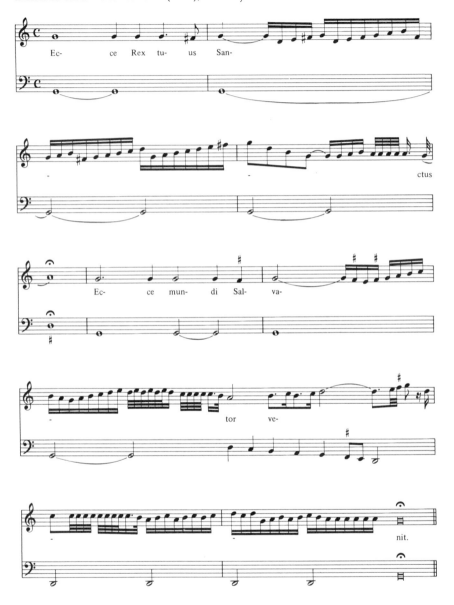

improvisation of the musical substance was left to the player of the
harmony instrument (organ, harpsichord, lute) since collective improvisation would surely have invited chaos. What really happened in such
cases we simply do not know. Today it will be up to the editor to fill such
gaps, possibly in a way that will leave room for some ornamental improvisation.

Returning to vocal music, the doctrinaire stance taken by the founding fathers of monody with regard to the primacy of the word could not last very long. Being the stronger partner, music soon rebelled against its subjugation to the word. Melodic blossoms began to spring up in arioso passages to relieve the dryness and tedium of endless recitative, and the places multiplied where appropriate textual clues were taken as occasion for ornamental passages. This evolution led by mid-17th century to the full emancipation of pure, singable melody, together with pure, playful ornament, in the so-called *bel canto* style of such masters as Cavalli, Cesti, Carissimi, and Stradella. For written-out specimens of *passaggi* by Cesti, see Ex. 32.5, from *Il pomo d'oro* from 1666.

EXAMPLE 32.5. Cesti (1666), *Il Pomo d'oro*, II, 14

This era produced its virtuoso singers and saw castrati rise to prominence and power. They claimed the right to often lavish improvised embellishments. Many composers recognized this right and consequently refrained from spelling out florid embellishments. They then intentionally wrote in an austere manner, relying on the singer's ability to improvise the necessary ornamental figurations. The *locus classicus* for such procedure became the evolving da capo aria where on the da capo return florid embellishments were expected but never spelled out. If written in a bare style, some small additions of *accenti* and *trilli* were in order already for the first part. The situation here was very similar to that of the simply written *airs de cour* and their two couplets.

When in the second half of the 17th century the violin sonata came into its own, followed soon by the concerto, analogous procedures were applied to their adagio movements. Written often in bare outline, the violinist was expected to flesh out the skeleton with ornamental figurations. In both aria and sonata the composer had the right to expect proper skills on the part of the performer while hoping that these skills would be used with good judgment and taste.

These hopes were not always fulfilled, however. The newly gained freedom, like any freedom, engendered abuse, and the never-too-rare species of performers who are vain and lacking in judgment often indulged in tasteless exaggerations that distorted many a composition. From now on we hear recurring complaints by composers who protest against such excesses.[6]

It is interesting that this second flowering of the *passaggi* in Italy came at a time when such large-scale embellishments had gone out of fashion in France, where principles akin to the monody were enthroned by the formidable Lully. From that time on lavish ornamental additions became associated with the Italian style as contrasted with the French style, in which ornamental additions were now mostly limited to the *agréments*.

Supplementing the Italian *passaggi*, many small graces were also in improvisatory use during the 17th century but did not appear in the score, since in Italy ornamental symbols did not come into use until the 18th century was well on its way. Only the trill symbol *t* had been in use for trill, mordent, and *trillo* from at least the beginning of the 17th century. But trills and mordents (*tremulo di sotto*) were frequently inserted without the prompt of a symbol. Slides and turn-like figures are shown in the many diminution treatises around 1600. Also, as reported in chapter 24, Bernhard had informed us around 1660 about four kinds of "Roman" one-note graces, all of which were anticipated; the (onbeat) appoggiatura made its perhaps first appearance in Bovicelli alongside the prebeat *Vorschläge* (on this, see chapter 23).

*Tosi.* On several occasions in this study reference was made to Pierfrancesco Tosi's important treatise of 1723, *Opinioni de cantori antichi sopra il canto figurato.* One of these references was to Tosi's description of rubato singing against a steady beat in chapter 9 (p. 94), another to his discussion of the various trill types in chapter 27 (p. 397), another brief one to his mention of the appoggiatura in chapter 23 (p. 315). Tosi also offers many enlightening comments on improvisation, though the lack of any musical illustrations is a considerable drawback.[7] He makes what may be the first theoretical statement about the embellishment of the da capo aria. In such an aria, he says, the first part should have only a few simple and tasteful ornaments in order to preserve the integrity of the composition; the second part should be given a little extra garnish to show more of the singer's ability; in the da capo, "whoever cannot vary and thereby improve what he has sung before is no great luminary [non è grand' Uomo]" (*Opinioni de cantori antichi*, 59–60).

The embellishments he has in mind, however, are apparently on a relatively modest scale and a far cry from what was being done at that time by many well-known singers. Belonging to an older, more conservative school, he heaps scorn on the excesses of the "moderns" and their offenses against the true art of singing. True taste, he says, resides not in constant velocity and in ceaseless and baseless roaming of the voice but in songfulness, in the sweetness of the *portamento*, the appoggiaturas, in the art and wisdom of the small graces (*passi*), the "unexpected deceptive play with note values within the strict movement of the bass." Such are, he says, the indispensable qualities of good singing, and they are absent in "extravagant cadenzas" (82). For this reason mainly, so it seems, he generally disapproves of cadenzas. He rejects them unconditionally in the middle of a piece, whereas he finds this "abuse" tolerable at the final cadence. Here, he says, the singer may insert a moderate flourish ("qualque moderato arbitrio") to show that the end is at hand, but he must not do so "outside of the regular measure, and without taste, art, or understanding" (87). He ridicules those singers who in a da capo aria will sing long *passaggi* at the end of the first section, much longer ones at the end of the second, and colossal ones at the end of the aria (81).

Interesting is Tosi's revelation (mentioned in chapter 15) that most of the *passaggi* were done nonlegato, with a moderate detachment so that the *passaggio* is neither too legato nor too staccato. The reason for this preference was presumably the ensuing greater clarity of articulation. The slur, he says, has only limited application in singing and should not encompass more than four notes.

He lists five types of small improvised ornaments (*passi*), "the most treasured delight of connoisseurs": the appoggiatura, the trill, the *portamento di voce*, the *scivolo*, and the *strascino* (111). As to the appoggiatura, he sees, as mentioned in chapter 23, the new fashion of marking it in the score as a slight of the intelligence of the singer, who should know where to place one and where not. Tosi does not explain the term *portamento*; Agricola, Tosi's German translator, however, understands it to mean the connection of pitches without interruption of the breath with a slight emphasis on each tone; *portato* rather than *portamento* is today's more common term for this type of articulation (the Germans call it *das Tragen der Töne*). *Scivolo*, meaning gliding, and *note scivolate*, meaning notes played with a sliding finger, refer most likely to the fast, anticipatory, upward gliding into a new pitch (i.e., the way the term *portamento* is most commonly understood today). The *strascino* (literally, dragging) is explained in an obscure paragraph (114–15)—that bewildered Agricola—from which emerges, so it seems, a rubato within a steady beat in combination with swelling and tapering of the voice.

Among other directives for the proper use of the small graces, Tosi says that they should be well spaced from one another and should never be repeated on the same spot.

Most significant in Tosi's presentation is the relatively modest scope he allows for *passaggi,* his general aversion to cadenzas, and his almost obsessive insistence on the integrity of the beat. In this conservative stance he was at odds with the upcoming generation of virtuoso singers—such as the legendary Farinelli—who indulged in elaborate *passaggi* and long cadenzas.[8] But Tosi was not alone in his pleas for moderation. Composers had generally little sympathy for the exhibitionism of singers and their ornamental exaggerations but were often incapable of asserting themselves vis-à-vis domineering vocal celebrities. There were exceptions in the case of a few strong personalties among the composers who managed to win the upper hand. Agostino Steffani, as reported by Hawkins, was extremely strict and apparently succeeded in asserting himself: "He would never admit of any divisions, or graces, even on the most plain and simple passages, except what he wrote himself, nor would he, with regard to his duets in particular, suffer them to be performed by any of those luxuriant singers, who had not sense enough to see the folly of sacrificing to the idle vanity of displaying their extent, or power, of voice, not merely the air, but frequently the very harmony of an author's composition" (quoted in Donington, *Interpretation of Early Music,* 156).

Yet, undeterred by such sporadic criticism, Italian virtuoso singers, led in the first half of the 18th century by celebrated castrati such as the above-mentioned Farinelli, indulged in highly florid *passaggi* and cadenzas that would have failed by a wide margin Tosi's conservative standards of restraint.[9] They were the "moderns" whom he had castigated and ridiculed for their excesses, yet their style was widely admired as the epitome of the vocal art. These were some of the famous singers whom Quantz had in mind when he wrote that in the first three decades of the century the art of singing has reached its greatest height (*Versuch einer Anweisung,* chap. 18, par. 56). Cadenzas became an unchallenged institution, though it seems that the finest artists limited their length to a single breath.

The Italian singers continued with their lavish and often extravagant embellishments throughout the rest of the century. Haas illustrates this point with a Cherubini rondo of 1784 as sung by Luigi Marchesi. It shows up to sixteen variants, all highly luxuriant, though each of nine given versions of the cadenza may have been singable with one—long—breath (*Aufführungspraxis der Musik,* 225–30).

*Handel.* Handel, italianate in ornamentation, may again be discussed in the frame of the Italian school. He was not nearly as strict as Steffani and indeed could not be, since a great deal of his music, both vocal and instrumental, was written in a manner that is patently unfinished and in need of ornamental completion by the performer. But we have reason to believe that he did not permit extravagance. We know from Burney that he ruled his establishment with a firm hand and rehearsed his singers individually at the keyboard. And most important, we have a few documents that point to Handel's preference for, or at least his satisfaction with, a remarkably moderate degree of vocal embellishment.

An autograph in the Fitzwilliam Museum in Cambridge (No. 252, pp. 11ff.) contains Handel's ornamental additions to his Italian cantata *Dolce pur d'amor l'affanno,* which he entered for the benefit of a singer. Of 148 measures, only fourteen contain additions written in little notes, and they are quite modest. Ex. 32.6a shows a few excerpts.[10] Furthermore, there are autograph additions to arias (from *Ottone*) that survive in the Bodleian Library in a manuscript first reported by James S. Hall and Martin V. Hall ("Handel's Graces"). Winton Dean elaborated on their findings in a monograph of 1976 and reprinted the arias with the additions in full score (while assigning—not always convincingly—metrical values to Handel's unmetrical insertions).[11] Again the additions are modest (with the exception of mm. 21–22 in "Affanni del pensier," where a lengthy melisma in siciliano rhythm is changed into running figures in sixteenth notes). Exx. 32.6b–32.6c show characteristic excerpts. As Dean points out in his preface, Handel supplied "little or nothing" at final cadences, "presumably" relying here on the singer. Yet the singer who needed guidance throughout the arias would seem to have needed it at cadences as well. Dean comments that Handel's additions never distort the "basic structure beyond recognition, and that Handel in general agreed with Tosi's well-known remarks on the subject" (Handel, *Three Ornamented Arias,* Preface).

*Instrumental Music.* The Italian vocal procedures understandably found their reflection in instrumental music, notably in works for the violin. As briefly mentioned before, adagios of sonatas and concertos, when written in skeletal style, were meant to be embellished.

It was mainly after 1700 that some composers occasionally spelled out diminutions, among them Vivaldi, Locatelli, Veracini, Bonporti, Martini; but hardly anyone seemed consistent. Thus we find for instance Vivaldi's notation running the gamut from skeletal to fully written-out diminutions, while most of his slow movements are in the middle range (to be called later the "first degree" stage) that allowed for further embellishment; similar notational differences are common with other composers.

EXAMPLE 32.6.   Handel

a. Cantata *Dolce pur d'amor l'affanno*

b. *Benche mi sia*                    c. *Alla fama*

About 1715, two years after Corelli's death, Estienne Roger published in Amsterdam an edition of the first six of Corelli's Violin Sonatas
Op. 5, with embellishments allegedly written out by Corelli himself (for
excerpts see Schmitz, *Kunst der Verzierung,* 55–61). The many long arabesques of this much-quoted version surprise by their luxuriance. Roger
North, an astute contemporary observer, bluntly condemned the publication as a fraud: "Upon the bare view of the print any one would
wonder how so much vermin could creep into the works of such a
master" (*Roger North on Music,* 161). Skepticism must have been expressed from various quarters because Estienne Roger felt compelled in
1716 to advertise an offer to show the Corelli manuscript and correspondence to any interested person. Since Roger, whose business practices
were not always above reproach, never to our knowledge produced the
documents, some doubts are still in order that the lavishness of the
coloraturas were a true reflection of Corelli's playing style.

Handel's chamber music too, like that of his Italian contemporaries, is often written in skeletal notation and is in need of embellishments, as are those slow movements that show some mild diminutions but nevertheless seem too bare to stand as notated. To give an idea of what might be needed for such movements, the *larghetto* from the well-known Violin Sonata in D Major (the only one preserved in autograph) may serve. Its first section is shown in Ex. 32.7 as written and as tentatively ornamented.

*Geminiani.* Geminiani's way of playing a Corelli sonata (Op. 5, No. 9) is preserved in a document that shows far greater reserve than the Roger versions and a better balance between structural and ornamental elements.[12] Since Geminiani, a student of Corelli's, was (according to Burney) notorious for his wild, undisciplined playing style (*General History*, 4:641), the ornamental reserve seems significant. The fast movements show considerable alterations that were almost certainly intended for the repeats: they are variations, not ornaments, and do not involve smaller note values.

Geminiani gave us other instructive examples of dual versions. His Sonatas for Violin and Bass Op. 1 were published in London in 1716 (and again ca. 1732) in the usual plain manner. In 1739 he reissued these sonatas "carefully corrected and with the addition, for the sake of greater ease, of the embellishments for the adagios." What is truly remarkable about this edition is the modesty of embellishments and with it the demonstration of how limited an amount of adornments can satisfy the stylistic requirements. A very brief but characteristic excerpt is shown in Ex. 32.8 (for two other excerpts, see *OrnB*, 559). In his (ornamented) sonatas of Op. 4 and Op. 5, Geminiani conveys the same lesson: their style is throughout the same as in Op. 1.[13]

*Tartini.* Tartini devotes more than half of his treatise to the problems of diminutions (*Regole*, 20–43). He calls them *modi*, which might be rendered as "figurations," and distinguishes "natural" from "artificial" ones (*modi naturali* and *artificiali*). The natural ones are those that even unskilled performers can insert spontaneously, whereas the artificial ones presuppose mastery of counterpoint. The natural ones, Tartini says, must not interfere with the melody nor form a discord with the bass, and this principle, to judge from the illustrations, seems to be the touchstone for the difference between the two types. In the natural ones, as shown in Ex. 32.9a, the skeletal notes remain in place while the figuration takes place *between* these notes, in interbeat space, hence affecting neither melody nor harmony. In the artificial *modi*, on the other hand, the skeletal notes may be replaced by pitches other than those of the chord, as we see in Ex. 32.9b for the first beat, or in Ex. 32.9d for the second beat. The Exx. 32.9b and 32.9c show the approximate range between the simple and the elaborate artificial *modi*.

Example 32.7.　Handel, Violin Sonata in D

EXAMPLE 32.8.  Geminiani, Sonata for Violin and Bass, Op. 1, No. 7

Especially important is Tartini's proposition that artificial figurations must not be introduced whenever the melody or a part thereof is either of such thematic significance or of such specific expression that it cannot be altered and must be rendered as written (29). Tartini also offers a number of illustrations for cadenzas, all of which are quite brief and consist of purely virtuoso flourishes; his examples of final cadenzas have an average length of eight measures (42–43).

More revealing still than Tartini's theoretical discussions are a few examples of entire ornamented movements that are preserved in his autograph. They are remarkable for their relative discretion. A twenty-measure excerpt of one such document (from the Capella Antoniana Collection) is given in *OrnB*, 563–64. Most of the figurations therein are of the natural type. Tartini's students and followers were not satisfied with the tasteful moderation of their master, and a rich collection of Tartiniana in Berkeley (Berk. B. E. 4) includes examples of immoderate embellishments. We find the same kinds of deplorable exaggerations in an illustration from Cartier's *École de violon* (ca. 1798) that shows a Tartinian adagio with sixteen versions of embellishments, most of them absurdly overladen (reproduced in Schmitz, *Kunst der Verzierung*, 131–33). Of such players Quantz says that they "overload an adagio with so many embellishments and wild runs that one would mistake it for a gay allegro, while the qualities of the adagio are hardly noticeable anymore" (*Versuch einer Anweisung*, chap. 18, par. 60).

EXAMPLE 32.9.  Tartini

a. "Natural Figuration"

b. "Artificial Figuration"  c.

d.

***How Much to Embellish.*** It is important to keep in mind that in the Italian style, from about the mid-17th to roughly the end of the 18th century, embellishments were obligatory in certain situations, foremost among them in the da capo return of an aria and in austere adagios of sonatas or concertos. To what degree this ought to be done, however, is a question that has no simple answer. It will help to think here in terms of an "ornamentation belt"—that is, a fairly broad range of legitimately possible levels of ornamentation, extending from a desirable minimum to a saturation point. Whenever composers did spell out some ornamental figurations the question arises whether what they wrote already satisfies stylistic demands or needs to be further embellished. And here we can distinguish "first degree" and "second degree" ornamentation, which correspond to budding and fully bloomed diminutions. As a rule of thumb, an adagio is skeletal if it contains no, or only very few, notes smaller than eighths; it has first-degree diminutions if it contains many sixteenth notes; it has second-degree diminutions if it contains a wealth of thirty-second notes or smaller values. The skeletal types were always in need of embellishment; the first-degree types may fulfill stylistic requirements in the lower range of the ornamentation belt, while further ornamental additions are optional and often desirable on repeats; the second-degree designs were in no need of further enrichment but on repeat could be somewhat varied.

# 33

# IMPROVISATION II: GERMANY

## German Followers of Italian Practices

It will be remembered that in the 17th century Italian small graces were widely adopted by German musicians in both north and south, Protestant and Catholic alike (see ch. 24, pp. 321–350). Whereas in the 18th century German musicians went their own ways in matters of the small ornaments, in matters of improvisation they continued to follow Italian models until roughly the advent of the Classical style. For the time span, then, of the 17th century plus about the first two-thirds of the 18th, the label of "Italo-German" seems justified for German improvisation, as it was for the 17th-century small graces.

One of the early German commentators and propagators of Italian practices was Praetorius. In 1619 he showed only the simplest patterns of Bovicelli's diminutions, but these were merely a preliminary exposition pending a projected extensive treatise on diminutions "in Praeceptis and Exemplis" (*Syntagma musicum*, 3:240). Unfortunately, he died before he could carry out his plan.

Herbst, who later in the century (1642, 1650, and 1658) based his treatise on Praetorius's work, also drew on Italian models to illustrate proper diminution practice, and he quotes extensively from Donati, Francesco Rognioni, and Banchieri (*Musica practica* [1658], *passim*).

The restrictions placed on diminutions by the Italian monodists found their reflection also in Germany. Crüger in 1654 inveighs against abuse of the *passaggi* and criticizes those who transgress the permissible limits for coloraturas "and obscure [the song] to a point where one knows not what they sing and cannot perceive, let alone understand, either the text or the notes, as the composer has set them." Instrumentalists, he continues, commit the same offenses, especially on the cornet and the violin, then adds (in a passage previously quoted): "it would be more praiseworthy and more agreeable to the listener if on the violin [instead of *passaggi*] they would make use of a steady, sustained, long bowstroke together with a fine vibrato [mit feinem Tremulanten]" (*Synopsis musica*, 189; *Musicae practicae*, 19).

Schütz's student Christoph Bernhard voices (around 1660) a similar appeal for moderation. Diminutions, he says, should be used only sparingly; otherwise they become difficult for the singer and annoying ("verdriesslich") for the listener. They must not move too high or too low, nor leave the tonality, nor create parallel fifths ("Ross-Quint"), octaves ("Küh-Octav") or unisons, nor destroy the harmony (*Von der Singe-Kunst*, pars. 36–39).

Important to note are a number of improvised ornamental formulas, miniature *passaggi* as it were, that were used in Italy and are known to us through German theorists who propagated them. Printz may have been the first to combine these patterns in a comprehensive presentation: starting with *Phrynis* in 1677 and continuing through a series of related treatises, he displays designs and terms that keep appearing in German tracts for over a hundred years up to Türk, at the end of the 18th century.

Among them is the *circolo mezzo* (Ex. 33.1a), meaning "half circle," a four-note figure of the turn family that can be either rising or falling. In either case the second and fourth tones are the same pitch. The two half circles can be combined to form a *circolo*, a full circle. The *figura suspirans* (Ex. 33.1b) is an anticipated turn; the *figura bombilans* (Ex. 33.1c) a pitch repetition of the *trillo* type; the *tirata* (Ex. 33.1d) the scalewise connection of two distant pitches; the *figura corta* a three-note formula (Ex. 33.1e) in dactylic or anapestic rhythm, that, as Printz tells us, in faster tempo may turn to triplets; and finally the *groppo*, (Ex. 33.1f), a turn embedded in a trill-like, though slower and sharper, alternation.

## *J. S. Bach*

In defiance of the prevailing convention, Bach wrote out his diminutions in regular notes and did so with a greater measure of consistency than he displayed in almost any other notational matter. Thus, we do not find in his slow movements the look of austerity so typical among Italian masters and their German disciples, where the lack of short note values betrays at first glance the need for ornamental additions. He had good reasons to do as he did. His rich harmony, dense texture, and fast

EXAMPLE 33.1.   Printz (1677, 1689)

a. *Circolo mezzo*          b. *Figura suspirans*          c. *Figura bombilans*
                                                            *(Bombo, Schwarmer)*

    *intendens    remittens*

d. *Tirata*

e. *Figura corta*

f. *Groppo*

moving basses presented far greater problems for the proper design of
diminutions than did the much simpler fabric of his Italian contemporaries, and of most of his German ones as well. Consequently, he was in
greater danger than anybody else to be ill served by improvising performers.

While we have the good fortune not to have to worry about inventing diminutions for Bach's written melodies, there are still spots where
the insertion of *passaggi* was probably or even certainly expected,
namely in some rests between phrases, on some holds, and on some
cadences. Such *passaggi* are not diminutions because they are not built
on an underlying melody; rather, they are brief cadenzas that can occur
in fast movements as well as in slow ones and seem welcome when the
music as written would create a sense of temporary stagnation or emp-
tiness that ought to be filled. Foremost among such contexts may be da
capo arias in which the cadence of the middle part is sometimes separated from the da capo by an awkward gap. Example 33.2a shows a case
in which there is an obvious need to fill with a transitional passage what
would be otherwise an embarrassing void. The responsibility of providing such continuity may fall on the singer, or on an obbligato instrument, or perhaps most frequently on the continuo player. Here the
continuo player seems to be the most likely person to supply a passage
perhaps of the kind shown in Ex. 33.2b. As to the body of the *da capo*
arias, Bach—at least in Leipzig—probably did not expect the repeat to be
ornamented since the arias were written for young students, and many
of these students, as he revealed in a memorandum, ranged from poor
to mediocre. For today's performances, a *modest* embellishment of a *da
capo* by small graces might not be improper.

In purely instrumental music, the places in which the insertion of small cadenzas appears to be needed are less frequent, but they do sometimes occur. One such spot from the First Sonata for Gamba and Clavier is shown in Ex. 33.2c, with the suggestion of a minimal embellishment in Ex. 33.2d.

EXAMPLE 33.2. Bach

a. BWV 3/3

b. BWV 3/3

c. First Sonata for Gamba and Clavier, BWV 1027/1

d.

Perhaps most striking, however, is the well-known case of the two adagio chords that are inserted between the two fast movements of the Third "Brandenburg" Concerto (Ex. 33.3a). To play the measure as written, as a naked progression of chords, might have made sense if the chords were meant as a simple harmonic link between the movements, but such is not the case. Both corner movements are in G major; but the chords represent subdominant and dominant of the relative minor and are hence disconnected at either end. They have to be treated as a separate entity that provides, in extreme condensation, the contrast of a slow movement. To support this musical function, a degree of embellishment is needed. Example 33.3b is meant only to give a very rough idea of what might be done (by the leading violinist) as a minimum.[1]

EXAMPLE 33.3. Bach, Third "Brandenburg" Concerto, BWV 1048

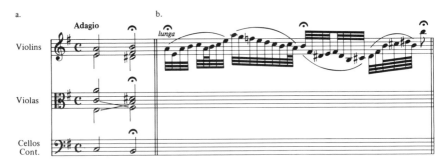

The *doubles* in the English Suites (for the Courante of the First Suite and the Sarabandes of the Second, Third, and Sixth) represent a special case in the framework of improvisation because they have given rise to the idea that they provide models for impromptu ornamentation of other, maybe all, of Bach's dance pieces on their repeats. Such assumption seems unjustified. True to their French models, these *doubles* are more in the nature of variations that involve not only the melody but the whole texture. Even in the Sarabande of the Second Suite, where only the top line is given in the *double,* its version leans more to free variation than to pure ornament in view of the substantive, expressive quality of the new melody, which has a structural ring and lacks the lightweight figurations of true improvisatory ornaments. It is also noteworthy that the first versions of these dances (e.g., the Sarabande from the Sixth Suite) would never have appeared in such austere shape had it not been followed by the written-out *double.* A comparable austerity will be hard to find in any other of Bach's slow movements. These considerations alone suggest that these specimens from the English Suites were not intended to serve as models for improvisation in other dance movements of Bach's. The same is true of the *doubles* in the Partita in B Minor for Unaccompanied Violin: they too are pure variations with hardly an intimation of ornamental character.

Next we need to consider improvisation of the small graces, the *agréments.* Bach sometimes notated them carefully and more or less completely, but sometimes much more sketchily. The most careful notation is to be found in the few scores that he readied for publication and in certain instrumental works for which he prepared fair copies. At the other pole are the compositional scores of cantatas and related works, written hurriedly when Bach was concerned with the essence rather than with surface niceties. Diminutions were too important a matter to be left out even in hastily written scores, but the figuring of the bass and the notation of small graces was at best fragmentary if not left out altogether. The omissions were then remedied by the editing of the parts that proceeded with Bach's supervision and active participation. In vocal works for which the score has survived but not the original parts, it will consequently be indicated to add small graces in proper sites.

Especially interesting are the cases of successive versions of the same work at different ornamental levels. The Inventions and Sinfonias are a good example since the whole set comes in multiple levels. The first version, which is included in Friedemann's *Clavierbüchlein,* is on the whole the simplest with regards to ornaments. Then in 1723 Bach wrote the famous fair copy (P 610). In the first version of this copy, Bach added a few graces but also left some out. At a later date, Bach added more ornaments to P 610 with a distinctly different black ink, among them the shower of some thirty mordents and ten trills in the Invention in E Flat, which before had only a single cadential trill, and the lavish embellishments added to the Sinfonia in E Flat, which before had nothing but a cadential trill in measure 12. Other additional ornaments can be found in slightly later copies made by Bach students; since some of these are identical, though made by different individuals, they may well have reflected Bach's own performance or directives.

Such multiple-level variants raise the question of whether the earlier simpler versions represented an incomplete notation and were never meant to be performed as written. Most likely the answer lies in the previously mentioned concept of an "ornamentation belt"—that is, a range from a desirable minimum to a still acceptable maximum of ornamental additions. The early versions of the Inventions and Sinfonias may be near the lower border of the belt, but they are not outside of it. Though some of the more lavish embellishments in the students' copies can probably be traced to Bach, they show only what may be done on occasion and not necessarily what ought to be done routinely.

There are, finally, some cases in all types of Bach's music—as in that of his contemporaries—in which it is necessary to add certain ornaments, especially trills on cadences in which the trills are often not marked but understood.

The chief problem of ornamental additions in Bach's works centers on repeats or da capos, the classic places where ornamental enrichment had become a widespread convention. It is a fair assumption that on such repeats a measure of alteration would be welcome. Sometimes a different registration on harpsichord or organ, a change of dynamics in other media, a different articulation such as an introduction of slurs where there were none before, or the reverse, might be all that is needed to inject a desirable element of diversity. Often, however, it will be advisable to change the level of ornamentation in some way. In sections well marked with graces, some or all may perhaps be omitted the first time and rendered only on the repeat; where there are few to begin with, new ones can be introduced. Once in a while, in movements not already saturated with diminutions, even a few new diminutions could be added if it were done with discretion and good judgment. The performer needs to do what is necessary while being wary of exaggerations that would overburden a piece instead of embellishing it.

## *Telemann*

Telemann left us three instructional collections in dual notation, two of sonatas and one of trios.[2] They represent what may well be the most helpful introduction to late Baroque diminution practice because they strike a happy balance between austerity and luxuriance. They show respect for structural notes, which are not obscured and remain intact in their proper places. In the rather rare cases in which another note takes the place of a structural one, it usually represents another chord tone. Since these collections are readily accessible, the brief extract given in Ex. 33.4a might suffice to give an idea of their style. In the trios we find an enlightening illustration of embellishing a cadential pattern often found in Handel: a series of chords separate by rests, as shown in Ex. 33.4b.[3]

## *Quantz*

Quantz expressed his admiration for the Italian singing style, which he says is profound and artful; it moves and astonishes, engages the musical intelligence, is rich in taste and rendition, and transports the listener pleasantly from one emotion to another (*Versuch einer Anweisung*, chap. 18, par. 76). He shared his employer's enthusiasm: Frederick the Great lavishly embroidered Italian arias. One such specimen of a Hasse aria with the king's embellishments is reproduced in Schmitz (*Kunst der Verzierung*, 121–25).

Quantz deals at length with diminutions, which he considers to be indispensable for Italian and other non-French music.[4] In first formulating general principles he stresses the importance of the written, structural notes, which must not be obscured and as a rule ought to remain in place. If occasionally another note is substituted, it must be one "from the harmony of the bass," and the regular note must be sounded immediately afterwards (*Versuch einer Anweisung*, chap. 13, par. 7). Diminutions must not be applied until after the melody has been heard in its simple shape; otherwise the listener will not be able to identify the

EXAMPLE 33.4. Telemann

a. Sonata No. 1 (1728)

b. Trio No. 2

diminutions as such (par. 9). Quantz sees a danger that all-too-rich diminutions will deprive the melody of its capacity to "move the heart." Instead of indulging too freely in diminutions, he urges players to render a simple melody nobly, clearly, and neatly (par. 9).

As some 16th-century writers had done, Quantz presents his didactic material first in the abstract, in the form of brief melodic and cadential formulas, whereupon he incorporates these formulas (identified by numbers) into the continuum of a whole adagio movement in dual notation, both as written and as embellished. The opening measures of this adagio were given in Ex. 19.4 because of their implication for phrasing. There it was pointed out that Quantz's musical examples as they were printed in his book are incomplete because Quantz supplemented them with verbal comments about their dynamic shadings, for which he had inadequate notational symbols. Here, because of its importance for improvisation, a further section of this embellished adagio is shown in Ex. 33.5, where again I supply the dynamic markings according to Quantz's verbal directives (in his chap. 14, par. 42). From it we gain a vivid impression of Quantz's improvisational style, which in its finesse of phrasing almost assumes a mannered quality.

Quantz's chapter 15 on cadenzas contains many interesting and astute comments.[5] The object of the cadenza, he says, is to surprise the listener unexpectedly once more at the end of the piece. There should thus be only a single cadenza in any one piece: to sing two or three in an aria—which can turn to five with a da capo—is an abuse (par. 5). "Cadenzas must stem from the principal sentiment of the piece and include a short repetition or imitation of the most pleasing phrases contained in it" (par. 8). "You must not roam into keys that are too remote, or touch upon keys which have no relationship with the principal one." A short cadenza must not modulate at all, while a longer one may modulate to subdominant and dominant. One may go from major to minor but only briefly, and then promptly return to the principal key (par. 14). Vocal and wind cadenzas must be performable in one breath. String cadenzas may be longer, but here too brevity is preferable to "vexing length" (par. 17).

## A New Trend

While many German musicians, like Quantz, continued to adhere to the Italian fashion of rich improvisatory diminutions, these procedures encountered a powerful challenge in the aesthetic attitudes that, issuing from the Enlightenment, were hostile to the arbitrariness of singers and players alike. This new trend found a powerful leader in Gluck, who, like Lully a century earlier, strove to free dramatic singing from arbitrary accretions and who, as a director, was strong enough to assert his will. This new way of thinking found its reflection in several important treatises, among them those of C. P. E. Bach and Leopold Mozart.

EXAMPLE 33.5.  Quantz (Table XVIII)*

*Dynamic marks added according to Quantz's verbal direction. "***f***" and "***p***" often stand for "***mf***" or "***mp***" respectively ("mezze/tinte")

**C. P. E. Bach.** Though Philipp Emanuel does not reject diminutions out-right—as Gluck was to do presently—he shows little interest in them and explains why they need not be discussed. They depend, he says, on taste and style and are too subject to change; in clavier music they are often written out, and besides, in view of the sufficient number of small graces (his *wesentliche Manieren*), one can easily dispense with them (*Versuch über Art das Clavier* [1753], chap. 2, sec. 1, par. 7). He does, though, devote a few lines and a few illustrations to the embellishment of fermatas (sec. 9, pars. 18–22). Observe that these are not diminutions but small cadenzas, which, as he himself had said, are improvised compositions, not ornaments.

A few years later, in the preface to his *Sechs Sonaten für Klavier mit veränderten Reprisen,* he speaks of the necessity for variation ("das Verändern") in the repeat. But here, as the music shows, he has in mind a reshaping of the melody, not the insertion of diminutions. We find no breaking up of the melody into smaller note values, the true mark of diminutions; often the variant has fewer notes than the original.

**Leopold Mozart.** The shift in opinion is even more palpable with Leopold Mozart because he so clearly parts company on this issue with Tartini, whom he follows so closely in all matters of small ornaments. Leopold has little use for diminutions and mentions only the standardized small patterns of the *groppo,* the *circolo mezzo,* and the *tirata.* And these he says must be used only in solo playing, and then only "in great moderation, at the right time, and *only* for the sake of varying passages that occur several times in succession." Those are hard conditions for even these miniature patterns (*Versuch einer Violinschule,* chap. 9. pars. 18–22).

## Persevering Diminutions

The nascent antidiminution movement, manifested in the stance of Gluck, C. P. E. Bach, and Leopold Mozart, was a portent of weighty changes that were to come to full fruition in the Classical era. But in the meantime, many composers and theorists in the German-speaking territories continued in both the practice and the advocacy of rich Italian-type diminutions. One important source for late galant diminution practice in Germany is a huge manuscript volume containing thirty-three violin sonatas by Franz Benda (BB, Mus. MSS. 1315/15). They are written throughout in double notation: the original and the embellished versions for the slow movements, the original and the variants for the repeats for the fast movements. The first of these sonatas—one of only two in the volume written in triple notation (with both simpler and more elaborate figurations)—is reproduced in Schmitz (*Kunst der Verzierung,* 135–39), and a fragment of Sonata No. 2 appears in *OrnB,* 570. Generally the diminutions are much more florid than Quantz's and Tartini's but still at least one step removed from the mentioned excesses found in Cartier's *École de violon* and in the Tartiniana collection at Berkeley.

The continuation of the Italianate diminution practice until the late part of the 18th century is attested to by the treatises of Hiller, Türk, and Tromlitz. Johann Adam Hiller, in his *Anweisung zum musikalisch-zierlichen Gesange* of 1780, offers an embellished aria in dual notation: "Arie mit willkührlicher Veränderung," written first in what we have called first-degree diminutions, is repeated with highly florid second-degree ones (135–40). The term *willkührlich* (arbitrary) indicates its improvisatory nature (the aria is reprinted in Schmitz, 141–143).

In his *Klavierschule* of 1789, Daniel Gottlob Türk devotes the third section of chapter 5 to improvised diminutions and formulates a few principles, some of which deserve to be summarized (references will be to this section).[6] Only such passages ought to be embellished—and then only on their repeat—that would not please sufficiently and hence be boring if repeated literally (par. 23). The embellishments must fit the character of the piece, must be at least as good as the original, and must avoid repetitiousness; they must not sound belabored and should be rendered in an easy-going, relaxed fashion; and all embellishments must be based on the given harmony. Like Tosi before him, Türk strongly emphasizes the need to respect the integrity of the beat (par. 24). Türk follows these principles with an illustration that shows part of an adagio movement with rather lavish diminutions (par. 25).

Although Türk deals with cadenzas in an earlier section of chapter 5, he adds little that is noteworthy to what Quantz had written on the subject. Somewhat unusual is his demonstration of bad cadenzas that illustrate in schoolmasterly fashion nearly twenty odd violations (from a to q) against his stated principles. More valuable is the very first section of chapter 5, which discusses fermata embellishments, including lead-ins and transitions.[7]

# Haydn

In Haydn's instrumental music ornamental figurations appear to have been fully written out already in works of the early period, such as the keyboard sonatas or string quartets of the 1760s. While small graces may certainly be inserted here and there in these works, there seems little if any place for added diminutions. While cadenzas continued to be a requirement in concertos, where they were indicated by a fermata on the $\frac{6}{4}$ tonic chord followed by a trill on the dominant, the need for at least brief cadenzas turns up in at least two keyboard sonatas and in several early string quartets. Specimens are the adagios of the Sonata in A Flat (Hob. XVI: 46/2), measure 77, and of the Sonata in G (Hob. XVI:39/2), measures 58–59. Among string quartets, no less than five of the set of six of Op. 9, as well as a few later ones, have in their slow movements the telltale signals for cadential inserts. The *largo* of Op. 17, No. 6, calls for *two* cadenzas, the first in measure 16, from supertonic to dominant, and the second in measure 38, as shown in Ex. 33.6, from dominant to tonic.

EXAMPLE 33.6.   Haydn, String Quartet, Op. 17, No. 6/2

Lead-ins are often required additions, notably in rondo movements when a fermata is written before the reentry of the main theme. Such lead-ins are most frequent from dominant to (prevailing) tonic, but there are many exceptions. For a spelled-out lead-in, see Ex. 33.7 from the String Quartet Op. 50, No. 1, or for a longer one see the Piano Sonata in E Flat (Hob. XVI:49/1), measure 131.

EXAMPLE 33.7.   Haydn, String Quartet Op. 50, No. 1/4, Lead-in)

Near the end of slow movements in Haydn's string quartets, up to and including Op. 50 of 1787, there are often two fermatas following one another that do not seem to call for a cadenza-like insert but rather for a brief embellishment. For an illustration, see Ex. 33.8a, from the andante of the String Quartet Op. 33, No. 6, with a figuration to be inserted of perhaps the kind suggested in Ex. 33.8b.

EXAMPLE 33.8.  Haydn, String Quartet, Op. 33, No. 6/2, Fermata embellishment

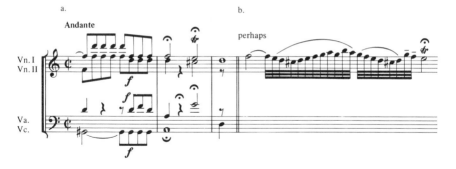

In Haydn's vocal, as opposed to his instrumental, music, there are up to about the year 1785 more openings for occasional florid embellishments, notably in his works written for Italian singers, such as his oratorio *Il Ritorno di Tobia* of 1774, which is filled with huge da capo arias (some of which Haydn shortened in a revision of 1784) and in which the da capo sections certainly elicited melismatic embellishments. For one dal segno tenor aria (Tobia) from this oratorio, we have Haydn's own added ornamentation and a dual version of a cadenza. Reprinted in the Henle edition (*Joseph Haydn: Werke,* vol. 28, 1), the embellishments are quite modest and mostly of the formulaic type and show greater animation only in a few measures in which the written melody is somewhat slow-moving, as in the excerpt shown in Ex. 33.9a. One of the two cadenzas that Haydn added to his ornamented version is given in Ex. 33.9b.[8]

The two German oratorios of Haydn's late years contain no more formal da capo arias, and added diminutions were not welcomed by Haydn. Giuseppe Carpani, the Italian translator of *The Creation* whose version was performed on April 4, 1801, presumably under Haydn's direction, writes in a memoir: "This music must be executed with simplicity, exactness, expression, and decorum, but without [added] ornaments."[9] In the same book by A. P. Brown from which I have quoted Carpani, we read that Haydn himself told his biographer Albert Christoph Dies how Demoiselle Fischer "sang her part with the greatest delicacy and so accurately that she did not permit herself the least unsuitable addition," by which, according to Dies, Haydn "meant cadenzas, ornaments, Eingänge, and so on." With good reason Brown infers that "Haydn wished for few added embellishments" (*Performing "The Creation,"* 44–46).

There are, however, in these late oratorios a number of fermatas at cadences that call for at least a brief embellishment. We find some such embellishments penciled into one of the four sets of original parts for the *The Creation.* Though these additions, as Brown cautions, may have been entered at any time during the 19th century while this specific set

(*Tonkünstler Parts*) was still in use, a specimen such as the one shown in Ex. 33.9c can nevertheless serve as a good model of what needs to be done; and besides, it may have been authentic.

We see how the mentioned split in the German-speaking territories between continuation of the Italian-style diminution practice (Quantz, Hiller, Türk) and its de facto abandonment (Gluck, C. P. E. Bach, L. Mozart) found its dramatic maturation in the music that to us matters most, in Haydn and, as we shall now see, in Mozart.

## Mozart

Concerning unwritten ornaments, a few words should first be said about the appoggiatura convention because it affects nearly every page in Mozart's operas, arias, and songs. This issue has recently given rise to a lively controversy.

A convention fully valid for Mozart that presumably went back to the 17th century allowed a singer to insert a stepwise falling—not rising—appoggiatura whenever a feminine ending was written with tone repetition. Contrary to some editors' opinions, this applies to questions as well as to declarative sentences. Unfortunately, several volumes of the NMA are filled with suggestions for —inappropriate—upward-leaping or upward-stepping appoggiaturas for questions.[10] The insertion of an appoggiatura was most frequent in recitative and in those cases in which a drop of a third precedes the feminine ending, when

♩♩♩ was often sung ♩♩♩ . The convention was not limited to the recitative, but in arias and other closed numbers such inserts were less often expected, partly because an appoggiatura was often spelled out, partly because more often than in recitative a tone repetition was intended to be sung as written. Inasmuch as tone repetition can be forceful as well as humorous, it was up to the singer's judgment to decide whether to add or not to add would better reflect the meaning of the words.

The recent proposition that in Mozart's time every feminine ending *had* to have an appoggiatura, and that tone repetition was not an option, cannot be maintained.[11] A number of notable contemporary theorists make it clear that appoggiaturas were by no means obligatory; among them, and perhaps most important, is Salieri, who when speaking of the recitative in his *Scuola di canto* of 1816 states that "appoggiaturas when not written, are arbitrary, and depend solely on the proper taste."[12] The addition of unwritten appoggiaturas continued in every single case to be a matter of music-dramatic judgment.

In his youth Mozart wrote many da capo arias as well as through-composed ones in skeletal style, all of which call for added embellishment. Luckily, Mozart left us fine examples of a semi-da capo aria "with

EXAMPLE 33.9.   Haydn

a. *Il Ritorno di Tobia*

b. *Il Ritorno di Tobia*

c. *The Creation*, No. 30

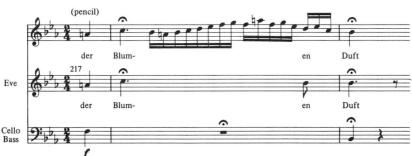

spelled-out *gusto"*—meaning with ornaments, variants, and cadenzas (for extensive excerpts, see *OrnM*, 231–33 and 235–38). The diminutions are rather modest, consisting mostly of formulas (such as the *circolo mezzo*). Only the cadenzas take freer flights yet stay clearly within the one-breath limit.

In the works of his maturity, however, Mozart wrote out all the figurations he wanted: starting from *Idomeneo* at the latest, no diminutions need or ought to be added to Mozart's text.

Vocal cadenzas (fermata embellishments) are another matter. As pointed out before, they are not diminutions and need to be added to many fermatas in arias that Mozart wrote throughout his life. They were a definite requirement for fermatas at the *ends* of arias, which we still find for the last time in *Idomeneo* (for instance in Idomeneo's aria "Fuor del mar"). For the great operas and arias of Mozart's last decade the problem focuses on fermatas in *mid*-aria. Such fermata embellishments can have the function either of extending the phrase, then concluding it ("end embellishment"), or first extending the phrase, then leading into the next one ("transitional embellishment"). Whether either of these is indicated is a matter of judgment. In many cases Mozart fortunately gives us an important graphic clue by the way he notates the fermata. Whenever he writes the latter with a wide arc that covers more than one note, or rest, and notably when he extends it over a whole measure, as he so often does, we can be sure that he wished for an embellishment. For an illustration, see Ex. 33.10a from Fiordiligi's aria "Come scoglio immoto resta" in *Così fan tutte*, with, in Ex. 33.10b, a tentative suggestion for its (end) embellishment. This aria is unique in that it has no less than eight of these wide-arched fermatas, all of which call for a measure of ornamental elaboration.[13]

EXAMPLE 33.10.   Mozart, *Così fan tutte*, K 588, I, 14

Unfortunately, so far only the NMA has been reasonably consistent in reproducing this important graphic variant of the fermata (without, however, always drawing the proper interpretive conclusions from this design). While the wide fermata always calls for an embellishment, a small one-note type may also call for it, but then it will be a matter of taste and judgment whether an embellishment is in order or not.

In Mozart's instrumental music too there are many occasions in which improvised additions are expected. There are the lead-ins (*Ein-*

*gänge* in Mozart's own terminology) that prepare the entry, and more frequently reentry, of a theme, again most typically in rondos. Moving mostly from dominant to (prevalent) tonic, they may consist—as Mozart's written-out specimens show—of a simple scale passage, whether diatonic, chromatic, or in broken thirds, or they may be more elaborate and approach cadenza size (as for instance the one in the finale of the Piano Concerto in E Flat K 271, m. 149, given in Ex. 33.12a). Though labeled "Cadenza," it is a nonthematic lead-in from dominant to tonic. Every so often Mozart will signal the need for an ornamental insert, for instruments as well as for the voice, be it a lead-in or an end embellishment, with the broad fermata, as shown in Ex. 33.11a, from the Piano Concerto in D Minor, and Ex. 33.11b, from the Violin Concerto in D, K 218. In the first case a lead-in is needed; in the second case there are two broad fermatas; the first for an end embellishment leading to the high D, the second, a lead-in to the repeat of the rondo theme.

EXAMPLE 33.11.    Mozart

a. Piano Concerto in D Minor, K 466/3

b. Violin Concerto in D, K 218

For two authentic lead-ins that could serve as models, the first, given in Ex. 33.12a, is the one just mentioned from the Piano Concerto K 271/3. It consists of a descending scale passage, extended by a few brief reversals of motion, followed by an ascending, accelerating arpeggio. The second (Ex. 33.12b), from the Piano Concerto in A Major K 385p (414)/3, is a simple scale passage, partly diatonic and partly chromatic.

Cadenzas in Mozart's piano concertos are a standard feature of every first, of many third movements, and, up until K 453, of some second movements as well. Their cue is a fermata on or after the $^6_4$ tonic chord, followed by a fermata on the dominant trill. Fortunately, we have numerous cadenzas that Mozart wrote out for the benefit of his sister,

EXAMPLE 33.12.  Mozart

a. Piano Concerto in E-flat, K 271/3

b. Piano Concerto in A Major, K 385p (414)/3

students, or friends, and these cadenzas give us an invaluable insight into Mozart's improvisation practice and into what specifically he wanted and did not want of a cadenza. These cadenzas have several features in common that provide us with an important framework for preparing cadenzas for those works in which none survived.

They are all rather short and concise, averaging for the first movement between twenty-five and thirty-five measures. They quote one or more themes and show them in a different light, either by melodic development (spinning out or fragmentation) or by brief harmonic digressions, but they never modulate into distant keys or engage in complex polyphonic elaborations. A good part of each cadenza, roughly one-half, consists of nonthematic virtuoso figurations, and each one ends in a trill on the dominant seventh chord leading into the coda.

Most of the cadenzas written for Mozart's concertos during the 19th and 20th centuries, beginning with those of Hummel and Hoffmann, are much too long and are technically and often stylistically incompatible with the main body of the work. Only recently have a few artists felt the need to return to the conciseness and relative simplicity of Mozart's own models.[14]

Violin cadenzas should be even shorter because the instrument lacks the piano's range and harmonic depth for sustaining interest without resorting to acrobatic feats that are out of line with Mozart's style. With even greater force this applies to winds that lack the violin's capacity for double or triple stops.

Mozart's piano concertos are a special case. He wrote many of them for his own use and did so often under great pressure of time. Whereas he wrote the orchestra parts with great care, he frequently only sketched in the solo part in quasi-skeletal form to serve as an *aide-mémoire,* which he filled out in performance by his improvisation. Sometimes the need for such filling in is obvious, at other times a careful evaluation is required to determine whether, in view of what happens in the other parts, a greater animation of the solo line seems permissible or even necessary. For the Concerto in D, K 451, which Mozart wrote for his own use, we are fortunate in possessing a document showing the ornamentation he supplied (for the benefit of his sister) of an eight-measure phrase in the *andante* that was originally written in skeletal notation. Though much quoted, it is reprinted here because of its importance (see Ex. 33.13). Significant about this ornamented passage is the simplicity of the elegant embroidery, which leaves all the key notes of the "skeleton" in place.

EXAMPLE 33.13.   Mozart, Piano Concerto in D, K 451/2

K 451/2

Whenever a phrase has a similarly lean look that is not compensated for with lively action in the orchestra, a measure of ornamentation will be desirable.[15] In so doing we must use Mozart's brief model as a guide, not the often all-too-extravagant elaborations and Lisztian paraphrases that Hummel and some other early 19th-century authors indulged in.

Another vexing issue is the question of embellishments in repeats. Da capo arias are rare in Mozart, and the few he wrote date mostly from before 1771. The dal segno aria, in which the repeat starts in the middle of the A section, had a somewhat longer life span in his works, but it too disappeared from the works of his maturity. Certainly in the da capo arias some embellishment was a stylistic requirement and is likely to have applied to the dal segno types as well, provided their original version had a skeletal look.

The real problem lies with the repeats indicated by repeat marks and with those of recapitulations and rondos. Here modern opinions differ widely, ranging from the need or at least the license to make generous ornamental additions (Robert Levin) to great reserve (Charles Rosen). Mozart was a legendary improviser, and it is likely that in performance his unceasing inspiration prompted him to embellish phrases on their repeat (and maybe also on their first statement). If, say, on a repeat mark, a soloist were to add here and there a small grace, a trill, a slide, a turn, or another modest melisma, it would be unobjectionable if done with discretion and taste. Before we make ornamental additions, however, we must remember that repetition is the most important element of formal design in music—as it is in architecture—and that a need for variety arises only when repetition breeds monotony. Often, of course, our great masters wrote out variants on repetition. Such variants, as Mozart himself wrote, for instance, on the returns of the theme in the Rondo in A Minor K 511, have been cited as evidence for the need to introduce comparable additions to other rondos in which the written repeats are literal. This argument is dangerous because the A-minor rondo is not typical. It is slow and deeply personal with tragic overtones, while most other rondos are vivacious and outgoing. A slow melody is less able than a fast one to hold up under several literal repeats and is therefore in greater need of gentle variants, which Mozart here as in other comparable situations fully spelled out. In contrast, a lively theme is more likely to have its identity disguised by ornamentation, and in a rondo the basic identity of the refrain is the essence of the form. Hence any additions that a performer may feel ought to be added have to be very modest.

The same is true of recapitulations in sonata form. Here we have some interesting evidence from Mozart himself. Whereas in instrumental music he often resorted for recapitulations to the shorthand device of referring the copyist to a sign from which a number of measures are to be copied, on other occasions he spelled out the recapitulations in full. He did so, for instance, in the last three symphonies, where lengthy sections are written note for note without the slightest change (thus, for example, in the first movement of the Symphony in E Flat, thirty-nine measures of the exposition; or in the first movement of the "Jupiter" Symphony, the first twenty-three measures). From this we can gather not that any embellishment is necessarily out of place but that it is not a stylistic requirement comparable to the embellishment of a da capo aria or of a wide-arched fermata.

All in all we have good reason to approach the embellishment of Mozart's repeats with discretion and humility.

---

Improvisation is arbitrary, and while it may be amenable to some general guidelines it cannot be subjected to specific rules. In general terms it can be said that for the Baroque and galant eras a bare-looking melody, vocal or instrumental, does not represent Classical simplicity but rather incomplete notation that needs to be filled in by ornamental additions. How much to add is a question that has no simple answer. We have suggested the concept of an "ornamentation belt" ranging from a necessary minimum to a still tolerable maximum. The illustrations given from Handel and Geminiani show how little is sufficient but also what seems near-minimal requirements for a da capo or a repeat. On the other hand, a maximum is reached when further additions would totally obscure the underlying melody. The modern performer who does not combine a gift for melodic invention with a sure sense of historical style will do well to exercise great reserve and aim at the lower border of the "ornamentation belt." A careful study of Telemann's *Methodical* Sonatas is certain to be helpful.

For Bach and those Frenchmen who consistently wrote out the diminutions they desired, we need not be concerned about this matter. For Handel, Vivaldi, Telemann, and most of their contemporaries, on the other hand, we do have to be concerned.

For late Haydn and the mature Mozart the main areas of concern are lead-ins, fermata embellishments (both vocal and instrumental), cadenzas, and to some extent the desirability of adding embellishments to repeats. For Mozart, in addition, there is the problem of identifying unfinished portions in those piano concertos he wrote for his own use and filling them out with diminutions. For most of these occasions we have authentic models that give us guidance.

By and large it will be advisable for modern performers to use their best taste and judgment and exercise reserve, in awareness that it is better to err on the side of modesty than of extravagance.

# Abbreviations

| | |
|---|---|
| BB | Deutsche Staatsbibliothek |
| BG | *Bach Gesellschaft* edition (Leipzig, 1851–1899) |
| BL | British Library |
| BN | Bibliothèque nationale |
| *DDT* | *Denkmäler deutscher Tonkunst* |
| *DDT*, N.F. | *Denkmäler der Tonkunst in Bayern*, Neue Folge |
| *DTÖ* | *Denkmäler der Tonkunst in Österreich* |
| *EM* | *Early Music* |
| *Essays 1982* | Frederick Neumann, *Essays in Performance Practice* |
| *Essays 1989* | Frederick Neumann, *New Essays on Performance Practice* |
| GMF | Archives of the Gesellschaft der Musikfreunde, Vienna |
| *Grove 6* | *New Grove Dictionary of Music and Musicians (6th ed.)* |
| *JAMS* | *Journal of the American Musicological Society* |
| K.00 (00) | Köchel catalogue, 6th ed. (numbers of 1st ed. in parentheses) |
| *KB* | *Kritischer Bericht* (of *NBA*) |
| LC | Library of Congress |
| *MGG* | *Musik in Geschichte und Gegenwart* |
| *MQ* | *Musical Quarterly* |
| *NBA* | J. S. Bach's *Neue Ausgabe sämtlicher Werke*, Leipzig and Kassel, 1954– |
| *NMA* | W. A. Mozart's *Neue Ausgabe sämtlicher Werke*, Salzburg and Kassel, 1955– |
| ÖNB | Österreichische Nationalbibliothek |

| | |
|---|---|
| Opéra | Bibliothèque de l'Opéra, Paris |
| *OrnB* | Frederick Neumann, *Ornamentation in Baroque and Post-Baroque Music* |
| *OrnM* | Frederick Neumann, *Ornamentation and Improvisation in Mozart* |
| P 00 | BB Mus. Ms Bach P 00 |
| RM | King's Music Library in BL |
| Schmitz | Hans-Peter Schmitz, *Die Kunst der Verzierung im 18. Jahrhundert* |
| St 00 | BB Mus. Ms Bach St 00 |
| *WAM* | *W. A. Mozarts Werke,* Leipzig, 1876–1905 |
| *WTC I or II* | J. S. Bach, *Well-Tempered Clavier* |

# Notes

## Introduction

1. I have discussed these developments in greater detail in the first two chapters of my *Essays 1989*. For an in-depth study see Harry Haskell *The Early Music Revival: A History* (New York, 1988).

2. The term "early music" which is obviously vague, first referred to music up to and including Bach, then up to Mozart; now it reaches to Berlioz and Chopin, and is well on its way, so it seems, to engulf Wagner and Brahms.

3. "L'appoggiature ancienne," in *L'interprétation de la musique française aux XVII-ème et XVIIIème siècles* Paris 1974, 91.

4. For a detailed critique of his views see my *Essays 1989*, Chap. 9.

## 2. Tempo and Proportions During the Transition to Modern Notation

1. For an interesting, if perhaps unusual case, see the ritornello in Monteverdi's *Orfeo* that precedes and follows Orfeo's song "Vi ricorda." In his article "Anent a Ritornello in Monteverdi's Orfeo," *Musica Disciplina* 5 (1951): 213–22, Willi Apel records eight different rhythmic interpretations to which he then adds his own ninth version!

2. ". . . deroselben [i.e. the 'signa veterum'] Varietet nicht allein keinen sondern *usum*, sondern auch nichts anders ist, als eine verirrung und verwirrung, dadurch nicht allein die Jugend in den Schulen, sondern auch offtmahls geübte *Musici Vocales & Instrumentales* in *Capellen perturbirt, remorirt*, auch wol gar *confundirt* werden" (ibid., 3:53–54).

3. For just a few examples see *Kleine geistliche Concerte* II, 6 ("Habe deine Lust"), where Schütz writes "tarde" at the final change from $\frac{3}{1}$ to $C$ ; *Symphoniae sacrae* I, 5, where one measure after the start in $C$ meter he writes "presto" and the same again later in the piece; *Symphoniae sacrae* I, 10, secunda parte, "presto" upon the words "amica mea, columba mea," followed by "adagio" on the words "O quam tu pulchra es"; *Symphoniae sacrae* I, 17, secunda parte, at $\frac{3}{1}$ "allegro" followed at $C$ by "adagio."

4. Arthur Mendel, "A Brief Note on Triple Proportion in Schuetz," *MQ* 46 (1960): 67–70. See also Heinrich Schütz, *A German Requiem (Musicalische Exequien)*, ed. Arthur Mendel (New York, 1957), i–xx.

## 3. Flexible Tempo After 1600

1. The manuscript additions were first published in English translation as *Elements or Principles of Music,* trans. and ed. Albert Cohen (New York, 1965). The cited passage is on p. 62.

2. Lois Rosow, "The Metrical Notation of Lully's Recitative," in *J.-B. Lully, Actes/Kongressbericht,* ed. Jérôme de la Gorce and Herbert Schneider (Laaber, 1990), 405–22. The cited passages are on p. 411.

3. "Qualche volta si usa un certo ordine di procedere, nelle compositioni, que non si può scriuere, come sono, il dir piano, & forte, & il dir presto, & tardo, e secondo le parole, muouere la misura, per dimostrare gli effetti delle passioni, delle parole, & dell'armonia . . . , & la compositione cantata, con la mutatione della misura è molto gratiata, con quella uarieta, che senza uariare, & seguire al fine" (Nicola Vicentino, *L'antica musica ridotta alla moderna prattica* . . . [Rome, 1555], fol. 88*v*).

4. See on this Luigi Ferdinando Tagliavini, "The art of 'not leaving the instrument empty:' Comments on early Italian harpsichord playing," *Early Music* 11/3 (July 1983), 299–308.

5. "Perche il sonare a queste Opere . . . si debba primieramente cercar l'affetto di quel passo, & il fine del Autore. . . . Si deveno i principij cominciarli adagio à dar maggior spirito, e vaghezza al seguente passo & nelle cadenze sostenerle assai prima che si incominci l'altro passo. . . . Conviene in alcune durezze fermarsi con arpeggiarle acciò che riesca più spiritoso il seguente passo" (Girolamo Frescobaldi, *Il primo libro di capricci canzon francese e recercari* . . . [1624], Preface).

6. ". . . l'objet dominant [de la musique française] est le sentiment, qui n'a point de mouvements déterminés, et qui par conséquent ne peut être asservie par tout à une mesure régulière sans perdre de cette vérité qui en fait le charme" (Rameau, *Observations,* p. VII).

## 6. Tempo Words

1. In an article entitled "Tempo and Dynamic Indications in Bach Sources" (in *Bach, Handel, Scarlatti: Tercentenary Essays,* ed. P. Williams [London, 1985]), Robert L. Marshall presents a table of "Tempo and Affect Designations in the Bach Sources," in which he lists no fewer than forty-five different designations along with the frequency of their appearance. Twenty of the forty-five occurred (or rather were found) only a single time, fourteen between two and five times, and only six more than twenty-five times. These six are the basic terms: *adagio, largo, andante, allegro, vivace, presto.*

2. A detailed tabulation of tempo words, as used by individual composers in the 17th and 18th centuries is offered in Herrmann-Bengen, *Tempobezeichnungen,* Annex, Tables 1 and 2.

## 7. The Final Ritardando

1. Daniel Friderici, *Musica figuralis* [1624], Regula 20. "Gegen Ende des Gesanges, in *penultima consonantia* . . . sollen alle Stimmen aushalten und ein

sanftes, feinmessig gezogenes *Confinal* machen, und nicht alsobald das *Final* dem Gesange anhängen. Denn solches den Zuhörenden gar verdrießlich und unangenehm zu hören vorkommt. Und nimmt auch dem Gesange ein gutes Theil der Lieblig- und Anmutigkeit hinweg, wenn man alsobald den Gesang abbricht und kurz abreist."

## 8. Tempo of Dances

1. Louis-Léon Pajot was General Postal Director in France and a physicist-inventor. His report is in *Histoire de l'Académie Royale des Sciences,* Année 1732, *Mémoires* (Paris, 1735), 182–95.

   Pajot's report is mentioned by Schulz (s.v. "Tact" in Sulzer's *Allgemeine Theorie* of 1778–79, where Pajot is referred to as "D'ons Embray." Among modern authors who report on some or all of these sources are Georg Schünemann (who insists on calling Choquel "Choquet") in his *Geschichte des Dirigierens* (Leipzig, 1913); Rosamond E. M. Harding, *Origins of Musical Time and Expression* (London, 1938); Curt Sachs, in *Rhythm and Tempo* (New York, 1953), 314–15; Eugène Borrel, *L'interprétation de la musique française (de Lully à la révolution)* (Paris, 1934), 185; Hellmuth Christian Wolff, "Das Metronom des Louis-Léon Pajot 1735," in *Festskrift Jens Peter Larsen* ed. Nils Schiørring, Henrik Glahn, and Carsten E. Hatting (Copenhagen, 1972), 205–17.

2. A recent fashion of playing these minuets, when marked "Allegretto"—or not marked at all—at a speed that would evoke the designation of "Vivace" is just as misguided as the opposite extreme, favored by a few older conductors, of playing them stodgily in "maestoso" mode. The speeders believe to have found a rationale for their action in some metronomizations by Hummel, Czerny, and Anton Reicha. Hummel is on such occasions usually touted as "the Mozart student" which is to confer on him high authority. He studied with Mozart at age eight for one year only and later disqualified himself as an authority on Mozart interpretation with outlandish and tastelessly lavish ornamentations of some slow Mozart movements (e.g., of the C-minor concerto).

   Surely there were faster minuets that could be beaten in one and slower ones with three distinct beats. The typical tempo was allegretto for the faster type, moderato to andante con moto for the slower one (such as the Minuet from *Don Giovanni*). True, the late Haydn in his string quartets introduced some very fast minuets that were truly Beethovenian scherzi and marked them "Presto ma non troppo" and even "Presto." But the point is, when Haydn wanted a truly fast minuet, he knew how to mark it.

   Very revealing in this connection is Beethoven's definition of "Tempo di Menuetto" in his Eighth Symphony, which he, notorious for his fast metronome markings, fixed at $\downarrow$ = 126: beaten in three, not in one, in a tempo that is the ideal realization of the "Allegretto" idea—only moderately lively, quite decisively not an allegro, let alone a vivace or a presto. When we ignore Mozart's and Haydn's tempo words for the sake of some fashionable theory, we do so at the risk of serious misrepresentation.

   Regarding the controversy, see William Malloch, "Toward a 'New' (Old) Minuet," *Opus* 1 (Aug. 1985): 14–21 and 52; Malloch, "Carl Czerny's Metronome Marks for Haydn and Mozart Symphonies," *EM* 16 (1988): 72–82; Frederick Neumann, "How Fast Should Classical Minuets Be Played?" *Historical Performance* 4 (1991): 3–13.

## 9. Rhythmic Alterations I: Artistic License and Defects of Notation

1. Lodovico Zacconi, *Prattica di musica,* I fol. 56r: "le dette figure s'accompagnano con alcuni accenti causati d'alcune ritardanze & sustentamenti di uoce que si fanno col torre una particella d'una figura & attriburla all'altra."

2. The book is now available in facsimile (New York, 1973). The illustrations are reproduced in Oliver Strunck, *Source Readings in Music History* (New York, 1950), 385, and in Edward Dannreuther, *Musical Ornamentation* (London, 1893), 1: 35–36.

3. These fragments were intended as supplements to Loulié's treatise *Eléments ou principes de musique* (Paris, 1696), which Rameau recommended to students of music. They were first published as inserts in the English translation of the treatise by Albert Cohen, *Elements or Principles of Music* (Brooklyn, 1985), 67.

   Regarding another notational irregularity involving an excess of beams, notably in Couperin and Gigault, see *Essays 1982,* 92–93, and 130–31.

## 10. Rhythmic Aterations II: The So-Called French Overture Style

1. In order to illustrate the opaqueness of this passage, I am quoting its substantive parts (with my comments inserted in parentheses) in the translation of William J. Mitchell [*Essay on the True Art of Playing Keyboard Instruments* (New York, 1949), 157]).

   "Short notes which follow dotted notes are always shorter in execution than their notated length. Hence it is superfluous to place strokes or dots above them."

   (On the face of it, Bach seems to speak here of a sharp articulation for the short notes, one that is understood without the need to specify it with the staccato symbols of dots or strokes. It is likely, however, that he had a late entry, an overdotting, not just a premature stopping, in mind when mentioning the deviation from the notes' "notated length"; we can gather that much from two of six examples he shows as well as from the second passage in question here.)

   "Figure VII illustrates their execution."

   (This Figure VII shows six brief illustrations, given here as simple rhythm patterns:)

(What Exx. a–d are to show about their execution is unclear. Dolmetsch writes in the form of a direct quotation [one of his two added sentences]: "The short notes at Exx. (a), (b), (c) would all be played at the same rate." This would-be translation has no basis in Bach's text. Example (e) does suggest overdotting for the sake of assimilation in a purely harmonic progression.)

"The asterisked example shows us that occasionally the division must agree with the notated values" (Zu weilen erfordert die Eintheilung dass man der Schreib-Art gemäss verfährt [*]). (A better translation would be: "occasionally the relationship of the parts requires literal rendition [of the dot]." The asterisked example shows a contrapuntal relationship that calls for exactness of the dot. It is this exactness listed as *occasional* need, along with the overdotted Ex. (e), that suggests the overdotted meaning of the first sentence.)

"Dots after long notes or after short ones in slow tempos, and isolated dots, are all held [werden insgeheim gehalten]"

(Here again there is ambiguity: "to hold a dot" can mean to hold it tenuto fashion for its full length, or it might mean to hold it beyond its literal value.)

"However, in rapid tempos prolonged successions of dots are performed as rests, the apparent opposite demand of the notation notwithstanding."

(This translation is inaccurate: "Kommen aber, zumahl in geschwindem Tempo, viele hintereinander vor, so werden sie offt nicht gehalten, ohngeacht die Schreib-Art es erfordert." Bach does not speak of inserted rests but quite certainly of shortening the value of the dots: "However, in rapid tempos prolonged successions of dots are often not held [for their full length] regardless of what is indicated in the notation." This underdotting is also confirmed in the second passage in question here. Now if "not holding" means underdotting, which it almost certainly does, then "holding the dot" in the previous sentence would have to mean exactness, yet Bach may have meant "holding longer."

(We see that this whole paragraph is infelicitously worded, and I can only repeat my recommendation of relying for Bach's ideas on the second passage, quoted on p. 100.)

2. To list just one telltale sign of its continuing, wide-ranging influence: in 1988, Richard Maunder, in his revisionist edition of Mozart's Requiem calls—unbelievable as it might seem—for choral and instrumental double dotting in the "Rex tremendae" (*Mozart's Requiem,* 153 and corresponding instructions in the score). Here we see unmistakably the long arm of Dolmetsch.

3. Michael Collins, "A Reconsideration of French Overdotting," *Music & Letters* 50 (1969): 111–23; John O'Donnell, "The French Style and the Overtures of Bach," Parts 1 and 2, *Early Music* 7 (1979): 190–96; 336–45.

4. It is the eighth note value of the dot after a quarter note that would have to be lengthened by one-half in order to change the single into a double dot. See chapter 11 for the nature of *inégalité* and for the pertinent rules about when the latter applies and when not (esp. p. 121).

5. In spite of Reichardt's caution not to deviate by a hairbreadth from the letter of the score, Neil Zaslaw believes he can extract a principle of overdotting from that author's text (*Mozart's Symphonies,* 486–89). I don't think this is

correct. Dotted notes, Reichardt writes, "call for a particular and precise performance." If they occur in a sequence, illustrated by a passage of dotted sixteenth notes ( ♩♪♪♩♪♪ ) , "then one need only be particularly aware that the shorter notes must be performed as short as possible, in order to give the longer notes so much the more weight" (quoted by Zaslaw, 486). Anybody who has had experience working with strings as a teacher, coach, or conductor will know that to achieve and maintain a strict 3:1 rhythm in such a passage with detached notes in a *tempo ordinario* is very difficult. Only by the sound pedagogical admonition to "play the short notes as short as possible" can one hope to achieve the literal rhythm. In vivace or presto even a modern virtuoso orchestra has to compromise on the rhythm by underdotting (as C. P. E. Bach was quoted for the keyboard); overdotting is practicable only in slow tempo. Johann Heinrich Koch, who mentions such mild overdotting or "somewhat lengthening the dot" (noch etwas länger aushalten), limits it to slow tempi and marks "Grave" over his illustration of dotted sixteenth notes (*Musikalisches Lexikon,* col. 1181). Reichardt reconfirms his principle of literalness when, two paragraphs later, he writes that "Each dotted note must be held right to the end of its value, in that way distinguishing itself from the note that is followed by a rest" (quoted by Zaslaw, 487). "To the end of its value," not beyond the end.

6. A book by Stephen Hefling dealing with overdotting and the *notes inégales* will come out too late to be considered here. I shall comment on it after its publication.

## 11. Rhythmic Aterations III: The notes inégales

1. For a complete tabulation of these meter/note-value relationships see my *Essays 1982,* 24–25, or "The French *Inégales,* Quantz, and Bach," *JAMS* 18 (1965): 322–23.

2. These fragmentary supplements were first published as inserts in Etienne Loulié, *Elements or Principles of Music,* trans. and ed. Albert Cohen (Brooklyn, 1965). The design for the *lourer* is on p. 67.

3. For a detailed discussion and documentation see my "French *Inégales,*" 335–43, or *Essays 1982,* 34–40. See also George Houle, *Meter in Music* (Bloomington, Ind., 1987), chap. 6.

4. In an article entitled "The Notes Inégales Revisited," in *Journal of Musicology* 6 (1988): 137–49, I detailed my objections to David Fuller's arguments favoring *inégalité* for Bach. In his answer, "Notes and *Inégales* Unjoined: Defending a Definition," in *Journal of Musicology* 7 (1989): 21–28, he tries to defend, with more wit than persuasiveness, his idea of overlapping dotted notes and *notes inégales* but fails altogether to address the *central* issue of my thesis: that the principles of the French convention do not apply to the music of J. S. Bach.

## 12. Binary–Ternary and Related Rhythmic Conflicts

1. We do find once in a long while a composer writing, as by serendipity, the quarter plus eighth-note ♩ ♪ in triplet meaning, though mostly without the

telltale number 3. That happened usually in the middle of a series of triplets, where the context almost forced the composer's hand. For an example see Bartolo's aria "La vendetta" (*Le nozze di Figaro*), mm. 61 and 65, both times on the word *garbuglio* in the middle of an extended triplet patter. But apart from such exceptional occurrences, it will surprise some readers to learn that the symbol with the number 3, as a standard notational device, was still unknown to Beethoven, Schubert, and Chopin. Brahms may have been the first major composer to have used the symbol systematically.

2. *Fitzwilliam Virginal Book*, ed. J. A. Fuller-Maitland and W. Barklay Squire, 2 vols. (Leipzig, 1894–99); reprint (New York, 1963), 1: 162, staves 2 and 3. This passage appears in the facsimile page of the manuscript reproduced facing the title page of the volume.

The manuscript of this collection, whose latest item—by Sweelinck—dates from 1612, was presumably completed in 1619.

3. For an interesting specimen, see Kerll's Toccata No. 2, in *DDT* N.F., 2/2; see also p. lxxiii (Revisionsbericht).

## 13. "Terraced" and Transitional Dynamics

1. The biography, which is reprinted in Hans T. David and Arthur Mendel, *The Bach Reader*, rev. ed. (New York, 1966), 293–356, is based primarily on information gained from Wilhelm Friedemann and Philipp Emanuel Bach. The reference to the clavichord is on p. 311.

2. Hermann Finck, *Practica musica* (Wittenberg, 1556), bk. 5, fol. Ss IIIv: "si in initio cantus, elegans fuga occurrerit, hanc voce clariore et explanata magis proferendam quam alioqui usu receptum est, et sequentes voces . . . simili modo enuntiandas esse: Hoc in omnibus vocibus, cum novae fugae occurrunt, observandum est, ut possit audiri cohaerentia et omnium fugarum systema."

3. "Qui si commincia piano assai / si dividono le viole in trè corpi rinforzando sempre / e si fanno entrare à un corpo per sino al più forte / Volta una battuta: uno doppo l'altro, mà insensibilmente devono entrare dal piano al fortissimo." A photocopy of the MS is at the Library of Congress (M1500 S446A2 Case).

4. The "doux" rather than "très doux" for the violas is due to the small number of players of the "parties de remplissage."

## 14. Dynamics in Notation

1. For an overview of these conflicting ideas see M. Jacob Adlung, *Anleitung zu der musikalischen Gelahrtheit* (1758; reprint, ed. H. J. Moser, Kassel, 1953), 773–81.

## 15. Vocal Articulation

1. Pierfrancesco Tosi, *Opinioni de' cantori antichi e moderni . . .* (Bologna, 1723), 31. The detached ones require the kind of "moto leggierissimo della voce in cui le note, che lo compongono sieno tutte articulate distaccamento, affinchè il Passaggio non sia, nè troppo attaccato, nè battuto soverchio."

## 16. Instrumental Legato

1. "Ego cum Lippio, Haslero & aliis in hac sum opinione; omnes ligaturas intricatas esse semovendas . . . et illarum loco hanc virgulam ⌣ usurpandam esse."
2. The *Bebung* is a vibrato-like pitch oscillation produced by rhythmically increasing the pressure on the depressed key while the tangent remains in touch with the string, thereby raising and lowering the pitch.

## 17. Instrumental Detachment

1. Wilhelm Trendelenburg, an eminent physiologist, has demonstrated these vibrating patterns with ingenious photographs in his classic study, *Die natürlichen Grundlagen der Kunst des Streichinstrumentspiels* (Berlin, 1925), 27–28.
2. "So muss nothwendig jedes Stück mit einer gewissen Mässigung gelind angegriffen, und mit solcher Art genommen werden, dass auch der stärkeste Strich die bereits schon in Erzitterung gebrachte Seyte ganz unvermerkt aus der wirklichen in eine andere Bewegung bringe. Diess will ich durch jene Schwäche verstanden haben, von welcher par. 3. schon etwas erinnert worden."
3. Dated March 3, 1760, the letter is reprinted, along with translations into French, English, and German, in G. Tartini, *Traité des agréments de la musique,* ed. E. R. Jacobi (Celle and New York, 1961), 130ff.

## 18. Special Articulation Problems

1. For this reason Robert D. Riggs's statement that the stroke always "means separated and, only if the context implies, some degree of accentuation" is unconvincing ("Articulation in Mozart's and Beethoven's Sonatas for Piano and Violin," Ph.D. diss., Harvard University, 1987, 206).
2. On the basis of the *NMA*'s editorial strokes, the La Salle Quartet played every upbeat in this piece with a strong accent, whose unbalancing effect was enhanced by a rubato hesitation.

## 19. Theory of Phrasing

1. Nancy Kovaleff Baker, in her fine translation of H. C. Koch's treatise on composition of 1787, renders *Einschnitt* as "incise" and does so specifically in order to encompass both meanings: a segment and its dividing line. She sees an asset in the double meaning, yet such equivocation, as every equivocation, is a liability, not an asset. William S. Newman uses the term "incise" in the same double meaning in his book on the interpretation of Beethoven's piano music (*Beethoven on Beethoven: Playing His Piano Music His Way* [New York, 1988]) and assigns to it a very large role.
2. Johann Peter Sperling, *Principia musicae* (Budissin, 1705), 72: "ein Zeichen, dass alldorten der Text einigermassen endiget: wird *comma* oder *virgula* gennant. Solches wird auch gefunden, bey Endigung eines Affectûs, welcher mit

einem Termino Musico (als *piano, presto, tardo*) ist angemercket gewesen, und gehet gemeiniglich alldorten ein anderer *Affectûs* an."

3. Mattheson had published this discussion almost verbatim two years earlier in his *Kern melodischer Wissenschaft* (Hamburg, 1737) as Chap. 5. I refer here to the *Vollkommene Capellmeister* because it is available in a facsimile edition (Kassel, 1954) and in an English translation by Ernest C. Harris, (Ann Arbor, 1981).

4. Chap. 14, Table 17, comments in par. 41. In E. R. Reilly's translation (*On Playing the Flute* [London, 1966]), the table is incorporated in the text, 169–70, comments 176.

5. Kirnberger's main discussions of phrasing are in *Die Kunst des reinen Satzes in der Musik* (Berlin, 1774–79), 2: 137–53, and in his article "Einschnitt" in Sulzer's *Allgemeine Theorie der schönen Kunst* (Leipzig, 1771–74).

6. The articles on music in Sulzer's *Allgemeine Theorie der schönen Künste* were started by Kirnberger, who wrote them alone up to "Modulation"; from there on Schulz, who was his student, collaborated with Kirnberger until, beginning with letter "S," Schulz became the sole author.

7. Heinrich Christoph Koch, *Versuch einer Anleitung zur Composition* 3 vols. (Leipzig, 1782–95), 2: 361–62. Koch uses the term in Kirnberger's sense as a subdivision of the larger unit of "Abschnitt." Koch's use further compounds the confusion of terms and is not helped by the English translation of "Einschnitt" as "incise" with its double meaning of segment and caesura.

8. I am referring in the following mainly to the excellent study by Albert Palm, *Jérôme-Joseph de Momigny: Leben und Werk* (Cologne, 1969), which has the advantage of having pulled together Momigny's ideas from various publications. Page numbers on Momigny refer to Palm.

9. For the units of phrasing Lussy uses the terms *rythme* for the equivalent of an alexandrine line, *hémistiche* for half of a line, and *incise* for a small section of a hemistich. *Incise* is again doing double duty by signifying both the very small, just-mentioned, melodic segment and the caesura that separates it.

## 21. Problems of Musical Ornamentation

1. A modern school of thought denies an absolute polarity of structure and ornament. It sees the relationship between the two categories as constantly shifting depending on the time span involved. The same note that is structural over the time span of, say, a quarter note, can become ornamental over the time span of a whole note, and so on with increasing time spans. Although of value for theoretical analysis, I believe this relativistic theory is unhelpful regarding performance of 17th- and 18th-century music.

2. Giuseppe Tartini, *Regole per arrivare a saper ben suonar il violino*, Ms. Venice; reprint (Celle and New York, 1961), 5, justifies the use of symbols for appoggiaturas. The symbols alert the performer to the need for a different treatment: whereas a regular, nonornamental note on the strong beat carries the metrical accent and often calls for a reinforcing trill, an appoggiatura should start softly, then swell and taper before it falls onto its principal note. Geminiani, Quantz, and Leopold Mozart give similar descriptions.

3. See *OrnB,* 9–12, for many references to this effect. Here I present just two, separated by a century and a half. Jacopo Peri, in the preface to *Euridice* of 1600, speaks of embellishments "that cannot be written, and if we do write them, cannot be learned from the writings" (e vagezze, e leggeadrie, che non si possono scrivere, e scrivendole non s'imparano dagli scritti). Rameau writes in *Code de musique pratique* (Paris, 1760), 13: "I give no examples of *roulades,* trills, and *ports de voix* because youth needs teachers in all these matters" (Je ne donne aucun example de roulades, trils & ports de voix, parceque la jeunesse a besoin de Maîtres dans tous les cas de la méthode).

4. See on this misunderstanding the above quote (p. 5) by Antoine Geoffroy-Dechaume, who spoke of the "inanity of ornament tables" (l'inanité des tables) that offer only a single transcription of any ornament while each is capable of a great variety of execution.

## 24. One-Note Graces III: Germany

1. László Somfai, "An Introduction to the Study of Haydn's String Quartet Autographs," in *The String Quartets of Haydn, Mozart, and Beethoven,* ed. Christoph Wolff (Cambridge, Mass., 1990), 40.

## 25. Two-Note Graces: The Slide

1. For examples, see the aria "Erbarme dich" from the St. Matthew Passion (BWV 244/47, m. 7 and parallel spots); or the aria "Zerfliesse, meine Herze" (Molt' adagio) from the St. John Passion (BWV 245/63, m. 1 and parallel spots; mm. 119–21).

2. For an example, see Cantata No. 94/7, pervasively.

3. For illustrations, see *OrnB,* Ex. 21.1.

4. D'Anglebert's models of Exx. 25.2a and 25.2c, as mentioned, seemed to exist in a French near-vacuum: no Frenchman adopted them and neither did Bach.

5. See for illustrations *OrnB,* Exx. 20.3 and 20.4.

6. For similar instances, see the St. Matthew Passion, no. 47, mm. 22–23, as well as at the dal segno; Cantata No. 8/2, mm. 19–20; Cantata No. 62/2, mm. 28–29; Cantata No. 69/5, mm. 20–21; Cantata No. 82/1, mm. 169–70; Cantata No. 115/2, mm. 17–18, etc.

7. What part J. C. Bach had in the writing of the book is difficult to know. There is, however, no reason to doubt his participation, as some scholars have done. The fact that the book was published a few years after Johann Christian's death in 1782 does not preclude the latter's cooperation. Ricci was a fairly successful composer whose works were published in Amsterdam, London, and Paris.

## 26. The Trill I: France

1. The nature of Marais's trills was misunderstood by some scholars on account of several cases in which he writes out in regular notes what appears to be a trill that starts with the auxiliary and keeps metrically emphasizing it. These

figurations are not trills, however, because they are played with separate bows for each note. They are related to the turn and have no evidentiary value for the interpretation of the trill symbol. Jean Rousseau explains the execution of these designs in *Traité de la viole* (Paris, 1687), 97–100.

2. For the latter, see Pierre Claude Foucquet, in his Couperin-indebted ornament table of *Les caractères de la paix* (Paris, ca. 1750), the *cadence et redoublé*.

3. François Dandrieu's model of the *tremblement lié* is given in the prefaces of the *Premier livre de pièces de clavecin* (Paris, 1724) and of the *Premier livre d'orgue* (Paris, 1739).

4. Jean-Antoine Bérard, *L'art du chant* (Paris, 1755), 115; Jean Blanchet, *L'art ou les principes philosophiques du chant* (Paris, 1756), 118. The two books are nearly identical. Blanchet sued Bérard, a well-known singer, for plagiarism.

5. L'abbé Pierre Duval, *Principes de la musique pratique par demandes et par réponses* (Paris, 1764), 63. Earlier in the book, speaking of trills in general, he had stated that they "must always" start with the upper note. This contradiction is another reminder to be skeptical of sweeping rules that speak of "must" and "always."

6. *Tremblement feint* was a term often used to signify a minuscule trill of one or two alternations at the end of a long appoggiatura support.

## 27. The Trill II: Italy and England

1. Quantz, in his autobiography (in Marpurg's *Historisch-Kritische Beyträge zur Aufnahme der Musik,* vol. 1 [Berlin, 1754], 197–250), speaks admiringly of Faustina's virtuosic passage work, including tone repetitions articulated in the fastest tempo with the clarity of an instrument (240–41). Quantz had never before heard this technique, which indicates that it had but few practitioners left. It is possible that the staccato tone repetitions in the Queen of the Night's second aria in *Die Zauberflöte* may be late descendants of this art.

2. The Italian-oriented German Wolfgang Michael Mylius had specified in 1685 that the trill symbol can stand for either trill or mordent (see below, p. 000).

3. In the introduction to the first volume of his edition of Scarlatti's sonatas for Le pupitre, Kenneth Gilbert arrives at the same conclusions summarized here, of prevalent main-note trill, of mordent meaning for both the term *tremulo* and for trill symbols preceded by a rising *Vorschlag,* referring for documentation to the very same spots I had pointed out (before him) in *OrnB,* 352–55.

4. Carlo Testori, *La musica ragionata . . .* (Vercelli, 1767), 143 and Plate 20, Fig. 103; Vincenzo Manfredini, *Regole armoniche . . .* (Venice, 1775), 26–27; Vincenzo Panerai, *Principi di musica . . .* (Florence, ca. 1775), 8; Antonio D. R. Borghese, *L'art musical ramené à ses vrais principes . . .* (Paris, 1786), 122 and Plate I, No. 12 (for illustrations see *OrnB,* 350–51).

5. Theophil Muffat's MS (BB 9160): *Suite des pièces pour le clavecin composées par G. F. Händel et mises dans une autre applicature pour la facilité de la main. Par Theophile Muffat 1736.* (In the right upper corner: "Ex libris Theophil Muffat.")

## 28. The Trill III: Germany

1. Fuhrmann, as mentioned before, wrote two treatises, *Musicalischer Trichter* in 1706 and *Musica vocalis* ca. 1715, which overlap in part and will be distinguished by their dates. This example is given in 1706, 64–66 and 1715, 44–45.

2. It is interesting that, as early as 1908, Adolf Beyschlag flatly denied that C. P. E. Bach's rule had to apply to Bach (*Ornamentik*, 129). He may be the only important author to have done so. Edward Dannreuther in 1889 did believe in the rule but weakened it by six substantial exceptions (*Musical Ornamentation* 1: 165–166).

3. As early as 1866 Franz Kroll in his BG edition pointed out that "it is not to be assumed that the trills on such long held-out notes ought to start with the auxiliary according to the rule" (*BG*, 24:230).

4. As convincing as may be the logic of main-note starts in these and similar contexts, the belief in the upper-note rule is so deeply rooted with a number of scholars and performers that they will resort to remarkable devices in order to escape the grip of such logic. Paul Badura-Skoda reports the amusing instance of Gustav Leonhardt's recomposing Bach's text for a recording of the Fugue in A Minor of *WTC II* in order to escape the need of starting a trill with the main note (*Bach Interpretation*, 386–87)!

5. Here for once it makes sense to speak of the *Schneller* as "inverted mordent."

6. Remember the full anticipation of Couperin's *tremblement lié sans être appuyé* and *tremblement détaché* and its reaffirmation by Père Engramelle. But outside of the rigid but rather narrow realm of C. P. E. Bach's and his followers, we need no theoretical confirmation for any ornamental designs that make musical sense in a field that was wide open to imaginative improvisation.

7. Georg Philipp Telemann, *Sonate metodiche à violino solo o flauto traverso*, Op. 13 (Hamburg, 1728); *Continuation des sonates méthodiques* . . . (Hamburg, 1728).

8. For Hiller, see Johann Adam Hiller, *Anweisung zum musikalisch-richtigen Gesange* (Leipzig, 1774), 167ff.; *Anweisung zum musikalisch-zierlichen Gesange* (Leipzig 1780), 68; *Anweisung zum Violinspielen* (Grätz, 1795), 47.

9. Georg Simon Löhlein, *Clavier-Schule* . . . (Leipzig and Züllichau, 1765), chap. 6; *Anweisung zum Violinspielen* . . . (Leipzig and Züllichau, 1774), 46.

10. The well-known Haydn scholar László Somfai, for instance, in 1982 included the trill with the turn, the mordent, the slide, and the arpeggio as "onbeat position ornaments" and illustrated the trill's execution in this manner: ▪▪▪▪ ("How to Read and Understand," 28). His ideas are followed by most "early music specialists" and many mainstream performers who want to follow the "rule" as they know it. More recently, however, in 1988, Sandra P. Rosenblum voices reservations on the question. While still favoring the upper-note start, she lists circumstances in the works of Haydn and other Classical composers in which a main-note trill start is indicated (*Performance Practices*, 245–49). My own findings about the incessant use of the main-note and the grace-note trill during the whole course of the 18th century (as detailed in *OrnB* and *OrnM*) may have played a role in such new orientation.

11. For their transcriptions the editors have used both tape recordings and, for the 1793 and the later undated clock, an impression of the cylinders that allowed an exact reconstruction of melody and rhythm. The music examples are reprinted here with kind permission from the Henle Verlag.

12. Haydn did not write into the score the mordents that are shown on the line of Haydn's autograph text. Instead, he wrote a directive at the end of the piece that every time the theme occurs, the half note has to receive a mordent ("muss bey jedweder Halben Notte folgender Halbe Mordent kommen") and illustrates it thus: , adding that this theme occurs sixteen times. The clock of 1793, as seen on the top line of Ex. 28.30a, has a *Nachschlag* instead of a mordent. The undated clock corrected the mistake and shows the mordent for every one of the sixteen entries of the fugue theme.

13. Paul Badura-Skoda, "Mozart's Trills," in *Perspectives on Mozart Performance,* ed. R. Larry Todd and Peter Williams (Cambridge, 1991). In the essay Paul Badura-Skoda still assumes that "Mozart began normal trills with a quick upper-note start" and views other designs as exceptions, however numerous (3). In addition to legitimizing main-note and grace-note trills, he stresses the importance of the *Pralltriller,* which now merges with the three-pitch *Schneller* by always starting with the main note. He could find no evidence that Mozart, Haydn, or Beethoven ever used the four-note *Pralltriller* that is "so dear to our harpsichordists" (19). He shows instances of anticipated trills (Exx. 48, 49, and 60), points to the occasional time-imposed substitution of turns for trills (24) and of *Vorschläge* for *Pralltriller* (23), and cites approvingly my "test" for the trill's start as a good "rule of thumb."

## 30. The Mordent

1. The BG and most older editions have trills instead of mordents in the second part. The NBA has corrected this mistake, which was due to a misreading of the symbols.

2. The passage is the inverted counterpart to the descending appoggiatura that resolves into a trill, shown in Ex. 28.15.

3. It is worth noting that Leopold Mozart sees the French *pincé* as falling into the same prebeat-implying dynamic pattern: "I may say," he writes, "that the mordent or the so-called French *pincé* approaches the principal note very softly and quickly, almost nibbling, pinching, or picking the latter but immediately letting go" (*Versuch einer gründlichen Violinschule* [Augsburg, 1756], chap. 11, par. 8, n).

4. For the versatility of the "Haydn ornament," see *Essays 1989,* chap. 7, esp. 97–104.

## 31. Other Ornaments

1. Where, as in Exx. 31.7f–31.7g, little unmetrical notes are used to indicate the turn, they replace a symbol.

2. For more details on Haydn's turns, see *Essays 1989,* chap. 7, 79–100, and chap. 8, 109–13 and 117–119.

3. The reason for the limitation to lengthy arpeggios is not quite clear; the rhythmic integrity of the melody can be impaired even by shorter arpeggios that are started on the beat, if less damagingly so.

4. This omission in all models in tables belongs to what Hugo Riemann has already been quoted as calling *vergessene Selbstverständlichkeiten* (forgotten matters of course). By having forgotten, many modern scholars are led astray.

5. In the String Quartet Op. 71, No. 1 (Hob. III:69), second movement, m. 41, all four instruments have on the first beat a siciliano rhythm with a *sforzando* written under the first note. The latter is preceded in the first violin by a three-note arpeggio, in the cello by a two-note arpeggio, in the second violin and viola by upward-leaping *Vorschläge.* Surely all four instruments need to pronounce the first *sforzando* note at the same time; this is possible only when the preceding ornaments of one, two, and three notes are all anticipated.

6. *Regole per accompagnar sopra la parte.* Ludwig Landshoff was the first to draw attention to this manuscript, which he tentatively dated around 1700 ("Über das vielstimmige Accompagnement," in *Festschrift zum 50. Geburtstag, Adolf Sandberger* [Munich, 1918]).

7. The usual left-hand string vibrato is produced by the pivoting of a finger while keeping its place on the string, in a motion activated by the shaking of the hand from the wrist or, in an alternate technique, from the elbow. The horizontal component of the resulting motion produces the pitch vibrato, but intensity and timbre oscillations frequently enter when a vertical component of up and down complements, and on occasion even replaces, the horizontal, pivoting component. A pure vertical finger motion that alternates milder and stronger pressure and originates in the knuckle, produces by itself a minimal pitch variation but a noticeable one of intensity and timbre. The greater pressure extends the surface of the fingertip that depresses the string and thereby ever-so-slightly raises the pitch. But at the same time, the stronger pressure hardens the surface of the finger tip and produces a louder sound and a harder timbre. The effect of the character and profile of the stopping agent on intensity and timbre can best be observed on the open string, which, bowed the same way, is notoriously louder and brighter in tone color than the stopped pitches because its stopping agent is the sharp wooden edge of the top nut at the scroll end of the string. By the same token, a bony finger placed steeply on the string will produce a harder, louder sound than a fleshy, fat finger placed flatly, touching with the cushioned part. The horizontal and vertical components can be mixed in all possible ratios and, combined with the anatomy of the finger and its steeper or flatter placement, can produce an infinite variety of vibrato sounds. Since the intensity and timbre oscillations are a by-product of the vibrato motion, they will totally coincide with the pitch oscillations and add an extra dimension to its effect.

8. This passage, which I showed in *OrnB* (Ex. 45.4), is also reproduced in Stewart Carter's recent article "The String Tremolo in the 17th Century," *EM* 19 (1991): Ex. 9. Carter holds that Cesti was the first to introduce the wavy line symbol for the bow vibrato and that before that time this kind of vibrato was

either indicated by slurred repeated pitches or marked with the words: *tremolo con l'arco*. Carter lists and quotes a number of such occurrences, beginning with Biagio Marini's *La Foscarina: Sonata a 3, con il tremolo* (43–51).

9. For more illustrations, see *OrnB*, 519–20. Greta Moens-Haenen tries to argue that Bach's wavy-line symbol for voice and melody instruments indicates not a vibrato but a half-tone upward glissando analogous to the *coulé du doigt* of the French gambists (whose symbol happened to be not a wavy line but a check mark: ✔; *Das Vibrato*, 242). For several reasons Moens-Haenen's interpretation is unconvincing to the point of being incongruous. The horizontal wavy line was a widely used vibrato symbol in France, Italy, and Germany, from at least the mid-17th to at least the late 18th century (still used by Gluck and Gossec among others), and it was a logical choice since its graphic design evokes an oscillating motion. Whereas for the gamba a half-tone glissando makes sense because the distance traversed is noticeable, for the voice and the violin such a glissando would be practically imperceptible; and to mark something that inconspicuous with a special symbol would make little sense, least of all with a sign that has had common currency for the vibrato and is graphically illogical for a glissando. Already Danoville in his gamba treatise of 1687, while explaining the half-tone glissando, says that the gamba is the only instrument fitting for that grace and that the violin strings are too taut to permit its effective rendition (*L'art de basse de violle*, 43). Moreover, we must not forget Bach's emotion-laden words that for the voice suggest tremor rather than a smooth, near-imperceptible glissando. Moens-Haenen herself admits that at least in one example (which I had shown in *OrnB*, Ex. 45.8h) a glissando is impossible between the repeated words "tot, tot, tot" (*Das Vibrato*, 247). The glissando interpretation is infelicitous.

10. He speaks of "Klavier," which to him means clavichord, not, as I mistakenly assumed in *OrnB*, the fortepiano.

11. Robin Stowell gives a detailed account of Leopold's remarks on the vibrato in *Violin Technique and Performance Practice in the Late Eighteenth and Early Nineteenth Centuries* (Cambridge, 1985), 203–6.

12. Ellen Harris has tried to present such evidence in her essay on the voice in the Baroque era (*Performance Practice*, ed. Howard M. Brown and Stanley Sadie [New York, 1990], 2: chap. 5). In my article "The Vibrato Controversy," *Performance Practice Review* 4, No. 1 (Spring 1991): I have endeavored to show that Harris's attempt was not successful. See this article also for more detail on the vibrato controversy.

13. While trying to establish only minimal use of the pitch vibrato in Baroque music, Moens-Haenen (see n. 9) seems also to judge by what we *know* rather than by what we *hear*. She is ambivalent about the innate vibrato of the voice. She does not deny its existence outright but tries to make it appear insignificant "in case it might exist." First she finds the question whether the voice vibrates spontaneously ("von Natur aus") difficult to answer but admits that one must consider the "possibility" of a "very small" natural vibrato (*Das Vibrato*, 11). Later she hedges again by speaking of a "possibly existent" (eventuell vorhandenen) natural vibrato, which would have to lie "considerably below" a conscious "ornamental" vibrato whose range and intensity is small to begin with (31). Caruso's vibrato, whether we call it

"ornamental" or not, was anything but small: as revealed by electronic analysis of his records, in moments of great intensity it reached the extraordinary amplitude of a whole tone! It was of course the phenomenon of "sonance" that transformed these "impurities" of a legendary sound.

## 32. Improvisation I: France and Italy

1. For more illustrations of *airs de cour* by Boësset, Moulinié, Bacilly, and d'Ambruis, see *OrnB,* 32, 33, and 527–28.

2. When after Lully's death the use of the symbols spread, several second editions of his works and a few posthumous first editions show ornamental additions mainly of the *port de voix* and slide types.

3. Among the more important treatises are: Dalla Casa, *Il vero modo di diminuir* (Venice, 1584); Bassano, *Ricercate, passaggi et cadentie* (Venice, 1585); Diruta, *Il Transilvano* (Venice, 1593); Bovicelli, *Regole, passaggi di musica* (Venice, 1594); Conforto, *Breve e facile maniera . . . a far passaggi* (Venice, 1593 [1603?] year illegible); Richardo Rogniono, *Passaggi per potersi essercitare nel diminuire . . .* (Venice, 1592); Francesco Rognioni (son of Richardo, with different spelling), *Selva de varii passaggi* (Milan, 1620).

4. For more illustrations, see *OrnB,* 533–34, and Howard M. Brown, *Embellishing Sixteenth-Century Music* (London and Oxford, 1976).

5. Letter to Aless. Striggio, December 18, 1627 (see *The Monteverdi Companion,* ed. Denis Arnold and Nigel Fortune [New York, 1972], 77).

6. In 1672 Gio. Maria Bononcini pleads with his performers not to disfigure his music and gives as the reason: "because today there are some [performers] so little informed of that art of tasteful embellishment that in singing or in playing they want with their disorderly and indiscreet extravagances of bow or of voice to change, indeed to deform, the compositions (even though these were written with every care and conscientiousness) in such a manner that the authors have no choice but to beg those singers and players to content themselves with rendering the works plainly and purely as they are written" (*Sonate da chiesa a due violini* [Venice, 1672], Preface).

7. Tosi's translators have supplied them throughout the volume with often very questionable results (as was shown for instance in connection with the trill).

8. For illustrations see Robert Haas, *Aufführungspraxis der Musik* (Wildpark-Potsdam, 1931), 185–87; Hans-Peter Schmitz, *Die Kunst der Verzierung im 18. Jahrhundert* (Kassel, 1955), 76–93; and Charles Burney, *A General History of Music, from the Earliest Ages to the Present Period,* (1789; reprint, New York, 1957), 4: 437–44, 461–62).

9. A whole aria by Farinelli's brother, Rioccardo Broschi, with Farinelli's diminutions and cadenzas is reprinted in Schmitz, *Kunst der Verzierung,* 76–93; seven cadenzas to an aria by Geminiani Giacomelli (one of four arias that Farinelli had to sing daily for the ailing Spanish King Philipp V) are reprinted in Haas, *Aufführungspraxis der Musik,* 185–87.

10. I am indebted to Professor Alfred Mann for the reference and a photocopy of the autograph.

11. G. F. Handel, *Three Ornamented Arias,* ed. Winton Dean (London, 1976).

12. John Hawkins, *A General History of the Science and Practice of Music,* new ed., 2 vols. (London, 1853), 2:904–7; reprinted in Schmitz, *Kunst der Verzierung,* 62–69.

13. At the other extreme we find a Dresden manuscript showing four versions, all extravagant, of embellishments to a Vivaldi concerto. Arnold Schering speculated in 1905 that Pisendel was the author and that the embellishments might reflect Vivaldian practices ("Zur instrumentalen Verzierungskunst im 18. Jahrhundert," *IMG* 7 [1905–6]: 365–385. Walter Kolneder, in *Aufführungspraxis bei Vivaldi* [Leipzig, 1955], 56, supports Scherings hypothesis as "likely"). A brief sample of this MS is given in Haas, *Aufführungspraxis der Musik,* 204.

## 33. Improvisation II: Germany

1. Some modern performers compose here a lengthy fantasy of almost movement length. This does not seem to be either necessary or fitting. Bach did not expect anybody else to do the composing for him. What he had a right to expect were some nonthematic flourishes.

2. Georg Philipp Telemann, *Sonate metodiche* for violin or flute and continuo (Hamburg, 1728); *Continuation des sonates méthodiques* (Hamburg, 1732; modern ed. of both volumes, Kassel, 1955); *3 Trietti metodichi e 3 Scherzi* for two flutes or violins and continuo (Hamburg, 1731).

3. An ornamented movement from Telemann's sonatas and a movement from the trios are reproduced in Hans-Peter Schmitz, *Die Kunst der Verzierung im 18. Jahrhundert* (Kassel, 1955), 106–9.

4. Johann Joachim Quantz, *Versuch einer Anweisung, die Flöte traversiere zu spielen* (Berlin, 1752), chaps. 13 and 14 deal with diminution, chap. 15 with cadenzas.

5. I am following here Edward R. Reilly's excellent translation of Quantz's treatise: *On Playing the Flute* (London, 1966).

6. Türk's treatise is available in a modern English translation by Raymond H. Haggh (Lincoln, Nebr., 1982).

7. See on this Robert Levin, "Instrumental Ornamentation, Improvisation, and Cadenzas," in *Performance Practice,* ed. Howard M. Brown and Stanley Sadie (New York, 1990), esp. 284–89, where he reprints some of Türk's examples of such embellishments.

8. A detailed report by Ernst Fritz Schmid on this ornamented aria ("Joseph Haydn und die vokale Zierpraxis seiner Zeit, dargestellt an einer Arie seines Tobias-Oratoriums"), presented at the International Haydn Conference in Budapest, September 17–22, 1959, was published in the Proceedings of the Conference (Budapest, 1961), 117–29. I am indebted to Prof. A. Peter Brown for having drawn my attention to this report, which he kindly sent me along with several other items of great interest regarding Haydn's compositional processes.

9. Guiseppe Carpani, quoted in A. Peter Brown's fascinating book *Performing Haydn's "The Creation": Reconstructing the Earliest Renditions* (Bloomington, Ind., 1986).

10. On this, see my articles "A New Look at Mozart's Prosodic Appoggiatura," in *Perspectives on Mozart Performance,* ed. R. L. Todd and P. Williams (Cambridge, 1991), esp. pp. 92–94 and 114–15, and "Improper Appoggiaturas in the *Neue Mozart Ausgabe,*" *Jl. of Musicology* 10 (Fall 1992): 505–521.

11. Will Crutchfield, "The Prosodic Appoggiatura in the Music of Mozart and His Contemporaries" *JAMS* 42 (1989): 229–274; "Voices" in *Performance Practice,* ed. Howard M. Brown and Stanley Sadie (New York, 1990), 2: 298–30. For an answer see Neumann, "A New Look at Mozart's Prosodic Appoggiatura," 92–116.

12. Regarding the theorists, see *OrnM,* chaps. 12 and 13, esp. 186–90; Antonio Salieri's *Scuola di canto in versi/e i versi in musica a 4 voci/il tutto composto da me Ant.Salieri,* autograph MS in the Library of the Gesellschaft der Musikfreunde, Vienna, shelf mark 915.

13. The NMA edition of *Così fan tutte* (ed. Faye Ferguson and Wolfgang Rehm) misunderstood in this aria (as well as elsewhere in this opera) the important cues of the wide fermatas. In only five of the eight cases the edition says that "a brief embellishment may be sung" instead of "ought to be sung," and in three other cases (mm. 60, 62, and 64) no mention is made of a desirable insert. Two whole-measure fermatas in Ferrando's aria "Un' aura amorosa" are also ignored, and so are many more in this opera.

14. Among the best modern cadenzas are those by Paul Badura-Skoda and by Marius Flothuis. Philip Whitmore published a very interesting monograph on the cadenza (*Unpremeditated Art: The Cadenza in the Classical Keyboard Concerto* [Oxford, 1991]). Though its purpose is to trace the history of the cadenza rather than to advise on how to invent one, chap. 8, on Mozart's cadenzas, contains information helpful to performers who wish to prepare their own.

15. For some examples of such phrases and their suggested embellishment, see *OrnM,* chap. 16.

# Bibliography of Sources Cited

Adlung, Jacob. *Anleitung zu der musikalischen Gelahrtheit*. Erfut, 1758. Reprint (ed. by H. J. Moser), Kassel, 1953.

Agincour, François d'. *Pièces de clavecin*. Paris, 1733.

Agricola, Johann Friedrich. Review of Löhlein's *Clavier-Schule*. In *Bach Documente* 3: 206. Kassel, 1972.

——. *Anleitung zur Singkunst*. Translated from P. Tosi's *Opinioni de' cantori,* with extensive commentaries in different print. Berlin, 1757. Reprint (ed. by Erwin R. Jacobi), Celle, 1966.

——. *Schreiben an Herrn . . . [sic] in welchem Flavio Anicio Olibrio sein Schreiben an den critischen Musicus an der Spree vertheidiget. . . .* Berlin, 1749.

Agricola, Martin. *Musica instrumentalis deudsch. . . .* Rev. ed., Wittenberg, 1545. Reprinted in *Gesellschaft für Musikforschung,* Jahrgang 24, vol. 20, Leipzig, 1896.

Ahle, Johan Georg. *Musikalisches Frühlings-Gespräche*. Mühlhausen, 1695.

Ahle, Johann Rudolf. *Brevis et perspicua introductio in artem musicam. . . .* Mühlhausen, 1673. (New enl. ed. by his son, Johan Georg Ahle, titled *Kurze doch deutliche Anleitung zu der . . . Singkunst . . . ,* Mühlhausen, 1690.)

Albrechtsberger, Johann Georg. *Anfangsgründe zur Klavierkunst*. MS. XIV 1952, GMF.

Alembert, Jean le Rond d'. *Elémens de musique, théorique et pratique, suivant les principes de M. Rameau*. Paris, 1752.

Allanbrook, Wye Jamison. *Rhythmic Gesture in Mozart*. Chicago, 1983.

Ambruis, Honoré d'. *Livre d'airs . . . avec les seconds couplets en diminutions. . . .* Paris, 1685.

Anglebert, Jean Henri d'. *Pièces de clavecin*. Paris, 1689. Facsimile, New York, 1965.

Apel, Willi. "Anent a Ritornello in Monteverdi's Orfeo." *Musica Disciplina* 5 (1951): 213–22.

——. *The Notation of Polyphonic Music, 900–1600*. 5th ed. Cambridge, Mass., 1953.

Azaïs, Pierre-Hyacynthe. *Méthode de musique,* Paris [1776].

Babitz, Sol. "A Problem of Rhythm in Baroque Music." *MQ* 38 (1952): 553–65.

Bach, Carl Philipp Emanuel. Preface to *Sechs Sonaten für Klavier mit veränderten Reprisen*. Berlin, 1760.

——. *Versuch über die wahre Art das Clavier zu Spielen.* . . . 2 vols. Vol. 1: Berlin, 1753; 2d ed., 1759; 3d enl. ed., Leipzig, 1787. Vol. 2: Berlin, 1762; 2d ed., Leipzig, 1797. Facsimile, Leipzig, 1957. English translation (translated and edited by William J. Mitchell), New York, 1949.

Bach, Johann Christian, and F. Pasquale Ricci. *Méthode pour le forte-piano*. Paris, ca. 1786.

Bach, Johann Sebastian. *Neue Ausgabe sämtlicher Werke*. Leipzig and Kassel, 1954–.

*Bach Dokumente*. Supplement to NBA, vol. 3. Leipzig and Kassel, 1972.

Bacilly, Bénigne de. *Remarques curieuses sur l'art de bien chanter.* . . . Paris, 1668. 2d ed. (with new preface), 1679. Facsimile, Geneva, 1971. English translation (translated and edited by Austin B. Caswell), Brooklyn, 1968.

——. *Les trois livres d'airs . . . augmentez . . . d'ornamens pour la methode de chanter.* Part 1. Paris, 1668.

Badura-Skoda, Eva, and Paul Badura-Skoda. *Interpreting Mozart on the Keyboard.* London, 1962.

Badura-Skoda, Paul. *Bach Interpretation: Die Klavierwerke Johann Sebastian Bachs.* Laaber, 1990. English translation in preparation by Oxford University Press.

——. "Beiträge zu Haydns Ornamentik." *Musica* 36 (Sep./Oct. 1982): 409–18.

——. "Mozart's Trills." In *Perspectives on Mozart Performance*. Edited by R. L. Todd and P. Williams. Cambridge, 1991.

——. "A Tie Is a Tie Is a Tie." *EM* (1988): 84–88.

Banchieri, Adriano. *Cartella musicale nel canto figurato.* . . . Venice, 1614. Reprint, Bologna, 1968.

——. *Conclusioni nel suono dell'organo*. Bologna, 1609.

Bassano, Giovanni. *Ricercate, passaggi et cadentie.* . . . Venice, 1585.

*Die Bedeutung der Zeichen Keil Strich und Punkt bei Mozart*. Edited by Hans Albrecht. Kassel, 1957.

Bedos de Celles, Dom François. *L'art du facteur d'orgues*. Vol. 4. Paris, 1778. Reprint, Kassel, 1966.

Beethoven, Ludwig van. *Letters*. 3 vols. Collected, translated and edited by Emily Anderson, New York, 1961.

Bérard, Jean-Antoine. *L'art du chant*. Paris, 1755. Facsimile, Geneva, 1972.

Bernhard, Christoph. ((1)) *Von der Singe-Kunst oder Manier;* ((2)) *Tractatus compositionis augmentatus;* ((3)) *Ausführlicher Bericht vom Gebrauche der Con- und Dissonantien;* all three preserved in MSS, first published as: *Die Kompositionslehre Heinrich Schützens in der Fassung seines Schülers Christoph Bernhard.* Edited by Joseph Müller-Blattau. 1st ed., Leipzig, 1926. 2d. ed., Kassel, 1963. English trans. by Walter Hilse. *Music Forum* 3 (1973): 1–196.

Berthet, Pierre. *Leçons de musique . . . pour apprendre à chanter sa partie à livre ouvert*. 2d ed., Paris, 1695.

Beyer, Johann Samuel. *Primae lineae musicae vocalis.* . . . Freiberg, 1703. 2d ed., Dresden and Freiberg, 1730.

Beyschlag, Adolf. *Die Ornamentik der Musik.* Leipzig, 1908. Reprints, Leipzig, 1953 and 1970.

Blanchet, Jean. *L'art ou les principes philosophiques du chant.* Paris, 1756.

Bodky, Erwin. *Interpretation of Bach's Keyboard Works.* Cambridge, Mass., 1960.

Bollioud de Mermet, Louis. *De la corruption du goust dans la musique françoise.* Lyon, 1746.

Bononcini, Giovanni Maria. Preface to *Sonate da chiesa a due violini,* Op. 6. Venice, 1672.

Borghese, Antonio D. R. *L'art musical ramené à ses vrais principes.* . . . Paris, 1786.

Borrel, Eugène. *L'interprétation de la musique française (de Lully à la révolution).* Paris, 1934.

Bourgeois, Loys. *Le droit chemin de musique.* Paris, 1550. Reprint, Kilkenny, 1982.

Bovicelli, Giovanni Battista. *Regole, passaggi di musica.* . . . Venice, 1594. Facsimile, edited by N. Bridgman, Kassel, 1957.

Boyden, David. "The Violin Bow in the 18th Century." *EM* 8 (1980): 199–212.

Boyvin, Jacques. *Premier livre d'orgue.* . . . Paris, 1689.

———. *Second livre d'orgue.* Paris, 1700.

Brijon, C. R. *L'Apollon moderne, ou le développement intellectuel par les sons de la musique.* Lyon, 1780.

———. *Réflexions sur la musique, et la vraie manière de l'exécuter sur le violon.* Paris, 1763. Reprint, Geneva, 1972.

Brossard, Sébastien de. *Dictionnaire de musique.* . . . Paris, 1703. Reprint, Amsterdam, 1964.

Brown, A. Peter. *Performing Haydn's "The Creation": Reconstructing the Earliest Renditions.* Bloomington, Ind., 1986.

Buelow, George J. "A Schütz Reader: Documents of Performance Practice." *American Choral Review* 27, no. 4 (Oct. 1985): 3–34.

Burney, Charles. *A General History of Music, from the Earliest Ages to the Present Period.* London, 1789. Facsimile, New York, 1957.

Buterne, Charles. *Méthode pour apprendre la musique vocale et instrumentale.* Paris, Lyon, and Rouen, 1752.

Butt, John. *Bach Interpretation: Articulation Marks in the Primary Sources of J. S. Bach.* Cambridge, 1990.

Caccini, Giulio. *Le nuove musiche.* Florence, 1601 [i.e., 1602]. Reprints: Rome, 1930; New York, 1973.

Callcott, John W. *An Explanation of the Notes, Marks, Words, &c Used in Music.* London, 1793.

Carissimi, Giovanni Giacomo. *Ars cantandi.* Augsburg, 1689. (Extant only in German translation.)

Carter, Stewart. "The String Tremolo in the 17th Century." *EM* 19 (1991): 43–59.

Cavalieri, Emilio de'. *Rappresentatione di anima et di corpo.* Rome, 1600. Facsimile, Bologna, 1967.

Chambonnières, Jacques Champion de. *Pièces de clavessin.* Paris, 1670. Facsimile, New York, 1967.

Chaumont, Lambert. *Pièces d'orgue sur les 8 tons.* . . . Liège, 1696.

Choquel, Henri-Louis. *La musique rendue sensible par la méchanique.* . . . Paris, 1759. New ed., 1762. Reprint, Geneva, 1972.

Clementi, Muzio. *Introduction to the Art of Playing on the Pianoforte.* London, 1801. Facsimile (ed. by Sandra P. Rosenblum), New York, 1974.

Clérambault, Louis-Nicolas. *Cantates françoises à I et à II voix.* Book 1. Paris, 1710.

Collins, Michael. "The Performance of Sesquialtera and Hemiolia in the 16th Century." *JAMS* 17 (1964): 4–28.

———. "The Performance of Triplets in the 17th and 18th Centuries." *JAMS* 19 (1966): 281–328.

———. "A Reconsideration of French Overdotting." *Music & Letters* 50 (1969): 111–23.

Conforto, Giovanni Luca. *Breve e facile maniera . . . a far passaggi.* . . . Rome, 1593 [1603?].

Cooper, Grosvenor, and Leonard B. Meyer. *The Rhythmic Structure of Music.* Chicago, 1960.

Corfe, Joseph. *Treatise on Singing.* London, [ca. 1800].

Corrette, Michel. *Les amusements du Parnasse: Méthode . . . pour apprendre à toucher le clavecin.* . . . Paris, [ca. 1749].

———. *L'ecole d'Orphée, méthode pour apprendre facilement à jouer du violon.* . . . Paris, 1738.

———. *Méthode pour apprendre aisément à joüer de la flûte traversière.* . . . Paris, 1735.

———. *Méthode . . . pour apprendre en peu de tems le violoncelle.* . . . Paris, 1741.

Couperin, François. *L'art de toucher le clavecin.* Paris, 1716. Enl. ed., Paris, 1717. Reprint, New York, 1969.

———. *Pièces de clavecin.* 4 vols. Paris, 1713–30.

Crüger, Johann. *Musicae practicae praecepta brevia . . . : Der rechte Weg zur Singkunst.* . . . Berlin, 1660.

———. *Synopsis musica.* . . . Berlin, 1630. Enl. ed., 1654.

Crutchfield, Will. "The Prosodic Appoggiatura in the Music of Mozart and His Contemporaries." *JAMS* 42 (1989): 229–74.

Dadelsen, Georg von. "Die Crux der Nebensache: Editorische und praktische Bemerkungen zu Bachs Artikulation." *Bach Jahrbuch* (1978): 95–112.

D'Agincour. See Agincour.

Dahlhaus, Carl. "Zur Geschichte des Taktschlagens im frühen 17. Jahrhunderts." In *Studies in Renaissance and Baroque Music in Honor of Arthur Mendel,* edited by Robert L. Marshall. Kassel, 1974.

Dalla Casa, Girolamo. *Il vero modo di diminuir.* . . . 2 vols. Venice, 1584. Facsimile, Bologna, 1970.

Danby, John. *La guida della musica instrumentale.* London, [ca. 1790].

———. *La guida alla musica vocale.* London, [ca. 1785].

Dandrieu, Jean-François. *Premier livre de pièces de clavecin.* Paris, 1724.

———. *Premier livre d'orgue.* Paris, 1739.

———. *Second livre de pièces de clavecin.* Paris, 1728.

D'Anglebert. See Anglebert.

Dannreuther, Edward. *Musical Ornamentation.* 2 vols. London, 1893–95.

Danoville. *L'art de toucher le dessus et basse de violle.* . . . Paris, 1687. Facsimile, Geneva, 1972.

Dart, Thurston. *The Interpretation of Music.* London, 1954. Reprint, New York, 1963.

Dauscher, Andreas. *Kleines Handbuch der Musiklehre und vorzüglich der Querflöte.* Ulm, 1801.

David, François. *Méthode nouvelle ou principes généraux pour apprendre facilement la musique et l'art de chanter.* Paris, 1737.

David, Hans T., and Arthur Mendel. *The Bach Reader.* Rev. ed. New York, 1966.

De la Barre, Michel. *Pièces pour la flûte traversière,* Paris, 1703.

De Lusse. See Lusse.

Demachy. *Pièces de violle.* . . . Paris, 1685.

Demantius, Christoph. *Isagoge artis musicae.* Ansbach, 1611.

Denis, Pierre. *Nouveau système de musique pratique.* . . . Paris, 1747. 2d ed., rev. and corr. under title *Nouvelle méthode pour apprendre . . . la musique et l'art de chanter . . .* , Paris, 1762.

Deysinger, Johann Franz Peter. *Compendium musicum oder fundamenta partiturae.* . . . Augsburg, 1763. 2d ed., Augsburg, 1788.

Dieupart, Charles. *Six suittes de clavessin.* . . . Amsterdam, [ca. 1702].

Diruta, Girolamo. *Il Transilvano.* . . . 2 vols. Venice, 1593–1609. Facsimile, Bologna, 1969.

Dolmetsch, Arnold. *The Interpretation of the Music of the Seventeenth and Eighteenth Centuries.* London, 1915. Reprint, London, 1944.

Donington, Robert. *The Interpretation of Early Music.* London, 1963. 2d ed., 1965. New version, 1974.

———. *A Performer's Guide to Baroque Music.* New York, 1973.

Dornel, Charles. *Pièces de clavecin.* Paris, 1731.

Durieu. *Méthode de violon.* Paris, 1796.

———. *Nouvelle méthode de musique vocale.* . . . Paris, [ca. 1793].

Dürr, Alfred. "De vita cum imperfectis." In *Studies in Renaissance and Baroque Music in Honor of Arthur Mendel.* Edited by Robert L. Marshall. Kassel, 1974.

Duval. *Méthode agréable et utile pour apprendre facilement à chanter.* . . . Paris, 1775. Reprint, Geneva, 1972.

Duval, L'abbé Pierre. *Principes de la musique pratique par demandes et par réponses.* Paris, 1764.

Emery, Walter. *Bach's Ornaments.* London, 1953.

*Encyclopédie méthodique, musique.* Edited by Jérôme-Joseph Momigny, Nicolas-Etienne Framery, and Pierre-Louis Ginguené. Paris, 1798.

Engramelle, Marie Dominique Joseph. *La tonotechnie.* Paris, 1775.

Falck, Georg. *Idea boni cantoris.* . . . Nürnberg, 1688.

Fantini, Girolamo. *Modo per imparare a sonare di tromba.* . . . Frankfurt, 1638.

Feyertag, Moritz. *Syntaxis minor zur Sing-Kunst.* . . . Duderstadt, 1695.

Finck, Hermann. *Practica musica.* . . . Wittenberg, 1556.

Fiocco, Joseph-Hector. *Pièces de clavecin.* Brussels, 1730.

Fischer, Johann Caspar. *Musicalisches Blumenbüschlein* . . . , Op. 2. Augsburg, [ca. 1696].

*Fitzwilliam Virginal Book.* 2 vols. Edited by J. A. Fuller Maitland and W. Barclay Squire. Leipzig, 1894–99. Reprint, New York, 1963.

Foucquet, Pierre-Claude. *Les caractères de la paix, pièces de clavecin.* Paris, [ca. 1749].

Francoeur, Louis-Joseph ("neveu"). *Diapason général de tous les instrumens à vent.* . . . Paris, [ca. 1772]. Autograph additions on ornaments, MS. 1843–1844, BN.

Freillon-Poncein, Jean Pierre. *La véritable manière d'apprendre à jouer en perfection du haut-bois, de la flûte et du flageolet.* . . . Paris, 1700. Facsimile, Geneva, 1971.

Frescobaldi, Girolamo. *Primo libro delle canzoni.* . . . Preface by Bartolomeo Grassi. Rome, 1628.

——. *Il primo libro di capricci canzon francese e recercari.* . . . Rome, 1624. Another ed., 1628.

——. *Secondo libro di toccate.* Rome, 1637.

——. *Toccate e partite d'intavolatura di cimbalo, libro primo.* Rome, 1615–16.

Friderici, Daniel. *Musica figuralis.* . . . Rostock, 1619. [3d] rev., enl., improved ed., 1624.

Fuhrmann, Martin Heinrich. *Musica vocalis in nuce.* . . . Berlin, [ca. 1715].

——. *Musicalischer Trichter.* . . . Berlin, 1706.

Fuller, David. "The 'Dotted Style' in Bach, Handel, and Scarlatti." In *Handel, Bach, Scarlatti: Tercentenary Essays.* Edited by P. Williams. London, 1985.

——. "Dotting, the 'French Style,' and Frederick Neumann's Counter-Reformation." *EM* 5 (1977): 517–43.

——. "Notes and *Inégales* Unjoined: Defending a Definition." *Journal of Musicology* 7 (1989): 21–28.

——. "Notes inégales . . ." In *Grove 6.*

——. "Notes inégales." In *New Harvard Dictionary of Music.* Edited by Don Michael Randel. Cambridge, Mass., 1986.

——. "Rhythmic Alteration—If Any—In Bach's Organ Music." *The American Organist* 27 (June 1987): 40–48.

——. "Trill." In *New Harvard Dictionary of Music.*

Ganassi, Sylvestro. *Opera intitulata Fontegara.* . . . Venice, 1535. Facsimile, Milan, 1934. German translation by H. Peter, Berlin, 1956. English translation (from the German) by D. Swainson, Berlin, 1959.

——. *Regola rubertina.* . . . Venice, 1542. Facsimile, Bologna, 1970.

Gasparini, Francesco. *L'armonico pratico al cimbalo.* . . . Venice, 1708. Facsimile, New York, 1967.

Geminiani, Francesco. *The Art of Playing on the Violin.* . . . London, 1751. Facsimile reprint (ed. by D. Boyden), Oxford, n.d.

———. *A Treatise of Good Taste in the Art of Musick.* London, 1749. Facsimile reprint (ed. by R. Donington). New York, 1969.

Gengenbach, Nicolaus. *Musica nova.* . . . Leipzig, 1626.

Geoffroy-Dechaume, A. "L'appoggiature ancienne." In *L'interprétation de la musique française aux XVIIème et XVIIIème siècles.* Paris, 1974.

Gervasoni, Carlo. *La scuola della musica.* 2 vols. Parma, 1800.

Gigault, Nicolas. *Livre de musique pour l'orgue.* . . . Paris, 1685.

Glareanus, Heinrich. *Dodecachordon.* Basel, 1547.

Gossett, Philipp. "The Mensural System and the 'Choralis Constantinus.' " In *Studies in Renaissance and Baroque Music in Honor of Arthur Mendel.* Edited by Robert L. Marshall. Kassel, 1974.

Grigny, Nicolas de. *Premier livre d'orgue.* Paris, 1699.

Haas, Robert. *Aufführungspraxis der Musik.* Wildpark-Potsdam, 1931.

Hall, James S., and Martin V. Hall. "Handel's Graces." *Händel Jahrbuch* (1957): 25–43.

Harding, Rosamond E. M. *Origins of Musical Time and Expression.* London, 1938.

Harris, Ellen. "Voices." In *Performance Practice,* 2 vols. Edited by Howard M. Brown and Stanley Sadie. London, 1989. New York, 1990.

Hartong [P. C. Humanus, pseud.]. *Musicus theoretico-practicus.* . . . Nürnberg, 1749.

Haskell, Harry. *The Early Music Revival: A History.* New York, 1988.

Hawkins, John. *A General History of the Science and Practice of Music.* 2 vols. London, 1853. Facsimile, New York, 1963.

Heinichen, Johann David. *Der Generalbass in der Composition.* . . . Dresden, 1728. English translation (trans. and ed. by George Buelow), Ann Arbor, 1961.

———. *Neu erfundene und gründliche Anweisung . . . zu vollkommener Erlernung des Generalbasses.* . . . Hamburg, 1711.

Helmont, Charles-Joseph van. *Pièces de clavecin.* Brussels, 1737.

Herbst, Johann Andreas. *Musica practica.* . . . Nürnberg, 1642. 2nd enl. ed. titled *Musica moderna prattica . . . ,* Frankfurt, 1658.

Hermann-Bengen, Irmgard. *Tempobezeichnungen, Ursprung, Wandel im 17. und 18. Jahrhundert.* Tutzing, 1959.

Hiller, Johann Adam. *Anweisung zum musikalisch-richtigen Gesange.* . . . Leipzig, 1774.

———. *Anweisung zum musikalisch-zierlichen Gesange.* . . . Leipzig, 1780.

———. *Anweisung zum Violinspielen.* . . . Grätz, 1795.

Hitzler, Daniel. *Extract aus der neuen Musica oder Singkunst.* Nürnberg, 1623.

Hook, James. *Guida di musica.* London, [ca. 1785].

Hotteterre, Jacques. *L'art de préluder sur la flûte traversière.* Paris, 1718.

———. *Premier livre de pièces pour la flûte traversière . . . avec la basse.* New ed. Paris, 1715.

———. *Principes de la flûte traversière, . . . de la flute à bec, . . . et du haut-bois.* Paris, 1707. Facsimile reprint (of 1710 Amsterdam ed.) with German translation, Kassel, 1941. (3d. ed., 1965.)

Houle, George. *Meter in Music.* Bloomington, Ind., 1987.

Hüllmandel, Nicolas Joseph. *Principles of Music, chiefly calculated for the Piano Forte or Harpsichord.* . . . London, [ca. 1795].

Jackson, Roland. *Performance Practice, Medieval to Contemporary: A Bibliographic Guide.* New York, 1988.

Janowka, Thomas Balthasar. *Clavis ad thesaurum magnae artis musicae.* . . . Prague, 1701.

Keller, Hermann. *Die Klavierwerke Bachs.* Leipzig, 1950.

——. *Die Orgelwerke Bachs.* Leipzig, 1948.

——. *Phrasierung und Artikulation: Ein Beitrag zu einer Sprachlehre der Musik.* 2d ed. Kassel, 1955. English trans. by Leigh Gerdine, New York, 1965.

Killian, Herbert. *Gustav Mahler: In den Erinnerungen von Natalie Bauer-Lechner.* Hamburg, 1984.

Kirkendale, Ursula. "The Source for Bach's *Musical Offering,* the *Institutio oratoria* of Quintilian." *JAMS* 33 (1980): 88–141.

Kirnberger, Johann Philipp. "Einschnitt." In Sulzer's *Allgemeine Theorie der schönen Künste.* 4 vols. Leipzig, 1771–74. 2d ed., 1778–79. 2d enl. ed., 1792–94.

——. *Die Kunst des reinen Satzes in der Musik.* 2 parts in 4 vols. Berlin, 1774–79. English trans. by David Beach and Jurgen Thym. New Haven and London, 1982.

Klotz, Hans. *Die Ornamentik der Klavier- und Orgelwerke von Johann Sebastian Bach.* Kassel, 1984.

Knecht, Justin Heinrich. *Kleine theoretische Klavierschule.* 2 vols. Munich, [ca. 1800].

——. *Vollständige Orgelschule.* 3 vols. Leipzig, 1795–98.

Koch, Heinrich Christoph. *Musikalisches Lexikon.* Frankfurt, 1802.

——. *Versuch einer Anleitung zur Composition.* 3 vols. Leipzig, 1782–95. English tr. and ed. by Nancy Kovaleff Baker. New Haven, 1983.

Koch, Heinrich Christoph, ed. *Journal der Tonkunst.* Erfurt, 1795.

Kolneder, Walter. *Aufführungspraxis bei Vivaldi.* Leipzig, 1955.

Kretschmar, Johann. *Musica latino-germanica.* Leipzig, 1605.

Kreutz, Alfred. *Die Ornamentik in J. S. Bach's Klavierwerken.* Frankfurt, 1950 (annex to the Peters Urtext edition of the English Suites).

Kuhnau, Johann. *Neuer Clavier-Übung erster Theil.* Leipzig, 1689. Modern ed. together with *Neuer Clavier-Übung andrer Theil* (1692), *DDT* 1/4, ed. by Karl Päsler, Leipzig, 1901.

L'Abbé le Fils [Joseph Barnabé Saint-Sevin]. *F   icipes du violon.* . . . Paris, 1761. Facsimile (ed. by Aristide Wirsta), Paris,  ⟩61.

Lacassagne, L'abbé Joseph. *Traité général des   émens du chant.* Paris, 1766. Facsimile, Geneva, 1972.

La Chapelle, Jacques Alexandre de. *Les vrais principes de la musique.* . . . 4 vols. Paris, 1736–[52].

L'Affilard, Michel. *Principes trés-faciles pour bien apprendre la musique.* . . . Paris, 1694. 2d ed., 1697. 5th and 6th ed., 1705.

Lambert, Michel. *Les airs de M. Lambert*. Paris, 1660.

Landon, H. C. Robbins. *The Collected Correspondence and London Notebooks of Joseph Haydn*. London, 1959.

Landshoff, Ludwig. "Über das vielstimmige Accompagnement und andere Fragen des Generalbasspiels." In *Festschrift zum 50. Geburtstag Adolf Sandberger*. Munich, 1918.

Lasser, Johann Baptist. *Vollständige Anleitung zur Singkunst.* . . . Munich, 1798.

La Voye Mignot. *Traité de musique.* . . . Paris, 1656.

Le Bègue, Nicolas. *Les pièces de clavessin*. Paris, 1677.

———. *Troisième livre d'orgue*. Paris, [ca. 1700].

Lécuyer. *Principes de l'art du chant.* . . . Paris, 1769.

Le Gallois, Jean. *Lettre de M. le Gallois à Mademoiselle Regnault de Solier touchant la musique*. Paris, 1680. Reprint, Geneva, 1984.

Le Huray, Peter. *Authenticity in Performance: Eighteenth-Century Case Studies*. London and New York, 1990.

Le Roux, Gaspard. *Pièces de clavessin*. Paris, 1705.

Levin, Robert. "Instrumental Ornamentation, Improvisation, and Cadenzas." In *Performance Practice*. Edited by Howard M. Brown and Stanley Sadie. New York, 1990.

Liverziani, Giuseppe. *Grammatica della musica*. Rome, 1797.

Loeillet, Jean Baptiste ("John"). *Lessons for the Harpsichord or Spinet*. London, 1709–15.

Löhlein, Georg Simon. *Clavier-Schule.* . . . Leipzig and Züllichau, 1765. 2d ed., 1773. 3d ed., 1779. 4th ed., 1782.

———. *Anweisung zum Violinspielen.* . . . Leipzig und Züllichau, 1774.

Lohmann, Ludger. *Studien zu Artikulationsproblemen bei den Tasteninstrumenten des 16.–18. Jahrhunderts*. Regensburg, 1982.

Lossius, Lucas. *Erotemata musicae practicae*. Nürnberg, 1558.

Loulié, Etienne. *Eléments ou principes de musique.* . . . Paris, 1696, and Amsterdam, 1698. Reprint, Geneva, 1971. English translation: *Elements or Principles of Music* (trans. and ed. by Albert Cohen), Brooklyn, 1965.

Lusse, Charles de. *L'art de la flûte traversière*. Paris, 1760.

Lussy, Mathis. *Traité de l'expression musicale*. Paris, 1874. 8th ed., 1904.

Mace, Thomas. *Musick's Monument.* . . . London, 1676. Reprint, 2nd ed., Paris, 1966.

Malloch, William. "Carl Czerny's Metronome Marks for Haydn and Mozart Symphonies." *EM* 16 (1988): 72–82.

———. "Toward a 'New' (Old) Minuet." *Opus* 1, no. 5 (1985): 14–21, 52.

Manfredini, Vincenzo. *Regole armoniche.* . . . Venice, 1775. Facsimile, New York, 1966.

Marais, Marin. *Pieces a une et a deux violes*. 1686.

———. *2nd [Second] livre de pièces de viole*. Paris, 1701.

———. *3me [Troisième] livre de pièces de viole*. Paris, 1711.

Marchand, Luc. *Pièces de clavecin avec accompagnement de violon.* . . . Paris, 1748.

Marpurg, Friedrich Wilhelm. *Anleitung zum Clavierspielen.* . . . Berlin, 1755. Reprint, New York, 1966.

———. *Anleitung zur Singcomposition.* Berlin, 1758.

———. *Des critischen musicus an der Spree erster Band.* Berlin, 1750.

Marshall, Robert L. "Tempo and Dynamic Indications in Bach Sources." In *Bach, Handel, Scarlatti: Tercentenary Essays.* Edited by P. Williams. London, 1985.

Martini, Jean-Paul-Égide [acc. to Fétis, a pseud. for Schwartzendorf]. *Mélopée moderne ou l'art du chant.* . . . Paris, [ca. 1791].

Marty, Jean-Pierre. *The Tempo Indications of Mozart.* New Haven, 1988.

Masson, Charles. *Nouveau traité des règles pour la composition de la musique.* Paris, 1699.

Mattheson, Johann. *Critica musica.* . . . 2 vols. Hamburg, 1722–25.

———. *Das neu-eröffnete Orchestre.* . . . Hamburg, 1713.

———. *Kern melodischer Wissenschafft.* Hamburg, 1737.

———. *Der vollkommene Capellmeister.* . . . Hamburg, 1739. Reprint, Kassel, 1954. English translation (trans. by Ernest C. Harris), Ann Arbor, 1981.

———. *Der wohlklingenden Fingersprache* II. Theil. Hamburg, 1737. 2d ed., Nurnberg, 1749.

Maunder, Richard. *Mozart's Requiem: On Preparing a New Edition.* Oxford, 1988.

Mazzocchi, Domenico. *Madrigali a cinque voce ed altri varij concerti.* Rome, 1638.

Mendel, Arthur. "A Brief Note on Triple Proportion in Schütz." *MQ* 46 (1960): 67–70.

———. "Some Ambiguities of the Mensural System." In *Oliver Strunk Festschrift.* Edited by Harold Powers. Princeton, 1968.

Mercadier de Belesta, Jean-Baptiste. *Nouveau systême de musique théorique et pratique.* Paris, 1776.

Merck, Daniel. *Compendium musicae instrumentalis chelicae.* . . . Part 1. Augsburg, 1695.

Mersenne, Marin. *Harmonie universelle.* . . . 3 vols. Paris, 1636. Facsimile, Paris, 1965. Comprises eight independently paginated treatises.

Mies, Paul. "Die Artikulationszeichen Strich und Punkt bei Wolfgang Amadeus Mozart." *Die Musikforschung* 11 (1958): 428–55.

Milán, Luys. *El maestro.* . . . Valencia, 1535.

Milchmeyer, Johann Peter. *Die wahre Art das Pianoforte zu spielen.* Frankfurt am Main, 1797.

Millet, Jean. *La belle méthode ou l'art de bien chanter.* Lyon, 1666. Facsimile, ed. by Albert Cohen, New York, 1973.

Moens-Haenen, Greta. *Das Vibrato in der Musik des Barock.* Graz, 1988.

Momigny, Jérôme-Joseph. *Cours complet d'harmonie et de composition.* Paris, 1806.

———. "Ponctuer." Article in *Encyclopédie méthodique, musique.* Edited by Jérôme-Joseph Momigny, Nicolas-Etienne Framery, and Pierre-Louis Ginguené. Paris, 1798.

Montéclair, Michel Pignolet de. *Nouvelle méthode pour apprendre la musique.* . . . Paris, 1709.

———. *Petite méthode pour apprendre la musique aux enfans. . . .* Paris, [ca. 1710].

———. *Principes de musique. . . .* Paris, 1736.

*The Monteverdi Companion.* Edited by Denis Arnold and Nigel Fortune. New York, 1972.

Mozart, Leopold. *Versuch einer gründlichen Violinschule. . . .* Augsburg, 1756. 2d ed., 1769. 3d ed., 1787. English trans. by E. Knocker, 2d ed., London, 1951.

Mozart, Wolfgang Amadeus. *The Letters of Mozart and His Family.* 3 vols. Translated and edited by Emily Anderson. London, 1938.

———. *Neue Ausgabe sämtlicher Werke.* Salzburg and Kassel, 1955–.

———. *Verzeichnüss aller meiner Werke vom Monath Febrario 1784 bis Monath [November 1791].* Autograph at the British Library. Facsimiles, Vienna, 1938, and New York, 1956.

Muffat, Georg. Preface to *Concerti grossi, 1701.* In *DTÖ* XI/2.

———. Preface to *Florilegium primum,* 1695. In *DTÖ* 1/2.

———. Preface to *Florilegium secundum,* 1698. In *DTÖ* 2/2.

Muffat, Gottlieb (Theophil). *Componimenti musicali per il cembalo.* Augsburg, [ca. 1736]. Facsimile, New York, 1967. Modern ed., *DTÖ* 3/3 (1896).

Murschhauser, Franz Xaver Anton. *Fundamentalische . . . Handleithung sowohl zur Figural als Choral Music.* Munich, 1707.

———. *Prototypon longo breve organicum.* Part 1. Nürnberg, 1703. Modern ed., *DDT* 2/18.

*Die Musik in Geschichte und Gegenwart.* 17 vols. Edited by Friedrich Blume. Kassel, 1949–86.

Mylius, Wolfgang Michael. *Rudimenta musices. . . .* Mühlhausen, 1685.

Neumann, Frederick. "Conflicting Binary and Ternary Rhythms, from the Theory of Mensural Notation to the Music of J. S. Bach." *Music Forum* 6 (1987): 93–128.

———. *Essays in Performance Practice.* Ann Arbor, 1982.

———. "The French *Inégales,* Quantz, and Bach." *JAMS* 18 (1965): 315–58.

———. "How Fast Should Classical Minuets Be Played?" *Historical Performance* 4 (1991): 3–13.

———. *New Essays on Performance Practice.* Ann Arbor, 1989, Rochester 1992.

———. "A New Look on Mozart's Prosodic Appoggiatura." In *Perspectives on Mozart Performance.* Edited by R. L. Todd and P. Williams. Cambridge, 1991.

———. "The *Notes Inégales* Revisited." *Journal of Musicology* 6 (1988): 137–49.

———. *Ornamentation and Improvisation in Mozart.* Princeton, 1986.

———. *Ornamentation in Baroque and Post-Baroque Music: With Special Emphasis on J. S. Bach.* Princeton, 1978.

*New Grove Dictionary of Music and Musicians.* 20 vols. Edited by Stanley Sadie. 6th ed. London and Washington, D.C., 1980.

*New Grove Dictionary of Musical Instruments.* 3 vols. Edited by Stanley Sadie. London and New York, 1984.

*New Harvard Dictionary of Music.* Edited by Don Michael Randel. Cambridge, Mass., 1986.

Newman, William S. *Beethoven on Beethoven: Playing His Piano Music His Way.* New York, 1988.

Nivers, Guillaume-Gabriel. *Livre d'orgue.* . . . Paris, 1665.

———. *Méthode facile pour apprendre à chanter la musique.* 2d ed. Paris, 1670.

Nopitsch, Christoph Friedrich Wilhelm. *Versuch eines Elementarbuchs der Singkunst.* . . . Nördlingen, 1784.

North, Roger. *Roger North on Music.* Edited by John Wilson. London, 1959.

O'Donnell, John. "The French Style and the Overtures of Bach." Parts 1 and 2. *EM* 7 (1979): 190–96; 336–45.

Ortiz, Diego. *Trattado de glosas sobra clausulas.* . . . Rome, 1553. Modern ed., with German trans. by M. Schneider, Kassel, 1924.

Pajot, Louis-Léon. [Report]. In *Histoire de l'Académie Royale des Sciences, Année 1732, Mémoires.* Paris, 1735.

Palm, Albert. *Jérôme-Joseph de Momigny: Leben und Werk.* Cologne, 1969.

Panerai, Vincenzo. *Principi di musica.* . . . Florence, [ca. 1775].

Pasquali, Nicolo. *The Art of Fingering on the Harpsichord.* Edinburgh, [ca. 1760].

Penna, Lorenzo. *Li primi albori musicali.* . . . 3 vols. Bologna, 1672. 5th ed., 1696.

*Performance Practice.* 2 vols. Edited by Howard M. Brown and Stanley Sadie. London, 1989. New York, 1990.

Peri, Jacopo. Preface to *Euridice.* Florence, 1600.

Petri, Johann Samuel. *Anleitung zur praktischen Musik.* . . . Lauban, 1767. 2d enl. ed., Leipzig, 1782. Reprint of 2d ed., Giebing, 1969.

Piani, Giovanni. Preface to *Sonate a violino solo e violoncello col cimbalo, op. 1.* Paris, 1712.

Picerli, Silvero. *Specchio primo di musica.* Rome, 1630.

Pisa, Agostino. *Battuta della musica.* . . . Rome, 1611.

Plantinga, Leon. *Clementi, His Life and Music.* London, 1977.

Playford, John. *An Introduction to the Skill of Musick.* London, 1654. 7th ed., 1674. 12th ed., 1694.

Praetorius, Michael. *Syntagma musicum.* . . . 3 vols. Wolfenbüttel, 1614–19.

Printz, Wolfgang Caspar. *Compendium musicae signatoriae et modulatoriae vocalis.* . . . Dresden, 1689. 2d ed, Dresden and Leipzig, 1714.

———. *Musica modulatoria vocalis.* . . . Schweidnitz, 1678.

———. *Phrynis Mytilenaeus oder satyrischer Componist.* . . . 3 vols. 2d ed., Dresden and Leipzig, 1696.

Purcell, Henry. *Choice Collection of Lessons.* London, 1696. Facsimile, New York, 1978.

Quantz, Johann Joachim. "Herrn Johann Joachim Quantzens Lebenslauf von ihm selbst entworfen." In F. W. Marpurg's *Historisch-kritische Beyträge zur Aufnahme der Musik,* vol. 1. Berlin, 1755.

———. *Versuch einer Anweisung, die Flöte traversiere zu spielen.* . . . Berlin, 1752. English ed. (trans. by Edward Reilly), entitled *On Playing the Flute,* London, 1966.

Raison, André. Preface to *Livre d'orgue, contenant cinq messes.* . . . Paris, 1688.

———. *Second livre d'orgue.* . . . Paris, 1714.

Rameau, Jean-Philippe. *Code de musique pratique.* Paris, 1760. Facsimile, New York, 1965.

———. *Nouvelle suites de pièces de clavecin avec des remarques sur les différents genres de musique.* Paris, [ca. 1725].

———. *Observations sur notre instinct pour la musique.* . . . Paris, 1754.

———. *Pièces de clavecin en concerts.* Paris, 1741.

———. *Pièces de clavecin avec une méthode pour la méchanique des doigts.* . . . Paris, 1724. Reprint, New York, 1967.

———. *Premier livre de pièces de clavecin.* Paris, 1706.

Ratner, Leonard G. *Classic Music.* New York, 1980.

*Regole per accompagnar sopra la parte.* MSS., Biblioteca Corsini, Rome.

Reichardt, Johann Friedrich. *Briefe eines aufmerksamen Reisenden die Musik betreffend.* Part 1. Frankfurt and Leipzig, 1774.

———. *Über die Pflichten des Ripien-Violinisten.* Berlin and Leipzig, 1776.

Reidemeister, Peter. *Alte Musik: Praxis und Reflexion.* Wintherthur, 1983.

Reincken, Johann Adam. *Hortus musicus.* . . . Hamburg, 1687.

Rellstab, Johann Carl Friedrich. *Über die Bemerkungen eines Reisenden.* . . . Berlin, 1789.

Riemann, Hugo. *Musik Lexikon.* 3 vols. 12th ed. Mainz, 1959–67. Supplement: *Ergänzungsband, Personenteil.* 2 vols. 1972–75.

———. *Vademecum der Phrasierung.* Leipzig, 1900.

Riepel, Joseph. *Anfangsgründe zur musikalischen Setzkunst.* 5 vols. Vols. ("Chapters") 1–3, Frankfurt and Leipzig, 1752–57; vol. 4, Augsburg, 1765; vol. 5, Regensburg, 1768.

Riggs, Robert D. "Articulation in Mozart's and Beethoven's Sonatas for Piano and Violin." Ph.D. diss., Harvard University, 1987.

Rodolphe, Jean-Joseph. *Solfège ou nouvelle méthode de musique.* . . . Paris, [ca. 1784].

Rognioni, Francesco. *Selva de varii passaggi.* . . . Milan, 1620. Reprint, Bologna, 1970.

Rogniono, Richard. *Passaggi per potersi essercitare nel diminuire.* . . . (Part 2 titled *Il vero modo di diminuire.* . . .) Venice, 1592.

Rose, Gloria. "Agazzari and the Improvising Orchestra." *JAMS* 18 (1965): 382–93.

Rosenblum, Sandra. *Performance Practices in Classic Piano Music.* Bloomington, Ind., 1988.

Rosow, Lois. "French Baroque Recitative as an Expression of Tragic Declamation." *EM* 11 (1983): 468–79.

———. "The Metrical Notation of Lully's Recitative." In *J.-B. Lully, Actes/Kongressbericht.* Edited by Jérôme de la Gorce and Herbert Schneider. Laaber, 1990.

Rousseau, Jean. *Méthode claire, certaine et facile, pour apprendre à chanter la musique.* . . . 2d ed. Paris, 1683.

————. *Traité de la viole.* . . . Paris, 1687.

Rousseau, Jean Jacques. *Dictionnaire de musique.* Paris, 1768. Facsimile, Hildesheim, 1969.

Rudolf, Max. "Ein Beitrag zur Geschichte der Temponahme bei Mozart." *Mozart-Jahrbuch* (1976–77): 204–24.

————. "Inner Repeats in the Da Capo of Classical Minuets and Scherzos." *Journal of the Conductor's Guild* 3/4 (Fall 1982): 145–50.

Sabbatini, Luigi Antonio. *Elementi teorici della musica.* . . . Rome, 1789–90.

Sachs, Curt. *Rhythm and Tempo.* New York, 1953.

Saint Lambert, Michel de. *Nouveau traité de l'accompagnement.* . . . Paris, 1707.

————. *Principes du clavecin.* . . . Paris, 1702.

Salieri, Antonio. *Scuola di canto, in versi, e i versi in musica.* 1816. MS. 915, GMF.

Samber, Johann Baptist. *Manuductio ad organum.* . . . Salzburg, 1704.

Santa Maria, Tomás de. *Arte de tañer fantasia.* . . . Valladolid, 1565.

Scheibe, Johann Adolf. *Der critische Musicus.* Leipzig, 1745.

Scheidt, Samuel. *Tabulatura nova.* Hamburg, 1624.

Schering, Arnold. "Zur instrumentalen Verzierungskunst im 18. Jahrhundert." *Sammelbände der Internationalen Musikgesellschaft* 7 (1905–06): 365–85.

Schickhardt, Johann Christian. *Principes de la flûte.* . . . Op. 12. Amsterdam, [ca. 1730].

Schiedermair, Ludwig. *Die Briefe W. A. Mozarts und seiner Familie,* 5 vols. Munich, 1914.

Schmelz, Simpertus. *Fundamenta musica cantus artificialis.* . . . Yresee, 1752.

Schmitz, Hans-Peter. *Die Kunst der Verzierung im 18. Jahrhundert.* Kassel, 1955.

Schubert, Johann Friedrich. *Neue Singe-Schule.* . . . Leipzig, [ca. 1804].

Schulz, Johann Abraham Peter. "Ouverture"; "Tact"; "Vortrag." Articles in Sulzer's *Allgemeine Theorie der Schoenen Kuenste.*

Schünemann, Georg. *Geschichte des Dirigierens.* Leipzig, 1913. Reprint, Hildesheim, 1965.

Schütz, Heinrich. Preface to *A German Requiem (Musicalische Exequien).* Edited by Arthur Mendel. New York, 1957.

————. Preface to *Historia der . . . Auferstehung.* Dresden, 1623.

————. Preface to *Psalmen Davids.* Dresden, 1619.

————. Preface to *Symphoniae sacrae II.* Dresden, 1643.

Schwandt, Erich. "L'Affilard on the French Court Dances." *MQ* 60 (1974): 389–400.

Schweitzer, Albert. *J. S. Bach, le musicien-poète.* Leipzig, 1905. Enl. German trans., 1908. English trans., 1911. Reprint, Wiesbaden, 1960.

Sénecé, Antoine Bauderon de. Lettre de Clément Marot, à Monsieur de xxx touchant ce qui s'est passé à l'arrivée de Jean Baptiste de Lulli aux Champs Elisées. Cologne, 1688.

Signoretti, P. *Méthode contenant les principes de la musique et du violon.* 3 vols. The Hague, 1777.

Simpson, Christopher. *A Compendium of Practical Musick*. London, 1667.

——. *The Division-Violist: or, an Introduction to the Playing of a Ground*. . . . London, 1659. 2d ed., 1667.

Siret, Nicolas. *Pièces de clavecin*. Paris, [ca. 1716].

——. *Second livre de pièces de clavecin*. Paris, 1719.

Somfai, László. "How to Read and Understand Haydn's Notation in Its Chronologically Changing Concepts." In *Proceedings of the International Joseph Haydn Congress*. Edited by Eva Badura-Skoda. Munich, 1986.

——. "An Introduction to the Study of Haydn's String Quartet Autographs." In *The String Quartets of Haydn, Mozart, and Beethoven: Studies of the Autograph Manuscripts*. Edited by Christoph Wolff. Cambridge, Mass., 1980.

Speer, Daniel. *Grund-richtiger . . . Unterricht der musicalischen Kunst*. . . . Ulm, 1697.

Sperling, Johann Peter. *Porta musica, das ist: Eingang zur Music*. . . . Görlitz and Leipzig, 1708.

——. *Principia musicae*. . . . Budissin, 1705.

Spitzer, John, and Neal Zaslaw. "Improvised Ornamentation in Eighteenth-Century Orchestras." *JAMS* 39 (1986): 524–77.

Stierlein, Johann Christoph. *Trifolium musicale consistens in musica theorica, practica et poetica*. . . . Stuttgart, 1691.

Storace, Bernardo. *Selva di varie compositioni*. Venice, 1664.

Stowell, Robin. *Violin Technique and Performance Practice in the Late Eighteenth and Early Nineteenth Centuries*. Cambridge, 1985.

Strunk, Oliver. *Source Readings in Music History*. New York, 1950.

Sulzer, Johann Georg. *Allgemeine Theorie der schönen Künste*. 4 vols. Leipzig, 1771–74. 2d ed., 1778–79. 2d enl. ed., 1792–94.

Tagliavini, Luigi Ferdinando. "The Art of 'Not Leaving the Instrument Empty': Comments on Early Italian Harpsichord Playing." *EM* 11 (1983): 299–308.

Tarade, Théodore-Jean. *Traité du violon*. . . . Paris, [ca. 1774]. Facsimile, Geneva, 1972.

Tartini, Giuseppe. *Regole per arrivare a saper ben suonar il violino*. . . . MS. Conservatorio di musica "Benedetto Marcello," Venice. Facsimile published as a supplement to the German, French, and English publication, *Traité des agréments de la musique*, edited by E. R. Jacobi, Celle and New York, 1961.

Telemann, Georg Philipp. *Singe- Spiel- und Generalbass-Übungen*. Hamburg, 1733–34. New ed., edited by Max Seiffert, Berlin, 1914.

——. *Sonate metodiche*, Op. 13. Hamburg, 1728. *Continuation des sonates méthodiques*. Hamburg, 1732. Modern edition of both volumes. Kassel, 1955.

Testori, Carlo Giovanni. *La musica ragionata*. . . . Vercelli, 1767.

Thielo, Carl August. *Grund-Regeln wie man . . . die Fundamenta der Music und des Claviers lernen kan*. . . . Copenhagen, 1753. (Published anon. under the autogram C. A. T., it is, according to Fétis, an abridged trans. of Thielo's *Tanker og Regler fra Grunden af om Musiken . . .* [Copenhagen, 1746].)

Tigrini, Orazio. *Il compendio della musica*. Venice, 1588.

Tosi, Pierfrancesco. *Opinioni de' cantori antichi e moderni o sieno osservazioni sopra il canto figurato.* Bologna, 1723. Facsimile as suppl. to J. F. Agricola's *Anleitung,* ed. by Erwin R. Jacobi, Celle, 1966. English translation by John Ernest Galliard: *Observations on the florid song.* London, 1742.

Trabaci, Giovanni Maria. *Secondo libro de ricercare, & altre varij caprici.* Naples, 1613.

Trendelenburg, Wilhelm. *Die natürlichen Grundlagen der Kunst des Streichinstrumentspiels.* Berlin, 1925.

Troeger, Richard. *Technique and Interpretation on the Harpsichord and Clavichord.* Bloomington, Ind., 1987.

Tromlitz, Johann Georg. *Ausführlicher und gründlicher Unterricht, die Flöte zu spielen.* Leipzig, 1791. English translation (trans. and ed. by Ardal Powell), Cambridge, 1991.

Türk, Daniel Gottlob. *Klavierschule.* . . . Leipzig and Halle, 1789. 2d ed., 1802. Reprint of 1st ed., Kassel, 1962. English translation (trans. and ed. by Raymond H. Haggh), Lincoln, Nebr., 1982.

Vincentino, Nicola. *L'antica musica ridotta alla moderna prattica.* . . . Rome, 1555.

Villeneuve, Alexandre de. *Nouvelle méthode . . . pour apprendre la musique.* . . . Paris, 1733. 2d ed., 1756.

Vogler, Georg Joseph, Abbé. *Kuhrpfälzische Tonschule.* Mannheim, 1778.

Wagner, Richard. "Ueber das Dirigieren." In *Gesammelte Schriften und Dichtungen,* vol. 5. Leipzig, 1883. 4th ed., 1907.

Walther, Johann Gottfried. *Musicalisches Lexicon.* . . . Leipzig, 1732. Facsimile, Kassel, 1953.

——. *Praecepta der musicalischen Composition* [1708]. Edited by Peter Benary. Leipzig, 1955.

Westrup, J. A. "Rezitativ." In *MGG.*

Whitmore, Philip. *Unpremeditated Art: The Cadenza in the Classical Keyboard Concerto.* Oxford, 1991.

Wiedeburg, Michael Johann Friedrich. *Der sich selbst informirende Clavierspieler.* Vol. 2. Halle, 1767.

Wolf, Georg Friedrich. *Kurzer aber deutlicher Unterricht im Klavierspielen.* Part 1. 3d enl. ed. Halle, 1789.

Wolff, Hellmuth Christian. "Das Metronom des Louis-Léon Pajot 1735." In *Festskrift Jens Peter Larsen.* Edited by Nils Schiørring, Henrik Glahn, and Carsten E. Hatting. Copenhagen, 1972.

Zacconi, Lodovico. *Prattica di musica.* . . . Venice, 1592. Facsimile, Bologna, n.d.

Zarlino, Gioseffo. *Le istitutioni harmoniche.* Venice, 1558.

Zaslaw, Neal. "The Compleat Orchestral Musician." *EM* 7 (1979): 46–57.

——. *Mozart's Symphonies: Context, Performance Practice, Reception.* Oxford, 1989.

# Index

Coloraturas. See Ornamentation, melismatic
Comédie Française, 34
Conforto, Giovanni Luca, and trill, 396
Contredanse, 74
Cooper, Grosvenor, 88
Corelli, Arcangelo, 514; and concerto grosso,
159; dance rhythms, 74; ornamentation
notation, 295, 524–525; Violin Sonatas,
Op.5, 218, 524–525
Corfe, Joseph, and trill, 406–407
Corrente, 78–79
Corrette, Michel, and articulation, 226; and
dynamics, 165; and mordent, 461; and
notes inégales, 132; and trill, 387
Coulé, 303–311, 381, 492, 511. See also Arpeggio; Tierces coulées; Trill
Couperin, François, and arpeggio, 488–489,
492–493; and articulation, 201, 203–204,
221, 223; and double dot, 98; and dynamics, 160; on French and Italian notation,
132; and improvisation, 514–515; and mordent, 459–460, 466; and notes inégales, 128,
132–134; and ornament table, 383–386,
459, 488, 565; and ornamentation, 307–308;
phrasing marks, 264–266, 271; Pièces de
clavecin, 133–134, 204, 264–266, 355, 383–
388, 447–448; and rhythm notation, 558;
and slide, 355–356, 448; tempo, 40, 49,
65; and tierces coulées, 492–493; and trill,
383–388, 391–392, 421, 426, 427–428,
447–448, 451, 474, 566; and turn, 474
Couperin, Louis, 40; and double dot, 98
Courante, 78–80, 110
Cramer, Carl Friedrich, and vibrato, 509
Crotch, William, 109
Crüger, Johann, blackened triplets, 142; and
improvisation, 530–531; and mordent, 465;
and ornamentation, 322, 530–531; and
slide, 361, 363; and trill, 409; and trillo,
506; and vibrato, 506
Cuzzoni, Francesca, and vibrato, 504
Czerny, Carl, 203, 206; and keyboard articulation, 246; and minuet tempos, 557

Da capos, and improvisation, 519–521,
528–529, 532, 535, 540, 543–544, 546,
550–551
Dadelsen, Georg von, 189, 248
D'Agincour, François. See Agincour, François
d'
Dall'Abaco, Evaristo Felice, binary vs. ternary rhythms, 143
Danby, John, and trill, 405–406
Dance music, articulation, 200, 207; character
of, 79–81; and improvisation, 534; influence of, 74; meter, 75–77, 79–81, 110; and
ornamentation, 534; and phrasing, 279,
281; rhythms, 74, 79, 81–82, 88, 110, 115,
217; tempo, 65, 69, 74–82. See also names
of individual dance types
Dandrieu, Jean-François, and mordent, 461;
and ornament table, 387–388, 461; and
trill, 382, 387–388, 565
D'Anglebert, Jean Henri. See Anglebert, Jean
Henri d'
Dannreuther, Edward, 125; and trill, 566
Danoville, and glissando, 569; and mordent,

458; and port de voix, 304; and vibrato,
500–501
Dart, Thurston, 9–10; and French overture
style, 112–113, 116–117, 119
Dauscher, Andreas, and trill, 433–434
David, François, and mordent, 461; and Vor-
schlag, 308
Dean, Winton, and Handel's arias, 523
Deis, Carl, and vocal articulation, 195
Demachy, and mordent, 458
Demantius, Christoph, and mensural nota-
tion, 24–25; and meter and tempo, 58; and
vocal articulation, 191
Denis, Pierre, and meter and tempo, 46–47;
and slide, 354
De Rore, Cipriano, 22
Des Prez, Josquin, 18, 137
Destouches, André Cardinal, tempo, 76
Deutsche (dance), 74
Deysinger, Johann Franz Peter, and trill,
431–432, 434
Dies, Albert Christoph, 543
Dieupart, Charles, 118; and arpeggio, 488;
and mordent, 458; and trill, 382; and turn,
474; and Vorschlag, 306
Diminution. See Ornamentation
Diruta, Girolamo, and keyboard articulation,
200–202, 231; and ornamentation, 312; and
slide, 357–358, 363; and trill, 396, 403
Dolmetsch, Arnold, 2, 9–10; and Bach's
trills, 413; and French overture style, 9,
109–113, 116–119; and notes inégales, 9,
125, 559; and rhythmic alterations, 89
Donati, Ignazio, and ornamentation, 530
Donington, Robert, 10, 99; and Bach's trills,
413; and French overture style, 113, 116–
117; and improvisation, 517; and notes inégales, 127–128, 130
D'Onzembray. See Pajot, Louis-Léon
Doppelvorschlag. See Anschlag
Dornel, Charles, and legato notation, 205;
Pièces de clavecin, 205
Dotted rhythms, 89, 93, 96–107, 109–119,
126–133, 558–560; and appoggiatura, 337;
and articulation, 249–250, 558; and slide,
363–366, 369–370; synchronized with trip-
lets, 96–97, 103, 107, 151–154; and trill,
402, 405, 416, 427, 429–430; and turn, 473,
482–486; and Vorschlag, 345, 348. See also
French overture style; Lombard rhythms;
Notes inégales; Pointer
Durieu, and articulation, 230–231; and trill,
390–391, 393
Dürr, Alfred, and notes inégales, 126
Duval, L'Abbé, and mordent, 461; and notes
inégales, 128; and trill, 389
Dynamics, and accents, 161, 163, 188; and
Anschlag, 371–372; and appoggiatura, 344;
and articulation, 188; and balance, 182–
184; definition of, 157; and improvisation,
516, 535; interpretation of, 4, 6, 173; and
melody, 175–176, 180–182; and mordent,
459, 463, 469–470, 476, 567; notation of,
159, 161, 163–177, 180–182, 184, 538–539;
and ornamentation, 294, 298, 314, 319; and
phrasing, 259, 267, 274, 280–281, 283, 289–
290; and rhetorical principles, 162–164;

Dynamics (*continued*)
and rhythm, 88–89, 91; and slide, 352; and solo vs. ensemble performance, 159, 161-162, 183–184; and tempo, 171, 174; terraced, 157–162, 180, 184; and texture, 158–159, 162, 178; transitional, 157- 158, 160–168, 180, 184; and trill, 441–442, 455; and turn, 473, 476–477, 480; variations in, 36–37; and *Vorschlag*, 301, 340–341. *See also* Accents; *Messa di voce*

**Early** music, 555; interpretation of, 3–5; revival of interest in, 1–2; and scholarship, 4. *See also* Authenticity (in music performance); Historical instruments; Performance practice; names of individual countries, composers, and performers of early music
*Early Music* (journal), 9
*Eingänge*, 542, 546–547, 551
Einstein, Alfred, and Mozart's dots and strokes, 233–234
Elvers, Rudolf, and dots and strokes in *NMA*, 234
Emery, Walter, and Bach's trills, 413, 424
*Encyclopédie méthodique, musique*, and ornament table, 392–393
English music, binary vs. ternary rhythms, 139–140; dance music, 74–80; dotted rhythms, 101; influence of Handel, 407; influence on music of other countries, 401; meter and tempo, 47–48; *notes inégales*, 114, 125; ornamentation, 295, 317–319, 404–405; and slide, 360–361; tempo words, 65; and trill, 404–407; and vibrato, 498, 504, 509. *See also* names of individual composers and theorists
Engramelle, Marie-Dominique-Joseph, and articulation, 223; and *notes inégales*, 129; and trill, 386, 392; and turn, 474
Erb, James, 193
Expression, and agogic accents, 89; and appoggiatura length, 341; and articulation, 188, 190, 198, 212, 245; role in interpretation of music, 6–8; and tempo, 6, 39, 41; and vibrato, 502, 504, 506

**Falck,** Georg, and dynamics, 165; and mordent, 465; and slide, 361, 363; and trill, 410; and *trillo*, 410
Fantini, Girolamo, and dynamics, 164; and *messa di voce*, 217
Farina, Carlo, and vibrato, 503
Farinelli. *See* Broschi, Carlo
Faustina. *See* Bordoni, Faustina
Fermatas, 71–73, 227, 328, 484, 511, 540–543, 546–547, 551, 571
Feyertag, Moritz, and trill, 410; and *trillo*, 506; and *Vorschlag*, 324
Finck, Hermann, and binary vs. ternary rhythms, 142; and transitional dynamics, 161
Fingerings, and articulation, 190, 201, 253–255; keyboard, 5, 190, 201, 252–255; violin, 254
Fiocco, Joseph-Hector, *Pièces de clavecin*, 388; and trill, 388

Fischer, Therese, 543
Fischer, Johann Caspar, and mordent, 465; ornament table, 412, 465; and trill, 412–413
Fischer, Johann Christian, 508
*Fitzwilliam Virginal Book*, 139, 360, 404
Flothuis, Marius, and Mozart's cadenzas, 572
Forkel, Nicolaus, 160
Form (musical), and vocal music, 22
Foucquet, Claude, and legato notation, 205; and ornament table, 391, 565; and trill, 391–392
Framery, Nicolas-Etienne, 273
Francoeur, Louis ("aîné"), and improvisation, 514
Francoeur, Louis-Joseph ("neveu"), and trill, 393
Frederick the Great, and ornamentation of Italian arias, 536
Freillon-Poncein, Jean Pierre, and mordent, 459, 471
French music, *Anschlag*, 370; *acciaccatura*, 495; appoggiatura, 334; arpeggio, 487–488, 490, 492; articulation, 198, 201, 217, 221, 223; binary vs. ternary rhythms, 139, 144; bowing style, 111, 114–115, 198, 217–218, 223; dance music, 74–80, 110–111, 115, 159, 217; dotted rhythms, 98–102, 110–111, 113–116; flexible tempo, 40; and gamba music, 458, 462, 474–475, 500–501, 569; and improvisation, 297, 511, 514, 520, 551; and influence of Italian music, 514; influence on music of other European countries, 132–133, 311, 321, 325, 340, 413, 422, 443–444, 449, 465; instrumental music, 40, 198, 501–502; keyboard music, 221, 381–383, 404, 413, 415, 427, 451, 456, 462, 487, 490, 514; lute music, 296, 306, 488, 500, 514; meter and tempo, 45–47, 58–59; and mordent, 399, 458, 462–463, 470; *Nachschlag*, 310–311; *notes inégales*, 113–114, 120–127, 129, 131- 133; ornamentation, 296–297, 301–303, 313, 321, 325–326, 370, 422, 427, 511, 514, 520, 551; performance style, 379; recitative, 34–36; rhythms, 9, 25, 58–59, 95, 131–133, 217; *ritardando*, 71; slide, 352–358, 362, 564; tempo words, 65, 67; trill, 376–379, 381–383, 387–394, 404, 411–413, 415, 427, 443–444, 446, 448–449, 451, 456, 566; and *trillo*, 503; and turn, 472–475; use of metronome devices, 75–76; violin fingerings, 254; and vibrato, 498, 500–502, 509, 569; and vocal music, 511; *Vorschlag*, 310–311, 313. *See also* names of individual composers and theorists
French overture style, 5, 100–102, 108–119
Frescobaldi, Girolamo, 20, 125, 411; binary vs. ternary rhythms, 140; and improvisation, 517; and instrumental music, 38–39, 517; and metrical notation, 27; and ornamentation, 517; and polyphonic style, 517; and *ritardando*, 70, 73; and *rubato*, 127–128; and tempo, 15, 25, 27, 38–39, 65, 81; and trill, 396, 403
*Works*
*Secondo libro di toccate*, 140
*Toccate e partite*, 396

527, 532–533, 538, 540–543, 546–549; and
da capos, 519–521, 528–529, 532, 535, 540,
550–551; and dance music, 534; and dynamics, 516, 535; and *Eingänge*, 542; and
fermata, 540–543, 546–547, 551; and harmony, 515, 531, 538, 541; and instrumental
music, 513–515, 517–518, 520, 522–525,
527–528, 531–535, 540–541, 548–549; and
*messa di voce*, 516; and mordent, 516, 520;
and *Nachschlag*, 310; and ornamentation,
293, 296–297, 321, 366–367, 510–551, 566;
and *port de voix*, 515; and *portamento*, 521;
and rhythm, 516–517; and slide, 515, 517,
520, 550; and texture, 531; and trill, 516–
517, 520, 550; and *trillo*, 516–517, 519–520,
531; and turn, 520, 531, 550; and vocal music, 511–513, 515, 519–523, 528, 530–532,
535, 538, 543–546, 550; and *Vorschlag*, 302-
303, 323, 517, 520
Indy, Vincent d', 2
*Inégalité*. See *Notes inégales*
Instruments, historical. *See* Historical instruments
Italian music, *acciaccatura*, 495–498; *Anschlag*,
370; articulation, 198, 201, 217, 221, 224;
binary vs. ternary rhythms, 139, 143; bowing style, 111, 198, 217–218; dance music,
78; dotted rhythms, 101; and *galant* style,
333; and improvisation, 297, 513, 515–520,
522, 528–532, 538, 540–541, 544; and influence of French music, 313; influence on
music of other European countries, 41–42,
201, 295, 319, 321–322, 361, 365, 404, 409,
411–413, 427, 443–444, 464–465, 504–505,
514, 517, 530–531, 538, 540; instrumental
music, 38–40, 198, 517–518, 523, 528; keyboard music, 221, 411; mordent, 314, 399,
401, 404, 412, 420, 434–435, 443, 457, 462-
467, 478, 495, 517; and *Nachschlag*, 311;
*notes inégales*, 114, 125, 132; ornamentation,
295, 298, 312–315, 319, 321–323, 326, 357–
359, 515–520, 522, 528–532, 538, 540–541,
544; recitative, 32–33, 35; rhythmic notation, 25, 58, 132; role of performer, 408;
and *Schneller*, 466–467; and slide, 357–359,
362–363, 370; style of, 217–218, 321, 513,
536; tempo words, 65–66; and trill, 395,
398–404, 409, 412, 420, 426–427, 434–435,
443–444, 451, 462, 465–467, 516; *trillo*, 395,
503–504, 516; triplet notation, 95; and turn,
475; vibrato, 498, 502–503, 509, 569; and
vocal music, 515, 522, 528, 530, 536; *Vorschlag*, 313–317, 323, 329, 334. *See also* names
of individual composers and theorists

**Jackson**, Roland, 10
Janowka, Thomas Balthasar, and ornamenta-
tion, 362
Joachim, Joseph, and bounced detachment,
219, 234
Jommelli, Nicolo, and dynamics, 161, 167
Jonas, Oswald, and Mozart's dots and
strokes, 234
Joseph II (Emperor), 203
Josquin des Prez. *See* Des Prez, Josquin

**Keiser,** Reinhard, and articulation notation,
230; recitative, 34; and slide, 362

Keller, Hermann, and Bach's trills, 413; and
keyboard articulation, 245–246; and
Mozart's dots and strokes, 234; and terraced dynamics, 158
Kerll, Caspar, binary vs. ternary rhythms,
140; and improvisation, 517; Toccata No.
2, 561; and trill, 411–412, 414
Kirkendale, Ursula, 163
Kirnberger, Johann Philipp, 72, 563; and
meter and tempo, 48–49; and *notes inégales*, 133; and phrasing, 261–262, 269, 563
Kittel, Caspar, influence of Italian music, 321
Klotz, Hans, 10; and Bach's trills, 413
Knecht, Justin Heinrich, and organ articulation, 202, 221; and trill, 433–434
Koch, Heinrich Christoph, and accents, 176–
177, 179, 367; and *Anschlag*, 478; and *ca-
lando*, 171; and dotted rhythms, 560; and
French overture, 114; and phrasing, 271–
272, 276, 278, 285, 562; and *sforzando*, 171;
and slide, 367; and tempo words, 68; and
trill, 432, 434, 444; and turn, 478–479, 484;
and *Vorschlag*, 341
Kolneder, Walter, 169, 571
Kretschmar, Johann, and mensural notation,
24
Kreutz, Alfred, and Bach's trills, 413; and
Mozart's articulation marks, 234
Krieger, Johann Philipp, recitative, 34
Kroll, Franz, and trill, 566
Kuhnau, Johann, and slide, 361–362; and
triplet notation, 95

**La Barre,** Michel de, and compound trills,
447; *Pièces pour la flûte*, 447; and *Vorschlag*
notation, 306
L'Abbé le Fils, and articulation, 230; and
trill, 390–392; and *Vorschlag*, 309
Lacassagne, L'Abbé Joseph, and mordent,
461; and trill, 389–391
La Chapelle, Jacques Alexandre de, and
compound trills, 448–449; dance tempi,
76–78; and *notes inégales*, 128; and slide,
354; and *Vorschlag*, 309
L'Affilard, Michel, and improvisation, 513;
and mordent, 459, 471; and *Nachschlag*,
310–311; and ornamentation, 304–305, 308;
phrasing marks, 264; and *port de voix*, 304–
305; and slide, 353; and tempo markings,
75–77; and trill, 381, 391
Lalande, Michel-Richard de, tempo, 37
Lambert, Michel, and improvisation, 511–512;
and ornamentation, 511; and trill, 377–378
Landowska, Wanda, 2
Landshoff, Ludwig, 568
Lang, Paul Henry, and *ritardando*, 70
La Salle Quartet, 562
Lasser, Johann Baptist, and mordent, 478–
479; and turn, 478–479
Lasso, Orlando, 18, 21
Lasso, Roland, 139
La Voye Mignot, and metrical notation, 30
Lead-ins. See *Eingänge*
Le Bègue, Nicholas Antoine, and arpeggio,
488, 493; and mordent, 458; phrasing nota-
tion, 264; and trill, 382; *Troisième livre
d'orgue*, 264

Leclair, Jean Marie, and improvisation, 514
Lécuyer, and tempo, 35, 71; and trill, 392–393
Le Gallois, Jean, and clavecin articulation, 201
Legato articulation, 188–189, 197–213, 221–223, 225; vs detached style, 188, 190–194, 200–203, 218, 221–222, 241–242, 246–246, 249–250, 254–255
Le Huray, Peter, and keyboard fingerings, 253; and *notes inégales*, 132
Leonhardt, Gustav, and Bach's trills, 566
Le Roux, Gaspard, 40; and mordent, 458; and ornamentation, 306–307; *Pièces de clavessin*, 447; and trill, 382, 446–447; and turn, 474
Levin, Robert, and improvised ornamentation in Mozart's repeats, 550
Lippius, Johann, and legato notation, 205
Liverziani, Giuseppe, and trill symbol, 403
Locatelli, Giovanni Battista, Concerto for Four Solo Violins, 401; and "Italian mordent," 401; and ornamentation, 314, 523; and slide, 357–359; and trill, 401
Locke, Matthew, and transitional dynamics, 165, 168
Loeillet, Jean Baptiste, and trill, 383, 391
Löhlein, Georg Simon, 94; and *Anschlag*, 372; and appoggiatura, 339; and arpeggio, 494; and compound trills, 453–454, 456; and mordent, 470; and *Schneller*, 431; and soloistic overdotting, 100; and trill, 431; and turn, 478; and *Vorschlag*, 339
Lohmann, Ludger, 202; and articulation, 193–194, 246
Lombard rhythms, 93, 247–248, 320, 357, 361–363, 517, 564
Lombardini, Maddalena, 218, 402, 430
Lossius, Lucas, and binary vs. ternary rhythms, 142
Loulié, Étienne, and *chronomètre*, 75; and dotted rhythms, 102, 128, 558; and improvisation, 513; and meter changes in vocal music, 35; and mordent, 459; and *Nachschlag*, 310–311; and *notes inégales*, 128, 132; ornament table, 353; and ornamentation, 304, 513; and slide, 353–354; and trill, 380–381, 383, 391; and *Vorschlag*, 318
Loure, 80, 110
Lübeck, Vincent, and trill, 411
Lully, Jean-Baptiste, 111, 123–124; bowing style, 209; dance rhythms, 74; dotted rhythms, 98, 116, 118; dynamics, 159; and improvisation, 511, 514–515, 520, 538; metrical notation, 26, 35; *notes inégales*, 123; operas, 511; and ornamentation, 303, 511, 513, 515, 520, 538; recitative, 34–35, 42; tempo, 47, 76, 78; and trill, 377–378, 511, 570; and "trio" in dances, 159; and vibrato, 502

*Works*

*Armide*, 378
*Isis*, 502
*Proserpine*, 78, 118
*Roland*, 35
Lusse, Charles D., 502
Lussy, Mathis, and phrasing, 262, 275–276, 289, 563

Mace, Thomas, and articulation, 198, 214–215; and mordent, 464; and ornamentation, 319; and phrasing, 260; and slide, 360; and tempo, 40; and trill, 405; and use of metronome devices, 75; and vibrato, 500; and *Vorschlag*, 319
Madrigal style, 21, 24, 36, 38, 42, 57
Maffei, Marchese Scipio, and transitional dynamics, 161–162
Mahler, Gustav, and tempo, 15–16
Mandyczewski, Eusebius, 277
Manfredini, Vincenzo, and mordent, 463–464; and trill, 402, 463–464
Mann, Alfred, 570
Mannheim school, 161, 167–168, 180
Marais, Marin, and articulation marks, 198, 226; and dynamics, 165; and improvisation, 515; and mordent, 458–460; and trill, 380, 446–447, 564–565; and turn, 446–447, 475; and vibrato, 501
Marchand, Luc, *Pièces de clavecin avec accompagnement*, 355–356; and slide, 355–356
Marchesi, Luigi, 522
Marenzio, Luca, 18
Marie-Thérèse (wife of Louis XIV), 78
Marini, Biagio, *La Foscarina*, 569
Marpurg, Friedrich Wilhelm, *acciaccatura*, 494, 498; and *Anschlag*, 371; and arpeggio, 489, 494, 498; and dotted rhythms, 98, 101; and *galant* style, 326; and keyboard articulation, 222; and meter, 60; and mordent, 469; and *Nachschlag*, 335, 340; ornament table, 366, 453; and ornamentation, 71, 326, 335; and phrasing terminology, 262; and *Schneller*, 431; and slide, 366; and tempo, 49, 60, 71; theoretical writings applied to other composers, 326; and trill, 428–429, 431, 433, 444, 453, 456; and vibrato, 507; and *Vorschlag*, 335
Marshall, Robert L., and Bach's tempo words, 556
Martini, Jean-Paul-Égide [acc. to Fétis, a pseud. for Schwartzendorf], and trill, 432, 434, 444
Martini, Padre, 402; and ornamentation, 523; and slide, 358–359; and trill, 400, 403; and vibrato, 503
Marty, Jean-Pierre, 11, 61–63, 67
Masson, Charles, and dance music, 79–80; and meter and tempo, 45, 47
Mattheson, Johann J., 161, 324; and *acciaccatura*, 497; and the application of rules, 12; binary vs. ternary rhythms, 144–145; and dance music, 75, 79–80; and metrical stress patterns, 86; and mordent, 468; on phrasing, 262, 266–267, 269, 272; and tempo, 37, 49, 75, 79; and trill, 412, 427
Maunder, Richard, and Mozart's Requiem, 559
Mazzocchi, Domenico, and dynamics, 164
Mei, Girolamo, 32
Meissner, Joseph, and vibrato, 505, 508
Melody, and accents, 176–177, 179; and articulation, 187, 198, 212, 246, 254; and dynamics, 175–176, 180–182; and interpretation, 3, 82; and rhythm, 85, 88. *See also* Phrasing

Ornamentatino (*continued*)
340, 345–346, 391, 404, 510–511, 514, 517, 519–520, 523–529, 531, 534–536, 538–541, 544, 546, 550–551, 570; and rhythm, 88–89, 93, 104–105, 293–294, 298, 319–320, 328; and *ritardando*, 71–72; and role of performer, 294–295, 297, 332, 350; in solo vs. ensemble performance, 99, 297; and style of music, 297; and tempo, 52, 71, 294, 298–299, 314; and vocal music, 293, 297, 303, 313, 322, 344, 511–513, 515, 517, 519–522, 530–532, 535, 538, 543–546. See also *Accent*; Accents; *Anschlag*; Arpeggio; *Chûte*; *Coulé*; Grace notes; *Messa di voce*; Mordent; *Nachschlag*; *Notes inégales*; *Port de voix*; *Portamento*; *Schneller*; Slide; *Tierces coulées*; Trill; Turn; Vibrato; *Vorschlag*
Ortiz, Diego, and slide, 357

**Pachelbel,** Johann, and trill, 411
Pajot, Louis-Léon, 557; tempo markings, 76–78
Palestrina, Giovanni Pierluigi da, 21; binary vs. ternary rhythms, 137–138
*Works*
*Ave verum*, 515
*L'homme armé*, 137–138
Panerai, Vincenzo, and trill, 402
Pasquali, Nicolo, and harpsichord articulation, 201–202
Passacaglia, 79–81
*Passaggi. See* Ornamentation, melismatic
Passepied, 80–81
Penna, Lorenzo, and trill, 396
Performance practice, as a scholarly discipline, 2; contemporary literature on, 9–11; early writings on, 4–7, 10, 38
*Performance Practice Review* (journal), 9
Performer, role in interpreting music, 1, 81–82, 136
Pergolesi, Giovanni Battista, and *Vorschlag*, 314
Peri, Jacopo, 32; and ornamentation, 564; and *Vorschlag*, 313
Petri, Johann Samuel, and articulation, 222, 230; and compound trills, 453–454; and dotted rhythms, 101; and meter and tempo, 50; and metrical stress patterns, 87; and *rubato*, 94; and trill, 431–432
Philipp V (King of Spain), 570
Phrasing, 6, 180, 259–290, 538, 562–563; and accents, 262, 272, 274–276, 280–281; and articulation, 188, 190, 198, 207–209, 212, 254–255, 259, 279–283; and dance music, 279, 281; and dynamics, 259, 267, 274, 280–281, 283, 289–290; and harmony, 259, 265, 269, 273–274, 276, 285–286; and instrumental music, 260–261, 263–264, 267, 270, 276, 279–289; notation of, 167, 263–267, 270–271; and rhythm, 88, 259, 283–289; and role of performer, 269–272, 274; and style of music, 278; terminology of, 261–263, 266–274, 277; and texture, 259, 278–279, 286–289; and vocal music, 260, 263–264, 267, 270, 272, 276
Piani, Giovanni Antonio, and dynamics, 165–166; Violin Sonatas, Op. 1, 165

Picerli, Silvero, and binary vs. ternary rhythms, 141–142
Pisa, Agostino, 141
Pisendel, Johann Georg, and dynamics, 161–162, 167; and Vivaldi concerto embellishment, 571
Pistocchi, F. A., 94
Planchart, Alejandro E., and mensural notation, 23, 25–26
Playford, John, and Simpson's ornament table, 318, 360, 404; and slide, 360; and trill, 404–405; and vibrato, 504
*Pointer*, 128–129, 132
Polyphony. *See* Texture
Porpora, Nicola, 342; and slide, 358–359
*Port de voix*, 200–201, 302–311, 318, 377, 521, 570; and beat placement, 318, 448; and improvisation, 515; with mordent, 302–303, 305–306, 308–309, 445, 458–461
*Portamento*, 222, 225, 344, 402, 521; and beat placement, 366, 370; and improvisation, 521
Praetorius, Michael, and binary vs. ternary rhythms, 142; and dynamics, 36–37, 162–163; and expression, 6–7; influence of Italian music, 321, 409, 530; and keyboard fingerings, 252; and legato notation, 205; and mordent, 409, 465; and mensural notation, 24–25, 58, 60; and motet vs. madrigal style, 22–23, 36, 57–58; and ornamentation, 321- 322, 530; and *ritardando*, 70; and slide, 361, 363; and tempo, 27, 36–37, 57–58, 60, 67, 81; and trill, 409–410; and *trillo*, 409–410, 505; and vibrato, 505, 508
*Pralltriller*. See *Schneller*
Printz, Wolfgang Caspar, and improvisation, 531–532; and metrical stress patterns, 86; and mordent, 465; and ornamentation, 531–532; and *ritardando*, 71; and trill, 410; amd *trillo*, 506
Proportions (metric), 19–21, 23–27, 31, 57–58, 65, 137
Prout, Ebenezer, 109
Purcell, Henry, dotted rhythms, 113; *King Arthur*, 504; embellishment notation, 295, 318–319; ad slide, 360–361; and trill, 404–405; and vibrato, 504

**Quantz,** Johann Joachim, and accents, 91, 179; and accented dissonances, 178–179; and accompaniment, 183; and *Anschlag*, 371; and appoggiatura, 316, 328, 330, 333, 335–337, 563; and art of singing, 522; and articulation, 219–220, 230, 245–246; and bowing styles, 110–111, 114, 217; and cadenzas, 538, 541; and dotted rhythms, 99–100, 105, 109–111, 115, 119, 366; and dynamics, 163, 171, 174, 182–183, 538; and expression, 6–7; and French dance music, 79–81, 115; and French performance style, 132–133; and grace note, 336–337, 343–344, 416; and improvisation, 514, 527, 536, 538–539, 541, 544; and Italian singing style, 536; and melodic accents, 179, 272; and mordent, 469; and *notes inégales*, 124–126, 129, 133; and ornament tables, 366, 430; and ornamentation, 326, 527, 536,

Quantz (*continued*)
538–539, 541, 544; and phrasing, 267–268, 272, 538; and slide, 366–367; and solo vs. ensemble performance, 99, 109–110, 115, 183; and staccato notation, 228, 230; and tempo, 50, 75–76, 78; theoretical writings applied to other composers, 4, 125, 326; and trill, 429–430, 432–434, 444; and *trillo*, 565; and triplets clashing with dotted notes, 96; and turn, 477, 484; and upbeat contraction, 118; and vibrato, 507; and *Vorschlag*, 309–311, 330, 335–337, 340, 429–430

Quitschreiber, Georg, and vibrato, 504

**Raison,** André, and arpeggio, 488; and double dot, 98; and mordent, 458; and organ articulation, 200; and *ritardando*, 71; and *Vorschlag*, 306

Rameau, Jean-Philippe, 304; and arpeggio, 488–489; articulation, 201, 203, 223, 227–228; clashing rhythms, 144; and dance music, 81; and double dot, 98; and dynamics, 166–167; and keyboard music, 460; and *Luftpause* notation, 167; and mordent, 460–461; and *Nachschlag*, 311; and *notes inégales*, 133–134, 144; and ornament tables, 307–308, 387–388, 433, 460; and ornamentation, 564; recitative, 35, 40, 42; *ritardando*, 71; and tempo, 40, 81; and trill, 382, 387–389, 433, 448–449; and turn, 474; *Vorschlag*, 307–308

*Works*
*Achante et Céphise*, 167, 561
*Cinq pièces*, 308
*Hippolite et Aricie*, 166
*Les Paladins*, 167, 227–228
*Pièces de clavecin en concerts*, 71, 133–134, 144, 307–308, 433, 461
*Zoroastre*, 166–167

Ratner, Leonard G., 74
Recitative, 22, 164, 515; and *acciaccatura*, 495; and appoggiatura, 332, 342–343, 544; and dynamics, 161; and improvised ornamentation, 519, 544; and tempo, 32–36, 42–43

Reicha, Anton, and French performance style, 132–133; and minuet tempos, 557
Reichardt, Johann Friedrich, 161; and dotted rhythms, 559–560; and keyboard articulation, 202; and orchestral precision, 115, 559–560; and ornamentation, 339–340
Reidemeister, Peter, and articulation, 199, 221
Reincken, Johann Adam, and dual nature of *tremolo*, 410; and trill, 443
Rellstab, Johann Carl Friedrich, and articulation in accompaniment, 221
Retard. See *Ritardando*
Rhetoric and musical performance, 162–164
Rhythm, 85, 88–89, 126; and accents, 176, 179, 188, 272, 276; and *Anschlag*, 371 and appoggiatura, 295; and arpeggio, 486, 488, 491–492, 494, 568; and articulation, 88, 188, 190, 248–250; in dance music, 74, 88, 217; and dynamics, 88–89, 91; and improvisation, 516–517; intepretation of, 3, 17, 90–91; and melody, 85, 88; and meter, 27–28, 85–86, 88, 131–132, 135–137; and mor-

dent, 457, 459, 462, 465–466, 468; notation of, 95–107, 126, 130–131, 136–140, 145, 153–154, 558; and ornamentation, 88–89, 93, 104–105, 294, 319–320; and phrasing, 88, 259, 283–289; and slide, 352, 357–359, 361–370; in solo vs. ensemble performance, 99, 104, 114–116, 126–127; and *style luthé*, 40, 319, 361; and tempo, 88, 106, 154; and texture, 135; and trill, 418, 421–422, 424, 431, 436, 445, 455; and turn, 473, 476, 480–483; in vocal music, 42, 130; and *Vorschlag*, 301, 307–309, 328–331, 342, 345–346, 348. *See also* Accents; Binary rhythms; Dotted rhythms; Lombard rhythms; *Notes inégales*; *Rubato*; Syncopation; Ternary rhythms

Ricci, F. Pasquale, 564; and ornamentation, 340, 367, 478, 484
Riemann, Hugo, 91, 245, 568; and phrasing, 275–278, 290
Riepel, Joseph, and phrasing, 267
Rigaudon, 80
Riggs, Robert D., and Mozart's dots and strokes, 233–234, 242, 562
*Ritardando*, 69–73, 259; and ornamentation, 71–72
Rodolphe, Jean-Joseph, and trill, 392–393
Roger, Estienne, 524
Rognioni, Francesco, 357; and Lombard rhythms, 517; and ornamentation, 312, 516–517, 530; and slide, 357–358; and transitional dynamics, 163; and *trillo*, 517
Rogniono, Richardo, 517; and slide, 357–358
Romanticism and the early music movement, 1
Rore, Cipriano de. *See* De Rore, Cipriano
Rose, Gloria, and improvisation, 517
Roseingrave, Thomas, and French mordent symbol in Scarlatti, 399
Rosen, Charles, and improvised ornamentation in Mozart's repeats, 550
Rosenblum, Sandra, 11, 198–199; and trills, 566
Rosow, Lois, 35
Rossi, Michelangelo, and improvisation, 517; *Toccate e corrente d'intavolatura d'organo e cimbalo*, 30; and trill, 396
Rossini, Gioachino, and dynamics, 168
Rousseau, Jean, 565; and meter and tempo, 46; and mordent, 458, 461; and *Nachschlag*, 310–311; and *port de voix*, 303–304, 458; and trill, 379–380, 391; and turn, 475; and vibrato, 500–501; and *Vorschlag*, 303–304
Rousseau, Jean Jacques, and dance music, 79–81; and expression, 7; and French vs. Italian rhythmic notation, 132; and *notes inégales*, 129, 132; and phrasing, 269; and *port de voix jetté*, 303, 309; and role of performer, 81, 269; and tempo words, 68; and trill, 389–391; and *Vorschlag*, 303, 309
*Rubato*, 41, 89, 92–95, 99, 125–127, 133, 137, 259, 516, 520, 522
Rudolf, Max, 11

**Sabbatini,** Luisi Antonio, and trill, 402–403
Sachs, Curt, 19, 76–77; and *notes inégales*, 125–126, 131; and *ritardando*, 70

Trio (dance form), 159–160. *See also* Minuet

Triplets, 142; blackened, 138–139, 142; notation of, 560–561; and *notes inégales*, 131; synchronized with dotted rhythms, 96–97, 103, 107, 151–154. *See also* Ternary rhythms

Troeger, Richard, and keyboard articulation, 201, 222

Tromlitz, Johann Georg, and articulation, 220, 230; and improvised ornamentation, 541; and soloistic overdotting, 100; and trill, 432–434, 444; and vibrato, 507–508

Türk, Daniel Gottlob, and accents, 179, 208; and *acciaccatura*, 498; and *Anschlag*, 372; and appoggiatura, 340; and arpeggio, 490, 494; and articulation, 204, 222–223, 230; and cadenzas, 541; and dynamics, 174; and expression, 41; and improvisation, 531, 541, 544; and meter, 61; and mordent, 470; and *Nachschlag*, 340; and ornamentation, 531, 541, 544, 571; and phrasing, 262, 271; and *rubato*, 94–95; and slide, 367; and soloistic overdotting, 100; and tempo, 50, 62, 68; and trill, 431, 433–434, 444, 454; and triplets synchronized with dotted rhythms, 103–104; and turn, 478; and vibrato, 507; and *Vorschlag*, 340, 372

Turn, 436, 470, 472, 566; articulation, 198, 250, 475, 477–478, 480; and beat placement, 313–314, 362, 462, 472, 474–478, 480–482, 484–485, 531; in cadences, 475; and dotted notes, 473, 482–483; and dynamics, 473, 476–477, 480; and improvisation, 520, 531, 550; and instrumental music, 474–476; notation of, 313, 470, 472–486, 531, 567–568; and rhythm, 473, 476, 480–483; speed of, 462, 473, 475–477; starting pitch of, 473–475, 482, 484–485; and tempo, 473, 476, 478, 483; terminology of, 462, 472–478, 531; with trills, 373, 387, 395, 442, 445–456, 474, 566

Unverricht, Hubert, and Mozart's dots and strokes, 234

Van Helmont, Charles-Joseph, *Pièces de clavecin*, 388; and ornamentation, 388; and trill, 388

Veracini, Francesco, binary vs. ternary rhythms, 143; and "Italian mordent," 401; and ornamentation, 523; and trill, 401; and vibrato, 503

Viadana, Lodovico, mensural notation, 58

Vibrato, 5, 198, 294, 472, 498–499; and expression, 502, 504, 506; and intensity, 501–503, 568; and keyboard music, 206, 505–507, 509, 562; notation of, 415, 461, 501–504, 506, 568–569; and pitch, 498–499, 502–503, 506–507, 568–570; speed of, 501; and string music, 499–509, 568–569; terminology of, 498, 500–504, 506; and vocal music, 499–509, 568–569; and wind music, 499, 501–502, 505, 507–509. *See also* Trill

Vicentino, Nicola, and tempo, 36, 64

Villeneuve, Alexandre de, and *notes inégales*, 129; and slide, 353; and *Vorschlag*, 308–309

Vinci, Leonardo, and *Vorschlag*, 314

Violin fingerings. *See* Fingerings, violin

Vivaldi, Antonio, articulation, 248–249; binary vs. ternary rhythms, 143; dynamics, 160, 169; and *notes inégales*, 133; and ornamentation, 295, 315, 523, 551, 571; and trill, 400; and vibrato, 503

*Works*
Bassoon Concerto in A Minor, 400
*L'incoronazione di Dario*, 143
Violin Concertos, C Major, 143; D Major ("del Guardellino"), 400; G Major, 143

Vogler, Georg, Joseph, and ornamentation, 340; and trill, 431, 434, 444

Volumier, Jean Baptiste, 133

*Vorschlag*, 300–303, 316, 322–338, 340–345, 348, 350, 351–352, 367, 429–430, 439, 443–444, 472, 498, 567; articulation, 206, 250, 331, 345; and beat placement, 301–310, 312–319, 321–326, 329–348, 350, 367, 372, 383, 463–464, 517, 520; and dynamics, 301, 340–341, 371–372; and harmony, 301, 307, 316, 328–331; and improvisation, 517, 520; and keyboard music, 302, 308, 310; and mordent, 445; notation of, 302–309, 312–320, 324–325, 326–340, 342–347, 367, 383, 399–401; and rhythm, 307–309, 328–331, 342, 345, 369; and tempo, 309, 339, 348; and texture, 328; and vocal music, 310, 313. *See also Anschlag*; Appoggiatura; *Coulé*; Grace notes; *Port de voix*; *Schneller*; Slide; Trill

Wagner, Richard, 555; and role of melody, 182; and tempo, 15, 81

Walther, Johann Gottfried, and *accent*, 310; and *acciaccatura*, 497; and Grigny's organ book, 354; and metrical stress patterns, 86; and mordent, 497; and *notes inégales*, 133; and slide, 362; and trill, 412–413; and vibrato, 506; and *Vorschlag*, 324–325, 329, 324–325

Walther, Johann Jakob, and staccato articulation, 225–226

Weber, Carl Maria von, 340

Westhoff, Johann Paul von, and dynamics, 169

Whitmore, Philip, and cadenzas, 572

Wolf, Georg Friedrich, and articulation, 202, 230; and dotted rhythms, 101

Words and music, 22, 27–28, 32–37, 42, 58, 65, 162–164, 235, 238, 247, 515, 517, 519

Zabern, Conrad von, and vocal articulation, 191

Zacconi, Lodovico, and binary vs. ternary rhythms, 141; and *ritardando*, 70; and *rubato*, 93; and tempo, 36; and vibrato, 502–503

Zarlino, Gioseffo, and binary vs. ternary rhythms, 140; and dynamics in vocal music, 182

Zaslaw, Neil, 11, 115, 559–560; and vibrato, 508–509

Zimmerman, Ewald, and Mozart's dots and strokes, 234

*Zwischenschlag*, 300–301, 326, 332, 338, 340, 351